Jean Paton and the Struggle to Reform American Adoption

Jean is about to break the sealed "birth certificate" at the conclusion of the "Red Tape Ceremony" that took place at the 1989 American Adoption Congress's conference in New York City. From left to right: Don Humphrey, the AAC's legal adviser at the time; Nancy Horgan, Rhode Island birth mother and adoptees' rights advocate; Joe Soll, founder of Adoption Crossroads; the AAC's president Kate Burke.

JEAN PATON
and the Struggle to
Reform American Adoption

E. Wayne Carp

The University of Michigan Press
Ann Arbor

Published in the United States of America by
The University of Michigan Press
Manufactured in the United States of America
⊗ Printed on acid-free paper

2017   2016   2015   2014   4   3   2   1

A CIP catalog record for this book is available from the British Library.

Library of Congress Cataloging-in-Publication Data

Carp, E. Wayne, 1946–
    Jean Paton and the struggle to reform American adoption / E. Wayne Carp.
        pages   cm
    ISBN 978-0-472-11910-3 (hardback) — ISBN 978-0-472-02990-7 (ebk)
    1. Paton, Jean M., 1908–   2. Adoption—United States—History.   3. Open adoption—
United States—History.   4. Adoptees—United States—History.   5. Birthparents—United
States—History.   6. Social workers—United States—Biography.   I. Title.
HV875.P36C38   2014
362.734092—dc23
    [B]
                                                            2013036411

To the memory of Jean M. Paton

Contents

Abbreviations

Unless otherwise stated, all manuscript sources are from the Jean Paton Papers in possession of the author. Similarly, unless otherwise stated, letters without a folder name can be found in the folder with the person's last name first, followed by the last name. For example, a letter from JP to Katherine Gordon can be found in the folder: Gordon, Katherine, Jean Paton Papers.

ABS	Jean Paton, *The Adopted Break Silence: The Experiences and Views of Forty Adults Who Were Once Adopted Children.* Philadelphia: Life History Study Center, 1954.
ALMA	Adoptees' Liberty Movement Association
BN	Blue Notebook, Jean Paton Papers
BJ	Bonnie Jacobs [Margaret McDonald Lawrence]
Carp, *Family Matters*	E. Wayne Carp, *Family Matters: Secrecy and Disclosure in the History of Adoption* (Cambridge, MA: Harvard University Press, 1998).
CM	Correspondence with Magazines
CUB	Concerned United Birthparents
FF	Florence Fisher
FR	FOCUS Release, Blue Notebook, Jean Paton Papers
JP	Jean Paton
JPP, UF	Jean Paton Papers, Department of Special Collections, George A. Smathers Libraries, University of Florida, Gainesville
LHSCR	Life History Study Center Release
MAC	Mary Anne Cohen
OV	Ruthena Hill Kittson [Jean Paton], *Orphan Voyage.* New York: Vantage Press, 1968.
ON	Orange Notebook, Jean Paton Papers
The LOG	*The LOG of Orphan Voyage* mimeograph, (1967–1981)
PR	*A Proper Response: To the Situation in Adoption* (1993–1998)
USCB	U.S. Children Bureau Papers, Record Group 102, National Archives II, College Park, MD
VWBP	Viola Wertheim Bernard Papers, Long Health Sciences Library, Columbia University, New York

Preface

This study began inadvertently in 1993 while I was writing *Family Matters: Secrecy and Disclosure in the History of Adoption*. Out of curiosity, I asked Jean Paton whether she had retained any correspondence from her days as an adoption activist.[1] She replied that she had many boxes of correspondence that told the entire history of the adoption reform movement.[2] Little did I know at the time that this was a vast understatement.

Three years later, I contacted Jean again in connection with my next project, a history of the adoption reform movement, because I suspected that she had played a major role in that story. I asked her how much correspondence she had retained over her lifetime of movement activities and whether she would give me permission to use it.[3] She evaded my question about the size of her correspondence but gave permission for me to conduct "responsible research" into her files.[4] I replied that I now intended to write a full-scale "life and times" biography of her, which I hoped would make a contribution "to the history of adoption, social work, and the larger realm of U.S. social history." I added that I would like to travel to Harrison, Arkansas, to interview her and once again asked her to give me some sense of the size of her files.[5] In a subsequent letter, Paton mentioned ten boxes of correspondence, which she agreed to mail to me. She also agreed to be interviewed.

In June 1998 I traveled to Harrison and interviewed Paton for one week. I discovered a diminutive, feisty woman with twinkling blue eyes, a great sense of humor, and a hearty laugh. In answer to my myriad questions, Jean reveled in bringing out reams of correspondence, official documents, old newsletters, and newspaper clippings—like a magician pulling rabbits out of a hat—to the squeals of delight and amazement of her audience of one.[6] At once, I recognized three things: how invaluable these sources were, the real possibility of their forming the basis of an important work of history, and how utterly ignorant I had been of the true history of the adoption reform movement.

This study is based primarily on Jean Paton's correspondence, which she sent me over the course of several years after I interviewed her in 1998. Although I had immediately recognized the value of her correspondence from what I had seen in Harrison, I could hardly have imagined the extent of it: it was a biographer's Eldorado. Jean had made an onion-skin carbon copy of every letter she ever wrote over a period of fifty years—filling some fifty or more boxes—and had carefully filed away almost every sheet of paper in a complex system of file folders. Paton's own writings range from a discussion of being suckled at the breast of her mother for the first four months of life to discussions of every aspect of adoption reform to reports of her health weeks before her death. In between are drafts of memos, essays, and articles she never published, reviews of her books and media notices of her travels, account books, typewritten notes of books she read, a detailed diary she kept between 1950 and 1953, memos of every phone call she received related to adoption reform, and even sixty-year-old college papers. Just as important for this study, Jean kept every letter, Christmas card, search group's newsletter, and solicitation she ever received. These materials include inquiries from triad members (adult adoptees and birth mothers[7]) seeking advice about how to reconnect with their original families, triad members requesting guidance on how to organize search and reunion groups, and correspondence from publishers, editors, and congressmen. Except for me (and Jean, of course) no one has read this enormous corpus of Jean Paton's work.

In May 2009, I returned to Harrison and interviewed June Schwantes, Jean's life companion for nearly forty years. During that visit I obtained dozens of Jean's photos and even more of Jean's correspondence and publications, including a complete run of the invaluable *The LOG of Orphan* Voyage, collected in two unmarked loose-leaf binders, which had been left behind in her office. Without these two thick binders, chapters 2–8 of this study would have been woefully incomplete. Finally, in October 2010, I received Jean Paton's library, where it had been stored for a decade in the attic of her friend, Ms. Chris Lee. The library contained almost one thousand books on a wide variety of subjects, although the bulk of the collection dealt with orphans. All of these materials— Paton's correspondence, her library, and photos—along with transcripts and tapes of all the interviews I conducted with Jean and others relating to this project will eventually be housed in the Social Welfare History Archives, Elmer L. Andersen Library, at the University of Minnesota.

Jean Paton and the Struggle to Reform American Adoption is primarily a work of original research that advances knowledge—the scholarship of discovery. The main goal of this biography is to introduce Jean Paton, the mother of the adoption reform movement and the social movement she pioneered, to the millions of people who have no knowledge of her or of it. She is unknown primarily because the materials for writing her story remained in her possession and were never accessible to researchers or the public. In addition, outside of a few chapters in books on the history of American adoption, there exists no full-scale history of the adoption reform movement. Consequently, in this book I quote liberally from Paton's unpublished correspondence, writings, and oral interviews because they have never been heard before, and because I want to respect Jean's exhortation that "Everyone except the adopted has been talking about adoption."[8] I believe it is important that her words be heard directly, not filtered or interpreted by a third person.

By extensively using Jean Paton's huge archive of materials, combined with oral interviews with her and her life companion June Schwantes, and other influential adoption reform activists, *Jean Paton and the Struggle to Reform American Adoption* represents the first biography of this pioneering reformer and offers an original contribution to the history of the movement. In doing so, I hope to restore Jean Paton's place in history as a figure as important to the adoption reform movement and the transformation of American adoption as the Reverend Martin Luther King, Jr., is to the civil rights movement and Betty Friedan and Gloria Steinem are to the women's rights movement. That said, I want to emphasize that this not a definitive biography of Jean Paton. In light of Paton's substantial archive, there are more than enough materials for numerous additional studies, such as a demographic profile of Paton's correspondents, their gender, race, age, region, and religion, or a study of the relationships between Paton and the hundreds of search organizations that she nurtured, advised, and corresponded with. Doubtlessly, additional studies will also follow from this one, interpreting Paton in different ways, perhaps minimizing her adoptive status and instead stressing her sexual orientation.

In this book I place Jean Paton within a historical context that inevitably reveals her early doubts, occasional missteps, combative quarrels, and an intense need for recognition—bordering on compulsion—especially toward the end of her life. Taking stock of her character with all of its shortcomings in no way diminishes the compassion, humanity, and empathy she exhibited throughout her life; nor does it denigrate her tremendous accomplishment as the pioneer of adoption reform and the engineer of many of the milestones of that movement. It simply sets the historical record straight and lets us see the woman for who she was. In her youth and early adulthood, Paton overcame many difficulties, which I disclose here for the first time, yet her intellectual curiosity and strength of character withstood the adversity she faced from within and without. When Jean was clearly on the wrong side of a reform issue, giving credit to others in the adoption reform movement who deserve it is simply the right thing to do. Her contentiousness in the arena of adoption reform—some might call it sticking to one's principles—was both her strength and weakness. Pioneering a social movement of identity politics for adopted people, she inevitably, like the leaders of every other social movement, alienated both friend and foe.

In *Jean Paton and the Struggle to Reform American Adoption*, several prominent themes stand out. First, Jean's adoptive status was a determining factor throughout her life. From adolescence through early adulthood, Jean wrestled with what Erik Erikson called an "identity crisis," manifesting itself in what he described as a "confusion of values." In Jean's case, the crisis was especially visible in her chosen profession of social worker. She found that it failed to provide what she needed, a lifelong, belief system she could attach herself to completely and without reservation.[9] She soon found that elsewhere, in Christianity and in the reform of American adoption. A second theme is that the mother of the adoption reform movement was made not born, the product of intellect and hard-won experience. Jean began her pioneering reform work late in life, forty-three years of age. Moreover, once she found her inspiration, that the stigma of illegitimacy was the root evil for adult adoptees and unmarried mothers, she vacillated for many years deciding who should be the primary focus of her efforts. Finally she threw all of her energies to helping adult adoptees. A third theme is that Paton pioneered a system of identity politics for adult adoptees, viewing them as a marginalized people. All of her writing, art, and poetry were designed to make adult adoptees think of themselves first as adopted people— and view themselves as men or women, black or white, homemaker or wage earner as secondary to their identity.[10] A fourth theme is the difficulty of pigeon-holing Jean Paton into the categories of current politics. In some ways she was liberal, championing juvenile justice, civil rights, and adoption reform. In her eighties, Paton advocated abolishing adoption itself and replacing it with guardianship. In other ways she was conservative: she opposed abortion, supported the traditional family over the adoptive, distrusted legislators, and showed little enthusiasm for the rights of adult adoptees. In bridging these seeming contradictions, it is best to understand Paton as fundamentally apolitical, acting from a deep Christian humanitarianism and empathizing with the oppressed and marginalized.

The biographer's perennial problem is that of the subject's memory. How much can the biographer trust the subject's memory of events; and, as the subject ages, how much do those memories become distorted or even forgotten? Having read Jean Paton's correspondence, I am impressed with the consistency and accuracy of her memory. Her seminal experiences in social work, for example, which she wrote about to many people when she was in her mid-thirties, she repeated over the years in many different venues, largely without distortion, into her eighties. Nevertheless, wherever possible, I have sought corroboration from other sources. However, when I was incapable of verifying Jean's statement from an interview, such as her belief that her mother sang Brahms lullaby to her during the first four months of her life, I refrained from including it in the text. By contrast, the memory of many of Paton's most important correspondents, major figures in the movement, I found to my surprise to be often inaccurate. When I discussed historical events in which Paton and these other activists were involved decades earlier, citing the primary source material—their own letters, for example—they often did not recall writing the letters or had no memory that the event or conversation had taken place.

Given this discovery, I made two decisions. Where there was a conflict between the primary source material and the later memory of a historical actor, I have relied on the primary source. (This is standard practice in writing history.) Second, and perhaps more controversial, I have conducted extensive interviews, but only with the most significant historical actors whose lives intersected with Paton's. The reasons for restricting the number of oral interviews are threefold. First, because the memories of some of the actors were so unreliable I decided it would be unproductive to pursue further contact. Second, the accuracy and completeness of the Paton records in my possession were so extraordinary that oral interviews would add little to the historical record that was not already known. Third, because this study had already been over ten years in the making, interviewing another twenty or thirty people would have added many more years to this engrossing undertaking, which has already gone on too long. It is time that the American people have a fuller knowledge of this remarkable reformer. Whether the decision to limit the number of oral interviews was erroneous only future studies will reveal.

Finally, a note about organization. The first eight chapters of this book are a chronological narrative of Jean Paton's life and her adoption reform activities. But with the entrance of adoption activist extraordinaire Florence Fisher onto the scene in the early 1970s and the resulting explosion of the adoption reform movement, strict chronology is less useful, as it would deteriorate into a mere chronicle of Jean Paton's numerous reform activities on many fronts. Chapters 9–13 thus take a more topical approach, with separate chapters on the rise of the adoption search movement in the 1970s, creation of birth mother and adoptee search groups, the debate over sealed adoption records, Paton's role as an ombudsman, and the creation of the American Adoption Congress. These are just some of the adoption-related activities that Paton was simultaneously involved in during the last decades of her life. The last two chapters and epilogue resume the chronological narrative.

A year before Jean died, she closed one of her letters to me with this sentence: "Best wishes to you in all your undertakings, and may they also reek with truth, as have mine." In writing this book, I have tried to live up to Jean Paton's admonishment.

After more than a decade of work on this project, I am very happy to thank the many people who encouraged, helped, and remained steadfast in their belief that the book would be finished someday. First and foremost, I cannot express deeply enough my debt of gratitude to Jean Paton for granting me unconditional use of her massive archive answering dozens of my questions, and blessing my request to set aside her story for several years to write a book about Bastard Nation—The Adoptee Rights Organization. I am also thankful to Molly Johnson, Jean's close friend, literary executor, and longtime adoption activist. She continued to cooperate wholeheartedly in this enterprise after Jean's death in 2002 and has continued to have faith in the completion of this book.

Many activists in the adoption reform movement have contributed to this book by agreeing to be interviewed, critically reading parts of the manuscript, donating personal materials, permitting me to quote from their correspondence, and generously providing me with important information about people and events connected to Jean Paton. Needless to say, they are not responsible for any errors of fact or judgment that remain, but they made this a much better book than it would otherwise have been. I especially want to thank Lee Campbell, Mary Anne Cohen, Lorraine Dusky, Florence Fisher, Jim Gritter, Pam Hasegawa, June Schwantes, Joe Soll, and Alice Syman.

I wish to acknowledge my debt to the institutions, colleagues, and friends who have helped to make this book possible. The bulk of research and writing of this book was made possible by the generous financial support from the president and provost of Pacific Lutheran University, in the form of liberal sabbatical leaves and Regency Advancement Awards. I am also deeply grateful to Dale E. Benson for endowing the chair I hold at PLU, which provided me with substantial release from teaching responsibilities. A grant from the National Endowment for the Humanities in 2002 allowed me to devote an uninterrupted year of research and writing. Librarians and archivists around the country supplied me with important sources. I wish to thank Stephen E. Novak, Head, Archives & Special Collections, Augustus C. Long Health Sciences Library, Columbia University Medical Center, New York City, for guidance with the Viola Wertheim Bernard Papers, as well as the following archivists: Michael Edmonds, Head,

Digital Collections & Web Services, Library-Archives Division, Wisconsin Historical Society; Florence M. Turcotte, Literary Manuscripts Archivist, University of Florida Libraries; and Sarah Wilkinson, Archives Assistant, Mount Holyoke College. I am also especially indebted to PLU's interlibrary loan librarian, Sue Golden, who throughout this long period quickly obtained countless books and articles from around the world.

A portion of chapter 4 was published under the title "Jean Paton, Christian Adoption, and the Reunification of Families," in *The Journal of Christian Legal Thought* 2, no. 1 (May 2012): 20–22. A portion of chapter 5 was published under the title "The Atheist and the Christian: Madalyn Murray O'Hair, Jean Paton, and the Stigma of Illegitimacy in the 1950s," in *Journal of the Historical Society* 12, no. 2 (June 2012): 205–27. A portion of chapter 10 was published under the title "A Revolutionary in the Making: Jean Paton and the Early Decades of Sealed Adoption Records, 1949–1977," *Adoption & Culture* 3 (2012): 33–62. I am grateful to the editors to reprint portions of these articles here.

LeAnn Fields was everything an author could possibly hope for in an editor. We live in a risk-averse world where university presses, not to mention trade and commercial ones, tend to publish biographies of already famous people: Abraham Lincoln is the subject of 15,000 titles, and more arrive every year. As a result, a biography of Jean Paton had a hard time finding a publisher. Several university presses turned it down often with the comment, "we never heard of her." I also heard that the book would have an allegedly small market, there being only approximately five million adopted people in America. LeAnn recognized immediately the potential of the "baggy monster," convinced its author that the original manuscript was way too long, and then fought tenaciously for its publication. Without her empathy, vision, and determination, this book would not have been published.

The book has been improved enormously by colleagues and friends who generously gave their time and insights. To them, I am deeply grateful for reading all or substantial portions of the manuscript: Audrey Eyler, Mark Jensen, Beth Kraig, Steve Mintz, Phillip Nordquist, and Paula Shields. Doug Oakman's advice on early Christian theology was particularly valuable. Two anonymous readers for the University of Michigan Press improved the manuscript with helpful queries and suggestions. Donna Bouvier, senior production editor at Harvard University Press, worked her usual magic in copyediting my manuscript into a readable book.

My greatest debt is to my wife, Paula Shields, and it is a particular pleasure finally to be able to thank her here. Thanks for listening, for always being there, and for sustaining me all these years.

Introduction

On March 27, 2002, Jean Paton, age ninety-three, died suddenly of a heart ailment at the North Regional Medical Center in Harrison, Arkansas. A Canadian obituary described Paton's signal contribution: "'In the beginning was the Word,' and the first 'word' of adoption reform was spoken by adoptee and social worker Jean Paton in the 1950s."[1] In her fifty-year struggle to reform American adoption, Paton, the mother of the adoption reform movement, gave adult adoptees a voice and provided them with a healthy self-image, facilitated thousands of meetings between adult adoptees and their families of origin, fought tirelessly to open sealed adoption records, and indefatigably explained the adoption experience to a wider public. To achieve these goals, Paton founded in 1953 the Life History Study Center, the first research institution dedicated to advancing the interests of adult adoptees and birth mothers and pioneered the first voluntary mutual consent adoption registry. In 1961, she established the first adoptee search organization, Orphan Voyage. Paton was also the author of two pathbreaking books, *The Adopted Break Silence* (1954) and *Orphan Voyage* (1968), as well as a newsletter, *The LOG of Orphan Voyage*. These publications not only kept subscribers up to date with the latest news in the world of the adopted but more importantly moved them to question their assumptions about illegitimacy, adoption, and the larger social and historical forces at work in American society. Her ceaseless activity created the preconditions for the explosive emergence of the adoption reform movement in the 1970s. When that social movement emerged, with its demand to open sealed adoption records, Paton played a prominent role in the formation of the first national organization for birth parents, Concerned United Birthparents, and was instrumental in the creation of the first national organization for adult adoptees, the American Adoption Congress. Along the way, she was joined by a new generation of outstanding adoption reformers, most prominently Florence Fisher, Mary Anne Cohen, Lee Campbell, Lorraine Dusky,

Betty Jean Lifton, Pam Hasegawa, Penny Partridge, Annette Baran, Reuben Pannor, Sandy Musser, Joan Wheeler, Ken Watson, and Dirck Brown, with whom she worked, advised, and quarreled. By the 1970s, Paton emerged as an influential presence on the national and international stage. She participated in national adoption reform protests and campaigned to open sealed adoption records and abolish adoption. Congressional committees sought her advice, and she corresponded with members of Congress. She was invited to participate in international debates on opening adoption records and inspired reformers spanning the English-speaking world. She received awards and tributes, but none pleased her more than the sobriquet bestowed on her, as early as 1981, as the "mother of the adoption reform movement."

To truly appreciate how Paton transformed American adoption, we must first understand what adoption was like before the early 1950s when she founded the Life History Study Center and published *The Adopted Break Silence*. Then, American culture contained both conservative and liberal elements, stigmatizing and valorizing the institution of adoption and triad members (birth parents, adoptees, and adoptive parents). Americans' cultural definition of kinship stigmatized adoption as socially unacceptable. Social workers had to overcome widespread popular prejudice toward adoption, in order to convince prospective adoptive parents that taking a child into the home was not abnormal. During the late nineteenth and early twentieth century, a broad segment of the American public believed that adoption was an unnatural action that created ersatz or second-rate families. Americans often heard physicians give their imprimatur to statements, such as "the normal biologic relationship of parent and child is more satisfactory . . . than an artificially created one."[2] Magazine articles printed variations on the theme, denigrating adoption by stating that, "though it is better to be adopted than institutionalized, no adopted relation is likely to be as good as a natural one."[3] The very language underscored the inferior nature of adoption: in popular discourse, adoptive parents were always juxtaposed with "natural" or "normal" ones.[4] Discriminatory laws reinforced the notion that the adoptive relationship was inherently flawed. Jurists regularly ruled in inheritance cases, for example, that adoption violated the legal principal of consanguinity or blood ties. In practice, this meant that adopted children did not have the same inheritance rights as birth children. In other cases dealing with disputed custody rights of adopted children, both courts and legislatures favored birth parents' appeals to restore their children to them.[5]

Medical science contributed to popular cultural prejudices against adopting a child by yoking adoption with the stigma of illegitimacy.[6] After 1910 the rise of the eugenics movement and psychometric testing linked adopted children to the social pathology of their unmarried parents, particularly criminality and inherited mental defects, such as feeblemindedness. Adopted children were thus burdened with a double stigma: they were assumed to be illegitimate and thus tainted medically *and* they were adopted, thus lacking the all-important blood link to their adoptive parents.[7] Would-be adoptive parents were implicitly warned to be wary of adopting children. In the year before Jean Paton was born, Amos W. Butler, secretary of the Indiana Board of State Charities, stated in his presidential address at the National Conference of Charities and Corrections a common belief: "In many of the orphans' homes a large number of the children come from feeble-minded parents. Some such, who show little or no defect, are placed in family homes; others are held to await developments."[8] By the 1950s, eugenic warning had been medicalized into psychoanalytic tenets and incorporated into the Child Welfare League of America's influential *Standards for Adoption Service*. It stated that unwed mothers "have serious personality disturbances [and] need help with their emotional problems."[9] Social workers resolved these "problems" by separating the unwed mother from her child, placing the child for adoption, and ensuring that if the mother ever returned to the agency for information, she be denied access to it.[10]

Despite the pseudoscientific stigmatization of adoption, the institution became immensely popular with the American public as illegitimacy rates soared, a consequence of loosened social bonds during World War II, and continued their upward flight for the next fifty years.[11] The adoption of infants became the social work "solution" to the postwar problem of illegitimacy, an unintended consequence of the baby boom. Beginning in the mid-1940s, the baby boom was both cause and effect of a profound change in the national culture that tied personal happiness to an ideology of domesticity and the nuclear family. Parenthood during the Cold War became not only popular but also a necessity. The media romanticized babies, glorified motherhood, and identified fatherhood with masculinity and good citizenship.[12] Wartime prosperity, a postwar pronatalist climate of opinion, and medical advances in infertility diagnosis combined to produce a remarkable increase in the number of applications to adopt a child.[13] In less than thirty years, the number of adoptions had grown nearly ninefold, to 142,000.[14]

The demand by this new interest group—white, middle-class, and childless couples—was immense, far exceeding the number of available children. By the mid-1950s one expert estimated that of the four and half million childless couples, fully one million were seeking the approximately 75,000 children available for adoption.[15] Subtly and overtly, social workers and maternity home officials pressured unwed mothers to place their babies for adoption, now considered "the best solution" to the "problem" of illegitimacy.[16]

Part and parcel of "the best solution" was the steady process of sealing adoption records. Sealing adoption records, whether by the courts, legislatures, adoption agencies, or bureaus of vital statistics, was a relatively recent policy. For a century before the 1950s, adoption records—birth certificates, court records, and agency case files—had been open in the vast majority of states and accessible to adult adoptees and even to birth mothers. When Paton traveled to Detroit to request her birth certificate in the Probate Court for Wayne County, for example, the clerk handed her the papers. He also offered her the use of a room to examine them, where, privately and in a relaxed setting, she discovered her natal mother's full name.[17] "There was no rigmarole then," Paton observed. "You were allowed to see your own paper in a kindly procedure."[18] Many years later, she characterized it as "a warm, accepting experience" and "quite simple and quite humane."[19]

Beginning in the second half of the twentieth century, however, secrecy became the norm. State legislators, influenced by adoptive parents, haphazardly enacted laws sealing court records, making them inaccessible to triad members. Paton personally experienced the effect of these laws. In 1942, when she returned to the Probate Office a second time to look at the legal record of her adoption, a clerk told her "in a clipped fashion" that she "would have to see the judge about that." Paton "felt—spontaneously—that I had been struck across the face with a riding crop." She remembered the event as the "most humiliating experience of my life."[20]

Denying access to adoption agency case records was also a slow but more complicated process, resulting from a combination of factors including the changing demography of adoption agencies' clientele, adoption caseworkers' often uncritical embrace of psychoanalytic theory, and social workers' increasing professionalism. Not all these factors operated simultaneously but each had its effect. Changes in the age and marriage status of birth mothers contributed to adoption agencies' turn to a policy of secrecy. Postwar unwed mothers' youth, their children's illegitimacy, and the quick separation of mother and child (as caseworkers increasingly followed British psychiatrist John Bowlby's advice on how to avoid "maternal deprivation") seemed to erode their special claim to receive family information.[21] As for those unwed mothers who wanted to keep their children or maintain contact with them, social workers echoed psychoanalyst Helene Deutsch's observation that "the least mature among unmarried mothers are the very ones who often fight to keep their children."[22] Consequently, social workers invoked a generalized neuroticism to deny birth mothers access to family information. Similarly, they began to interpret adult adoptees who searched for their parents of origin as "very disturbed young people" and "sick youths," a perspective grounded in the psychoanalytic concept of Freud's family romance fantasy. Social workers interpreted this tenet of psychoanalytic theory to mean that searching for birth parents was pathological and, by extension, represented the failure of the adoptive process.[23]

Moreover, adoption agencies almost immediately began to view secrecy as a professional attribute providing them with a competitive edge over unlicensed and private adoptions. In their uphill battle to sway public opinion in general and adoptive parents in particular of the benefits of regulated adoptions, agencies touted the advantages of secrecy. As early as 1944, California's Department of Social Welfare identified as one benefit of using an accredited agency its "ability to conceal the identities of the natural parents and the adopting parents from each other, thereby eliminating the possibility of the natural parents interfering or causing embarrassment to the child at a later date."[24]

Jean Paton's most notable achievement was to provide adult adoptees with a self-definition, instill pride, create a self-conscious community, and eventually generate political action. She accomplished this by assuming the role of ombudsman for adult adoptees, creating an institutional framework through the Life History Study Center and Orphan Voyage in support of a counternarrative to America's cultural framework of defining adoption solely in terms of children. Instead, through constant reiteration, she argued that adopted children grew up and became adults who demanded to reconnect with their natal families in order to regain their psychological health. Thus, Paton's foundational philosophical tenet and institutional expression challenged both American society's prejudices against unwed mothers and social work policies and practices that systematically stigmatized triad members, legally separated natal parents from their children, and sealed adoption records. Paton's ceaseless toil in the wilderness of the '50s and '60s laid the institutional and ideological groundwork for the better-known adoption reform movement of the 1970s.

The polestar guiding her philosophy of adoption reform was that the stigma of illegitimacy was responsible for the difficulties adoption triad members faced and behind the wrongheaded policies of social workers. Birth mothers' grief, adult adoptees' psychological difficulties, adoptive parents' denial, social workers' obsession with secrecy: all were a product of society's refusal to accept the fundamental importance of the genetic family connection. This foundational insight, based on Paton's own experience and reinforced by her omnivorous reading in science, history, philosophy, and literature, was one source of her moral outrage and her skepticism of such proposed adoption reforms as legislation to enact adoption registries, confidential intermediary systems, and open adoption.

From the beginning of her days as an adoption reformer to the day she died, Paton demanded as a sine qua non for adoption reform that adult adoptees have a voice in every decision made about them. This was the essence of her criticism of psychoanalytic and social work studies: they were undertaken without adult adoptee input. An essentialist at heart, Paton also distrusted any study not conducted by an adult adoptee. Experiential knowledge of the world of the adoptee would become her touchstone for the genuineness and accuracy of any expert study.

Erik Erikson hypothesized that "great" figures in history internalized the problems of their age, and in resolving these problems, transform the culture. That argument, I think, sheds light on Paton and her influence. In addressing her own identity issues, she imagined a better world and went out and made this vision a reality. She succeeded in raising adult adoptees' consciousness of themselves as a valuable, marginalized group, as well as society's consciousness about adoptees' needs. Paton's solutions to the problems of adoption triad members were unique. They were filtered through her deep belief in Christianity; the ideas of American psychoanalyst Abram Kardiner; and the writings of Simone Weil, a French philosopher, Christian mystic, and social activist. Her creation of the Life History Study Center and Orphan Voyage were the means to reform American adoption without resorting to legislation: communication with triad members to facilitate reunions with original family members based on the Christian beliefs of forgiveness and reconciliation. In this way, Paton sought to heal the psychological damage done by the stigma of illegitimacy, sealed adoption records, and the separation of natal parents from their children. She never deviated from her goal of encouraging adult adoptees and birth mothers to take control of their lives and enrich the society that so cruelly turned its back on them.

Patron's struggle to reform American adoption was never easy and yielded infrequent victories. For the first twenty years she made few allies and faced resistance at every turn. Paton was opposed by leaders of the Child Welfare League of America and state and county social workers, rebuffed by commercial publishers, ignored by the mainstream news media, and disparged by judges in the law courts. The opposition did not let up in the 1970s with the emergence of the adoption reform movement, led by the indomitable Florence Fisher and other adoption activists. If anything, it complicated Paton's efforts, for now she had ostensibly strong allies who disagreed with her ideas and competed for leadership of the movement. In the last two decades of her long life, Paton grew increasing bitter as a newer generation of leaders honored her in the breach, shut her out of the centers of power, and ignored her advice, which remained as controversial and cogent as ever. We should not be surprised by Paton's disenchantment with the adoption reform movement and its leaders. As the eminent psychiatrist Robert Coles, has observed, "those who want to change a society are no more immune to despair and sadness and anger and a sense of futility than the rest of us."[25]

This, then, is Jean Paton's story: one courageous woman's struggle to overcome American society's prejudice against adult adoptees and women who gave birth out of wedlock, reverse social workers' harmful policies and practices concerning adoption and sealed adoption records, change laws prejudicial to adult adoptees and birth mothers, and, finally, to bend to her will through force of argument the many allies who opposed her ideas in the adoption reform movement. It all began in 1951 with the founding of the Life History Study Center. But first we must learn how Jean Paton became the person who successfully challenged the culture's focus on the adopted child and pioneered a social movement to reform American adoption.

I

The Search for Identity

I think of my adolescent years .... Those near me, in relationship with me, who might
have helped, simply did not know what I was saying. Wants to know her mother? She
has a mother.

—JEAN PATON, 1990

Of all of Jean's Paton's childhood memories, the happiest were of riding in the
car with her handsome Scottish-born father, Thomas Woodburn Paton, a
prominent Ypsilanti, Michigan, general practitioner, when he called on his patients. She looked forward to these rides with her father and treasured their
companionship. Jean would usually remain outside the sick person's house on
warm days but would go into the farmhouse if it was cold and wait in the kitch-
en while her father disappeared into the bedroom. Jean also spent many hours
in her father's office, familiarizing herself with medical instruments, reading
magazines, and "looking at the peculiar pictures" in the *Journal of the American
Medical Association*. In this way, she acquired at a young age a sense of what
doctors did, though she later admitted, "I didn't see the hard aspects of it." She
recalled many decades later that she spent so much time with her father that it
was bound to give her a conviction about what to do when people were in trouble. Jean would follow in her father's footsteps, by making "house calls" either in
person or by mail to assist troubled members of the adoption triad (adult adoptees, birth mothers, and adoptive parents).[1] As she said, "you just get in your car
and go out to help them, which, of course, is what I eventually did in my work."[2]

In both private and public statements, such as the one above, Paton
projected a consistent self-image that made it appear that she was almost pre-
destined to be the mother of the adoption reform movement. In Paton's telling,
she had acquired from her earliest days a hatred of human suffering, initially

from watching her first adoptive father die of liver cancer and later from accompanying her second adoptive physician father on his medical rounds. In this way, Jean developed a deeply ingrained duty to help others. Moreover, Paton's "own experience in orphanhood," she wrote, gave her a "special advantage"[3] because she "knew the special language" of both the foster children in boarding homes and babies who were expected to be placed in adoptive homes,[4] thus making employment in social work a logical, if not an inevitable, career choice. In 1951, Paton related, she left social work for graduate work in science at the University of Pennsylvania, and two years later in 1953, established the Life History Study Center in Philadelphia to explore the world of the adult adoptee and to offer her findings to her chosen profession.[5]

These infrequent accounts that Paton told others about her past personal experience, from childhood into her adolescent and young adult years, form what developmental psychologists refer to as a person's *narrative identity*. It is the story that "people construct and tell about themselves to define who they are for themselves and for others."[6] They organize, unify, make coherent, and give purpose to a life that might otherwise feel splintered and diffuse.[7] Paton's narrative identity presented an integrated and unified purpose to her life that stressed empathy for the ill, service to others, and a special talent for self-sacrifice for her adopted brothers and sisters. Paton's narrative identity—the facts that made up the story of herself—was not false. But the road Paton traveled to that point was far more convoluted and uncertain than she suggested. And it omitted much. That she accomplished so much makes the story all that more remarkable.

Jean Paton was born Ruth Edwina Emerson on December 27, 1908, at 3:45 p.m. in Detroit's Women's Hospital. Her twenty-three-year-old unwed mother Emma Cutting chose Jean's middle name to honor her "favorite lady doctor" in the maternity home.[8] Emma was born of English stock, the oldest girl in a family of eight. She was a serious-looking young woman, with piercing eyes, thick eyebrows, and a high forehead, graced with a generous mop of thick, dark hair. And, like Jean, her mother was short, just 4 feet 9 inches.[9] Like most young women in the first decade of the twentieth century, Emma was not well educated, having quit school in the fifth grade. At age twenty-three, deeply in love with James Kittson, a man seven years her senior, later described by Paton as "rootless, good-natured and restless," Emma became pregnant for the first and only time, by the alleged bastard son of James Jerome Hill, and builder of the Great Northern Railroad.[10] Approached by Emma's father to rectify this blot on the Cutting name, Kittson agreed to marry Emma, but refused to live with her and settle down. Unwilling to agree to such an arrangement, her father sent Emma to the Women's Hospital in Detroit, where she nursed Jean for four months. They were lonely months for Emma: the father of her baby did not visit her, nor did members of her sturdy English Methodist family except for her younger, independent sister, Viola. Emma nursed and loved Jean intensely as only a mother who had been rejected by both her lover and her family could. Several months before, the Cutting family had already made these decisions for her. Emma was to come home without the baby, tend house, and help raise the younger children. A bastard child was not welcome in the Cutting home. Giving up Jean for adoption was a painful emotional experience for Emma,[11] but she had no choice. In addition to the burden of parental disapproval, Emma had no financial support. Years later, after she had married, Emma asked her mother what had happened to her baby. Her reply was, "She's dead."[12]

The Women's Hospital did not place children for adoption. Baby Ruth was placed in a temporary home by the Children's Home Society of Michigan until she was adopted on May 10, 1909, by Harry and Millie Dean, a housepainter and his wife, who lived in Detroit. The Deans renamed the baby Madeline Viola Dean. Baby Madeline lived with the Deans for only two years. At age forty-four, Harry Dean contracted liver cancer and died on May 6, 1911.[13] The last six months that Madeline lived under the Deans' roof were filled with illness and the smell of death. Some seventy years later, Paton believed that her first adoptive father's death had left her with "an undying and fierce hatred of the spectacle of human suffering."[14] Impoverished by her husband's death, Millie Dean was unable to support Madeline. She returned the child to the Children's Home Society of Michigan, which again placed Madeline in a foster home in Ypsilanti, Michigan, a small city of 15,000 people thirty miles west of Detroit.[15]

Madeline stayed in that foster home for seven and a half months. During that time, she was displayed to a prospective adoptive couple, who rejected her because they wanted a boy, a surprising decision because little girls were favored by most adoptive parents.[16] This latest rejection, though unintended and undertaken with some delicacy, was doubtless not lost on the child and must have served to intensify her insecurity and sense of abandonment. Sometime after the visit of that couple, however, a woman noticed Madeline playing in the yard, discovered she could be adopted, and said, "I'll take her."[17] On December 11, 1911, Thomas Woodburn Paton, age forty-two, and Mary M. Paton, neé Picket, of Ypsilanti, adopted Madeline and renamed her Jean Madeline Paton.

Jean thrived in her new home. The Patons were solidly middle class and were much better off than the Deans had been. They lived in a large, imposing, Victorian house, located on 122 Normal Street, and at the time of Jean's adoption had just purchased a new EMF automobile for Dr. Paton to use in making house calls over the muddy, rutted roads in and out of Ypsilanti.[18] Mary Paton had been a teacher, and probably had been made to quit her job as a condition of her adopting Jean, a common adoption agency practice during the first half of the twentieth century. Mary taught Jean to read, and at an early age Jean became a precocious reader. When she went to kindergarten, the teacher called upon her to instruct the other children how to read. Although she read a lot, however, Jean was hardly a bookworm. She climbed trees and houses under construction and had many playmates. She roller-skated and bicycled all over town.[19] In July 1921, at age twelve, Jean went to Camp Arbutus in Mayfield, Michigan, where she enjoyed swimming, canoeing, and, like all summer campers, pleaded with her parents for more "dough" and more letters from home.[20] Back home that fall, a car struck Jean while she was racing a playmate to school. Her father ran to the scene and carried her home. It was not a serious accident, but as a result Jean forever had a scar on the back of her head and a little bump on the side of her forehead.

Overshadowing the myriad events of an active twelve-year old was Jean's abrupt discovery that she had been adopted. The Patons, like most adoptive parents during the first half of the twentieth century, were reluctant to tell Jean of her adoptive status. Probably, they feared that they would lose her love. Knowing that someone would eventually find out that Jean was adopted and possibly of illegitimate birth—it was impossible to keep such a secret in a small town like Ypsilanti—Mary put out her own positive story first: Jean's mother, Emma, was a member of Detroit's high society; her father, James, was a musician in the Detroit symphony orchestra.[21] But she never volunteered the information of the adoption to Jean. That was left to a female playmate, who taunted Jean one day across the street from her house with the comment "You're adopted, ya know?" Jean ran home and asked her mother if it was true. Although visibly upset by the sudden turn of events, Mary forthrightly admitted it. And although Jean was able to glean some information about both her first adoptive and her birth parents now and then, the Patons were reluctant to speak directly or at length of these matters to her ever again.[22]

Angry, Jean did not allow the incident to rest there. She marched over to the home of the girl who had taunted her and complained to her mother. Looking back almost eighty years a more mature Jean Paton reflected that it "didn't particularly help . . . but that's the way I reacted then."[23] She believed that the way she handled it was "sort of silly." But the incident was significant. Although Jean claimed that finding out about her adoption in such an abrupt fashion did not surprise her and denied going into a state of shock over the sudden revelation of her adoption status, she was aware "that something had happened."[24] Exactly what that "something" was is open to differing interpretations. Some medical experts would later call it "genealogical bewilderment"—lifelong feel-ings of rejection, confusion, abandonment, and low self-esteem as a result of not knowing one's genetic parents.[25] This might explain Jean's intermittent lack of self-confidence and inability to stay on task even as she thrived in her adoptive home. But just as likely, Jean was experiencing Erik Erikson's "identity crisis," manifesting itself in what he identified as a "confusion of values." These feelings had repeatedly tugged at Jean's subconscious and would manifest themselves in various ways throughout her adolescence and young adulthood. Earlier in life, having just learned the letters of the alphabet and connected them to her new home, Jean went out to the back step, took a hammer and a nail, and pounded the letters "JEAN PATON" to that back step. She also built in her imagination a fantasy world, "a very big world, which of course supplemented the certainty that I felt in this home."[26]

Paton's feelings of emotional confusion intensified as she entered adoles-cence and young adulthood, a product of her precocity and her adoption. A child prodigy, she skipped several grades, graduating from the Ypsilanti school system in 1924 at age sixteen. As a result of her multiple promotions, Jean had few friends her own age and became a loner. She also began to manifest behav-ioral problems in school and at home. In her senior year of high school, she was unable to turn in her final history project. Only a threat from the teacher to withhold Jean's diploma compelled her to hand in the assignment. Around this time, questions about her adoption, never answered satisfactorily by her adoptive mother, which had been gnawing silently at the back of Jean's mind, suddenly burst forth. Jean ran away one night "to find out who I am." Then, just as suddenly, Jean's restlessness about her birth origins went underground again when she came home the next day. Jean's erratic and errant behavior worried the family.

After her high school graduation, Jean chose to commute by trolley to the University of Michigan rather than live away from the family and attend Mount Holyoke College in Massachusetts, where she had been accepted. But by the end of the first year of college, "the old avoidance thing raised its head again." Jean found herself having trouble getting her papers in on time and unable to finish courses. As a result, Jean believed that her "social development . . . was retarded."[27]

Paton's parents decided that a change of environment might help. In 1926, eighteen-year-old Jean finally went off to Mount Holyoke College, but instead of performing better, she found herself "completely blocked, unable to attend classes." Paton lasted at Mount Holyoke only until Christmas. Jean returned home "terrified at the prospect of life ahead of me."[28] She remembered her time at the college there as "pure hell."[29] Her father got Jean a job in a local library, where she was content. But, of course, her college career had been interrupted. During the Christmas season, Jean received a card from Ann Young, her Mount Holyoke astronomy professor, encouraging her to make something of her life. Jean took to heart this advice from such an august authority figure. She "read everything in the *EncyBrit* in my home, never before having bothered with it," thus beginning her lifelong autodidacticism. She then proceeded to devour the nonfiction books at the library where she was employed, working her way through the disciplines of sociology, psychology, history, biography, and literature. (About all the reading she did at that time, she admitted later, "it's a little hard to believe, but it is the truth."[30]) But even as Jean voraciously devoured whole disciplines in her reading, she was emotionally miserable and had no understanding why.

Aware of his daughter's problems, Dr. Paton became persuaded that Jean needed to know more about her natal parents and began on his own to make inquiries about them. He asked a local minister to help, but when the minster got close to locating them, Thomas Paton ordered him to desist. Jean was of aware of her father's actions, including his calling off the search. She later characterized her family's failure to carry through on the search for her natal parents, especially her birth mother, as one of the "only two things that went wrong" with her life.[31] Thomas Paton's decision not to search profoundly alienated Jean from her father. She never mentioned him again in her correspondence, not even when he died, approximately twenty years later.[32]

Next year when Jean returned to Mount Holyoke, her resistance to going to classes and finishing assignments resurfaced. Instead of attending to her studies, Jean spent much time on the athletic field, playing baseball and soccer, captaining one or both teams. Counseling for her attendance problems failed, and Jean again dropped out of school.[33] Much later in life, with greater perspective, Paton characterized her difficulties at Mount Holyoke as those of a "bewildered adopted person" brought on by "inhibition of the normal growth of the brain, and failure of a strong sense of identity."[34]

With the financial support of her father, Jean made yet another try at college, heading for the University of Wisconsin in 1928 to study economics and sociology. But her difficulties followed her there. Again she found that her inner demons prevented her from engaging in the vigorous life of the mind that her professors demanded. In 1929, at the end of the academic year, she traveled to Pennsylvania to work at the Children's Aid Society of Philadelphia. This position was, Paton said later, "my port of entry into social work . . . after a miserable failure at college." Jean had just turned twenty-one, and she was "utterly inadequate to the task" of functioning as a social worker. She received quite a bit of help from Elizabeth DeSchweinitz, her first supervisor, who also broached the idea of therapy. When DeSchweinitz asked Jean if she could afford professional treatment, Jean lied and said no, thus postponing it, as she intended. After floundering as a social worker for several months, Jean decided to return to the University of Wisconsin. Three years later, in 1932 she received her bachelor's degree cum laude.[35] Looking back, Paton blamed the extraordinary length of time she spent at college on an unidentifiable "psychological blockage to get myself to classes," which resulted in her failing some courses.[36]

Paton had the bad luck of graduating from college in the midst of the Great Depression. With no jobs available, Paton did the only sensible thing: she returned to the University of Wisconsin for her master's degree. In graduate school, the "soft" side of the social sciences began to take second place; sociology no longer had pride of place. Instead, she concentrated on economics, with an emphasis on statistics.[37] When Paton finished her degree in 1933, there were still no jobs, but she managed to find employment at the university doing economic research in the Department of Rural Sociology. When that position ended in December 1934, the enterprising Paton kept herself afloat by working in a Madison hardware store as a bookkeeper.[38]

As the Depression deepened and President Franklin D. Roosevelt's New Deal created numerous federal agencies to deal with the nation's economic crisis, the demand for college-educated government workers increased steadily. In mid-1935, Jean's first real employment opportunity opened up. She left her bookkeeping job and went to Washington, D.C., to work for the federal government as a junior economist. During her first year in the nation's capital, Paton worked for the U.S. Labor Department's Bureau of Labor Statistics, and from 1936 to 1938 she worked for the U.S. National Labor Relations Board (NLRB)'s Research Division. Among her duties was writing research papers on labor relations that the NLRB lawyers used in arguing cases before the Supreme Court. Paton was extremely proud that in one of the Supreme Court's cases, *NLRB v. Jones & Laughlin Steel Co.* (1937), the judge writing the majority opinion used one of her phrases.[39]

Although war loomed in Europe and President Roosevelt wrestled with another downturn in the economy—the "Roosevelt recession" of 1937–1938—Paton took little interest in world or national politics. This is a trait that would never change. She rarely noted world or national events later in life except as they affected adoption reform. Instead, as Paton became increasingly unhappy with her life that year, she became preoccupied with two issues that would bedevil her for the next sixteen years: her career and her identity.[40] Recalling her discussion and the advice of Elizabeth McCord, her first supervisor at the Children's Aid Society of Philadelphia, Paton decided to go into therapy with Jessie Taft, who had been at the forefront of Progressive Era child reform and the professionalization of social work and who by the 1930s was one of the nation's most prominent female social workers. Taft would prove to be influential in Paton's life. Born in 1882 in Des Moines, Iowa, Taft grew up in a comfortable, middle-class home. In 1913 she became one of the first women to receive a doctorate from the University of Chicago, where she majored in psychology and philosophy. In 1934, after an impressive career working at a variety of top-level social work positions, she became a full-time faculty member at the School of Social Work at the University of Pennsylvania. By the time Taft arrived at the university she had been living with Virginia P. Robinson, a child educator and author, for five years, and they had adopted two children, a girl and a boy.[41]

Paton began a therapeutic relationship with Taft on a weekly basis at first. Sometime later, Paton underwent several weeks of intensive therapy with Taft, after she "almost broke down." Her memory of what took place in the therapy sessions was sketchy, but Paton did remember that she gave Taft a considerable amount of poetry and took up sculpture some years later on Taft's recommendation.[42] Paton also recalled that she "was scared stiff all the time." The buried secret and the unanswered questions, which had unconsciously consumed her off and on ever since her adoptive father had abandoned the search for her birth parents, continued to haunt her. Paton did not realize that this was the problem at the time. Taft did her best, but Paton thought her case hopeless and did "not think anybody could have reached me."[43]

Paton separated from Taft at the end of 1938, and on Taft's recommendation went to teach for one year at the Bank Street School in Greenwich Village, a center of progressive research on child development.[44] While at Bank Street, Paton saw Otto Rank, an Austrian psychoanalyst and one of Freud's closest colleagues for twenty years, for analysis three times.[45] Paton's short therapy sessions with Rank were efficacious. Almost twenty years later, she remembered him as being "very kind and generous to me in the days of my utmost bewilderment, and he helped me take a necessary step ahead."[46]

Influenced by Taft's prodigious intellect and the productive time she spent with the children at Bank Street, Paton began to sense that perhaps she should seek a career in social work. In 1939, she applied and was accepted as a student at the University of Pennsylvania School of Social Work.[47] Along with course work, Penn's School of Social Work prepared its future social workers with extensive training in fieldwork. For the first two years of her graduate study, Jean traveled by train to Richmond to work as a caseworker with foster children waiting for placement in adoptive homes at the Children's Home Society of Virginia. In the following academic year, 1941–1942, Jean worked for the Child Welfare Services of Mifflin County, Pennsylvania. In the very first article she ever wrote, published in *Survey Midmonthly*, the "bible" for two generations of social workers, Paton described her duties and the reasons for the successful meetings between herself, as a social work representative, and the three county commissioners, the political arm of Mifflin County.[48] In this short, dense article, in occasionally obscure language, written at the very beginning of her professional career, emerge several themes that would characterize Paton's intellectual thought, advice, and adoption reform activism for the rest of her life.

Paton recounted how she had brought before the three Mifflin County commissioners what she considered the region's most pressing child welfare issues. The commissioners' job was to approve or reject funding. Paton praised the method by which the commissioners went about this task, emphasizing their lack of a routinized course of action. In contrast to the rigidity of social work decision making, Paton declared, "there was no rigid order of procedure. The Commissioners had no folder, no list. One thing led to another." This resulted in much give and take in the discussion between Paton and the commissioners, which allowed trust to be built between the two parties; they realized they shared a common goal: the problems of child care and the preservation of the family. Paton then raised a question: how did the commissioners, elected by the people and focused on the immediate interests of their constituents—crop yields and taxes—cooperate with Paton, "an outsider and a professional appointee, none too close to most of the matters for which they were responsible?" Unity was possible, according to Paton, because the commissioners were "able to bring in their humanity, their practical wisdom, and their genuine concern for children." Paton found in the commissioners' humanity all the support she needed, which was far superior to "professional skill or any theory about what a child welfare program ought to be."

In fact, the county officials taught her many things—in particular, that child welfare services could not be considered separately from the larger community, that they were an integral part of it. Moreover, the county commissioners worked from a divided motivation. They acted out of a generous impulse to enrich the lives of children but also managed the community's misfortunes and administered an approximation of justice to citizens who misbehaved or, as Paton opaquely wrote, to "a portion also of its sin." The two motivations sometimes were contradictory, Paton noted, but any problems could be overcome if the officials' job performance were based "in the institutional fabric of the community, its moral judgments, its spontaneous desire to mitigate disaster, and its love of children." But such a humane, just approach to resolving community problems was a thing of the past. According to Paton, in the present day, social workers were inclined to "mete out the justice of God, by process of scientific method; to find disaster only an opportunity, or worse, a 'challenge to case work'; and to dilute our love for children by interpretation and diligent belaboring of their maladjustments." Nevertheless, Paton offered hope that if sound public officials—men drawn from "good family responsibility"—could be found to support a sensible child welfare program, the vices of present-day social work could be eliminated.

The target of Paton's article was professional social work policy and practice, particularly its reliance on casework and its claim to a scientific methodology. Here also in the article is a hint of the distrust that would eventually lead Paton to her belief that the social work establishment conspired to keep her research from being accepted and from finding a wider audience in the public; to her virulent dislike of psychoanalysis and anything that smacked of therapy; to her scorn for social work studies of adult adoptees conducted by experts who were not members of the adoption triad. Here, too, is an idealized, conservative vision of "the beloved community" as an organic entity whose citizens shared an emotional connection and where individuals' needs were fulfilled.[49] Paton would found Orphan Voyage and later the American Adoption Congress in a futile attempt to create a community based on these principles out of the population of adult adoptees who were searching for members of their original family. Finally, here, too, is evidence that embedded in Paton's innermost being was religion, a belief in the love of a Christian God, which manifested itself in language unbecoming a modern social worker: Paton writes of "sin" and "the justice of God." In this early article can be seen much of the mind-set that would later color Paton's understanding of adoption reunions.

2

The Birth of a Reformer

It seems possible that by getting some material from adopted people I might make an original contribution to the field.

—JEAN PATON, 1953

The overt rejection of professional social work would take another ten years. In 1945, Paton finally earned her MSW from the University of Pennsylvania's School of Social Work and qualified as a psychiatric social worker.[1] Two years later, she was employed at the New Hampshire Children's Aid Society.[2] During her year there, Paton made another meaningful decision that would have far-reaching consequences. Acting upon Taft's earlier suggestion to pursue artistic endeavors, Paton took lessons in sculpture from Maria Kostyshak, "a very interesting young woman of Russian extraction, a painter herself" at the Museum School in Manchester, and discovered that sculpture "was natural for me. It came like water flowing out of my hands."[3] From then on, creating art from clay became a lifelong passion, never a hobby; Paton's art work always serving the cause of adoption reform. After her time in New Hampshire, Paton took a job at the Department of Public Welfare in Baltimore, Maryland.

Paton's experiences as a social worker during the 1940s made a lifelong impression on her. It had always been clear to Paton that she "did not fully understand the emotions of the normal family," but during her time at the Philadelphia Child Guidance Clinic, she wrote Louise Whitfield, chief psychiatric social worker at South Carolina's Greenville Mental Health Clinic, she came to realize that her "best work was with persons whose families were 'fringe.'"[4] During four of those years, Paton focused on the identity needs of children in boarding care. She talked with the children about their past, their families, and the reasons why they had been separated from their parents. In every case, Paton recollected several decades later, the child was comforted, and "their presenting symptoms, as one says, cleared up."[5] Paton felt she knew how to talk to foster children. She "rejoiced," she wrote, "when I gave them enough background information to take a lot of the worry out of their faces." Her joy stemmed both from compassion for her young charges and from the "great happiness to find my place in the scheme of things."[6]

Late in life, Paton remembered an incident that took place during her work in New Hampshire with a four-year-old foster child who wet her bed. Each Thursday, Paton took the child to the visiting psychiatrist. After a few weeks the child quit the habit. The psychiatrist, realizing that the change in the girl's behavior had little to do with him and the brief time he had spent with her, asked Paton, "*What did you do?*" Paton instinctively understood that the child was worried about being separated from her parents and told the psychiatrist that she told the girl that she had a family and that "someday you will be in touch with them." Paton believed that "it helped her stop wetting the bed."[7] She also recounted another case, that of a foster child who, Paton discovered, had an aunt. She was determined that the little girl meet her aunt, even though the boarding mother objected to the idea. Paton won out and arranged the meeting; afterward the boarding mother confided to Paton, "I am glad she went. She is so much happier."[8] Such incidents reinforced Paton's belief that she had a special connection with foster children and orphans.

Arranging the surrender of infants from birth mothers, however, Paton found gut-wrenching; it made her miserable and filled her with guilt. She managed two of these surrenders during her years in social work, and she never forgot them, asserting that "the nature of that experience is a social death." One of the surrenders occurred at the New Hampshire Children's Home Society. The unmarried mother had freely relinquished her daughter. In Paton's office, after she had signed the papers, the mother asked her, "Would I ever know if anything happened to her?" Paton answered in the customary way, according to agency policy, which was to say, "No." As she recalled years later, however,

> The moment the words were out of my mouth, I said to myself, "What is going on here? We are playing funeral, and no one is dying." Perhaps if I said it out loud, my whole life would have been different, but as it is I have had to expiate keeping that understanding, that moment of insight to myself. But it has reassured me whenever there was any chance for doubt, that the total surrender is very wrong.[9]

Nearly fifty years later, Paton was still haunted by having taken a child from an unmarried woman, leaving her crying and grief-stricken and then sometime later seeing "the worker carrying the baby, she all smiles, to some potential adoptive couple. I realized the terrible contrast. Some things have stayed with me forever."[10]

It was Paton's experience with unmarried mothers, observing the stigma surrounding having a child out of wedlock, that formed the core of her study of adoption. The holistic approach to adoption that she eventually embraced—a family systems approach that included the entire adoption triad and her fierce opposition to the solutions later proposed by adoption reformers—can be explained by her single-minded, even obsessive, belief that the root of all the problems in adoption stemmed from society's condemnation of the unmarried woman and her child. It became the chief focus of her studies, dwarfing at times even adoption. As early as 1949, while she was at the Baltimore Department of Public Welfare, Paton sent an article on adoption to *Good Housekeeping* magazine. To the editor of the magazine, Paton presented herself as an expert based on her own personal experience, her professional knowledge from several years in child placement, and her observations "which I have made, maturely more interestedly, in unsought and unsuspected places."[11] This last comment, in Paton's typically private, oblique language, could only have given the editor pause. What in the world did this mean? No doubt, Paton was referring to the close relationships she established as a social worker when talking with foster children. It would not be the last time Paton's inexperience with an influential publications gatekeeper sabotaged her efforts to see her ideas in print.

Paton summarized the article she was offering for submission as addressing the question "What is the problem of the adult illegitimately-born?" Her answer was, "a lack of knowledge and contact with the natural parents."[12] In the article, which the editor promptly rejected,[13] Paton acknowledged that society had progressed from an older attitude toward illegitimacy, which consisted of "brutal unquestioning condemnation" of birth parents and their children. The modern viewpoint, she admitted, had mitigated to some degree the "pain and tragedy inherent in a countering of human mores." These mitigating factors appeared on "four fronts" and included increasing tolerance in those who sat in judgment of the illegitimate, modification of the stigma of illegitimacy through secrecy in public records, provision of a measure of counsel to birth mothers, and the placing of children in adoptive homes. But, asked Paton, cannot we do more? For "illegitimacy is an affront. The most wise and weathered of us cannot accept an act which places a human child outside the spontaneous protection of society. We must be without feeling, must be ourselves abstracted from society, if this violation of codes passes over us easily." For this reason, Paton believed adoption was a necessary institution and declared that it must not be denied to the child.[14]

But adoption in its present form, according to Paton, was still not the answer and had to be reformed. The plain fact was that children grew up and matured. "We are, by now, dealing with adults." Both birth parents and adult adoptees were returning to courts and adoption agencies seeking to find each other. Both institutions, she declared, were confused and made uncomfortable by such requests; in turn these adults, "because of the strains and difficulties of adoptive life, bear within themselves gross immaturities" and thus depended on adoption agencies to take responsibility for reuniting adult adoptees with their families of origin. Paton thought it neither possible nor right, however, that adoption agencies should engage in reunions. What was needed was a central point of clearance not connected to a court or agency, where birth parents and adult adoptees, at the age of twenty-five or older, could come and register the facts about themselves, together with a request that they be notified when both parties had registered and been matched. Her solution, although she did not label it as such, was in essence a voluntary mutual consent adoption registry. Paton also addressed the concerns of adoptive parents, assuring them that reunions would not destroy their relationship with their children; on the contrary, their basic insecurities would be assuaged.[15]

Almost simultaneously with her submission to *Good Housekeeping*, Paton wrote to the editor of *Mental Hygiene*, including a piece entitled "Adoption Comes of Age." It criticized an earlier article by Arthur L. Rautman that had implicitly justified contemporary adoption agencies' policies of withholding family information from adopted persons.[16] Paton's solution to the problem of interested parties accessing information was novel. For pragmatic and moral reasons, Paton absolved child-placing institutions from any responsibility for arranging meetings between adult adoptees and family members and did not envision enlisting public opinion in the cause of adoption reform. Because Paton was acutely sensitive to adoptees' powerlessness, she believed they must not appeal to social workers or public opinion for permission to search; they must take responsibility for their own lives, by creating an institution independent of traditional authorities to facilitate searches for parents, siblings, or, in the case of birth mothers, for the children they had relinquished. To that end, Paton called for a "central point of clearance," which would allow birth parents and adult adoptees to register identifying and nonidentifying information about themselves "together with a request that each be notified when both have registered and been matched."[17] This article was also rejected.

But her idea would not die. The next month, Paton wrote a letter to the editor of the *New York Times* denouncing the belief that adult adoptees and their birth mothers should remain "dead to one another" their entire lives. She modified slightly the proposal she had articulated for *Mental Hygiene* suggesting instead the central point of clearance could be adoption agencies, where adult adoptees and birth parents could "come and request being put in touch with each other."[18] Paton would soon establish the Life History Study Center to be that central point of clearance.

Before Paton opened the Life History Study Center, she would experience the most tumultuous three years of her life. Fortunately, she kept a weekly diary from January 1950 through September 1953, which reveals a woman oscillating between hope and despair, striving for self-improvement, and searching for happiness and self-esteem in the form of success: in her job, art, poetry, writing, and love life. Never again would Jean Paton express her innermost emotions so nakedly on paper.

When 1950 dawned, Paton had been out of work for two months, a period of time she termed a "job crisis."[19] With high hopes, she had applied for a position with the Family and Children's Society of Baltimore County, where she had been interviewed by the director and asked if she would like to do adoption work. She replied that she did not think it possible "as long as there is a sealed adoption record."[20] By the third week of January, Paton was becoming impatient to learn whether she had been hired. She finally heard from her prospective employer on January 28 with the news that she would start work on February 1. Paton found "considerable reassurance in being welcomed back to the fold." Yet she couldn't help expressing her ambivalence about social work: "May it sustain and not devigorate me." The following day, overwhelmed by the plethora of phone calls and "new faces and voices and personalities," her old habits kicked in, and all of her new hopes and plans became "vague like soup."[21]

While waiting, Paton filled the month with the kind of activities that would typically occupy her for the next several years. She revised a sculpture, *Burial of the Dead Self*, and completed another, *Wave Motion*; she wrote poetry; she regularly traveled to Philadelphia for socializing with her female friends; and she read incessantly, always seeking the possibility of making an original contribution to knowledge.[22] Paton also wrote extensively. Early in January, she dashed off another letter to the editor of the *New York Times*, ostensibly in defense of socialized medicine, but in reality a plea for socialized social welfare.[23] During much of what she called her "applied time," Paton worked on a major social work paper. Yet this consummate intellectual expressed ambivalence over intellectual work, and this indecisiveness made her impatient with getting on with her life. In general terms, her distress stemmed from the age-old existential question: what was she to do with her life? Paton was torn between the life of the mind and social work in the field, with real people. Referring to her paper, Paton wrote: "How absurd to expect a mere bit of writing to sustain a general life purpose but it must—something must. It is time I came upon a sustaining purposeful work and let it carry what has had heretofore to be in my own belly and my own immediate habitat."[24] Paton's life was also filled up with more trivial matters: caring for stray cats, chastising noisy neighbors, and attending successfully to what might have been a slight case of eczema on her right elbow.

Paton turned forty-one in December 1949, and between February and June 1950, she pursued life energetically. She had always been athletically inclined and though she ceased swimming and fencing, which she had earlier enjoyed, she continued biking.[25] Paton also found immense satisfaction in singing and was quite talented, even entertaining the idea of becoming a soprano soloist. She noted that an added incentive for singing was that it lessened her desire to smoke.[26] As she would for the rest of her life, Paton read at a frantic pace, devouring fiction and nonfiction books on a bewilderingly array of subjects, ranging from aesthetics, botany, and politics to history, anthropology, and psychoanalysis. On the latter topic, she became "immoderately irritated" at Helene Deutsch's two-volume *The Psychology of Women: A Psychoanalytic Interpretation* and pronounced it "terrible; psychiatric equals psyche-theatric."[27] Paton's apparently eclectic taste in recreational reading concealed the onset of a lifelong method of reading with a larger purpose in mind. For example, while reading Carl Van Doren's biography of Nathaniel Hawthorne, she discovered a definition of the skill required in interviewing clients in a passage Van Doren quoted from *The Scarlet Letter*. She concluded that Hawthorne knew so much about social work because he made "Art out of suppression."[28] Paton seldom read purely for pleasure; she would systematically extract useful information to advance the cause of adoption reform.

In mid-February 1950, Paton found that she was suddenly at peace with herself, which consisted of "mostly a feeling, a certainty of having stepped out into the world after a long amorphous condition." She continued, "Is this not what the forties can bring? Such extending happiness as I know is unusual." Paton was quick to explain that her happiness was not composed of "exultant moments," but "only brief excursions from an almost complacent course." The signs Paton enumerated were extremely modest, but of immense importance to such a self-conscious woman. She mentioned that her speech was slower, her words more expressive of herself; she was less guarded, more aware of others.[29] To her astonishment, a wave set had resulted in an unprecedented successful control of her hair.[30] Summing up her new disposition, she wrote, "I feel firmed up, realized, opened out, slightly fortyish, and through with fooling around."[31]

At least one significant event contributed to Paton's newfound state of mind. In January 1950 she met a woman named Dorothy Mattison in Philadelphia during a New Year's party and became infatuated with her.[32] Philadelphia was the nation's third largest city, and Cherry Street in the heart of Center City, where Paton lived, was the home of a substantial gay, lesbian, and multicultural population.[33] Contemporaries remember that lesbians rarely frequented gay bars. Instead, they went to parties. As gay activist "Mark Kendall" recounted, lesbians "had a very well-developed social network and they entertained in each other's homes."[34]

Gabriel Garcia Marquez warned his biographer that "Everyone has three lives, a public life, a private life, a secret life."[35] One of the very few secrets in Paton's life was her relationship with Mattison. Aside from June Schwantes, Paton's life companion of forty-plus years, Paton never mentioned another person with such emotion. Because of the risky and unorthodox nature of the relationship, Paton never committed to paper any identifying information about Mattison—she never mentioned her age, class, religion, likes or dislikes; aside from mentioning her last name once in the diary and her full name in the acknowledgments of her 1954 book *The Adopted Break Silence*, she referred to her simply as "DM" or, more commonly, simply as "D." Paton's recourse to secrecy is best explained by historian John D'Emilio: "In mid-twentieth-century America, homosexuals were well advised to keep their sexual preferences secret. Discovery virtually guaranteed that a man or woman would be ostracized by family and friends, denied most means of earning a decent living, and consigned to a marginal existence."[36] Lesbians were often sent to mental institutions.

We may never know whether it was love at first sight. But we do know that at their first encounter Paton was quite taken with Mattison. She found her "most stimulating, a creative person still much berserk and full of energy."[37] The use of the word "berserk" deserves comment. In the hundreds of thousands, perhaps millions, of words Paton wrote over a period of fifty years, she never used the word "berserk" again. I contend that the word signified to her the flash of connecting—in historian Martin Meeker's words, the "moment of emergence from the isolation and invisibility into which most who would later identify as homosexual or lesbian are born."[38] The point at which Paton recognized her own sexual preference for women was returned in the gaze of Dorothy Mattison. Certainly the strong emotion she felt toward Mattison was demonstrated immediately after Paton began her new job in February. She wrote letters to Dorothy and visited her several times in Philadelphia. After one of these weekend visits, Paton's uncharacteristically poetic entry for March 5 ended with a question decidedly unrelated to social work: "The chills and fevers of uncertainty, are they greater within or without the lover's arms."[39]

Paton's ardor went unacknowledged during the first three weeks of March, when Dorothy failed to phone or write. Anxiously, Paton noted that she "waited to hear from D and didn't."[40] In her despair, Paton acknowledged an inner strength she had not known she possessed: a part of herself that was "strong and well and can love."[41] The recognition of her capacity to love another person made her "feel younger, almost young."[42] Paton observed that Dorothy was having "a profound effect" on her. During those three weeks, she began to fantasize about Mattison, noting that she "sensed her so very present, in voice, manner and appearance."[43]

April marked a watershed in Paton's relationship with Mattison and in her life generally. After a weekend visit in late March, which Paton described as "living quietly surrounded by ghosts of passion," she visited Mattison again in the first week of April and returned home aglow "in happiness and relatedness," viewing everyone she met on the street as a potential friend.[44] The reason for this newfound happiness was Paton's decision "to risk giving and so received. What more can one ask of any week but that it shake the roots of an existence."[45] She counted it as the beginning of "the actuality of a new life."[46] A week later found Paton confused. She got down on her knees, perhaps in prayer, and "discovered it possible in myself not to demand fundamental security from another person."[47] But by April 18, Paton recorded that her fantasy life was growing the more she thought of the real events in her life. She was frequently overwhelmed by "the complete astonishment of being loved and wanted."[48] This feeling made a mockery of her old insecurity.

While Paton's relationship with Dorothy Mattison at the beginning of January sparked her happiness, continuing success in professional work and in her art strongly fueled it. While making progress on a major class paper, entitled "In the Circumstances of the Case,"[49] Paton also dashed off a manifesto, published in the May issue of *Social Casework*. In this letter she audaciously demanded that the profession stop producing countless social work articles that began "with a generalization and end with a case." She called for some sector of the profession or an individual member "discontented with the undefinitive forms in which these research projects have been presented" to have the architectonic vision to organize, edit, and describe the magnificent body of social work research that already existed to create definite forms, which in turn would provide a base for further research and possibly "a definition of the professional task."[50] Paton had circulated a copy of her letter before sending it off to the editor. Later, at a dinner held for alumni of the University of Pennsylvania's School of Social Work, where Jesse Taft and Virginia Robinson spoke, Paton received multiple congratulations for her *Social Casework* letter. Nevertheless, even in the face of these best wishes, Paton could not shake off her doubts about the importance of intellectual versus experiential knowledge. She wondered why "my writing has more value to [professionals] than my day to day work which supports me, and which seems more like real work all the time."[51]

Paton's duties as county administrator at the Baltimore Family and Children's Society had also emerged more clearly out of their earlier "obtrusives and uncertainties." In mid-March, while her supervisor, a Mrs. Blake, was on vacation, she eagerly anticipated defining a new, more favorable working relationship with her boss and asking for her own permanent office, where she could "express something contemporary and vital."[52] Paton was gratified in winning these concessions and felt "more respect from the rest of the staff." Her attitude toward her profession was also given a lift; she noted that she now "saw that social work is worthwhile as well as requiring something extra in the worker."[53] By April, she felt her job was "beginning to click."[54]

Paton continued to enjoy deep satisfaction from her sculpture and poetry. Weekly she cast a variety of clay figures ranging in skill from simple ashtrays to complex human forms. She wrote an illustrated do-it-yourself book on working with clay sculptures, and sent it off to a publisher while she thought about organizing a one-woman exhibition of her work.[55]

Paton had definite ideas about art and sculpture. In April 1950 she wrote a short letter to editor of the *Baltimore Evening Sun* denouncing modern artists who caused people "to feel bruised as if they had been pushed down the cellar stairs." Paton believed that "people have a right to ask of artists some encouragement in their lingering belief that life contains both beauty and intelligibility."[56] Paton's artistic values aligned with the 1930s imperative that art be socially responsible. Her letter to the editor expressed her negative response to the postwar development of abstract expressionism, which "found an increasing preoccupation with new concepts of form and space rather than the communication of meaning through familiar content."[57] For Paton, art was a tool for social and political change—in her case, adoption reform.

Paton's sense of well-being began to unwind in the spring of 1950. Between May and October 1950, her relationship with Dorothy Mattison ended fitfully and mysteriously. When Dorothy once again ceased communication during the first three weeks of May, Paton was desolate. On May 19, she wrote in her diary, "It is hard to keep myself on an even keel. Yet planning for myself is planning for us. What is she doing?"[58] The next day, Paton heard from Dorothy, but within a week Paton was dejected again. On June 4, she noted that "all last week was a terror—no ground, no clarity, no rightness, hard work, indecision except that it was a difficult week. I did not write to my love."[59] Over the next four months, Paton's diary remained silent about their relationship.[60] On October 10, when Paton next mentioned Mattison, the tone of her entry had greatly changed. She planned on spending the weekend in Philadelphia, and wrote that she "may or may not see Dorothy—and how she will appear to me after this intervention, or I to her, is anybody's guess."[61]

As her relationship with Mattison deteriorated, Paton's unhappiness with social work also increased, to the point where she decided to leave the profession. This was not an easy decision, and Paton came to it in fits and starts. In May and June, her activities still demonstrated a commitment to the profession. In May, she expressed satisfaction with her responsibilities at the Baltimore Family and Children's Society, where she used a functional approach to interviewing. She believed that such a technique got to the roots of a certain case work problem with significant results. She concluded, "From now on, so help me, there will be more of this new approach, and I hope plenty of chips will be falling."[62] The following month, Paton put pen to paper and vigorously defended the profession of social work. She had been prompted to do so when she took strong exception to the prominent sociologist Pitirim A. Sorokin's recently published book, *Altruistic Love: A Study of American Good Neighbors and Christian Saints*, which, along with several methodological shortcomings, she criticized as denigrating social workers. On June 26, she wrote Sorokin personally, declaring that she believed it "utter nonsense to exclude all the activities of this profession by the sweeping, uncomprehending judgment that we are all officious, cold, heartless, and formal—or if we are not so, our agencies make us so, despite our desire."[63]

Nevertheless, even as she passionately defended her profession, Paton began to show a few small signs of dissatisfaction with it. As she finished her first paper on the social work profession entitled "In the Circumstances of the Case," and submitted it to the editor of the *Social Work Journal*, she mused that she would rely less often on science and psychiatric statements because she had "believed for some time that total psychiatry [was] waning."[64] In the same week, after listing various Franklinian virtues to improve upon—"develop greater integrity, scrutinize use of time more carefully," increase frugality in budgetary matters, and more regularity in evening library visits—Paton inwardly rebelled and complained: "Why is it so necessary to program oneself?" The obsessiveness of watching herself so closely she likened to "constant hand washing in a sickly atmosphere."[65] The lack of money began to bother her, too. As a social worker, Paton had always lived on a shoestring budget. She now "looked at the dollars straight on" and decided that her lack of income was constricting her choices.[66] Paton recorded that her assets amounted to $734.47, with $322.00 in her checking account, but estimated that her balance after Christmas would be $475.00.[67] What alternatives were there? She contemplated leaving family social work after one more year, during which she would study community sources in the library. What then? Paton entertained the idea of a career teaching social work at a college located near a good graduate school in social work, anthropology, or sociology.[68]

During the summer of 1950 Paton neglected her diary, distracted by the Philadelphia heat, and focused on writing poetry. In the next four months, preoccupied with taking care of her adoptive mother and perhaps with the aftermath of her fractured relationship with Mattison, Paton wrote sporadically on such topics as the healing properties of sculpture and art therapy, the latter the result of working as an art therapy volunteer in the State Hospital in Catonsville, Maryland, the previous winter.[69]

In early April, Paton finally heard from David G. French, the editor of *Social Work Journal*, who rejected the manuscript.[70] French declared that he did not believe that Paton would find a market to publish her paper, for two reasons. The first problem was that it was "a highly personal document" in which Paton had presented "an integrated statement of the task of the social worker in an agency in relation to the client, agency, and society, as you see it." In an age of empirical social work research, French's criticism of Paton's paper being too "personal" had merit because, surprisingly for such a well-read person, she had not included a single footnote or referenced any authority in the field in the entire manuscript. His second criticism revolved around Paton's writing skills. French's strictures deserve to be quoted in full because they represent a fair assessment of Paton's writing style, a problem that would plague her the rest of her life and that explains why publishers later repeatedly rejected her book manuscripts and many readers did not understand what she self-published.

> The other thing is the rather unusual vocabulary you use in presenting your material. It is essentially poetic in its flavor, and the figures of speech demand a good deal of close attention on the part of the reader. The whole approach to your subject matter is so unique, furthermore, that you have had to devise expressions of your own which are *not* part of the everyday vocabulary of the social worker.

Paton was cursed with the agenda of a social scientist and the mind of a poet-philosopher, who invented neologisms to express her best reform ideas.

The end of the relationship with Mattison, the rejection of her long paper, and her growing dissatisfaction with social work coincided roughly with Paton's eventual decision on July 3, 1951—arrived at over a period of twelve hot and humid Philadelphia days—to leave her chosen profession and move to the field of social medicine, with an emphasis on research.[71] A month before, Paton had turned to Mary K. Bauman, an alumna of the University of Pennsylvania who ran the Personnel Research Bureau in Philadelphia, which guided its clients into training programs and jobs they were best suited for.[72] Paton initially sought out Bauman for help in finding "some new vocational direction, after an expanding sense that my present vocation of social work had lost significance for me."[73] She directly attributed her resolution to leave social work to anger at "having been so long and so deeply embedded in a crust of professional activity which contains errors."[74] But the "errors" that so angered Paton did not have anything to do with adoption policy or sealed adoption records. Instead, Paton's unhappiness with social work was an intellectual one, and it was not hers alone. The problematic nature of the profession dated back to 1915, when education reformer Abraham Flexner read his influential paper "Is Social Work a Profession?" before the National Conference of Charities and Correction and answered his own question in the negative.[75] In terms that echoed Flexner's criticism that social work failed to meet the criteria of a genuine profession because unlike other professions, such as medicine, law, and the ministry, she wrote, it appeared "not so much a definite field as an aspect of work in many fields." Paton lamented that social work was "a response to failures in other professions as much as a positive and continuing means to social cohesion."[76]

Bauman administered to Paton the Strong Vocational Interest Test for Women to measure and evaluate what careers fit her abilities, preferences, and interests and also her potential for additional education.[77] Paton achieved her highest scores in the categories of artist, dentist, laboratory technician, and physician. She recorded her lowest grades in the category of English teacher, social science teacher, YMCA secretary, life insurance saleswoman, buyer, housewife, elementary teacher, stenographer–secretary, business education teacher, and physical education teacher.[78] The career assessment test impressed Paton with its validity, and it gave her confidence that her mind, "despite poor vocational use, had remained healthy, and could be entrusted with long and difficult work."[79]

But Paton had already made up her mind that she would apply to graduate school at the University of Pennsylvania. She loved Philadelphia, where she "always felt most at home, and I still think of that as the place."[80] Her application was accepted but as she toured the campus and registered for classes she occasionally groaned aloud from embarrassment at her inability to feel any joy at leaving social work and beginning a new endeavor.[81] In her diary Paton re-corded the continuing struggle she was still working through, that of shifting from her motive to leave social work—its lack of an established intellectual and scientific core or skill—to finding "the true continuing motive," which was not simply her own self-development. For Paton, the fundamental question to be answered was a socially pragmatic one: "whether or not scientific knowledge can be beneficial, or even whether it has pertinence for human endeavors, which appear to be unsusceptible to science."[82]

On August 30, Paton announced to Mary Bauman that she had complet-ed her final day in social work. She thought it "resembled a 21st birthday" and "wanted some kind of ceremony." She also was gratified when a friend of hers, who earlier had raised objections to Paton's new program, came by and told Paton that she now thought that Paton was headed in the right direction. Paton concurred, and told Bauman that she had lost the feeling of confusion that had surrounded her; now she was simply perplexed by the intellectual challenges before her.[83]

By October 1951, Paton was enrolled in a graduate lab course in physiologi-cal chemistry, trudging up four flights of stairs twice a week to class, and dis-covering that she was so out of shape that she could hardly make it up to the top floor. As a consequence, Paton permanently quit smoking. She also took a seminar in the Sociology Department in social research.[84] She fretted over the perennial issue of all graduate students, finding a topic; as she put it, "Where the idea comes that starts a study is most obscure to me." But unlike many other students, Paton was concerned that because social research was such a nebulous discipline, even if one found a topic, it would be "quite removed from every day affairs and problems" and thus from policy. Paton was a thoroughgoing pragma-tist and reformer: knowledge had to be socially useful.[85]

As Thanksgiving approached, Paton felt dejected. The holiday was a family affair, which made her feel left out. As November drew to a close, her gloomy cast of mind spilled over into her seminar studies; she observed with the "great-est discouragement and disgust" that everything that was written about health turned out to be about sickness. Health statistics especially disappointed Paton because they did not "reveal much beyond common sense or what superficial acquaintance with health laws or policy statements would reveal."[86] She was focused on health studies because for her seminar topic Paton had chosen to re-search nutrition studies. In the evenings, she went off to one her favorite haunts, the Philadelphia Public Library's periodicals room, where she read intensely on the subject. She concluded that health personnel functioned in a cold, imper-sonal manner. As the project neared completion, Paton's disenchantment with her course of study increased. Her research confirmed to her that home econo-mists were more concerned with the science of their subject—CHO, fats, and proteins—than with the social and human side—food habits and preventive methods of keeping healthy. Thus, Paton was confronted by the same intellec-tual problem that was bedeviling her since she left social work, though she now framed it in a different way. She asked in despair, "How can social scientists have anything of importance to say, when emerging social problems so urgently place themselves within the body and are, thus, under the authority of the medical man, and/or the psychiatrist." Paton concluded that all the sociologist could hope for was to work in a subordinate position on a team of researchers until sometime in the future, when "he presents his own organization and knowl-edge." Still, Paton held out a modicum of hope for herself: it might be possible that "there are obvious errors and failure (and perhaps successes) that are not entirely under the sway of the established biological disciplines." Ever the real-ist, however, she noted that locating them was like hunting for a treasure with a dowsing rod.[87]

As 1952 began, Paton glimpsed a solution to the problem of uniting the dis-ciplines of biology and sociology, which greatly excited her. In early February, during her second semester at Penn, she enrolled in two courses: genetics and animal distribution—the geographic distribution of animal life on the Earth, the study of which is called zoogeography. In one her classes discussing mos-quitoes, "of all places," Paton experienced "the most original idea I ever had!" The professor had assigned the class the task of what Paton called "a simple translation," which was to "take the idea of taxonomy, and see its usefulness in biological science, its penetration into all areas of theoretical growth, and com-prehension, also just plain communication help" and apply it to people. Such an exercise was calculated to result in a taxonomy of the human species. Paton quickly "drew up seven sub-species, which about covers it. And I can see how they merge and differentiate, how they are formed and changed; and many fruit-ful possibilities lie in their development."[88]

Her professors were not impressed with Paton's "most original idea." She observed that both the botany and zoology departments thought her exotic and "were a little astonished to have a social worker" in their midst.[89] Nevertheless, Paton was impatient for recognition and felt "science" was too rigid in accept-ing her new thoughts. She looked outside Penn for like-minded colleagues and support for her ideas. In early February, Paton traveled to Wagner College on Staten Island, New York, to attended a lecture by botany professor William Sei-fritz. In a subsequent letter, she used his presentation of two slime molds to il-lustrate the relationship between them and her theory "of stages in development of human character."[90] Seifritz was enthusiastic and encouraging. In response to her idea of the interdisciplinary nature of social work and science, he remarked, "This is just how I, too, feel about it. The chemists won't listen and the philosophers dream. You are the intelligent in-between one."[91] Paton considered this letter "rather special, as I remembered it quite well, and did not want it to disappear."[92] Throughout the semester, she continued to write to academics outside of the University of Pennsylvania for support of her original idea.[93]

With the onset of summer, Paton's "personal business in Michigan" began to take on a significance that would change her life. Beginning in September 1950, she had been "summoned to Michigan by the clear inability to wash my hands of mother and her property," and the necessity of caring for her. She began commuting regularly by plane to Michigan, and assumed the role of nurse, doctor, and housekeeper.[94] The irritation clearly detectable in her tone combined with the responsibilities of a dutiful daughter, characterized the complicated relationship Paton had with her adoptive mother. She was deeply grateful for the cover story her mother had put out to the community while she was growing up that her natal parents "were splendid folks,"[95] because "it surely protected me from the breath of the Stigma" [of illegitimacy].[96] As a result, it instilled in Paton a respect and admiration for her natal parents, a lesson she never forgot. But aside from this positive element of her adoptive experience, in later years, she rarely mentioned her adoptive mother, and when she did, it was never in affectionate terms. To one correspondent, the best she could say was that Mary Paton "was not a cruel woman, just an unhappy one."[97] To another, Paton wrote that she "ran away from [her] mother's domination, which I could not deal with directly."[98]

In late 1950, Mary Paton died, and her will, or lack of one, presented problems. No contemporary evidence survives that provides clear information about the will. A hint of the trouble brewing, however, can be glimpsed in a letter Paton wrote to Bauman in May 1952, mentioning that Paton's late April visit to Ypsilanti had been unpleasant. In her typically convoluted syntax, Paton told Bauman that it was "a new experience to have enemies; of all that life has conveyed, that never came before. Presumable the possibility of inheritance often does just that."[99] At the time Paton wrote this, in the early 1950s, thirty-six of the forty-eight states, including Michigan, allowed adult adoptees the right to inherit from their adoptive parents if they died intestate; but even where the law gave the adult adoptee the right to inherit from the adopter, sometimes unscrupulous or greedy relatives contested the will on the basis that the adult adoptee was not a blood relative and thus had no standing in law.[100]

Something like this happened to Paton. In her letter to Bauman, she was referring to distant relatives of Mary Paton, who had moved to California expecting to inherit from Paton's mother's estate. When they discovered they would not, they threatened to sue. Paton believed that even if she prevailed at law the case would be appealed, so she was not counting on being provided for in the near future. Eventually, as time for the suit approached, it was settled out of court, probably in January 1953—though exactly when the case was settled is not clear.[101] Paton was awarded $40,000, principally in stocks and some bonds (equivalent to $321,948 in current dollars); at the time the case was settled the median annual income for a female householder without a spouse was $2,455.[102]

Paton failed to mention or minimized the role her adoptive mother's inheritance played in allowing her to pursue her life's vocation of adoption reform, but future events suggest otherwise. In January 1953, when it appeared certain that she would inherit from her adoptive mother, Paton gave notice to her summer job at the Pennsylvania Association for the Blind at Bethlehem that she was quitting, began house-hunting in Philadelphia, and went back to Penn to continue her education.[103] She enrolled in an anthropology class, a prehistory course, and perhaps a linguistics or genetics class.[104] Being the autodidact that she was, Paton also enrolled in a mathematics refresher course by correspondence with Edmund C. Berkeley and Associates Consulting Services and revived her German language skills in order to read German anthropologist Ilse Schwidetzky's most recent book.[105] In early March, Paton moved into her new house—which cost around $5,000—in Center City, at 222 North Hicks Street in Philadelphia.[106] Her indecision about branching off into adoption reform was evident as late as August 1953, when she wrote to Columbia University's co-chairman, Professor Goodwin Watson, expressing an interest in enrolling in its new doctoral program in social psychology and relating her educational qualifications in detail.[107]

But at the same time that Paton was applying to graduate school—the summer of 1953—she was writing to her Mount Holyoke friend Mary McConaughy the thought that "a study of adopted adulthood might be possible, and that I would try."[108] Paton repeated this claim throughout her life, and it was consistent with her desire, especially strong at the start of her adoption reform career, to be recognized as an intellectual. As she reported fifteen years later in *Orphan Voyage*, Paton had said to McConaughy, "It seems possible that by getting some material from adopted people I might make an original contribution to the field."[109] But she was also deeply discontented with several aspects of adoption practice, and this is what drove her to begin her experiment as a pioneer in adoption reform. In 1955, responding to a direct question from one of her correspondents, Paton declared that the "immediate reason" for entering into the business of reforming American adoption was because she was "getting fed up with all the 'chosen child' talk," which seemed to her "a roundabout way of telling a child that he is loved."[110] Paton did not believe that a child needed a special vocabulary about this topic, and more to the point, "the fact that he is 'chosen' will not look so lovely when he is older." In addition, Paton was concerned with the increasing closure of adoption records and her dislike of that effort by adoption agencies to match the child and adoptive parents "to such a degree of perfection that they might as well as be of natural relationship." A final motive for her decision to enter into reforming the practice of adoption was personal. Paton resented that "nobody took me seriously about my curiosity about my natural family, nor [thought] it worth looking into."[111] The result of Paton's intellectual ambition, reformist impulse, and private dissatisfaction was the Life History Study Center, the first self-help institution dedicated to reforming American adoption.

3

The Life History Study Center

The Life History Study Center is an experiment in communication. It is not an agency. It is a sort of agglutination of aliveness among people who are restive within adoption.

—JEAN PATON, 1955

On August 24, 1953, Jean Paton placed a four-by-six-inch brass signplate on her front door, ordered business cards, and sent out publicity material announcing the start of the Life History Study Center, which she stored on the third floor of her home.[1] Over the years, Paton gave several reasons why she chose this name for the first organization devoted to adult adoptees. In 1968, in her book *Orphan Voyage*, Paton related that on April 28, 1953, on a ten-day train and bus trip to Florida, she jotted down the name "Life History Study Center" on some brief notes, which later formed "the roots of a conscious plan toward a project by which I hoped the many threads of my life might be gathered together."[2] Thirteen years later, Paton told adoption activist Sandy Musser that she had used the term "Life History" because it was the one unifying concept in all the science courses she had taken at the University of Pennsylvania.[3] But probably the most accurate reason was one Paton gave in the opening pages of her path-breaking first book, *The Adopted Break Silence*, written shortly after the Center opened. There, she wrote that she selected the name to emphasize "the view that adoption—among other human institutions—is a process which influences an individual life for many years beyond its initiation," a novel idea in the 1950s.[4]

From the start, Paton viewed the study of adult adoptees and the Center as inextricably tied together. In the first three-panel leaflet Paton produced for the organization, she stated a foundational and radical concept for her interest in the adult adoptee. She declared that "the time has come for us to stop thinking of adoption in terms of infancy and childhood only, and to recognize and take into account the adulthood and special problems of this group of people." A corollary to this idea, one also unique to Paton, was that family systems theory (she would have blanched at the term) was the best approach to take in understanding the "special problems" of the adult adoptee. Such a theory postulates that individuals in the family cannot be understood in isolation from another—in other words, families are systems of interconnected and interdependent individuals, none of whom can be understood in isolation from the system. Although Paton never stated her approach as formally as that, she made it clear in her leaflet that her efforts to understand the adult adoptee were not confined to that single group but also included the other members of the adoption triad: the adoptee, "a first parent [and] an adoptive parent."[5]

Paton's method to study the problems of the adult adoptee, the leaflet stated, would be to use the existing population of adult adoptees and learn from them about their experiences and present attitudes. To this end, Paton announced that notices were being placed in magazines asking interested parties to respond. Those who replied would be sent a questionnaire, with the data resulting from the surveys to be used for broader research projects and for "consultation in adoption life situations." True to her principles, Paton anticipated that her research would not end with the publication of her study, but that her research would be grounds for helping her "subjects." Further evidence of this goal was Paton's pledge to create a voluntary mutual consent adoption registry, an idea she had suggested as early as 1949. She pledged to study "the practicality and need of a central registration service to provide communication between natal parents and their adopted adult children, when mutually desired."[6]

Paton wasted no time in beginning the research project that would become her pathbreaking book, *The Adopted Break Silence*. In August, after inquiring about the rates, Paton placed the following notice in the *Saturday Review of Literature* classified advertisements (Personals): "WERE YOU ADOPTED before 1932? Your experience may assist research in adoption from point of view of experienced adult. For details write: LIFE HISTORY STUDY CENTER, 222 N. Hicks St., Philadelphia 2, Pa."[7] The ad ran for seven weeks between September 19 and November 14, 1953.[8]

Paton then set about preparing the groundwork for the research report. Her Penn class in social research proved quite useful in this endeavor. She first developed, in "an afternoon of intense concentration," a five-page questionnaire that probed not only the factual information about adult adoptees—date of birth, place of birth, sex, race, date of adoption—but also more controversial subjects, such as their attitudes toward their first parents and adoptive parents.[9] Paton's instructions on the questionnaire were expansive and encouraging. She urged the respondents to write in their own prose style, to use their own ideas, and to elaborate at length on any point, even if it was not specifically asked on the questionnaire. Moreover, Paton removed the customary distance between researcher and subject by providing them with an incentive to participate openly. She reminded them that "your answers are pioneering ones; that previous adoption studies have rested primarily on the attitudes of others than adoptees." Paton wanted to infuse her respondents with the same energy and importance that she felt for asserting adult adoptees' voice in their own affairs.[10]

The Life History Study Center questionnaire promised respondents that their answers and identities would remain confidential. Although adult adoptees were not in danger of losing their job or being arrested, as homosexuals experienced, the revelation of adoption status in the 1950s carried enormous stigma and concomitant guilt and shame for all members of the adoption triad: adopted persons for their purported illegitimacy, birth mothers for giving birth out of wedlock and their failure to live up to the ideal of motherhood, and adoptive parents for their infertility. Paton assured her respondents that "strict anonymity is being safeguarded in the writing." She further promised that she had "taken every possible care to . . . not [reveal] your identities. Names have been removed from the questionnaires and replaced by numbers. When the report is issued, the name-number cards will be placed in a safe-deposit box in the name of the Life History Study Center."[11] Even these pledges of confidentiality failed to soothe the fears of some adopted people. One person declined to complete the questionnaire, stating that in her personal circumstance it was more important to be discreet. Nevertheless, she assured Paton that "there exists no doubt in my mind that your project is a valid and honest one, and I am sure your personal and professional integrity is without question."[12]

While Paton developed her questionnaire, she moved rapidly to mechanize the arduous program of the central registration service, the Reunion File. On September 30, Paton wrote to Remington Rand, one of the nation's biggest makers of information processing technology, and requested a meeting with its System Consultation Service to discuss help for adult adoptees and their original parents "by means of a central registration service." Specifically, she wanted to know if the company could guarantee confidentiality for the participants and, once the system was operating, whether it would be easy to match up a large number of registrants.[13] Paton also began outlining the specifications for her registration service, which would consist of an announcement, the creation of an information sheet and reply form, the registration application itself, and an acknowledgment form from Paton.[14]

Paton was astute and relentless in creating or finding opportunities to pub-licize her work. Initially, on behalf of the adoption reform project, she relied on her social work background to influence a professional audience and gain legitimacy for her Center. Reaching out to her old social work contacts, Paton approached Helen Hubbell, head of Pennsylvania's Rural Child Welfare orga-nization, where Paton had worked for a year, and sent her some Life History Study Center leaflets, which Hubbell distributed among her staff.[15] In the same vein, Paton wrote Margaret Wagenhals, assistant editor of *Mental Hygiene*, re-minding her that they had corresponded in 1949 and 1950, when Wagenhals had rejected Paton's critical review of Arthur L. Rautman's article on adoption. She now asked if Wagenhals might be more favorable to publishing a similar article now that she was engaged in a new situation.[16] But Paton also sought out fresh avenues of publicity: she wrote to the editor of the *Saturday Evening Post*, describing her new adoption project and requesting an interview to discuss the possibility of the magazine's publishing an article on the Life History Study Center, with its focus on adult adoptees. She assured him that the subject had never been discussed before, yet the issue was increasingly popular, "due to the fact that adopted babies are growing up, there are more of them each passing year, and enough of them are distressed about their problems."[17]

Paton also publicized the work of the Center by communicating directly with adult adoptees who responded to the *Saturday Review of Literature* ads. Paton treated the respondents as stakeholders, not subjects or clients, to whom she had a responsibility to report on the progress of the study. More than that, Paton conceived of adopted people not just as a minority group but as a unique community of like-minded individuals with whom she strongly identified. She took her respondents into her confidence and treated them as equals; together they would struggle against a hostile, unadopted world. Through her periodic writings, which she first called "Notices," then "Releases," and which later would evolve into her newsletter, *The LOG of Orphan Voyage*, Paton raised the con-sciousness of adult adoptees while at the same time kept them updated about the Center's activities and her own personal life. Instinctively, before the digital age, Paton created the role of blogger.

On November 15, Paton mailed a progress report to those adopted people who had responded to the initial September ad in the *Saturday Review of Lit-erature*, because she "thought some contact between us might be good." The four paragraphs of the report created a sense that the Center was the hub of impor-tant activities and that the adopted community had a vital stake in contributing to its success. Paton related that she recently traveled to Washington, D.C., and discovered that the Center had already come to the attention of people in the social work field, including the U.S. Children's Bureau. State agencies, such as the Pennsylvania Welfare Department, also showed an interest in the Center, though cautiously. In addition, Paton herself was contacting state civic groups, public relations individuals, and a freelance writer. She also hoped to see in person, either at the Center or in their homes, those adopted persons who were within traveling distance. She concluded by assuring her readers that their "vital and important materials" would someday amount to something.[18]

Paton wrote again to her adoption community on Thanksgiving Day, thankful that she was "not wrong in my guess that you existed and you would respond if I called out." This second report updated her readers on the progress that had been made. Paton had received sixty replies from all over the United States, including an adoptive parent and four adoption agencies. She promised to begin reading their questionnaires in mid-December and then write the study. Breaking down the barrier between researcher and subject, she requested that "if you can think of some form of encouragement, send it. It will be needed." Turning to the central registration service, Paton informed her respondents that it was still in the "prospectus state." To gain experiential knowledge of the process, she was personally contacting the persons she believed were her birth parents. Paton drily commented afterward that "this will keep me forever from saying to any applicant for Registration Service that it is easy to do." She had decided on the registration system after gaining absolutely no acceptance from the established, respected, unadopted people she had confided in. Yet to her, it seemed to be "the only answer to much unfinished adoption business." She closed the report by first praising the respondents' courage in taking part in the study and then asking them to send her any new thoughts they may have had, reminding them "that the work is only started." She asked, "What do you plan to do about adoption? Are you aware of the adopted around you? And do you have anything for them? If so, maybe I can help you do it, as you have helped me."[19]

As Paton admitted, she did not meet with much success from people who were not adopted. Nothing came of her plans to use her social work contacts to establish a base within an institutional setting. She ruefully noted to a correspondent that if she could solve the problems of adult adoptees in such a manner, she would never have left social work. Consequently, instead of establishing "a regular project," Paton would continue "on the wildcatting basis."[20] The *Mental Hygiene* editor, Wagenhals, wrote back to say that she remembered Paton but did not encourage her to resubmit her article.[21] Similarly, within four days of submitting her materials, Paton received a rejection letter from the *Saturday Evening Post.*[22] Undaunted, Paton immediately wrote to the editor of the *Ladies Home Journal*, offering an article on the adoption project underway at the Life

History Study Center, again with the same result. The editor replied frankly that the article did not "sound like Journal material, and we regretfully cannot be hopeful." She suggested that Paton "submit the completed manuscript to a magazine more in a market for such a piece."[23]

It is not surprising that Paton's proposal for an article about the reunion of adult adoptees with their first parents did not appeal to the editors of popular magazines. Such a piece boldly challenged the bias in American culture on pronatalism and adoption. During the 1950s baby boom, popular magazines such as the *Saturday Evening Post* published optimistic, upbeat articles illustrated with smiling family members, with titles such as "We Like Lots of Children," "We Want Her for Always," and "We Adopted a Daughter."[24] The articles targeted female readers and celebrated the altruism of adoptive parents, the happiness that a child brought to the family, and the safety of adoption.[25] With the new emphasis on secrecy in adoption, coupled with the psychoanalytic diagnosis that unmarried mothers were neurotic at best or pathologic at worse, the last thing potential adoptive parents wanted to hear was that adopted children would grow up to search for their original families. Moreover, Paton explained that the Life History Study Center's mission was to reach out to the adult adoptee and adoptive parent and to learn from them "the consequences of this special culture of having four parents, the two sets being separated quite rigidly."[26]

Paton's conceptualizing adopted persons as a "special culture," or minority group, was similar to that of the gay emancipation movement taking place simultaneously in Los Angeles, where gay activists were struggling to convince society that homosexuals were a minority group based on their sexual behavior, rather than a problem of individuals characterized by moral weakness, sin, or pathology. But while gay activists sought to persuade the general public that homosexuals were moral, upstanding, and psychologically healthy citizens, Paton's goal was the opposite: to convince people that popular magazines' projection of happy adopted children was inaccurate and to assert that adoptees grew up to become deeply troubled adults.[27] Against America's strong cultural belief in pronatalism and adoption, it is not surprising that Paton's article was repeatedly rejected.

Paton also had little success, though for different reasons, when she next turned to several major New York book publishers in an effort to have her study of adoption research published so she could reach a popular audience. Here, at least theoretically, she had a better chance of success because the number of serious books, as opposed to articles, about adoption one could count on one hand. But Paton's inexperience in the world of commercial publishing was evident when she first approached Charles Scribner's Sons. In lieu of a customary book prospectus, she send the Press a vague cover letter; the Life History Study Center leaflet; and a thirty-page, double-spaced poem entitled *The Adopted.*[28] Within two weeks, Paton received a polite rejection letter from Scribner's.[29] Less than a month later, on December 4, Paton repeated her mistake, sending a poem instead of a book prospectus to the Macmillan Company, with the same results.[30] At this point, rejected by two major commercial publishers, Paton gave up and decided to self-publish. She wrote to a printer and on December 16 received an estimate of $407 for 500 copies and $537 for 1,000 copies for printing a book of seventy-two pages.[31] For the rest of her life, with ever-growing resentment, Paton never mastered the art of the book submission.

Paton made another effort to publicize her work through a Hollywood celebrity, Art Linkletter, who at the time was the western chairman of the Adopt-a-Child Program, which was involved in caring for international orphans in their own countries.[32] An autobiographical article in the December 1953 *Woman's Home Companion* revealed that the Canadian-born Linkletter, who had risen from poverty to riches, was adopted. However, his parents had concealed his adoption from him, and his discovery of the truth from some old letters traumatized him. He also stated in the article that he knew who his "real parents" were and they knew him, "and we respect each other and say nothing."[33] Linkletter's primary message in the article was "never lie to a child," especially if he is adopted.[34]

Even though Paton's views differed in certain respects from Linkletter's— most notably in his reluctance to contact his natal parents—Paton wrote Linkletter hoping that he would be interested in the Life History Study Center material she had enclosed. She appealed to him as one adopted person to another, hoping that he might respond to her concern that adoption procedures had been shaped only by the unadopted. She told Linkletter that she would be pleased to receive anything he might want to write.[35] There is no record that he ever replied.[36]

By the time Paton attempted to publicize her project, she had a clear idea of the methodology she would use in the study of *The Adopted Break Silence.* A hint of her method can be gleaned from the subheading printed on the Life History Study Center's letterhead, "Research in Life History, and in Art-Science Therapy." Paton's explicit resistance to social science objectivity was spelled out in a month-long correspondence she had with the then little-known H. David Kirk. A Canadian sociologist, Kirk later wrote a groundbreaking book, *Shared Fate: A Theory of Adoption and Mental Health,* which described the way adoptive parents coped with their "role handicap," a phrase he used to describe the difficulties inherent in raising adopted children.[37] At the time of his correspondence with Paton, Kirk had recently completed his dissertation at Cornell University and was an instructor in social science at State Teachers College, part of the state university system of New York. He wrote Paton on September 16, 1953, stating that someone had brought to his attention her *Saturday Review of Literature* advertisement in the "Personals" section, and informing her that he had just completed a two-year study of "community values and beliefs which impinge on members of adoptive families." His next study, he wrote, would involve the gathering of life history data. Kirk wondered, in light of their shared interests and efforts, if they could collaborate or at least mutually supplement each other's work. Obviously curious, he politely asked to receive additional information about the nature of Paton's research.[38]

Five days later, Paton sent Kirk both her preprinted form letter and the questionnaire, which she realized would reveal her flawed methodology. Defiantly, she wrote, "I am making no effort to be statistically valid, and insert a note of bias from the beginning." She believed that the value of her study was in something she called its "pre-pilot" quality, "its way of reaching people, its enlisting their initiative, and its complete flexibility to develop along the lines indicated by their responses." Paton must have known that another name for her "pre-pilot" methodology was a self-selected sample, for she acknowledged that it could not be amalgamated with "the sort of thing that fellowships are granted for," referring to Kirk's mention that he had received a grant for his study from the U.S. Public Health Service. She held out the hope that she was wrong, and deferred to his experience, mentioning that she had already received three replies to the *Saturday Review of Literature* advertisement. Paton was confident that there were a great many more people who would write her, and that "their wise, adult attitudes will express something very important in this field."[39]

Kirk responded by proposing that they meet to discuss their mutual interest in adoption.[40] On September 29, Paton replied. She expressed a desire to read Kirk's paper, but she was not interested in a meeting. Paton believed that their approach to the subject was incompatible. As she put it, "the legitimate want to put aside the flesh; the bastard-adopted want to put it on! The service I want to build may implement the latter. The former seems quite impossible!"[41] From the very beginning of her adoption reform activities, Paton drew a sharp distinction between the ability of those who were legitimately born to conduct adoption research and those born out of wedlock and adopted, believing that the former were inherently incapable of researching the adopted population.

Kirk did not respond for two months to Paton's rebuff, though it was not because he took offense at her assertion that the legitimately born were inherently unqualified to conduct adoption research; rather, his job as a lowly instructor kept him so swamped that he barely had time for research. When he finally replied in early December, he made every effort to overcome her skepticism "about the feasibility of some cooperative research activity on our part." He strongly disputed that her goals were different from his. He expertly translated Paton's almost biblical pronouncements as the "wish to be of service primarily to adoptees who are in search of their identity and natural family connections, as well as to make discoveries about the particular kinds of experience which such persons have as adults." Kirk then presented the purpose of his research, which he defended by stating that although they appeared to be organized primarily around social theory, they were also policy oriented, designed "to serve the welfare of adopters and adoptees." He again earnestly pressed Paton to meet with him about adoption issues, suggesting that by virtue of their "different training and personal experience we would each have considerable to give the other."[42]

Paton, in her response, grudgingly acknowledged that each of them could influence the other's work and finally agreed to meet. She then launched into an extended defense of her methodology and the motivation for her study. Paton informed Kirk that she had "a serious background in the social sciences and social research, with much mathematics at one time or another," and thus was fully aware of her faulty methodological approach. She explained that her questionnaire was drawn up very quickly, "out of the high points of my own personal experience, with readings from my years in child placing." This grounding in her own experience had proven useful. Paton had been glad to discover that all her respondents shared her personal experiences. Furthermore, she told Kirk candidly, her motivation was "not to study per se, but in all that I do to help release the energies bound up in adopted people because of irresolution and non-integration of the double parentage." She hoped that by keeping her procedures close to modern currents in adoption research, she would not go "too far off base." She was confident, moreover, from the benefits she witnessed from her "straight-dealing" with children about their origins, that adults would profit also.[43] Paton's reliance on her own adoption, reunion, and social work experience, interwoven occasionally with her vast book knowledge, was characteristic of the advice she provided for the rest of her life to triad members and adoption reformers.

Paton expressed sympathy as well for "the genuine adoptive parent," who, she stated, was neither responsible for the problem nor able to cure it. Instead, Paton believed a completely new definition of the institution of adoption was needed.[44] In a subsequent letter responding to Kirk's request that she elaborate, Paton explained that a new definition of adoption would entail "making it possible for all four parents to have co-existence."[45] For this to happen, a major change in the attitudes of adoptive parents would have to take place; specifically, they had to believe in the existence of their children's natal parents and convey this information to their adopted children, in accord with their wisdom and emotional maturity. However, Paton noted, adoptive parents were handicapped in this goal by the failure of social workers to provide them with adequate information. This is why her "Registration Service" was necessary—not, as some might think, as an assault upon adoptive parents, but for the greater integration of adopted persons, who, she believed, lacked it. Not wanting Kirk to suppose that she was labeling adult adoptees psychologically damaged, she quickly added that although adopted persons lacked familial integration, they "none the less form a courageous and compassionate group of people" whom she regarded most highly and counted herself among their number.[46] The correspondence with Kirk reveals many of the intellectual tendencies and personality traits that would be repeated throughout Paton's career: an unscientific methodology based primarily on personal experience, a lone-wolf attitude toward collaboration with others coupled with a possessiveness of her original ideas, a fervent belief that adopted people were psychologically damaged by the closed system of adoption, and a propensity to romanticize the inherent qualities of orphans and adopted people.

After corresponding with Kirk, Paton sat down to write *The Adopted Break Silence*.[47] By March 1954, she had completed the introduction and the first two chapters and anticipated that the publication would be ready for sale by midspring.[48] Like many other authors, however, she was overly optimistic about her timetable: she was still writing in late July, revising in August, and reading galley proof in October.[49] The book went on sale on November 10. Still, it was a remarkable feat.

What Paton had once been envisioned as a pamphlet had turned into a pathbreaking 180-page book. *The Adopted Break Silence* presented adult adoptees speaking in their own voices, accompanied by the extensive analysis of an adopted person. Before Paton, there had been many books about adopted babies, especially around the theme of the "chosen" baby,[50] but only a few books by adult adoptees, and these were autobiographical works, such as Carol Prentice's *An Adopted Child Looks at Adoption* and Eleanor Gallagher's *The Adopted Child*.[51] Paton deliberately eschewed writing an autobiography because she had previously attempted to convey her ideas about what she believed to be undesirable aspects in adoption policy—the growth of secrecy in adoption records, the failure to recognize the existence of adult adoptees, and the erasure of birth parents from the memory of the adoptive family—and discovered that unadopted people viewed her beliefs as a product of her own personality development, with no broader application. Paton knew this was inaccurate but realized that she could never demonstrate the universal truth of her beliefs by writing an autobiography.[52]

The first sentence of *The Adopted Break Silence* explained the book's title and purpose: "Everyone except the adopted has been talking about adoption."[53] The preface then set forth one of the most important tenets of Paton's outlook on adoption reform: only birth parents and adult adoptees could solve their own problems. This rock-solid belief, from which Paton never deviated, was the natural corollary to Paton's essentialist view that only adopted persons were capable of researching accurately the adoption community. It would turn her into a ferocious critic of social workers, confidential intermediaries, and, eventually, even the American Adoption Congress. Paton arrived at this belief from generalizing about the way unadopted people refused to accept as worthwhile her desire to search for her birth parents. Elaborating, Paton explained that lonely people found the loneliness of adoptive persons nothing special; people unhappy with their own birth parents saw little value in searching for birth parents; and those who had psychological problems failed to see a special hardship in the separation of parent from child. These psychological "obstacles to the understanding of adoption" were so widespread in the unadopted population, Paton declared, they "cannot be moved." Instead, birth parents and adult adoptees had no recourse but to look to themselves, shake off their paralyzing silences and secrets, and speak out.[54]

In the book's introduction, Paton addressed the purpose of her study: to present adult adoptees' speech and their thoughts and to allow for a dialogue, partly among themselves and partly with outsiders. Her eloquent description is as revealing of herself as of her respondents:

> Their speech is unaccustomed. It has been in fragments heretofore, and often disputed. They may disagree, and on many points may not have made up their minds, but they have spoken seriously and sometimes with pain. It is speech that is charged with deep feeling, sometimes for and sometimes against adoption. It is often the language of people who have become lonely and sensitive to human injury. It is rarely joyous, and is seldom self-assured, but it measures the values of living.[55]

Unfortunately, the eloquence was infrequent. Part of the problem was that the social scientist rather than the artist dominated the early pages of Paton's book. At the very outset, she declared, "No attempt is made to do more than to describe these reports, to organize the facts and attitudes which they contain, and to suggest a few thoughts."[56] From the very start, with the section "What Is Adoption?" Paton's study, thick with description, was not always cogent. Providing no legal definition of adoption, Paton gave her own definitions, alluding to the separation of the birth and the adoptive parents, the ambivalence of having two sets of parents, and stressing the adult adoptee's inability to know anything about the birth parents, which led to wasteful illusions. She did, however, acknowledge the variability of the definition, and when she presented eleven consecutive quotations from respondents as being representative, not one of them spoke to the issue. Instead, the majority confessed confusion or an inability to be of assistance, while simultaneously expressing willingness to help and praising Paton for undertaking such an important project.[57] Similarly, the next four sections or chapters, covering thirty-nine pages, were dry-as-dust demographic and statistical information on the respondents' date of birth, place of birth, reason for adoption, intermediate placement, occupation, marital status, and the like. Here, Paton the taxonomist was in her element, breaking down each category into its most minute elements, but for the reader, even the adult adoptee, it must have been hard work.[58] Eventually Paton herself acknowledged a problem. Almost three decades later, she wrote, "I must say I wish my first book had not been so concentrated in its style and writing. . . . I tried to get all things into it, [because I] had become so weary of superficial and partial treatments of adoption. I think I succeeded in a way, but it did make for difficult perusal."[59] Although Paton expressed disappointment about the way the book read, she retained a sense of humor about it. She once remarked that a woman from Mill Valley, California, had referred to her book as "*The Adopted Break Wind!*"[60]

Near the end of the book, Paton provided a few hypotheses or generalizations, which shed light on her beliefs about the nature of adult adoptees and their search for their birth parents. She suggested that two primary factors determine the extent to which an adult adoptee would desire to seek out original family members. One was "the amount of security he finds in his adoptive home and family through his developmental years," and the other was his own self-development, though Paton admitted that the two were interrelated. As long as these two factors were high—that is, the more secure and emotionally mature the person—the less inclined the adult adoptee would be to search. However, even in a situation where an adult adoptee felt very secure, death or illness of one or both adoptive parents could lead to the desire for searching. Where the adoptive home lacked security, however, the adult adoptee's efforts toward self-development tended to be accompanied by a move toward the birth parents. By self-development Paton meant significant events in the life course, such as going off to college, joining the military, marriage, parenthood, and the death of the adoptive parents.[61]

A second hypothesis, which Paton never repeated again publicly or privately, was that "the extent of the participation of the adoptive parents" determined an adult adoptee's degree of success in searching for his or her birth parents.[62] Conversely, the more the adult adoptee operated independently of his or her adoptive parents, the more likely the problem he or she began with would remain after completing the search. Underlying both of these hypotheses was the axiomatic assumption that all adult adoptees would at some point in their lives, to a greater or lesser extent, express curiosity about their birth parents.[63]

It was only in *The Adopted Break Silence*'s last section, entitled "Evaluation of the Institution," that the book came alive, containing some of Paton's most provocative and original ideas. Paton redefined the purpose of adoption; it was not simply to rear a child, because there were alternative methods to adoption for that. Nor was the purpose of adoption to solve the problem of infertility. Though she believed that these two factors were desirable consequences, the successful maturation of the child or the satisfaction of the adoptive parents were not the only functions of adoption. For Paton, the purpose of adoption was to repair the rupture in the culture "which had been established in terms of family and continuity of generations."[64] Although Paton did not state it explicitly, the "larger purpose" of adoption—the repairing of a rupture in the cultural fabric—was nothing less than the reuniting of the adult adoptee with his or her family of origin.

Exemplifying these themes, Paton included three illustrations. The book's frontispiece was a photograph of her sculpture entitled *The Adoptive Character*. Paton had discovered that working with clay helped her think and get in touch with her feelings about adoption reform.[65] She explained the meaning of the frontispiece in a letter printed in the *Western Journal of Surgery, Obstetrics and Gynecology*: "The non-belonging adopted is shown; also the burdened family soul. Adoption problems exist only in relationship to the general human problem. When the latter is denied, so is the former obscured."[66] A second illustration, "Don't Forget," was a drawing by a six-year-old girl on the day of her adoption. The final illustration was a photograph of a second sculpture of Paton's entitled *The Search*.

Another original idea of Paton's revolved around the idea that children should be "matched" with their adoptive parents based more on their own experiences rather than simply on physical or mental characteristics.[67] She elaborated on this concept in a separate document, where Paton codified and expanded on her methodology, which she labeled the "life history method" of adoption. She identified three differences that made her life history method superior to the inadequacies of older, specialized methods used in the disciplines of psychology and social work. The first difference had to do with professional social work's practice of adoptive "matching." Paton sought to replace the traditional method of matching the physical characteristics of the infant with the adoptive family with matching "the experience of the adoptive family with that of the background of the child." This would have two benefits: it would facilitate the adoptive parents' ability to understand the child's background, and it would allow the child, when he matured and wished to understand his own past, to have a preview of what his original parental home must have been like. But what did Paton mean by experience? She did not mean socioeconomic status, though recent research has demonstrated that, more often than not, women who relinquished their children for adoption came from a lower socioeconomic and educational background.[68] The examples Paton provided in *The Adopted Break Silence* revolved around the adopted child's experiential knowledge of orphanhood and adoptive parents' analogous experience with death in their own family. What was crucial was that *"there should be some resemblance between the family experiences which lie between them as they come from two different directions into one home—together."*[69] Conversely, a child who was born out of wedlock should not be placed in a family whose genealogy stretches back, unbroken by divorce, for many generations because it would be difficult to find common ground for understanding when the child, now grown, wishes to search for his birth family.[70]

Second, the life history method made it unnecessary to study an individual's life in great detail or have a large number of cases to arrive at valid generalizations. Paton attributed the efficacy of her methodology to the fact that the evidence considered "are all integrated factors inherently, and it is not necessary to correlate them since they belong together." Probably borrowing from Rankian therapy, with its emphasis on relationships,[71] Paton asserted that with her approach "no proof is asked for by this method but rather *signs of relationship* (self reported, at that) within an organic whole." The goal of her life history method was to discover original concepts to explain the relationships. If the concepts were discovered, Paton asserted, it was "unnecessary to have thousands of instances to show the living process as it expends itself in the individual."

The final difference of the life history method was that it was beneficial if the investigator "had a predominance" of this type of experiential knowledge "in his own life history." By this Paton meant that an adopted person had an advantage in researching other adopted people because they shared the same inherent feelings and understanding. Paton recognized that this sort of subjectivity was "anathema to the objective approach in the social sciences." In several places in *The Adopted Break Silence*, Paton confessed that the study was not a representative sample. Nevertheless, she dismissed any potential criticism by asserting that her essentialism was "an irreplaceable source of knowledge." Paton went so far as to assert, "the life history method concepts cannot be derived from the outside." In other words, researchers who used the life history method had to be drawn from the ranks of the adoption community. This attitude, which Paton maintained throughout her life, partly explains her fervent disapproval and criticism of any adoption research conducted by professional researchers, such as Arthur Sorosky, Reuben Pannor, and Annette Baran.

Paton next turned her attention to the future of the Life History Study Center. In January 1954, she had written to her first supervisor at the Children's Aid Society in Philadelphia in 1928, Elizabeth de Schweinitz, informing her of the Center's activities and declaring, "I hope to continue for a long time in this effort to build something strictly for and by the adopted, including I should add adoptive parents."[72] By mid-April, Paton had decided to expand the Center's activities beyond adoption research to include a fee-based consultation with adult adoptees.[73] In July, Paton redesigned the Center leaflet, changing the title to "The Adoption Project of the Life History Study Center" from "The Program of the Life History Study Center." The revised four-panel leaflet spoke of Paton's new confidence and pride in the endeavor. The front cover now clearly stated that the Adoption Project directed "attention to the adult years of those who were adopted children" and offered "study and referral services to adopted individuals and to others."[74] The rest of the leaflet forthrightly detailed Paton's perspective on several issues concerning adoption policy. The Center's greatest apprehension was the growing social work policy of enforcing the separation of birth parents and the adopted child, which was "both mistaken and generally needless." Paton also enunciated the principle that adoptive parents should give their children information "on the matter of being adopted, why, and further aspects as age and wisdom" permit, including knowledge of their birth parents, notwithstanding that such knowledge "may be seen, at the time, a handicap and an affront to their self-esteem." Paton affirmed that adopted people were fully capable of adjusting to the truth. Finally, she affirmed the need for careful adoption placement polices.

The leaflet next presented the new services that the Center was prepared to offer. Following an inquiry and a review of the situation, Paton offered a referral service to adoption agencies or other local resources. She would review an applicant's adoption history "in light of the experiences reported to us by others," and would also comment briefly on adoption matters, "as we feel we can be of service this way." Pointedly, and in contrast to her later policy and practice, Paton announced that fees would be charged by agreement and paid at the time that service was accepted. Throughout her life, she would be a stickler for financial accountability, and the leaflet emphasized that all the money raised from the sale of publications and services would be applied to the Center's future growth, after expenses had been paid.

In addition, the leaflet listed a series of services that Paton anticipated providing in the future. These included collecting and identifying the names of people willing to be contacted by others in their neighborhoods, consulting with people interested in researching or writing on adoption, and making what Paton labeled "field trips" away from the Center, where she would offer her services in person. The leaflet also advertised the imminent sale of *The Adopted Break Silence* as "the first full-scale publication of the Center" containing "an analysis of 40 men and women, living in 15 states, aged 23 to 68, who have experienced many different kinds of adoption from best to worse." The study promised to present the reason why some adopted adults searched for their original families and others did not, as well as how much they knew about their background and whether their adoptions were successful or not, and why. The leaflet promised that all personal, identifying information received by the Center would be held in complete confidence.

In August, Paton still faced the daunting task of finding a publisher for the now-completed manuscript of *The Adopted Break Silence*. Early in her writing of *The Adopted Break Silence*, Paton made a stab at getting the book published; perhaps she was being playful in sending out a feeler to W. B. Saunders Company, a respectable Philadelphia publisher of medical textbooks and monographs. Without even including a résumé or discussing her qualifications, she simply asked in a two-sentence letter, "Would you be interested in a little Kinsey on the subject of adoption?"[75] Paton was well aware that Saunders had won out over heavy competition to sign Alfred C. Kinsey's *Sexual Behavior in the Human Male*, which had become a best-seller; she may have hoped that lightning would strike twice.[76] Saunders' managing editor, John L. Dusseau, however, politely turned Paton down, pointing out that although he was sure her project was one of unquestionable value and interest, its appeal "must be to the lay public rather than to the medical profession." In fact, Dusseau informed Paton, Kinsey's type of book was the sole exception in the company's history.[77] After this single rejection, Paton solved the problem of publication herself. She simply looked in the Philadelphia yellow pages, located a nearby printer, and asked the company to publish a first edition of 1,000 copies. According to Paton, it was an informal affair, with the company even helping her with some of the proofreading. The printing costs came to nearly $3 a copy.[78]

Beginning in August and continuing through the fall, Paton worked tirelessly, mailing prepublication publicity for *The Adopted Break Silence*.[79] In August, she sent a two-page flyer, initially to the Free Library of Philadelphia, where she did so much of her reading and research; to the College of Physicians and Surgeons, because she still viewed herself as a medical researcher; and to the Philadelphia Art Alliance, for Paton still considered herself an artist.[80]

In September, Paton mailed another batch of 250 prepublication leaflets to the original list of people who responded to the ad in the *Saturday Review of Literature*. The first page of the flyer boasted that "no such revealing source of new insights on adoption has ever before been offered," warned the reader that it "was a serious book, not for one-sitting reading," and contained a form for advance orders. The second page of the flyer contained an annotated table of contents of the book.[81] On August 30, she dispatched a letter to her hometown paper, the *Ypsilanti Daily Press*, explaining why it might be interested in taking note of her work.[82] A week later, she received her first newspaper notice, a piece in the Ypsilanti paper headlined "Adoption Study by Miss Paton to Be Released." And, although her letter had never mentioned her connection to the city, the story identified Paton as "a former Ypsilantian."[83] By September 5, Paton had initiated mass mailings of an order form for *The Adopted Break Silence* to 700 new names that had come to her attention since placing the ad in the *Saturday Review of Literature*, 265 adoption agency members of the Child Welfare League of America, 65 Pennsylvania child care agencies, 70 libraries, 40 schools of social work, 120 Planned Parenthood offices, and an undisclosed number of psychology and sociology departments on the East Coast.[84] After securing a directory of American psychologists, Paton sent out an additional 300 flyers to East Coast practitioners, as well as another 143 to child guidance centers around the country, 120 New York City psychiatrists, and the Louise Wise adoption agency.[85]

On October 9, Paton's industrious efforts to promote her book before its publication paid off with a notice by Dr. Paul Popenoe, a proponent of eugenics, father of modern marriage counseling, and author of an immensely popular syndicated newspaper column, *Modern Marriage*. He quoted Paton's statement that adopted people should not be singled out by being denied knowledge about their birth parents and the circumstances surrounding their adoption, "insofar as they are mature enough to maintain their life responsibilities in the face of what may seem to be, at the time, a handicap, and an affront to their self esteem," a none-too-subtle reference to their illegitimacy. He also quoted Francis Bruce

Strain, an authority on child development, who declared that those placed for adoption had the right to know they were adopted and also the right to know their own ancestry. Popenoe asked that readers who had been adopted write to him about whether they felt harmed by having learned the truth about their parentage. He in turn provided his readers with the name and address of the Life History Study Center, and though he purported to only want to "get the facts," it was obvious that he favored Paton's and Strain's position.[86]

As a result of Popenoe's column, which had appeared in New York's *Buffalo Evening News*, Paton received a letter from the Reverend Oren Lorenz of the United Brethren Church. He wanted to know whether to tell their adopted married son, age twenty-three, about the identity of his birth parents, which was on a birth certificate in their possession. Lorenz also wanted Paton's opinion about the wisdom of making an investigation of the birth parents, without anyone knowing why the information was wanted. Lorenz believed that perhaps it was best if the birth parents knew the identity of their son.[87] Lorenz's letter was the first inquiry from someone who was not a social worker asking Paton for advice about search and reunion. It was typical of the way triad members would hear of Paton's service and initiate contact: through mention of the Life History Study Center or, later, Orphan Voyage, in newspaper or magazine articles.

And Paton's reply was also typical of what she would say as she struggled with the complexities of her new pioneering role as adoption reformer, slightly defensive and hedged with qualifications. She first told Lorenz that his questions were difficult, the Center was young, and the service for helping adult adoptees was in the development stage. She then described her hypothesis about the deleterious effect of withholding information from adult adoptees, outlined the genesis of her soon-to-be-published book, and stated that she was enclosing a description of it. In describing the registration service, she forthrightly stated that "there are undoubtedly many situations where contact would not be happy" but quickly added that she had ways of guarding against such an outcome. And although she said that the service was for young or older adults, she reiterated her frequently voiced belief that "a person must be mature enough to make his own application for [it]; both mature and at a time of life when the information and contact [was] important and needed." Based on his youthful age, Paton discouraged Lorenz's son from seeking such contact immediately. She suggested instead that he be told of the Center's existence and "when— and if—he should want to contact me," Paton would be happy to assist him. At this early stage, Paton did not believe that adult adoptees had a universal urge to search for their birth parents, as she would at a later date. In closing,

Paton seemed to waffle in her advice. She enunciated what would become one of her most important tenets: that what helped an adopted person the most was the process of searching—"it was the trying, in the most responsible way"— that aided the adult adoptee in the quest to overcome psychological and social handicaps. But Paton undermined this positive advice by again suggesting that Lorenz's son due to his youth "may be satisfied now with what he has."[88]

On November 10, 1954, *The Adopted Break Silence* officially saw the light of day. In the same month, Linus Pauling won the Nobel Prize for chemistry; the Dow Jones Industrial Average closed at an all-time high of 382.74, the first time the Dow had surpassed its 1929 peak level reached just before that year's crash; and a small group of animal lovers established the Humane Society of the United States. Paton paid no attention to these newsworthy domestic events. Instead, she continued to drum up publicity. As *The Adopted Break Silence* rolled off the press, Paton sent out almost 200 advance copies to professional people, libraries, clinics, and reviewers. Each participant in the study also received a copy free of charge.[89] In addition, Paton took every opportunity to correspond with academic authors about their work, in order to share her knowledge of adoption and advertise the book. For example, after reading his article "Some Clinical and Cultural Aspects of Aging," she wrote to David Riesman, University of Chicago sociologist and author of *The Lonely Crowd*.[90] Riesman had distinguished "three ideal-typical outcomes" of aging for individuals past midlife, which he labeled the "autonomous, adjusted, and anomic reactions to aging." The forty-five-year-old Paton delighted in his positive assessment of both autonomous and anomic older individuals who enjoyed life by resisting "the culture's strictures and penalties imposed on the aged," either through inner psychological resources of renewal or through outer resources of work or power.[91] She informed Riesman that a number of the respondents of *The Adopted Break Silence* fell into that older age category. Most important, Paton declared, she concentrated on older adopted adults because adoption was a lifelong experience that could not be understood in a short span of time. It was "the very aging process that we go through—in so far as we acknowledge it—that awakens new insights about the importance of natural parents."[92] This insight lay behind Paton's emphasis that the most successful reunions were undertaken by mature individuals in their later years.

Paton's assiduous efforts to publicize *The Adopted Break Silence* initially generated a spark of interest. Riesman thanked Paton for her reaction to his article and stated that he "was very much interested to learn of your work." He also said he had forwarded her enclosure about the Center's work to his colleague, Professor Martin Loeb, an expert in the field of adoption.[93] Paton found "singularly gratifying" a letter from Deloris N. Murray, who read about the book in the *Du-luth News Tribune*, Minnesota, and declared that "it was about time the adopted break the silence and having broken it keep up the din until something is done about the inhumane way we are 'protected' from knowledge of our heritage."[94] On January 20, 1955, Paton was invited to participate in a panel discussion on a popular New York City evening radio show, *Psychologically Speaking*, addressing the topic "How It Feels to be Adopted."[95] Five days later, King Features Syndicate, a major distributor of columns, comic strips, and other material to newspapers, sent out a review of *The Adopted Break Silence*, which summarized the book's major findings, including Paton's disagreement with placement experts over their practice of denying the need of adopted adults to search for their birth parents.[96] She also received a letter from Dr. Marie Skodak, a highly respected adoption researcher, who had read the study and expressed interest in perhaps being a collaborator in Paton's next study.[97]

On the whole, however, Paton's efforts to publicize her book failed to pay large dividends. The response from academia was decidedly mixed. Constance Carr, editor of *Childhood Education*, the organ of the Association for Childhood Education International, apologized after almost five months for mislaying Paton's letter and materials relating to *The Adoption Break Silence*. Carr informed Paton that it was unnecessary for her to send a review copy since the possibility of the book's being reviewed was "very remote."[98] Taken aback, Paton sent a copy of Carr's letter to a friend for her opinion of it. "Hazel" declared that it was "the classic example of academic snobbery born of professional insecurity." She assured Paton that she did not recognize even one of the names of the board of directors on the letter's masthead and counseled her to ignore them.[99] Paton had somewhat better luck with individual faculty members. Ernest Osborne, professor of education at Teachers College, Columbia University, requested a review copy of *The Adopted Break Silence* to use in his syndicated newspaper column "The Family Scrapbook"; Paton readily assented.[100]

Perhaps most disappointing was the generally frosty response Paton received from professional social work organizations. As early as August 1954, she wrote to Edika Lauer of the Child Welfare League of America, informing the organization of the study, providing specific information about the eight adoption agencies involved in some of the adoptions reported, and requesting a directory of members.[101] She received an immediate reply from Henrietta L. Gordon, information and publications secretary and an expert on adoption policy and practices, who, in addition to giving Paton information on how one might purchase such a directory, sharply questioned Paton about the study. In a sentence dripping with suspicion of private, uncommissioned studies and an attempt at prepublication censorship, Gordon asked Paton "whether you have been in touch with agencies which you list in your letter to Miss Lauer, whether any of them had an opportunity to preview your manuscript, and if none of them have read it, who did read it in advance."[102] A month later, making no reply to Gordon's queries, Paton informed her that she was enclosing a preview of the study for her perusal.[103] In the same month Mary D. Paasch, the librarian for the Family Service Association of America, rejected outright Paton's request for a directory of its member agencies, citing the organization's policy that its directory not be used for commercial purposes. Paasch did, however, suggest to Paton that she send her a copy of the book for review.[104] Similarly, Madelyn C. Waterbury, administrative assistant for the American Association of Social Workers, informed Paton that the group did not give out its list of "chapter chairman," but she too recommended that it could be reviewed for the *Social Work Journal*.[105] Ultimately, Russell H. Kurtz, the book review editor of the *Journal*, judged that Paton's book merited only a bare-bones "Brief Mention," which meant that just the facts of publication—title, author, publisher, number of pages, and price—were printed.[106] In reply, Paton wrote that she was "very happy" that the journal even mentioned her book, but she confessed that she was "a little distressed at there being no street address"; without such information, Paton explained, interested customers would be unable to purchase her book.[107]

Perhaps discouraged by the mixed but meager response, Paton returned to the publicity trail and in February mailed out flyers to mental health personnel and members of the American Association of Theological Schools. Each version was tailored to appeal to its respective constituency. The 1,300 mental health flyers for mental health specialists emphasized the obligation of those professionals to provide services for adopted persons to live healthier lives.[108] The edition for members of the ministry, numbering only 75 copies, stressed the cleric's counseling function regarding adoptive parents and children and suggested that *The Adopted Break Silence* was an indispensable source to understanding the attitudes of the respective parties and potential problems that might arise in later years.[109] By 1958, *The Adopted Break Silence* had sold over 1,000 copies.[110]

Paton then made preparations to undertake her second study, in which she would interview adult adoptees in Michigan and reunite with her first mother.

4

On the Road

Often my labors seem non-existent. I once explained to a friend that half of my time
is taken up just standing good for the basic idea of the Center, as if I lay there in the
dark like the little Dutch boy with his finger in the dike, but in this case my finger is
to keep the thing open.

—JEAN PATON, 1955

As early as January 1954, even before she began writing *The Adopted Break
Silence*, Paton was "planning an additional field trip into the middle west."[1] At
the beginning of December 1954 Paton sent out the formal notice, announcing
that she was undertaking a second adoption study, "To Be Chosen: The Family
Life of the Adopted," which fourteen years later would be published as *Orphan
Voyage*.[2] In this announcement Paton identified the area for study as a midwestern state, which she chose because many U.S. adoptions had first occurred
there. She provided several reasons for embarking on a second study so soon.
Besides wanting "to fill some of the lacks in the first one," Paton also wished
to elaborate on some of the material in *The Adopted Break Silence*, such as an
examination of the developmental struggles of older adult adoptees, under the
guiding hypothesis that there existed "a universal appetite for security within
Society."[3] In late December, Paton issued a second announcement, which offered more precise reasons why she decided to undertake a second study. Several people had been interested in knowing more about Paton's personal views
and experience on the subject, a few of the study's respondents had expressed an
interest in identifying additional aspects of the "adoptive character," and "there
were criticisms of the sample."[4]

Having decided by January 10 that Michigan would be her destination,
Paton sent an announcement, similar to the one placed in the *Saturday Re-*

view of Literature, to many Michigan newspapers, large libraries, and every county public-welfare department. It was headed "Adoption Study by Michigan Woman," and its first sentence read, "Men and Women who were adopted before 1910, and who are living in Michigan, are being sought out by the Life History Study Center in Philadelphia."[5] The announcement went on to state that "Miss Jean M. Paton" had been born in Detroit and raised in Ypsilanti and since the fall of 1953 had been studying adoption "from the point of view of the adopted." This second study would differ slightly in its methodology from the first: Paton would venture out on a "field trip" and conduct personal interviews.[6] The announcement stated that "Miss Paton" would arrive in Michigan in the late winter or early spring to talk with adult adoptees, giving the address of the Life History Study Center for people to contact if interested. A follow-up announcement sent to those who responded included the now familiar questionnaire, but Paton did not intend to rely on the written responses because she planned to interview all of the participants. By this time, Paton had also decided that she would make two trips to Michigan, the first during the last four days of February, when she would stop at Lansing, Bay City, and points in between; and the second in late March, to the northern part of Michigan.[7] Paton's arrival was made easier by several notices in Michigan newspapers.[8]

Paton had an additional reason for heading to the midwest, and specifically Michigan, for a second adoption study. She had decided that it was time for her to search for her own birth mother. The issue had haunted Paton, off and on, for a long time, but she had delayed searching for multiple reasons. Having been raised in a good family who protected her from the stigma of adoption and illegitimacy, Paton was not driven to make a search. In addition, she did not want to offend her adoptive mother while she was alive.[9] After her adoptive mother's death in 1950, Paton longed to reunite with her birth mother but had still delayed because "I usually wound up deciding that she would not feel the same way." Still, she was lucky: although her birth mother had falsified the family name on Paton's original birth certificate the Patons had supplied it to her. It was Cutting.[10] Paton consulted Detroit's Polk city directories and found her mother's name listed twice at the family address where they had lived since 1900, but lost the trace in 1932.[11] Unbeknownst to Paton, that year her mother's sister Viola had married and moved into the house with a new family name. In 1954, not knowing that family members still lived there, Paton had driven by the house and almost knocked on the door to inquire about her birth mother.[12]

The same year, Paton wrote to a couple she thought were her birth parents. Though she was mistaken, the experience was life-changing and gave her insight into the nature of reunions between adult adoptees and their birth parents and the concept of forgiveness.[13] Energized, but confronted by countless people in the Detroit directory with the family name of Cutting and not having the stomach to do it herself, Paton hired a private investigator for $35 to write what she described as "cursory" letters of inquiry.[14] The letters said simply that Paton had been born in that general family and wanted to see the house where some of them had lived, adding that she had been raised by others. The letter went on to state that Paton would come by on a certain afternoon and hoped the person would be home.[15] On February 18, 1955, a week before leaving for Lansing, the investigator reported to Paton that he had found Viola and that she was still living at the old family address with her husband and a child.[16] Paton dropped to her "knees in thankfulness that someone in my natural family was alive and could be approached." At the end of February 1955, Paton went off to Lansing to begin interviewing adult adoptees for her second book and to reunite with her first mother.

In Lansing, Paton interviewed eight adult adoptees, six in their homes and two at her hotel. After completing the interviews, each of which lasted nearly two hours, she drove 125 miles north, in a snowstorm, to Bay City, just below Lake Huron, and over the next couple of days interviewed a few more adopted people.[17] Overall, she had been received well, though for the most part the interviews merely confirmed what Paton already knew experientially.[18]

This second adoption project of Paton's, however, took a backseat to what turned out to be a pivotal event in Paton's life: the reunion with her birth mother. The first step that led up to this momentous episode was Paton's meeting with her aunt Viola, who years before had compromised her own dream of becoming an attorney because of her father's opposition and had instead become a court reporter.[19] Before their meeting, Paton sent her aunt flowers; on her arrival she was met by a sympathetic Viola, who opened the door "dabbing at the corner of her eye with her handkerchief."[20] Paton knew from that moment on that it all was going to be alright, though one of the only things she could remember was her aunt asking her, "You are Emma's girl, aren't you?" Additional conversation revealed that Jean's mother was still alive, living outside Detroit, and, most important, would very much want to meet with Jean. Viola ventured to act as an intermediary, saying that she would contact Jean's mother through a neighbor's phone and get back to her the following day.[21]

Thus it transpired that Jean Paton, age forty-seven, met her first mother, Emma, age sixty-nine, on a springlike day in early March 1955. On hearing the news from Viola of the return of her daughter, Emma cried all night. The next day, as Emma and Jean sat together on the sofa in Emma's home in Richmond, Michigan, about forty-four miles north of Detroit, Emma was still tearful and in a state of shock.[22] But they were tears of joy. Emma was jubilant to see her daughter, whom she thought of as simply returning home after an extended absence. Jean had a completely incorrect image of her mother in her mind's eye and was initially taken aback by Emma's height— a mere four feet, nine inches to Paton's height of five feet— and educational attainment, having reached only the fifth grade, and not the least bit intellectual.[23] Paton exaggerated the contrast between her and her mother, declaring that "here am I, always have been, conscious of a prodigious array of talents, always able to do whatever I tackled."[24] But with time, Paton discovered similarities: both mother and daughter liked to "dance a jig about the room, and to teach a little child to dance," and both loved to sing.[25]

During her brief stay, Jean discovered that soon after her birth, her mother had married a tinsmith, Eddie Steiner. With the exception of a detached retina in one eye and cataract operations on both, her mother was in good health. Her illiterate husband, however, was nearly blind from glaucoma. With Eddie unable to work and without Social Security, the couple were on welfare.[26] Paton asked her mother to reveal the identity of her birth father, but Emma was ambivalent: she both feared and hoped that Jean would find him. On the one hand, it was a painful and buried memory, which Emma resisted digging up and she dreaded that Jean might bring him home. On the other hand, Emma still loved him.[27] In the end, Emma gave Jean his name.[28] Emma's feelings for her former lover were confirmed for Jean in another way that she found both a blessing and a shock. As Jean was leaving, Emma kissed her as if Jean were her husband. Paton declared many years later to a correspondent, "believe me no one before or since ever kissed me so."[29] Now, knowing her father's name, Paton followed up on this lead before she left Michigan. She visited with Miriam Buncher in the Social Service Department of Detroit's Women's Hospital, where she was born, and inquired about her background.[30]

Paton did not meet any other family relatives aside from Viola and Emma. Her other aunt, Dolly, made it clear that Jean was persona non grata, and the rest of the straitlaced Methodist family shared Dolly's prejudices about Emma's child born out of wedlock. During their visit, over tea, Emma informed Jean that her family had called her illegitimate. The concept was so fraught with shame, Paton recalled, that her mother sputtered on the word and almost choked on it. In an attempt to reassure her, Paton smiled at her mother and said, "yes, that's the word." She wanted her mother "to think I did not disapprove of how I came into this world."[31] Paton believed that it was only then that her mother was "absolved of her long, long, guilt."[32] Paton attributed her relatives' prejudice not only to religious bigotry but also to the fear that she might have her eye on an inheritance. They were unaware that Paton was financially independent, and she did not think it important to convey that fact to them.[33]

Paton returned home during the first week of March. Her reunion with her mother, which she described as a "strange and potent experience," made a deep and lasting impression on her.[34] To one correspondent, she reported that she was "still pinching myself" but went on to declare that the simplest way to explain the effect of the reunion was that "I feel sewed up." To another, she wrote, it was "wonderful beneath knowing," to find one's mother; as there were "no more specters, no more fantastic living, no more paralysis of will for avoiding the deepest desire of nature."[35] To Paton's delight, a correspondence sprang up immediately between them. She also received a report from Miriam Buncher concerning her start in life at Women's Hospital, but it failed to shed any new light except the date when Emma entered the home.[36]

In mid-April, Paton returned to Michigan for a second visit with her mother and noted the transformative changes from her first visit. Emma was over her shock. She took Jean with her for walks all over the neighborhood and introduced her newfound daughter to her friends, wanting people to know who she was, since Emma had had no children with Eddie. Emma was also much more social. Eddie took her to church, and she had joined a club for the elderly. Her husband had built a yard table and benches, and Emma was planning a lawn party for all her new club friends.[37] Revealing her pride in her daughter, Emma wrote Paton asking for copies of the Detroit newspapers that carried stories of the Life History Study Center, so she could show them to some of the women in her church.[38] She also would "be glad to meet your lady friend" and "hoped that they would like each other."[39] Emma wrote Jean that she was aware that "my relations don't like the way I had my girl," but revealing one source of Jean's spunk, she added, "I should worry, we got each other."[40] In July, her mother wrote her that "I don't worry or cry anymore."[41] Paton was "very deeply happy" about her mother's alteration.[42]

One lesson she drew from this experience was that reunions could be therapeutic; but at the same time it reinforced her belief that they were for mature adult adoptees. It seemed to Paton that there was "no other true restorative for the natural mother (in illegitimate cases particularly) than the child who was surrendered" returning at a time of life when he or she "has something to give and does not come running for a solution to some life problem."[43]

Paton also felt better and kicked herself for waiting so long to reunite with her birth mother. She felt she had gained psychological strength from the experience. Paton mused that she had lost that "vague ghost of a 'mother,'" and would no longer have to wonder "about people I meet on the street and resemble, being told that I look so much like so-and-so."[44] Paton was told that for the first time she seemed to have a sense of humor. A former Baltimore supervisor in social work noticed that immediately and blurted out, "You've changed! You never used to laugh at yourself."[45] Moreover, Paton believed that the reunion with her mother had strengthened her in two additional ways. Nearly thirty years later, she wrote one correspondent that it made her "realize at long last that I had been conceived and born quite like other people" and also that her mother had given her "a sense of my personal human history and genetic history."[46]

Paton universalized her reunion with her mother, making it the basis for advice she gave to correspondents who sought her help. A month after reuniting with her mother, Paton advised one Massachusetts woman who had been adopted that reunions should not take place until "the child is adult and mature" because "one has to be mature to make reconciliation work." Rationalizing her own delayed search, Paton informed the woman that that was the prime reason why it took adult adoptees so long to begin searching.[47] Similarly, when Betty Tschopp wrote, asking about how she should approach her birth mother, Paton recommended using an intermediary to write letters to her relatives, as she had, and even gave Tschopp a script for the intermediary to use.[48] Paton also postulated an inherent, inescapable resentment between the birth mother and the adoptive mother, based on the fact that the adoptive parent had raised the child. She pointed to her own birth mother, who only with difficulty, and some years later, was able to call her Jean, a name Emma had not given her.[49] Another reason her reunion had turned out so well, suggested Paton, was the fact that her birth mother had loved her birth father and had told her husband about the daughter she had relinquished for adoption. But such a fortuitous situation did not always exist.[50] Paton counseled one of her correspondents, a male adult adoptee, that he had to be content not knowing everything about his natal family. Like all adopted people, he would have "to add things up at the end, and find there is a piece missing." She told this correspondent that her mother had provided her with her father's name and a few other facts in letters about him but had been reluctant to convey anything more. And although she could surmise some things, "I do have nothing more."[51] In the future Paton would do an immense amount of reading in science, literature, history, social work, and the social sciences, but she would continue to ground her advice to triad members in her own life experiences.

After visiting with her mother, Paton embarked on the main purpose of her second trip to Michigan, to interview the adult adoptees that she had been unable to meet during her first trip because of the distance involved and the new ones who had recently heard about her work. Just before she left, Paton sent out another round of flyers announcing the sale of the second study of adult adoptees. Now calling the publication "I Went to Michigan," Paton would write it between May and September 1955.[52] As before, she placed notices of her arrival in local newspapers. Again, her way was paved by a notice in the *Oxford Leader*, announcing her arrival in Michigan to interview adult adoptees, "a source of important information."[53] She received another favorable write-up in the *Detroit News*, including a small photo. The article painted a picture of Paton as a sober reformer with impressive professional credentials who was daring to challenge adoption agencies' practice of "overlooking one universal instinct: the desire of every person to know who he is, who his ancestors were."[54] During this second Michigan trip, instead of staying comfortably ensconced in various hotels and venturing out to the immediate neighborhood as she had done before, Paton visited fifty adult adoptees in twenty-five communities scattered throughout the entire state.[55]

Although Paton promised to publish the results of these interviews within months, they did not appear until 1960, and then only as a mimeograph; they reappeared again in 1968, as part of *Orphan Voyage*, Paton's second self-published book. Their merit lay mostly in Paton's ability to give voice to the heretofore silenced adult adoptee population. The thirty-five-page section, made up of mostly verbatim accounts of the experience of adult adoptees, contained several notable observations.[56] Paton identified for the first time the presence in adult adoptees of "The Ghost," which she defined as "a sign, a symbol, a suggestion of the absent natural relative. It may be only the fruit of one's imagination or it may be eventually a revelation of reality. But in its ghostly state it is just enough of something seen or heard to suggest the presence of another person and leave disquiet in its wake."[57] Ghost experiences, Paton believed, prompt adult adoptees to search for their original families. Never one to sugarcoat the adoption experience, she described three cases of searches that were unsuccessful and laid out the complex reasons why.[58] In this section, Paton's tone was clinical, her analysis psychological, and as a whole, she declined to provide any adoption reform prescriptions.

In contrast to Paton's formal writing, her comments in newspapers reveal a more passionate, committed activist. In particular, on April 28, 1955, in the Menominee, Michigan, *Herald-Leader* an extensive interview between its editor, Jean Worth, and Paton provides the best insight into Paton's thinking on a wide range of adoption reform issues. In answer to Worth's questions, Paton criticized adoption agencies' policy of sealing adoption records (because it would bring "problems in adulthood that would be very hard . . . to solve"), the inability of social workers to understand the difficulties of adopted people (because they themselves were not adopted), the inadequacy of the "chosen baby" story (because when the baby grew up the adult might think, "what was the matter with my family that it didn't want me?"), and the lack of professional social work literature looking at the adult adoptee (because "literature on adoption stops short at [age] 10 or 12").[59]

Paton was deeply affected by her Michigan interviews. Even though the adult adoptees she met were friendly and treated her well, she harbored within herself a deep well of insecurity and disappointment, a result of the resistance she had met with in the past two years; only a conscious effort to steel herself against these feelings had kept her working at the Life History Study Center. Consequently, each new door she approached in Michigan created in her feelings of being rebuffed, a readiness to take offense, and a self-consciousness to fight against such a destructive pattern. As Paton later confessed, "Too many years of silence have left their mark." On the evening of April 24, in just such a bleak mood, Paton contemplated not taking the long, troublesome auto ferry to Michigan's Upper Peninsula to continue the interviews and instead returning to Philadelphia. She even began composing the letters of apology that she would write upon her return home. But then she suddenly recognized what was happening and changed her mind. Contrary to acting on her fear, "I was doing something quite normal and ordinary. The changed behavior was so intriguing to me that I lost my hesitation and made arrangements at the motel office to be awakened early enough to get aboard the ferry."[60] It would be a gross exaggeration to conclude that Paton totally lost her fear of being rebuffed by this single triumph over her demons at the motel on the shore of Lake Michigan; her numerous sudden cancellations of meetings throughout her life attest to that. But successful events such as her boarding the ferry in late April 1955 bolstered Paton's confidence and energized her in the short run.

In her first Life History Study Center "Release" upon her return to Philadelphia, Paton confided to her readers that the previous release had been somber in tone, but "now I am encouraged." Paton translated that encouragement into a variety of activities that showcased her newfound self-assurance and vigor. In the next seven months—from May to December—she blitzed professional groups such as Pennsylvania child-caring institutions and New Jersey social councils with flyers advertising *The Adopted Break Silence*.[61] In addition, she continued to reach out to the educated lay public by sending out flyers to booksellers, church workers, private schools, and libraries and placing ads for the book in the personals column of magazines that ran the gamut from *Popular Mechanics* and *Pennsylvania Farmer* to *Cupid's Destiny* and the *Christian Register*.[62] By August 1955, as a result of her salesmanship—sending out review copies and sales in the

United States, Canada, and overseas—Paton had run through the first printing of 1,000 copies of *The Adopted Break Silence*, and she announced that the book was going to be reprinted "with a few improvements," including a higher grade of paper and saddle-stitched binding, though the appendix, which had appeared in the first printing, would be dropped.[63]

At last Paton's entrepreneurial efforts paid off, and she began to receive the public recognition she greatly coveted. A variety of professional organizations, mass-market magazines, and newspapers began requesting review copies of *The Adopted Break Silence*, including the Child Study Association, the National Council of the Young Men's Christian Associations, *Reader's Digest*, and the *Boston Globe*.[64] In the wake of Paton's return to Philadelphia, advice columns and feature articles on the Life History Study Center as well as reviews of *The Adopted Break Silence* also began to appear in newspapers. In May, the Life History Study Center was mentioned favorably by the self-promoting, best-selling author of eugenics and popular essays Albert Wiggam in his syndicated column, *Explore Your Mind*. In answer to the question "Should adopted children [*sic*] be told about their natural parents?" Wiggam answered yes, because it gave them self-understanding and some knowledge about their heredity, something the amateur eugenicist believed "everyone should know more about." As his authority, he cited the Life History Study Center study of forty adult adoptees. And, though he did not mention Paton's name or the Center's address, he urged his readers to write the Center with their questions.[65] Similarly, in November, Philadelphia's largest newspaper published a long, favorable piece about the Center in its women's section, presenting Jean as "a small, gentle, soft-spoken women," a part-time sculptor, and a former professional social worker with several college degrees who had given up her salaried position to open a place for adoption research and service. Paton came across as a remarkably articulate and straightforward reformer. To the question why she quit her social work job, Paton replied that she did so because "adoption agencies tend to withhold identification information about adopted children." They operated under the inaccurate assumption that "once the adopted person reaches adulthood he will have no interest in his past or forebears." Paton declared, "The adopted adult wants to know, for better or worse, the who, what, and why of his ancestry." Without that knowledge, she continued, the adopted person would be plagued with problems as an adult. In a prescient statement, Paton predicted that "the needs of the adopted person will grow sufficiently so that in five or 10 years it will become a social problem."[66]

In the wake of Paton's third field trip to Baltimore and the District of Columbia between August 1 and 3,[67] several newspaper stories, including one in the

Evening Star and another in the *Washington Post*, publicized Paton's activities and the Life History Study Center. The story in the *Washington Post*, written by a staff member of Yale's Clinic of Child Development, the prestigious Gesell Institute, was a review of *The Adopted Break Silence*, which it described as "just the kind [of book] that people interested in adoption have long been waiting for." Undoubtedly, the most gratifying aspect of the review to Paton was its characterization of her study as a piece of "scientific literature," although the piece also mentioned the book's lack of "one overall answer" and its failure to give advice or make many predictions. Still, the review concluded by declaring that the book "provides extremely worthwhile reading."[68]

Other signs of recognition included a friendly letter from H. David Kirk, now an associate professor at McGill University's School of Social Work in Montreal, Canada. He wanted to reconnect with Paton, first, by ordering a copy of *The Adopted Break Silence*, which he "was very anxious to see," and second, enclosing a paper he had written. Kirk also mentioned that he had attended the Child Welfare League of America's (CWLA) conference in Chicago six months earlier, heard that she was in attendance, and searched, but could not find her. He continued to be interested in her work and hoped that Paton would keep him informed about it.[69]

After cordially acknowledging his letter, Paton broached a subject that would be a source of lifelong bitterness: professional social work's rejection of her work. She informed Kirk that she had not attended the Chicago CWLA meeting, adding chillingly, "I have no connection with the League. There has been no invitation to me nor a request from me. Our worlds are rather separate." Paton had attended previous meetings but had been treated like a "ghost," as she invariably discovered from one or another of the professional social workers in attendance. She also welcomed Kirk's reaction to *The Adopted Break Silence* and predicted that he would see now why in the past they had differed. In Paton's opinion, family background was destiny: in her background was the birth and the adoptive family, while in Kirk's was the "normal family." Their respective experiences were so essentially different that "we cannot possibly see it [adoption] the same way." There was only one thing they had in common, "as do all adopted people and adopted parents: hunger." Paton explained that what she meant was that adopted people hungered "to belong to the race, by joining the natural family," while adopted parents hungered to belong "by being inseparable from their adopted children." With a hint of triumphalism, Paton concluded, "Only one of these hungers can be satisfied directly."[70]

Paton's dynamism and focus carried over into her work on adoption at the Life History Study Center. In June, she wrote a 1,500-word letter to the editor, which was published in the 1955 issue of the *Western Journal of Surgery, Obstetrics and Gynecology*, on the subject of unmarried mothers and the way society ignored the topic of illegitimacy. She argued forcibly that the consequences of such cultural silence resulted in adopted persons becoming invisible, timid, and alienated from society.[71] Paton also fired off a letter to the editor of *Women's Home Companion*, offering to write a feature article detailing her recent field trip to Michigan.[72] Similarly, she wrote a letter expressing "complete agreement" with an article by psychiatrist Iago Galdston that was highly critical of the social work profession for its inability to solve the problems it was created to alleviate.[73] Paton viewed the primary problem of adopted people and their families as "certainly a religious question" revolving around "the problem of forgiveness in the face of deep schism." She was doubtful, however, that social workers could be sufficiently educated or that the social work profession contained sufficient wisdom and understanding to solve the problem. Paton proposed that the solution to the problems Galdston suggested lay in the organization and research of the Life History Study Center, which she described as "an experiment in communication. It is not an agency. It is a sort of agglutination of aliveness among people who are restive within adoption."[74] In addition, she planned a fourth field trip for two weeks in October, taking her through the states of Indiana, Ohio, and Pennsylvania.[75] After delaying for a year, Paton finally set up her post-adoption registration service, the Reunion File, and sent out an announcement in October that her service was designed "to assist and guide adults who are seeking adult family members from whom they were once separated by adoption." She restricted the service to adult adoptees above the age of thirty-five, conforming to her theory that only mature adoptees could benefit from a reunion, and promised that their identity would be kept secret.[76]

Paton also found time to revise the Life History Study Center's leaflet. In comparison to the first one, issued two years earlier, with its tentative reaching out to the adoption triad, her revised leaflet projected a confident tone and provided clear explanations for the Center's existence, purpose, and relationship to members of the triad, professionals, and laymen. Paton now explained that the Center was created as a result of the flawed nature of adoption, which resulted in making "many adopted people feel isolated, unwanted and lonely to an extent that few realize." She believed that a "partial cure" was possible through individual action; but before taking the first step, "a place of belonging" was needed—namely, the Life History Study Center, which Paton now described as "a bridge between the adopted and other people," whose purpose was to encourage cultural understanding. More specifically the function of the Center was "a communications network and a storehouse of information." And for the first time Paton bestowed upon herself a title, referring in the third person to the Center's "director," who communicated by correspondence and field trips, and occasionally more formally "by releases and pamphlets."

The leaflet next turned to relationships with triad members and professional social workers where Paton set minimal expectations for successful interactions. Above all else, adult adoptees required patience because of how difficult it was through mere letter writing to "unravel the mystery of their origins and particularly in breaking the fantasy of their natural parents." To supplement the inadequate slowness of communication and alleviate adult adoptees' impatience, the director planned on establishing additional personal contacts through field trips. For adoptive parents, the paramount requirement was that they interact with the Center "if the problems of their children" were to be solved. To this end, the director would meet with groups of adoptive parents at their request. For birth parents, Paton acknowledged contact with a few and deflected criticism by denying any intention to "stir up groundless hope." But in no uncertain terms, the director declared, the Center believed that "the fiction of eternal abandonment of babies" should never have begun. Paton encouraged "patient natural parents" to correspond with her. For the professionals, Paton still had hope that they could be reached and reformed. She admitted that she had left the profession of social work and thus appeared to be isolated from professionals, but she assured her readers that adoption social workers were "only too eager to learn the facts and to reconsider—if necessary the views they have formed without the facts." Evidence of social workers' open-mindedness lay in the increasing correspondence and interviews the director was receiving from that quarter. Paton valued the contact of all persons of "proved sympathy and understanding" of the adoption problems she described and encouraged the participation of laypeople in public policy questions. The leaflet also included a comely headshot of Paton, accompanied by a detailed listing of her educational and social work credentials.[77]

All of Paton's enterprising activity came to a screeching halt in June 1956, when she abruptly announced that she was leaving Philadelphia and relocating the Life History Study Center to Ojai, California, where she stayed for the next two years.[78] When Paton had finally completed the move from the East to the West Coast and settled in her new home, she brought up for discussion the issue of pain in adoption. It was her effort to mitigate pain that led Paton to voice her first concrete proposals for adoption reform, all the while denying that she was a reformer. Paton began her discussion of the pain adult adoptees experienced by denying that they had a single, unified kind of pain; instead, she asserted that "the amount of pain behind adoptions varies a great deal. It is as varied as the situations which produce the need for adoption; and it exists in equal measure in situations where adoption does not result." In fact, it had much in common with other human pain, which was why people were so sensitive and awkward about adoption. But Paton asserted that adult adoptees experienced a special pain, which she described as "the loss of the integrated goal, the plucking out of commonness, segregation from race." Perhaps Paton sensed that her definition was unclear. She elaborated, but as so often happened as she delved philosophically deeper into a subject, her prose became more abstract and opaque.

> The question which so many adult adopted people ask, "Who Am I?" expresses the loss of the integrated goal; the poetics and other spiritual essays of the adopted express the detachment from the common; and the compulsive marriages, often to a lowly spouse, express the desire to blend with race somehow. And, in a more common form, there is the unassertive manner, the compensatory vocation, the failure ever to break from the parental hearth.

Paton admitted that on the surface one could never know whether there was pain in any of these lives, unless one communicated directly with them. The interviewer had to be extremely skillful, posing the right questions, in a quiet manner, and had to be able to listen carefully to what was being said. If the interviewer was oversensitive to pain he would see it everywhere; if he was undersensitive, he would deny that it exists. Paton identified *The Adopted Break Silence* as a study where the interviewer had such skills and where her questions "evoked a long-standing situation of pain in many instances." In fact, Paton located the resistance to her work in the degree of pain it identified in adult adoptees, causing readers to either shudder at the sight or deny her work's statistical validity.[79]

Paton was much clearer on "the real causes of enduring pain among adopted people." These she identified as "repression and overburden." By "repression," Paton meant the psychological damage adopted children experienced when their parents refused to answer their questions about their origin. By "overburden," Paton was referring to the behavioral and psychological problems springing from the initial repression in the child. Paton was quick to admit that many adoptions succeeded, some adoptive parents adjusted to their infertility, and (much more rarely) an unmarried mother went through life happy and productive. But in all of the successful cases that Paton was aware of, children knew the origins of their birth, the adoptive parents did not deny their infertility, and the unmarried mother admitted the reality of her status. These facts, Paton believed, were important evidence in the fight to reduce the pain of adopted persons.

What was to be done? Or, as Paton put it: "How in all this hurly-burly of pain can anybody bear to live from day to day?" She denied the possibility that any sort of "very wide-scale" reforms could reduce the pain she described, but she did believe some small steps could be taken. Paton suggested that birth certificates be abolished and in their place the state should issue identity cards. By employing such a democratic and honest process, Paton believed that two sources of pain would be eliminated. With citizens possessing identity cards "no one would feel set apart by having a special certificate." This change would also stop the falsification of birth certificates, which "played havoc with the biological facts of life." Paton, however, held out little hope for acceptance of the identity-card idea. She noted that "people are horrified at the suggestion, and do not stop to give it consideration." Another step that could be taken would be to set up a registration service, i.e., Paton's Reunion File, to facilitate searches for adult adoptees to reunite with their birth families. Such organized assistance would reduce greatly the decades-long uncertainty about the original family that gripped adopted people. Paton also recommended the institution of an educational program for infertile couples to teach them that the prospect of childlessness was not shameful and that a childless marriage could be satisfying. She advocated abolishing the word "sterility" or confining its meaning to voluntary infertility. Moreover, consistent with her worldview that social work must focus on the adult and not the child, Paton decried the enormous amount of discussion about the black market in children. She instead called for discussion about "the human situation of illegitimacy," and she demanded that society "show a little true feeling for the unmarried mother." This entailed evaluating the question of illegitimacy from the single mother's point of view and answering the following related questions: How much did it matter to the unmarried mother how her baby was taken from her? And how did she live afterward? The latter question, Paton asserted, was the really important issue; yet it was never mentioned.

Despite Paton's strong position as an advocate for reforms to existing adoption laws, language, and treatment of members of the adoption triad, she denied that she was a reformer. She claimed that the Life History Study Center was simply a communications agent, and the director's activities were always guided by that limitation. The advantage, in Paton's opinion, of this stance was that

> she can be one person, with no sense of being a Cause; she is simply a technologist and engineer, with sympathy and understanding, to be sure, but primarily she works as a craftsman without feeling she must be a Reformist, yet believing in the revolution that can occur in an individual and within his relationships,

once he starts to solve his adoption problem and become a child of nature—at whatever age.

In short, Paton was a radical individualist, a person temperamentally averse to political and social solutions to what she defined as the primary problem of the adult adoptee: "the distortion of personality that results from the peculiar trauma of adoption, which in turn derives from the lack of any form of reality relationship between adopted people and their natural parents."[80]

Although Paton used the phrase "the peculiar trauma of adoption," she emphatically denied that she ever had any notion that adopted people were "worse off than others"; in this, she parted company with future psychotherapists, such as Marshall Schechter, who believed that adult adoptees were over-represented in clinical-care populations. In fact, Paton asserted, she had never explored such a question in her research. Rather, she had discovered a psychological "stumbling-block," not universally shared, but suffered by "a large part of the adopted population, which would prevent their further development." This stumbling block, Paton went on, was not the result of the original separation from the child's birth parents. Instead, Paton maintained, the adopted person's block stemmed from the fact that their absent birth parents were "socially dead and there is no greater or seemingly more impossible labor than to revive the socially dead." This was why illegitimacy—Paton referred to it as "the whole cultural ritual of repression"—took its toll on the adopted person. Adoptees, powerless in the face of the culture's repression, hurled "themselves uselessly in their hope to become integrated human beings." The result: the adopted became voiceless despite being usually highly educated and aware of their psychological difficulties, while the unadopted discussed their problems endlessly and futilely. In addition, the unadopted groups in the population, such as the institutionalized child and the stepchild, were listened to and consequently experienced "less, if any, social death."[81]

Try as she might to deny she was a reformer, the Life History Study Center's "Releases," which Paton instituted in 1955, are evidence of her reforming zeal. Most noticeable about Paton's Releases was their conversational tone. Like many modern bloggers, Paton treated her audience not only as equals—she never talked down to them—but as a community of brothers and sisters who were united in a battle against oppressive forces, personally interested in the day-to-day struggles of their leader, Jean Paton. Consequently, the Releases were an assortment of confession, lecture, and information, revealing many of Paton's innermost thoughts about adoption and news of her future plans.

Paton's Releases became an ideal medium to advocate for the reform of

American adoption. She often seized upon a current event in popular culture—whether movie, play, or book review—to advance the cause of adoption reform. Although not much of a filmgoer herself, Paton used the movie *Anastasia* (1956), a historical drama starring Ingrid Bergman, Yul Brynner, and Helen Hayes, to criticize current adoption polices. The review barely mentioned the movie, which revolved around the identity of a young, confused woman in the 1920s who is influenced by Russian expatriates into passing herself off as the Grand Duchess Anastasia Nikolaevna, daughter of the murdered Tsar Nicholas II of Russia. Paton changed the focus to the "rough going" *The Adopted Break Silence* had met from the "established public thought of today," that adoption professionals were capable of skillfully placing a child with adoptive parents and successfully creating an adequate substitute family for everyone concerned. Consequently, if the natal parents interfered or even thought about the child they had relinquished to adoption, the social work community presumed that there was either something wrong with the adoption or in the "life experience" of the person who brought the issue up. Adoption theories and policies built by analogy on the experiences and psychology of the natal family were mistaken. As a result, wrote Paton, if an adopted person returned to an agency seeking answers to the question of "who am I?" or "where did I come from?" he is "viewed as a nuisance and a misfit. He is patronized, told to 'come off it,' to busy himself with something more important, like a naughty child." The public, Paton complained, is only interested in the adoptable child or the recently adopted child.[82]

But Paton asserted it was possible to look at things very differently, as illustrated in the film *Anastasia*, which depicted the plight of a woman who, without free access to all the documents needed to function in the culture, suffered a failure of identity. A majority of adopted people were in the same situation. Because they lacked knowledge of their birth parents, a large percentage of adult adoptees failed to develop as psychologically healthy individuals. Still, adult adoptees were intelligent people, "with probing minds and sufficiently broad life experience," who were not satisfied to remain in ignorance by the taboo of silence that society placed on their parentage. Many therefore searched quietly for their original families, with varying degrees of success. They often met with impossible obstacles, which took many forms: "closed or altered records, discouraging officials, fearful friends and relatives." To complete a search in the face of such formidable barriers often took much courage or stubbornness. Paton did not believe the situation had to remain the way it was. Her solution was to demand one simple change: "Do not make the natural parents play dead." Optimistically, she believed that if this social work policy of denying the existence of first parents was discontinued, adult adoptees' identity problems could be solved, because identity was not something handed to a person but "established by him, by his own efforts and serious choices. He cannot choose with the dead. But with the living he can." Paton's contribution to helping adult adoptees help themselves was the Life History Study's central registration service, which would facilitate reunions between mutually consenting parties. At this early date, Paton believed that a successful reunion had the power of relieving both parties of "the pervasive burden of fear and resentment which presently beclouds so many adoptions, and could assist many in assertion, feeling of belonging, and steady sense of union."

Paton concluded the review by declaring that the only thing that would be lost by following her advice would be "the Chosen Child Culture," a practice she had disliked for a long time. The Illinois Children's Home and Aid Society was using the concept as early as 1916 in short stories in its newsletter to advise adoptive parents on how to tell children about adoption. Typically in these stories, the mother would inform the youngster that "an adopted child means a chosen child . . . you were chosen out of all the world full of babies. We didn't have to take you. We took you and kept you because we loved you, and wanted you." Inevitably, the story would have the child one-upping a playmate by declaring proudly that he had been chosen, while his friend's parents had to take him.[83] When Paton refuted this notion in 1956, she undoubtedly was referring to Valentina P. Wasson's *The Chosen Baby* (1939), a national best-seller recommended by the U.S. Children's Bureau, agency professionals, and popular magazines. The slim volume provided an identical storyline of the adoption for adoptive parents to read to their child at bedtime, advising them to tell their child that he or she was specially "chosen."[84]

As part of her reforming agenda, Paton understood the need to build a mass following or at least attract as many adult adoptees to her beliefs as possible. But she also had a genuine desire to keep her audience minutely informed about the Center's accomplishments and her own future plans. Paton accomplished this not only through her Releases but also through annual reports, the first which was issued in August 1956. It revealed that Paton felt a tremendous responsibility to her readers, and she apologized for its lateness. She particularly wanted her readership to know that the Center was growing larger all the time through dint of the hard efforts of the director, a title she now regularly used. More than 400 adult adoptees, adoptive parents, social work professionals, and others currently subscribed to the Center's mailing list. The Center now possessed a library, containing directories and professional literature, and a mimeograph machine for issuing releases and other materials, such as the Center's leaflet and flyers for *The Adopted Break Silence*, which was going through a second printing.

The Center also contained an extensive system of files, including its mailing list; an increasing number of the director's reading notes; and an annotated bibliography. Readers could also order reprints of Paton's other publications, including her interview with the editor of the Menominee, Michigan, *Herald Leader* and the "1200 words of intense commentary on adoption by J.P." from the *Western Journal of Surgery, Obstetrics and Gynecology*.[85]

The annual report included notes on Paton's many projects in development. She was writing up a bibliography and dictionary of terms useful in studying adoption and working on her second study, "I Went to Michigan," which she reorganized and retitled "Three Trips Home." In addition, Paton was assembling materials for a new study to be called "The Adoption Fantasy"; and if demand was sufficient, she would consider writing a sequel to *The Adopted Break Silence*.[86] For the uninitiated, Paton noted that "from time to time, the director gets in her car and travels to near or distant points, usually having contacted, in advance, persons on the mailing list, and arranging with them for interviews." In fact, she announced an ambitious cross-country field trip that would start in September and cover ten states and fourteen cities.[87] Most important of all to the director's growth in knowledge was the correspondence carried on with adult adoptees who communicated their problems to the Center. Paton asserted that their correspondence represented the evidentiary data base upon which she clarified her thinking because it contained "the processes (never twice alike) they pass through, the feeling they have, the pains they have known, and sometimes the triumphs of success."[88]

In addition, Paton used the annual report and Releases to make her readers stakeholders in the Center's activities. She asked for volunteers to help her with "chores" such as addressing envelopes; to agree to be interviewed; and, more significantly, to participate as "field participants." The latter Paton defined as adult adoptees whom she knew well, who were thoroughly knowledgeable about the Center's activities, and who were in touch with other adopted persons or had referred such people to Paton. The director envisioned these people as assuming certain responsibilities for a local area.[89] Here was the origin of Paton's "network of people," her "underground railroad," which, in lieu of chapters or groups, she would cultivate in order to connect adult adoptees with each other.

Paton humanized herself through the Center's annual report by discussing events in her personal life and also revealing her deepest feelings—of doubt, anger, happiness. She rhapsodized about Ojai's overpowering beauty and its benevolent climate. So happy was Paton in her new home, with its agreeable weather and her vegetable garden, that she admitted that it was only with some reluctance that she was planning her next nationwide field trip with its physical rigors. She spoke of her health and revealed that her "lame right arm" was now on the mend and that her work was better organized, suggesting perhaps that the director had been slightly disorganized earlier.[90]

Paton confessed that the work was very slow and listed her accomplishments in chronological order:

1953–54   Preparation of The Adopted Break Silence
1954–55   Promotion of The Adopted Break Silence
1955–56   Development of concepts beyond adoption
1956–57   Study, consultation, writing

Paton's sluggishness, she averred, was not unique. She believed it was characteristic of adult adoptees, and she could provide endless examples. She also held that behind the sluggishness in adopted people lay the virtue of great endurance, and if the lethargy were rooted out, the result would be "an unusually effective individual."[91] Paton dramatized her new discoveries in adoption as analogous to Galileo's conviction on a charge of heresy when, in the face of the Church's disapproval, he championed the view that the Earth rotated around the sun. She spoke darkly of "fears and uncertainties," of unnamed "rebuffs" that resulted in "the adoption propaganda bombardment" ringing in her ears. But, she assured her readers, though the task was slow, difficult, and fearful, she would persevere and get the job done.[92]

5

Religion and Reunion

It has seemed to me that the religious aspect of adoption is in the fact of forgiveness and the grace of God, as these make possible relief from the otherwise impossible burdens of illegitimacy and prohibition of contact between natural parents and adopted children.

—JEAN PATON, 1959

The years 1957–1960 were the most intellectually fertile ones of Jean Paton's life as her intensive reading melded with her experience as an adopted person, social worker, and Christian. Paton produced a new adoption reform program, which she named "Reunion," and new concepts crucial to her understanding of adoption reform. Her voracious reading habits did not prevent Paton from attending to the practical matters of marketing her written work and conducting adoption interviews. In January 1957, she placed another ad in the Personals section of the *Saturday Review of Literature*, alerting potential readers to the preparation of her latest publication, "Three Trips Home."[1] A month later, she devised and sent out a detailed questionnaire on what she had termed the adoption fantasy.[2] In April, Paton mailed a press release to Canadian newspapers, calling on adult adoptees born before 1935 to volunteer for a study of adoption. She continued to promote *The Adopted Break Silence*, sending review copies to publishers and journal editors who requested them and mailing flyers, which publicized favorable reviews of the study.[3] One review, in the syndicated newspaper column *Child Behavior* by psychologist Louise Bates Ames and Dr. Frances Ilg, cofounders of the Gesell Institute of Child Development, which called the study "extremely worthwhile reading," brought in 700 inquiries.[4]

In October, Paton also found time to undertake a field trip to Southern California to interview fifteen people.[5] The interviews with adult adoptees produced little new material. However, one unintended consequence of her California visit was that she learned at a public function that social workers disliked her book. Paton noted that they believed that *The Adopted Break Silence* "was an attack upon the profession of social work." She dismissed their criticism. It was "a small and most grudging view," she wrote, adding that "the book is an attack upon myself, and I have profited from it."[6] Still, their disapproval rankled Paton and would have far-reaching consequences, giving her an explanation for why her work was ignored and laying the groundwork for her future animus against the profession.

By May 1958, Paton had moved about eighty miles east of Ojai, to Acton, California, a small residential community located in the rugged Sierra Pelona Mountains.[7] There Paton began reading extensively. As in her earlier reading, she showed a remarkable appetite for interdisciplinary study, including history, religion, politics, psychology, science, genealogy, anthropology, and sociology.[8] During this intense period of study, one concept—Christian adoption—came to dominate Paton's intellectual landscape, without which it is impossible to understand her life's work.[9] This idea drew upon Paton's intense religiosity, which was initially sparked in childhood. Ypsilanti was home to more than ten vibrant Christian denominations, and while growing up, Jean was a member of a fundamentalist Presbyterian church; she once even entertained the idea of becoming a missionary.[10] The church provided her with "a sense of God," who was "a presence throughout the world, and He was Love."[11] Paton believed that "this was a wonderful gift."[12] But her public schooling tempered her religiosity through critical thinking. She related how just before going away to college at age fifteen or sixteen, her minister gave her an antievolution tract. Once he was out of sight, Paton violently tore it up, "right through the binding." It took her "many years to repair the inner injury."[13] Sometime in her forties, however, as a result of what appears to be a conversion experience, Paton was "born again." She wrote to Richard Byfield, a minister of the Protestant Episcopal Church in San Francisco, "His presence shot through my many-tiered walls. I have been on my knees in gratitude more than one time since I began the Life History Study Center."[14] Paton incorporated the Christian beliefs of forgiveness and reconciliation into her ideas about adoption reform; these religious concepts came to define her understanding of intermediaries, search, and reunion.

It may be a surprise for many to learn that Jean Paton was a religious person or that religious tenets permeate her understanding of adoption reform, because from the mid-1960s on Paton spoke about her religiosity only rarely. There were several reasons for this. In the 1950s, Paton believed that the current generation of adopted children would not be religious in the future because the majority of them would have been raised in positivist or relativist families. She foresaw that "there will be nothing for the Life History Study Center to offer the adopted population, except that small segment which is still being reared in religious belief."[15] Later, Paton deliberately concealed her religious beliefs because she "realized how many people are offended by the slightest reference to God."[16] Eventually, she came to think that many adult adoptees were not believers because the sealed adoption record laws had destroyed their faith. As Paton put it, "if we cannot believe in our roots, we cannot believe in God."[17] In addition, as the Adoptees' Liberty Movement Association and other adoption search and support groups gained momentum in the early 1970s, Paton became preoccupied with "the warfare within the movement" and took less interest in issues that used to concern her, such as religion. But that Paton's religious beliefs remained central to her understanding of everything connected to adoption reform is demonstrated by numerous remarks scattered throughout her correspondence and publications.

Paton's understanding of Christianity revolved around a few basic concepts. Although unsure of God's ultimate purposes, she took from the Gospel of John that "his message [was] Love."[18] She believed Jesus was the adopted son of Joseph, and was a social orphan, which Paton defined as a person deprived of their original parents not by death but by social reasons.[19] Paton reprinted with approval a statement from a British Broadcasting Company program, *The Listener:* "And what of Joseph? Where did Jesus get his feeling about fatherhood if not from him? Yet throughout the whole of Christianity he has been represented as a simple, bewildered working man. Conventional Christianity, tied to the supernatural, neglects Joseph and Mary as the educators of Jesus."[20] Inspired by these words, Paton completed a piece of sculpture on the Holy Family, which "included Joseph, *and* the supernatural."[21] She thought that "only Jesus among all the founders of religions knew of and dealt with the ensnarement of official hostility toward outcasts and uncertain souls."[22] She especially liked to envision "the Messiah" as "'The Lamb of God—Despised and Rejected.'"[23] She noted, "It is perhaps even truer than has sometimes been suggested that the Christian Church belongs especially to orphans."[24] Thus, Paton held that Christianity related to the needs of adopted people. She recognized that the church was flawed and that it did not always live up to its origins, but "at least the ministry had a history and an ethic if only they would apply it."[25] The church for Paton was a much better alternative to professions like social work or psychiatry, which had "little to offer except a pretense of skills."[26]

In November 1955, one of Paton's earliest references to the religious aspects of adoption appeared in her review of Ralph Barton Perry's, *Puritanism and De-*

mocracy, in which she specifically discussed "Christian adoptions."[27] These had little to do with the specific practices of a Christian denominationally operated adoption agency. For Paton, at the heart of Christian adoption was the doctrine of forgiveness, and at the heart of any adoption was illegitimacy. As she advised one correspondent, "illegitimacy colors all adoption practice." It was responsible for why adoption records came to be sealed, and why adopted persons had a sense of inferiority, making them hesitant, which ultimately delayed their development in life.[28] According to Paton, "there was no cure for illegitimacy except for forgiveness." In a Christian adoption, birth parents were "no more evil than anyone else." To Paton, the "basic Christian message" was "Go and sin no more. There is forgiveness. If the practice and structure of adoption included forgiveness, the explanation to the child would be possible."[29] According to Paton, the problem of the stigma of illegitimacy could only be solved "in a society which has been formed by those related to God through the grace of forgiveness, and who express this in their social relations."

Paton admitted to Johanna G. Schenk, Director of Casework at Boston's Children's Friend Society, that no single person was an expert on the subject of forgiveness. Nevertheless, she modestly claimed to have pioneered the concept into the subject of adoption, though she suspected that "it was there from the first, surely."[30] Paton was right on both counts. Not only was Paton the first person to apply the idea of Christian forgiveness to an adoption reunion, viewing the meeting as both a psychological process and a performance in which both parties were considered injured and had to utter words of forgiveness to each other, but she was also a pioneer in hypothesizing a positive relationship between theological and therapeutic forgiveness.[31]

Paton's initial understanding of forgiveness was grounded in the teachings of Paul Tillich, one of the most influential Protestant theologians of the twentieth century. Dismissed in 1933 from the University of Frankfurt for his opposition to the Nazi movement, Tillich immigrated to America on the advice of Reinhold Niebuhr, who had offered him a position at the Union Theological Seminary in New York. In 1951, Tillich produced the first volume of his magnum opus, the three-volume work *Systematic Theology* (1951–63). Four years later, Tillich retired from Union Theological Seminary to accept the prestigious appointment of University Professor at Harvard. His popularity in the United States grew from his dynamic preaching and best-selling books, such as *The Courage to Be* (1952) and *Dynamics of Faith* (1957), which introduced theological issues and modern culture to a general readership.[32] In 1959, his somber visage graced the cover of *Time* magazine, as Tillich joined Reinhold Niebuhr and Billy Graham as heralds of a revival of religion in the 1950s, which was marked by "a sober, critical, Protestant, Christian worldview."[33] Tillich was a powerful, even mesmerizing preacher, and collections of his sermons were the most widely read of his works; three volumes of them were published. Paton took notes on the second volume, entitled *The New Being* (1955).[34]

On February 21, 1954, at the Unitarian Church of Germantown in Philadelphia, Paton had heard Tillich deliver a sermon on forgiveness.[35] As his text, he took Luke 7:36–47, which tells the story of Jesus eating at the house of one of the Pharisees. A woman, a known sinner, approaches Jesus. She washes his feet with her tears, wipes them with her hair, and then kisses and anoints them with oil. When the Pharisee objects to the sinner's deeds, Jesus rebukes him, comparing him to his detriment to the sinner, and gives him a lesson on forgiveness, summed up in the sentence: "Therefore, I tell you, her sins, which are many, are forgiven, for she loved much, but he who is forgiven little, loves little."[36]

For ten closely argued, dense pages of printed text, Tillich unpacked Luke's gospel message to the Germantown faithful. Among the major points Tillich made that Sunday was that the sinner was truly a sinner and the Pharisee a truly righteous man, and that Jesus did not reproach him for a lack of love toward Jesus or for a lack of righteousness. Rather, Jesus' censure was caused by the fact that little is forgiven to him.[37] "Only if this is clearly seen can the depth and revolutionary power of Jesus' attitude be understood," Tillich declared. "He takes the side of the sinner against the righteous, although he does not doubt the validity of the law, the guardians of which the righteous are."[38] Tillich continued by repeating Luke's message in easily understood language, careful to avoid any accusation that forgiveness was conditional: "It is *not* the love of the woman that brings her forgiveness, but it is the forgiveness she has received that creates her love. By her love she shows that much has been forgiven her while the lack of love in the Pharisee shows that little has been forgiven him."[39]

Paton was much taken with the next passage in Tillich's sermon, marking it with green pencil for emphasis: "And nothing greater can happen to a human being than he is forgiven. For forgiveness means reconciliation in spite of estrangement; it means reunion in spite of hostility; it means acceptance of those who are unacceptable, and it means reception of those who are rejected."[40] Forgiveness was unconditional. Tillich concluded his sermon with an examination of those he called "the righteous ones." He underscored that they really were righteous, but "since little is forgiven them, they love little." Their unrighteousness did "not lie on the moral level"; their unrighteousness consisted of thinking they did not need forgiveness. Thus, even their righteous actions were not warmed by love. "The righteousness of the righteous ones is hard and self-assured." Turning to why the righteous could not have helped the sinner and why Christians turn away from their ministers, Tillich answered in a sentence that Paton underscored in her copy of the sermon: "Because they seek a love which is rooted in forgiveness and the righteous ones cannot give."[41] Seven years later, echoing Tillich, Paton condemned social workers and professionals:

> The world of adoption and illegitimacy, the world, that is, which talks about these experiences and which has power over people of illegitimate birth, these people in power condemn and increasingly fail to forgive—or even to understand the nature of forgiveness—those who have sinned. . . . Social work and its allies in adoption and illegitimacy are deeply characterized by hardness of heart, and this condition becomes more and more aggravated with each passing year.[42]

More immediately, Tillich's sermon on forgiveness had a profound personal effect on Paton. After avoiding the issue for twelve years, Paton finally got up the nerve to write to a couple who she believed (erroneously) were her first parents. This experience gave Paton a kind of understanding that matched Luke's biblical message, as she later explained:

> The five days that followed the mailing of the letter preceded the answer, and had nothing to do with the answer. They were the direct and clear result of the breaking of a dam. All the years that I had held back this curiosity, all the piled-up impulses that none of the diversions had used up spent themselves fully and throbbingly in my body.
>   For two days I was too tense to feel anything. And then it came. For three days every few hours, there rose up from the bottom of my being sobs as deep as all creation and shook me—knowing and willing for them to come—until they were assuaged. Again and again, not painfully—for I was mature enough to welcome them—but everlastingly satisfying themselves, knitting themselves into all my tissues, making themselves forever inhabitants of my sensitivity and thus unforgettable, they came and went, so that to the end of my days there can never again persist in me any hardness of heart toward any natural mother of an adopted child. It was peace that came, at that small purchase price.[43]

Paton interpreted her sobs, which had begun even as she was writing the letter, as the result of her turning away from her mother, a "hardness of heart," as she called it. But when they were over, Paton had the courage to search for her mother, to seek forgiveness, and to forgive.[44] This incident was the source of her first insight into the concept of the need to be forgiven in reunions.

The concept of forgiveness also clarified for Paton many things she had earlier found puzzling. A lack of forgiveness helped explain "the resentments, sometimes hatreds, of many adopted people; the dreamlike existence in which the natural parents are forced to live; the hostility among many social workers toward the irregular [illegitimate] births."[45] Paton explained that certain adoption practices, especially the cutting off of kinship ties through legislation that sealed adoption records, induced adverse mental symptoms in triad members and discriminatory policies in social workers, "in which the only form of lasting relief [was] forgiveness."[46]

Ultimately, an adopted person could only become healthy and unalienated through searching for and reconciling with his natal parents. For Paton, there were "no matters in human life of greater importance than those which cluster about the experience of search."[47] But adult adoptees had first to be encouraged to search. Many of them dreaded the unknown,[48] feared rejection,[49] felt guilty toward their adoptive parents, or were prevented by the sealed adoption records system.[50] Quoting from the Gospel of Thomas, one of the earliest accounts of the teaching of Jesus outside of the canonical gospels, as an epigraph to a Life History Study Center Release, Paton wrote in October 1958 that "Jesus said: Let not him that seeketh cease seeking till he find, and when he findeth, he shall be disturbed and having been disturbed he shall marvel."[51] In quoting from this unorthodox gospel, Paton provided biblical sanction for adult adoptees to search for their natal parents, but she was also informing them that reunions were difficult affairs, filled with conflict. Ultimately, though, the struggle was worth it. Paton's experience had taught her that most adopted people who were "firm and persistent" waited until they were at least twenty-five years old or older to search.[52] Paton also believed that no mature adopted persons should begin to search for their biological parents unless they had "an underpinning of religious belief." Otherwise, they might find themselves without a secure base if the search were successful.[53]

The search was so significant in Paton's philosophy because, for her, a reunion, when done constructively with a natal parent, was the only way to overcome the adult adoptee's alienation—or, as Paton put it, referring to a successful search and reunion, "nothing fills the empty spot quite in the same way."[54] By 1978, instead of using the term "void" or alienation, Paton was using psychological language and medicalized the reunion issue, believing that "every adoptee feels rejection and experiences depression. This is to different degrees, but it is universal. And lifelong."[55] There was an inherent friction—a difference in basic vocabulary, their relationship to society, and their life histories—between adult adoptees and natal parents, partly as a result of the fact that the former were born illegitimate and the latter legitimate.[56] The timing of the onset of the trau-

mas was different, as were the signs and effects. The childhood of adopted people was clouded with inhibitions created by the sealed adoption records policy.
Their maturation was aborted, resulting in academic underachievement. Birth
parents, by contrast, usually managed to get through their teenage years, and
even later years, without these inhibitions imposed by society. "They do mature,"
wrote Paton. "Then it all goes up in smoke."[57] The pain the two triad members
experienced also differed. The pain birth parents felt was "grief compounded";
the pain adopted adults felt was "a feeling of exile and bewilderment, being under constant threat of losing what little identity one has."[58] Resentment in adult
adoptees was natural. Paton advised them that if they felt anger toward their
natal parent, they should redirect their bitterness "on the institutions and po-
tentates who brought it about, who brought about the prejudice, and the fancy
method of the sealed record." She asserted that "it is *not* a sin to give birth. That
is not what one forgives; one forgives a birthparent's misconception about her
behavior, and gives her a new mode." But the cure was still the same: "a successful
search and participation with others, removes the bulk of it, and gives us something to take its place."[59] Much of winning the battle of psychological health for
adult adoptees was the process itself: it was therapeutic in its effects; it healed
the inherent alienation resulting from the stigma of illegitimacy and the loss of
kin due to adoption

But what were the components of a constructive and successful search and
reunion? At the foundation of a positive reunion was reconciliation and forgiveness, terms Paton used synonymously. By reconciliation, Paton meant that
a reunion ultimately became a psychologically therapeutic experience. In her
view, the search was a process by which adopted adults hoped to find pieces of
themselves. But they would be looking for another person who had the same
urge. "If done in the spirit of reconciliation, out of a belief that such experiences can be integrating, we achieve more than the strangeness after it is over,"
she wrote.[60] One of the problems Paton envisioned in the relationship between
the adult adoptee and the birth parent was the lack of a clearly assigned role
for either of them in the process of reconciliation. The relationship had to be
created by them: "It's sort of pot luck." But Paton had no doubt about what attitude lay behind the relationship: "They have to heal each other. . . . No one can
really 'forgive' a birth parent except the child she had out of marriage. It is the
adoptee's job to do this forgiving."[61]

Paton's formulation of Christian adoption, highlighting reconciliation and
forgiveness and search and reunion, led to an announcement in June 1958 pro-
claiming a new program of the Life History Study Center, which she named
"REUNION."[62] The REUNION leaflet struck several new notes. First, its tone

was more confident and assertive, with fewer qualifications than marked Paton's earlier leaflets, in which she announced the Life History Study Center. Second, Paton emphasized the psychological damage among many in the adopted population caused by the lack of knowledge of their first families and "the frustration of their desire to know their own people." As a corollary to this statement, Paton asserted that it had been "clearly shown that a healthier personality results from successful and well-considered Search for kindred." This was the central point of Paton's concept of the therapeutic effects of reconciliation and reunion. Finally, the leaflet emphasized the importance of kinship, family, and heredity, which she was just beginning to study. She had not found much to read on these subjects, blaming the growth of the state for causing kinship to "go out of style" and holding responsible the prevalence of sex for making heredity disappear from people's consciousness.[63]

Separately, Paton announced the establishment of Hill House, the first of several attempts throughout her life to establish permanent institutions for adopted people—in this case, a refuge for people whom society had abandoned and who were desperate to connect with "their fellow man."[64] In dramatic language, Paton elaborated on their identity. The abandoned were "not the offender, but the innocent. Not the success, but the restless failure. Not the scholar, but the student. Here is a place free of status, unstratified, full of communication and inquiry." Anticipating skeptical responses both from people who were psychologically secure ("Is it not a chaos in the wilderness?") and from despairing people who had been abandoned ("Of what use can anything be?"), Paton provided readers with two functions she believed Hill House fulfilled. First, its orientation was to provide a cure—the experience of acceptance—for people who, through repeated, long-term social experiences of rejection in many relationships, felt "the resulting torments, the paralysis of will, the disbelief in self." Second, Hill House would be a physical place. Paton recognized that the abandoned were at a serious disadvantage. Other groups, whom society rejected because of their race or religion, were able to join together with ease because no obstacles were placed in their way to communicate with each other. But this was not the case for people who were rejected because of their illegitimate birth. Hill House would not only accept abandoned people but also enable them to find one another.

With her focus on abandonment, Paton's thoughts naturally shifted to her own family. In October 1959, she began using a pseudonym, Ruth Kittson, on flyers used to advertise some of her writings. The use of the surname Kittson was highly significant because it was the first time Paton used her birth father's name in public, and one of her reasons for doing so was that she was hoping to locate a half brother or sister.[65] Paton began searching for her birth father, James J. Kittson, almost immediately upon returning from her reunion with her birth mother in March 1955.[66] In the ensuing four years, she had made much progress. By 1957, she had discovered through city directories that her father had worked at Detroit's Burroughs Adding Machine Corporation. A query to Burroughs produced the information that he was a Canadian citizen, born in 1878, making him thirty years old when Paton was born.[67] Later investigations in Chicago directories revealed that he had held several jobs as a machinist. Paton learned that "he was a rootless unmarried man."[68]

Paton continued to search for her father's family. She contacted St. Paul, Minnesota, and Canadian librarians and priests; after her own search ground to a halt, she even hired a Philadelphia attorney to delve into the matter.[69] Her relentless pursuit of her father's family background was motivated by her suspicion, which took root as early as 1956, that he was the bastard son of James J. Hill, the great Canadian-American railroad mogul and builder of the Great Northern Railroad.[70] There was a connection between the two families. Norman W. Kittson, a wealthy, dour Scots-Canadian, veteran transnational fur-trader, and onetime mayor of St. Paul, became Hill's friend, mentor, and longtime business partner. In Kittson's honor, Hill even named his firstborn son James Norman.[71] In 1958, Paton continued to work gathering material on what she was referring to as her "Hill project."[72] Fifteen years later, Paton was still attempting "to unravel the background of my natural father, but to no avail."[73] Then suddenly, in September 1974, Paton wrote without qualification that Norman Kittson's daughter, Annie, who was unmarried, had had an affair with James J. Hill and gave birth to Paton's father, James J. Kittson. Paton never mentioned what documentary evidence convinced her that Hill had had an affair with Annie Kittson and was her grandfather. Nevertheless, the only thing left unsettled in Paton's mind was "what may have been done to cover it up." She advanced one theory: that "an unmarried man in the family adopted two boys, presumably my father and his brother, but then he died, and it seems their mother [Annie] took them again and lived with them in Detroit until her marriage." But she was unsure of this and commented on her hunch: "Perhaps this is a total confusion."[74]

Searching for her own roots never deflected Paton from the task of reforming American adoption. In August 1958, she announced the completion of what seemed to Paton the endless task of revising "Three Trips Home."[75] Sometime later, in a "Progress Report," Paton stressed that "Three Trips Home" was a very different type of work from *The Adopted Break Silence*. Paton explained that "Three Trips" highlighted the personal search of the author for her mother and father and identified for the reader the "processes which led to a successful discovery experience." It also promised personal interviews with a large number of

Michigan adopted adults and numerous quotations from professional, scientific, and literary sources.[76] In May 1959, Paton sent out an advertising flyer for "Three Trips Home," which stated that the manuscript had been submitted to a publisher, but like *The Adopted Break Silence*, no commercial publisher had accepted it. She mimeographed "Three Trips Home" and marketed it along with the poem *They Serve Fugitively* and "The Method of Benevolence," a compilation of the Life History Study Center's Releases for the years 1955–1959, under the title "Adoption in Existence: Three Studies"; each part sold separately.[77]

Paton's whirlwind efforts to publish, publicize, and sell her work on adoption came on the heels of repeated rejections from mass-market magazines, such as *McCall's*, the *Saturday Evening Post*, and the *American Mercury*.[78] She had submitted the story of her successful reunion with her sixty-nine-year-old mother and the resulting satisfactory four-year relationship with her. In her cover letter to the magazines' editors, Paton acknowledged that she was aware that her reformist approach to adoption differed greatly from theirs and the mainstream media, but defended it by noting that her research of the past six years supported its conclusion.[79] The rejection from the editor of the *American Mercury* was especially disappointing because, as she wrote in her cover letter, the magazine was "the only one in America, so far as I have been able to determine, which has ever carried a realistic article on the subject of adoption."[80]

Though disappointing, these rejections from commercial publishers never stopped Paton from publishing her own work. Occasionally, Paton sent out Life History Study Center Releases that, while appearing whimsical, contained sharp commentary on larger issues about adoption reform. In November 1958, for example, Paton addressed the question "How to Change the World."[81] With characteristic realism, Paton asserted immediately that it was unnecessary to try to change the world; it would change of its own accord. However, Paton said, if one wished to attempt such a feat there were two methods to choose from. In the first method, which she stated was the preferred one of the day, several individuals gathered together, discussed the issue, arrived at a progressive program, publicized and expanded the program, and then lobbied legislators until the group's program had been enacted into law. Paton ended her summation of this first method of changing the world with the cynical comment: "The consequences are familiar."

The second approach to changing the world, Paton informed her readers, was the one used at the Life History Study Center, and it differed from the first in almost every particular. Instead of beginning with several people, it originated in an individual's desire to change only oneself. It spreads into the culture "out of recognition that no one can have a unique problem." The people affected always represented a marginal group, created by social pressure, which resulted in dissatisfaction within each individual of the marginal group. It sought a minimum of publicity. At the outset, established sources of power, as well as publicity, were of little importance. Paton also provided a rare insight into her daily schedule, by way of supplying an example of a person following this second method, which she summed up as "a humdrum life":

A.M	6–9	Breakfast and correspondence
	9–10	Errands and housework
	10–12	Work on files
P.M.	12–2	Lunch and social contacts
	2–4	Yard work and clearing building lot
	4–5	Nap
	5–7	Dinner and social contacts
	7–10	Writing and study

She observed that although some days were more idle and others less so, as the years passed, the person changed and the job of changing the world was accomplished. Paton added that "the Supreme Court never so much as hears of it."

Here in microcosm Paton illuminated for the first time some themes that reflected both her strengths and her weakness in ultimately building her own mass movement for reforming American adoption. In Paton's endless dedication both to replying personally to every adoption triad member correspondent with empathy and advice and to her hard-driving regimen of reading and writing (modestly concealed under the phrase a "humdrum life") lay her true strength. Paton made a virtue out of failure, generalizing from her own experience to minimize the importance of publicity, which she initially had vigorously cultivated through a variety of media and the disciplines of academia and professional social work. Similarly, her experience with legislative bodies and their laws—ranging from sealed adoption statutes to falsified birth certificates—had left her with a deep suspicion of all government officials. In Paton's opinion, any attempt to use the state legislatures or courts for adoption reform was doomed from the start, especially when the problem afflicting adopted adults was far deeper than law alone. Paton's method of changing the world would transform many people's lives for the better, and sow the seeds for later adoption reform, but it proved ill-designed for a mass social movement, the likes of which would not appear until Florence Fisher and ALMA would burst on the scene like a lightning bolt. But this was more than a decade away, and in the world of social reform this seemed more like a century. While Paton was working hard on formulating the concept of Christian adoption, the world of single motherhood began to overwhelm Paton's dedication to adoption reform.

Fig. 1. Jean, adopted at age four-and-a-half months and named Madeline Viola Dean by her first adoptive parents, Mr. Harry Dean and his wife Millie.

Fig. 2. Jean and her second adoptive father, Dr. Thomas Woodburn Paton.

Fig. 3. Jean and her
second adoptive mother,
Mrs. Mary M. Paton.

Fig. 4. Jean on her
bicycle.

Fig. 5. Jean at age twenty-two.

Fig. 6. Jean at about age thirty. "Half way out of the fog; long way to go."

Fig. 7. Jean and June, her life companion of over thirty years.

Fig. 8. Jean with her first mother, Emma Cutting, in Richmond, MI, May 1967.

Fig. 9. Frontispiece from *The Adopted Break Silence*, "The Adoptive Character" Jean explained its meaning: "The non-belonging adopted is shown; also the burdened family soul. Adoption problems exist only in relationship to the general human problem. When the latter is denied, so is the former obscured."

Fig. 10. Florence Fisher, founder of ALMA in 1971. (Photo taken in 2010).

Fig. 11. Jean selling *Orphan Voyage* at an American Adoption Congress conference.

Fig. 12. Jean draped in chains on the "Orphan Voyage Float" protests sealed adoption records with adoption activist Ann Seitz in the annual Delta County, Colorado, parade, July 1983.

October 21 1983

The Editor
Daily Sentinel
Grand Junction CO

Dear sir

Four pastors of the Lutheran church in your area have proclaimed in your columns that adoption is a "compassionate" alternative to abortion. And as if that
were not enough, they also state that there are hundreds of childless couples
who can have their hunger for a child fulfilled if only women will sign away
their own flesh and blood, after nine months of gestation.

One should perhaps hesitate to dispute the statement of four pastors, but perhaps a Scotch Presbyterian can be permitted to try?

There is nothing "compassionate" about adoption under the provisions of the statutes of Colorado. Under these statutes an adopted person is never to have ancestry, is never to know how much of himself is rooted in what he has inherited from his forebears, and worst of all, he is not permitted the experience of
reconciliation with those who put him away. He will never know the experience
of forgiveness, giving it or receiving it.

A woman who gives a child to adoption does not shut herself off from the experience, though she may try to do so. She continues to experience grief and
guilt, which plague her through the years. Adult adoptees discover this, as they
mature, and as they succeed in finding their kindred people. We have seen their
grief, and have wiped away their tears.

That is, adoption can be a compassionate experience if no wall is put between
the adopted person and his kindred people. But the state of Colorado, in its
unwisdom, has put up this wall, and thus insured immaturity to the adoptee and
continued grief to the birthparent.

There are numerous adoptive parents who see this, and who do truly desire the
happiness of their children, and that of the birthparents. It can be achieved,
but only on the outskirts of the present laws. The purpose of adoption is not
to cure sterility, but to repair the social wound of illegitimacy, which requires
reconciliation between those who have been separated. Forgiveness is a Christian, not a legal, virtue. Surely the ministers realize this and know from the
Gospels which they preach that statute law is not necessarily the law of Christ.

Sincerely

Jean Paton
Orphan Voyage   Cedaredge CO   81413   Coordinator

Fig. 13. Jean Paton to the Editor, Grand Junction (CO) *Daily Sentinel*, October 21,
1983.

Fig. 14. Jean at the back door of her home in Cedaredge, CO.

Fig. 15. Jean, at work in her office in Harrison, AR, during the 1990s.

Fig. 16. Jean in 1993 on her eighty-fifth birthday.

6

Illegitimacy, Traumatic Neurosis, and the Problem of Affliction

> Illegitimacy colors all adoption practice.
>
> —JEAN PATON, 1966

During these years of intellectual ferment—the late 1950s—the concept of illegitimacy and the issue of single motherhood became an increasingly important thread, weaving in and out of Jean Paton's research, advocacy, poetry, and search for her birth father and his family. By 1961, failing to see any concrete results of her program for adoption reform, Paton discontinued her Life History Study Center Releases, suspended sales of her second publication, "Three Trips Home," and concentrated on making sculpture and fixing up her house. This temporary hiatus was followed by an intense period of intellectual study and creativity, which laid the foundation for Paton's belief in American psychoanalyst Abram Kardiner's theory of traumatic neurosis and French philosopher Simone Weil's concept of "affliction." Paton considered both concepts fundamental to understanding adult adoptees. But instead of immediately opening up a new chapter in Paton's efforts to communicate with adult adoptees and the larger culture, these ideas remained dormant. In the place of adoption reform, Paton created a new program, in late 1961, which she called "FOCUS," in an effort to communicate with the "illegitimate" and relieve the burden of grief carried by unmarried mothers. The shift in the Life History Study Center's program from adoption reform to fighting the stigma of illegitimacy and helping unmarried mothers was a slow process; at bottom, Paton saw illegitimacy as the root problem afflicting adult adoptees.

Paton had lived with the idea of illegitimacy for a long time. Given her religious upbringing and frequent Bible study, she must have been familiar with the story in the Book of Genesis of Ishmael, the bastard son of Abraham and his slave maid, Hagar. An angel predicted that Ishmael "will be a wild man; his hand will be against every man and every man's hand against him; and he shall dwell in the presence of brethren."[1] Other biblical passages copied the harsh treatment of Genesis on illegitimacy. Deuteronomy, speaking of bastards, provided that "even to the tenth generation none of his descendents shall enter the assembly of the Lord."[2] Nor did the sins of the mothers of illegitimates escape condemnation. The Book of Sirach stated that an adulteress "herself will be brought before the assembly, and punishment will fall on her children. Her children will not take root, and her branches will not bear fruit. She will leave her memory for a curse, and her disgrace will not be blotted out."[3] St. Paul in the New Testament echoed these attitudes, laying the groundwork for later Christian views on illegitimacy.[4]

Paton rejected these biblical admonitions, which were cruel and unjust on their face and contradicted her empathetic feelings for single mothers that had been forged out of the emotionally brutal experience of taking infants for adoption as a social worker. In 1949, as we have seen, while working as a supervisor for the Baltimore Department of Public Welfare, Paton sent to *Good Housekeeping Magazine* an article on adoption in which she denounced the treatment of unmarried mothers and illegitimacy.[5] Six years later, she followed up this rejected article with a 1,500-word letter to the editor in the *Western Journal of Surgery, Obstetrics and Gynecology*, criticizing social workers' unfeeling conduct with unmarried mothers and society's indifference to the topic of illegitimacy. Paton decried the toxic consequences of the cultural silence, which resulted in adopted persons becoming invisible, timid, and alienated from society.[6]

There was very little direct testimony from single mothers in the public realm. Although numerous studies of illegitimacy by Progressive Era reformers had been published thirty years earlier and some states had even enacted an American version of Norway's 1915 Castberg law, which recognized the inheritance rights between an illegitimate child and his father, unmarried mothers, fearing the stigma of illegitimacy, avoided public exposure. In 1957 Paton remarked to one correspondent that unmarried mothers were "even more silent, if possible, than the adopted." She could think of only one book that treated the subject, Nan Britton's *The President's Daughter*, a best seller from the late 1920s that told the story of Britton's long affair with a married senator from Ohio who would become the twenty-ninth president of the United States. In 1919, Nan Britton had a child, Elizabeth Ann, by Warren Gamaliel Harding.[7] Paton's strong belief that society discriminated against unmarried mothers would have been reinforced by reading on the first page of *The President's Daughter* that on June 10, 1927, the New York Society for the Suppression of Vice had arranged for the New York City police to prevent its publication by seizing and carrying off the zinc plates and printed sheets in the printing plant. An order from a New York magistrate's court almost three weeks later forced the Society to return the seized goods.[8] By 1957 Britton was one of only two single mothers with whom Paton corresponded.[9]

Along with the Bible and Britton's activism, a third major influence on Paton's thinking about the injustice of illegitimacy on single mothers was Madalyn Murray (later Madalyn Murray O'Hair), founder of the group American Atheists and best known for the lawsuit *Murray v. Curlett* (1963), which led to a landmark U.S. Supreme Court ruling ending the practice of government-sponsored prayer in American public schools.[10] Murray became so controversial that in 1964 *Life* magazine dubbed her "The Most Hated Woman in America," which she wore as a badge of honor.[11]

On the face of it, the atheist and the devout Christian had little in common, but in 1957, when Murray first contacted Paton, they both were better educated than most American women, well-versed in the Bible, and rebels against society's traditional social conventions.[12] However, it was their mutual loathing of society's treatment of single mothers and their professional experience with adoptions that brought Murray and Paton together. Murray first came to Paton's attention when she responded to an ad of Paton's in the *Saturday Review of Literature* in 1957 soliciting interviews with unwed mothers. This aspect of Murray's life is something that none of her many biographers has explored in detail. Murray, a single mother, had given birth to two out-of-wedlock children by two different fathers. During World War II, as a newly commissioned Second Lieutenant in the Women's Auxiliary Army Corps, she fell in love, had an affair with a young, dashing bomber pilot, Captain William J. Murray Jr., and became pregnant. Her first son, whom she named William J. Murray III, was born on May 26, 1946. Eight years later, on November 16, 1954, Murray gave birth to another out-of-wedlock child and named him Jon Garth Murray, though Captain Murray was not the father.[13]

As a single mother, Murray raised her family while attending college and law school. Her biographers have been content to describe these basic facts and immediately turn to the origins of Murray's atheism. But the correspondence between Murray and Paton reveals for the first time Murray's feelings of persecution as an unmarried mother long before she became persecuted for her atheistic views and also provides a new understanding for her decision to emigrate to the Soviet Union. The Paton-Murray correspondence also sheds light on the origins of Paton's lifelong concern for birth mothers, which few people are aware of.

After Murray's first letter of inquiry and Paton's reply, Murray sent Paton a four-page handwritten letter, ostensibly to request a copy of Paton's ground-breaking study of adoptees in America, *The Adopted Break Silence*. But the letter turned into a heady mix of biography, confessional, and commentary on illegitimacy—complete with bibliography. It was a letter the likes of which Paton had rarely, if ever, received from any member of the adoption triad. Murray forthrightly announced at the onset that she "gave birth to a bastard . . . & chose to keep him," referring to her first son, Bill.[14] Perhaps fearing Paton's strictures, she never mentioned her second son, Jon, either in this communication or, for that matter, in the two women's entire correspondence, which stretched over the next two years. Murray related how her out-of-wedlock pregnancy had led her to social activism. She told Paton that she had entered law school as a result of the frustrations she encountered in the legal fight "to win a name for my son," and that the ensuing court fight over the paternity of the child caused her to become interested in the issues of paternity and adoption while she was working as a probation officer. Over a period of two years, Murray declared, she investigated 700 private adoptions, and was now a caseworker at an "Eastern Family and Children's Agency"—the Family and Children Aid Society of Baltimore County—the same agency Paton had worked at six years earlier.[15] Murray was even replicating Paton's career path. She informed Paton that she was enrolled in a school of social work, studying to be a psychiatric social worker.[16]

Murray's candid revelations about her life as a single mother reinforced Paton's worst suspicions of the everyday humiliations society heaped upon single mothers. Murray wrote that by having given birth to a child out of wedlock, she had been "characterized as a whore, a feeble-minded unwed mother, a person acting hostile against parents, an unresolved Oedipal character . . . a masochist, a selfish person." But that was not the worst of it. Murray complained that she paid a high price for her indiscretions. She was forced to live and work under an alias. Ordinary activities to which other citizens never gave a thought tied her in knots. Murray lamented that she had to go through "a million machinations when insurance companies, schools, unemployment compensation boards, passport authorities, churches, etc. ask for my son's birth certificate." These situations required her to tell "a million lies" and assume "a million pretenses." Murray found her circumstances bitterly ironic: her casework supervisors praised her superior understanding of the unwed mother, "but would quickly have fired me if they had known why I could understand." The whole business was almost too much to bear; she had not revealed to her son his bastard status and dreaded his approaching maturity. Yet, she declared, "It was worth it & more." Moving from self-analysis to more academic matters, Murray provided Paton with a fourteen-book bibliography on the subject of illegitimacy, including Hawthorne's *The Scarlet Letter* and the Bible, "especially Deuteronomy 23:2."[17] In closing, she wrote that she used the name "*Mrs.* Madalyn Murray," calling the name "a pathetic device."

Paton's reply was unresponsive at the emotional level to Murray's personal plight as an unwed mother, offering few words of comfort or acknowledgment that they shared similar career paths. In promising to send her *The Adopted Break Silence*, Paton deflated her correspondent's expectations, saying it did not "deal with your immediate problem." Instead, Paton related to Murray at an intellectual level, earnestly commenting on selected works in the bibliography and suggesting a few of her own. She heartily agreed with Murray on the merits of *The Scarlet Letter*, viewing it as "one of the rare pieces of writing that reaches to the truth of bastardy." What Paton particularly liked about the book was its emphasis on the "importance of the mother's keeping her child—for her own self." In Paton's opinion, Pearl's mother was as important as any other person, and if she was successful in raising Pearl, it would ultimately benefit the child. Among the four texts Paton recommended was Nan Britton's *The President's Daughter*.[18] She mentioned her correspondence with Britton and offered to put Murray in touch with her. Paton recognized Murray's intelligence and signaled her desire to continue their correspondence.[19]

Murray replied enthusiastically, declaring that she "would love to contact Nan Britton." She had already purchased and read *The President's Daughter*, she told Paton, and was in total agreement with Britton's fundamental premise that there was a need for legal and social recognition and protection for all children born out of wedlock. However, Murray would add to Britton's reform agenda a need "just as great" for the "legal and social recognition and protection of all single *mothers* in the United States." And, she rhetorically asked Paton, what about the "frightened insecure fathers who find safety only in flight?" Murray thought it all "too big of a problem," but hoped to focus on one aspect of it.[20]

Almost two months later, in July, Murray wrote Paton another lengthy letter, in which she reported on the progress she was making on her research into illegitimacy, outlined her future plans, and discussed further her ideas about adoption and illegitimacy.[21] Of more interest to Paton were Murray's extreme views on adoption and personal experiences as a single mother. Murray believed that unless there was evidence of severe emotional or physical neglect children were better off with their birth families or relatives than in an adoptive home.

Paton agreed with such a view. But Murray went further. She felt "strongly that a woman or man who is physiologically incapable of having a child is psychologically incapable of having a child." In an era when a medically certified record of infertility was the sine qua non for receiving a child for adoption, Murray's statement was tantamount to abolishing adoption, a position that Paton did not hold at the time. Murray justified doing away with adoptions based on the psychological damage she believed was done to the children by forcing them to live in a home with parents who represent "breathing proof that they are unfilled humans, incapable of such a function as reproduction."

Turning to the subject of single mothers, Murray provided startling and depressing statistics from her experience as a probation officer in Harris County, Texas, while she was attending law school. For more than two years, she had investigated thirty adoptions a month, only three of which had been processed by licensed social agencies. She declared angrily, "*None* of the mothers were ever encouraged in any way to retain their children." Murray was incredulous that in such a large number of adoptions, not one adequate birth mother or relative could be found to care for the infant. She explained the situation this way: "Every conceivable pressure, economic, psychological, religious, legal, physiological, were [sic] brought to bear on them to give the child away." Recounting this tale of oppression reminded Murray of her own horrific experience, which she confided to Paton. At the hospital, while she was waiting to give birth, her physician asked if he could place the child with adoptive parents, who would give the baby a good home. Murray refused to discuss even the possibility of adoption with the physician, and he became quite angry with her. According to Murray,

> he did not cut me to prevent tearing and after Bill's birth did not repair me as he should have. When, after 10 agonizing days in the hospital this became apparent even to me, and my parents, the physician and I had a helleva round in which he told me that "The likes of you, need to suffer" and told me someone else could fix me up. I was taken home and another physician was brought in who corrected the damage somewhat. Bill was a forceps birth and when he was handed to me, he had a black eye, a broken nose, two deep forceps indentations on his forehead, deep scratches across the nose and eyes where the forceps "slipped" and a battered and puffed face.

Murray wrote Paton that she wondered whether this physical damage to her son Bill had been intentional. She suspected it had been no accident: if he had "been presented to doting adoptive parents," Murray alleged, he would have "arrived in better condition."

If her own experiences were in the past, Murray asserted, similar ones were still very much in the present. In her current position as a caseworker she had met twelve birth mothers who had relinquished their children for adoption within the past fourteen years. Every one of them was "overwhelmed with guilt and felt that their present troubles stemmed from the hidden sin of denying their motherhood." Although some of the birth mothers had attempted to search for their children, it was to no avail.

Paton's response to Murray's letter, written nearly two months later, was measured. She expressed shock at Murray's account about the physician, declaring that it was "hard to believe that doctors can be so cruel." But Paton refused to generalize from Murray's tragic episode to all doctors, stating that it was unfortunate that she had gotten the wrong one. Paton told Murray that she knew a woman doctor in Baltimore who seemed "really sympathetic with women who go through this experience, and believes that none of them wish to give up their babies." In addition, Paton threw cold water on collaborating with Murray, just as she had once shied away from cooperating with David Kirk. Diplomatically, Paton suggested that she herself did not reject adoption but rather "chose another, eventual point of entry" to assert her differences with professional social work. Another difficulty that Paton detected was that Murray was too personally involved with the issue of illegitimacy and wondered if that would influence her effectiveness.[22]

Although Paton's response was subdued, it had made a deep impression on her. One immediate effect was to galvanize Paton to organize the Sulphur Mountain Conference, which was to be a continuing program of the Life History Study Center focused on "the problems of illegitimacy."[23] The conference was necessary because Paton believed that the practice of adoption did not wipe out the problems of illegitimacy; reinforced by Murray's ideas, Paton felt that these problems may even be intensified in those born illegitimate who were not adopted. Paton's promotional materials specified that the participants would need to have experiential knowledge of illegitimacy. Just as Paton had learned how invaluable it was to interview adult adoptees, she now wanted to hear direct testimony from single mothers and their offspring. This time, though, she did not exclude professionals and social scientists. The initial reaction from people personally involved in illegitimacy was disappointing—no one responded— but Paton was heartened by some positive replies from institutions, such as the Booth Memorial Hospital in Oakland, California, and the Florence Crittenden Homes of San Francisco; Trenton, New Jersey; and Toledo, Ohio.[24]

For the first time, Paton blamed adult adoptees for failures in her program: specifically, the sluggish pace of getting the conference organized. This blame game would become a repeated motif in her correspondence and newsletters for the next five decades. She used it to explain almost everything that went wrong in adoption reform. Paton labeled the adopted population a "paralyzed people." She informed Murray that this psychological state consisted of "confusion resulting in paralysis that afflicts so many adopted people. It dulls their wits unmercifully—a full blown lobotomy I claim. And no one cares, for we need brains only for sputniks, and perhaps think we can do without the brains of the adopted, rather than resurrect their parents, anyway."[25] It would be wrong to take Paton's harsh judgment of adult adoptees at face value. On the one hand, it was Paton the frustrated reformer, not Paton the scientist speaking. Paton the reformer was always of two minds. She truly loved adult adoptees and idealized them as having something important to contribute to society. But she blamed society for separating them from their natal parents, resulting in psychological problems, some which she believed manifested themselves in passivity.

By March 1958, Paton's hopes of having a real conference with face-to-face meetings of people personally involved in illegitimacy had been dashed by the lack of response from would-be participants. She put the best face possible on the failure by announcing that the April conference on illegitimacy would be held by correspondence, with a report of the conference proceedings eventually to be mailed to all contributors.[26] This promised final report dripped with suppressed anger, as Paton provided those on the mailing list with a detailed description of those who responded and their excuses for not attending or their off-subject remarks.[27]

In spite of—or because of—the conference's failure, in the following months Paton's interest in the problem of the unmarried mother and illegitimacy intensified as relevant items crossed her desk and she gave more thought to the issue. In November 1958, Paton publicized the issue in a Life History Study Center Release. First, Paton revisited her dislike of psychiatry and took umbrage at psychiatric social work research conducted on unmarried mothers.[28] What prompted Paton's ire was a notice that the Boys and Girls Aid Society of Oregon had received $59,000 to study the personality of unmarried mothers. Paton predicted to her readers that the professionals had already made up their minds about the unmarried mother's personality, having decided it in "smoke-filled rooms (interdisciplinary conferences)." They would choose some selected cases to justify "the attitude of American official social work to the unmarried mother." As evidence, Paton quoted from Madalyn Murray's letter, concealing her identity by referring to her simply as a social worker who was herself an unmarried mother: "I have been characterized as a whore, a feeble-minded unwed mother, a person acting out hostility against parents, an unresolved Oedipal character . . . a masochist, a selfish person." Paton also directly quoted Murray's two years of investigative work as a probation officer, which revealed that "none of the mothers were ever encouraged in any way to retain their children."

A second item, which Paton cited extensively, was an article critical of the trend in psychiatric interpretation and the consequences for the unmarried mother. In Paton's opinion, it captured the zeitgeist perfectly. "Today," wrote Josie Svanhuit in *Canadian Welfare*,

> the "experts" generally attribute unmarried motherhood to unresolved parent-child conflict and say it is an "unrealistic way out of inner difficulties" of the mother. If the mother is abnormal it follows of course that she is not a fit person to raise her own child. Obviously then it becomes in the best interest of the child to be separated from her. Since illegitimate children are today practically the sole source of children for adoption . . . the coincidence of the rise of this latest theory with the Hollywood-inspired demand for children is disturbing.

Paton quoted Svanhuit approvingly as she noted that social workers violated casework's principle of self-determination when they attempted to convince the unmarried mother that "it was impossible if not absolutely immoral for her to plan to keep her own child." In other words, Svanhuit wrote disapprovingly, "she must be made to face the reality of the situation," and relinquish the child for adoption.[29]

As Paton focused on the problem of illegitimacy, adoption reform began to lose its urgency as she received, during the first four months of 1959, rejection slips from *American Mercury* and *McCall's*.[30] Another indication of Paton's gradual shift away from adoption reform occurred in April 1959. Paton announced that after three years of relative inactivity, she was resuming her field trips with an ambitious coast-to-coast schedule, stopping in seventeen cities, over the next six months.[31] Significantly, Paton never mentioned the word "adoption" or the phrase "adult adoptee."[32] Instead, she placed ads in the "Personals" columns of several local newspapers requesting to speak to persons born out of wedlock. Several months later, in July 1959, Paton signaled that the Life History Study Center was "expanding its services to adopted adults to include adults who have struggled with the problem of illegitimacy without the benefit of adoption, and who wish to share their knowledge with others in a similar predicament." She made it known that she would be available in Los Angeles to speak to those persons born out of wedlock, especially those "who have already reached a solution to their difficulties and who feel they have something to offer others who are still struggling."[33]

Paton's interest in these subjects was sparked by the renewal of her correspondence with Madalyn Murray after more than seventeen months of silence.
Over a period of several months in 1959, Murray wrote Paton a series of letters relating her woes as an unmarried mother. She began by discussing her
troubles at Howard University's Graduate School of Social Work, dramatically
announcing that she had quit psychiatric social work. Elaborating, Murray declared she had rebelled against the "'Mother Superior' system of supervising"
that was symptomatic of the "total illness" of the social work profession, which
preached an odious ideology against unmarried mothers.[34] She wrote:

> It appears to me that it is a perversion of our animal nature to force human
> beings to do what a cow would not do: give up its young. Even a dog licks her
> own pups. There is no animal, of any level, which does not recognize its own.
> Imagine the brainwashing, the stress, the distortion of natural instinct (I use the
> word advisedly) which forces the mother to give up the child.

Murray had been brought to this emotional pitch by listening to a psychiatrist from Washington, D.C.'s St. Elizabeth's Hospital deliver a lecture repeating
what had become by then the standard interpretation of the unmarried mother:
that having a child out of wedlock was a symptom of individual or family pathology. Murray had taken careful notes of the lecture and quoted verbatim
what the psychiatrist had said about single mothers. "They come in, have children & leave. They are psychopaths with no real feeling. They are the ones (who
give up their children). I would incarcerate in some prison or reformatory. They
have so little capacity to relate." Murray concluded that "social workers are the
pall bearers for the victims of our culture."

In February 1959 Murray was expelled from Howard after receiving a negative evaluation for telling off her supervisor.[35] According to Ann Rowe Seaman,
one of Murray's biographers, Murray was expelled as a result of her objections to
the racism among Howard University's African-American supervisors.[36] Murray's July 18 letter to Paton provides different, and perhaps more convincing, details of the expulsion. She declared that she was "honored" to have been expelled
because it grew out of the context of her revulsion at social workers' treatment
of single mothers. The triggering event was her "radical, heretic & social ideas—
fundamental of which was: each human spirit has dignity and equality with
each other human spirit, and we owe each other understanding and acceptance.
The social worker too often is the enforcer of culture, the persuader to bow to
authority, the manipulator, the craven misfit who forces 'the poor unfortunate' to
live up to artificial standards which the worker herself cannot reach."

Murray then declared that the stigma of illegitimacy had made her own life not just difficult, but impossible. She questioned the value of removing the word "illegitimate" from a birth certificate when the child had to take the surname of the mother. She related in detail the horrendous consequences that occurred despite Progressive Era reformers' best efforts:

> Then, require name, mother's *maiden* name & father's name, for school, employment, army, church, boy scouts & ad infinitum? How does the child explain? How does the parent explain? Then make the showing of birth certificates mandatory for school, for the draft, for insurance policies & (so help me) for Little League!! One need hardly start out with guilt, as it is poured on—& poured on—& poured on, until one acquires it, & its attendant fears.

Disgusted with social work, Murray informed Paton that she had returned to the law. She was now employed as an attorney for the Department of Health, Education & Welfare's Social Security Administration, adjudicating claims for disability. But the status of single motherhood continued to weigh her down. Within three days of being on the job, she was asked to fill out forms for an FBI security clearance. Scared to death of being found out, she related to Paton that she worked "in quiet desperation, fear rising as the telephone rings now & then, for the repeat pattern will come. The F.B.I. will find (oh horrors!) that I am an unmarried mother, a social leper, not fit for decent H.E.W. employees association & I will be dismissed." Still, even through her fear, Murray thought the situation somewhat absurd: "Who the hell would have thought F.B.I. clearance was needed for a non-security position . . . & who would have thought Little League Baseball would want a birth certificate . . . & who would have thought a Work Permit for my son to cut grass (as a private entrepreneur) this summer would require a birth certificate???? and on & on & on."

Murray was torn between her anger at the injustice of officialdom and the urge to mourn the apathy of those who did nothing to change the status quo. To the former, she vowed to "defy them" and "look them squarely in the eye & try to educate them by my demeanor, my handling of the situation, my understanding of their viewpoint." But inside, Murray wept and her heart broke. For the latter, "the apathetic throng" who dared not speak, Murray had no words; she could only grieve.

Paton's response five days later seemed distant, expressing a sympathetic comment only in passing about Murray's "deep pains." Instead, Paton commented on her dislike of Little League baseball when she was growing up, preferring spontaneous, pick-up games, where she had "a whale of a good time." She also expressed her aversion to urban areas, declaring that "we have lost a great deal since we became citified." Paton said she had difficulty advising Murray on what to do because her "reasonable militancy" was so much different from her own, stemming from different pains. Paton noted that no one had been deliberately cruel or unkind to her, so far as she knew. On the whole, for all of her troubles, she had to conclude that life had been rather kind to her. This response seems a bit disingenuous, since Paton's ability to empathize with the oppressed was acute. Perhaps Paton, who on occasion could be fairly conservative, was put off by Murray's militancy. In any case, the best that Paton could do in the way of help was to suggest that Murray come west, to Acton, "an unbelievable outpost of the old ways of life, and a very beautiful spot, California," where she could help with the Life History Study Center program and Paton could help her.[37] Paton did not mind subordinates; she had difficulties with reformers of equal or superior talents.

When Murray wrote again in August, she updated Paton on her job at the Social Security Administration, where she had become much more fatalistic. She anticipated being fired, sooner or later, "*when* it occurs, not if." Returning to the subject of single mothers, she reiterated that she was back to working on two books related to illegitimacy, which had been interrupted by her studies at Howard University. Her latest idea was that single mothers had to publicize their plight, stand together, face the nation, and say, "We are proud to be mothers and our children are a credit to us and to the nation." Nothing was accomplished, Murray insisted, "by hiding, by feeling shame or fear." By conducting themselves in such a humiliating manner, single mothers were unable to mobilize support, spread understanding, or acquire acceptance. She insisted that America needed to become aware of the problems of single mothers and that they were "natural human beings, with natural human problems." Murray exclaimed, "Damn it, the point has come when alcoholics, syphilitics, dope addicts, juvenile delinquents et al are sympathetically handled in the mass media of newspaper, magazine, T.V. & radio . . . so why not unmarried parents?" Then, softening her tone, she said the one thing she had learned in social work study was "not to damn the absconding male. Maybe he has more problems than the woman!" Murray explained that women were forced to confront and cope with the problem of their pregnancies while the male in his flight perhaps incurred even deeper psychic scars. Looking at what she had just written, Murray exclaimed, "I *never* thought I could feel sympathy there, but I do! Ah growth!" Paton made no reply to this letter.[38]

Soon after receiving Murray's letter, Paton proposed a novel solution to the problems faced by unmarried mothers. Although the general hospital was slightly more humane than the old maternity home, where for decades unwed mothers had been shunted out of sight by their parents to hide their shame, she criticized hospitals for not meeting the needs of single mothers. Specifically, Paton believed that the hospitals pressured unmarried mothers to surrender their babies for adoption because so many childless couples wanted them. She suggested "that what these women need is a special Crèche, a small equipped hospital for infant delivery," free of the pressure to relinquish their children for adoption. Paton, however, envisioned more than a friendly environment for unmarried women. Her idea for the "special Crèche" included the institution being staffed by alumnae, who would return to help the newcomers, share their knowledge, and assist the newly unwed mothers in planning for the future after leaving the crèche. Finally, Paton hoped it would be a place where the unmarried mothers'"babies could return for purposes of reconciliation at maturity." Thus, the crèche would serve two purposes in a single institution: it would lessen the tragedy of unwed parenthood; and, by encouraging reconciliation in later life, adoption would become a far less stressful experience.[39]

On October 20, Murray wrote Paton again, identifying the letter as a "progress report from the embattled grass roots." She told Paton that she had been called into the office of the Civil Service Investigation Division to hear that she "had engaged in infamous, immoral & notoriously disgraceful conduct by reason of having an illegitimate child." As a result, Murray was unworthy of associating with civil servants. When the officials asked her to respond to the charge, Murray was defiant. She told them, in a tone that was neither self-justifying nor seeking pity, that she was proud to have given birth to her child and reveled in the "honor and fulfillment which comes from motherhood." The officials said her case would be reviewed. Murray believed that "she had one chance in about 190 million of being retained on the civil service list," and that she would be fired in two to four weeks.[40]

Murray then wrote Paton that she was thinking of emigrating to the Soviet Union. Her biographers have suggested several reasons for Murray's eventual application in 1960 for Russian citizenship in preparation to emigrate, ranging from unhappiness with family to dissatisfaction with work or long-term affiliation with communists and radical political groups.[41] But Murray's letter to Paton adds another dimension. Rather than its being an escape from family complexities and employment difficulties or a special fondness for Marxism, the initial attraction of the Soviet Union for Murray was that she would be "acceptable there as an unmarried mother." America's prudishness was wearing her down, she wrote to Paton, so she was "*very seriously* thinking of going to a country whose cultural climate is not so rigorously puritanical as ours." But she was not quite ready to go yet. Murray again asked Paton about employment possibilities in California, stating that she needed an income of about $6,000 a year to maintain herself and her family. Not surprisingly, she rejected any notion of working in the field of social work.[42]

Paton's response five days later was sincere and direct, but neither sympathetic nor encouraging. Although she had given Murray's predicament much thought, Paton prefaced her remarks by stating she had little in the way of specific advice since they had never met and her history and problem differed so much from Paton's. Still, after rereading Murray's letters, Paton had arrived at a "strange diagnosis": Murray was in the wrong line of work. Neither the law nor social work suited her. Recounting her own positive experience, Paton suggested that Murray contact Mary Bauman in Philadelphia at the Personnel Research Center and get herself vocationally and mentally tested, "as a way of getting a new direction." Paton assured her that "it was a good way to improve one's routing." She provided a mixed message when it came to encouraging Murray to come out to California, first saying that employment opportunities were good, then undercutting that assertion by admitting she spoke only from hearsay. Paton then unintentionally insulted Murray by suggesting that she could get a job as a secretary until things worked out, but again put a damper even on this humble program by asking her why she would come out to California without knowing the purpose of the trip in the first place. She then threw cold water on the entire idea of traveling to California for employment: she would be glad to do what she could for Murray, "but it might not be very much, and you might feel that you should never have come out." In response to Murray's trial balloon of defecting to the Soviet Union, Paton rejected the idea out of hand. The Soviet Union struck Paton "as a land of despair, and only a despairer would find it a homeland." She understood what Murray meant by "our intensive Puritanism," but did not think it a serious problem because "it is breaking up."[43]

If Paton was not enthusiastic about encouraging Murray's move to California, her sympathy for single mothers remained fierce and unabated. Two months after receiving Murray's latest missive, she fired off what she called her "annual Christmas letter," which was published by the *Los Angeles Times* on December 24, 1959, under the heading "Remembered." It began:

> In remembrance of today's forgotten women, the one who has given her child to adoption, never to hear of him again.
>
> To such mothers, to those who grieve, may I send assurance that not everyone had forgotten them, especially not their children, many of whom when grown, think of them with growing wisdom and in the spirit of forgiveness.

Those of us, who are less than perfect can never understand the reason for this lifelong punishment for what is, often enough, scarcely a sin, certainly not the mortal one.[44]

Paton later saved a note from one admirer, who had written after reading her letter, declaring that he appreciated the fine work which he knew she had dedicated her life to and wanted to tell her that "Remembered" was "beautifully expressed."[45]

As Paton continued to be intensely interested in the lives of single mothers, she was becoming increasingly dejected at the lack of progress she encountered in her efforts at adoption reform. Part of the problem, Paton believed, was social workers' opposition to her efforts to change adoption policies. Almost immediately after publishing *The Adopted Break Silence*, "the rebuffs and hostilities" began growing apace. But it was in California in 1957 that she received "the Basic Blow from the very people whose ways and teachings had led, I thought, into the work of helping, which work was now finding expression in this pioneer effort."[46] In 1968 she repeated to one correspondent the charge that the social work profession viewed *The Adopted Break Silence* as an attack on the profession.[47] The following year, a chance encounter one evening at a relaxed gathering of social workers brought home the accuracy and staying power of her decade long suspicion. A social worker, upon being introduced and hearing Paton's name, exclaimed, "'Oh, you're the one who is attacking the profession!'"[48] The comment stunned Paton. From this incident, Paton concluded that "this message had been put on the social work network in California, reinforced by the interpretation that I was beset with an unresolved oedipal complex." Paton believed that she was receiving massive resistance from the profession because of her message that social work should rethink the policy of sealed adoption records, which, Paton asserted, clinical evidence demonstrated was a cause of "disturbances" in the adopted population.[49] In Paton's mind, she was being blackballed by the entire social work profession.

She responded to this failure to communicate effectively with the adoption community in variety of ways. In June 1959, Paton discontinued the mimeographed Releases, the lifeblood of the Life History Study Center, except for occasional publications on special subjects. Discouraged, she wrote to one North Dakota correspondent, "It finally seemed that their time of principal usefulness was over. For there is a limit to what an individual can accomplish."[50] Sales of her subscription to "Adoption in Existence" were almost nonexistent; subscribers were cancelling the third installment of her poem, *They Serve Fugitively*. Paton could not understand it, although she detected a pattern. To one correspondent, she lamented, "People go with me just so far, and then they turn away. It is hard to take."[51] She was also wearied by the continuing hostility of social work professionals, whom she partly blamed for the rejection of her counsel for radically reforming adoption practices. For the time being, she put the Life History Study Center program aside and immersed herself in other activities, primarily fixing up her house up. She also chopped her own wood to feed the stove in the winter. Paton thought it a strange life after being a city person for so long. But she now thought she would be unable "to bear the particular stresses which have come over me without this plain and simple life. Perhaps it is just my small town childhood coming to expression."

Some of these "particular stresses" had to do with the fact that Paton was going through menopause—what she called "that Great Change."[52] She felt sluggish and sleepy; a day's work felt like it took a week, but she said it was nothing to complain about.[53] She continued to feel weary, but attributed it to a pulled abscessed tooth and the complicated sale of her property in Acton.[54] At a deeper level, Paton had become sick at heart at the lack of progress she was making in adoption reform. Despite all of her efforts to give voice to adult adoptees and change the culture of American adoption, she had nothing to show for seven hard years of work. There was so little response for subscriptions to "Three Trips Home" that in June 1960 Paton withdrew volume 2 from sale. The announcement caused consternation among some of Paton's loyal readers, who interpreted the action as a signal that Paton was quitting adoption reform. Several wrote urging her "not to give up the ship"[55] and to continue "to educate the U.S. in the truth about us."[56]

Paton published these letters from her supporters and answered them with a three-page reply, explaining the nature of her struggle. She had become convinced of the impossibility of striking hammerblows against the problem of "illegitimacy and its effects on adoption." Not that she was incapable of doing so, Paton hastened to add, but it was just a "fact that I am not a militant person, I am not conflicted, I am not bitter." She admitted that on occasion she got angry and sometimes cast invective, but she would do this only because the person deserved it. Refusing to accept the mantle of revolutionary or even reformer, Paton declared, "Basically I am an artist. Conflict buries an artist, and ultimately if the artist is strong enough, any conflict is overcome. And not by compromise or by adjustment." But it was not just her self-conception as an artist and her nonmilitant temperament that kept Paton from meeting the problem head-on. The very way Paton conceptualized the problem prevented her from mounting a political crusade against it. As she put it, "Suppose I wished to attack. Whom could I leave untouched? Who does not contribute to this problem of adopted people? I should have to attack the whole population." Paton thought this idea absurd. What Paton meant by "attacking society" was asking it "to include in its bosom the illegitimate—which it can never do."

But if Paton would not attack, neither would she surrender. Instead, she explained that her plan was "to communicate with any and all who are interested, to consolidate and integrate their views and to re-present them to others." This had been her way of proceeding whenever she was in doubt about her programs. Communication for Paton did not mean issuing pronouncements from on high but listening to "something far livelier": the speech of those afflicted by the stigma of illegitimacy. Or, as she epigrammatically put it: "My speech includes the ear."

In October 1960, reflecting her dejected mood, Paton labored hard to produce a new leaflet, "Reunion and Identity." It revealed that she no longer thought first of transforming society but instead would concentrate on the individual, exposing the vast intellectual and experiential distance she had traveled in the two years since issuing her leaflet, "Reunion."[57] She backed away from the Life History Study Center's ambitious program of help by eliminating from the new leaflet, "Reunion and Identity," mention of all the services it had promoted for adult adoptees. Paton appeared to be retreating into herself. The connection to a broader world, suggested in the first leaflet with its emphasis on the importance of kinship, the wider family, and heredity, had disappeared. In its place Paton identified a new program, "Identity," which she described as "an offshoot of Reunion." She wanted adult adoptees "secure in their sense of themselves" to provide the public, through Paton's Identity program, with "reports of the pathways to personal security." Paton was particularly interested in learning who helped these adopted people at critical points in their life to develop a sense of identity, what they saw as the source of their change in attitude from resentment to generosity, and how they acquired their aptitude for difficult tasks and their "growth in consistency in plans and steadiness in pursuit of them." In short, Identity appeared to be a self-help program that might enable Paton to reaffirm her own security in a period of self-doubt. After an initial flurry of interest, in the end few people responded to the new program, and it died quickly as Paton recognized that the issue of illegitimacy was where her true interests lay.

Madalyn Murray's work difficulties brought home the problems of unmarried mothers forcibly. Murray had never responded to Paton's advice that she seek vocational counseling. But one year after Paton's letter suggesting vocational counseling, on October 20, 1960, she wrote her final letter to Paton, dramatically recounting her termination from the Social Security Administration.[58] Murray had thought that she had been vilified, maligned, and abused earlier in her life—but being fired—"the nightmare"—was the worst experience in her life. Murray had appealed her termination three times and spent a small fortune on attorney fees. But most disturbing were "the hours of humiliating & degrading questioning concerning my sex life." Murray detailed the third degree she endured at the hands of federal officials:

> Have you ever been questioned for six hours at a time with a light shone in your face? Have you ever, under oath, been asked when you last had sexual relations, and with whom? Have questions been asked of your neighbors dripping with such innuendo that the neighbors have ostracized you? Has your son had his school mates questioned? Have you had male business acquaintances approached and asked concerning their "relationship" with you?

As a result of her "disqualification for Federal Service," Murray stated that she had been blackballed and was unable to find employment anywhere. Indeed, she had even been denied unemployment insurance. Murray conceded that the government had a right to fire her, yet she could not believe that it had "a right to brand me with such stigmata that a future is precluded me." She concluded defiant as ever: "They can all go to hell. I am proud of my actions, of my life & of my son who stands by my side." Paton never replied to Murray.

But Paton was now preoccupied with the idea of helping single mothers. To her readers she floated a trial balloon: "It is conceivable to move into illegitimacy entirely, and leave adoption (per se) behind." Paton added that she thought that such a change in approach would be more honest, but anticipated even more trouble and thus hesitated to act. Another direction, Paton suggested, would be to develop Identity, but she rejected this path as a major focus, viewing Identity as a program that would continue as a long-term project no matter which way she went. Still, even though she was "persona non grata with most of the professionals," Paton held out hope that there were two "important areas," which she did not identify, that showed interest in her work.

Paton felt liberated by the possibility of changing course and began to view her work on adoption in a more positive light. She declared that the winter of 1960–61 marked "the turning point in the life of the Center."[59] In just a few months, she had experienced "a whole series of breakthroughs," which she attributed to her total commitment to adoption reform and the cumulative effect of seven years of experience. Resorting to a musical metaphor, she compared her breakthroughs to "a kind of accelerando, to be followed perhaps by largo, scherzo, maestoso." One the most important breakthroughs related to methodology. Instead of berating herself for not achieving results quickly, Paton now asserted that a slow pace was not only advantageous to investigating the life course of the adult adoptee, but necessary, even a virtue. She contrasted her measured and deliberate methodology of correspondence over an extended period of time, which eventually produced some success, to social work's dynamic and pressure-filled interviews with clients lasting over five years, which were seen as "chronic, unfavorable, as failures." Paton dismissed the idea that her methodology was a product of her idiosyncratic personality. Instead, she preferred to believe that the unhurried nature of her work to overcome society's inflicted wounds was inherent in the subject matter. It seems reasonable to conclude that Paton was viewing this particular "methodological breakthrough" through Panglossian glasses, rather than admitting her failure to make progress in reforming American adoption practice. Paton's acceptance of the slow pace of reform is perhaps another reason she never successfully organized a mass social movement.

At the start of February 1961 Paton announced a second intellectual breakthrough, which she this time accurately deemed "essential in understanding adopted people and their adult problems."[60] It centered on the idea of "traumatic neurosis," a concept developed by Abram Kardiner, an American psychoanalyst and one of the founders in 1930 of the New York Psychoanalytic Institute, the first psychoanalytic institute in the United States. Kardiner's first notable contribution to psychoanalysis revolved around the question of the impact of culture on personality; his work had a major influence on the emergence of the "culture and personality field" in anthropology and is now considered a precursor of the object relations theory and ego psychology in psychoanalysis. Earlier, however, between 1922 and 1925, Kardiner had worked at the U.S. Veterans Hospital in the Bronx, New York, where he encountered scores of "shell-shocked" and "battle-fatigued" soldiers who manifested sensorimotor dysfunctions, including tremors, spastic paralysis, paraplegias, and speech disorders. Kardiner labeled these disorders "traumatic neurosis," a term first introduced into psychiatry in 1898 by Hermann Oppenheimer to describe long-term emotional disturbances arising in the wake of military action or railroad disasters.[61] Freud constructed his theory of neurosis on the model of traumatic neurosis, but stressed the psychosexual stages and instinctual trends as the factors that set off the trauma.[62] Kardiner's experience in the Veterans Hospital convinced him that wartime traumatic neurosis was a defensive mechanism to ward off trauma, which sometimes destroyed the individual's adaptive capacity. Thus he contradicted Freud, insisting that the traumatic neurosis of war was not a conflictual illness, but the result of an adaptive failure between the ego and the environment. In this way, Kardiner reintroduced the concept of traumatic neurosis into psychoanalytic theory.[63]

As early as 1956, Paton had been attracted by Kardiner's war work on traumatic neurosis. After reading Kardiner's *War Stress and Neurotic Illness*,[64] Paton wrote him, observing that she had noticed the problems and behavior of adopted people resembled those of the soldier. Paton confessed that she was neither a psychiatrist nor steeped in psychiatric literature, but she was nevertheless convinced that the standard neurotic diagnosis was incorrect. She enclosed a leaflet and some introductory material from the Life History Study Center about her program and asked for his assistance.[65] Paton received no reply. In 1959, however, after developing her thought more fully on the subject, she wrote again. Paton told Kardiner his distinction between traumatic neurosis and the Freudian notion of character neurosis was "indispensible in understanding adopted adulthood and the special problems in such lives which are originated under the general heading of Search."[66]

Paton described her breakthrough in more detail in her 1961 Release, "Clinical Aspects of Adoption," which discussed Kardiner's book. She prefaced her discussion by noting that psychiatric offices and clinics were filling up with adult adoptees, and suggested that it would "be the gravest misfortune if there were a misunderstanding of the nature of their 'neurosis.'"[67] However, Paton had concluded that was the case: most clinical treatment of adult adoptees was guided by a false analogy, and nothing could come from such practices except "the intensification of the distress of adopted people [and] continued failure in their lives." She grounded her belief in the inadequacy of psychoanalytic treatment in two sources. The first came straight out of Kardiner, closely following the New York psychoanalyst's rejection of Freud. As Paton wrote:

> I am specifically persuaded that the problem which matures in adoption adulthood is a problem which results *not* from libidinal distortion, *not* from classical forms of neurosis, but that it is the result of a traumatic event, that it expresses the development of traumatic neurosis, that it can be cured only by methods which apply to the cure of traumatic neurosis.

Paton provided an example from *War Stress and Neurotic Illness*. Kardiner described the wife of a military patient, who placed a picture of the soldier's buddy on a table near his bed. Paton then quoted Kardiner's comment that "It is probably another way of undoing the whole traumatic incident, because it assures him that his buddy did not die." By analogy, Paton observed that adopted people were unconsciously burdened with the belief that they had killed their natal parents. For adult adoptees, Paton declared, " Search unravels this"—the Search was the equivalent of the picture of the soldier's buddy.[68]

The second source of her confidence in the correctness of Kardiner's theory of traumatic neurosis was Paton's own experience. Not only were the traits Kardiner described of traumatized soldiers similar to the ones that Paton had observed in troubled adult adoptees (though she admitted that the soldiers' trauma was more extreme), but her own troubles and her own cure rested on similar events. She now viewed her sessions with Jesse Taft and Otto Rank as either therapeutic failures or ineffectual because of incomplete treatment. Her cure, a product of Search, came out of a nontraumatic, nontherapeutic approach. Having established beyond a doubt within her own mind the correctness of her position, Paton ended her discussion with a typical zinger: "Let us begin. What are we waiting for? The Parousia?"

Paton would continue to believe in the concept of traumatic neurosis for the rest of her life. Here, finally, was the empirical, intellectual proof, reinforced by experiential knowledge, that Paton needed to support her long-standing animus against psychoanalysis. It is also the key to understanding the apparent contradiction of Paton's opposition to psychological explanations and psychiatric treatment for adult adoptees' problems while simultaneously maintaining that adoption practices caused psychological problems, or, put another way, Paton's habit of repeatedly excoriating adult adoptees for their immaturity, passivity, and infantilization while also asserting that adoption was the cause of their maladjustment. What a number of adoption activists and practitioners have misunderstood is that in Paton's intellectual world, these psychological traits were caused by social practices—the stigma of illegitimacy, the sealed adoption record, and the refusal to allow adopted children knowledge of their original family by the age of twelve—not psychological trauma caused at birth by being separated from their mothers. Thus, the cure also had to be social—the Search—not therapy. These "breakthroughs" on the subject of adoption—methodological and theoretical—were the culmination of several years of intense thought in Jean Paton's life. Rather than opening up new roads and the beginning of new adoption studies, however, they represented the end of Paton's focus on the subject.

Symbolically, Paton's shift away from the subject of adoption was accompanied by her decision to move away from Acton, California, to Hillsboro, New Mexico. She purchased a small adobe house as a home for Reunion, packed her belongings in mid-May, and arrived in Hillsboro "on or about" May 20.[69] Paton was attracted to Hillsboro for a variety of reasons, which she summed up succinctly: "A generous landlord, good neighbors, quiet nights, no jets or other aircraft flying near, people who like to see sculpture and talk about their own crafts, lousy TV and no FM and so on. Also people who are excellent conversationalists." Hillsboro was also more isolated and primitive than Acton, which appealed to Paton.[70]

Paton's third intellectual breakthrough was the incorporation of Simone Weil's concept of "affliction" into her fundamental understanding of adoption. Weil was an eccentric French philosopher, Christian mystic, and social activist, and active in the French Resistance during World War II. She wrote extensively about the individual's relationship to the state and God, the spiritual short-comings of modern industrial society, and the horrors of totalitarianism.[71] As a youth, she had been an advocate for workers' rights and the poor. She was by turns a Marxist, a pacifist, and a trade unionist. A brilliant intellectual, Weil found new insights in the misery of daily life, "driven by her constant desire not to separate herself from the misfortunes of others."[72] Thus between 1934 and 1935, Weil showed her solidarity with the working class by performing back-breaking, dangerous, and degrading labor incognito in several Paris factories and at a Renault plant, working a milling machine until ten o'clock at night until she was again dismissed.[73] Supporting the Republicans, she went off to fight in the Spanish Civil War in early 1937 and later joined the French Resistance during World War II. Although born into an agnostic family of Jewish descent, Weil experienced religious ecstasy in Assisi, in a chapel frequented by St. Francis. In 1938 she wrote that "the Passion of Christ" had "entered into my being once and for all."[74] Her mystical beliefs resembled Roman Catholic theology, though she was never baptized. After her family fled the Nazi occupation of France, Weil refused to remain safe with her family in the United States. She returned to France to work as a writer for the Free French in London in 1943, contracted tuberculosis, and died refusing food, a choice she conceived as an act of solidarity with her starving countrymen. Doctors ruled her act of self-mortification a suicide.

Weil took everything to extremes; few can match her passion, intensity, or risk-taking. The numerous biographies of Weil reveal that there were many sim-ilarities between Weil and Paton. Paton, of course, never burnt as brilliantly or acted so precipitously.[75] For example, Weil was almost pathologically receptive to the sufferings of others without restriction, while Paton was acutely aware of them, as she grew older, only in unmarried mothers and adult adoptees, and late in life, adopted children. Both women, though, had a visceral instinct for equality and justice. Both had many friends, and both were also argumentative, breaking off friendships brusquely over questions of ideology or policy. Neither woman would compromise her principles. If, as Francine du Plessix Gray writes, Weil felt "an unstinting intellectual responsibility to the world," Paton felt as strongly, but as time passed, restricted it to members of the adoption triad, especially the adult adoptee.[76] Weil glorified the proletariat; Paton, the social orphan. Neither woman's writing was easy to understand. In her school days, Weil's instructor warned, to no apparent effect, to "be on guard against over-abstruse reflections expressed in almost impenetrable language." Aside from her newsletter, *The LOG*, Paton's literary output was often opaque, sprinkled with philosophical allusions and neologisms. Both liked to make Franklinian lists exuding moral and intellectual gymnastics. At the girls' Lycee at Bourges, Weil's dedication and kindness earned her the nickname "La Simone" or "Mother Weil" from the students in her philosophy class; for similar traits, admirers bestowed upon Paton the affectionate sobriquet the "mother of adoption reform." But there were important differences, too. Weil's closest friends were men; Paton's confidantes were women. Weil was sickly, anorexic, and plagued with punishing migraines. For most of her life, Paton remained in robust health. Weil's parents provided crucial support for Weil in times of need. Paton was remarkably self-sufficient. Weil's religious thought can be placed in the tradition of radical Christianity, in the fellowship of Martin Luther King, Jr., and Daniel and Philip Berrigan. Paton's Christianity, though infusing her conception of adoption reunions, remained personal and ecumenical.

Paton first encountered Weil's thought in 1956 when she read *The Need for Roots*, written just before Weil's death and translated into English in 1952.[77] The book addressed France's past, analyzing the spiritual and ethical reasons for France's defeat by the Nazis in order to lay out a roadmap for the country's postwar future. Weil attempted to convince the leader of the French Resistance, Charles de Gaulle, to form a contingent of nurses that would serve at the front lines. In using the metaphor of "rootedness," she attempted to enumerate the "needs of the soul" in order to prevent the development of demoralizing uprootedness. Weil's analysis of these needs, as Robert Coles has observed, "amounts to a remarkable conservative manifesto, a powerful statement on her part with respect to politics and social institutions. The categories are themselves instructive to consider—order, private property, honor, hierarchism, obedience."[78] Weil's conservatism was echoed in Paton's later insistence that her emphasis on the preservation of the natal family; that is, preserving the connection between the adopted person and the birth family was not radical, but conservative. Similarly, Paton's expression of disdain for the "rights" of adopted persons in the debate over sealed adoption records strongly resembled Weil's discussion of the priority of obligations over rights.[79] Reinforcing Paton's scorn for the notion of adoption "rights" was another piece by Weil, which Paton read and took extensive notes on. Entitled "Beyond Personalism," it equated rights with force and argued for the superiority of justice over rights.[80]

But it was Weil's concept of affliction, most fully articulated in her book *Waiting for God*, that had the most profound effect on Paton. As result of her experience on the assembly line, which "reinforced her belief that suffering was the only road to spiritual growth," Weil developed her concept of "affliction."[81] She wrote of her transformative experience to the Dominican priest Father Joseph-Marie Perrin:

> After my year in the factory . . . I was, as it were, in pieces, soul and body. Until then . . . I knew quite well that there was a great deal of affliction in the world, I was obsessed with the idea, but I had not had prolonged and firsthand experience with it. As I worked in the factory . . . the affliction of others entered into my flesh and my soul. . . . What I went through there marked me in so lasting a manner that still today when any human being whoever he may be and in whatever circumstance, speaks to me without brutality, I cannot help feeling . . . that there must be a mistake. . . . There [at the factory] I received forever the mark of slavery. . . . Since then I have always regarded myself as a slave.[82]

Paton declared that adoption and affliction were synonymous and that "the study of adoption was the study of affliction." Believing thus that it was incumbent upon anyone concerned about adoption to understand the concept of affliction, Paton used a Life History Study Center "Release" to quote a long passage from Weil's essay "The Love of God and Affliction":

> There is not real affliction unless the event that has seized and uprooted a life attacks it, directly or indirectly, in all its parts, social, psychological, and physical. The social factor is essential. There is not really affliction unless there is a social degradation or the fear of it in some form or another . . . .
> Affliction is something specific and impossible to describe in any other terms, as sounds are to anyone who is deaf and dumb. And as for those who have themselves been mutilated by affliction they are in no state to help anyone at all, and they are almost incapable of even wishing to do so. Thus compassion for the afflicted is an impossibility. When it is really found we have a more astounding miracle than walking on water, healing the sick, or even raising the dead.[83]

Paton had only superlatives for Weil's analysis. She declared that "nothing" she had read compared to Weil's statement "for grasp and presentation." It came "as near to the description of the problem faced by people of illegitimate birth as anything" she had ever read, adding in an uncharacteristically immodest aside, "and you know how many sources I have searched." In future years, Paton would recommend *Waiting for God* as "splendid," the essay "The Love of God and Affliction" as "almost unique. Except maybe for the book of Job."[84]

Paton recognized that there were both negative and positive aspects to the concept of affliction. On the negative side, she informed her readers, ordinary people, no matter how skilled or dedicated they were, did not have the ability to grasp the problem they were dealing with. The positive side, Paton observed, was that affliction was "bound up with ultimate values, the resolutions of the polarities and disturbances of life." Paton cited Oedipus and Job as "men of affliction, and their tales have more meaning to more [people], and deeper meaning, than any others known to us."[85] Here Paton was alluding to Weil's statement that affliction was a "marvel of divine technique," which used suffering as a path way to beauty and reality.[86] As Francine du Plessix Gray has written, for Weil, "the transforming power of suffering is indispensable to understanding that the entire universe is 'the vibration of the word of God.'"[87]

This point cannot be overemphasized enough because of the confusion caused by Paton's frequent use of the concept when discussing the adult adoptee population. In its everyday usage, most people interpreted the term *affliction* as pain, suffering, or sickness. In such common understandings, a person wants to escape or be cured from a state of affliction. But at Weil's and Paton's hands, affliction became both a badge of distinction and the necessary means to a higher level of existence. The most serious example of the confusion that ensued as a result of misunderstanding Paton's use of the concept of affliction occurred in 1968. Barbara Grier, the newly appointed editor of *The Ladder*, the newsletter of the Daughters of Bilitis, the first national lesbian rights organization in the United States, invited Paton to write an article for the magazine.[88] In the course of writing the piece, which compared adult adoptees and lesbian groups, Paton repeatedly used the term "afflicted" and "afflictions," referring to the social handicaps of lesbians.[89]

Grier liked the article very much but warned Paton that readers' replies might be very hostile, from "fighters who will want to take your hide off in inch wide strips for the word 'affliction.'"[90] Paton found Grier's reaction to the word "affliction" interesting, and explained to Grier that "the word is now in disrepute, and there is almost nothing written on it" except the Book of Job and Simone Weil's *Waiting for God*. Weil's work, Paton declared, was "explicit, detailed," and, she presumed, "accurate on the subject." Grier was not to worry too much, Paton jauntily assured her: the *Ladder*'s complaining readers would be answered "with some of the best literate stuff that has ever appeared."[91] Grier replied that she did not mean to be overprotective or to suggest that Paton was unable to defend herself against critics. She was "fully aware of the range of your mind, just the

little I have seen makes me well aware you could take on a regiment and win."
Still, Grier felt it necessary to explain that "the word affliction, however, will take
on 'nigger' tones to some of my readers . . . who do not feel 'afflicted,' or rather
who do not wish to feel so . . . in either case, they will be just as angry."[92] Paton
gave some thought to Grier's strictures on the offending term, and three months
later confessed that concerning the word "afflicted," many people were mistaken
if they thought she meant "sick." She declared emphatically, "I *do not*." But she
did not offer to define it. Paton simply repeated that not much had been written
on the subject and that she would do some serious writing on it.[93]

Weil's concept of affliction on Paton was dramatic. In November 1961, she
announced that the Life History Study Center was planning to make "a pronounced shift in focus of its activities in the next several weeks." It would change
over "from looking at adoption to looking at illegitimacy."[94] The new program
would be known as FOCUS and would attack the issue from two directions.
Paton would seek out and talk to people, including unwed mothers. In addition,
she would mentor them "in program development," in order that they could ultimately take responsibility for dealing with their own problems. Second, Paton
would attempt to change the negative image of illegitimacy by collecting and
publicizing positive materials on illegitimacy that had "light, color, and hope."
Such publications, she believed, would make the experience of illegitimacy
"more bearable" for people unable to evade it or who choose to accept it "even
when they are offered the refuge of adoption." In January 1962 Paton announced
that the initial response to the new program had been greeted by "almost unani-
mous and even pronounced approval." She noted, with much satisfaction, the
sharp and surprising contrast between this heartfelt approval of FOCUS and
"the long, ah long experience of resistance, frown, and even insistent condemnation" of the Life History Study Center from social workers.[95]

To combat the negative image of single motherhood, Paton provided her
readers with ways that they could enlighten and empower themselves to combat the stigma of illegitimacy. She recommended that they set aside Freud and
read Jung; Freud was not applicable to orphans, while Jung was helpful, though
not the last word. When they read newspaper articles about adoption and illegitimacy, Paton advised them to read critically. They should always "look for
the voice of experience," by which she meant the voice of the adopted or "illegitimate" person. If the voice of experience was absent, Paton instructed them to
ask, "Whose voice *is* it?" She also advocated that her subscribers should study
great literature—the classics—and folktales, because almost without exception
"they describe alienation, exile, illegitimacy; or they are written by such persons." Paton believed that some operas were another fruitful source of similar

themes. She recommended that her readers listen to the heroine's aria in act 4, "Sola, Perduta, Abbandonata" (Alone, Lost, Abandoned), in her favorite opera, Puccini's *Manon Lescaut*, because it captured the pain that many adopted people must feel and thus would validate their feelings and provide them with comfort.[96] Finally, she encouraged her followers not to be disheartened that the problem of illegitimacy had been around for ages. It was no different from most other human problems in that respect. She assured them that there existed examples of people—role models—who have lived successful lives even with the same social problem. The lessons to be taken away, Paton advised her readers, was that they discover the details of these successful lives, make inquiries of others similarly situated, and begin to search.[97] With this sort of logic—finding and identifying "illegitimate" heroes, Paton hoped she might help destigmatize those born out of wedlock.

But Paton's new FOCUS lasted less than one year. In February 1962, a month after its establishment, Paton issued a single-sentence Release announcing that, on her physician's advice, both "Reunion" and "FOCUS" were being transferred to "inactive status" for six months, until September.[98] She later reported that she suffered from "accumulated fatigue and tension," one of the many emotional symptoms of menopause.[99] Her doctor's advice was not surprising. For centuries before the 1960s, female physiology equaled pathology.[100] But by the 1950s, physicians were being encouraged to listen to female patients and to let them know that their menopausal symptoms would eventually diminish on their own; and popular advice literature was also starting to see menopause "as a natural transition with few significant consequences."[101] In March and early April Paton returned to Acton, discovered the "magic result of a winter of California rains," and decided eventually to return to the first home of Reunion."[102] By May, Paton declared that her lethargic spirit, which had brought her work to a standstill, had lifted, and that she would be ready to resume her activities in the fall. But instead of continuing her work with birth mothers and children born out of wedlock, Paton returned to the problems afflicting adult adoptees and created Orphan Voyage.

7

Orphan Voyage

The reason I use the term Orphan Voyage is that adopted people lose their parents, although not by death, but by a social decision that they had no part of. We are a different kind of orphan.

—JEAN PATON, 1994

Orphan Voyage, "a program of mutual aid and guidance for social orphans,"[1] grew out of several profound insights that Jean Paton received while attending two presentations she heard in April 1962 while attending the Los Angles meeting of the Child Welfare League of America. The first presentation, by Dr. Genevieve Carter, a Southern California professor of social work, resulted in Paton's issuance in June of her only substantive piece on illegitimacy for the year. Carter suggested that because there were so many difficulties in the lives of adopted people that "'we' would have to learn to be satisfied with something less than average perhaps 'ninety-percent.'" Paton fired back: "No, illegitimacy is not inferiority." She declared that people of illegitimate birth were fully capable of a life filled with joy, hope, and fulfillment. Paton admitted that "the bastard" did not arrive at these things easily—it usually took three decades to complete the transformation—but illegitimacy was simply a fact, not something to be resented. Paton asserted that most of the problems of people of illegitimate birth arose from "a complete misunderstanding" of the social conditions in which successful and fulfilled lives could be achieved, and that this misapprehension was shared not only by illegitimates but by "nuclear social folk."[2]

But it was the conclusions that Paton reached from her criticism of Carter's single comment that were most startling and would have far-reaching results both for her own life and for adoption reform. She declared that the most valued service that any one person could do for another would be to explain these adverse social conditions and experiences in order to educate those "who despair, and to encourage those who understand but falter." Paton concluded that for these reasons, FOCUS intended "to shift itself from looking at illegitimacy to being in relationship with those who are on the way to fulfillment, developing ourselves and our resources out of this communication."

Related to this shift in outlook was an additional insight that Paton received at the Child Welfare League of America meeting from a second paper, this one delivered by Marshall D. Schechter, a Beverly Hills child psychiatrist in private practice.[3] Paton dubbed the paper Schechter read at the 1962 Child Welfare League of America meeting "the Schechter report." Writing to her FOCUS subscribers, Paton succinctly summarized Schechter's thesis, which, like an earlier published paper, revealed the existence of "an amazingly large-scale psychiatric problem in the population of adopted people."[4] Her initial reaction bordered on triumphal: "This was no surprise to yours truly." Paton, however, believed that this revelation must have been shocking to the hundreds of people in the audience. As an example of their astonishment, Paton reported that she had sat next to a San Francisco Welfare Department social worker, who throughout the presentation stoutly denied Schechter's remarks and was overheard by Paton to mutter under her breath that he must be "finding only what he was looking for."[5]

Initially, Paton viewed the paper in positive terms and was grateful to Schechter for supporting her position. She asserted, "A stone has been lifted; for no longer need I scream and point and insist and maintain to all who are in ear-shot, that this problem exists."[6] It was also transformative. The Schechter report, Paton stated, allowed her to resume the original plan for the Life History Study Center, which had been "long postponed" because of what she perceived as the crucial priority of the subject of illegitimacy. Now, however, that the professionals had "opened the Black Box of adoption," Paton could do what she wanted to do from the beginning: "to help some of my people."[7]

Paton cautioned her readers that now was not the time for complacency and equated the Life History Study Center's new service activities as being on par with the nascent civil rights movement. "Just because we live in the midst of talk about human rights, and the emancipation of submerged populations, and the freedom of minority groups—do not be confident that the problems of adopted people are about to be solved. They are the final minority, the enduring colonials, the silent folk who upon rare occasion speak."[8] The Schechter report and Paton's announced shift of focus away from illegitimacy and into service to the adopted population also signaled the solidification of the third phase of her adoptive identity, what Harold Grotevant has identified as "connections beyond the family, to friends, neighborhood, community, and culture."[9] These aspects of

Paton's adoptive identity were always present, but they were brought together in a harmonious whole in her new effort, Orphan Voyage.

On September 1, 1962, Paton announced in a preliminary statement the creation of Orphan Voyage.[10] A product of nine years of concentrated study of adopted adulthood in all its complexity, the new program would have three purposes. First, Orphan Voyage would continue to investigate and study adult adoptees. Second, it would provide help to them and others who felt abandoned by one or both of their birth parents. Elaborating on this point, Paton envisioned that the help was not to be a one-woman operation, but instead she would enlist those "who have had appropriate life experience" and were willing to help others. Always guarding against the arrogance of "experts" telling their clients what was good for them, Paton insisted that the form that any such help offered by Orphan Voyage would be "determined both by those who give and by those [who] receive" it. Paton was unable to abandon people born out of wedlock who were not adopted. She envisioned searching for them and offering help contingent upon understanding their needs. Paton conjectured that perhaps just being included in Orphan Voyage would be of some help to them. The third purpose of Orphan Voyage was to demonstrate to "the unadopted and legitimate" that the program's efforts were not a threat to or in conflict with their interests. Paton did not elaborate on what those interests were, but it is safe to say that she was directing her remarks to adoptive parents and social workers in an effort to break down the opposition of these groups that were preventing adopted persons from connecting with their natal families. She counseled her readers that patience was of the utmost importance, because they had embarked upon a new human experience: nothing less than giving social orphans "a direct voice" at the table where their fate was decided.

Ten days later, Paton announced to her readers, "The voyage is underway."[11] To another correspondent, she stated that the Voyage had "lifted anchor. It will probably be as slow as a barge trip, but on the other hand we are going where nobody ever went before."[12] Paton reported that she had recruited a dozen like-minded souls who were "spread all over the map" and that although the number seemed small, "We are enough." Paton went on to outline her own role in Orphan Voyage. She was going to continue to study and publish work on adult adoptees, confront the California welfare bureaucracy, and begin to accept referrals from social orphans and others and transfer these to her twelve newly joined members. She asked these dozen to inform her if they were willing to have Paton refer to them people who lived nearby. She wanted these adult adoptees in need to have someone personally to assist them, since Paton would be geographically far away. Here was the essence of Orphan Voyage: Paton would act as the central contact point—the coordinating engineer—of a huge referral system, sending out messages to her agents located across the United States to personally aid social orphans.[13]

At least initially, Paton did not envision search and support groups in Orphan Voyage chapters—it was to be a single-group, one-on-one operation. Nevertheless, Paton spoke the language of community. In private, she enjoyed using an extended nautical metaphor to express the egalitarian, affectionate community she anticipated creating. To potential Voyager Leona Bayer, Paton wrote, "If you want to participate in the Voyage, you have to come on board, maybe swab the decks, stand watch, or [do] other sometimes onerous, sometimes thrilling chores. Nobody on this ship except the crew!"[14] In public, Paton reported that she had planned for the first meeting of Orphan Voyage to take place at her home in Acton, but this was not to be. Instead, she carried on the initial organizing activities by letter. Ending her second communication to her twelve members, she stated that had they been present she would have had to make a speech. In such a case, she would have said:

> It is time, past time, but still not too late, to realize that the social orphan is not alone in this vast universe, but is kindred to many, many like himself. All he need do to ripen his life and receive his blessing is to open himself again to the day, to the years, and to his brethren.

Paton assured her correspondents that she was content with the organization's beginnings, and awaited their replies.[15]

From the very beginning, some people objected to Paton's use of the term "social orphan" and even the name of her organization, "Orphan Voyage."[16] On several occasions, she took time to clarify and defend her choice of terms.[17] To one correspondent, Paton wrote that after much study she realized that there was a great deal of significance in, and many types of, orphanhood. There was "the death orphan, the social orphan, the person born out of marriage, and combinations thereof."[18] All of these varieties of orphanhood had much in common, and their relationship to adoption lay in identity and creativity. She explained, "I firmly believe that adoption without natural identity stifles the creative life. Orphanhood promotes it."[19] On another occasion, Paton impatiently responded to the question of her use of the word "orphan" by declaring: "If we are not orphans, why are we in this work? We are seeking reconciliation with parents—or children—with whom we have lost. Is this not orphanhood?"[20] Paton explained that the name "Orphan Voyage" sprang from the combination of her personal experience of being so alone in her efforts to effect change in adoption and that throughout her life she was "indeed on a Voyage, and was increasingly attuned to the fact that others, in equal or even greater isolation, were on the same lonely course." To another correspondent, she simply stated that the reason she used the term Orphan Voyage was that "adopted people lose their parents not by death but by a social decision that they had no part of. We are a different kind of orphan."[21]

In December, feeling that she had not yet explained Orphan Voyage's purpose clearly enough, Paton issued another Release, "What Is the Orphan Voyage?"[22] Again, she used seafaring metaphors. It was time, she told those "who were on the Voyage and [those] who are interested in it from positions on the shore," to "open the sealed orders put into our hands as we lifted anchor and see what it is we are doing, where we are to go, and how we may complete the trip successfully." Paton playfully imitated the metaphorical form of one of her favorite books, John Bunyan's Christian allegory *The Pilgrim's Progress*, to inform her readers what their orders were:

> Proceeding cautiously but firmly from the point of departure: namely, Great Smog of Grief and Shame, pass beneath the over-weening cliffs of Authority and Profession, heed not the fragrant Air of Adjustment nor the Organ of Oblivion, but veer sharply into the Turbulence of Timidity and pass beyond into the Surrounding Sea. There in that audacious water, that unchartered mass, you will as crew discover each your Island of Identity.[23]

Proudly she informed her readers that Orphan Voyage now had its own letterhead, that it had received responses from the outside world, and that its members were gaining a sense of one another, though Paton admitted that they had not yet learned to work together, and presciently added that "perhaps we never will." She also announced Orphan Voyage's first big project, "Illegitimacy and the Artist," which, she explained, was "calculated to bring us beneath and beyond those over-weening cliffs."

Paton's life was seamless: her artistic endeavors were never an isolated activity; they always were created in support of adoption reform. An example of Paton's pragmatic use of art is evident in another Release sent the same day, December 11. In it she provided a rationale behind Orphan Voyage's 1963 work project, "Illegitimacy and the Artist": it would provide "illegitimates" with both a platform for self-esteem and validation from society.[24] For Paton, the fundamental problem that those born out of wedlock confronted their entire lives was "the guilt which they feel so deeply, and which nothing seems able to release them from." Paton believed that as long as "illegitimate" people felt guilty they would be helpless to fight their oppressors or grow to be fully formed human beings. They "cannot join forces, they cannot resist the wrongs done them, and they cannot develop their own lives out of their talents and toward their dreams." What was to be done? How could their guilt be removed? Paton rejected using the mass media because it was already saturated with the message, directed at parents, foster and adoptive parents, and even grandparents, that people born out of wedlock were innocent. Paton did not believe that was true. Nor did she believe that illegitimates desired innocence; she certainly did not. Their goal was "only to live out our lives with at least a show of self-determinism." To accomplish this objective and to prove to themselves, as well as to others, that persons born out of wedlock had a valuable contribution to make to society, Paton proposed to house in her new studio at Reunion a collection of materials on the theme "Illegitimacy and the Artist." By 1970, Paton had identified over 600 orphans in her exhibit notebook.[25]

Paton confessed that the idea of an orphan "character" and its relation to creative expression had grown on her gradually; she was unable to pinpoint the exact time it hit her. But she was acutely aware that Edward Albee was one of the original forty respondents in *The Adopted Break Silence*, "when he was a nobody (in 1953)." She then began noticing other creative orphans, such as the explorer Henry Morton Stanley, celebrated for the words he uttered to Scottish missionary and explorer David Livingstone upon finding him: "Dr. Livingstone, I presume?" To one correspondent, Paton observed that Stanley revealed himself to her in that famous phrase by using the "typical orphan subjunctive."[26] Decades earlier, when she worked as a social worker, Paton had discovered that she had a special gift for the language of adopted people. She had now developed a theory that orphans spoke a different language and that they formed a special community, separate from adopted people and those of legitimate birth. As Paton assured one correspondent some years later, "Yes, we orphans do think of each other, usually, as brothers and sisters. It is sort of because we speak the same language, and some of it is not the same language that other people speak. It is a little like meeting someone from our city when we are in a foreign country. We reach out warmly to them."[27] Paton believed it was this unrecognized linguistic difference between orphans and adult adoptees that prevented experts from effectively helping them. As a result, she informed another correspondent, there was "not much of an alternative to what Orphan Voyage was trying to do: set up communication lines, and some semblance of order and organization."[28]

As 1963 began, Paton again addressed the issue of Orphan Voyage's purpose. She began by noting what she considered the most galling criticism of her groundbreaking 1954 study, *The Adopted Break Silence*: that its participants were not typical of the adopted population. She quickly denied the critics' accusation that they were "relatively sick compared to most adopted people."[29] In fact, they were as relatively healthy as compared to the general population of adopted people, a fact that Paton stated that "will eventually be accepted." It was because social orphans past and present were healthy that "the Orphan Voyage is not a trip to oblivion, but an example for those who are to come." Just as John Winthrop aboard the *Arbella* in 1630 envisioned the Massachusetts Bay Colony to be a "city upon a hill" with the eyes of the world upon the Puritans, Paton imagined that the "homely detail" of the Voyagers' lives "will someday be an example to others" who have been stigmatized by illegitimacy or family breakup and "who wonder how to live—because they feel so different from their neighbors and friends." Paton recognized, however, that Orphan Voyage's potential as an exemplar was in the distant future, and that her failure to meet personally with the Voyagers through her field trip made her idea "a very lonely proposition." She thus implored her followers to substitute the examination of the lives of creative artists in lieu of a personal meeting with her. It was through the biographies and works of artists, Paton declared, that "you will find an echo to the life and conundrums that are in you."

Along with providing a rationale for Orphan Voyage's existence and a positive role for orphans and adult adoptees, Paton reassured her readers (and maybe herself) of the physical reality of the new organization and its many assets. As the new year got underway, she issued a Release providing an inventory of the many components making up Orphan Voyage. At Acton, there were three structures. The residence, where Paton lived, was a large room made of native stone containing a bedroom and a bath. The second building was an unattached office. Paton called it her "communications center." It had been converted from a six-by-eight-foot henhouse. Modernized, electrified, and insulated, it now housed files, a mimeograph machine, and a brand-new, expensive electric typewriter, the first of many. The third building, the new redwood studio, was Paton's "creative center." Paton proudly enumerated the other components making up Orphan Voyage: the library, the releases, the publications, the notebooks, and the correspondence.[30] This last, a new creation, Paton envisioned would contain correspondence with "people whose interests were separate from adult adoptees but who were simpatico with their pain." Paton explained:

> We are certainly not alone in the world with our problems and concerns. People everywhere who are oppressed, who are afflicted, who believe in life despite their suffering, who see a partial remedy in reaching out to one another, we are all in the same boat, in that Surrounding Sea.[31]

Returning to her idea of the positive role of orphans and adopted adults, Paton explained that the Surrounding Sea was where "the world sent its explorers and found its future. Suffering is not for nothing."

Paton also provided Orphan Voyage members with a glimpse of the emotional health of its creator, anticipating the personal revelations of future bloggers. She initially did this by giving readers a preferred history of herself, one that dramatized Paton's life and passed over the initial trial-and-error period when she began the Life History Study Center in 1953. Instead, Paton rhapsodized about what "a wonderful time" she had in the "little house in Hicks St., Philadelphia," sorting through her mail and mentally creating a relationship with her beloved adopted community, "at peace and aglow with a sense of clear and secure purpose."[32] But then, with the publication of *The Adopted Break Silence*, Paton recounted that she met with "rebuffs and hostilities," culminating in 1957 when, she cryptically declared, she "received the Basic Blow" the social work establishment's conspiracy to silence her. What was so galling to Paton was that these social workers had once been her mentors and colleagues. As a result of this unexpected attack, Paton portrayed herself over the next five year as declining in energy, overcome with "numbness and indecision" rather than, in actuality, experiencing a vital period of intellectual ferment, capped by a tireless campaign against society's stigma of illegitimacy and for the rights of birth mothers. However, continuing with her rewriting of history, Paton announced that with the birth of Orphan Voyage the "time of trial" appeared over. Once again Paton felt that she had found that "serenity which was such a wonderful experience in the early days." She hastened to add that not all the problems were solved, "but the bewilderment and uncertainty" was gone. In fact, she dared to suggest that "I found a shore on the other side of the Surrounding Sea," reminiscent of Martin Luther King Jr.'s passionate peroration on the night before of his assassination, "And I have *seeeen* the promised land." But Paton quickly brought herself back to earth by informing them that the Child Welfare League of America had rejected her request to exhibit her orphan collection.

Paton, at least at first, did not envision Orphan Voyage to be "an adoptee search and support group," as it is often (anachronistically) described. It was both less and more than that. At the outset, Paton continued to raise the consciousness and self-esteem of social orphans by disseminating research and media reports to the adoption community. The "search" aspect of Orphan Voyage, however, with its intricate network of trustworthy references and, later, Orphan Voyage branches developed a decade later and was a slow process, requiring years of painstaking networking. In the beginning, Paton continued issuing her Releases and resurrected older issues she deemed important, mainly concerning adult adoptees. In February 1963, Paton seized the opportunity presented by a cover story in *Newsweek* featuring Edward Albee, who already was being hailed as the playwright of the century and whose play *Who's Afraid of Virginia Woolf* had transformed Broadway, to put forward her Christian method of reunion.[33] She noted that the core of the *Newsweek* story discussed Albee's long-standing resentment of his birth parents for abandoning him, a fact the article suggested still motivated him. Paton wrote that his hostile attitude was typical of adult adoptees, but then suggested that it restricted him as an artist and predicted it would lead to his creative downfall unless he changed it. She observed that the majority of the public found this resentment acceptable; indeed, everywhere lauded it, "despite the fact that it is an emotion which is like sandpaper upon the self."[34] Moreover, these same people insisted that a person maintain the attitude of resentment, lest one be tempted to forgive one's birth parents, while yet knowing that all human beings are fallible. Paton looked upon this intractable attitude with incredulity and angrily rebuked the public: "The entire message of the Christian religion is completely shoved aside in this, the message of forgiveness." She went on to suggest that it was not even necessary to be "a professing and believing Christian to arrive at a position where forgiveness seems indispensible." It was only necessary to recognize that no other theoretical position would make it possible for the social life between the adult adoptee and the natal family to continue without violent interruption. Without forgiveness, Paton declared, "Nothing else will prevent erosion of relationships, nothing else will prevent revolutions, nothing is more revolutionary and yet at the same time more utterly conservative."

In support of this provocative statement, Paton advised her readers to consult the section in Hannah Arendt's book *The Human Condition* on forgiveness, and afterward to read the New Testament for "greater insight."[35] If Paton's Orphan Voyage members had followed her advice and consulted Arendt's *The Human Condition*, a complex and difficult work, they would have found Arendt affirming that "the discoverer of the role of forgiveness in the realm of human affairs was Jesus of Nazareth."[36] Arendt developed a line of thought asserting that forgiveness could be a necessary corrective against actions taken by men and made the radical suggestion that it was man's duty to forgive. This was because "trespassing is an everyday occurrence . . . and it needs forgiving, dismissing in order to make it possible for life to go on by constantly releasing men from what they have done unknowingly. Only through this constant mutual release from what they do can men remain free agents, only by constant willingness to change their minds and start again can they be trusted with so great a power."[37]

Arendt ended her discussion by citing approvingly Paton's favorite parable of Jesus eating at the house of one of the Pharisees, which Tillich explicated in his sermon on forgiveness almost ten years earlier.[38]

Paton continued her discussion of forgiveness and stated that every adopted person had a choice between resentment and forgiveness. She viewed this choice as both a great problem and a great opportunity. She thought it unfortunate that contemporary American society offered so little cultural material to encourage the creative solution of forgiveness, specifically mentioning Albee by name. But then, remembering Albee's penetrating piece *The Sandbox*, which Paton said "transcended his private emotions," Paton admonished the playwright to "Go Home. For our sakes as adopted people, for your own sake as a human being, forgive your parents!"[39]

Along with advocating Christian adoption, Paton again brought up one of her earlier Reunion projects, Hill House, which was to be a refuge for those who had been abandoned by society. The Hill House idea represented two aspects of Jean Paton's career that have not been given much emphasis. On the one hand, it illustrates how far Orphan Voyage was from being in its origins a prototypical search and support group. Paton firmly believed that none of her writings or field trips would be of much use "until there is built an actual place of refuge" for people who were oppressed by the social stigma of illegitimacy. Hill House was to be a place where these people "may come to know others who have had similar experiences . . . find true acceptance, . . . gain for oneself a wider perspective, and to dare to hope once more."[40] On the other hand, Hill House was only the first of several similar attempts—Paton House in the late 1980s was its successor—to erect permanent institutions to serve the needs of adult adoptees.

In addition to reissuing her original 1958 broadside announcing its existence and purpose, Paton in May 1963 sent out an invitation to participants interested in attending Hill House's first meeting, which eventually took place with three participants at one of their homes in El Norte, California.[41] Her confidence bolstered by talking with this small group of sympathetic and like-minded individuals, Paton was inspired to make more ambitious plans. She would meet with an attorney to draw up Articles of Incorporation for Orphan Voyage as a nonprofit venture (she could not resist adding, "Was it ever anything else?"). She also promised to keep writing, in response to the group's desire to have additional adoption study materials, such as introductory bibliographies."[42]

One of the first results of this promise was Paton's return to a subject she had touched on in 1956: the theme of the "chosen child."[43] By the 1960s, in addition to adoption professionals and Valentina P. Wasson's national best-seller

The Chosen Baby, the federal Children's Bureau, mass-market magazines, radio shows, and even Dr. Spock advised parents to tell their adopted children that they had been specially chosen.[44] Paton now took the opportunity to provide the first extended critical assessment of the concept. She began her critique by raising the question of why such a story was needed. Her answer was that, for a child, adoption was a very different thing from being born into a family. She noted that as a child grew up and entered into society, he or she encountered what Paton called "gaps in the culture," resulting in fears, which created "the special 'loneliness' of adopted people." Societal agents had contrived the word "chosen" as a convenient filler to paper over these developmental difficulties. Paton believed that the story had some benefits but asserted that that it was wrong on the part of adoption professionals to view it either enthusiastically or assume it answered every question concerning adopted children; in fact, the "chosen-status" assertion was a double-edged sword, containing a sting, by which she meant that it harbored many hidden negative connotations.

What was to be done? Instead of bestowing a chosen status on the orphan Paton suggested that a person should "*choose oneself.*" She thought that this task could be both useful and unifying of those born legitimate and illegitimate. But a person could not make such a choice "unless the history of one's self can pass in review at the moment of choice." Paton supported her radical idea by quoting a passage from Danish philosopher Søren Kierkegaard's *Either-Or*:

> The self he chooses contains an endless multiplicity, inasmuch as it has a history, a history in which he acknowledges identity with himself. This history is of various sorts; for in this history he stands in relation to other individuals of the race and to the race as a whole, and this history contains something painful, and yet he is the man he is only in consequence of this history. Therefore, it requires courage for a man to choose himself; for at the very time when it seems that he isolates himself most thoroughly he is most thoroughly absorbed in the root by which he is connected with the whole.... He repents himself back into himself, back into the family, back into the race, until he finds himself in God. Only on those terms can he choose himself.[45]

Eliminating the special designation of the chosen child, Paton optimistically thought, would force adopted people to inquire about the true history of their adoption. Such an action, she believed, would conform to the basic teachings of Christianity, which she summed up by quoting French philosopher and novelist Julian Benda, that only "he who has obliterated from his heart every feeling of difference between himself and other men" [was] a Christian."[46]

On September 2, Paton set up Orphan Voyage as a nonprofit corporation and began working on the organization's bylaws and ways to finance and promote it.[47] Like no other text, the bylaws shed new light on Paton's initial ideas about the purposes of Orphan Voyage. The five-page document outlined the corporation's objectives, membership categories, organizational structure, and programs. Perhaps the most significant and surprising piece of information about the bylaws, like Sherlock Holmes's dog that didn't bark, was its silence about adoption reform or sealed records. Curiously, not one member of the adoption triad was mentioned; nor were the words "adoption" and "adopted." Paton appeared to be still in the grip of older ideas that dominated her mind in the late 1950s: succor for the social orphan and the illegitimate. Article I of Orphan Voyage's bylaws, "Objectives," stated that the purpose of the organization was "to promote the interest and welfare of those persons born in illegitimacy and to encourage communication and understanding between those persons and the general public."[48] It would be guided in its principal activities "by definite programs and policies" listed in Article VII; these were dominated by orphan-related activities, whether it was "Gathering Life History," which occurred "whenever an orphan speaks freely," or "The Works of The Orphan," described as "an exhibit program to gather and present works of artists either themselves orphans or expressing the reality of the orphan life."[49] Other programs once designed for adoption triad members, such as the Reunion File for matching triad members, were now bundled under the new program KINDRED, designed for "socially-separated adults." Paton's field trips also even failed to mention triad members.[50]

Thematically, many of the programs in the bylaws functioned as support groups, reminiscent of Alcoholics Anonymous or the consciousness-raising efforts of 1970s' women liberation groups. Paton labeled one of the programs "Retreat," and designated her own home as one. Its purpose was "to put courage and hope into the hands of those who feel little but emptiness, or perhaps a hard stone wall before their faces and who have therefore shrunk back from living contacts." Another program Paton called "Relationships." This she conceived of as the "most delicate and important part of the work": to maintain "the vital ties among the participating orphans."[51]

Active participation by the membership was another theme that ran throughout the bylaws. Membership was not restricted to adult adoptees or orphans, or even socially separated adults. Article III of the bylaws announced that membership was open to any adult interested in the objectives of the corporation, subject to the approval of a majority of the authorized corporation's directors. However, membership was a dynamic activity, demanding participation in the life of Orphan Voyage. Members were expected to be stakeholders in the organization. The bylaws declared that the members were obligated to frequently review Orphan Voyage's programs, contribute writings for publication, offer their homes "as a retreat for social orphans," and be especially sensitive to the feelings of rejection that many orphans harbored.[52]

The role of "the director," of Orphan Voyage, as the bylaws referred to Paton, reflected her ambivalent sense of leadership, commitment to its members, and participatory democracy. On the one hand, there was no question about who was in charge. The director controlled Orphan Voyage's communications, publicity, field trips, and finances. However, the bylaws also stated that the director was "not an authority over others." Paton viewed her mandate from the members as "a demand to reach society and to persuade it." But it was not unilateral. She expected, and the bylaws stipulated, that those designated as "Assistants" would stand in judgment of her actions, serving as a check on her measures. Paton expected assistants who lived near the headquarters to meet frequently with her, at a minimum once a month, in order to give and take responsibilities from the director. Ultimately, the bylaws foresaw a time in the future when the direction and responsibilities of Orphan Voyage would shift from a largely one-person operation onto the shoulders of the membership.[53] Nevertheless, on the role of the director, the bylaws were meant as counsels of perfection; they were never realized in practice. Paton was temperamentally incapable of compromising with people who disagreed with her fundamental principles, which would lead to bitter disagreements with future adoption activists.

While still working on the bylaws Paton went off on her September field trip to St. Paul, Minnesota, which she said was the "most rewarding."[54] Over a whirlwind weekend at the end of the month, she contacted professional adoption workers and attended a convention of 100 "alumni" from the New York Foundling Hospital.[55] Through Jeanette Kammen, a longtime correspondent, extraordinary collector of books on orphans, and typist in the St. Paul Welfare Office, Paton met with two of the social work staff.[56] One of the social workers, James Haugan, had been an original participant in *The Adopted Break Silence* and a recent correspondent. His interview was quite gratifying; he favored searching for one's birth parents and for adult adoptees to make their own decisions about this process.

Immensely satisfying to Paton was her meeting with a group of adult adoptees who had been foundlings. It had been a long time since she had had the opportunity to talk to "adult adopted people about their search interest." Paton happily reported that it was "just like old times." Some of the foundlings carried indenture forms, others "made-up" birth certificates. She informed them of a new service that she was starting, KINDRED, which would assist people with their search. The highlight of the St. Paul visit was the Saturday-night convention banquet at which the "125 or so" foundlings celebrated their "homecoming." Three speeches were made: one by a foundling priest, who declared that his orphanhood provided him with the insight to help other orphans; the second by a social worker, who stated that the foundling conference now made her realize that adopted people grew up; and the third by Paton. She told the assembled guests that when new and difficult things needed to be done in society, there were two ways of accomplishing the task. The first was done by an individual, such as herself, "who goes out on her own into uncertainty and tried to find answers that only individuals can find." Other things could only be carried out by a group, "such as the Foundlings. They had to meet society more directly, using the individual, just as I need to use them." Here in embryo was Paton's idea of a self-help adoption community that would symbiotically assist and be assisted by her. Crowning the evening, the foundlings conferred upon Paton an honorary degree as the "Duchess of Verbs and Nouns."

Although she hardly needed it, Paton also received corroborative evidence of professional social work's reactionary attitude toward the idea of searching for original family members. She related that the day after the banquet, she spoke to an adoptive mother, who, over her husband's and her parents' objections, decided to come to Paton's hotel room to discuss various matters concerning her adopted child. She told Paton that her three Twin Cities social workers, graduates of the Wisconsin and Minnesota Schools of Social Work, had told her that "if adopted children are curious about their natural parents, it is a sign of something wrong in family relationships, or in the child's development." The mother declared that she did not believe them. Paton wholeheartedly supported her judgment. To Paton, "Childhood Curiosity, whether about natural parents or about sex, or about the sun turning about the earth, is not a sign of maladjustment but a sign of intelligence, and of a will not broken by skillful manipulators." Paton told this adoptive mother that "the reason for this unsound advice is that the profession of social work is trying to use adoption for purposes for which it is unsuited." That was why adopted people had "strains."

Upon returning to her home in California, Paton immediately placed the Duchess of Verbs and Nouns scroll on the wall over her typewriter to remind herself "to keep writing, for the words are welcomed and valued, if not by everyone, at least by the people whom I have elected to speak for." But she confessed to herself that she had come back to many problems, and lamented that helping people who have been crushed by social work policies was "one of the hardest labors ever devised by the Author of the universe." The next day Paton announced she was going to leave California and move to the Midwest.[57]

8

Orphan Voyage Moves South

It is illegitimacy that needs attention, far more than adoption.

—JEAN PATON, 1966

Paton's decision to move from California to the Middle West had its roots in her efforts to give some organizational shape to Orphan Voyage's rudimentary structure. She declared that more was needed than simply corresponding "with people in distress."[1] Orphan Voyage had to offer something more tangible. That was the prime reason Paton was moving to the Middle West. There she would "be better able to build a Place that will be a symbol AND a reality to those whose lives are otherwise going to go down the drain into the obscurity that only an abandoned orphan can know." Its location, closer to the eastern half of the United States was also a major consideration; California and even Arizona were simply too far away.[2] Paton began gradually selling off her California real estate, in preparation to establish "a new, and I hope more fulfilling Home for the orphans," in the Middle West.

What Paton referred to as the "Middle West" was in reality the Southeastern region of the United States. She had settled on moving to the rugged Boston Mountains area in north-central Arkansas. On November 30, she set off from Acton and eventually found a place she liked two miles from Hasty, Arkansas. The area she picked was a beautiful spot high on a bluff overlooking the Buffalo River with a spring below that was piped up to her house for drinking water.[3] Many years later, she remembered fondly hiking down to the spring to pull out the poke weed that clogged the intake pipe.[4]

Paton set out for Hasty on March 21, 1964. In short order after arriving on her forty-acre property, which she described as "nothing fancy," Paton converted or erected separate structures for "The New Hill House"; her studio, an ever-growing library, a meeting room, and an office; utility sheds for tools and vehicles; and a home to live in.[5] She quickly sent out application notices to prospective Orphan Voyage members describing who was eligible to join the organization, even assigning them roles.[6] Paton simultaneously sent out an announcement of Orphan Voyage's current projects. Heading the list, significantly, was "Art and Literature," which exemplified what other orphans had "thought, seen, written, and portrayed in works of art."[7] Next was "Communications," described epigrammatically as "to exist; to speak; to hear; to think." Rather than reuniting adult adoptees with their natal families, Paton's third project, "Service," was viewed in terms of her self-appointed role as an ombudsman. She defined it as "To stand guard against the extreme adversity of the social orphan, and to shelter him in his times of trouble." The fourth project, "Education," was not conceived as instructing adult adoptees in methods of search or political activism but rather "forming educated and creative orphans who will enrich their own and future societies."

In the four years, Paton resided in the Southeast—first in Hasty, later in Memphis, Tennessee—Orphan Voyage activities occupied a small portion of her time. Instead, she became absorbed in advocating for juvenile justice, civil rights, and against abortion. But initially, while Jean was setting up Orphan Voyage in Hasty, she met June Schwantes, who became her life companion.

Schwantes was ten years younger than Paton; she was born during the 1918 flu pandemic in Chicago's Swedish Covenant Hospital, where patients lying on mats filled every corridor.[8] From an early age, June dreamed of being a nurse, and a chance meeting with a missionary nurse to children in Africa reinforced her desire for such a career. After high school, and against her father's wishes, Schwantes fulfilled her childhood dream and graduated after three years of training as a nurse. She immediately enlisted in the Navy, serving stateside at the Naval Station Great Lakes in Chicago and the Naval Hospital in Norfolk, Virginia, before undertaking a tour of duty in the Pacific on a hospital ship, the USS *Bountiful.* Her time on board the *Bountiful* proved exciting: she encountered a typhoon, was hit by a floating mine, and witnessed from afar the two-detonation atmospheric nuclear test series that occurred at Bikini Atoll in July 1946.[9] After returning home to Chicago, Schwantes attended Wheaton College, a Christian liberal arts institution, and later Vanderbilt University, eventually earning a BS in Nursing. She then began working as a nurse at the Cook County Department of Public Health; but she wanted to do Christian missionary work. During her time at the Department of Public Health, Schwantes was approached by a nurse representing the North Arkansas Bible Mission, a voluntary partnership of dozens of churches for the purpose of mission work in northwest Arkansas.[10] Soon thereafter, Schwantes accepted the Bible Mission's offer of $100 a month and a car and became a nurse in an Arkansas county so poor that that it had no doctor. There June became a jack-of-all-trades: she "delivered babies, treated all kinds of illnesses, and even set the leg of a fawn."[11] In addition, she worked with children, taught Sunday school, and managed to find time to preach occasionally. Her dream of starting a children's camp resulted in the creation of Rock Haven Bible Camp, which still exists.

At some point, Schwantes had moved to Hasty. Her first impression of Jean Paton's presence in the small town was memorable. One day, June as usual had gone down to the general store to pick up her mail. Parked right in front of the building was a brand-new, kelly green Jeep with a large red ribbon tied in a bow on its hood. She asked the storekeeper, "Who in the world got that Jeep out there?" and was told it was "a new gal" who had just moved in. June asked her name and the storekeeper told her. But Jean herself was nowhere to be seen. Before leaving the store, June told the storekeeper, "I want to meet her. Tell her to come by the house." When Jean did not show up promptly, June took it upon herself to stop by Jean's place, and they became acquainted.[12]

Jean discovered that she and June had much in common.[13] June had been abandoned at an early age when her parents divorced; she had gone to live with her grandparents for three years and then rejoined her parents when they remarried. Both Jean and June were evangelical Christians, enjoyed reading the Bible, and attended Hasty's Sunday school, though June was more devout.[14] Both loved music; June was a member of a singing group, secretly known as the "Hasty Funeral Trio" because they sang at funerals.[15] The two women began to take trips together. Jean bought a boat and they sailed up and down the Buffalo River, sharing many intimate conversations. In short, they became friends. At age fifty-six, Jean, who had been feeling lonely and depressed, had finally found an intelligent, independent woman every bit her equal, who was adventuresome, capable, engaged in humanitarian causes, religiously committed, and with a sense of humor. Within a year they were living together and would continue to do so until Jean's death thirty-seven years later.[16]

How were two women able to live together in Hasty, Arkansas, and later in Memphis, Tennessee, and Cedaredge, Colorado, where bigotry against same-sex couples often took the form of hostility, ostracism, or outright violence— behavior the two say they never experienced?[17] Historically, as late as the first quarter of the twentieth century in Western civilization, female romantic friendship was commonplace: women spent all their time together, exchanged passionate letters, and vowed eternal love.[18] By the 1960s, lesbianism was viewed as a sexual perversity, but personal characteristics could trump ignorance and prejudice.[19] This appears to have been the case with Paton and Schwantes. In Hasty, before settling in with Paton, June had lived with another woman, who was associated with the Mission. June was a valuable asset to the community, which lacked a doctor. Moreover, the Rock Haven Bible Camp was esteemed by the parents and especially the campers, who, when they grew up, reminded the forgetful "Miss June" how important she had been to them.[20] Paton explained the lack of intolerance this way:

> No, that [intolerance toward women living together] has never been a problem to us. We are a couple of spinsters without family connection; that's kind of obvious with no children running around, no grandchildren. We're both busy in independent ways that people can understand. And my housemate is a very valuable person to most people because of her vast experience in nursing and in medical questions. That is what she has been giving her life to. And I have been giving my life to something which people may not understand as well but they know I'm busy with it. And I'm a reasonably generous person; I'm not hard to get along with. People don't have those kind of questions about us, or they don't voice that kind of question.[21]

Any discussion of two people of the same sex living together raises the question of sexuality because, in contrast to heterosexual relationships, theirs are defined by their sexual activity.[22] As Naomi McCormick has stated, "Because women's sexuality is socially constructed by men, contemporary sexologists are inclined to demand genital proof of sexual orientation. Before labeling her as bisexual or lesbian, most sex researchers expect a woman to have had genital relationships with other women."[23] However, research has shown that assumptions of sexual activity among lesbians can be mistaken. McCormick eloquently states their conclusions: "Female bisexuality and lesbianism may be more a matter of loving other women than of achieving orgasm through genital contact."[24] Paton and Schwantes fit this research profile: each affirmed their love for the other and scoffed at the suggestion of having sexual relations with the other.[25] If one must characterize their relationship, then a "Boston marriage"; that is, a romantic but asexual relationship between lesbians, best fits them.[26] Suffusing their partnership were the principles of Christianity found in Bible verse and gospel hymns, in particular the Gospel of St. John, with its message that the highest form of love was that of a friend for a friend.[27] It was the glue that kept the adoption reformer and the nurse inseparable.

Paton grew contented with the companionship of Schwantes, the folks at the Mission, and the beauty of rural Hasty, high on her bluff overlooking the Buffalo River. But there were aspects of Hasty that she could do without, particularly the winter deer season. As Paton complained with growing distaste to Lucille Hood, an adult adoptee and marriage and family relations counselor, with the arrival of deer season she was "surrounded by hunters and dare not take a hike in my woods! These men in Hasty go out in groups of six to eight, with their trucks and their dogs, and stake out the area. The deer have little chance except to stay hid in some remote area. Yesterday was an eight-pointer, and one of the men brought it to the house in his truck for me to admire."[28] With the hunters cruising up and down the highways, Paton thought it wise to stay at home, busying herself "with the usual assortment of things to do." These included commending Denis Johnston, author of a Jonathan Swift biography, for revealing that Swift was an adopted bastard;[29] writing up some notes on French Enlightenment political philosopher and orphan Baron de Montesquieu; and working on a book manuscript. Paton ruefully added that the only trouble with making progress on her adoption work was that she realized that she had "about six more books to write instead of one or two." That is why, she explained, she stuck to writing letters.

Of course Paton did much more than just write letters during her first year in Hasty. In celebration of the tenth anniversary of the publication of *The Adopted Break Silence*, which she described as "the first and still the only study of adoption by adopted people," Paton announced an open house at Orphan Voyage in order to show its work.[30] On display would be Orphan Voyage's library, works and paintings by "persons of unsocial birth or otherwise orphaned," and Paton's publications and sculptures.[31] A leaflet later referred to these offerings as the Art of Orphans Exhibit.[32] The open house would provide an opportunity for the public and the "orphans" to talk with each other.[33] Paton also composed a bibliography of literary and what she deemed "contemporary and comprehending" sources for understanding adoption, orphanhood, and illegitimacy.

In addition, Paton continued to use *The LOG* to enlighten Orphan Voyage members about her personal life. Under the revived stimulus of June's intense Christianity and companionship, Paton became "emboldened to write . . . more specifically about my Christian beliefs" and their relationship to Orphan Voyage.[34] Paton began by addressing the reputation of where she lived in Northwest Arkansas—the Bible Belt—with its disbelief in evolution, uncritical reading of Scripture, "extremism in religious emotion, [and] . . . repression of natural desires." She made no attempt to repudiate the region's fundamentalist character, though maintaining that she found "no anti-Christian bearing in evolution." In fact, living in the Bible Belt had encouraged her to reiterate her religious beliefs to Orphan Voyage members, which she had represented in earlier Releases and in her art. She worried that her work was being misinterpreted and thus felt it necessary to repeat that her religious convictions were genuine; she was not joking, or temporarily under an emotional delusion, or had changed her mind on the basis of new evidence. She assured her readers that she would never change her mind: "there will be no new evidence; it is all in, and I have looked at every bit of it."

Paton was alluding to the truth of Christianity and that she was born again. And thus, she asserted, she had no doubt about a few things. She was sure that her ability to find her mother, Emma Cutting, was blessed by God; that Emma felt blessed by her reappearance; and that the reunion would never have occurred except for the Christian beliefs instilled in her youth. Moreover, she maintained, "my seeking and finding her was an act in which both she and I were forgiven together—she for whatever guilt she had accepted for abandoning me; I for turning away from her all my life to that time. If such forgiveness is not a portion of Christianity, will one of you give it a better name?" She concluded, "Well, as I said, here I am in the Bible Belt, encountering witnessing Christians. I am associating myself with one of them in particular. The element of Christianity will in this way be encouraged to grow in the work of Orphan Voyage" and be the better for it. Paton added, "I do hope you will not look upon me as a dreary theologian, and will even feel some relief that I have been this explicit."

Four months later, Paton returned to the subject of Christianity because, she jocularly observed, of the tendency by some of the Orphan Voyage members to believe that she had lost her mind, some of whom regretted it and others who accepted the fact.[35] But whatever their opinion of Paton's mental state, she pointedly noted, none of them had suggested "an alternative to the Christian view of life as an explanation of or a basis for a changed life experience such as is referred to in the word, 'forgiveness.'" That was the heart of Christianity, and she was at a loss to see what else a person could believe in: indifference? skepticism? adjustment? futurism? Paton rejected these alternative perspectives and was glad that she had come to the Bible Belt, where she could practice her Christian beliefs more readily, though she admitted in a different fashion from her neighbors.

Paton then put forth the case for Christian reform. She was struck, as so many other reformers before and after her have been, by the gap between America's potential to deal creatively with human suffering and its failed reality. Her resulting jeremiad does justice to the Puritans:

Have we reduced human suffering—beyond the physical? Have we reduced crime, emptied our mental hospitals, rehabilitated the prisoner, helped the bastard and his parents? Have we made family life happier, emancipated women to a sense of wholeness, projected the joys of childhood into adult years, made old age a dynamic force in the culture, have we wiped away one human tear? No, we have not.

Paton identified the culprits: the professionals who confined these long-suffering, weeping people "to offices and institutions of expertise." The sufferers then became statistics, mere "data of social dislocation." Paton continued her indictment: "Research grows, the professions are understaffed, taxes climb to accommodate chronicity. The races march. Shots ring out."

In this singular act of proselytizing, Paton plaintively asked, "Why not consider Christianity?" She confessed that the main reason she had chosen Christianity as the primary means of reform was because non-Christian ways of helping—and by this she meant social welfare agencies and even mainstream Christian churches—were "too small in relation to the presenting problem. An elephant shrunken to a mouse." They were incapable of providing the adult adoptee with a deep recovery, characterized by "rebirth and revitalization on a new level," which Paton was convinced Christianity inherently offered, and which she had experienced herself in 1955 with her "breakthrough" reunion with her first mother. She did not hold that there had to be a choice between reason and religion, or as she put it, "exercising the intelligence and God." Paton believed the opposite was true. She wrote in conclusion, "If one will face affliction attentively long enough, and will exercise his intelligence the entire time, and will remain tender in his heart toward those who suffer, there can be no other outcome than God. After all, did not Jesus demonstrate all this to us?" It would be the last public statement Paton ever made on the subject of Christianity.

In April 1965, Paton announced abruptly that she was now living in Memphis and was being joined in the move "by a new friend . . . Miss June Schwantes."[36] Accompanying them was the adopted daughter of a Venezuelan missionary couple, colleagues of Schwantes, who wanted to attend a nursing school in Memphis.[37] The impetus to leave Hasty came from Paton, who had been the victim of a robbery, in which her family silver was stolen. Schwantes had been chafing for some time to leave the small provincial town in order to gain additional nursing experience and was happy to leave Hasty when she received word that she had been accepted as a supervising nurse at the Memphis City Hospital, a large medical institution.[38] They first moved into an apartment, but by May, Paton had purchased a large house in a good neighborhood. Paton boasted of its 400-square-foot living room and a tile roof to keep out the notorious Memphis heat.[39]

Paton found her new home "stimulating, in that many new things are going on here, there are great big plans for the future, and also many of the issues that are alive in our culture are going to be fought out here." Her initial enthusiasm for Memphis was prompted by the warm reception both her adoption work and her art received in the local press. She had attended a charity "Attic Sale" of old paintings at the Memphis Academy of Art and purchased four Audubon prints for $250, the top sale of the day. When Paton informed the salesperson that her interest in the Audubons was not just for themselves but because the artist was an orphan, the salesperson had contacted a columnist for the *Memphis Press-Scimitar*, who wrote an extensive article on Paton, providing readers not only with a brief biography of Paton's decade-long interest in adopted people but also an extensive report on her upcoming open house of the "Art of Orphans Exhibit" at Orphan Voyage. He quoted extensively from Paton's exhibit pamphlet, which explained that its purpose was "to acquaint the general public with the point of view of orphans in adulthood and encourage orphan adults to meet with others of similar history for mutual understanding and help." The article went on to name specific books and works of art that would be on exhibit and that had been created by orphans, including Annie Oakley, Charlie Chaplin, Carl Jung, Jonathan Swift, Charles Baudelaire, Edgar Allan Poe, Hans Christian Anderson, Leonardo de Vinci, Sophocles, Jean Racine, Friedrich Nietzsche, Charles Darwin, Edward Albee, and Erasmus.[40]

Paton was unavoidably caught up in the contemporary zeitgeist of the 1960s rights revolution, and its language permeated her writings during her three years in Memphis, giving it a militant cast absent from her previous work. She first cast her eye on juvenile justice reform. In May 1965, two cases that would revolutionize the constitutional rights of juveniles were moving up the appeals process to the Supreme Court. In *Kent v. United States* (1966), the Court held that youths in the District of Columbia were entitled to counsel before a juvenile court could waive jurisdiction and transfer their cases for trial to a criminal court. Furthermore, for first time since the juvenile court came into existence in Illinois in 1899, the Court expressed doubt about the constitutional status of juvenile proceedings. Fourteen months later that doubt changed constitutional law. In the decision *In re Gault* (1967), the Court held that children accused in a juvenile delinquency proceeding have the right to due process, counsel, cross-examination, and avoidance of self-incrimination. The majority of the Court famously declared that "neither the Fourteenth Amendment nor the Bill of Rights is for adults alone."[41]

Although these revolutionary constitutional decisions by the Supreme
Court were in the near future, Paton had read about the trend affirming juvenile procedural rights in the *National Observer*, a weekly national newspaper
that synthesized the week's events and current trends.[42] In a "Topical Release"
of May 1965 she noted that many people favored the legal position that juveniles
should be represented by a lawyer, just as indigent adults increasingly were.[43]
She quoted a Minnesota Probate Court judge, who observed that a juvenile
court could become so enamored by its helping philosophy and its staff of experts that it lost its judicial objectivity, which could only be restored through
representation by counsel. To this, Paton wrote "Amen." She then linked by
analogy the revolution in juvenile court work to social work in adoption. Paton
wrote, "there is a sense in which an adoption agency is a court of last resort
for all three parties to adoption, a court from which there is no appeal except
refusal of services, a court in which the individual has no representation." The
similarities did not end there. Juvenile courts were characterized by the lack of
juries and great secrecy. Thus, the public knew little except what it was told by
the court and adoption agencies. However, the inimical results of secrecy were
well known.

Paton declared that if certain legal rights of all parties in adoption were
recognized and represented by counsel, adoption would be transformed from
its current failed state. She proposed a series of rights, one for each party to
the adoption. Birth parents had "the right to earn the respect and forgiveness of
their abandoned children." This right was to be implemented through communication with the adopted person, with certain conditions attached. The birth
parents had to earn the right to communicate only after they went through a
period of social and emotional readjustment, which would prepare them not to
be destructive to anyone in the adoption. The adoptive parents had "a right to
attain security in a society of families." In order to implement this right, Paton
called for the "expansion of adoption" to include communication between the
adoptive and birth parents, but only after a period of preparation and "only to
a degree." Adopted persons had "a right to overcome the inevitable trauma and
schism inherent in their situations." This right necessitated a search experience
to satisfy the normal curiosity of each adopted person in order to allow him
or her to develop intellectually and psychologically healthy personalities. These
searches for original family members were to correspond with the maturity and
social experience of each individual, but such factors were not to be used to
prevent an adult adoptee from undertaking a search. Paton believed that all of
these "rights arose from constructive reactions to deep sorrows and failures of
human growth," principally child abandonment and infertility.

Paton asserted that she did not maintain that adopted people had a right to "happiness" or to a secure home, loving parents, or a good education. These were "rights to receive," which she rejected, in favor of "rights to do." Paton's "rights to do" were the rights to participate in creating one's own identity and humanity. Just as Paton had come to believe in the truth of experiential knowledge over random samples as the ultimate methodology, she bestowed upon her beloved adopted community the same right of taking their destiny into their own hands. A corollary to this belief was that adoption laws had to come from the bottom up. As she wrote, "It is our further belief that laws must ultimately derive from the experience of the people, not from the words of those who study the people."

Paton was reawakened to the issue of juvenile justice by a February 1967 article she read in a Memphis newspaper. It related how a father kidnapped his four daughters, who had been placed in the Porter-Leath Home, Memphis's oldest orphanage, because his ex-wife, receiving no child support from him, was unable to support them. He had been arrested and jailed. In his defense, the father claimed that he feared his children would be adopted, but regretted his impulsive action, vowing to gain custody legally if he was ever released from confinement.[44] Paton quickly visited with the superintendent of the Porter-Leath Home to hear more about the case. She learned that parental visitation was under the supervision of the juvenile court, which struck her as inimical to family relationships. She was also taken aback by the superintendent's lamentation that in the modern age there were no more orphans, meaning children without both parents. Paton then explained to him the nature of social orphans. As for the case of the four children kidnapped by the father, she was not optimistic; she believed that the children should not expect much from either parent.[45]

Never one to leave to others what she could do herself, Paton soon thereafter arranged to tour the Memphis Juvenile Court and its facilities and talk to Judge Kenneth A. Turner.[46] She found the institution to be an "orderly and reasonable establishment, one which should have meaning to those who come to it in trouble." Still, there was room for improvement. Specifically, Paton suggested to Judge Turner that in order to break the problem of recidivism among juveniles—from one generation to another, what Paton referred to as "Orphans breed orphans"—there was a need to create an organization of orphans. Only such an organization would have the necessary knowledge and self-interest to "break the repetition of the cycle of orphans."[47] Judge Turner thought Paton's suggestion excellent and stated that the court would be happy to cooperate in such a program. He invited Paton not to hesitate to call on him for assistance.[48]

Although Paton occasionally took time off from her reform activities and relaxed, she spent most of her time writing *The LOG of Orphan Voyage*, a kind of proto-blog consisting of whatever struck Paton as newsworthy or interesting. In 1966, *The LOG* revolved around the triumphal theme that her ideas and organization were not singular, nor was she alone—and, by extension, neither were Orphan Voyage members. In March, she happily announced her discovery of a 1964 article, "Genealogical Bewilderment in Children with Substitute Parents," written by the British psychoanalyst H. J. Sants, and liberally quoted from it. Sants mirrored Paton's ideas about adoption, including the notion that grafting children onto a new family could never be absolute because "roots in the natural family can never be severed without a trace"; that children, very often in adolescence, begin searching for clues about their first family; that secrets could never be indefinitely kept; and that "all children need to know their natural origins."[49] Paton also alerted her readers to a monthly publication from the National Council of Adoptive Parents entitled *ADOPTALK*, which carried an article discussing four points of view on searching for birth parents, including Orphan Voyage's. And she announced the existence of Adoptees Anonymous, a group in England, which Paton thought should more appropriately be named "Adoptees Non-Anonymous."[50] This organization's mission was to promote mutual understanding through group discussions of adopted persons and to inform the public of the difficulties adopted people face. Its main goal was to legalize the right of adult adoptees to search for their original families.[51] Another Englishman, a correspondent of Paton's, was advertising for adoption life histories. Simultaneously, a California female adoptee wanted to establish a local group of adopted persons who would share their experiences and help one another.[52]

Instead of interpreting these developments as the start of a dynamic social movement, Paton believed these new allies reduced the need for her to play an activist role in adoption reform; she would leave that to "the new hands" and would "move on to a new, and admittedly difficult facet" of reform. She declared, "it is illegitimacy that needs attention, far more than adoption." Strengthening her decision to curtail Orphan Voyage's focus on adoption was an epiphany Paton experienced about the institution's negative effects on the family. Throughout her career as an adoption reformer, Paton had never been anti-adoption; there existed "the good adoption," which, she believed, could be improved with communication between the birth and adoptive parents and the child. But in July 1966, after a visit from a young single mother who was attempting to make a decision about relinquishing her new baby, Paton found herself crystallizing what she described as a long-dormant, unconscious attitude about the toxic nature of adoption. Relinquishing a child damaged and reduced a birth family's capacity for love and warmth. This insight profoundly moved her. Paton reacted by "revolting at the casting out of a baby from its own people." She revealed that she had finally "lost the illusion of adoption." Paton felt that she had awakened from a dream "into a culture which is increasingly beset by orphanhood.—in all its forms—in all its destruction—without creation. The orphan, be he [Lee Harvey] Oswald, [Richard] Speck, Malcolm X, or suddenly orphaned [Charles] Whitman, or any other; in this destructive time he takes the reins. He is society now."[53]

As Paton once again redirected her attention from adoption to illegitimacy, she focused on abortion, asking her readers, "*How can persons of illegitimate birth hold up their head in a culture that wants to do away with births in this category?*"[54] Over the next two decades, the issue led Paton into conflict with a variety of groups who advocated the legalization of abortion. She had been receiving literature for several years from the Society for Humane Abortion (SHA), a California-based nonprofit organization founded in 1964, which advocated that a woman's decision to obtain an abortion should be treated just as any other surgical procedure: a private matter between a patient and her physician.[55] Now, in the spring of 1966, Paton was prompted to write the SHA twice, not to object to abortion per se, which Paton did not "feel harsh toward," but instead to protest its negative view of illegitimacy. The SHA, needlessly in her opinion, promoted and publicized abortion as an effective means to eliminate or reduce illegitimacy.[56] The following year, Paton filed away a *Washington Post* article that reported that a large majority of American psychiatrists favored liberalization of America's abortion laws. Underscored was a quotation by a psychiatrist that was said to be typical of the profession: "The maladjustment of orphans and adopted children is so extensive that no unwanted baby should be allowed to be born."[57]

In *The LOG*, Paton expressed herself more emotionally about abortion, asserting that "the violence of the present assault upon illegitimacy can scarcely be overstated. The abortion programs are attempting to sell their point of view by pointing out to the public that if there is enough abortion there will be a decrease in illegitimate births." Paton cited other social currents promoting the destruction of illegitimacy, including a book advocating the establishment of brothels to reduce illegitimate births and the birth control pill, which, she sarcastically noted, was "supposed to have the same beneficent result." In light of such prevalent negative attitudes, Paton asserted, it was no wonder that social orphans felt a profound sense of inferiority.[58]

But what could be done about it? Paton proposed the formation of the Committee for the Reconsideration of Illegitimacy. The members of this organization would become intimately associated with illegitimacy, and would reconsider its social stigma and its effect on the life of the orphan. The Committee's underlying philosophy was to make the nonorphan cognizant that his or her life was incomplete and that ultimately only the involvement and association of orphan and nonorphan would make life complete for both. The Committee's methods included challenging society's habit of stigmatizing illegitimacy, presenting society with the example of orphans cooperating with each other, demonstrating to the public the unique values orphans have given to the world, and forcing society to listen to what it had for too long turned a deaf ear to "the grief, the isolation, the fears of persons of innocent birth, but condemned to a sense of inferiority because of the nature of their birth."[59] Its ultimate goal was to make the lives of those born out of wedlock less socially handicapped. Paton called for the first meeting of the Committee in late September 1966 and sent out application forms.[60]

Simultaneously with the formation of the Committee for the Reconsideration of Illegitimacy and her epiphany of the destructive nature of adoption, Paton announced she was going to stop communicating with the membership of Orphan Voyage. Piqued at the memberships' lackadaisical response to her efforts on their behalf—by August, only four people had joined the Committee for the Reconsideration of Illegitimacy—she announced that she had recognized not only the truth about adoption but also the indifference of her readers. She would let them stew in their own juice: "I shall leave you to the reality of adoption and the reality of illegitimacy," Paton declared. "Perhaps my withdrawal from you will free you to actions heretofore only contemplated. I hope so." In the meantime, Paton informed the membership, she was going to write something more substantial about illegitimacy than a monthly Release, having immersed herself in the subject for the past fourteen years.[61]

Unfortunately, she never wrote her promised book on illegitimacy. Instead, in 1967 she republished "Three Trips Home." She had never given up the idea of seeing it in print between hard covers and distributed by a legitimate publisher, as opposed to the mimeographed copies she had run off a decade earlier. On several occasions between 1958 and 1962, Paton had sent the manuscript to publishers in New York City and also to a freelance writer in Los Angeles, only to have her hopes raised and subsequently dashed with "kind" rejections.[62] After failing to place the manuscript with a commercial publisher, Paton signed a contract with Vantage, a New York vanity press, and spent a good part of 1968 raising the money to pay the expense of publication.[63] The new book, she informed a few of her correspondents, would be called *Orphan Voyage*, a title chosen by the publisher, which Paton liked, though she had wanted to call it *Up from Bastardy*.[64]

Paton resented commercial publishers' rejection of her work, but she eventually came to regret her decision to self-publish. In 1976, when Lee Campbell, the founder of Concerned United Birthparents, complained bitterly about the inability of the movement to get books published unless one was a journalist or an adoptive parent, Paton replied that she had been rejected twice due to dubious claims by publishers over "questions of marketability."[65] Paton was sure that there was a market for her book and declared, "I am saddened by my inability to reach people by the Work."[66] Two years later, when Paton's hardback copies of *Orphan Voyage* began to run low, she had come to the conclusion that publication by a vanity press had been a "mistake in judgment." In mitigation of her error, however, she asked her correspondent, "But what can one do when one is in advance of the times?"[67] Nevertheless, when it came to publishing a paperback edition of *Orphan Voyage*, her past experience with commercial publishers was so dispiriting that she thought it would be a waste of time to contact them. Thus, in 1980 she once again personally published another 1,000 copies at a cost of $3,000 from a local printer.[68]

Paton's move to Memphis in 1965 coincided with the civil rights movement's shift into a more militant stage. That stage in the movement witnessed the outbreak of the Watts riots in Los Angeles, leading to a series of inner-city riots in the next two years, the disintegration and disillusionment of the mainstream civil rights movement and concomitant rise of Black Power, the formation of the Black Panther Party, and in 1968 the assassination of Dr. Martin Luther King, Jr.[69] During these years, Memphis was undergoing its own civil rights revolution.[70] In 1964, black Memphis students demonstrated in favor of the Civil Rights Act of 1964 and the desegregation of the prestigious Second Presbyterian Church. As the war in Vietnam escalated, black Memphisians protested against all-white draft boards; support for the Black Panther movement grew as low wages, long hours, unemployment and poverty reached new heights. Responding angrily to black militancy and the apparent support of businessmen to continue an interracial dialogue, white voters supported conservative Republican candidates.[71] The moral power of the civil rights movement was reinforced by the Warren Court's emphasis on the expansion of individual rights. Landmark decisions on voting, school prayer, criminal due process, libel law, pornography, and school and housing segregation signaled that "a Rights Revolution was at hand."[72] Memphis politics became increasingly polarized.

During 1967 and 1968, Paton forcefully embraced the zeitgeist of the civil rights movement, which would reach its boiling point in Memphis with Dr. King's assassination. Not surprisingly, the bulk of this period saw Paton absorbed in political debates about racial issues as she entered into the public realm to fight for the rights of black people.

But if Paton was liberal in matters of civil rights, she was always of two minds when it came to adoption issues concerning African-Americans. On the one hand, she rarely viewed the problems associated with adoption relationships in terms of race.[73] As Paton bluntly wrote one correspondent, "As far as I am concerned, the matters I deal with are not racial."[74] Underlying this belief was the assumption that most of her correspondents were white. But she never inquired about their racial status because she firmly believed there was "a great similarity in life experience between the white and black adoptee, of illegitimate birth, or whatever."[75]

Paton expanded on her beliefs in the early 1970s, when the Milwaukee Urban League inquired about Orphan Voyage's policy on transracial adoption. True to her philosophy of listening to the people at the bottom rather than dictating from the top, she replied that her policy was to "Wait for the adoptee to tell us." Paton's best guess, however, was that a black person who had been adopted into a white family might feel resentment toward people of his or her own race rather than the adoptive parents.[76] In response to another inquiry, from the Harlem, New York–based Institute of Afrikan Research, Paton said she was sure that sometime in the future, black people would desire the same help from her as white people.[77] In 1977, reacting to the publication of Joyce Ladner's book *Mixed Families*, Paton wholeheartedly agreed with Ladner that "to adopt a black child means that these parents have forfeited their rights to be regarded as a 'white family.'" But she saw no difference between the races. Applying Ladner's statement to white adopted persons, she "translated" it into what she called the Paton-Kittson Law: "Any family that adopts an illegitimate child has forfeited its right to be regarded as a legitimate family." The consequences of this law, Paton explained, was that all adoptive families must plan on contacts with the child's first parents and study extensively the culture of the adoption relinquishment in order to "provide the child with *both nurturing and racial belonging*, to the human *procreated race*."[78] On the whole, however, interracial social work matters did not concern her.

But if Paton ignored the racial component in adoption or believed it ultimately inconsequential, she had thought long and hard about the similarities and differences between black people and adopted people, even before she had come to Memphis.[79] One of her central ideas about the difference was that the skin color of blacks stamped them with an inescapable stigma, whereas those persons born illegitimate could escape society's badge of shame by remaining silent. But this fundamental difference did not mean the two groups did not share similarities. As Paton wrote, for an illegitimate person to remain silent was a poor solution because "the cure of adoption can aggravate his disease if it denies him his kindred." A decade later, Paton elaborated on this point. She claimed that adopted people were in the same position as "very white skinned black people" who had passed for white to avoid the stigma of racism. The difference was that adopted people could stay in their adoptive homes and not face discrimination. However, once they began to search for their original families, adult adoptees had to come to terms with the fact that they were born out of wedlock and were abandoned by their first parents.[80] Similarly, in the case of the black person, the cure—fighting the oppression of the white person—also contained symptoms of a disease. In the process of militantly protesting (here Paton was perhaps alluding to the rise of the Black Power movement), black people discovered that they too could oppress. She observed that some blacks did not mind this oppressor role, while others did and found it a poor solution.

In thinking about the cure for these two deep social problems, Paton often made comparisons between the two groups, especially concerning matters of adoption reform. She explicitly compared Orphan Voyage with the National Association for the Advancement of Colored People. Both institutions, she said, represented "some members of an underprivileged group who strive for a lifting of social repressions which are deeply felt and which leave strong impressions." Paton optimistically believed that the solution that she had seen in the black community was similar to the one she was so familiar within the community of adopted persons: "communication between those who seemed to have been separated by unscalable walls of custom and law." However, Paton's cure for the disease of racism and the stigma of illegitimacy was couched in a belief in gradualism. She admitted that the communication process was "small in scale" and successful only "in a relatively few instances," but believed that its momentum would grow and increase and that such a course of action would eventually destroy the barriers that society had erected. Paton believed that this gradual approach, "like water trickling under a dam against the inevitable," would result in "cures" for some.

Late in life Paton's gradualist, optimistic perspective broke down as she became discouraged about the prospects for successful adoption reform. She continued to admire black people's solidarity and skill at organizing demonstrations, and most of all their bravery in overcoming the terrors of racism that they confronted every day. She often juxtaposed their organizational expertise and courage to the detriment of the adopted population, who, in Paton's opinion, were disorganized to the point of anarchy, unable to cooperate with each other, and psychologically incapable of militant protest. Her criticism took many forms. She once observed, for example, that blacks were more angry than adopted people and envied them "the ease of their indignation."[81] To another correspondent, she declared, "Black people know affliction when they see it." She related how once, while sitting in the audience of an adoption workshop, she muttered the word "colonialism" within earshot of a black judge; he "shook with recognition," according to Paton. She was later informed that "ever after he opened records upon request."[82] On another occasion, thinking back on the civil rights movement, Paton enumerated the various sources of its success, including black churches, committed white people, and "the brave souls among their own number who stood up, walked, sat down, drank out of the public drinking fountains, etc. etc."[83] These actions revealed the nature of the problem of racism to everyone and focused the public's attention on solving it. In contrast, "we hurt folks go silently to our conferences, and in hidden quarters speak about our problems."[84] Paton admitted to her correspondent that there were some demonstrations, but lamented that the adopted population built nothing of permanence. She went so far to as to wish that all members of the adoption triad turned purple at the moment of the adoption. In such a world, they would have to deal with their affliction openly. Instead, "we have 'passed' from bastard to adoptee, and it doesn't show."[85]

Most significantly, Paton personally identified with enslaved blacks and their "affliction," as she called their pain and suffering. As early as 1962, she viewed the adopted population as "the final minority, the enduring colonials . . . . the despised, patronized, and abandoned," and warned her readers not to be confident, "just because we live in the midst of talk about human rights and the emancipation of submerged populations."[86] But it was in 1967, Paton wrote, while she was reading a series of articles about African slavery in the magazine *Transaction,* that she had had an epiphany that she too was a slave and was unsuited for such a status. Paton observed that "a large part of our maturation conflicts had to do with realizing softly that we were slaves." She did not know what she was going to do with "this crystallization," though she knew she would do something in order to "leave slavery behind."[87]

Both Paton and Schwantes had "an intensified awareness of the racial problem, even beyond what everyone else living in Memphis had" as a result of June's employment at the City of Memphis Hospital, where blacks predominated as both patients and employees.[88] Paton's sensitivity to the issue of race was heightened by the predominance of out-of-wedlock births in the Memphis hospital and their deleterious effect on the larger community.[89] She also received hate literature from several groups who opposed efforts to integrate Memphis. The White Rescue Service circulated a flyer among white Memphis citizens denouncing a charity group, the Shelby United Neighbors, for daring to place white children in a black orphanage. Referring to the charity as the

"Soviet United Nigras," it accused the charity of being engaged in a "plot against the White Christian community" to promote "a NAACP type operation" of "forced integration" by putting up for adoption white children in black families and black children in white families.[90] Similarly, Paton found on her doorstep a two-page circular, quoting the Bible, Thomas Jefferson, and Abraham Lincoln in support of the proposition that the "INTEGRATION OF THE RACES IS THE WORLD'S NUMBER ONE SIN!!!" and criticizing the idea that "All Men Are Created Equal."[91]

Paton expressed her distaste for this crude racism by replying to the publication of a letter to the editor from one "Albert R. Fox," who denied that Africans had achieved any level of civilization comparable to the white man, citing the supposed lack among black groups of domesticated animals, use of the wheel, the construction of stone or brick houses, sophisticated ships, or written language. Fox then praised the poor white immigrants who had advanced in the United States "by their own efforts and initiative."[92] Paton sarcastically requested time to answer "the ancient and nauseating argument about the Negro being inferior because while in Africa, he did not go around in a space capsule. Or words to that effect." She then agreed that important inventions seemed to have derived from whites, but quickly asked, "so what does that prove?" Paton then ridiculed the idea that singular inventions by whites had any effect on lifting the intelligence of the mass of Caucasians: "There are thousands, millions of people of exquisitely white skin who in full sight of a powerful modern technology and communication system, do nothing in the evenings but sit glued to a chair and look at the dancing screen of television, yawn, arise, sleep, arise, do a routine day, ride home, etc. and repeat it." As for Fox's Horatio Alger–like immigrants, Paton provided a realistic history lesson. She declared that when those poor people reached the shores of the United States, they died in droves in the miserable cities or, referring to the New York Children's Aid Society's orphan trains, their children were shipped to the Midwest "almost as slaves," setting a pattern for future abandoned children "of servitude to their benefactors."[93]

The issue of illegitimacy, however, was never far from Paton's mind. Because she knew that poverty was one of the root causes of why mothers relinquished their children for adoption, she continued to take a keen interest in this issue as well. In November 1965, she attended a Memphis Public Library program on local poverty.[94] She took many notes and asked why it was not possible to help people "in advance of government confirmation."[95] Two years later, the *Memphis Commercial Appeal* ran a two-part series decrying the city's failure to ease the plight of poor people, despite the nation's War on Poverty and the growth of slums, unemployment, and illegitimacy, which was compounded by the lack of both public housing and educational institutions.[96]

Paton spotted the paragraph on illegitimacy and wrote a long, critical letter to the editor in response.[97] She remarked that she had not realized that she had entered "the United States illegitimacy capital" when she moved to Memphis, but apparently it was true. That being the case, she described herself as "an insider" who worked with persons of illegitimate birth who had been adopted and offered Orphan Voyage's services to the city. Anticipating objections from those who might say that there was a great difference between those who had been born out-of-wedlock and those adopted, Paton declared they were wrong. The two shared a great similarity: "a sense of incomplete identity, a gnawing resentment, a feeling of isolation from society." Paton was convinced that these psychological states spawned violence. Like much of the media, she linked "family pathology," such as illegitimacy, with the explosive urban riots of the past several years.[98]

Paton proposed a remedy for illegitimacy, but not before first flatly ruling out simply prohibiting the practice through prescriptive or moralistic advice. She asserted that one had to be realistic with "innocent, living people" and not allow moral scruples to get in the way of acting charitably. Paton believed that the "illegitimate" person's resentments and isolation could only be overcome "by considerate and compassionate social behavior." As an example, she singled out a group of African-American women who were helping women who had given birth to a child out of wedlock. She suggested that such an example should be followed "by white women for white women."

Continuing to address illegitimacy as "the special problem" of the black population, Paton wrote that it was "an insult to a race to assume it cannot form family life." She asked whether society thought it was doing "the Negro a favor by giving him ADC [Aid to Dependent Children] without question" and then asked what the effect would be on fatherless, African-American children, admitted to integrated schools, where all the other children bore their fathers' names. Paton demanded that the entire concept of ADC be thoroughly revised because it was "quite wrong for society to subsidize illegitimacy." She asked that society discriminate between the motivations of single mothers: ADC was permissible for those women who wanted "to raise her child to happiness" as opposed to women who simply gave birth to children out of wedlock in order to receive a stipend from the government. Finally, Paton reiterated that she was sure that "the participation of those who are the problem" was absolutely essential to the success of solving the public problem of illegitimacy.

Paton attached to her letter to the editor a Release from Orphan Voyage entitled "A Modest Proposal," which amplified her suggestions about reforming ADC.[99] In order to receive ADC, Paton stipulated that the state should only support mothers who demonstrated a capacity "for love and appreciation of a child's need of a father"; multiple pregnancies were one sign of unfitness for the public benefit. These new criteria would not be applied retroactively; current ADC recipients would not lose their benefits. She also called for putting the birth father's name on all official records, including the child's birth certificate and school records, and using it in daily life. Paton's justification for this approach was that the child's father would become more meaningful to him or her and that the child's resentment, which was usually directed at society for failing to provide the necessary family background, would be redirected to where it rightly belonged: the missing parent. In addition, she called for opening sealed adoption records when a child reached the age of maturity. In this way, Paton asserted, the present-day harsh stereotypes of unmarried mothers could evolve into a more realistic image. Moreover, Paton also called for deemphasizing adoption, which she viewed merely as a panacea, since it did not reduce illegitimacy and might even increase it. Addressing the isolation of the fatherless family, Paton called upon religious institutions to extend "practical help and sustaining neighborliness," and for society to recognize and value positively "the courage and love" that these households fostered under adverse circumstances.

Paton returned from her self-imposed exile from Orphan Voyage in June 1967, ten months after departing in a huff. In her first communication to Orphan Voyage members since her departure, she made no mention of her engagement with the civil rights movement. Paton admitted that she had not the done the writing she had planned, but provided no explanation and made no apology; various projects had been consolidated, she informed her readers, and that was all to the good. Paton jauntily continued: "The decks are cleared, the ropes are coiled, the mast is ready for the sail and the wind can be felt in its first stirrings. If you want to take this little trip with me, the usual way of signing on for the voyage is at hand. Use it, I think it is going to be a an interesting year."[100] She then announced Orphan Voyage's agenda for the immediate future. Among the items she announced, the most significant was "the largest postponed plan of all": the start-up of the Reunion File. It was to be offered first to Orphan Voyage members and later to the public.[101] It marked Paton's renewed interest in adoption reform.

In September, Paton went on a field trip to Minneapolis, Minnesota. On one of her stops, she met with local adoption officials at the Lutheran Children's Friends Society, an adoption agency that recently had initiated a policy promoting reunions between adoptees and birth parents if all members of the adoption triad consented.[102] The chief advocate of the Society's new policy was Harriet Fricke, the organization's director of casework. As Fricke related before a meeting of the Open Door Society of Minnesota, an organization advocating the adoption of African-American children, the usual agency policy prohibited reunions between adult adoptees and birth parents. But when an adult adoptee recently came to the agency requesting help in locating his biological parents, the issue was brought up at a staff meeting and no one could explain why the prohibition was in place. After considerable debate, the policy of not permitting reunions was changed.[103] At her meeting with Paton, Fricke was quoted as saying that the Society's "policy puts us on the extreme left or radical edge on this question."[104]

Fricke was correct: at the meeting, which Paton attended, other adoption officials sharply disagreed with the Society's position. Ray Mondloh of the Children's Home Society of Minnesota denied that a reunion between an adult adoptee and his or her biological parents was of any use in solving a person's identity problems. He suggested instead that adoptive parents be given additional help to provide their children with a sense of identity of what it means to be adopted. Clayton Hagen of Lutheran Social Service of Minnesota agreed, asserting that "in modern society individuals had to construct their identity in terms of themselves, not their parents." Countering these statements, Paton set out a few basic facts. Adopted children had a deep need to know their first parents or at least something about them, she asserted. It was better to know even an extremely unpleasant truth, than to be left to wonder. Adult adoptees were uncomfortable about their status and felt guilty about requesting information about their first families, as if they were being disloyal to their adoptive parents. Clinching her argument, Paton provided evidence from her own personal history. She told the gathering that she had found her sixty-nine-year-old birth mother after a long search, though she only began her search after her adoptive parents had died. "The search and the meeting were upsetting experiences for me," said Paton, "but knowing her finally led to a greater sense of peace for me than anything I had ever felt before."[105]

The Minneapolis meeting with adoption officials garnered notable coverage in the local press. In addition to an article by Molly Ivins in the *Minneapolis Tribune*, another article, by Carol Roloff in the *St. Paul Pioneer Press*, provides a snapshot of Paton's beliefs in the late 1960s about the problems adopted people face. Paton asserted that throughout their lives most adopted persons were haunted by a ghost: their birth mother. She believed that virtually every adopted child felt a shock—traumatic neurosis—because of being separated from his or her first family. Paton also thought, long before it was asserted by other adoption researchers, that every adopted child had a natural, healthy instinct to discover something about his or her family history. She was certain that possessing such knowledge would not in any way damage an adopted child's adoptive parent relationship.[106]

Paton suggested several age-specific solutions to the problem of traumatic neurosis. Instead of recommending young children be reunited with their natal parents, Paton suggested what she called the "expanded family," in which "the adoptive parents know the natural parents and mention them to the child." She did not elaborate what it meant to "know" the natural parents, and thus there is some ambiguity about whether Paton meant a form of open adoption, where the adoptive parents physically met the birth parents and perhaps remained in contact with them, or merely received identifying information from the adoption agency and conveyed it to the child. In either case, the benefits were manifest: the child gained knowledge of his or her original family, and the adoptive parents "would no longer feel threatened or worry. The ghost would be gone." When an adopted person reached the age of twenty-one, Paton believed that adoption records should be made available. Adult adoptees needed to know their birth parents in order to develop healthy personalities. To that end, Paton offered a national registry—Orphan Voyage's Reunion File—for adult adoptees who wanted to get in touch with their birth families.

Suddenly, in May 1968, Paton announced that there was a fifty-fifty chance that she would move the headquarters of Orphan Voyage to Colorado by the fall. The reasons for her latest move are not entirely clear. She had initially moved to Memphis to be closer to her membership base and reiterated that the city still had a fine, central location for that purpose. But, Paton also asserted, Colorado was equidistant from Minneapolis and San Francisco, the two cities where Orphan Voyage members were most active. In the Twin Cities, members had begun to advertise the Reunion File and were thinking of opening a chapter of Orphan Voyage.[107] Other dedicated members, such as St. Paul native Jeanette Kammen, were hawking Paton's book *The Adopted Break Silence*.[108] Paton believed that such activities could add immensely to the effectiveness of the Reunion File and stated that she would pay the activists a visit.

But Memphis and Colorado were both centrally located in relation to Paton's membership base; the relocation to Colorado cannot be explained solely in terms of geography. Several other factors might account for the move. Paton exaggerated the interest and activism of Orphan Voyage members. Five months earlier, in January, Paton once again felt the need to appeal to her membership to participate actively in the program. There was also a hint that the program was adrift, bereft of new ideas. Having started up the Reunion File and put into motion the republication of "Three Trips Home" as *Orphan Voyage*, Paton plaintively wrote, "NOW I AM ASKING YOU what you want to do. Can I in some way encourage you to spread out more actively in the community? Is this not the greatest gift I can give you? Doesn't the world need you, and your understanding?" She then listed a number of ways that members could make a difference in the world. They could lend their names to the Orphan Voyage letterhead, write a letter to the editor of their local newspaper, distribute Orphan Voyage materials, begin a local branch of Orphan Voyage, contact legislators when laws affected adopted individuals. Paton assured her readers that she would be there to help if only they would initiate the project, adding "BUT YOU MUST BEGIN." With Orphan Voyage membership growing at such a slow rate, the location of the headquarters was at Paton's discretion.

However, perhaps what really pushed Paton out of Memphis was the assassination of the Reverend Martin Luther King, Jr., which occurred the month before she announced her possible move to Colorado. King had come to Memphis on March 29, 1968, in support of the black sanitary public works employees, who had been on strike for higher wages and better treatment. Hours before he spoke that day, violence and wild looting broke out, resulting in injuries to nine police officers and the arrest of hundreds of African Americans; many people were hospitalized, mostly teenagers. As a result, the Tennessee legislature declared the first state of emergency since Reconstruction in 1866, and 3,800 National Guard soldiers accompanied by armored personnel carriers rolled into the city. Six days later, King was gunned down. After King's assassination, riots broke out in Chicago, Detroit, Baltimore, Washington, and dozens of other cities.[109]

In the same issue of *The LOG* that Paton mentioned her pending move to Colorado, she made an oblique reference to King's death. She wrote, "Recent events in Memphis are all too well known to bear much repetition. Of course it was upsetting, distressing and provocative of thought."[110] Then, as if feeling that the assassination was somehow an indictment of the racism of all white people, Paton sought to clear herself of the charge. She wrote, "Negro people I have known in other places seem to have considered that I was not prejudiced against them, and I imagine they are good judges of that. So let it be." Ever the contrarian, however, Paton could not abide the ubiquitous righteous talk of the need for social justice in the wake of King's death. She wrote, "People talk about social justice as though it were a solution to something." Then, in the next sentence, which must have confounded her readers, unless they were schooled in the philosophy of Simone Weil, Paton declared, "Affliction is caused by justice, not cured by it." Then, undoubtedly thinking of her own life's work in defense of unmarried women and adult adoptees, Paton added, "Only creative compassion knows the answer. It doesn't make big progress but I am inclined to think it survives longer." Paton believed that compassion "was the very opposite of assassination. It is mercurial and cannot be possessed or programmed." Her response to widespread rioting was summed up in her epigrammatic statement "It is easy to express rage; and so difficult to look at grief." But in the end, for Paton, a person who valued quiet, privacy, and the tranquility and beauty of nature, civil rights politics and the turmoil of urban riots must have proved a needless distraction.

In October 1968, Paton and Schwantes drove a U-Haul from Memphis to the town of Cedaredge, sixty-five miles from Grand Junction, the largest city in western Colorado. Soon thereafter, Paton reported on her new location to the Orphan Voyage membership. She described Cedaredge as situated on the western slope of the Rocky Mountains, just under the Grand Mesa. She waxed eloquent about the acre of land their small house sat on, which commanded

> a very beautiful series of views in all directions. Particularly to the south and east the views are outstanding. We can see the valley of the Gunnison [River] as it empties from the Black Canyon. The San Juan mountains spread out before us, fifty to one hundred miles away. The Paonias [moths] greet us from the front door. Close at hand, a creek runs through our back yard, beckoning to us from dining, living, and bedroom windows. It pleases us and irrigates the fruit farms below us. Next spring, when the warm days return, we will spread out hammocks between the scrub oaks here by the creek and relax, at least from moment to moment.[111]

To other correspondents, Paton invariably described Cedaredge as "a beautiful place."[112] Paton admitted that she preferred to live out of the city.[113] The ability to live and work in nature added immeasurably to her pleasure of being in Cedaredge. Paton loved her "yard work," often "weeding the strawberry bed, listening to the creek, watching the birds."[114] She felt in tune with "streams and gardens and all else that goes with such" and mused that "perhaps all this is helpful to survival." It certainly renewed her spirit and allowed her to continue her work of reforming American adoption, whereas city life, she confessed, "would have broken my back by now."[115] Cedaredge would be her home for the next twenty-eight years. But Paton's peace of mind would be troubled in the coming years with the rise of the Adoptees' Liberty Movement Association, Florence Fisher, and the new adoption reform movement: a force she could not control.

9

The New Adoption Reform Movement

As to [Florence] Fisher's book, she has many inadequacies, she is self-centered, stage-struck, dishonest, and ultimately destructive. This is my seasoned view. Despite all the awakening she has brought about, it was coming anyway. She sure shoved me back to the back row.

—JEAN PATON, 1975

I've never met [Arthur] Sorosky, and I have mistrusted his motivation from the beginning.

—JEAN PATON, 1975

By an odd twist of fate, the two great pioneers of American adoption reform, Jean Paton and Florence Fisher, a forty-three-year-old adult adoptee and homemaker, were linked to a weeklong World Conference on Adoption and Foster Placement held in Milan, Italy, in September 1971.[1] Paton first heard of Fisher in early 1971 from New York City–based Family Court lawyer and adoptee Sidney Green.[2] Between March and May 1971, in frequent phone calls and letters,[3] Paton discovered that Fisher was deeply involved in fighting for the rights of birth mothers and adult adoptees. In fact, Fisher was engaged in two cases, the New York State "Baby Lenore" adoption case, in which a Colombian birth mother, Olga Scarpetta, brought suit to have the DeMartino family return her child to her;[4] and she was fighting against a bill brought forward by Republican Joseph R. Pisani, in the wake of Scarpetta's lawsuit, limiting the time during which a birth mother could revoke her agreement to let her child be adopted to thirty days.[5] As Paton wrote Fisher, "we can work together."[6] The New Yorker's activism deeply stirred Paton's hopes for adoption reform. In March, Paton confidently wrote Fisher, "this year 1971, I would characterize as one of breakthrough. I have been waiting for it for a long time." A month later, Fisher announced to Paton the creation of her new search group "under the following name: ALMA (Spanish for 'soul') . . . for aren't our souls negated by all the existing legislation?" ALMA was also an acronym for Adoptees' Liberty Movement Association. Fisher added that the organization was needed because "the sealed record mess started here in the East and it's about time we started a movement to change things."[7]

Paton must have raised an eyebrow at Fisher's assertion that an adoption reform movement was in need of founding—thus implying that none yet existed. Nevertheless, Paton remained optimistic during this three-month period and supported Fisher's activism by generously sharing her twenty years of knowledge and experience about the adoption reform movement and its principal activists. She mailed Fisher recent literature on opening adoption records and the stigma of adoption, sent the Orphan Voyage printed materials Fisher requested, provided her with pertinent background information on the people Fisher was to meet on TV programs, and put her in touch with key movement people, such as Chicago-based Margaret McDonald Lawrence and Minnesota social worker Harriet Fricke.[8]

Fisher's energetic activism resulted in an unprecedented outburst of publicity for the adoption reform movement. Her entrance onto the stage of the adoption reform movement is reminiscent of Virginia Woolf's famous claim in 1924 that "on or about December, 1910, human character changed."[9] After Fisher, the movement was never the same. Fisher told Paton how she lobbied New York State legislators, contacted the judge in the "Baby Lenore" case, appeared on numerous television programs, was interviewed by the news media, and placed an ad in the *New York Times* for adult adoptees who wanted to search for their original families, which had resulted in numerous responses.[10] In July, the movement received the most publicity to date, when reporter Theo Wilson wrote an in-depth, four-part series on the "Adoption Underground" in the *New York Daily News*, featuring both Paton and Fisher.[11]

Paton sensed a seismic change in the movement's leadership, methods, and strategy. Swiftly, in the wake of Fisher's spate of favorable publicity, her unalloyed optimism changed to "a state of terrible ambivalence." It was hard for Paton to "see others taking it all away from me." But her initial feeling of jealousy soon passed. The movement came before her own ego. After some reflection, Paton realized that no one was taking the movement from her. Militant leadership resulting in the growth of the new adoption reform movement was a positive development. She concluded, "I wish people would do it all over the country and perhaps they will."[12]

By August, Fisher and Paton were corresponding regularly. Fisher addressed Paton as "Jean dear" and poured her heart out to Paton, regaling her with both the joys and the difficulties of her newly acquired role as the adoption reform movement's leader. In one letter, Fisher wrote, "Tell me Jean, have you reached the point when the injustice of it all doesn't rip your guts apart . . . I haven't."[13] Paton replied, "Yes, I know what you mean by the effect on one's guts by the injustice of it all. I convert every ounce of that rage into program, writings, holding forth, and if ever there was a rage that paid off I guess it is this one. I have been angry at the sight of infliction of pain since I was a very small child. It's deep and eternal."[14]

During one of their many phone calls, Fisher informed Paton of her intent to attend the Milan conference. Although Paton longed to go, she was financially unable; in addition, she claimed that movement events were "ripening so fast," her presence was needed at home.[15] By August, however, Paton had written a conference paper, "The American Orphan and the Temptations of Adoption: A Manifesto," and sent it off to be read by one Dr. Cicorella, the moderator of the panel "Adoptive Family vs. Family of Blood."[16] He liked Paton's "flaming Manifesto" very much.[17] The paper began by paraphrasing Karl Marx's *Communist Manifesto*: "Orphans of the World, Arise! You have little to lose and much to gain if you will stand free, look about you and claim the rights that are essentially yours, as beings conceived, born, and mortal—as is the condition of all mankind."[18] But then almost immediately it lapsed into Paton's private vocabulary and romantic vision of orphanhood. In a literary style part poetic, part philosophical, and sometimes downright opaque, Paton argued for the "specialness" of orphans, decried their subsequent enslavement resulting in colonial status, and proclaimed the consequent need to protest. It concluded on a triumphant note that must have puzzled the delegates:

> We have climbed down to earth, bent down and kissed its actuality. We rise and walk away from the tent. We go outside into the unplanned and uncontriving world to seek our lands, our kin, our mortality and our hope. Limited now, mere mortals, we laugh. We look into the eyes of our fellow orphans, and prepare together to build a world where the orphan will never be called such a name again. He will be a member of the Brotherhood of Those Who Remain after the Disintegration, and will walk freely in and out of the margins of society. And he will be at peace.
>
> FOR the orphan who is able to climb down to the earth and belong to it again has in him a power to survive and therefore he dares to love. You who

still sit in the tent and applaud his flights of fancy, where will you be when the orphans have all gone away?[19]

Hearing of Fisher's intent to attend the Milan conference, Paton offered to write a letter of introduction to the program director and send her a copy of the "Manifesto."[20] Fisher offered to go in Paton's place and requested that she advise her "as what you want me to say, do, and send on whatever materials you want me to use, etc."[21] Paton agreed, and Fisher read Paton's "Manifesto" in Milan.[22] It was not until almost six months later, however, that Paton heard anything about the reception in Milan to her "Manifesto," and it came only after her direct request. Fisher gave Paton a gloomy report: "And your manifesto, which I felt in my guts, no one understood . . . it was too easily dismissed as poetically beautiful, but who but one of us could possibly feel it?"[23] What Fisher held back from Paton was the audience's boorish behavior while she read the "Manifesto": some walked out; others talked; no one paid any attention.[24] Still, at the end of 1971, Paton's optimism about adoption reform remained high. She had been leading the movement virtually alone for twenty years, but now she told a reporter, "I feel like the Dutch boy and the dike. I keep waiting for someone else to come along, and this year, I think someone has."[25]

Over the course of the next two years, however, Paton became increasingly troubled about Fisher's involvement in the adoption reform movement. Her ambivalence stemmed from a combination of pride, pragmatism, and principle. Paton had devoted twenty years of her life giving form and direction to reforming social work practices toward unmarried mothers and adoption, and she had the utmost faith in her own values, procedures, and organization, which had evolved experientially, with much thought. As she put it: "I have worked slavishly, grubbing, clerking, carding, typing, all these years. . . . I rejoice in what I have been able to birth, a real network of concerned people all across the country. And I bring them together, and they thrive."[26] As Paton's correspondents began to share their complaints about Fisher's personality and methods, Paton voiced her own disagreements with Fisher's pronouncements and actions. Part of the problem was the issue of who should lead the new mass social movement. Paton initially blamed herself for giving Fisher an inflated notion of her own importance. She believed that Fisher's exalted position originated when Paton gave her a platform in Milan—totally ignoring Fisher's report of the audience's failure to understand the "Manifesto" and Fisher's growing reputation and talent for leadership *before* the Milan conference.[27] At bottom, Paton ardently believed that she was the true leader of the adoption reform movement; Fisher was a valuable secondary figure and ALMA a subsidiary of the parent organization, Paton's own Orphan Voyage. As Paton wrote, ALMA was simply "the militant branch of Orphan Voyage."[28] And, even as she valued Fisher's militancy, Paton believed that, as a technique to bring about needed reforms in social work, it should only be resorted to judiciously.

A more important reason for Paton's growing uneasiness about her rival was Fisher's irresponsibility in aiding adult adoptees and in managing ALMA's financial matters. At the heart of the matter was Fisher's inability to respond to adult adoptees who were searching for their original family members. Paton realized that this problem was perhaps inevitable in light of Fisher's remarkably successful publicity campaign. An article in the December 3, 1972, issue of the National Enquirer illustrated the scope of the predicament: the story informed readers of Fisher's search for her own birth parents and her founding of ALMA, resulting in an outpouring of 5,000 letters to the organization for help. A follow-up article reported that the initial National Enquirer story generated an additional 2,600 letters.[29] This was one reason, Paton claimed somewhat disingenuously, that she herself had not gone "gung-ho for publicity," for she had "realized I could not at all meet even the beginning needs of a lot of correspondents."[30] But the fact remained: adult adoptees by the thousands were writing to Fisher, and she was not responding. Paton wondered why someone in ALMA was not taking charge of the situation.[31] Worse, Paton believed that Fisher was taking adult adoptees' money and spending it on herself.[32] But, Paton wrote, "She wouldn't think of it as stealing, since she has no sense of responsibility to the others, perhaps does not, cannot realize that the others really exist."[33] Despite all this, however, as late as 1973 Paton still "value[d] what she has accomplished, and think we all should. The fact that she is not a group leader should not distract us from that. I think ALMA should be able to handle the situation, and I don't want to interfere with its efforts."[34] Certainly Fisher harbored no ill feeling toward Paton. She sent her an autographed copy of her gripping, melodramatic book, The Search for Anna Fisher, which recounted her frustrating, but ultimately successful, twenty-year search for her mother.[35] Fisher inscribed the book "To Jean Paton, with love and hope for the future. Affectionately, Florence Fisher."[36]

Paton's ambivalent feelings toward Fisher were mirrored in her mixed evaluation of The Search for Anna Fisher. Paton praised it as "a good account of a single search." In addition, the book "gave a good picture of the negatives in New York City, whom many have met."[37] Paton was referring here to the lawyers, the doctors, the clerk of New York's Surrogate Court, and the nuns of St. Anthony's Hospital, all of whom stymied Fisher's search by refusing to give her information about her natal family.[38] But on the whole, Paton thought, "the book fell apart and was weak in too many places. I thought the ending was weak."[39] Specifically, she noted the book's "lack of otherness," by which Paton meant that Fisher manifested the inherent "problem of us orphans": narcissism. Paton believed that the leadership of the adoption reform movement needed to transcend what she saw as the intrinsic character flaw of orphanhood—egoism—and give something back to society. Paton had learned this feeling for others from her physician adoptive father "on his home visits and in his office" and from her "maternal [adoptive] mother, who was certainly warm and generous in nature."[40] Paton's criticism was both ungenerous and inaccurate. Fisher ended her book with an extended discussion of her growing involvement in adoption politics, beginning with New York's Baby Lenore case and her passionate defense of the rights of birth mothers and the creation of ALMA. All of these activities were examples of political activism in the service of others, not mere egoism.

Paton's criticism aside, *The Search for Anna Fisher* was a runaway hit. Newspaper reviewers cast the book in superlatives, writing, for example, that Fisher's meeting with her mother "takes one on a journey of intrigue that makes it nearly impossible to put the book down."[41] The reviewers also supported the rights of adult adoptees to obtain information about their first families and acknowledged the withholding of birth information and sealing of adoption records unjust and unjustifiable.[42] The book was picked up by *Readers' Digest* and by the Book of the Month Club. It also led to another round of television appearances for Fisher, most prominently on the *Today* show, hosted by Barbara Walters, herself an adoptive mother.[43] ALMA's membership quickly soared into the thousands, and from her base in New York, Fisher opened branches throughout the United States.

For Paton, 1973 was crowded with positive signs of adoption reform and her continuing influence as the leader in the movement. Paton's fight for the rights of birth fathers and service as an expert witness in two trials brought her recognition in legal circles around the country.[44] She noted favorably the burgeoning adoption reform events, reflected in frequent media reports from mainstream papers like the *St. Louis Post-Dispatch* and took pride in the numerous requests for her help from such organizations as the Kiwanis Club of Delta, Colorado, and the Phoenix, Arizona, Department of Public Welfare.[45] Perhaps nothing was more gratifying to Paton than social workers coming to her for advice. When in January 1973, Annette Baran, a social worker from Vista Del Mar Child-Care Service in Los Angeles, wanted to learn more about Orphan Voyage, Paton quickly mailed her some introductory materials.[46] Baran was working with Arthur D. Sorosky, a child psychiatrist and assistant clinical professor in the Division of Child Psychiatry at UCLA, and Reuben Pannor, director of social work and research at the Vista Del Mar Child-Care Service. Together, they had formed the Adoption Research Project. Six months later, Pannor informed Paton that he agreed with her ideas on sealed adoption records and hoped "their work would throw some much needed light on the subject and create a more open climate on the part of agencies."[47]

After so many frustrating years, Paton could not help express skepticism, not at the researchers' liberal beliefs toward opening adoption records but, as Paton put it, at "the actuality of it all." By this she meant it would a long time before "social work . . . appears before the legislature and asks for the unsealing of adoption records, opens their doors to reconciliation, [and] lets natural parents come in too."[48] She also revealed her doubts about whether Pannor, Baran, and Sorosky had the toughness to fight the phalanx of social workers marshaled against the sealed adoption record. She rhetorically asked Baran, "Are you sufficiently fortified against those who insist upon sealed records to do this?" and immediately answered her own question: "I can't believe that you are, yet." Pannor had mentioned to Paton that he had been in touch with Florence Fisher and hoped he would get together with her again when she returned to Los Angeles.[49] Irked by the reference to Fisher as an expert on adoption reform matters, Paton bared her long-simmering resentment to Baran: "My personal, unvarnished feeling is: Why don't they ask me to come and unload some of the encyclopedic knowledge and insight of the situation. After all, I have lived deeply in both the world of social work and the world of adoption, in the latter extremely widely as well as deeply. I am sixty-five years old, this December. Why wait till I am too old to walk."[50]

Although skeptical of their fortitude to fight for their beliefs, Paton commented favorably in July on the work of Sorosky and his associates. She was referring to the publication of a feature article in the *Los Angeles Times* on the militant nature of adult adoptees searching for their original family members.[51] It characterized the three Los Angeles professionals as working with "scientific detachment" on a study of complex adoption issues. They planned to present their findings at a meeting of the Academy of Child Psychiatry in Washington, D.C., in October, and called on birth parents and anyone else who had participated in a reunion to send them letters describing the experience. They optimistically predicted that "some break in the secrecy surrounding adoption will come through the courts and that adoption agencies ought to be prepared for the upheaval which is sure to follow." The story also introduced readers to Florence Fisher as "the person most responsible for the surge of interest in adoptees' rights" and described her twenty-year search for her mother and the founding of ALMA, whose membership now numbered 4,000.

All of these events—Florence Fisher's ascendance to the leadership of the adoption reform movement, the spectacular increase in media attention to the issue of unsealing adoption records, and the imminent opening of these records—had a dramatic effect on Paton. Although she was genuinely excited at "the rapid movement toward change in the adoption culture," Paton felt the "movement" had taken a wrong turn. She believed that her readers were wrong to think that unsealing adoption records was the ultimate victory against social work oppression, and she feared that they failed to recognize the consequences of their newly acquired freedom.[52]

What was to be done? Paton's answer was a bombshell. She announced, "I am turning my efforts in another direction." From now on, she stated, "The Museum of Orphanhood . . . will be the main focus of my endeavors." She elaborated, "It will be a nucleus for a new understanding of the way of life of the social orphan, his life history, his different characteristics, his contributions, and his destructiveness and his selfishness also, for we must look at the whole figure." Paton conceded that she would still answer letters and write educational materials, but could not resist taking her readers to task. Referring to the future educational materials she proposed to write, Paton stated that that "even you yourselves might be induced to read them that you can better understand yourselves. For on the whole I think that you have not taken much thought about yourself, having been bound up with the agonizing situation of social repression." Paton concluded by upbraiding her readers for not being as kind and generous to their birth parents as they ought to be.

Upon receiving the October 1973 issue of *The LOG*, Margaret McDonald Lawrence fired off the most scathingly critical letter Paton ever received.[53] Lawrence, a psychologist, educator, and adult adoptee, had first contacted Paton in June 1970 in response to an ad for *The Adopted Break Silence*.[54] She joined Orphan Voyage and discovered that she and Paton held similarly radical views on adoption reform. Lawrence, who had founded the Adoption Study Project, frequently advised Florence Fisher before Fisher founded ALMA.[55] Because they had become close friends and remained so until Paton's death, Lawrence was able to confront Paton about her veiled threat to quit the movement. She interpreted Paton's piece in *The LOG* as evidence that Paton had developed a Messiah complex, blaming adult adoptees for their own problems. In her letter, Lawrence addressed Paton as "Dear Moses," and in her first sentence advised Paton that it was "time you came down off the mountain." Attacking Paton's self-pitying tone, Lawrence wrote, "Twenty years ago there was no group of suffering adoptees who asked you to make it your life's work to free them. The decision to become a career orphan was your own." After acknowledging that Paton knew more about the effects of orphanhood on adult adoptees than anyone else in the country, Lawrence reproached her for blaming them for their timidity and inability to help themselves. Both she and Paton knew that "the psychology of anonymity and slavery is the unique problem of the orphan today. If this wasn't true, your expertise would be unnecessary." Rhetorically she asked, "Is it now appropriate for you to damn the rock when it was your own decision to try to move it?"

Lawrence next addressed the question of leadership and Paton's decision to quit the movement. She observed that it was "almost inevitable" that all those who devoted their lives to the "orphan movement" got "caught up in a concept of themselves as Messiahs. You are going to be the ONE. And you are going to lead us all to freedom in spite of ourselves." Quoting Paton's words back to her—that for the past twenty years she had "tilled the soil, but the fruit is borne elsewhere," a not too subtle allusion to Florence Fisher's rise to prominence—Lawrence asked sarcastically: "If you can't be THE One, you'll just pick up your marbles and go home?"

Paton did not reply for six weeks, which was highly unusual. But when she did, she initially took Lawrence's strictures in stride. It was natural, "of course," that "two individualists like ourselves" were "bound to have at least moments of difference, and we have had our first." But Paton was sure that "things will restore themselves without much difficulty," because they valued each other immensely.[56] As for quitting the movement, Lawrence was wrong, or rather she had not "read the fine print on that fateful LOG." In fact, Paton declared, she had more movement activities to do than ever before. She was involved in the fight to open adoption records in Iowa; she was "gallivanting" by bus to New Mexico, Utah, and Salt Lake City to inform state adoption officials about changes formulated by Sorosky and his associates; she was also planning to buy a small house nearby in Eckert, Colorado, because the cabin in Cedaredge was getting crowded and she wanted "to establish a work place for Orphan Voyage." She was also planning field trips to Wisconsin and Detroit.

After this litany, Paton addressed the issue of living away from populated areas on a mountaintop. "I know you think of me as being isolated," she wrote, but "no matter where I lived I would be isolated, so why not be where I enjoy it." For Paton, the need for isolation was not geograhical but a psychological state of mind, the inherent result of being an orphan. Having warmed up, Paton finally came to grips with Lawrence's accusation that she was indifferent to reforming

American adoption. Flatly denying it, she scolded Lawrence, "And don't *ever* underestimate the depth and extent of my commitment. If nothing else, you don't sock away some $1,500 annually in a project for twenty years only to give it up out of momentary pique."

While replying to Lawrence's attack, Paton found her relationship with Florence Fisher deteriorating to the breaking point. By 1974, much to Paton's dismay, Fisher, as head of the nation's largest and most influential adoption search group, had assumed undisputed leadership of the adoption reform movement.[57] ALMA's success spread quickly, sparking the creation of hundreds of other adoptee search groups across the United States, with names like Yesterday's Children (Illinois), Adoptees' Identity Movement (Michigan), and Reunite (Ohio).[58] By 1975, more than 3,000 adult adoptees and 1,500 mothers had returned to 155 adoption agencies searching for information about their families and children.[59]

As ALMA's fame and influence grew, Fisher's flaws became magnified in Paton's mind, eventually resulting in a final break. Paton began to find Fisher's extroverted style especially grating, and she began to make her feelings known in various ways. When asked by one correspondent if she considered herself militant, Paton no longer thought the quality worthy of an activist and, obliquely referring to Florence Fisher, equated it with hysterical characteristics. She replied, "This is a moot question. I am not an actress. I don't spend much time screaming." Paton agreed with her good friend Margaret Lawrence, who described Fisher's ideas about adoption relationships as simplistic and harmful to the movement.[60] Paton wrote that what differentiated herself from Fisher was that "I talk, sometimes incisively. I listen, a great rarity in this world of adoption. More to the point, I think. I know how complex adoption is."[61] Paton was also irritated by Fisher's neglect to give credit where credit was due. On the *Today* show, Fisher discussed the Reunion File as if the idea had been hers from the start.[62]

But much more disturbing to Paton were the many reports that Fisher neglected her correspondence with the adopted population. As Paton acknowledged, "one of the worst crimes is, I think, to let an inquiry lie without response, and I know without doubt that she does this, for people write to me stating they have written to ALMA and had no response."[63] Illustrating this point, Paton shared a letter from an ALMA member to another group:

Some of us are members of ALMA but that means that simply we have paid our dues and the information is somewhere in New York; correspondence with them is out of the question; assistance of any kind is not to be had though it is a place for one's data to sit and wait for the matching information to cross its path. Thank you for your prompt reply to our requests. Bless you for your kindness.[64]

Reports from Margaret Lawrence reinforced Paton's negative image of Fisher. In Illinois a new and energetic activist, Donna Cullom, had organized a local chapter of ALMA and declared herself president. On the strength of ALMA's appealing computerized matching system, Cullom signed up 100 people, raised $300 in dues, and forwarded the money to Fisher. But she received no acknowledgment from ALMA headquarters. Frustrated at the lack of response, Cullom asked Lawrence for an explanation. Lawrence told her, "There is no computer, there is no organization and only God knows where those dues go beyond Flo's telephone bill. And there is the constant threat of really serious trouble as Flo continues to ignore the legal requirements associated with collecting monies and keeping track of them!"[65] Alarmed and angry, Cullom disassociated herself from ALMA and started up her own adoption reform group, Yesterday's Children. When Lawrence told Paton of this incident, Paton declared Fisher "a thief and a destroyer" and vowed to have nothing to do with her anymore.[66]

A year later, in 1975, Paton repeated her denunciation of Fisher, again using the phrase "a thief and a destroyer." This time her words were prompted by what Paton believed to be Fisher's continuing effort to control the adoption reform movement by unprincipled means. Fisher's unforgivable behavior took two forms. First, according to Paton, ALMA claimed "it was the only place in North America that provided service to adopted people." Paton considered this an insult to the many hardworking and dedicated people in the movement, not only in the United States but also in Canada. She believed that activists "must give recognition to one another."[67]

Second, according to Paton, Fisher began setting up rival ALMA groups in areas where Orphan Voyage groups were already established in a deliberate attempt to siphon off Paton's members. A year earlier, Paton had complained to adoption activist and poet Penny Partridge that Fisher "cannot bear that any group anywhere is not an ALMA group, and wants to set up competing groups, as in Chicago and Detroit."[68] This tampering with her membership was the last straw for Paton. While still recognizing "the good that was accomplished by her simple and loud scream of rage," she could not forgive Fisher for "the fact that she tries to set up competing groups wherever there is one that does not carry the name of ALMA."[69] In Paton's eyes, ALMA had degenerated into "a total cult" of personality revolving around Florence Fisher.[70]

With such organizing tactics, Fisher had hit Paton where she lived. When it came to creating groups under the Orphan Voyage name, Paton had never before been possessive; in fact, she had been very laissez-faire, encouraging her adherents to strike out on their own. But the creation of rival ALMA organizations struck at Paton's means of livelihood. By this time, her inheritance had run low, and Paton was living mainly from money generated from subscriptions to *The LOG*.

The competition for leadership of the adoption reform movement and Fisher's sharp tactics began to wear on Paton. As early as 1973, Paton obliquely mentioned to one correspondent that, with "the new activity springing up all over in the adoption field, opening the new vistas" that maybe it was time "to shift my labors."[71] She began to complain of fatigue and threaten to retire. In 1975, she told Margaret Lawrence that every time she walked out to her cabin, she did so reluctantly, no longer wanting "to do the tedious, complex things that are there to be done, and which no one else seems to want to do."[72] In 1976, rumors swirled about her impending retirement. Paton assured one correspondent not to worry. She "would do more of other things, less grinding the mimeo and pounding the typewriter and filing and keeping of records of where people are."[73]

While Fisher was ascending to the leadership of the adoption reform movement and Paton flirted with retirement, Sorosky, Baran, and Pannor burst upon the public consciousness. During the period 1973–1975 Sorosky, Baran, and Pannor became the most prominent intellectuals of the movement and provided it with its social science perspective. Their intellectual orientation led them to play down Fisher's emphasis on adoptees' constitutional rights. Instead, they medicalized the sealed adoption records issue. They made adoptee identity conflicts central to the adoption reform movement by using the discourse of social science to demonstrate the therapeutic value of adoptee searches and reunions.[74]

Through popular magazines, such as *Psychology Today*, and major newspapers, most notably the *Los Angles Times*, Sorosky, Baran, and Pannor promoted the cause of open records. To an unprecedented degree, they disseminated to the public and the social work community the work that psychologists were doing in the area of adoption reform. Through the shrewd use of the public media, they became the best known experts on this subject. The influence and ubiquity of their studies on the adoption reform movement cannot be overemphasized. No other body of intellectual work treating the adoption reform movement would be so universally cited as accurately portraying the psychological dynamics of adult adoptees and birth parents. Between 1974 and 1978, Sorosky, Baran, and Pannor published eleven articles and a book, insuring wide circulation of their findings.[75] All advocated opening the adoption records, either by refuting the unfounded fears of birth parents, adult adoptees, and adoptive parents, or by announcing the positive results of a policy of openness. The three researchers single-handedly provided the adoption reform movement and other proponents of open adoption records with language and arguments that bore the incontestable cachet of social science and medical authority.[76]

During these years, Paton remained in close contact with Sorosky, Baran, and Pannor. In *The LOG*, she reproduced the six conclusions of a paper on adoption reform they had delivered in October 1973 to the American Academy of Child Psychiatry in Washington, D.C.[77] Paton had written Sorosky earlier that she found his team's conclusions "most satisfying."[78] But she was deeply troubled by the most important one of the six, which called upon adoption agencies "to accept the adult adoptee as a full client, who has the right to complete information and to the cooperation of the agency" and to act as "an intermediary between adoptee, birth parent and adoptive parent."[79] Paton believed that adoption agencies had neither the capacity nor the personnel to carry out the innovative tasks the adoption researchers had assigned them. Moreover, Paton objected to adult adoptees being labeled "clients." Quoting an adult adoptee from a recent issue of *The LOG*, Paton summed up her own well-known libertarian views: "I really do not want any of the professions, 'social work in particular,' to hold my hand. I want them to unseal the records and stay out of my business."[80]

A month later, in November 1973, the issue of intermediaries acting as a third party between triad members and their natal families flared again after Pannor sent Paton an account of the American Academy of Child Psychiatry meeting in Washington, D.C. The article stated that the major recommendation coming out of the meeting was a proposal to set up mediating boards, composed of professional social workers, to investigate each reunion that was desired between an adult adoptee and a birth mother and to make a decision after seeking permission from all parties involved. Paton was aghast at such a suggestion and thought it inconsistent with the study's conclusions. She wrote Sorosky that she could not possibly be involved with a study, "which would have such a colonialistic outcome."[81] Paton stated that Pannor had assured her he did not favor adoption agency intermediaries, but she wanted Sorosky to explain how such a statement had found its way into the article.

After receiving no reply for five months, Paton wrote again, prompted by a comment she had read in the May 1974 issue of *McCall's* magazine about the research being conducted by the Adoption Research Project.[82] The article stated that the researchers were hopeful that adult adoptees would become less interested in searching for their birth parents once adoption records were opened. Paton bluntly stated, "I doubt this very much." Instead, she believed that the quality of the search would change; by this Paton meant that the timing and the manner of searching would change. Adult adoptees, she predicted, would "no longer go through tortuous years of indecision and semi-paralysis, to say nothing of guilt." They would be able to begin their search much more easily and quickly. Paton also envisioned that opening the records would introduce mutuality into the search, because she assumed (wrongly) that the records would also be opened to birth parents. On the whole, Paton declared, "things would be much improved." But, she concluded, "as for saying that there will be a lessening of direct encounter between adoptee and natural kindred, I doubt this very much. And, Dr. S., I should know." This last sentence was one of the rare moments that Paton revealed her own healthy sense of self-worth. It also was a classic example of her methodology: experience was a sure guide to knowing the truth.

The next month, Sorosky replied to Paton with equanimity and respect. He ignored her concerns about social workers acting as intermediaries at the outset of the reunion process and her argument over the alleged reduction in the number of searches for birth family members once records were opened. Instead, Sorosky stressed to Paton the tremendous progress his group had made as a result of an article appearing in the May issue of *McCall's* magazine. The Adoption Research Project had received 400 letters after the article appeared, 40 of which described reunions. According to Sorosky, his group's research had concluded that in 80 to 90 percent of these reunions "the results have been psychologically beneficial to the adoptees and in nearly as many cases with birth parents." Sorosky told Paton that he and his colleagues were planning to publish their results in professional journals and popular magazines and include all their findings in a book, to be published a year later. He concluded by asking for continued contact and praising Paton extravagantly: "We look to you as the pioneer in the field and hope our findings will further the work you began over 20 years ago. If it wasn't for you this study would undoubtedly never have come to pass. The next time you are in L.A. we would like to spend more time with you sharing our thoughts."[83]

Paton wrote back immediately and thanked Sorosky for his "very friendly and ego-building comments."[84] She appreciated that Sorosky recognized the significance of her labors, saying she had been told, "on good authority, that I changed the adoption culture." But that did not deter her from again criticizing him. Paton pointed out that in his last letter he had mentioned the receipt of 400 letters from triad members, 40 of which related to completed reunions. Paton pointedly asked, "What happens to the other 360?" She told Sorosky that she had received a complaint from a Michigan correspondent who had written the Adoption Research Project and had voiced his frustration after not receiving a reply. This was one of the reasons, Paton wrote, she had never "sought massive publicity" because she "did not wish to awaken hope in a person I could not offer at least a crust, if not a whole loaf." She asked Sorosky, "Do you refer these people, and to whom?"

Sorosky found Paton's comments "very provocative and challenging."[85] He admitted that the publicity generated by their research "has its adverse effects" and that there was a danger "of awakening hope in a person whom we are not able to offer at least a crust, let alone a whole loaf." But the researchers did not conceive their role "as providing immediate assistance to these anguished individuals." Paton was mistaken if she thought that. Their role, Sorosky declared, was "to compile enough data to make our conclusions as objective and scientific as possible." As to the job of providing aid to adopted persons, "We will leave that to you and Florence."

Paton could hardly contain her anger at Sorosky's response. She was troubled, she wrote, "even perhaps offended" by it for two reasons.[86] First, Paton believed that any research in the area of "human affliction is not possible if one turns one's back on portions of it, because one does not have the time." One could not possibly understand the lives of adult adoptees, she stated, "unless you commit yourselves more deeply, take the plunge into our world." Paton had developed a hatred for soulless researchers and their studies as far back as her college days at the University of Wisconsin, when she studied under sociology professor Samuel Andrew Stauffer, who pioneered in developing survey research techniques, in particular how to measure attitudes.[87] Recalling Stauffer, she denounced "these people [who] care nothing for the pain and grief of those they study; they offer no help at all."[88] Second, Paton was upset by the role Sorosky had assigned himself—as scientific researcher—"leaving the grubby detail to help to me and Florence. With our consent? Did you not know that Florence does not answer her mail? Do you realize I have no secretary? That I am human, limited? If you ask so much of me, or thrust it on me, then at least you should send me the 300 letters. But I do not want them. What on earth can I offer, single individual that I am?" And then, ever curious, caring, and censorious, Paton added, "(What did you do with the letters?)."

Diplomatically, Sorosky never responded to Paton's somewhat contradictory and unanswerable accusations. He did continue to correspond with her, however, updating her on his activities, complimenting her, and sending offprints of the Adoption Research Project's latest publications.[89] One of the offprints, "The Reunion of Adoptees and Birth Relatives," presented adult adoptee reunions in a very positive light declaring that 82 percent of the participants "felt that they had personally benefited from the reunion."[90] It gave Paton full credit for initiating the adoption reform movement, quoted her approvingly, and cited four of her works in the bibliography. The article went out of its way to incorporate Paton's criticisms. It predicted that reunions were bound to increase in the future as a result of media publicity and help from activist groups. It also noted that some adult adoptees and birth parents opposed the mediating boards acting as intermediaries for reunions because they resisted having their lives controlled by outside parties.[91]

Paton, unfortunately, misread the article, perhaps because Sorosky had used negative phrases to describe adult adoptees, such as "profound loneliness and depression," "poor relationship with the adoptive parent," "youngster's manipulative powers," "bewilderment and confusion," "isolation and alienation," and "preoccupied with existential concerns"—though he usually qualified or contextualized these negative phrases and regularly concluded these remarks on an upbeat note.[92] Moreover, Paton herself had made similar critical statements about adult adoptees' behavior. Nevertheless, she was disturbed and distressed by the article and chose to attack Sorosky again.[93] "You people," she began, meaning therapists in general and psychiatrists and psychoanalysts in particular, were blinded by the "narrow certitudes" of the clinical approach, which resulted in seeing "nothing healthy whatever" about adult adoptees. How easy it was, she continued, to use these negative categories, especially since it led to quick publication of one's work. Rhetorically she asked, "How much harm have you done to see nothing but this sickness in what we do? I cannot tell you the depth of my reaction."

Three months later, Sorosky defended himself, the work of the Adoption Research Project, and the psychiatric profession.[94] He believed that Paton "had been unnecessarily distrustful of our efforts." He tried to gain Paton's support, which, he wrote, "would be very helpful in encouraging the various activist groups to send us cases to study," arguing that "your enemy is also our enemy, so we must be allies." He related how his group's work for adoption reform had been opposed by the Child Welfare League of America, adoption social workers, and even adoptive parents, who questioned their motives and sent them threatening letters. But as a result of their many presentations at the CWLA's regional and other professional meetings, Sorosky contended, social workers and other professionals and even adoptive parents were abandoning their outmoded stereotypical ideas and embracing Paton's point of view.

As for the psychiatric profession, Sorosky informed Paton—in a statement that revealed a remarkable ignorance of his own field—that she was entirely mistaken, that in fact it was "the one profession that has been entirely supportive" of adoption reform.[95] According to Sorosky, psychiatrists had never been involved in adoption issues in the past, and after discussing the subject with his

UCLA colleagues, they could not understand why it had never been brought to their attention before. Sorosky then flattered Paton in an aside: "They had never read your books, right?" He pleaded with her to support him and his associates at the Adoption Research Project. Sorosky confessed, "it hurts me that you above all should be inspiring resistance against our work." He attributed Paton's distrust to deep scars from her past, which made her have doubts that "a non-adopted group of researchers can have a honest sincere interest" in adoption reform. He hoped that a face-to-face meeting could resolve the conflicts between them. Sorosky ended with a compliment: "It is only because of our admiration for your work that we would like to gain your trust and confidence."

Paton replied to Sorosky immediately, extending an olive branch.[96] She hoped that a better relationship could be established and told him that their relationship was not as "bad as you think it is." But in the rest of the two-page-long letter she proceeded to lecture Sorosky on the culture of the adopted. He was "in error" to blame her for motivating the adopted population to resist the Adoption Research Project's blandishments to cooperate with it. Paton admitted that she had expressed honest reservations about Sorosky's conclusions. But, she declared, "I do not think I do people's thinking for them." The problem Sorosky faced, she informed him, was inherent in the adult adoptee's general character: they were naturally hesitant to commit themselves to anything. Lamenting Sorosky's ignorance and thinking back on her own twenty years of experience, Paton exclaimed, "If you did only realize how very difficult it is to find them, to hold them, to nurture them." Orphan Voyage, was built up "by dint of patient, personal, and persistent effort." Adult adoptees knew that Paton cared for them. "They know I understand, for I am one of them. They aren't interested in research; they are interested in becoming free people, in completing the arc of themselves."

Paton then shifted direction, raising a personal issue with Sorosky. She resented deeply his habit of referring repeatedly to her as an

"activist," whatever that is. I am a philosopher, a poet, an engineer, and I love these brothers and sisters whom I have found, perhaps the children I never had, and it is true that in my own way I will fight for them to the death, yet I do not fit under that label. I particularly do not want you bracketing me, unless you must, with Florence Fisher, who has, I believe, destroyed more than she has accomplished for the cause.

She also did not see the need "of continuing to study us little orphans as if the problem were not perfectly clear." Adopted people were "deprived of certain

essential human rights, and it is very generally known what effect this deprivation has upon the human character." What were these human rights? Paton
spoke of only one: the right to one's adoption records, the birth certificate. Paton
realized she seemed "unyielding," but she could not bear the thought that adopted people were referred to as "clients" nor that they should have to depend on
social workers as "intermediaries." As long as the Adoption Research Project's
studies contained such implications, "just as long I will be stiff necked."[97]

Sorosky had his defenders within the movement. One of them, adoption activist and writer Betty Jean Lifton, exchanged several letters with Paton, and in
one she championed Sorosky and his colleagues' 1974 *Journal of Youth and Adolescence* article. Paton would not hear of it. She declared to Lifton that Sorosky
was "on the side of the manipulators for he had never disavowed it [the article].
Now I know and turn away. He is just one more chain. The spectacle of all those
psychiatrists sitting together in Washington discussing our neurotic motives
makes me sick to my stomach. They make no distinction between character and
traumatic neurosis, and so provide the wrong prescription."[98] Lifton, who held
a doctorate in psychology and was married to the well-known psychiatrist and
human-rights advocate Robert Jay Lifton, replied that she thought Paton was
too hard on Sorosky. Lifton stated that she was happy that psychiatrists had
begun to take an interest in the problem of adult adoptees. It did not mean that
they thought adult adoptees were abnormal; psychiatrists study all of human
behavior. In fact, Lifton believed that the only hope for social work in general
and getting adoption records open in particular was for psychiatrists to discuss
the issue.[99]

Paton disagreed strongly with Lifton's assessment of Sorosky. She was
"repelled" by Sorosky's "colonialistic suggestion" that social workers act as intermediaries to reunions. It had the sound of "residual chains." At bottom, for
Paton, there was an unbridgeable divide between those who were adopted and
those who were not. Because Sorosky and his associates were not adopted, their
methodology was ipso facto suspect, indeed, inferior. As she put it, "they have
not a sufficient grounding in the realities of this life of adoption. They are far
too legitimate to comprehend, no matter how hard they try, and I think Sorosky
tries, all right. There is nothing wrong with him except his legitimacy."[100] Lifton
persisted in her praise of Sorosky.[101] Paton remained unpersuaded. Frankly, she
did not trust Sorosky: "He just looks upon me as a cheap and easy source of
names."[102] By August 1975, Paton wrote another correspondent, "I've never met
Sorosky, and I have mistrusted his motivation from the beginning."[103]

In the summer of 1975 Paton went public with her criticism of Sorosky.[104]
The final straw was a paper presented by Sorosky, Baran, and Pannor that ad-

vocated "regional reunion registries in which adoptees and birth parents can express their interest in a reunion with the other." In the paper, Sorosky accurately attributed to Jean Paton the origins of the idea of an adoption registry. He announced that a bill proposing just such an adoption registry was recently introduced in the California legislature. However, the paper radically deviated from Paton's original conception for the Reunion File. It suggested that to make the adoption registries effective, a "professional assistance and counseling board" would be created, "consisting of mental health specialists (psychiatrists, psychologists, and adoption social workers) and representatives from each of the adoption triad: adoptees, adoptive parents and birth parents."

What upset Paton was the utter blindness of the researchers to their own conclusions. Rhetorically, she asked: after studying adult adoptees' reunions for many months and concluding that they worked out just fine, why did Sorosky and his associates think that these people needed mental health assistance? Moreover, though the researchers claimed to be scientific and objective, nowhere in their analysis was there any evidence for the need for a counseling board. As Paton put it, the experts "go to great lengths to get what they consider scientific samples, yet when they get to findings and conclusions they draw it all out of their hats." She pointed to "the simple fact" that successful reunions had been going on for many years, "illustrating something which is valuable and beautiful, and which the professionals seem unable to value, even to *see*. There is nothing in all of their annals of professional help which equals the power and the beauty of your reunions when they work, when they are done right, and it is obvious from the accounts that many of you do know how to do them right." Paton had had enough. She thought that it was "pathetic that the professionals cannot see it."[105] Inadvertently, by explicitly calling for mental health assistance, Sorosky had questioned Paton's philosophy of the search with its emphasis on forgiveness, "natural" intermediaries, and reunions, thereby exacerbating her long-standing animosity toward experts.

For Paton, there was no inconsistency in her inclusion of a "natural" intermediary in the morphology of an adoption reunion and her fierce denunciation of Sorosky and associates for advocating the use of professional intermediaries to facilitate reunions. This was because Paton believed that under exceptional or unusual circumstances a person could benefit from the use of an intermediary, in order to make the process more efficient or to lessen the pain of the participants' initial contact.[106] The most common type of intermediary Paton had in mind was the private investigator, though she deplored those who charged adult adoptees exorbitant prices.[107] As usual, Paton based her policy on her own experience. As we have seen, she had paid a private investigator $35 to find her natal family, and he had contacted Paton's aunt, Viola, who eventually put her in touch with her first mother. Paton explained that she had used her aunt as an intermediary because she was a person "who knew the original circumstances, and the present situation."[108] With the growth of the adoption reform movement, Paton began referring to people who lent support during reunions as "natural intermediaries," counting in this group a spouse, adoptive parents, friends, or helpers in adoptee groups.[109]

Paton's initial objection to using professional social workers as intermediaries was due to their lack of expertise: few had any experiential knowledge of social orphanhood—that is, being born out of wedlock or adopted. She also believed they lacked knowledge of what it meant to reunite with original family members. On the latter point, she wrote her friend Margaret Lawrence, noting that social workers were mistaken about the emotional dynamics of a reunion. "They keep insisting that reunion is a brief experience," she declared, "and from it people go [on] to lead their own separate lives." Some do, she admitted, but social workers were wrong to think that a reunion had no consequences. On the contrary, adopted folks "meet people we like and with whom we have things in common, to say nothing of the other relatives we have." Paton believed these errors were inevitable because social work "decides everything in conferences of its own indigenous population. They can't seem to get the idea that [they] cannot discover it all by themselves, and must admit its clientele as peer into its councils." Until that happened, and Paton wondered out loud whether it would ever happen, "we outcasts must find our own world and our own hopefully mutual solutions."[110] Here she sounded once again two of her favorite themes: that adult adoptees must be included and given voice in any discussion concerning them, and that their best hope for success was to be found by helping each other, not depending on outsiders.

Paton later articulated additional reasons for her opposition to intermediaries, all of them related to adult adoptees. Essentially, she believed that intermediaries were superfluous. Adult adoptees were fully competent to undertake their own searches. When a social worker from Lutheran Social Services asked Paton what materials or information its adoption wing should supply returning triad members with, Paton replied that she did not believe that natal parents or adult adoptees needed much help in achieving reconciliation. She advised the social worker "that all an agency needs do, upon receiving these requests, is to go down to the closed files, draw out the information and present it to the person to whom it does indeed belong."[111] For Paton, the search and reunion process was a private affair; an intermediary violated the relationship between the adult adoptee and the birth parent, making the initial meeting inherently humiliating and demeaning.[112]

Most important, intermediaries short-circuited the very process necessary for achieving psychological health and a successful reconciliation and reunion. Having had their self-confidence undermined due to the stigma of illegitimacy and the sealed record, Paton believed that, for searchers, "there is only one cure possible, to engage in such actions as make us believe in ourselves at last."[113] In the face-to-face confrontation of adult adoptee and birth parent there were always fears to be overcome and even the occasional trauma. But Paton held that the presence of intermediaries deprived the adult adoptee from "walking through the fear which he experiences in a search. If he does not walk through it, he never overcomes it. . . . Adopted people who must use an intermediary in this process are never released from this fear."[114] It was a once-in-a-lifetime chance that had to be seized. Paton wrote, "What other opportunity does anyone have to overcome the ghosts and fantasies and in particular our fear of our own strength?"[115] To use an intermediary, Paton wrote a commercial adoptee search company, "to be told that one cannot do it by oneself, one cannot confront a person who gave birth without the way being prepared by some stranger, is to take from that person the one best chance of being free of inferiority and stigma."[116]

Nevertheless, the intermediary concept, first enunciated in the United States by Sorosky, Baran, and Pannor, began to take hold. In 1975, Joan Vanstone, a pioneer Canadian adoption activist, informed Paton of a report on a proposed new Ontario law to open adoption records. Paton approved the tone of the hearings and recommendations but denounced a clause providing for intermediaries, which, she predicted, "can and would lead to an unbearable tyranny."[117]

Closer to home, in August 1976 the Washington Adoption Reunion Movement (WARM) was created, an organization initially made up of adult adoptees and adoptive parents to discuss methods of searching for family members.[118] With input from adoptive parents, the group decided that adding a third party—an intermediary—would be prudent. County court judge Norman B. Ackley, himself an adoptive parent, became a regular participant at WARM meetings and the groups' mentor and ultimately undertook a review of the law governing adoption disclosure. In Judge Ackley's opinion, adoption records in the state of Washington, like those in many other states, could legally be opened "for good cause shown," thus leaving the decision to the discretion of the judge. Ackley took it upon himself to write a procedural format, which permitted adult adoptees in Washington to petition the County Court, and for the court to appoint a Confidential Intermediary to perform a search for the petitioner's family. In the summer of 1977, the first such petition by an adult adoptee was filed, and WARM's Confidential Intermediary system went into operation.[119]

A year later, in late July 1978, WARM subsidized Paton's trip to Washington State to present her opposition to intermediaries. She met with WARM's board in an informal setting, at a member's kitchen table.[120] Paton liked the people in the group, especially Eddie Rizk, whom Paton described as "a real asset."[121] But this did not prevent her from speaking her mind. Paton despised WARM's use of intermediaries. It horrified her.[122] Writing to Joan Vanstone, Paton questioned their motives: "I think some of us want to be social workers, as if that would make us more legitimate, or a bit less a bastard."[123] What particularly galled Paton about WARM's employment of intermediaries was that they were drawn from the ranks of the adopted. She could not imagine herself in such a role. If a judge approached her, Paton wrote Eddie Rizk, offering her the names of birth parents with a request that she make initial contact, she would turn him down. "It is a physical fact that I would feel a deep revulsion to be an intermediary by fiat—or any other way, except in some sort of exceptional situation." Paton recalled how decades earlier, as a social worker she had been offered a job, which she needed, to make adoptive placements. She returned home and could not even swallow as she mulled over the offer. The next day, she rejected the job, saying, "I can't do it under the sealed record."[124] For Paton, any reliance on intermediaries was tantamount to remaining in servitude to social work, maintaining a master-slave relationship. It was incomprehensible to Paton why adult adoptees voluntarily placed themselves in such a position.

> I just can't understand how anyone in the population, who has been sensitive to the importance of being released from our chattel status, can do anything which even smells of chattel status. And even for an adoptee to take the role of approach to the birth parent, in place of the hungering adoptee, is a perpetuation rather than a release from this chattel status.[125]

The movement, riven by hostile divisions already, Paton declared, was now divided by those who believed in "uncompromising freedom, and those who accepted an offer of an intermediated search."[126]

By 1976, the increasing intervention of social workers as intermediaries and counselors in the lives of adult adoptees in search of their first families reignited Paton's long-standing visceral dislike of experts and professionals. As she commented to one correspondent, "I am so disgusted with social work in adoption, and in counseling generally."[127] Throughout the year, her correspondence was filled with anger against professional social workers, striking out at their ig- norance of matters pertaining to adult adoptees. To Betty Jean Lifton, Paton complained that, with rare exceptions, "none of the professionals even know the language" of adopted people.[128] To another triad member, she lamented that "the professionals do not know the first thing about human affliction." In Paton's opinion, this was the fault of social workers' woefully deficient education. She denigrated the MSW program, observing that "two years of special courses in college" were not equivalent to the experiential knowledge that came from being born out of wedlock and being adopted.[129] Reiterating her point to Lee Camp- bell, the president of CUB, Paton asked, "What do they know?"[130]

Paton suggested that social workers needed to be reeducated. To Campbell she advanced the idea of providing them with a training session and make them pay for it.[131] Paton elaborated on this point to Michael Haag, an adult adoptee and doctoral student in social psychology at the University of California, Santa Cruz. At a panel session of the American Psychological Association, a female social worker had stood up after the presentation and, referring to sealed adop- tion records, explained that social workers, including herself, had just done what they were told to do all those years without thinking. She concluded by saying, "I'm sorry." Paton commented, "When regret and remorse are expressed, then I trust them, otherwise I do not. I know it is difficult to face the guilt of having damaged so many souls, but it is what they did. And, I will not forgive them until they say they are sorry, and act accordingly."[132]

This lack of trust—Paton viewed it as duplicity—underlay much of her anger. To Haag, Paton observed "how sweetly some social workers speak of opening records. But it is almost universal that they never take a stand against the seal."[133] Similarly, Paton expressed strong misgivings about changes in the law or adoption policy initiated by professionals because "they still think of us as inferior people, and our position does not really matter to them as much as their convictions about their own abilities."[134] Although agreeing initially with her Canadian friend, adoption reformer Joan Vanstone, that the Child Welfare League of America "presumably" showed "a change of heart," citing an editorial in its journal *Child Welfare*, Paton was "skeptical about it." She explained that the editorial's real purpose was "to amass a lot of money to do research on the problem, calling on all the professions." Rhetorically, she raised her old question, "Why do they never wish to call on us?"[135]

This was really the crux of Paton's bitterness toward social workers: her democratic ethos could not stomach the elitism of social work's pretension to knowledge they did not possess. She railed against the idea of "one person sitting in front of a desk and pretending to know more than the one they are advising." Instead, adopted people, not social workers, were the key to the success of adoption reform. Paton asserted that her ideal—"the way it should be"—was "doing for one another . . . mutual and self-respecting and other-respecting."[136] Indeed, she was hopeful that the stirring of reform around the country was evidence that adopted people were "structuring a new profession." By volunteering and helping each other, Paton declared, "it was the story of the Good Samaritan all over again."[137] Adopted people and only adopted people had the knowledge and power within themselves to help each other.

Closely linked to Paton's dislike of social workers was her criticism of adoption agencies. Unlike today's activists, Paton did not define adoption records as only birth certificates. She understood that adoption agencies were the custodians of important records containing vital information about family history. But she expected nothing from agencies "except sticky fingers," bureaucrats who refused to provide adult adoptees with the information directly.[138] According to Paton, their reluctance stemmed from the fact that they were too full of their public image as custodians of sealed records.[139] She disagreed with those in the movement, such as CUB president Lee Campbell, who believed that a strong program of education would change adoption agencies' policies. Instead, Paton counseled that the only kind of pressure that would be effective would be the activities of CUB members who reached out with a helping hand to "young women in birth trouble."[140] Paton also resented the large amount of funding adoption agency research was receiving to study adult adoptees. She questioned why agencies needed eight months to study adoptees since, she observed sarcastically, "they have had a couple of decades of refusal" and presumably knew everything there was to know already.[141] Not until Paton saw "some signs of real remorse and guilt on the part of the people who have shackled so many" would she believe that adoption agencies were serious about adoption reform.

First Florence Fisher: because of her, Paton's leadership in reforming American adoption had been lost, her income weakened. Then Sorosky and his research associates: because of them, the movement was being destroyed from within by the spread of intermediaries and the strengthening of the social work establishment's intrusion into the lives of adult adoptees. It was galling; it was depressing. Paton felt like escaping from it all. In September 1977, rumors of her retirement again swirled around reform circles. The following month, in *The LOG*, Paton publicly affirmed the reports of her "probable retirement," which she said would occur in September of 1978.[142] She assured her readers that her successor would only be a person who had proven to be trustworthy over long years of experience and in whom Paton had complete confidence. She even went so far as to detail the qualifications the person needed to become her successor. Yet not two pages later, Paton all but retracted her retirement. Under the heading "Changes During the Year of Transition," she declared that Orphan Voyage was not shutting down, and concluded, "There is no thought in me to dismantle this operation but to begin to place out some of its several functions on quite competent shoulders, and to help these new servants of the cause to stand firm."

Paton's talk of retirement was just that: a momentary outburst born of frustration and stress. In the six months that followed, there was little evidence that Paton was withdrawing from her crusade to reform American adoption. As adoption agencies began to support legislative efforts to enact voluntary mutual consent adoption registries, Paton continued to denounce their motivations and urged her readers not to support the legislation. In 1978, on the twenty-fifth anniversary issue of the Life History Study Center, she provided the reasons why in a short history of adoption agencies' policies and practices toward sealed adoption records.[143] Paton first observed that for decades, social work "loved the sealed record form of adoption and worked under it without the slightest sign of protest." Only now, when adoption agencies saw adult adoptees "breaking the chains" that kept them away from their first families, were they open to reform. But don't be fooled, Paton warned. Social workers only wanted "to control you and mediate a reunion." She accused many of them of not even believing in reunions and deliberately setting out to sabotage them. As proof of their duplicity, Paton charged that "if social work believed in reunion, they could begin at once, without any change in the laws." She suggested that adoption agencies could announce publicly the creation in their offices of Bureaus of Reconciliation and welcome adult adoptees to come in. No adoption agencies acted on her suggestion to establish Bureaus of Reconciliation.

Nor did Paton's admonitions, criticism, and idealism have any effect on slowing down the momentum of using intermediaries in adoptee search and reunion efforts. WARM's confidential-intermediary program in Washington State, for example, prospered. By 1980, WARM had contacted 800 persons and had facilitated approximately 350 reunions or contacts with birth parents or siblings. Thirty-five judges in the state worked with WARM to open files, with Judge Ackley himself mandating the opening of 277 files.[144]

Paton responded to WARM's growing success by counseling adoptees to avoid WARM. When her advice was successful, it affirmed her resistance to WARM and the value of self-conducted reunions. In 1982, she wrote Margaret Lawrence that she had received much satisfaction from a young library student who had just completed a successful reunion with her mother. The student had phoned Paton and said, "I am so glad that you said I did not have to go through WARM; I have done something I didn't have any idea I could do, and I am now so fulfilled and complete. It just feels wonderful."[145] Seven years later, Paton's opposition to WARM had only strengthened. In January 1989, she noted that WARM had claimed that their intermediary system would demonstrate that reunions work, and that adoption records would then be opened. Paton couldn't resist a little jibe: "Well, ha ha, it hasn't happened that way and it is not about to."[146]

10

Organizing the Movement

> Somehow letters from the mothers always tend to make me cry, much
> more than the adoptees.
>
> —JEAN PATON, 1976

> Orphans are not group people.
>
> —JEAN PATON, 1978

Although the East Coast news media, such as the *New York Times* and the
Washington Post, generally ignored the adoption reform movement, the hometown paper of Arthur Sorosky, Annette Baran, and Reuben Pannor, the *Los
Angeles Times*, frequently ran feature articles and TV movie reviews on the subject.[1] The *Los Angeles Times* was also the first paper to feature, as news, what
would become a staple of mass-circulation magazines and, later, TV talk shows:
the search and reunion of adult adoptees with their natal parents. The testimony of social scientists supported these dramatic, reality shows. Both adult
adoptees and birth parents were portrayed as having to overcome enormous
obstacles that were always being thrown in their way.[2]

The combination of drama, self-help, and demand for individual rights in
adoptee autobiographies and search and reunion news stories was tailor-made
for mass-circulation magazines. Even before Florence Fisher and ALMA burst
on the scene, mass-circulation magazines sensed the potential market and occasionally ran stories about adopted persons searching for their birth parents.
In 1971, for example, *Seventeen* dramatically recounted an adopted girl's difficult
odyssey in an unsuccessful search for her birth mother.[3] But beginning in 1974
and continuing through and beyond the decade, mass-circulation magazines
such as *McCall's*, *Parents Magazine*, *Reader's Digest*, *Seventeen*, and *Good House-*

keeping provided its readership with articles entitled "Who Are My Real Parents?," "The Adopted Child Has the Right to Know Everything," "Search for a Stranger," and "We're a Family Again." Thematically, they dramatized the plight of adult adoptees who were prevented from discovering their family heritage, championed the right of adult adoptees to view their adoption files, and featured successful search and reunions. Many of these stories showcased Fisher and ALMA or Sorosky and his associates' research results, giving only a short paragraph to Paton and Orphan Voyage.[4]

Despite the brevity of the mentions of Paton and her organization, the mass media's coverage of the adoption reform movement produced hundreds of requests for aid. A single article in the June 1974 issue of *Cosmopolitan*, recounting an adopted woman's long and difficult but ultimately successful reunion with her birth mother, resulted in Paton's being flooded with over 500 letters and quite a few phone calls, about a third of them from mothers who had relinquished their babies for adoption two to ten years earlier.[5] The heart-wrenching letters put Paton "through the wringer."[6] The cruel way these mothers had been treated continued to astonish and wound her.[7] Envisioning a world of semi-open adoption, Paton asked adoption researcher Arthur Sorosky why these women couldn't be sent verified reports of their children's condition in the years after they were adopted. Facts such as these, she believed, were what birth mothers most wanted. Paton could not think of any "civilized reason for withholding" such information.[8]

Paton was unique among adoption reform activists in the 1950s and 1960s to defend natal mothers against the stigmatization of society. Paton's support for them came out of her holistic understanding of the importance of kinship and heredity within the adoption triad, her social work experience, her reunion with her own natal mother, and her natural empathy for the oppressed and marginalized. In the 1970s, birth mothers' troubles were never far from her mind. In 1971, she fired off a letter to New York's governor, Nelson Rockefeller, congratulating him for vetoing a bill enacted by the legislature, which would have limited the time from six months to thirty days after which a mother could no longer revoke her agreement to let her child be adopted.[9] In 1974, on trips to Michigan and Wisconsin, Paton met with birth mothers who had joined adult adoptee search groups. She assured one correspondent that they suffered grievously from the separation of their children and offered her a diagnosis. Their pain stemmed "not so much from a bewilderment of identity but a grief which can well up from a very deep place."[10] Paton's concern for natal parents was increased by her awareness that there was "considerable hostility in the adoptee population to natural parents (often they do not realize it) and natural mothers sense it (if they do not imagine it)." For this reason, Paton believed, many birth mothers did not participate in the efforts to reform American adoption.[11]

Their failure to become involved in the movement, Paton thought, was also exacerbated by Florence Fisher and ALMA, whose policy, she believed, discriminated against birth mothers from active participation in searches.[12] Paton was not entirely correct, however. No matter what Fisher's policy was toward birth mothers in ALMA's New York headquarters, she had no control over the hundreds of ALMA chapters across the country, and many of these supported natal mothers in their search for their children. The Southern California chapter of ALMA, for example, celebrated the reunion of birth mothers with their daughters; it also published the mothers' letters advocating the value of reunions.[13] Similarly, the Massachusetts chapter of ALMA, meeting for the first time in May 1975 in Lexington, included birth mothers in its membership, though it made clear that it would not assist them with their search until the child was eighteen years of age.[14] By 1980, even Fisher's New York headquarters was celebrating birth mother reunions.[15] Nevertheless, Paton never changed her opinion that Fisher and ALMA were prejudiced against birth mothers.

In the summer of 1975, as the adoption reform movement's steady drumbeat to open adoption records accelerated, Paton disagreed strongly with adoption activists who maintained that only adult adoptees should have access to their adoption records. She believed that "everyone named on the records should have access to them, not only at their maturity, but at all times." She exhorted other activists not to exclude anyone, adding, "Let the mothers have access to records, too."[16]

Her long-standing empathy with birth mothers, the outpouring of letters she received as a result of the *Cosmopolitan* article, her personal meetings with distressed birth mothers, and the mothers' virtual exile from accessing adoption records troubled Paton immensely and cried out for a solution. What acted as a catalyst for Paton was an intensive six-month correspondence with Mary Anne Cohen, a twenty-nine-year-old Lexington, Massachusetts, birth mother. In 1969, after her firstborn son had spent a year in foster care, Cohen relinquished him to adoption. As the years passed by, she grew desperate to know what had happened to her son—she thought she was going crazy—but it had never occurred to her that adoptees had any need to know their birth parents. In 1971, she heard Florence Fisher on the radio, joined ALMA in 1975, and soon thereafter heard about Jean Paton and Orphan Voyage from a member of a group called Adoptees in Search. Cohen immediately wrote Paton, and was amazed when she wrote back.[17] Mutual admiration quickly ensued. Cohen found Paton sympathetic to birth mothers—unlike Fisher, who, Cohen felt, held grudges. Cohen later credited Paton as being "the first to touch and inspire me" in her "career" as an adoption activist.[18] For her part, Paton was "well impressed" with Cohen's deep empathy with the desperate plight of natal mothers longing for their lost children, commended her to other correspondents as a person with "much fire in her writing," and published her poetry in *The LOG*.[19]

Cohen's correspondence was instrumental in triggering Paton's first thoughts about an organization for birth mothers.[20] In September 1975, she asked Cohen, "Do you think there should be somewhat separate facilities for the natural parents? Not completely separate, but that they should have something of their own department in the movement? I think so more and more." By November Paton's ideas had matured and were moving toward an independent birth mother's organization. She announced that starting in 1976, Orphan Voyage would develop "a network of natural parents who have given children to adoption." Paton envisioned Orphan Voyage facilitating introductions of birth parents to one another, helping them construct a message to society, and building bridges with adult adoptees. Nevertheless, Paton stressed that the birth parent network would not be an auxiliary of Orphan Voyage; it needed "a degree of independence" from the adoptee population "in order that its own clear voice can be heard." Paton wanted "the silence of the natural parent to be broken for the same reason that I wanted the voice of the adoptee to be heard, *his* silence broken." What she fervently hoped was that "all under the stigma of society might become healed through mutual effort."[21]

Paton's plan to develop a communications network for birth parents took a new turn in February 1976. She was inspired to change direction after receiving in the mail an enclosure entitled "Letter to My Sisters" from Cohen. "Letter to My Sisters" recounted how Cohen had telephoned a local mental health center with an inquiry about starting up "a support group for women who have given up children to adoption." She had initiated the call after talking to another woman who had become "emotionally crippled, incapacitated, by her reaction to the loss of her child." The man who answered the phone was puzzled, replied vaguely, and offered little help; he never before had such a request. His response bewildered and infuriated Cohen. She lived in a highly educated, "psychology-conscious" area, where self-help groups abounded. Cohen enumerated them for her readers: "infertility, homosexuality, senior citizens, new parents, women who have had abortions, divorces, diseases, and of course groups for adoptive parents." It then dawned on her why the mental health specialist had a right to be surprised:

because it was the first time he had received a request from a ghost, and only the undertaker provides services for the dead! Each time an adoption is finalized and the birth records sealed, a mother is symbolically buried; her pain becomes invisible and irrelevant to the society that has forgotten her. Our grief is the grief of ghosts, scratching with transparent noiseless fingers at the windows of those who fear to look us in the face.

Cohen blamed social workers, who refused to recognize birth mothers' grief and guilt, leaving them without any rights once the relinquishment papers were signed. They hid behind the rationale that birth mothers had freely chosen to give their children for adoption. For if social workers admitted the legitimacy of birth mothers' grief and their responsibility for these women's lifelong pain, it would shatter the myth that after nine months of pregnancy and the birth experience that the mothers' memories and concern for their children disappeared without a trace. With the rise of the adoption reform movement, however, "our children, the adoptees, have come out of hiding to demand their rights [and] the silence of natural parents is the last nail holding together the rotten structure of deceit, secrecy, and subjugation on which too many adoptions have been based."

Cohen called on birth mothers to "conquer our shame and fear and turn to each other for the strength and comfort society refuses to provide." She was hopeful for the future, and mentioned Paton's plans of beginning a contact and support network "just for us." But Cohen had her own ideas about how such a network would be implemented. She closed "Letter to My Sisters" asking for birth parents to write her with their "ideas, needs and experiences." She was interested in practical suggestions on how birth parents could reach each other and who among them had "skills in writing, art, media, counseling, group leadership that could be of use."[22]

In February 1976, stirred by Cohen's "Letter," Paton mailed it out in a "Special Release" to the subscribers of The LOG, with a cover letter announcing that she had changed course. Rather than opening up a communications network within Orphan Voyage for natal parents, she was going to leave the development of the program up to Cohen and those who joined her in the new venture. Paton pledged her help, when called on, "but the essential guidance will come from the population of natural parents."[23] Paton had faith in the ability of natal parents to manage their own affairs. In fact, she had a higher opinion of birth parents than adult adoptees when it came to activism, which was another reason Paton was now giving them particular attention. In her opinion, natal parents

were more "active, motivated, and though afraid, they have a reason to search—
they know their child was alive."[24]

Paton's faith was not misplaced. In July 1976, Lee Campbell, a Massachusetts birth mother and friend of Mary Anne Cohen, placed a notice in the *Boston Globe* soliciting responses from individuals who relinquished their children
to adoption and wanted to discuss their experiences. The newspaper notice resulted in a meeting of four individuals at a Cape Cod church and the creation
of a national birth parent group, Concerned United Birthparents (CUB).[25] The
newly formed organization held its first meeting on July 18, with eight members
"either present or having sent their regrets," and proceeded to enact bylaws, se-
lect a board of directors, and settle on the corporation's officers.[26] The bylaws
stated that CUB's primary function was "to promote the general mental health
and welfare of birthparents located throughout the United States." CUB envisioned achieving its purpose through politics and education. It would lobby
legislative bodies to enact laws and policies that would provide for the needs of
birth parents and promote "open adoption, an alternative adoptive process to
the present closed adoption." In addition, it pledged to work with professional
social workers to deal with the problems of birth mothers and to dispense information revealing "the feelings and needs" of birth mothers to adoption agencies,
media outlets, and adoptive parents' groups as well as to birth parents and their
families.[27] Significantly, although birth mothers longed to know how their children were doing, searching for them was not mentioned in the bylaws.

Securing her name and address from Cohen, Paton wrote Lee Campbell
in August 1976 offering her assistance, and a long and fruitful correspondence
ensued.[28] Campbell immediately replied with a fact-filled letter, characterizing
CUB's progress as a "serious, dedicated, and purposeful" organization.[29] She
defined "birthparents," a neologism coined by CUB to assuage adoptive parent
fears:

> One word; no hyphenation. We hope that, psychologically, once we are known
> under a consistent title, adoptive parents will feel less ambiguous. "Birthparent"
> is a particularly good title for it invokes reminiscences of "grandparent," etc. A
> minor point but one which does cause needless consternation among adoptive
> parents.[30]

Campbell then provided Paton with CUB's philosophy. She assured Paton
that CUB "was not necessarily against adoption, per se"; under certain circumstances it could be a viable alternative. However, CUB was against "the present

form of closed adoption" because it left the impression "that birthparents have no feelings worthy of consideration, that they are, in fact, baby machines, and incubators." CUB needed to educate society and adoptive parents that birth parents were not the "enemy," but real people. According to Campbell, birth parents felt that "we have a right to know the end of our story; to know the children we begat as one adult to another, as can any butcher, baker, and candlestick maker." To this end, Campbell proposed that adoption agencies be required to institute a type of open adoption by accepting from birth parents a "Release of Protection," a CUB-invented form that released them from state laws of anonymity and that required adoptive parents to reveal to the child upon attaining the age of majority the identity of his or her birth parents.[31] In this way, adoptive parents would no longer be able to keep the adoption a secret from their children, and children, upon reaching their majority, would be informed of the identity of their birth parents and that the birth parents favored a reunion.

Paton modestly replied that she was not competent to evaluate CUB's structure, but hastily assured Campbell that she was in full agreement with most of it. This did not keep her from raising some questions, particularly about the role of social workers. In particular, Paton was "concerned" about the inclusion of professional social workers in any constructive role involving natal parents, perhaps alluding to CUB's proposed Release of Protection form. She questioned social workers' competence to perform their required task. Paton believed that CUB would have to hold training sessions for the social workers and suggested that they "charge them for it." She confessed, "I am hard of heart towards them. I see how much severe damage they have consented to in their practices for so many years, and have been unwilling to review their policies. They have let themselves be blinded, and still show no remorse."[32] Undoubtedly thinking of Sorosky and his research associates, Paton said that she deeply mistrusted their sudden show of interest in the welfare of adopted persons.

In her reply, Campbell acknowledged Paton's strictures about social workers, but continued to be hopeful. She admitted that social workers had lied and manipulated her in the case of her own son, Michael. But Campbell excused social workers' behavior on the ground that they were ignorant of birth mothers' pain and ongoing suffering because none of the mothers had ever returned to an adoption agency and informed them. That was CUB's mission now. Campbell was an optimist. She had faith that social workers were human, too, and could be touched, eventually. She boasted, "I know I have turned on a few light bulbs within their dimmed tunnel-brains all by myself. This is one of my greatest satisfactions."[33]

In 1977, Paton continued to object to Campbell's assumption that if only

CUB were able to educate social workers, they would begin to treat birth parents more fairly, as human beings. Paton insisted this was chimerical thinking. She warned Campbell, "Agencies belong to society and are paid by society. They will never quite understand what they have done that is wrong, and so they will never change it." Birth mothers instinctively knew about the inequities of the adoption process, and thus, according to Paton, CUB birth mothers had within themselves the power "to make something new that was not there before." The best method to accomplish their goals of reforming adoption was for CUB members "to reach out helping hands to young women in birth trouble, and find resources for them."[34] A year later, in response to Campbell's request for feedback on CUB's Round Table on Adoption, which included six nonnegotiable rights for birth parents, Paton voiced doubts whether "adoption is any kind of a solution."[35] The more she thought about it, the more Paton was coming to the conclusion there needed to be a structured or institutional arrangement to help parents keep families together. Paton advocated working harder on "an open adoption plan because the sooner that is arrived at, the sooner we come to destroying adoption as we have known it."[36]

Throughout its early years, Paton was a strong supporter of CUB, repeatedly encouraging and praising it. When Campbell pointed out CUB's limitations—a paid membership of less than 100; a mailing list of a mere 162 persons ("Please remember we're only babies," she said defensively)[37]—Paton was quick to contradict her, declaring "that was a large number of people." She reminded Campbell that quite a lot could be accomplished by just a few.[38] Continuing to reassure her, Paton insisted, "Don't be discouraged by the immense numbers put out by other organizations. They were often figments of someone's imagination. The real work in this movement is being carried on by a handful of people. As always when human affliction is concerned, many are called, few are chosen, but they create beautiful things for the future."[39] A year later, Paton congratulated Campbell on CUB's growth and confessed to a certain degree of envy at the organization's youth and vigor. Feeling her age, she lamented that "it is sometimes terrible to be in my seventieth year" with diminished energies. Nevertheless, it gave her great pleasure to view "so much solid work" being done.[40]

During CUB's early years, it was often consumed by the explosive issues of whether birth mothers should search for the children they had relinquished for adoption and at what age the children should reach before beginning the search. At the heart of the issue was the policy of secrecy in adoption. Social workers defended the policy of secrecy on the basis that the adoption process would crumble if birth parents invaded the privacy of adoptive parents and contacted their minor children. Adoptive parents had a morbid fear of birth parents reclaiming their children and needed to be reassured that this would never happen. The social work policy of secrecy supplied this reassurance. In its early years, CUB leadership recognized the significance of that dynamic and sidestepped it publicly, by officially remaining neutral on the issue of searching for children or encouraging the practice. Its newsletter, the C.U.B. Communicator, for example, proclaimed: "CUB IS NOT A SEACH GROUP."[41] However, the issue was complex, made so by a distinction CUB leaders made between search and contact. To CUB, search and contact were not the same thing, and could occur years apart. "Search" was a process, in which CUB members faced a series of decisions: the initial decision was whether or not to search. If one decided to search, then there were additional decisions to make: if, when, and how to make contact to the adoptive family or child.[42]

Some early CUB members preferred to wait; others who had found their minor children made early contacts. Mary Anne Cohen, made a personal decision, at least initially, against contacting her son at that time or anytime soon. He was a young preteen, too young, she thought, by many years for any direct contact, and she had misgivings about contacting the adoptive parents. As she expressed her concerns to Paton: "I'm not going to risk harming my son or ruining my chances of an eventual relationship with him by moving too soon. Also, I have great reservations about contacting the adoptive parents, ever. I think it should be up to [my son] to decide, when he is an adult, whether to tell his parents I have contacted him since he knows them and I don't."[43]

Others, such as Lee Campbell also chose her own personal path about her search and, later, sought early contact. In the C.U.B. Communicator, she divulged she knew the whereabouts of her minor son, Michael, and had driven past his house once, where she felt "warmth, gratitude, and a strange déjà vu indescribable something."[44] Knowing her leadership status as CUB's president served as a guide to the membership, in September 1977, Campbell took a vote on the question of whether an officer of CUB who either contacted a minor child or the adoptive parents of a minor birth child should resign. The vast majority of those voting viewed the issue as a personal venture and rejected the idea of mandatory resignation.[45]

Five months later, in February 1978, Campbell phoned her son, who was by then fifteen years old. She posed as a pollster, and discovered that he wanted to know about his birth parents. Angry that Michael's adoptive parents had told him she was dead even though they had been informed three years earlier that Campbell was alive, she decided after four months of pondering to contact him. In June, she went to the supermarket where Michael was employed and had him carry her grocery bags to the car. Campbell introduced herself as the pollster who had called him earlier and provided him with the business card of a search group, which he accepted reluctantly. Three months later, as Campbell confided to Paton, she still had not heard from him and was at her wits' end. Campbell sought Paton's advice. Should she contact Michael directly and rely on his strength to make his parents understand the necessity of his need to know his birth mother? Or should she circumvent her son and have "an adoptive mother of four" whom Campbell had "grown to love greatly" act as an intermediary and write his adoptive parents? Or perhaps it was better to just wait. This was the most difficult option. "I may expire doing it, but if it's best for Michael, I will expire!!" What should she do?[46]

Paton strongly believed that adopted children should have contact with members of their natal families at the age of twelve.[47] She chose that age out of admiration for an old Michigan social work practice in which adoption workers visited the adoptive home at twelve "to make sure the child knew he was adopted."[48] Paton's belief in this practice was reinforced by her reading G. Stanley Hall's classic work *Adolescence*, which emphasized the importance of age twelve for the onset of major changes in youth.[49] Paton later gave two different explanations of how she had come to embrace this principle. In August 1976, she claimed she had awakened one morning with the "absolutely clear conviction that all adopted children should have real contact with kindred at the age of 12."[50] But in November 1977, Paton contradicted herself, stating that she had mentioned the idea of an adopted child having contact with a member of the kinship family by the age of twelve "some time back" to a Columbia, Missouri, reporter.[51] However Paton came up with the idea, she never wavered from her conviction that twelve-year-old adopted children needed contact with their original families.

Paton justified her belief in contact with minor adopted children in a variety of ways. First, birth mothers needed this communication to alleviate their suffering. Paton never doubted that birth mothers were afflicted beings, in the Weilian sense, and even though Paton believed in the high value, even necessity, of reunions for mature adopted persons, she could not see how birth mothers could bear to live without knowing whether their children were dead or alive.[52] Paton believed that their getting in touch with and securing knowledge of their children would prevent them from being institutionalized in mental hospitals or committing suicide after relinquishment, events of which she had personal knowledge.[53] She also defended the age of twelve for minor adopted children to have communication with their biological kin on the grounds that it was imperative that they have "first-hand knowledge of their roots, voices, faces, sounds, and mannerisms." Only then could these children know that they had a history.[54] Just as important as the positive knowledge of history was for the healthy development of the adopted child was the avoidance of the negative consequences that resulted from lack of contact. Upon entering adolescence, Paton contended, adopted children began to fill with fantasy and conflict, which led to running away, suicide, and delinquency and laid the groundwork for adult misbehavior and underachievement.[55] For Paton, "reality was the name of the game."[56] To wait for the age of majority, as many inside and outside the movement cautioned, was too late; it postponed "what needs to be done now."[57] Consequently, Paton objected whenever she heard the age of eighteen being bandied about as the only legitimate time to make contact. "I am troubled by that magic age of 18," Paton wrote Campbell, "which seems to get in the way of communication, whereas in reality, the adopted person needs help before that age."[58]

As a rule, however, Paton was against surreptitious meetings with minor adopted children. Before Campbell confided in Paton about contacting Michael, Paton matter-of-factly told Campbell that "none of us wish to get the reputation of helping mothers of 'under-age adoptees' search for them." When informed separately of several instances of birth mothers who, under false identities, went into adoptive parents' homes and stole photos of their children, Paton doubted that the women were helped by stealing the pictures. She had no doubt that they were expressing a deep psychological need, but concluded that "it is no cure" for their suffering.[59] What then was the proper method of contact? Paton insisted that there had to be meetings between the two sets of parents before the birth parent reunited with the child, and that these meetings be based on respect, at a minimum, and on love, if possible.[60] But what if such a meeting with adoptive parents were impossible? Then "one must wait." Paton, did, however, leave the door open by suggesting that there were exceptional circumstances when contacting minor adopted children was permissible.[61]

Paton, never too optimistic, was acutely aware of the difficulties involved in such a get-together. For any meeting to take place, Paton believed that both parties had to reduce their fear of each other.[62] Even when both sets of parents agreed that contact was in the best interest of the young adopted child, Paton refused to predict a happy outcome. She was in fact unsure, even pessimistic, about the initial meeting. If all went well, then children would be receptive to meeting their birth parents. When Paton heard of these occasional successful visitations, she expressed great happiness.[63] But she believed that in many cases children would resent the birth parents and resist visits. This was a natural reaction stemming from bewilderment at why they had been given up in the first place, and was a high hurdle to overcome.[64]

When Paton replied to Campbell's letter asking for advice on how to proceed with her own son, she adhered to her principles. She found it troubling that the adoptive parents had told Michael that Campbell was dead. Paton believed that Michael had to learn that she was alive "before the image of a dead mother gets too deep inside him." The only thing she advised Campbell to do, however, was to have her contact Michael again, "tell him that his mother is alive, and that he can someday go to an agency for the information about her. And then go home and pray."[65] She also suggested that Campbell contact Michael's pediatrician. Perhaps he could act as an intermediary. Paton even recommended waiting until Michael was eighteen, when he could be considered an independent adult. Instead of focusing on contacting underage minors, Paton proposed that CUB focus on birth mothers' pain and labor on what she called "a workable solution."[66] Paton's conservative advice to Campbell that she not reveal herself to her son and postpone the reunion, must have been a bitter pill for Campbell to swallow.[67]

The letters Paton received as a result of the June 1974 *Cosmopolitan* search article not only galvanized her into channeling her enormous energies into supporting CUB and birth mother activities; it also resulted in her first and only attempt to form local search groups. This might appear to contradict the claims of some, including the present writer, that Orphan Voyage "was the first adoptee search organization."[68] But a closer look reveals that, in Paton's mind, at least, Orphan Voyage was not an organization that actually searched for individuals. It was instead a center for search assistance and support. In this it was different from adoptee groups such as ALMA, for example, which explicitly promised to help its members to search for family relatives and fight politically for open adoption records. In addition, Paton's vision had never included the formation of branches of Orphan Voyage.

Paton believed that part of the reason for her aversion to groups and cloning Orphan Voyage had to do with something inherent in her personality. To Clare Marcus, head of the Canadian Adoption Research Group, Paton admitted, "I am not a group person, by nature. I have never had a group but simply connected to people through communication."[69] Part of her distaste for affiliate groups was owing to her leadership style, which had always been intensely individualistic—"a genius with a thousand helpers."[70] As she explained to co-founder of the Adoption Forum in Philadelphia, Penny Partridge, "my focus is on the individual, because my life consists principally of them, daily, from all over the country, far from any group in most cases, and I rely so much on individual help for them, people not associated with groups but very able and committed people." Paton coupled her commitment to individuals with an aversion for hierarchy, a love of equality, and personal humility. She was simply stating the obvious when she exclaimed to another friend, "I do so strongly believe in democracy and in helping people to learn to walk on their own that I am disinclined to indulge in manipulation."[71] In 1971, sensitive to the inequality inherent in her title, Paton announced her demotion from Director to "merely a Co-ordinator."[72]

Instead of Orphan Voyage chapters, Paton developed a network of people "who had been tested, corresponded with, referred to."[73] She elaborated to Houston, Texas, search group leader Peggy Dorn: "the best analogy I know is the underground railroad which was used to free the slaves."[74] Paton provided a detailed paradigm of how such a network began and grew. It was always initiated from below, and began with a personal letter or telephone call. In the example Paton provided, a Midwest adoption reform network started in 1972 with a phone call from Laverne McCurdy of Clinton, Wisconsin. His wife, who had relinquished her baby for adoption shortly before they were married, was depressed and craved knowledge of the child. Seeking the information, McCurdy visited the Milwaukee adoption agency that had placed his wife's child. The social worker advised him to consult a psychiatrist. Instead, McCurdy called Paton for advice. Later that year, Paton visited the McCurdys in their home. Mr. McCurdy informed her that he had discovered where his wife's child lived but had not made contact. McCurdy was angry at the adoption agency's refusal to release any information and became convinced that the policy of sealed adoption records was unjust. He wanted to do something about it.[75]

Around this time, Paton's good friend and adoption activist Margaret Lawrence moved to Chicago. Paton introduced her to McCurdy. Together, they planned a series of actions. The local newspaper published a sympathetic story about the plight of adopted adults' inability to access their records; a local state legislator introduced a bill permitting open records; the same local newspaper printed the many letters to the editor it received; and a debate began about opening adoption records. With all the favorable publicity, McCurdy was invited to appear on radio and TV talk shows. He began to facilitate reunions. McCurdy attempted to solicit adult adoptees to reunite with their natal families, but the local media rejected his attempt to advertise. Undaunted, he placed a sign on his car asking people with an interest in reunions to contact him. In early 1974, McCurdy started a group called "Truth Seekers in Adoption." He assisted in a difficult reunion, which the papers publicized widely. As a result, McCurdy's group became known far and wide.[76]

At the same time, another adoptee group was forming under the leadership of Donna Cullom, who had been introduced to the adoption reform movement by ALMA. Cullom's story of her search for her mother was picked up and widely publicized by the *Chicago Tribune*. Cullom, too, started an adoptee search group, called "Yesterday's Children." Paton, who was corresponding with Cullom, introduced her to Lawrence and, together with McCurdy, there now existed a formidable and functioning solid front of adoption reform in Chicago. None of these groups took the name of Orphan Voyage, nor did they consider themselves branches or chapters of Orphan Voyage.

However, with the onset of adoption reform activism in the early 1970s, Paton's attitude toward groups connected to Orphan Voyage began to change. Part of the reason for the change was due, paradoxically, to thoughts of retirement.[77] She never mentioned her fatigue to Orphan Voyage members. Instead, Paton framed the issue as one of preparing for the future by shifting responsibility for producing *The LOG* and maintaining the Reunion File from her shoulders to those of the membership.[78] Forming affiliate groups to Orphan Voyage, Paton felt, would be one way to slowly reduce her enormous workload.

In addition, three other problems could be solved by bringing groups into the orbit of Orphan Voyage. Paton made a sharp distinction between groups in urban and those in rural areas. People in urban areas could easily find help by reaching out to a nearby group or another experienced person, aided by herself, the coordinator. But many adult adoptees who needed help lived outside of cities, and they could only be served by a connection to an active headquarters. Simply referring such a person to ALMA or even Orphan Voyage, in a routine way, was insufficient because the individual then had to be referred a second time to get a local contact. The result, according to Paton, was that many outside of urban areas gave up the search.[79] In addition, there remained the problem of life after the reunion. Paton saw a need for adult adoptees to share the various ways in which they and their two sets of parents learned to live together "no longer in secrecy but in openness." These accounts, Paton told her membership, would be published in *The LOG*.[80] Centralization was a necessity for both of these tasks.

In addition to the opportunity provided by the deluge of letters from the *Cosmopolitan* article, and Paton's own weariness and practical considerations of organization, Paton's embrace of groups was prompted by necessity. The increased burdens of time, money, and energy caused, ironically, by the very success of the adoption reform movement and the concomitant multiplicity of adoption rights organizations required Paton to explore the idea of Orphan Voyage chapters. For Paton, the large number of organizations proliferating throughout the United States was a double-edged sword: they portended a breakthrough in the movement, which she welcomed; but the immediate result for her program was confusion and chaos. Through her network of people,

Paton had confidence that when she referred someone, the recommendation would have value. The explosion of adoptee groups, however, ruined the network's stability. Paton despaired that she "had no sense whatever of what these groups to whom I am referring people have to offer, where they are at."[81]

Canadian adoption activist Joan Vanstone commiserated with Paton. She wrote, "I know it must be annoying to you who have toiled so long and hard to see anarchy arising in the various groups."[82] Vanstone, founder of the support group Parent Finders, informed Paton that the Canadian groups had avoided the problem because "all have the prefix of Parent Finders—thus denoting unity and strength of numbers."[83] Vanstone had scored a bull's-eye: what bothered Paton the most about the proliferation of groups in America was the habit of adult adoptees asking for help when they lived right in the midst of an area that contained a search group. The problem, according to Paton, was that "they look in vain for the name Orphan Voyage in their local directory."[84] Paton thought it was "high time for the movement to give up having such cute names for each new group, so that they can never be found. Alcoholics Anonymous knows better. An alcoholic knows where to turn. He opens the phone book, and looks for AA in the yellow pages, and he finds it. Little old lady Paton has been carrying on this labor for a long time, and it is time for grown up adoptees to devise a substitute, and make it work."[85] In their efforts to establish an identity, groups forgot their function, which was "to help somebody. To help them find help." Paton grumbled, "This having each group a separate name is the pits."[86] It was like "sewing without a knot in the thread."[87]

Paton operated on a shoestring budget. She confided to one correspondent that her income in 1972 was only about $500, and that she was nearing poverty.[88] By 1974, she had discontinued subsidizing Orphan Voyage, curtailed her field trips, and was hoping that people who found her useful would subsidize her travel.[89] As a result, Paton said, she needed members who would subscribe to *The LOG*, but "not on a wholesale basis. I think am not in a position to give sufficient response. But prefer to grow on a slower but solider basis."[90] Group affiliation with Orphan Voyage appeared to be a solution to this problem. The sticking point was the reluctance of adult adoptees to pay dues to two organizations. Paton believed that adult adoptees did not appreciate the importance of a central headquarters. Moreover, they wanted help but had a hard time paying for it. She held that it was "part of the dependent characteristics that many adopted people develop." One way Paton proposed to circumvent adult adoptees' disinclination to pay dues was for a certain percentage of all group membership income to go to Orphan Voyage.[91]

Finally, implicit resentment at ALMA's success provided another basis for Paton's turn toward forming Orphan Voyage chapters. Disliking the professionalization that she saw creeping into the movement, Paton put forward an alternate program for the future, which for the first time included affiliate groups. Writing in *The LOG* in June 1972, she first exhorted her readers to clear away what she considered the wrong emphasis. Adult adoptees should not waste time on the errors of professional social workers, except as their activities affect them, and to "attempt a degree of self-protection." Nor should adult adoptees take pride in any professional learning about the realities of the life of the adopted person. These issues should not be the focus of adult adoptees' actions. Instead, they should live out activities which would provide them with a stronger and more permanent sense of identity, and "which will have value not only to us but even to society."[92] The program for achieving this goal consisted of five components: a Reunion File and the development of adoptee groups; a Museum of the American Orphan, for educational and therapeutic purposes; a physical headquarters, such as at Cedaredge; a network of communication; and a medium for self-expression and mutual understanding: *The LOG of Orphan Voyage*.[93]

Except for the mention of affiliated groups, the new Orphan Voyage program appeared to be more of the same: the genius with a thousand helpers, and Orphan Voyage writ large. But in explicating how the new program would function, Paton made plain that she wanted to shift responsibility from herself onto the rank and file. For one thing, Paton served notice that she would no longer be producing *The LOG*. Instead, "you should before too long be taking this over," envisioning local groups rotating the task on a regular basis.[94] More generally, Paton looked forward to an open, independent program in which adult adoptees were actively engaged in supporting themselves within groups. The reward: "You will no longer be clients, dependents, children."[95] By September 1975, Paton announced that there were thirty small groups affiliated with Orphan Voyage, which she characterized variously as "a change in direction" and "a breakthrough."[96]

Unfortunately, Paton's new organizational structure to create groups affiliated with Orphan Voyage was doomed to fail. At the heart of the enterprise were two contradictory impulses warring within the coordinator. On the one hand, Paton wanted to create an organization characterized by some form of participatory democracy—groups run by its members, without a formal chain of command and with decision making direct and consensus oriented.[97] On the other hand, because of the chaos of mushrooming groups that she observed all around her, Paton needed to dominate these very same people because standardization was desperately needed,[98] even though she was temperamentally unfitted to exercise centralized control. She never understood this intractable contradiction.

Paton quickly discovered the impossibility of her task. As early as February 1976, Paton announced that "my own hopes of having people sign group agreements had proven an impossible dream."[99] But she never recognized the contradiction within herself. Instead, Paton blamed the failure of her plan on the groups themselves and the defects of adult adoptees. She complained to Florida adoptee Karen Rowland that the poor response she received from groups to the idea of coordinating with Orphan Voyage stemmed from adoptees' independence and the belief that they could "do it all by themselves."[100] Such behavior—going it alone, focusing on their own problems—resulted in groups dividing their strength, failing to cooperate, and working at cross-purposes. Paton cited "publicity-prone" ALMA as a prime example of this tendency, complaining that its members were prohibited from referring "to Orphan Voyage, yet it has copied everything I (and some others) have said and done, with no credit at all."[101] Similarly, to Texas-based Peggy Dorn she wrote, "my own problem, with FF, is at a distance, and yet whenever a group mentions OV she does her best to discredit."[102] In addition, individual groups were preoccupied with internal fights and jealous conflicts. On the whole, Paton thought that the problem was inherent in adoptees: "we orphans are not good group people."[103]

Adult adoptees, Paton felt, were their own worst enemies. As individuals, they tried to dominate, a problem that according to Paton was endemic in the movement and that resulted in groups splitting up.[104] She singled out for condemnation the "Florence cult," which paralyzed the will of adult adoptees, who were unable to leave or disobey Fisher's rules.[105] In addition, adult adoptees were too egotistical, and this resulted in power struggles over leadership, another problem endemic to adoptee reform groups. Sometimes, Paton pointed out, these personality clashes built up over time and occurred in stages: an individual spoke before a microphone, and then began to think that he spoke for the group; pretty soon, he believed he was in charge of the whole group. In Paton's experience, a crisis occurred in every group every two years, and revolved around just such a point of conflict.[106]

Conversely, some groups split because a competent leader would be challenged from within. Nancy Sitterly, Connecticut coordinator of an Orphan Voyage chapter, threatened to quit because of "dissension among the ranks—from a few who have done little or nothing to help." Sitterly explained to Paton that she had single-handedly run the group, putting out the newsletter, organizing the searches, and spending over $1,000 of her own money. But a few dissidents, according to Sitterly, who were capable of stirring up a lot of people, "want to be more organized thus giving them more power." She equated an organization with officers and a secretary and treasurer's report as a social group, not a search group. Sitterly wanted none of it: "I have done it all—and I don't want to take orders from anyone." Sitterly made no apologies: "The bottom line, Jean, is that I am not a 'group' type personality."[107]

Paton sympathized with Sitterly. In her reply, she confessed that she was "not a group person, either" and added, "I think the more authentic people among us are not." Moreover, Paton told Sitterly, she had witnessed the same behavior dozens of times, inevitably in the second year of the group's existence. But she was incapable of offering Sitterly any concrete advice on how to solve the problem. Instead, Paton first claimed insufficient knowledge of the particular circumstances of Sitterly's group: "Without knowing what you have tried I cannot even attempt to evaluate what comes next." Then she tried to console Sitterly by noting that she was emulating Paton herself, in that she was a strong person who took over a group and poured money into it. But Paton immediately undermined any benefit of conferring such a special status on Sitterly with a layer of self-pity: "I worked like a dog, and still do, at the things I had started and no one seemed able to take over, but felt that I had a special responsibility since I had started things, and could not, and cannot, drop it. I have the incessant demand in my correspondence, and now receive over 2500 pieces of mail a year (yesterday I received 13)." And, sounding a theme that would only get louder as time passed, Paton wrote, "my greatest burden is the fact that others in the movement have come along (as you now confront) wanting the notoriety and the credit, taking over my ideas, my labors, as if they were doing the same or better! This is much harder for me to bear than the slings and arrows of the world, which I can understand, sort of." For Paton, her only recourse was "to continue what I saw in front of my face to do and somehow it has proven to be a solution." And that was her implicit advice to Sitterly: emulate the master, and soldier on in the face of adversity. In sum, Paton wrote Sitterly, "I am sure you will arrive at what is right for you, and what is right for you is right for us all."[108]

By February 1976, rather than admit publicly she had failed to bring the chaotic groups into Orphan Voyage's orbit, Paton accepted reality and put before the membership a federal concept of the relationship of Orphan Voyage to the groups. Writing in *The LOG*, she acknowledged that "actually orphans are not group people. In their essential nature they are solitary, more so than most."[109] Therefore, Paton declared that a network of small groups corresponded best with the nature of orphans, though at certain times and for special purposes they were capable of acting in concert "in a massive way" before returning to their small groups again. But small groups were not self-sufficient: there was poor communication between the groups, and there were areas where groups did not exist. Thus, there was also a need for large groups, though Paton did not elaborate on this idea, except to say rather cryptically that they existed "for purposes which only large groups can address themselves profitably." Furthermore, Paton stated, "Orphan Voyage works under these concepts."

Five months later, however, to her private correspondents Paton was far less sanguine, announcing that she had "come to the conclusion that adoptees at least are entirely unable to form groups that will last."[110] In September, Paton declared, she had given up on groups "as such."[111] To Agnes Ingram, Paton stated, "I have rather quit on the ideas of having 'groups' as they have so many problems and seem unable to lift themselves over the rims of their teacups."[112] She also expressed a pessimistic view of adult adoptees' ability to cooperate. To Mary Doyle, Paton quoted her favorite philosopher, Simone Weil, suggesting that adoptees had an intrinsic incapacity to work together:

> And as for those who have themselves been mutilated by affliction, they are in no state to help anyone at all, and they are almost incapable of even wishing to do so. Thus compassion for the afflicted is an impossibility. When it is found we have a more astounding miracle than walking on water, healing the sick, or even raising the dead.[113]

Paton would instead continue to concentrate on her network of individuals, whether they belonged to a group or not, and concentrate on "building my underground railroad," which now included about sixty individuals, "because it works and because it is going to be needed for a long time."[114] Now Paton believed that her network was superior to groups, which "get quarrelsome, fight for 'power,' and do nothing but break apart over and over." Paton would continue doing "the grubby job of keeping in touch with people, believing in them."[115] What this meant in practice was doing what she had been doing for the past twenty-three years: working quietly and persistently with a personal touch— never using form letters—on the actual problems of adult adoptees and dealing with any complications that might come to her attention in the aftermath of difficult reunions.[116]

Despite her failure to centralize control over the groups, Paton remained optimistic. In September 1976, she thought the movement "as a whole" was doing very well.[117] In a major statement to the Orphan Voyage membership, Paton announced that the movement no longer simply consisted of a few outstanding personalities operating in a few urban area groups. Throughout the country new leadership was springing up, centering on different groups of people—birth parents and even adoptive parents. Paton approved of this new diverse population of reformers and predicted that these different groups would someday come together and build something new. She believed that "this is our best hope."[118] Adding to Paton's positive outlook was her scheduled trip to Toronto, Canada, on September 26, where she was to participate in an hour-long debate on television before a live audience on the right of adult adoptees to have information about their families.[119]

II

Sealed Adoption Records

If the word "rights" were not in the dictionary we might be better off. We would then be fighting for the things that matter most, roots and relatives and pride.

—JEAN PATON, 1982

Jean Paton's participation in what was billed as "The Great Debate" by the Toronto television station that produced it came about after a visit in August 1976 with Joan Vanstone, a Vancouver activist and founder of Canada's adoption search group, Parent Finders. Unable to attend, Vanstone suggested Paton as her replacement. Paton looked forward to the debate, believing that it would have important consequences.[1] She also appreciated the respect accorded her: not only did the debate sponsors pay her a $350 honorarium plus all expenses, but Canadian adoption search groups took Paton out for meals while she was in Toronto, and one member drove her back from her hotel to the airport.[2] In the aftermath of the debate, Paton felt she performed well and spoke with feeling. One highlight that stuck in her mind was that "a young man in the audience said 'amen'" when she finished speaking.[3] Nevertheless when the moderator, Pierre Berton, polled the audience at the end of "The Great Debate," few had changed their original position in favor of Paton: the concluding vote was 51 in the affirmative and 24 in the negative. On the whole, Paton's argument that adult adoptees had an absolute right to knowing who their birth parents were was not particularly effective. She was too discursive, spent too much time on historical issues, and failed to provide persuasive answers as to why adoption records should be opened.[4]

Although Jean Paton left voluminous records attesting to her activism regarding adoption reform, we know surprisingly little about her position on the issue of sealed adoption records. Later in life she was hailed by adoption activists as pioneering "our national movement to open sealed adoption records."[5] But in fact her views on this subject evolved and changed over time. In the first decades of her activism between 1949 and 1970, Paton's beliefs reflected the era of her own upbringing. Because adoption records were open before the 1950s, her correspondents were unconcerned with gaining access to them. Consequently, Paton concentrated on the psychological healing of adult adoptees through the mechanism of a national mutual consent adoption registry, the Reunion File. In the 1970s, her thinking evolved in accord with the fresh leadership and concerns of the newly energized adoption reform movement. Though still skeptical of the immediate beneficial results of open records, Paton promoted others' efforts to open adoption records and eventually added her own voice to theirs. By the early 1980s, she had wholeheartedly embraced the notion of opening adoption records unconditionally. This chapter explores Jean Paton's evolving position on this issue, an aspect of her adoption activism that is still largely unknown.

Between 1949 and 1970, Paton seldom expressed opposition to sealed adoption records. However, on occasion, as in 1963, on a field trip to St. Paul, Minnesota, when she spoke to a convention of 100 "alumni" at the third annual convention of the New York Foundling Hospital, she did. A newspaper account of the event quoted her as saying, "The sealed record almost completely prohibits a person from finding out his real background. He is turned away and feels resentful. As soon as the record is sealed, society has entered into the situation. And the adopted person feels he can't fight society by himself—he becomes an outsider." Her solution to the problem of sealed adoption records was not to advocate political action, but to help people locate relatives "lost to them by adoption, divorce, or to other social separations" through use of her matching Reunion File, the first national voluntary mutual consent adoption registry.[6]

Nor did Paton write many letters advocating that adoption records be open. Of the thousands of letters she wrote between 1949 and 1970 advocating adoption reform, in only four did she express opposition to sealed adoption records, and she mentioned the topic only rarely in *The LOG*.[7] One typical Paton letter, to the editor of the *Denver Post* in 1969, blandly recommended Orphan Voyage's Reunion File as an alternative to the sealed record.[8] Conspicuously missing from Paton's thinking during these early years was an appeal to the mass media to persuade adoption agencies to open their records or, failing that, to mobilize public opinion to pressure legislatures or the courts to repeal the laws sealing adoption records.

Why did Jean Paton pay so little attention to the issue of sealed adoption records between years 1949 and 1970? There are three primary reasons. First,

Paton had grown up in an era when adoption records were not sealed and had successfully accessed her court record. Consequently, the policy of closed records meant little to her personally. From the enactment of America's first adoption law in 1851, in Massachusetts, until roughly the 1950s, adult adoptees could legally access their adoption court records and agency records, and until the 1960s and 1970s, their birth certificates. When in 1917 Minnesota lawmakers passed the first statute containing a clause making adoption court records confidential, it was the public, not adoption triad members, who were excluded from viewing their records. Because of the stigma of shame and scandal that surrounded adoption and illegitimacy during the first quarter of the twentieth century, these legislators intended to bar access of these records to potential blackmailers, who might threaten adoptive parents with telling the public about the child's adoption, or nosy neighbors, who might discover the child's illegitimacy. Before the 1950s, nearly half of the states had no confidentiality clauses in their adoption statutes.[9]

Similarly, before the 1950s, adult adoptees had little difficulty in accessing their files from adoption agencies. State statutes remained silent on the regulation of adoption agency files. It was left by default to the discretion of the agencies' executive directors and social workers, who cooperated with birth parents and adopted adults who returned to agencies requesting both nonidentifying and identifying information. The Children's Home Society of Washington even conducted searches for adult adoptees who were looking for original family members. Social workers also routinely provided adoptive parents with information about their child. And adopted adults could also access their original birth certificates, even after they had received an amended one. By 1948, although nearly every state in America had embraced the idea of issuing a new birth certificate upon receiving a court-ordered decree of adoption, the laws stipulated that the original birth certificate could be accessed upon the demand of the child when he or she came of age, at the request of his or her birth or adopting parents, or by order of a court of record.[10]

In addition, when Paton conducted research for both *The Adopted Break Silence* and *Orphan Voyage*, she solicited the views of adult adoptees who had been born before 1910 and 1932, respectively.[11] The result was that the problems of the adult adoptees Paton came to know in the 1950s and 1960s hardly ever had to do with a failure to access adoption records. For Paton and those adult adoptees, the root problem was not the sealed adoption record but the stigma of illegitimacy. Her chief preoccupation was to address all of illegitimacy's attendant psychological problems—shame, fantasy, resentment, passivity—and formulate what she believed to be its cure: a reunion with kindred, facilitated through forgiveness and reconciliation. Thus, on the rare occasion in the 1950s when Paton mentioned sealed adoption records, she did so to make the psychological point that closed records would cause the adult adoptee "problems in adulthood that would be very hard for him to solve."[12]

Second, Paton's experience with her own records made her doubt their value. They reinforced her tendency to view the problems of adopted people in terms of psychological problems and to assume that those problems would be solved through reunions. In the mid-1950s, Paton requested and received from the Michigan Department of Health her original birth certificate. It reaffirmed what she already knew: that her mother, Emma Cutting, had named her baby Ruth Edwina. But to Paton's surprise, Paton herself was "not a Cutting!" Her name on the birth certificate was "Ruth Edwina Emerson" and her mother's name was "Cassie Emerson." Paton knew that her mother went by the name "Cassie" in the Home and imagined that officials there "changed Emma to Emerson, and that was that. What fun they had changing names around."[13] On a more serious note, Paton wrote to Madalyn Murray O'Hair lambasting her original birth certificate for not only displaying "illegitimacy, but also the usual blankness on other details, as to father. Furthermore, my mother's name was fictitious."[14] The lesson Paton undoubtedly took away from accessing her original birth certificate was that such records were nearly worthless in providing information about one's original family because they inevitably lacked pertinent information and were filled with lies.

Third, and perhaps most important to Paton, her organization Orphan Voyage provided an alternative to opening adoption records: a Reunion File. As we have seen, Paton first broached this idea in "Adoption Comes of Age," in an unpublished article from October 1949. She elaborated on it a month later in a letter to the editor of the *New York Times*.[15] In 1953, Paton resurrected the idea of a national mutual consent voluntary adoption registry at her Life History Study Center, which would be the central point of clearance. She started a program she called "Reunion," where persons could join a program for "Mutual Registration" based on a "Matching File" to reunite with original birth family members.[16] In the 1950s, in a burst of enthusiasm, Paton wrote to IBM to explore the idea of computerizing the Reunion File, but never followed through.[17] Paton kept returning to the idea in the following fifteen years, but she could not afford to publicize the program, nor did she have the energy to overcome an unenthusiastic public.[18] By the late 1960s, she had become conditioned to accept "gradual growth" in the Reunion File.[19]

The second phase in the evolution of Paton's position on opening sealed adoption records, stretched from 1970 to roughly 1977, and coincided with the birth of the adoption reform movement and the creation of the 1970s reform groups, such as Florence Fisher's Adoptees' Liberty Movement Association (ALMA), Donna Cullom's Yesterday's Children, and dozens of others. Although, as with Paton, seeking original family members was central to the mission of these search groups, these new organizations focused on what they saw as the solution to their problem: opening adoption records.

The 1970s saw the buildup of a critical mass of adult adoptees who had grown up in a world of sealed adoption records in the twenty-five years following World War II. Unlike their prewar counterparts, these younger adult adoptees were denied easy access to their adoption records.[20] Sealed records thwarted their greatest desire: to reunite with their families. Florence Fisher continually thundered at the outrage. Fisher didn't ask that the records be opened; she *demanded* that they be opened, using the language of rights: "In the United States," said Fisher, "the adopted adult at any age is denied the right to see the records [of] his birth and adoption."[21] In the first issue of the newsletter for Yesterday's Children, Cullom made clear the organization's goal: "OPEN RECORDS FOR ALL ADOPTEES OF LEGAL AGE." The publication also contained the names and addresses of Illinois' federal, state, and local legislators, with instructions "to write, and let them know how you feel about the sealed records."[22] By contrast, Paton rarely used *The LOG* to instigate a writing campaign to political officials. She believed that adult adoptees were wrong to think that unsealing adoption records represented the ultimate victory against social work oppression.[23]

Paton foresaw two problems once the records were unsealed. The first revolved around the role of social work. Although Paton was unsure of the details, she was certain that social workers would have a hand in shaping the fate of adult adoptees' lives in the wake of the opening of the adopted records. Paton was prescient of the future: state functionaries would operate confidential intermediary systems and voluntary mutual consent adoption registries, dominated by the psychology of pathology and attachment. She predicted that "the professions, social work in particular, are going to have their hands in yours as you confront your destiny." Paton continued, "If you are not ready, you will be guided, make no mistake."

The second problem was far more serious: Paton predicted that, having achieved freedom, adult adoptees would find themselves no better off than before—or, as she put it, "in the same situation, after the sealing is removed." As Paton had been advising for decades, and a major reason why opening adoption records had never been a strong priority for her, the root of adult adoptees' problems was psychological, due to the fact of their illegitimacy and the resulting cultural silence and repression. Once the records were unsealed, she stated, adult adoptees "will be confronted with [their] own resistance to reunion, [their] own repression of the longing to know your antecedents, [their] own childish resentment against the original parents who surrendered [them] to adoption."

Consequently, Paton continued to work assisting the search for kindred with the aid of references from Orphan Voyage, helping the plight of children born out of wedlock, and fighting the injustice suffered by birth mothers. These activities continued to be central to her conception of adoption reform; demands to unseal adoption records only occasionally appeared in her correspondence and public statements thereafter. Between 1970 and 1977, for example, Paton kept up a steady stream of letters to public officials, academicians, editors of newspapers, and popular magazines. She addressed dozens of letters to recipients, from the editor of *Women's Day* and American psychologist Rollo May, to media personality Barbara Walters, Governor Nelson Rockefeller, Supreme Court Justice William Rehnquist, and President Jimmy Carter. Only two of her letters during this time advocated opening adoption records, and not one of them used the term "rights."[24]

Nor did Paton often address the subject of opening adoption records in her public statements. In 1972, a *St. Louis Post-Dispatch* reporter characterized ALMA and Orphan Voyage as "two national movements that would abolish the existing practice of sealing the birth records of adopted children." However, in the article, Paton said nothing about unsealing adoption records. Instead, she denounced sealed records for adding a stigma when adoptees already felt the burden of illegitimacy.[25] This was typical of Paton's approach to the issue: she chose to emphasize the psychological damage caused by the sealing of adoption records rather than to propose a political solution of opening them.

Paton was skeptical of political solutions to the problems besetting adult adoptees. Her Orphan Voyage publications seldom mentioned lobbying state legislatures or filing "rights-based" lawsuits to repeal sealed adoption records statutes, although Paton frequently urged adopted persons to return to adoption agencies and request information. At the heart of Paton's aversion to reform legislation was her clear, long-standing suspicion of the motives of lawmakers. In 1975, she wrote adoption reformer Joanne Small that "when I see adoption legislation as being presented now to legislatures, as in Ohio for example, it is so damn complicated, I think the best thing to do is wipe out all adoption legislation, leave matters to ethics, morality, and natural law, and set up effective groups."[26]

For tactical reasons, some adoption search organizations also failed initially to mount campaigns to access adoption records. As Florence Fisher noted,
ALMA had *"never* advocated any *legislative* change" to state laws, because if
"we try to change the law State by State the adoptees who are being hurt by
the present laws would all be dead and buried before the States would open
up unconditionally."[27] But by late 1975, Fisher had changed her mind, and she
began thinking about challenging the constitutionality of the sealed adoption
law in the U.S. Supreme Court. If successful, such a suit would have the effect of declaring all state laws sealing adoption records unconstitutional.[28] In
May 1978, ALMA filed a class-action federal lawsuit in the U.S. District Court
for the Southern District of New York and lost.[29] A year later, on appeal, the
U.S. Court of Appeals for the Second Circuit addressed and rejected each of
ALMA's constitutional arguments.[30]

Paton was dubious of lawsuits in general and skeptical of ALMA's in particular. In August 1976, she wrote CUB member Mary Anne Cohen that she
had heard talk of Fisher's lawsuit for several years but doubted whether Fisher
would spend the money.[31] Paton took a wait-and-see attitude toward the lawsuit. Almost a year later, however, she thought ALMA's lawsuit a strategic error.
While the ALMA case was on appeal before the U.S. Court of Appeals for the
Second Circuit, Paton expressed pessimism to her friend Margaret McDonald
Lawrence about its outcome, even if ALMA emerged victorious. Paton believed
that if the Court ruled favorably, rather than opening all state adoption records
unconditionally as Fisher anticipated, the state legislatures would rewrite the
confidentiality clauses of their adoption statutes to require adoption registries
or confidential intermediary systems. When that happened, Paton predicted,
"we would have to go through the whole process over again." She rhetorically
asked, "What is to gain from her case?"[32] She also thought the case a tremendous waste of money, that the funds could have been used much more constructively.[33] Paton's growing animosity toward Fisher, compounded by her belief in Fisher's alleged corruption and rivalry for leadership of the movement,
undoubtedly colored her negative views on the lawsuit. By 1979, her evaluation
of Fisher was unequivocal: "she is a destroyer, she will destroy everything she
touches."[34]

Paton's skepticism stemmed from her larger vision of the complexity of
adoption reform. Paton never accepted that it could be reduced simply to expertise in searching. The movement needed to sustain adult adoptees who had no
other place to turn. Paton envisioned a community of adopted persons, helping
each other and working out their own fate as the only solution to the problems

they faced. As she said in a letter rejecting the appeal to rights and suggesting that Fisher's lawsuit was an error, "the thing that is going to save us all is our own work together."[35]

In the early 1970s, Paton focused on her Reunion File, an alternative to opening adoption records. With the birth of the new adoption search movement and especially in light of the publicity Paton received from Theo Wilson's four-part series on the adoption search movement in the *New York Daily News*,[36] letters poured in to Orphan Voyage from birth mothers seeking the children they had relinquished for adoption. Paton viewed the surge in interest by birth mothers as "a real possibility for the Reunion File to get into operation."[37] In November 1974 she noticed that her reunion scheme was gaining popularity, "as if the idea had sprung up to them out of the earth," not only among adoption researchers such as Arthur Sorosky and his associates but also among search groups such as ALMA and Canada's Parent Finders.[38] Paton seized the opportunity. By the summer of 1975 she was ready: she announced in *The LOG* that the Reunion File was formally open. She was convinced that it would be "sufficient to bring people together, provided they can learn of the FILE and get themselves entered into it. No matter where they lived."[39]

Within two years, however, Paton was having doubts about the efficacy of adoption registries in general and the Reunion File in particular. Writing to one of her New Zealand correspondents, Bill Lumley, Paton said she was of two minds. On the one hand, she believed that the adoption registration system "can do a lot of good" if it was continuously well publicized and if birth parents and adult adoptees registered in great numbers.[40] On the other, she was dissatisfied with adoption registries because the system induced passivity. When an individual registered and then was told there was no match or was refused the information sought, the adult adoptee was inclined to become dejected and give up searching.

Paton also began to sour on her own creation, the Reunion File, as she ran into the same serious problems that had bedeviled her when she tried to organize local groups under her control. As usual, she saw ALMA as the thorn in her side, the group that exemplified these issues. In 1971, ALMA was one of the first search groups to set up a registry, the ALMA National Reunion Registry. It was a study in contrasts with Paton's Reunion File. In Orphan Voyage's membership application, Paton prepared adult adoptees for a realistic reunion experience by explaining that some took place spontaneously, some by accident, others by a formal plan, and "in still other cases, years of feverish search bring no result."[41] In contrast, Fisher's ALMA Registry emphasized results. Its newsletter, *The ALMA Searchlight*, announced that if there was "a 'match-up' between you and the person you are seeking you will be notified immediately," suggesting quick results.[42] A regular feature in the newsletter was a section under the heading *"THE SEARCH IS OVER!!!"* containing stories of successful, in some cases nearly miraculous, reunions.[43] As ALMA's membership soared, its registry also grew. By 1975, the group had four volunteer search consultants and genealogists on its staff.[44] A year later, ALMA announced that its registry was now "INTERNATIONAL."

At first, Paton was less bothered by Fisher's exaggerated emphasis on the ALMA registry's success than she was by her failure to give Paton credit for inventing it. She knew that the emotion was childish, but she resented "the fact that Flo and her group have taken my idea of the Reunion File without any acknowledgement."[45] Moreover, she was skeptical of ALMA's idea of computerizing the registry. Paton believed that computers were an unnecessary expense, involving costly processing time and also would take an inordinate amount of time. In contrast, Paton believed that ordinary file cards used in a manual system would give you the answer "in less than a minute."[46] In the short term, Paton concluded, file cards would suffice, though they were "not very glamorous."[47] More important, Paton was offended by the fact that Fisher was using the registry to make a lot of money.[48]

But the biggest problem with adoption registries was simply that there were too many of them (in 1977, Paton put the number in the United States at fifteen). The lack of centralization, Paton complained, resulted in duplication and wasted effort, and created divisiveness in the movement.[49] She also questioned the motives and ability of some of those in charge of running competing registries. Paton feared that they were using "the idea of the File for special purposes." She listed three such motives: (1) to "avoid facing the problem," by which she could have meant any number of things, including failing to confront the stigma of illegitimacy head-on or circumventing the therapeutic purpose of conducting one's own search; (2) to "Make money; Feel like a Messiah," a not-so-subtle jab at Florence Fisher's commercialism and publicity-seeking persona; and (3) "a quick, material answer to a human being in grief," an oblique reference to ALMA's failure to provide the personal, hands-on attention to adopted adults that was Paton's specialty. To Orphan Voyage's membership, she provided a detailed description—half boasting, half self-pitying—of the painstaking work necessary to maintain the Reunion File:

> it is fussy and meticulous work, not to be performed by volunteers, not to be sitting in somebody's home-office, vulnerable to a change of heart on the part of

that person, unsupervised, financed by hit and miss contributions, and sometimes held as possessively and fiercely as a cub by a mother bear.

The latter complaint was undoubtedly directed at CUB. Paton had recent-
ly protested to Lee Campbell that she, Paton, referred many birth mothers to
CUB, thereby losing the possibility of their joining Orphan Voyage and enter-
ing their name into the Reunion File. This was a disaster because, as she asked
Campbell, "how are your file and mine to make a match if they are separated?
This is the perennial question."[50]

Moreover, Paton was upset by genealogist, historian, and researcher Emma
May Vilardi's offer of not charging for her International Soundex Reunion Registry.[51] This was ironic, since Paton was especially scathing in denouncing Fisher
for commercialism. In 1977, however, Paton viewed the issue in ethical terms:
having the search done for free undermined the moral fiber of adult adoptees,
who were "already troubled by dependency in their character." For indigent
adoptees, however, Paton never charged. She prided herself that Orphan Voyage gave "members responsibility and did not take it away from them." If she had
thousands of members, like ALMA claimed, the culture of adoptee dependency
would have been transformed.[52]

Four years later, Paton's complaint about the Soundex registry changed to
one of personal economics. The lure of being able to access a registry for free
had proven irresistible to adult adoptees, as Paton noted ruefully. It had not only
pulled "the rug from under Florence," but it had also "pulled the rug out from
under me, for I have no memberships through the movement, no participation
in the File from the movement, no *LOG* subscriptions except from group leaders (sometimes)."[53] Three months later, in December 1981, Paton saw the writing
on the wall. She wrote one correspondent that her "next move will be to give
up the OV Reunion File. It's silly to be competing with a free file, Emma's, but
I am proud, and don't quit easy."[54] The future brought no relief. From a mere
500 registrations per year, the Soundex registry in 1982 was averaging nearly
4,000 registrations annually, with 74 matches.[55] A November 1983 "Dear Abby"
column, which endorsed Vilardi's Soundex registry, produced 4,500 letters in
the following three days; two months later, the number had soared to 9,000.[56]

Her growing dissatisfaction with her own Reunion File and adoption
registries in general led Paton at last to begin to turn her attention to unsealing adoption records. The change was not apparent in anything Paton said in
public; she continued to say little about the issue during the 1970s. But in the
pages of *The LOG*, items relating to unsealing records grew in number and
prominence. For example, as early as November 1974 Paton reprinted from the

journal *California Pediatrician* Dr. Joseph H. Davis's piece, "Who Am I?—The Adoptee's Search for Identity." Davis was Chief of the Department of Pediatrics in California's Palo Alto Clinic and a member of the American Academy of Pediatrics' National Committee of Adoption and Dependent Care.[57] He had become involved in adoption reform after reading Florence Fisher's *The Search for Anna Fisher*. In "Who Am I?" Davis first presented adult adoptees' "problem" in seven postulates, three of which were of primary important. As they grew up, Davis suggested, adopted persons irrespective of their adoptive family relationships "have a compelling desire to learn their natural identity." Also, when adult adoptees are denied access to their birth records, they feel second-rate. Finally, sealed adoption records deprived adult adoptees of a natural right: escape from a contract they entered into when it was impossible for them to give their consent to its conditions. Davis then presented five "recommendations," invoking his authority "as a pediatrician and a member of the American Academy of Pediatrics, whose motto is 'For the Welfare of Children.'" The most important of these proposals for adult adoptees was his urging that citizens should support the reform efforts of adopted adults "*Who Have Reached Maturity* to gain access to court and agency records to learn their identity." Davis also advocated that citizens should support legalizing the opening of adoption records when the adopted person reached maturity.[58] These were radical proposals, and they represented an important milestone in adoption reform because Davis was one of the first professionals outside of adoption circles to befriend the movement.

Although Paton did not often advocate opening records through legislative or legal procedures, beginning with Davis's piece she opened *The LOG* to others who did. In February 1975, *The LOG* devoted several pages to announcing that Donna Cullom's group, Yesterday's Children, had filed suit in U.S. federal court "to gain the right of every adoptee to have access to the records of his own birth and adoption."[59] Paton endorsed this move, noting that it would affect all adopted persons because it was based on the unconstitutionality of sealed adoption records, unlike earlier cases, which had been founded in the psychological need of single adoptees to know their original family members. She explained that the lawsuit, *Yesterday's Children v. Kennedy*, was built around the idea that adult adoptees who were denied access to their adoption records were deprived of their rights accorded by the First, Fifth, Ninth, Thirteenth, and Fourteenth Amendments to the Constitution.[60] However, the district court abstained from deciding the case, and the Seventh Circuit upheld the abstention.[61] *Yesterday's Children v. Kennedy* was the first class-action case arguing for adoptee access to adoption records. It exemplified the search movement's wide-ranging and creative legal arguments based on the idea of "rights."

Paton's *LOG* followed the developments in the Yesterday's Children's law-suit closely,[62] and she continued to highlight news items about sealed adoption records. In the summer 1975 issue she printed a suggestion by William Rice, a professor at the University of Wisconsin Law School, that "any person over the age of fourteen" and any parent or guardian should be permitted to examine all court records or judicial proceedings that related to his own or his ward's birth and family status.[63] This was followed in the next issue by a report from Joan Vanstone, national director of Parent Finders in Canada, about her success in presenting the case for opening sealed adoption records to the Child Welfare League of America conference and on several local radio shows.[64] In the October 1975 issue, Paton recommended to her readers a law article that affirmed adopted adults' right to know their family heritage, calling the legal doctrine that he or she show "good cause" before a judge permitted access to the records "unfair and unnecessary."[65]

Four months later, in the February 1976 issue of *The LOG*, Paton surveyed legislative developments on adoption records in the various states. She reported that "the big thing taking place right now" was that several states, including Colorado, Florida, Missouri, Ohio, and New York, were considering opening sealed records to adoptees when they reached the age of eighteen. Openly disputing the opponents' argument that such an action would destroy the privacy of the birth parents, Paton pointed out that that this had not kept Finland, Scotland, and England from opening birth records to adoptees. She suggested wickedly that there was "something about the American male, I think, that doesn't want to admit an inconvenient child. Of course that isn't the way they put it."[66]

In the February 1977 issue of *The LOG*, Paton raised a new issue: the notion of retroactivity. This was something that the opponents of opening adoption records usually relied on, arguing that by opening adoption records retroactively, either the state or adoption agencies would be breaking promises that they entered into with birth parents to keep the adoption confidential. Paton was one of the few activists who could remember a time when the records were unsealed and open to triad members. Informed by a Denver adoption agency executive that the records could not be opened "because we can't break promises," she replied, "You broke promises when you sealed them." Paton reported that the executive acknowledged that this was true, and he mused that maybe the records of people who were adopted before they were sealed would be allowed access to their records. Paton proceeded to advise adult adoptees that if they were adopted in states that did not seal original birth certificates at the time of their birth, they should be able to access the information.[67]

A month later, in a mimeographed communication to an unidentified state legislature that was considering revision of its adoption law, Paton proposed an age-graded system of opening adoption records as a necessary first step in the transition to a system of open adoption. For birth parents and persons adopted before records were sealed, she suggested, the records should be opened and the state should notify the parties of this development. Similarly, records should be opened to adult adoptees twenty-five years or over. Finally, Paton recommended that adoption records be open to adoptees eighteen to twenty-five years of age whose adoptive parents stated that "the matter had been covered in home discussions."[68] Though they were subordinated to her proposal for setting up a system of open adoption and they were never published, these strong recommendations demonstrate that Paton was embracing more fully the movement to open adoption records.

Yet Paton was still was unable to bring herself to propose publicly a concrete method to open adoption records. In the June 1977 issue of *The LOG*, under the heading "A CHALLENGE TO SUPERFICIALITY IN THE MOVEMENT," Paton declared, "We need to begin to say that the sealed record is *wrong* in a country given to freedom. We need to say that the sealed record was a *mistake*, persisted in by professionals, augmented by publicity, and motivated by something other than the well being of the affected population."[69] She called for understanding the psychological problems caused by sealing the records and crafting precise solutions. But in her entire, manifesto-like pronouncement, Paton failed to suggest a political or legislative solution. Instead, she repeated her customary criticisms of the movement and admonished adult adoptees to build their own services to each other, to grow emotionally, to think nationally rather than locally, and to stop fighting among themselves "before complaining about society and its sealed records." In the same issue, however, Paton printed items strongly in favor of open records, including a letter from members of a Tennessee Catholic diocese calling on the church "to unseal adoption files by changes in the law."[70]

During the 1970s, Paton's view of her work and the adoption reform movement vacillated from heady optimism to disappointment. In 1976, she remarked to one correspondent that she believed that "the entire adoption world is cracking open."[71] Similarly, she wrote to an adoption reformer that "the adoptee movement is growing so beautifully, even the self-interested ones cannot dim it."[72] Two years later, to another correspondent, Paton compared the remarkable progress that had been made in recent years to the 1950s and observed that she was "perhaps over the spectacle of the sealed record, for I know it is on the wane, and I also know how the open records movement will not cease."[73] Yet the 1970s also inaugurated what would be an ongoing lament of the failure by movement leaders to accord her the recognition she believed was due her. More than once, she would remark, "most of the things I have suggested have been taken up, and no credit given to me."[74] She would occasionally temper these bitter observations with a grudging admission that she was "glad to see things get done." But just as quickly, Paton undercut her generous remarks by belittling the main thrust of what ALMA or Yesterday's Children was doing to open adoption records, declaring, "There is not much initiative in the movement beyond trying to do a court case, trying to put up a show with the legislature."[75]

Paton also seemed of two minds when it came to legislative action. Though she wanted state lawmakers to open adoption records, she never really believed they would. As she wrote to Missouri adoption reformer Betty Wheeler, "It seems to me all the legislatures are going to put through some form of legislative approach to us, keeping us in thrall to the professionals, giving us as little as possible."[76] Linked with Paton's feeling of being unappreciated was Paton's deepseated belief that she was not supported by the adult adoptees she so loved—this despite the fact that few were as dedicated to the cause of adult adoptees as was she. Paton believed the work was just too demanding for most: "it is hard work," she wrote, "grubby with details, without pay, requiring hours every day, requiring a degree of giving of myself that is really almost too much for anyone."[77] In addition, money issues haunted her throughout the 1970s. Poverty stalked Orphan Voyage, dooming Paton's attempt to organize local groups and coordinate them with the leadership of Orphan Voyage. Although pessimistic about the direction of the movement, Paton never gave up on her "troubled people."[78] In July 1978, she spoke to public welfare workers "on the sealed adoption misfortune, telling them that "they had done wrong."[79] But for the most part she left it to other adoption reformers to work on the issue of sealed records. Instead, Paton's reform efforts in the late 1970s and early 1980s focused on finding a solution to the problem of the proliferation of adoption registries.

12

Ombudsman

I know what happened in adoption, and I know why. I think of it as a tragedy, but also I believe that adoption can at long last recover, and I will do whatever I can, as long as breath is in me, to help it come to pass.

—JEAN PATON, 1978

As early as 1954, Paton assumed a new role, one which she performed for another forty-eight years: that of unelected, self-appointed ombudsman, acting as an intermediary, watchdog, investigator, spokesperson, and defender of the adoption community. No issue was too small (the use of the word "adopt" in connection with highways or pets) or too large (perceived miscarriages of justices in social work, court proceedings, or congressional legislation) for Paton to sit down at the typewriter and dash off principled advice objecting to an action or practice.

In February 1954, Paton broke away from writing *The Adopted Break Silence*, and for the first time became involved in a matter of public policy about adoption through a court case. The legal dispute came to Paton's attention when an adult adoptee, Ruth Oliver Hill, literally knocked on Paton's door in Philadelphia.[1] Hill informed Paton that as a result of the death of John Tschudy, the Wisconsin Department of Welfare was in the process of removing the Tschudys' adopted child, Jeffrey, from the widow, placing the child in a foster home. Mrs. Tschudy had brought suit in the Columbia County Court in Portage, Wisconsin, attempting to retain custody of Jeffrey. Paton and Hill traveled to Madison, Wisconsin,[2] and on February 2 wrote the presiding judge, Alton Morrison, to protest the welfare department's action. Citing their special interest in the case—"having been adopted children"—Paton and Hill protested on two grounds the Department of Welfare's action. First, they doubted that a successful adoption had to conform to such a rigid social work standard, referring to a two-parent household. Second, they believed that the removal of the child during his early childhood simply because of a normal family misfortune was psychologically damaging. It was a threat to the child's permanent sense of security and to all adoptive placements. In support of their second claim, the letter mentioned the Life History Study Center's research project , which was providing compelling evidence, despite its limited sample of adult adoptees, that the "'best environments' do not necessarily make for the best security for adopted children" because psychological security for young children, and thus security for the adult in later life, did not depend on wealth and social position. It was, rather, the result of love, affection, and a feeling of belonging. They doubted whether "little Jeffrey could ever find compete security in another foster home, no matter how carefully it might be chosen."[3]

In mid-February, after he had rendered his decision, Judge Morrison replied to Paton and Hill. His opinion mirrored some of their ideas, but nevertheless he felt compelled by the law to uphold the Department of Welfare. Sympathizing with Paton and Hill, the judge commented that the welfare officials were not free in their approach because they were responsible to their superiors, and as a result, "their thinking becomes warped." He wished the two women continued good luck in their endeavors.[4] Paton did not let the matter rest. On August 1, immediately after finishing *The Adopted Break Silence*, she again wrote Judge Morrison, informing him that her findings confirmed her original belief that adopted children raised by widows had turned out favorably.[5]

A year later, on November 4, 1955, again acting in her new role as ombudsman for the adoption triad, Paton fired off a letter in response to a newspaper article, which described how, at a session of the National Council of Churches' conference on social welfare, representatives deplored the black market in babies. Playing on the term "black market," Paton advocated "the more fundamental green market." She explained that a green market was one "wherein all participants in adoption thrive through the years." Although admitting that it may be necessary for an unmarried woman to relinquish her child to adoptive parents, Paton declared that it should not "mean a lifetime of sorrow and worry about this child of her flesh and mishap." She then asked how the pain and ages-long stigma was to be removed. This was possible, she answered, "under Christian concepts" and the Life History Study Center's Registration Service, which could be used "for reconciliation and reunion at appropriate times. Only in this way can it be possible for the natural parents of an adopted child to find complete forgiveness, and for the child and adoptive parents to fully participate in the Christian form of love." Paton invited the pastors to address this problem in their counseling, and suggested that she was available for advice if they wished to write her.[6]

Many of Paton's most significant ombudsman activities, however, occurred at the national level. Throughout her career, she never hesitated to contact Congress about adoption issues. As early as 1964, she had protested the insufficiency of a Senate bill criminalizing black-market adoptions, saying that the bill failed to get at their root causes.[7] The following year, she objected strongly to a bill introduced by U.S. representative Clement Zablocki of Wisconsin, the Adoption Opportunity Act of 1965, which permitted taxpayers to deduct $1,250 of adoption expenses.[8] In ten closely reasoned, typed pages, Paton pointed out the inadequacies of the bill, ranging from the meagerness of the tax deduction and its implicit encouragement of black-market adoptions to its inability to alleviate the stigma of illegitimacy and its potential costliness.[9] How had such a bad bill come about? Paton blamed government bureaucrats, in league with self-interested professional adoption agencies, which had failed to consult the people most affected by it: the illegitimate. She proposed that Zablocki start fresh with a more positive agenda and made three suggestions that he should include in the new program. First, birth certificates should be standardized in such a way that would help a child in his or her early social encounters, but without falsifying the document. Second, in order to overcome the social stigma of illegitimacy, hope must be given to birth parents by preparing them for a reunion with their relinquished children when the adopted children have become adults. Third, the criteria for selecting adoptive parents must be reformed, so that they be chosen on the basis of their ability to identify with a child's social background, rather than on what social workers consider a criterion of what is "normal" or "standard."

Zablocki replied, thanking Paton for her letter. But he demurred from her critique that his bill failed to attack the wider problem of illegitimacy and its obligation toward the child born out of wedlock, declaring, "that was not my purpose. My aim was to give equitable treatment to adoptive parents, while at the same time providing a measure of incentive for those who might wish to adopt but are prevented because of the cost involved." He also chastened Paton for not being a practical, political compromiser, like himself. Zablocki's "admittedly-limited approach" had a good chance of being enacted, while her "more inclusive assault" would go down to defeat.[10] It was a lesson that Jean Paton never learnt.

Paton quickly responded to Zablocki, rejecting his strategy of political compromise. Instead, she tied the cause of adopted people to the identity politics of the 1960s. "For years we have tried to help, some of us, the worker, the negro, the poor. We are beginning to learn that the only effective results come from

these people themselves. Why not with the illegitimate? Should you not consider them first, and believe you do not understand until you hear from them?"[11]
Instead of a tax deduction, which forced adoptive parents to assume the burden
of the cost of adoption, Paton suggested the radical proposal that all adoption
expenses be socialized and that the national government assume payment.[12]

Almost a decade later, in 1975, Paton struck up a correspondence with both
Senator Alan Cranston, who was holding hearings about black-market babies,
and Senator Walter Mondale, chairman of the Subcommittee on Children and
Youth, who was holding hearings concerning the Opportunities for Adoption
Act. To Senator Cranston, she reiterated that the solution to the traffic in babies
for adoption was opening the adoption records. "In this way," she wrote, "most
of the greed would be sweated out of the process." Opening the records would
also be therapeutic, healing the "deep wounds of separation." Little harm would
be done. Moreover, from a historical perspective, the records had been opened
for "many, many decades before the recent era of manipulation and experiment,
which have ended so disastrously for so many." Paton also hit upon another favorite theme: the lack of participation by members of the adoption triad in decisions that affected them. She suggested that Cranston not confine the witnesses
appearing before his committee to a few social workers and adoptive parents.
Instead of experts and adoptive parents, Cranston should include those with
experiential knowledge of adoption. She recommended that he put representative adult adoptees, adoptive parents, and birth parents in a room and let them
hammer out a solution that they could all agree to. In this way, Paton declared,
"reality and mutual consideration would at last enter into the practices of adoption." She also sent Cranston copies of *The LOG*.[13]

In mid-July 1975, Paton began receiving detailed reports on both Cranston's
and Mondale's congressional hearings from Joanne Small, an adoption reformer
and coordinator of the Washington, D.C.–based search group, Adoption in
Search (AIS). Small was hopeful of influencing adoption reform by creating
a national lobbying organization and pressuring congressional committees to
open adoption records. Her primary assumption was straightforward: the committees craved national publicity, and the adoption activist groups would give
it to them. Small understood that Paton did not support the idea of a national
adoption lobby, but she explained that the idea had come from Paton herself,
when she had suggested that AIS was in a particularly advantageous position to
keep a watch on Congress. She hoped that Paton would at least consider testifying as a witness before the committee. To emphasize that need, Small closed
her letter with a quotation from Elizabeth Cole, the Director of the Permanent
Families for Children Unit of the Child Welfare League of America, which must

have reinforced Paton's belief in the obtuseness of professional social workers. Cole was quoted as saying, "The adoption triangle then is composed of biological parents, adoptive parents, and agencies."[14] Small also forwarded a letter she wrote to Senator Mondale on the same day, wherein she upbraided him for referring to adult adoptees as "adopted children" and called upon the committee to include adult adoptees as active participants.[15]

Paton's own views on advising national institutions, such as the U.S. Children's Bureau or HEW, or on appearing before congressional hearings was a complicated mixture of pessimism, hope, cooperation, and hubris. Typically, she somewhat disingenuously told adoption reformer Nancy Schmitt in 1977, she did not seek national publicity, and then bragged that she got "more than a little without trying and it keeps me more than busy." Just the other day, Paton related, she had watched *Good Morning America*, which ran a "rather sugary reunion story, and decided to write David Hartman and tell him why he should get me on his program." However, when Schmitt suggested that she might serve on HEW's advisory board to the Office of Adoption Information Services, Paton replied that "HEW would scrape the barrel before they would appoint me." Still, she mused, it was a possibility: Senator Cranston knew of her work through *The LOG*, although she doubted he actually read it. And, she added, other senators had referred people to Orphan Voyage. When Paton contemplated alternative candidates for the HEW spot, such as Florence Fisher, she exclaimed, "Heaven help us." In her judgment, Paton declared, she could not "really think of anyone better qualified" than herself.[16]

A year later, eager to provide national leaders with her expertise, Paton sent a statement supporting in vitro fertilization (IVF) to HEW's Ethics Advisory Board, which was holding public hearings on the subject across the country. Decades earlier, the issue had not been controversial. Thus, in the 1940s, IVF was seen as a technological miracle; by the 1960s however, conservatives viewed it as morally suspect, a threat to the traditional family, and by the 1970s it was a political minefield.[17]

Paton had intended to speak in person at the National Ethics Advisory Board's public hearing on December 8, 1978, in Denver, but adverse weather conditions prevented her from attending. The one-page statement she sent the Board sided with liberals on the question of IVF treatment, not out of sympathy for childless couples but for the conservative reason of the superiority of the biological over the adoptive family. Paton began her statement by making a sharp distinction between surrogate motherhood and IVF. Although modern contract surrogacy had just recently emerged around 1976, the informal practice had been around a long time.[18] Undoubtedly, Paton was also familiar with examples of surrogate motherhood from the Bible, in the Book of Genesis.[19] She declared that surrogacy was only a short step removed from adoption; therefore, not only was her testimony germane to the subject but there was a parallel in that both experiments were "destructive of human beings who were reared out of these processes." Such a statement bordered on being anti-adoption, which Paton was not; she was only highly critical of its adverse effects on triad members. Thus, she immediately qualified her assertion by noting that any child could be raised lovingly by a caring substitute parent, but added, "he cannot properly mature without a distinct and true knowledge of his progenitors, and a sense, therefore, of belonging to the chain of the human race." And while adoption retarded the maturation of the adult adoptee, a woman who relinquished her child to strangers was "partially destroyed for the rest of her years." Having criticized surrogacy and established the primacy of the biological family and the weakness of the adoptive one, Paton finally came out in favor of IVF, stating she had no objections to it, if the embryo was "retransplanted into the womb of the woman." What was crucial to Paton was that the procedure did not break "the genetic chain" and that no secrecy be involved. If these prerequisites were observed, Paton was confident that a child born under such circumstances would have "a secure sense of self and his ancestry."[20]

Over a three-month period, the Ethics Advisory Board read reports from scholars in the fields of reproductive science, ethics, theology, law, and the social sciences, received more than 2,000 pieces of correspondence, and conducted extensive hearings at which 179 individuals testified. In its final report, the Board concluded that it was "acceptable from an ethical standpoint to undertake research involving human in vitro fertilization."[21]

Another opportunity for Paton to make her voice heard at the national level offered itself in connection with HEW's 1980 proposed Model State Adoption Act and Model State Adoption Procedures.[22] The Model Adoption Act originated in Congress's effort to fulfill its mandate authorized in the Child Abuse Prevention and Treatment and Adoption Reform Act of 1978.[23] Section II of the law required HEW to appoint a Model Adoption Legislation and Procedures Advisory Panel, composed of eleven to seventeen members, broadly representative of groups, adoption agencies, and "persons concerned with and having expertise in adoption."[24] In June 1978, not surprisingly, Paton wanted very much to be appointed to the Advisory Panel. She wrote several officials in the U.S. Children's Bureau soliciting the position, detailing her qualifications and sending reading materials on the subject of adoption.[25] One of her correspondents, U.S. Children's Bureau Deputy Associate Commissioner Susan Weber, telephoned her with the information that candidates' names for the Advisory

Panel had already been submitted to Secretary of HEW, Joseph Califano, and that she was not on the list.[26] Paton immediately wrote Califano, offering herself for service on the panel and attaching an annotated résumé.[27]

The résumé was a remarkable document for its boastful earnestness. In addition to what Paton termed "relatively objective qualifications"—educational institutions of higher learning, occupational experience in social work, and activities as coordinator of Orphan Voyage (field trips, articles, TV appearances, newsletters, and "incessant daily correspondence")—she immodestly informed Califano that she possessed rare personal qualities, one of which verged on total objectivity: "an ability to communicate, listen, and to hear" and "to reproduce, without distortion or reinterpretation what people say." In addition, she had an unshakable conviction of the strength of human beings combined with an undying and ferocious hatred of human suffering, which she traced to watching her first adoptive father's painful death. Yet this hatred did not unbalance Paton's reason; instead it motivated her to understand a social problem and to do something constructively about it. For example, confronted with the sealed record in adoption, Paton built a successful network—"which I call an underground railway"—consisting of dedicated and intelligent adult adoptees, nationwide, whom she and others could call upon for help. People who received this help at a critical time and in the right way, Paton assured Califano, "go on to constructive reconciliation with their original kindred." Moreover, Paton reassured the secretary that at heart she was a conservative, stressing that she believed "in the value of the family as an institution," justifying her stance by pointing out that everyone born out of wedlock shared her conviction because "we know better than anyone else how empty life can be without it." Paton also told Califano that she believed "in the fundamental, the supreme value of reconciliation." She concluded by assuming a worldly-wise attitude, assuring Califano that she had survived all of adoption reform's temptations, anxieties, and mental depressions. Furthermore, Paton told him that although she thought of adoption "as a tragedy," she was convinced that it could be reformed, and pledged that "I will do whatever I can, as long as breath is in me, to help it come to pass."[28]

On August 1, Califano thanked Paton for her interest in serving on the Model Adoption Legislative and Procedures Advisory Panel.[29] Ten days later, when he announced the panelists, it is not surprising that her name did not appear. Paton's ardent desire to be of help had led her to arrogant boasting. Her statement of having total objectivity was enough for any Washington cabinet member to be wary of selecting such a person to serve on the Model Adoption Advisory Panel.

Among the members Califano appointed were three representatives from advocacy groups: an adoptive parent, Laurie Flynn, president of the North American Council on Adoptable Children; a birth parent, CUB president and founder Lee Campbell; and an adult adoptee, Adoptees in Search founder Joanne Small.[30] It was an able group. The advisory panel's guiding principle was openness, which was particularly noticeable in their work on adoption records, where the Model Act repudiated the traditional notion of secrecy. The panel members stated their position candidly: "It is the philosophical position of the Model Act that secrecy is not and has never been an essential or substantive aspect of adoption." Moreover, the Model State Adoption Act asserted, "modern attitudes and realities of adoption no longer support the cloak of secrecy upon which sealed records laws were based."[31] Consequently, the sections governing all adoption records—court files, birth certificates, and even adoption agency records—opened them to adult adoptees.[32]

As originally proposed, the Model State Adoption Act's recommendation for adoption records can almost be envisioned as a legislative coup d'état, an end run around all opposition to sealed adoption records legislation. Had it been approved without changes and subsequently adopted by the states, the adoption reform movement's leadership could have declared unconditional victory. But that was not to be. Standard operating procedure required that HEW solicit commentary from the public. It received thousands of written comments, of which 82 percent opposed the Model State Adoption Act in general; 90 percent of adoptive parents objected to the open records provisions.[33] In March 1980, the CWLA's leadership also found fault with the proposed legislation, contending that the proposed model statute went far beyond its mandate and made numerous unsound recommendations, especially concerning adoption records. It proposed substituting it with Minnesota's recently established adoption registry, which permitted a meeting only after both parties had agreed to share identifying information.[34]

Although Califano had passed over Paton as a panelist, she followed the proceedings closely. In May 1980, Paton took the seventy-seven-page Model State Adoption Act (MSAA), which had been published in the *Federal Register*, to a nearby motel, and over the period of a week wrote an extensive critique, which she considered "timeless."[35] On the whole, Paton found the MSAA woefully inadequate. In a cover letter she wrote to accompany her comments, she wrote, "I do not accept it, and this very fundamentally."[36] She even criticized the adoption activists' success in securing the opening of adoption records because "anyone in the adoptee movement knows that it is not sufficient to examine a birth certificate to accomplish a reunion."[37] Paton pointed out that the MSAA's philosophy of permanence, which mandated that the states either prevent foster care placement, reunify children with their families, or place them in adoptive homes, cited "as the greatest value to the child," was at odds with an eventual reunion with the child's birth parents once he or she came of age. It was the philosophy of permanence, according to Paton, which was the reason why the MSAA explicitly rejected the idea of the creation of a mutual consent voluntary adoption registry: it would facilitate reunions, making them less difficult and more frequent.[38]

But Paton's strictures against the flaws of the sealed adoption records' clauses took up a fraction of her criticism of the MSAA. At the heart of Paton's concerns, and taking up most of her ten-page critique, was how the document affected both the institution of adoption "under the seal" and triad members.[39] She was especially critical of the way the MSAA treated birth mothers. Paton deplored the failure of social workers to provide birth mothers with any detailed or balanced counseling about the alternatives available to them, such as to keep their child by providing services to them in their own home or temporary care in a foster home with a future plan to reunite the child with the original family. These options were deliberately omitted, Paton lamented, and adoption with its philosophy of permanence was the only choice recommended. Ultimately, Paton placed the blame on a structural problem in society's institutions: the birth mother had no alternative but to turn to an adoption agency for help; the state provided no other alternative agency that stood "foursquare for the preservation of family ties."[40] The result "often enough" was the relinquishment of the child, who was placed in an adoptive home.

For the creators of the MSAA, adoption of the child marked the successful end of the process. For Paton, adoption signified only the beginning of a failed utopian project. She was upset that the MSAA was silent about the first eighteen years of the child's life after his or her adoption. Paton believed that children needed specific and realistic knowledge about their natal family; but the MSAA could never achieve this goal merely by mandating the careful recording and preserving of the child's biological heritage and opening it "to him at the magic age of eighteen." For one thing, all of the family information came primarily from the child's natal mother, "so that only a limited and unverified picture of the larger family is available." The second weakness of the MSAA was that the information conveyed to the adoptive parents consisted, in Paton's view, of almost meaningless detail. "Your mother had blue eyes, was 5 feet 3 inches tall and liked sports. Does anyone really believe this is a biological heritage?"[41] The result of the flawed adoption disclosure plan in the MSAA was therefore psychologically disastrous and would create a crisis of identity for the young adoptee:

He will have no maturing understanding of the circumstances of his adoption, will not learn to consider his parents real of fallible humans, cannot therefore ever accept them in a maturing wisdom; and the perilous consequence is that he will not understand himself, or accept himself.[42]

Paton envisioned an open adoption as the one solution to this problem because it would permit the "two sets of parents to communicate with each other"; but the Model State Adoption Act prohibited it.[43]

Ultimately, Paton faulted the MSAA for not getting at the root of the problem, which was adoption itself and its underlying philosophy of permanence, grounded in utopianism. It refused to recognize human frailty, "human misery, human breakdown, and society's own contribution thereto," in its dream of permanence and perfection.[44] Paton was appalled at the repetition of the word "permanence" in the MSAA, "as if by recitation of a word, like the turning of a prayer wheel, the desideratum of permanence would be achieved."[45] Rather than fund the MSAA, with its elaborate bureaucracy of social workers and complicated legal processes, the public, Paton asserted, would be better served by discovering the social reasons for the problems of the adult adoptee population caused by out-of-wedlock birth, extramarital pregnancy, divorce, the failure of society to provide day care, and infertility of married couples. Unfortunately, Paton phrased the last sentences of her critique in her characteristic style, with its own special vocabulary, taken from Simone Weil, so that her meaning became obscure and was probably lost on many of her readers:

> The interests of society at large are not served by funding and elaborating massive plans for deprived elements in the population on the basis of a philosophy. The interests of society are served by adherence to a life understanding of and a developed wisdom about the nature of human affliction and what is required for its healing. The members of the population of adoption are people who bear the condition of affliction, which always expresses a degree of social alienation. In adoption the affliction comes about through illegitimate birth, through extra-marital pregnancy, marital breakup, or personal failure before the responsibilities of child care, and through the childlessness of some married couples. Are not all these injuries both to society and to the individuals concerned?[46]

Paton was convinced that adult adoptees were not going to be healed by the MSAA, which she scorned as "a massive and cumbersome (and expensive) effort to substitute for what cannot be substituted for, to build a superstructure of professionalism tied in with courts and record repositories to insure that a few words, 'philosophy of adoption' and 'permanence' can bring to heel a perpetual human problem, yet somehow not only failing to accomplish it but also exacerbating it." Instead, Paton declared that adult adoptees, having in common the condition of affliction, would be healed by reaching out to each other in a generous manner because they truly wished to be healed. Keeping in mind the "beloved community," Paton affirmed the "inherent tendency of afflicted people to help one another in their strange, almost incomprehensible but human fashion."[47]

Three months before writing her critique of the MSAA, in February 1980, Paton became involved in a third encounter with congressional legislators. She received a phone call from Jackie Parker, an aide to Carl Levin, a Democratic senator from Michigan. Levin, a Harvard University Law graduate, had worked in Detroit liberal politics and had been elected to the Senate in 1978. He immediately became involved in adoption affairs, coauthoring in 1980 a provision in the Adoption Assistance and Child Welfare Act that removed the disincentives to adopting special needs children in foster care by continuing the foster care subsidy after the child was adopted.[48] Levin also proposed in 1980 an early version of what would become the Adoption Identification Act—the national computerized adoption registry—but his proposal was rejected by the Senate.[49] According to Paton, Parker told her that Senator Levin wanted to set up a national reunion file "as a way of getting around the intense opposition to open records."[50] At first Paton was skeptical of the proposal, but the more she talked to Parker and the more she heard about Levin, the more she "liked the sound of things."[51] Paton believed that Levin had "the interests of the adoptees at heart," and recommended its support to her correspondents.[52]

A month later, after reading two drafts of Levin's proposal for a computerized national adoption registry, Paton wrote Parker with four recommendations. Paton pointed out that the proposal's phrase "costs of the search" gave the mistaken impression that adoption registry officials would carry out an active search. She suggested that the clause be rewritten to state that the expense would cover the "cost of the computerization." She also recommended that adding the birth weight and time of birth to the computer's list of matching items would facilitate reunions. Paton questioned as well the wisdom of keeping the information on file for only three years. She reasoned that more time was necessary to acquaint people with the adoption registry's existence, and argued that it would not cost any more to keep the information for the extra time. Finally, noting that the adoption registry was to be operated by HEW officials, Paton questioned their trustworthiness. She based her fear on having just received and read the MSAA. Paton noted the contradiction in that document between its philosophy of permanence and the philosophy of reunion and reconciliation, which could only be viewed "as an interruption to that permanence and therefore as a blot on the idealism in the plan." She suggested that perhaps the adoption registry should be placed in a different government department, such as Justice or Interior.[53]

The hearing for Senate Bill 989, the Adoption Identification Act of 1981, took place eighteen months later, on July 23, 1981, before the Subcommittee on Aging, Family, and Human Services of the Committee on Labor and Human Resources. At the hearing, Senator Levin proposed a national voluntary clearinghouse—a national computerized database—for the millions of adoptees and birth parents who were looking for each other.[54] It was to be established as a three-year pilot program, its cost not to exceed $800,000, which Levin characterized as "minimal."[55] According to Levin, a national clearinghouse was necessary for a variety of reasons. It was clear that state and private adoption registries were incapable of doing the job of successfully matching the millions of people searching for each other. In support of this position, Levin quoted Paton, whom he referred to as "the mother of the adoptee movement":

> The various reunion or matching files of adoptee groups at ALMA, Orphan Voyage, and International Soundex, the numerous small files are little match for the problem, presented to a population within adoption which number close to two-and-half-million people. We need to assist people who have a mutual desire to meet after the separation by adoption by a computerized identification center of a national scope supported and carried on in such a way that it can be a permanent starting point for people who would otherwise have to flounder or fail.[56]

Rather than emphasize the inefficiencies of the local registries, however, Levin highlighted the pain and suffering that triad members felt and the necessity of treating them with thoughtfulness and compassion. He also stressed that the national registry would balance the interests of all members of the triad by protecting the confidentiality of adoption records. Repeatedly, Levin assured committee members that the national registry was purely voluntary, that a match between consenting adults age twenty-one and over had to be made before any information would be released, and that no adoption records would be unsealed.[57]

Paton did not appear as a witness before the committee, though it was not from want of trying. A month earlier, in June 1981, she had written a letter to the Chairman of the Subcommittee on Aging, Family, and Human Services, Jeremiah Denton, expressing her interest in testifying on behalf of the bill, "to assist in the process of reconciliation between mature adults who had been separated by adoption."[58] Paton enclosed a four-page pamphlet she had written in 1975, "A Basic Guide to the After-Adoption Reunion Experience," which was the most extensive statement she ever made on the subject. The pamphlet is directed at the adult adoptee but makes hardly any mention of rights, adoption legislation, intermediaries, or adoption registries. Although never mentioning religion, it has the metaphorical and literary overtones of John Bunyan's *The Pilgrim's Progress*. Instead of Bunyan's cataloging the journey of Christian, a man who is seeking his salvation on a pilgrimage to Heaven, Paton lays out the often difficult and confusing path an adopted person must travel in order to feel the joy of reconciliation and reunion. The search for original family members begins in the effort to repair a deep and severe injury—a feeling of emptiness and uncertainty—which has been "inflicted by no visible weapon, and leaves no visible scar," Paton referring here to the sealing of the adoption records. It is only in this sense that reunions are confusing. Paton then shifts to an extended metaphor of patching up a roof to make her point: "One can feel ridiculous setting about repairing a roof which has not been torn by wind and hail and which appears to be intact. Who would climb a ladder to repair such a roof?" But the process of healing begins in the very act of climbing the ladder, for "we" are complicit in the injury of social separation because of our refusal to deal with it. "As we climb that ladder we see that in fact there is something wrong with the roof, and we hope, rung by rung, that we can do something about it." Paradoxes reign: reconciliation is a universal good, but it is prohibited by law and frowned upon by the culture. Paton asked rhetorically, "Is it not strange that a culture should discourage repair?"[59]

But the voices of discouragement and prohibition were not universal; there were supportive voices springing up everywhere, making adult adoptees rejoice and strengthening their resolve. Consequently, "the emptiness lessens, the uncertainty shifts to something livable, like a plan, a road map, something organized and real." Whereas in *Pilgrim's Progress*, Christian reunites with his old friend Faithful and other characters, such as Ignorance and Hopeful, and have many adventures, Paton introduces only one other person to her narrative, a fellow adult adoptee "who has travelled the reunion path and come through rejoicing and rid of the excess of fear and repression." Just as Christian is overwhelmed by doubt at the River of Death and almost drowns, the searching adult adoptee in Paton's narrative is struck by doubt at the "terrible contrast" between the joy of the reunited traveler and his own fear and bewilderment. Wracked by suspicion and disbelief, Paton's traveler begins to wonder "if life is really going to permit us to experience joy? Can life go on without that heaviness of bewilderment? Can we ever expect to wake each day without it, ever again?" Thus Paton has brought the traveler to a point where he has to make a choice between two different paths: "one dominated by fear and bewilderment or the possibility of joy and the return of joy." Ever the realist, Paton tips the scale in the direction that she wants the traveler to go. She explains that joy is an emotion that comes and goes, but if fear and bewilderment become dominant, they remain with a person every moment of their lives. Paton concluded by stating that these questions might be difficult for philosophers, but not for adult adoptees. The answer was "'yes' to reconciliation and its rewards."

When Senator Denton failed to choose her to testify before the subcommittee, Paton sent a statement, urging passage of Levin's proposal for a national computer adoption registry. She adduced three reasons that a federal presence was necessary "to promote reconciliation." First, Americans were a highly mobile population, and triad members often moved away from the place where they were originally adopted. It was impossible for the individual states to "legislate for citizens spread about the entire country."[60] Second, because adoption records were sealed they presented most adult adoptees and birth parents with many obstacles: ignorant of knowing where the adoption took place, they were prevented in many cases from initiating even a private search; and even where adoption records were accessible through legal means, "they were falsified." Third, it was only fitting that the federal government provide a remedy for the misery that sealed adoption records had caused because it was "the United States Children's Bureau, which since the mid-1940s has spent large sums in promoting the sealed-record form of adoption through field work and central publicity."[61]

Paton also included with her statement an enclosure containing ringing approval of the MSAA from the General Assembly of the Presbyterian Church, passed at its annual national convention. It was a far more radical document than Paton's own statement. Citing biblical examples, the inequities of secular law, and even the endorsement of social work, the General Assembly of the Presbyterian Church went on the record "supporting the rights of adult adoptees to receive, upon request, copies of their original birth certificates and court and agency records pertaining to their adoption." In addition, it endorsed Title V of the MSAA, which would grant adult adoptees all of their adoption records.[62] Both of these documents were included in the subcommittee's proceedings of the hearings and later published. When Joseph D. Harrington, chair of the AAC legislative committee and a leading authority on state adoption registries, forwarded Paton a copy of the hearings, she thanked him for allowing her to see for herself that her statement had actually been printed. Recognition from an established authority was an unusual experience for Paton. She explained, "I have had such a dose of being shoved aside, for whatever reason, that I get the 'orphan syndrome' expecting rejection. No matter what we experience in the way of acceptance, the old patterns tend to continue."[63]

Levin's emphasis that the national computerized adoption registry be carefully designed to avoid intrusion into the life of adult adoptees or birth parents or "violation of constitutional privacy rights," and to prevent the unsealing of records, was a calculated preemptive strike against several witnesses, including William L. Pierce, president and chief executive officer of the National Committee for Adoption, who appeared before the hearing in opposition to the bill.[64] In the end, influential senators from both sides of the aisle objected to Levin's bill as an unwarranted intrusion of the federal government into matters best left to the states; it died in committee.[65] A year later, Levin sent Paton a form letter thanking her for her support and promising to reintroduce an identical bill in the following session of Congress.[66]

Between Paton's endorsement of Levin's national adoption registry in 1981 and its reintroduction in 1988, Paton turned her back on the entire notion of adoption registries. Several developments were responsible for Paton's about-face. Beginning in the late 1970s, state legislators established voluntary mutual consent adoption registry systems, following the precedents set by ALMA, CUB, and the International Soundex Reunion Registry. As early as 1982, Paton reacted negatively to this trend in adoption reform. She disapproved adamantly of those state adoption registries, such as Louisiana's, which subjected adult adoptees and birth parents to mandatory counseling. She also deplored the unfortunate tendency in states that set up adoption registries for search groups to disintegrate and fade away. Instead of collapsing, Paton urged search group members to hit the streets, ringing doorbells and advertising the existence of the registries to insure that everyone used them.[67] By 1985, adoption registries had become the most popular solution to the demand for open records, with sixteen states enacting them.[68]

Paton had an additional reason to dislike them. In 1986, she had learned from a New Zealand adoption reformer, Mary Iwanek, that adoption registries were a ploy used by the opponents of adoption reform to circumvent opening adoption records. This bit of information made a strong impression on Paton. Writing to Margaret Hutchinson-Betts, cofounder of the Vermont search group Parents for Private Adoption, Paton contended that the same situation existed in the United States. In addition, she complained that after establishing adoption registries, lawmakers "then say not to bother them for anything more. And since there are no provisions for advertising the Reunion File, it is a secret burial place for hopes."[69] Paton would in the future refer to adoption registries as "tombs."[70] Referring to her own Reunion File, she went so far to declare that "sometimes I regret that I ever conceived it." She concluded that she now feared that Levin's national adoption registry would set up "a professional superstructure and thus it will be a heavy and dead hand. I am against it, now, until the records are open. Then, and only then, should it be implemented."[71] But she now despaired of seeing even this development. By 1986, Paton observed, "groups meet about open adoption, intermediaries, and adoption registries, but somehow I no longer hear a voice that says 'Open the records,' as we used [to] hear."[72]

Two years later, when Senator Levin's aide Jackie Parker again contacted Paton to support a national computerized adoption registry, she raised objections. Responding to Parker in February 1988, Paton repeated some of her earlier reservations about the registry. She was consumed with "realistic dread" of the innovations the Department of Health and Human Services officials would add to the registry, such as counseling and intermediary services. Paton concluded on a discouraged note:

> Please remember, Jackie . . . I am weary. I approach my eightieth birthday, and my funds for my use, and for Orphan Voyage, are extremely limited. I am grieved by the destruction of my people, and chagrined that my 35 years of endeavor have brought little fruit.[73]

Nearly six months later, on June 30, prompted by reading the Registry bill in the *Congressional Record*, Paton wrote Senator Levin in an attempt to explain her change of heart. She took pride in the fact that she did "mother" the first reunion file, "pulling it out intact from my innards as long ago as 1949 (in a letter to *Mental Hygiene* magazine)." But experience had shown her, she wrote, that reunion files had been used in the United States, Canada, and New Zealand as a way to stave off opening adoption records. Paton acknowledged that Levin acted from good motives, that it took courage to introduce the bill, and that he had high hopes for it. Sadly, she concluded, "I wish I shared those hopes, but I no longer can, because of what I have seen."[74] Paton next turned her reform efforts to the chaos of local adoption groups by creating a national organization for adult adoptees.

13

The American Adoption Congress

I am a realist, an engineer by every instinct, and I want to continue to build bridges, to give people hope, to show them there is a way to greater integration and enjoyment in their lives.

—JEAN PATON, 1975

The AAC is a disaster, and I am not sure if anything will revolutionize it.

—JEAN PATON, 1983

As early as July 1968, Jean Paton began thinking about forming a national organization of adopted people. She had been led in that direction by a question from one of her correspondents, who asked, "When will we be able to have a national convention of adoptees? I am sure that day will come." In response, Paton issued a call for volunteers to serve on a committee to make arrangements for just such a convention.[1] Nothing ever came of the idea, however. And although seven years later, in February 1975, Paton had again mused that "someday all the organizations will get together," it was a letter of Bill Deautriell's sent to her by Karen Rowland that triggered additional thought about such a national organization for adult adoptees. Deautriell, a New York adoption reformer who worked with ALMA's Florence Fisher, admired greatly Paton's work in Orphan Voyage.[2] He had joined Orphan Voyage in 1973, volunteered to serve on its board of directors soon thereafter, and started a local chapter of Orphan Voyage in 1975.[3] He had written to Rowland expressing his concern about a successor to Paton, asking, "Do you think she should consider some plan and arrangement for the continuation of her noble and urgent work, if she should become incapacitated or retire from the tremendous duties of Orphan Voyage in the future?" Deautriell went on to tell Rowland that Paton had admitted to him that her dream of centralizing local adoption search groups had been a failure. It was this comment of Paton's, Deautriell stated, that "prompted the utopian idea" for him to establish a National Adoptees and Orphans Society.[4] Rowland viewed Deautriell's suggestion of competing with Paton traitorous and replied that she was unconcerned about the future. Privately, Rowland told Paton she would never join such an organization as he proposed.[5]

Thus, in mid-March 1976, with local adoption search groups resisting Paton's idea of affiliation with Orphan Voyage and talk of a national organization for adult adoptees in the air, Paton also began entertaining the notion of such a project.[6] She had no illusions about its creation, and little confidence of its success even if it managed to get off the ground, because the idea had three strikes against it. First, Paton believed that adult adoptees distrusted the idea of a national organization because of Florence Fisher's poor leadership of her national group, ALMA; as a result, Paton felt that "most people who have experienced ALMA [were] disgusted. It has degenerated into a commercial operation."[7] Second, she believed that the individualistic tendencies characteristic of adult adoptees would prevent cooperation, and their dependency and lack of realism would prevent them from engaging in the hard work necessary to keep such an organization functioning. She pithily summed up the issue: "people will not work. This is especially true of adoptees, but they love to see themselves in print."[8] Third, there was the major problem of overcoming the provincialism of the individual adoptee reform organizations, with "every little group thinking it is a national organization."[9] Nevertheless, despite the obstacles, as she wrote to Edith Ward at the end of April 1976, "something has to be done to nationalize the service."[10]

In the spring of 1978, the sixty-nine-year-old Paton announced to the readers of *The LOG* her plan for a national conference, a sort of constitutional convention. She had asked Orphan Voyage member Anne Silber, an adult adoptee, author, and civil rights crusader, to invite some forty committed and knowledgeable people from the Orphan Voyage mailing list to deal with the problem of the fragmentation of the adoption reform movement and the lack of coordination among the many local groups. She assured her readers that "I shall have little to say about decisions that are reached. It is yours." In addition, Paton dropped a bombshell by revealing that she would be stepping down as coordinator.[11]

Paton's next comments revealed what she had in mind for the future national organization. She suggested that perhaps the conference planners would decide what do about her resignation, but that "any alternative person had better come out to Cedaredge and spend a week or two engaging in the work before they take on the commitment, for there is no way of explaining what is required."

There would also be many detailed questions about ownership of the files and where they would be ultimately located. Apparently, Paton was thinking that a national organization would simply be somebody else running Orphan Voyage. She again assured her readers that she would not let go of the operation until adequate preparation had been made, but after that point, "I will not interfere."

At about the same time, Paton took stock of the adoption reform movement on the occasion of the twenty-fifth anniversary of the founding of her Life History Study Center. She did so in a special issue of *The LOG*, which provides several additional clues to both why Paton showed a newfound interest in promoting the idea of a national organization for adult adoptees at this time and what shape the new organization might take. In one statement, "Mediation of a Coordinator in the Spring of 1978," Paton revealed her belief that she was a failure: all of her efforts in the movement had fallen short or were disintegrating. She had worked so hard for so many years, she said, and had figured out what adult adoptees needed above all else, which was a means of communication. She had provided that to the community of adult adoptees by writing away incessantly at her IBM typewriter.[12]

But all had come to naught. She summarized her expectations and failures in three fields: the Reunion File, birth mother groups, and adoptee search and support groups. Paton lamented that she had invented the Reunion File, originally created in the hope that it would strengthen human relationships, but instead adult adoptees used it as a way to avoid relationships. She observed that after submitting their names and dates on cards, adult adoptees believed they had no other responsibilities or obligations. Paton bitterly concluded, "So I saw my Reunion File go down the drain of superficiality and impersonality. And I grieved." Turning to birth mothers, Paton credited herself with both recognizing that they needed a voice for themselves and for getting "them familiar with each other." Their organizations were presently strong and making progress, but Paton anticipated that the experts and professionals would take them over and reinterpret their message, making it unrecognizable. She had also tried to encourage adoptee search and support groups to affiliate with Orphan Voyage, the better to learn the benefits of mutual cohesion and the value of strength in numbers. "But," Paton said, "they began to quarrel among themselves, split, divide, express their hostilities improperly." They really did not want to subordinate themselves to anyone; they just wanted to be "mutual among themselves." Paton, the indomitable adoption reformer, summed up her thoughts on her failed efforts with the melancholy observation: "So there is not much left for me to do except collect my thoughts, put out a *LOG* in the fall which will bring you up to date on events." But deep down, Paton hoped that nationalizing the movement might be a way to control and salvage all of the projects she held so dear, but were on the verge of failing.

In the same issue of *The LOG*, Paton again announced her retirement.[13] But almost immediately, Paton disregarded her statement of retirement and threw herself into devising a plan to nationalize the movement to attain the goals she saw slipping away from Orphan Voyage. What Paton intended was to gather together a small group of longtime, competent leaders, who were "continuously concerned and with some perspective and balance," to "set forth what needs to be done." She identified by name Mary Ramos, Joan Vanstone, Margaret Lawrence, and said she could think of eight or ten more.[14]

But Paton's plans quickly went awry. The letter Anne Silber sent out at the end of March 1978 set in motion a process that took on a life of its own, with results very different from those Paton had in mind. Rather than inviting an elite number of activists to meet and discuss a national conference, Silber first solicited advice from fifty-one reformers in five areas: Where should the conference be held? When? For how long? Who should be invited? And what should the agenda be?[15] By early May, twenty-seven adoption reformers had replied, representing themselves as well as such groups as the Adoption Study Project, A.I.M (Always in Me), the Adoption Forum of Philadelphia, Search, and Parent Finders. Many expressed their enthusiasm and wholehearted support for the idea of a national conference, declaring that they were willing to go "anywhere—anytime."[16] Several replies were perfunctory, answering the questions in a bare-bones fashion,[17] while others went on for several typed, single-spaced pages, making preconference organization suggestions and outlining in great detail what its goals and agenda should be.[18]

In late May, Silber wrote a form letter to the respondents, expressing her gratitude for their "open, sensible, sincere, and down-to-earth" replies and summarizing their consensus opinions to her questions.[19] The group favored meeting in Kansas City, with Washington, D.C., mentioned several times. They also heavily favored a meeting sometime in late September through mid-October. In regard to the format, most of the respondents supported plenary sessions with speakers, followed in popularity by small workshops and some open discussions. Some of the most frequently mentioned agenda items included "Search methods, Open Records, Open Adoption, National Registry, and a 'Clearinghouse' type of operation to keep abreast of legislative problems." Silber asked for additional comments and informed the respondents that she would finalize the plans by the end of June.

By October, that small elite proposed by Paton mushroomed into several regional meetings of adoption reform groups. In that month, sixteen West Coast adoption reform groups, calling themselves the Western Conference, proceeded to lay the groundwork toward a National Adoption Convention in Washington, D.C., the following spring. Its theme, "Unity—Trust—Understanding," became the theme for the National Conference. At the Eastern Conference, which was held on December 2 and 3 in Philadelphia, Nancy J. Schmitt along with Sharon Forbes, hammered out the national conference program. By then Schmitt, founder and president of the Adoption Research Council, and Virginia Rader, the D.C./Maryland branch coordinator for Concerned United Birthparents (CUB), had become the national conference coordinators. With the addition of Canadian and Mexican triad members, the conference became international.[20]

In correspondence with Schmitt, Paton's idea for the structure of the national organization came into sharper focus: it was to be Orphan Voyage on a national stage. What Paton had failed to do on her own—have the adoption search and support groups affiliate with Orphan Voyage voluntarily from below—she would now attempt from above. She looked to colonial America for inspiration: "I think the only way I can understand what is now going on is to think hard of what this country went through when it had 13 colonies." However, the means she counted on to achieve this end backfired. Paton claimed that she wanted to stay out of the planning and delegate the work in order to "give people a chance to make something of this opportunity."[21]

But it was not to be. Rather than acting as trusted "navigators," in harmony with Paton's plans, the planners at the regional conferences went their own way. Nothing emanating from the regional conferences convinced Paton that the planners recognized the practical problems involved in creating a national group. Instead, she complained, all they talked about was "organization and profess empty words." When Schmitt mentioned the new name for the national organization—the American Adoption Congress, which the planners had agreed upon—Paton dismissed it outright, with the argument she had voiced many times before: new names were not necessary. Instead, she declared, they should stick with the name Orphan Voyage, just as "in Canada, they do not waste time on making new beginnings everyday or year; they don't all like the name of Parent Finders, but recognize that it has a history and value because of its history." She showed more of her hand to Schmitt by declaring that she favored "a board of 7–9 people." If the upcoming convention did not produce such a group, Paton said, "I will appoint one for Orphan Voyage, and at the same time announce a new off-shoot of Orphan Voyage to express its plans for the next decade." The American Adoption Conference, to Paton's way of thinking, was to be Orphan Voyage writ large. As for the resistance to Paton's ideas that she sensed were coming out of the regional conferences, Paton explained it away: "basically people don't like Orphan Voyage because they resist being social orphans." Such obstructionism was inherent in the adoptee character. Fatalistically, she concluded, it could not be changed, though she believed it could only "be faced, overcome, and even triumphed over."

Schmitt replied respectfully, but with a sharp rebuke. She assured Paton that everyone knew that it was Paton who had sparked the idea of a national organization and was responsible for what was being done.[22] She denied that there was any truth to Paton's accusation that "everything I suggest, people take up, and then claim they have done it."[23] On the contrary, Schmitt vowed, she knew of no one claiming the idea of creating a national organization as their own. But she minced no words, telling Paton, "We cannot have the reorganization and continuation of Orphan Voyage as a single goal."

Schmitt continued, countering each one of Paton's objections. She agreed with Paton that "we are social orphans," but the problem to be overcome was not "a name" but the competition among all of the different adoption search and support groups. Yes, Schmitt said, the thirteen colonies are to a degree analogous to the present situation, but we have to deal with ninety-two colonies with three or so major groups: ALMA, Yesterday's Children, and Orphan Voyage. And, although all these organizations' leaders were in Paton's debt, Schmitt forcefully declared, "they cannot and will not give their allegiance to a group affiliated with any other group already in existence. Pride, power, and principles are at stake!"[24] She tried to convince Paton that in light of the strong personalities and competitive nature of the groups, the organization of the nascent American Adoption Congress was being kept deliberately simple, as a democratic association of many independent groups. Contrary to Paton's idea of top-down leadership, Schmitt resorted to a different historical analogy and stated the simple truth: "The Congress cannot run these groups. And if the largest groups refuse to join then the same fate which befell the League of Nations will befall us." She asserted that no one would attend the conference if it were seen as a simply a meeting to further the ends of Paton's Orphan Voyage. Schmitt pointed out that Paton had spent twenty-five years perfecting the goals and platform of Orphan Voyage. It was time to give the other groups some room to grow within the adoption reform movement. In regard to the board of the American Adoption Congress, Schmitt told Paton that it had already been decided that for the first conference the board would be composed of the regional coordinators and Anne Silber. Schmitt concluded her letter as she had begun, attempting to assure Paton of her esteemed place in the history of the movement and mollify her bruised ego, but resolving that Paton not get her way:

What is happening is happening in many ways because of your leadership—but it can't happen in your name. O.V. is part but not the whole movement. Originally O.V. and you gave the rest of us a starting place. You have not been forgotten and you are given credit for more than you probably realize. Please bear with us as we try to do the work of unifying. Only then can we celebrate and you can accept the glory and thanks you deserve.[25]

Paton's reply to Schmitt revealed her divided mind. She struck out against practices by adoption activists she disagreed with, yet repeatedly pledged cooperation. Defiantly, Paton declared that she had no intention of appeasing Donna Cullom of Yesterday's Children or Florence Fisher in their practice of censoring what publications their members could read. "I have not given my life and inheritance and years of lost peace just to make soft noises that will not annoy Donna or Florence." Taking aim at Fisher, Paton asserted, "I don't see why I should bow out because she won't acknowledge my existence. I am not that masochist anymore." Melodramatically, she added, "Should the whole cause be lost for this?" suggesting that if Paton did not speak her mind at the upcoming meeting the adoption reform movement would come crashing down. But immediately following each paragraph complaining about particular leaders, Paton assured Schmitt that she thought the D.C. meeting would produce much good and she would cooperate, "with the momentum that I—as so much else—initiated." After pledging her loyalty, however, Paton closed her letter stating, "But I am also laying my own plans to see to it that the truth of our grief and subjection is given the light of day, and that the caring network (this is what OV is) gets further opportunity"—suggesting that her promise of support could just as easily be interpreted as a threat to push forward with her plan to nationalize Orphan Voyage.[26]

In the five months before the convening of the first American Adoption Congress, conference coordinators Nancy Schmitt, Virginia Rader, and Sharon Forbes threw themselves into a whirlwind of activities. They saw to it that hotel reservations were made, speakers invited, panels and workshops organized, meal tickets and banquet arrangements secured, sightseeing trips planned, and package deals for conference participants worked out. Rader was responsible for press coverage. Financial and accounting matters were assigned to Ned Ballengee. Linda Burgess helped finalize local arrangements.[27]

Not everything went according to the original proposal.[28] The coordinators had hoped to get Alex Haley, author of the popular book and TV miniseries *Roots*, as a keynote speaker, but apparently he was unavailable. More important, behind the scenes, considerable discussion had occurred at the western and the midwestern regionals over the question of whether there should be any "special recognitions" at the conference. According to Margaret Lawrence, Yesterday's Children founder Donna Cullom had opened the midwest regional with a statement that the coordinators had decided that "there would be no tributes at the conference and no recognition of any one individual adoption leader's work." Lawrence, who was present, responded to that statement. She thought it was a good idea, with one exception: Jean Paton. Lawrence asserted that "there was no way you could hold a national conference and not make a singular tribute to Jean Paton." Cullom strongly opposed the idea of a special tribute to Paton. She argued the point on the basis of equality: it was unfair to the other leaders. When the discussion ended, the midwest regional participants voted unanimously for a tribute of some kind, though the regional coordinators rejected the additional suggestion of a gift from everyone. Cullom carried her anti-tribute fight to the Philadelphia Forum, attempting to keep the group from even discussing the issue, but failed: it voted unanimously to honor Paton.[29]

In February 1979, Schmitt and Rader mailed out invitations and registration forms for the upcoming AAC conference. The organization was defined as consisting of "autonomous groups and individuals who wish to establish a network to effectively change the present structure in adoption." The registration form gave the location of the hotel and described the workshops and business meeting. It also announced the AAC officers: the National Coordinator was Anne Silber, and the Directors were Margaret Lawrence and Jean Paton.[30]

Silber wrote Paton in February, keeping her apprised of the modifications to the conference agenda. The only remaining task, she continued, was to draw up the constitution and the bylaws. Silber said she was asking everyone for input on the formation of the bylaws. She requested Paton's help on the project and suggested that they meet in person.[31]

In spite of Paton's sharp differences about the name, structure, and purpose of the new organization, she responded positively in March 1979 to Silber's request and took it upon herself to write bylaws for the AAC. In a short preamble to the bylaws, Paton stated that their "general purpose" was to assist "people in the population of adoption to find relief from the oppressions of the sealed record." The bylaws themselves were comprehensive, covering membership fees and categories, the election of officers, the Reunion file, referrals, newsletters, publicity, legislative matters, legal matters, educational functions, and the relationship between the national AAC and the regional affiliates. Paton suggested that the bylaws were a work in progress, not chiseled in stone, and presented them in a two-column format to permit readers to make suggestions alongside the proposals. But, belying her flexibility, she added that she "would not want to be associated with an organization whose bylaws were markedly different from these which are submitted."[32]

In the same month, Paton also demonstrated her commitment to the AAC by mailing the conference invitation and registration form to her *LOG* subscribers with a ringing endorsement. She declared that although the conference was very expensive, its value was "inestimable" and "was an opportunity which should not be missed." But Paton downplayed the importance of the workshops and other activities. For her, the significance of the first AAC conference was that it build her beloved community of adult adoptees. The "most important thing" about the conference was "learning to know one another and TO TRUST ONE ANOTHER." Why was this important? First, it was necessary to impress "the legitimate world" with the adoption reform movement's solidarity. Second, the trust was necessary to "work on things that have got to be worked on if we are to survive and succeed in freeing those who really want to be free, and who still need our help, very much."[33] Thus, from the very beginning, Paton and the AAC's major organizers disagreed about the purpose of both the conference and the organization.

On the morning of May 4, 1979, the American Adoption Congress kicked off its four-day inaugural conference at the Bellevue Hotel in Washington, D.C.[34] Slightly more than 200 members attended from at least thirty-two different triad search and support groups, with the big four—ALMA, CUB, Orphan Voyage, and Yesterday's Children—having the most members present. The first three days were filled with workshops and discussions on the most burning issues concerning the adoption reform movement: "Search Training"; "Post Search"; "Legislation and Intermediaries"; Physical, Social, and Emotional Needs in Adoption"; "Economics of Adoption"; "What Is 'Good Cause' for Opening Sealed Adoption Records"; "The Rights of Privacy with Personal and Professional Accountability."

Throughout it all, Jean Paton was the center of attention. On the conference's opening night, held at the Georgetown University Law Center, the AAC's Board of Directors—Nancy Schmitt, Margaret Lawrence, and Jean Paton—was introduced, along with the Regional Coordinators.[35] Immediately following, four keynote speakers addressed the conference, with Paton leading off.[36] A standing ovation greeted Paton's introduction.[37] The following Saturday morning, Paton spoke at the "Legislation and Intermediaries" session, and in the afternoon at the "Rights of Privacy" panel. That evening, at the conference banquet, she received a moving tribute prepared by Margaret Lawrence and Linda Burgess. The next day, Paton was a member of an eight-person panel assigned the task of questioning members of HEW's Model Adoption Legislation and Proceedings Panel, whom the AAC had invited to meet with them. This was followed in the evening by a two-hour after-dinner affair, billed as "A Talk with Jean Paton," in conjunction with a cheese and wine party. Jean had the spotlight to herself. On the last day of the conference, members were encouraged to attend a meeting of the Model Adoption Legislation and Proceedings Panel, which was considering the subject of open records.

In Paton's eyes, the conference was a huge success. She thought it was "a splendid experience" for the conference-goers. There was "much, much fraternity, sorority, [and] hugs all the time, warm and glowing smiles, expressions of satisfaction for having come."[38] As for her own participation, the conference was unprecedented. "I never had an experience like that before," she declared to Orphan Voyage members.[39] It was the first time that Paton had found herself in the company of so many dedicated adoption reformers, and she enjoyed immensely being recognized as the pioneer of the movement. "People looked at me with a sort of awe, for they knew I started it all, and I was recognized at the banquet with great enthusiasm and given a silver ladle."[40] When the audience gave her a standing ovation, Paton recounted that she "never felt so loved in my life."[41] Other good news included her appointment to the AAC's board of directors and the presence of over twenty ALMA members who were eagerly looking to join.[42] Paton distributed and sold many "Bastards are Beautiful" buttons, which were "proudly worn."[43] Many conference goers shared Paton's positive assessment. Susan Darke, coordinator of Happenings, a Massachusetts adoption search and support group, exclaimed, "WOW, what an experience, and one I will never forget." Darke added that "the biggest thrill came in meeting Jean Paton. Although we have worked together for almost five years now, it was the first time I saw the woman behind the name. She is everybody's mother. She gave birth to a nation of adoptees and because of her we now stand recognized."[44]

Other attendees, however, were less enthusiastic. Rae Johnson, southern regional coordinator and a member of Orphan Voyage, left the conference with mixed emotions. Although Johnson confessed that she found the workshops "extremely helpful," the speakers "intelligent," and the face-to-face meetings "terrific," she feared that there was too much dissension revealed to those who were unaware of such disagreement, and that this revelation did much harm to the movement. "We fought among ourselves; we treated our speakers with disrespect by not letting them speak their piece, then asking of discussion afterwards. We plotted and planned and threatened behind closed doors, almost giving people the *right* to call us children for life. It *was* childish." According to

Johnson, one of the biggest areas of contention was the issue of whether to use intermediaries in searching for natal family members. The conference resolved the issue in favor of allowing each group to decide for itself.[45]

Paton objected to this decision. Writing in *The LOG* immediately after the conference, she declared that her position on intermediaries had been "crystal clear" for a long time: "no obligatory intermediary, only one chosen, and even then used very rarely by the seeker." Paton's objection to leaving the question up to a group to decide centered on taking the decision away from the individual, leaving the adult adoptee with no voice. This was an intolerable situation. "We have been voiceless too long. This is our problem. What on earth would induce any of us to muffle the desires of those we seek to 'help'? What has come over people? Do they want to be social workers. If so, they should leave the movement and not subject people to their uncertain motivations."[46]

Paton's disagreements with and protests against the AAC at the very outset of the organization's birth would multiply and continue for the rest of her life. Reconstructing the whole story now, unfortunately, is difficult: important activists, such as Donna Cullom, have passed away; others cannot be located; memories of participants have faded; Paton's correspondence is thin and cryptic during this period; and most of the records of the AAC are lost or unavailable. But it is possible to reconstruct some broad outlines about the early development of the AAC and the resulting factional divisions. What emerges from the surviving evidence is that right from the start Jean Paton and Margaret Lawrence were at odds with the regional coordinators on how to run the organization. Within two weeks of the end of the conference, Lawrence wrote to Dirck Brown, one of the three western regional coordinators, practically accusing him of staging a coup against the newly appointed board of directors, consisting of herself, Paton, and Schmitt. In particular, she upbraided Brown for scheduling the next AAC national conference without notifying the board.[47] Lawrence's accusation was as inaccurate as it was unfair. Not only had representatives of the western region notified the board of directors of their intention to host the next national conference in Santa Monica, California, in May 1980 but board member Nancy Schmitt had sent a questionnaire to the AAC membership requesting them to give approval for the meeting in Santa Monica and also asking them to express their preference for biannual national conferences of the entire AAC with annual regional conferences.[48]

Lawrence was opposed to any meeting being held so soon after the one in D.C. There were more important things to accomplish, what she considered "the real things," such as establishing the AAC's structure and organization in different regions of the country. For both Lawrence and Paton, the issue of ad-

ministrative processes, defined by written bylaws, the democratic electoral process, and, and as we shall see, financial accountability, was a cardinal principle
that took precedence over anything else.[49] Again, some of Lawrence's charges
were inaccurate and unfair. Immediately after the inaugural 1979 AAC conference, for example, the board of directors appointed a committee to draft bylaws.[50] Perhaps Lawrence's dissatisfaction stemmed from the AAC's refusal to
accept the bylaws that Paton had written.

Paton was in agreement with Lawrence about the need for the AAC to have
a set of formal bylaws. She also fervently believed that they should be distributed to as many people as possible. Otherwise, she wrote Virginia Rader in September 1979, "There will be no effective AAC." Individual membership was the
key to success, and Paton reiterated the importance of nullifying the influence
of groups within the organization, though she was pessimistic about achieving
this goal.[51] Regional director Colleen Hogan sent a rejoinder to Paton's charges
of political intrigue and conspiracy at the AAC conference. She pointedly and
correctly told Paton that the business of writing up the bylaws had not been assigned to the initial directors. Instead, the bylaws committee of each region was
given this assignment, and the bylaws had been submitted to Nancy Schmitt
before August 6, according to committee directions.[52] Paton paid no heed to
Hogan, and in November noted to Nancy Sitterly that the AAC had not made
much progress, due to the perennial problem of getting people to work coop-
eratively over great distances. She informed Sitterly that her patience had worn
thin. As a result, she was going to contact some of her own more responsible
correspondents to enlarge their network—Paton had in mind dividing the
country into six districts—and take over the responsibility for helping adult
adoptees in need. She asked Sitterly if she was interested in joining her in this
endeavor. In effect, by proposing a shadow organization either alongside or on
top of the AAC, Paton appeared already contemplating abandoning the organization should it fail.[53]

During 1981, the constant infighting over AAC political developments coupled with Paton's daily managing of Orphan Voyage began to take its toll. As
the New Year dawned, Paton announced to a correspondent that she had "no
personal life at all anymore."[54] She had sent out hardly any Christmas cards for
the past two years. Paton blamed "the work for this, draining out all personal
life and relationships." She was exhausted, at her wits' end: there was so much
routine work to do, "which should not be done in a routine way. I see no way out
of it." Earlier plans to delegate the work to other people were not working out;
people made promises, but few kept them.

A few months later, Paton informed Jay Swearingen, founder of the Tampa,

Florida, branch of Orphan Voyage, that she was healthy, but "I have had burn-out for some time." She announced that she was going to stop publishing *The LOG*. She was trying to "lift the load" from her back by only writing letters, which helped her unwind and "be herself again." Paton confessed, "It has been a long, long ordeal, with many painful times, and many discouragements." Yet she could not let go of the work completely. There would always be "the mail and phone calls, and a desire to respond"; she would substitute pamphlets for *The LOG*. Paton thought the course of adoption reform was irreversible, but asserted that she was "going to resume my own life, there is no alternative."[55] Toward the end of the year, she confided in Swearingen that she continued "to feel quietly desperate." Both the mail and her age increased. Paton hoped to assemble a committee to begin to take over Orphan Voyage's functions, but the plan was not put forward in any detail.[56]

While Paton was contemplating reducing her workload during 1981, the AAC held a national conference in Kansas City, Missouri, May 27–31. Paton attended and was awarded an honorary lifetime membership in the AAC.[57] She also presented a paper, later published in her pamphlet series, entitled "The Adoption Colony." It set out the idea that by the 1950s (rather than the 1930s, as she had once written), liberal theorizers, denigrating the "permanent value in kinship systems which mankind had developed over millennia," decided to experiment on the "Broken Family" and cure its ills through "the healing arts." The experimenters tried foster care, which was a failure, so "their labors moved sideways to adoption," where the child's psychological problems could be delayed and where family restoration could be prevented. The problem of illegitimacy offered the social practitioners another opportunity "to build a new Society, by the pursuit of adoption." When criticized, the "social practitioners" resisted intensely. Thus, the kinship family continued to be weakened and attenuated by this liberal social experiment, which was supported by legislatures and judges. Paton ended her paper not with a call to arms to open adoption records, but with an opaque, lyrical call for blood kinship:

> There is, however, a faint hope of survival. The principal supporting plan—sealed adoption—has produced a viper in its bosom. Some would so term it. Others might say it is an element of survival, an instinctual thrust of basic value coming up out of the innocent mouths of the principal victims of the institution—the adopted. This voice, this plea, this protest asks for kindred. The question then is: Can they be found and can a connection be made, and can the healing take place?[58]

In addition to papers and workshops, AAC '81, as it was dubbed, put the finishing touches on unifying the national organization. Representatives from the nine national regions met and "emerged from their respective meetings—bleary-eyed and exhausted—in the wee hours of the morning, but nonetheless smiling triumphantly" in having elected officials and ratified the proposed bylaws.[59] Jean Paton had been left out of the deliberations.[60] Penny Callan Partridge, adult adoptee, poet, and cofounder of the Adoption Forum of Philadelphia, was elected the first president of the AAC, and Tom Allington, the president of a Kansas City, Missouri, adult adoptees organization, vice president.[61] The AAC also voted to publish its first newsletter, using the medium of the *Open A.R.M.S. Quarterly*, an adoptee search newsletter published by Bob O'Dell out of North Platte, Nebraska.[62]

The fall 1981 issue of the *Open A.R.M.S. Quarterly* reprinted President Partridge's acceptance speech. She began by defining and explaining the AAC's purposes. It was a coalition of individuals and groups throughout North America who were to coalesce and grow together, and who cared about "making adoption more open" in a variety of ways. The AAC was also an organization of self-education about adoption openness, dedicated to educating the adoption community and the general public on the same topic. Looking to the future, Partridge viewed the upcoming twelve months as a "setting up" or a "trying out" year. Progress would be determined by how many people joined and actively supported the AAC. The biggest dream of the board of directors for the future, Partridge told her listeners, was increasing the AAC's membership. By the summer of 1981 the organization counted 100 individual members and had collected over $1,000 in annual dues. Partridge announced that in addition to the $10 regular individual membership fee, the board had initiated more membership categories, including $20 for "Sustaining Individual Members" and $150 for "Life Individual Members." Moreover, there was a minimum $25 fee for "Affiliate Organizations" and, for those groups who could afford it, a $150 fee to become a "Sustaining Affiliate Organization Member."[63]

In July, Paton wrote Partridge a two-page litany of suggestions and complaints.[64] She began with her old bugbear of objecting to the AAC's group membership category: it discouraged individual dues, said Paton, and obscured the relationship between the individual and the national organization. In contrast, an individual membership gave the person an opportunity to know firsthand the AAC's goals and accomplishments, which was of the utmost importance. Paton also urged Partridge to create a formal budget in order to clarify how much money the AAC had on hand and to anticipate future revenues and expenditures. She also suggested that the AAC seek tax-exempt status. In addition, Paton denounced the exorbitant expense of the annual meeting, estimating the cost to the AAC at $20,000, a complaint she would frequently repeat. Instead, she proposed that there be three regional meetings—in the West, Midwest, and East—every other year and a national meeting in alternate years.

Paton's "greatest priority," however, was for the AAC to set up a clearing house and referral system. What she meant was the AAC had to take over the job Orphan Voyage had been doing for the past twenty-eight years. In fact, Paton stated that one of her original motives for suggesting a national conference was "to iron out the referral process and set up something of a clearing house." But she had not been on the program committee, and thus nothing had been done about it. Yet, as she had always believed, this—providing service to the hapless individual adoptee who had no place to turn—had to be the heart of the AAC, and it was the key to the organization's success, as it would increase the membership. Finally, Paton pushed for an education committee that would be strictly focused on educating the adult adoptee, not the general public, at least at the outset. "When we know who we are, and what we want to do, then and only then will we have something to educate the world with." Paton closed the letter by asking Partridge to "please forgive this hard-headed, warm-hearted gal who is so weary of doing so much drudgery, and waiting for you kids to take hold." She asked the new AAC president not to view the letter "as criticism but as hope."

Paton never received a reply to her July letter to Partridge. But the AAC issue continued to fester in her mind. Six months later, Paton wrote another letter to Partridge and sent copies to forty other people.[65] Paton was angry, and in her letter, she vented her frustration. The AAC had ignored "the principal issue," which was "the freedom of the adopted person to grow into a true maturity with knowledge of his roots presented to him at an early enough age for them to be incorporated into his psyche in a positive and constructive way." Paton did not elaborate on how the AAC should implement such a policy. Furthermore, the AAC's efforts to gain access to adoption records by the age of majority did not meet the adult adoptee's real need. Nothing about the AAC pleased her: it wasted money, the bylaws needed reconsideration, the voice of the adult adoptee was suppressed, and the people who did the real work [Jean Paton?] were "largely unhonored, uncompensated (except by satisfaction), and have no voice in the plans for the Congress." In short, Paton declared, the AAC had "no stated plans, no stated purpose, no reliance on the really important people among us, [and] no honor or consideration to those who have carried the load for the last five years."

Three weeks later, Paton wrote Jay Swearingen, saying she imagined that her letter had set the phones buzzing. She believed that the response would be mixed: about a half-dozen people, perhaps more, would agree with her; unnumbered others were "probably petulantly angry" at her allegedly "disruptive criticism." The important point, Paton stated, was the bylaws that she wrote in 1979. They set forth the purposes of the AAC: service to all individuals and groups; the criterion, helpfulness. But, she lamented, no one in the AAC cared.[66]

In March 1982 she again wrote Swearingen, stating that she now looked upon the "AAC as a bunch of largely undisciplined people."[67] With the announcement of the fourth AAC conference in San Antonio, scheduled for June 3–6, Paton decided not to go. In attendance would "be only the snarling old guard."[68] But by April 5, she had changed her mind about attending because, as she told Parent Finders board member Mary Jane Brinkos, it represented an opportunity for like-minded people to associate with each other. That was why she would not attend the seminars or workshops: so she could have time to talk to others.[69]

With the AAC San Antonio conference looming, Paton decided to send "the board members or whatever they are, a brief series of analyses of the situation," which would provide them with a basis for discussion when she met with them. In her first letter to the AAC board members, Paton's central concern was to demand that the board reconsider the purpose of the organization, which she totally mischaracterized: "The AAC is a loosely-knit grouping of afflicted people in our society who are struggling to become whole, by their own means and the help of anyone they are able to find. They discover they are not alone, and at the same time they discover reconciliation, and the importance of kinship, and the fact of human heredity, all these special discoveries are needed by society, by a society which has gone awry in its overemphasis on the individual and at the same time on the State." Paton had always differed from other adoption reform activists in her emphasis that adult adoptees had a unique contribution to make to society and that society needed them. She believed that the mission of the adoption reform movement was to educate society through conversation, which had been going on for a long time through media accounts of reunions, letters to elected representatives, talks with adoptive parents' groups, and other such activities. It was the daily labor of search and reconciliation, framing a narrative based on the value of kinship and heredity, that would ultimately release adult adoptees from the oppression of sealed adoption records. She insisted that the AAC was best conceived "as a service organization of afflicted people who acknowledge their affliction, who reach out into the world for something more satisfying and comforting, and who have made the immense discovery that illegitimacy is not a permanent condition, if it is overcome by reconciliation."[70]

The following week, Paton sent off a second letter to members of the AAC board, this time on the subject of underage searching.[71] Here Paton called adoption under the sealed records system "a social death," harming both adopted people in their maturity and birth parents during their long years of not knowing about the child they relinquished. Paton was of the opinion that the AAC was "a movement without focus" unless the organization formulated a policy to spare "our brethren" the pain "we have been through." Such a policy, declared Paton, must begin in the adoptee's childhood in order to help both the adult adoptee and the birth parent. She placed the principal responsibility for facilitating the relationship with the birth parents on adoptive parents. The AAC's job should be to prepare adoptive parents to expect an approach from the natal parent at some time after the adoption.

Paton fired off a third and final letter to the AAC's board members two weeks before the San Antonio conference. She specified five things that the AAC needed to put into place: a statement of purpose for workers in the field, priorities for the board, budget prospects in light of the priorities, program evaluation, and setting standards. Paton concluded by declaring that in some ways the AAC had fallen down on the job, but in other ways it had performed a miracle. However, the age of miracles had passed, and it was time to face the reality of the situation. "No one in their right mind" was going to donate "a lot of money or even a little mite until we can say clearly what we stand for and how we are going to go about it."

Paton's suggestions were clearly at odds with the AAC's mission. But she was wrong in accusing the organization of being without direction. At its first meeting, the board of directors announced that it had filed articles of incorporation with bylaws, applied for federal tax-exempt status, and appointed Betty Jean Lifton director at large to apply for grants and Joseph Harrington chairman of legislative affairs.[72] By December 1981, the board announced that it had retained the firm of Harris Ragan Management Corporation, which would design a fund-raiser in support of a campaign to open adoption records, and that it had formed a committee to support open adoption.[73] In March 1982, Harrington reported on various state legislative bills affecting adoption records and the effort by William Pierce and the National Committee for Adoption to craft a Model Registry Bill regarding adoption, which in Harrington's opinion was "as bad a bill as one could think (25-year-old minimum age for adoptee, permission of both birth parents for information to be released on any parent, and counseling for both parties, adoptee and birth parent)."[74] The following month the AAC announced that it had retained Leon Freidman, a New York lawyer, to work pro bono as legal advisor to the AAC.[75] Clearly, Paton and the AAC's board of directors had different visions of what the organization's mission should be.

Paton left Cedaredge in June 1982 for the AAC conference in San Antonio with some hope for reform. Although not many AAC board members had responded to her letters, few raised any serious objection.[76] Paton thus believed that her three letters, sent in advance to AAC board members analyzing the organization's problems, would provide the basis for their discussions in San Antonio. In addition, Paton looked forward to talking at her conference book stall with like-minded activists, such as Jayne Askin, whose book *Search: A Handbook for Adoptees and Birthparents* Paton admired.[77] At the conference, Paton dramatized the plight of adult adoptees one day by walking around the Hyatt Hotel on the River Walk wearing chains surrounding her body.[78] In addition, the AAC leadership honored Paton by conferring on her an "honorary lifetime membership."[79] But on the whole, the San Antonio conference left a sour taste in Paton's mouth. On Hyatt stationery, she melodramatically wrote, "This organization has come very close to destroying itself by refusing to let true disagreements come to the surface where they might be resolved," an oblique reference to her inability to meet with the AAC board of directors to air her grievances.[80]

Paton remained silent about her experience at San Antonio for almost fifteen months, a highly unusual amount of time for her not to discuss with others, either publicly or privately, major events in her life. Finally, in September 1983, in one of the only comments Paton made about the San Antonio conference, she stated that she had "felt repulsed by some people in AAC." She was unable to identify them but suggested to Patty O'Gorman, founder of the group Liberal Education for Adoptive Families and one-term director of the AAC's Midwest Region, that these individuals were motivated out of jealousy or resentment of her criticism of the organization. Paton claimed that the worst consequence of their hostility was not its effect on her ego, which was only temporary, but that these people rejected her "assets to the movement," which she itemized as "Ideas, practices, [and] engineering ways to get things done." Rejecting her, Paton wrote, was self-defeating. She believed that movement people were hurting themselves as well as other triad members by doing so. Paton understood the psychology of these people, but it grieved her "to see the movement falling into the hands of people who talk strong but whose hearts are cold."[81] Even the AAC's bestowal of a second Honorary Lifetime Membership award rang hollow. When she received notification of the honor, along with a scroll, from AAC president Sophie Elvert, she could not help pointing out that she had received the same award in Kansas City a couple of years previously and that her name was again misspelled, adding, "my name has never been spelled correctly." She scornfully commented, "So much for history."[82]

During the first six months of 1983, Paton received several reports of serious factional fighting among the AAC leadership, with charges and countercharges of corruption and false statements being hurled about.[83] Paton's disenchantment with the AAC grew deeper. With Jay Swearingen, Paton began to explore the possibility of starting up a national newsletter, to fill the void left by her discontinuance of The LOG and the AAC's neglect of the issue.[84] By June 1983, she wrote to one correspondent, "the AAC is a disaster, and I am not sure if anything will revolutionize it."[85] Paton was not prepared to break totally with the AAC—which, after all, was her own creation—but she was close.

Six months later, in January 1984, Paton wrote her good friend Joan Vanstone, "I despise the AAC."[86] The source of this vehement declaration would hardly be surprising to people who knew of Paton's visceral dislike of professionals and experts, but it was a new attack on the AAC's actions: its love of professionals corrupted the organization. Instead of emulating Orphan Voyage in helping adult adoptees search for their kindred, AAC leaders "preferred sitting on the laps of professionals, and pretending to be almost-social workers."[87] To Jayne Askin she complained that the AAC had become "make-believe social workers, semi-professionals. It is a farce, but of course it is also tragic, as the people who want help are still writhing in the pit not knowing where to take hold."[88] Paton likened the leaders' activities to "playing Statue. . . . You strike a pose, each person does, and someone decides which is the best one."[89]

Again, Paton's criticism was unwarranted. She seemed to forget or ignore what she had written in her 1979 bylaws for the AAC. Although the 1979 bylaws stated that membership was open to "any adoption triad member seeking reunion with another person from whom he was separated by adoption" or "any group" involved in search efforts, Paton also included in the bylaws a category labeled "Associate Memberships," which allowed in the AAC "any individual, although not of the adoption world, who wishes to participate if only by membership in the work of the Congress."[90] No one in the AAC replied to Paton to remind her of her own words.

From Paton's perspective, even the AAC's program had become subverted by the infiltration of social work. In July 1984, the word "bonding" jumped out at her from the program of the AAC regional conference, which was to be held in September in Albuquerque, New Mexico. As she read the program, Paton wrote Sally File that she "could scarcely believe what I was seeing, professionalism gone rampant." She suggested to File that she was thinking of wearing a black armband or perhaps widow's weeds to express her "utter sorrow."[91]

Nevertheless, despite Paton's disenchantment, she continued to attend AAC national conferences. She eagerly invited her good friend, New Zealand adoption activist Mary Iwanek, to the 1986 national conference in Milwaukee.[92] Iwanek accepted Paton's invitation. After several years' correspondence, it was their first meeting in person. Iwanek found both the conference and Paton "absolutely wonderful." It was the first time Iwanek had attended such a large gathering of adult adoptees and birth parents, and she found it extremely valuable to talk and listen to the participants. She also came away feeling proud of the progress New Zealand had made in opening adoption records. In comparing the two countries, she came to realize that "we in New Zealand, although a small country down under, were not behind in our thinking and practice." She was, however, "somewhat shocked" about the degree to which private enterprise was involved in the search process in the United States and the concomitant high costs involved for those who wanted to trace their families of origin. Iwanek could not help thinking that the professional searchers might be caught up in a conflict of interest: as long as people were making a living from searching, they probably would not put much effort into changing a law that would negatively affect their income. Also off-putting to Iwanek was what she saw as the conservative nature of "the professionals" at the conference. She wrote, "if those attending were the liberal thinkers I would hate to think what some of the others are like.[93]

Paton shared Iwanek's feelings about the conference, but for her all the value came from meeting Iwanek. She told her that she had thought of her many times, and especially at the high moments of the conference, which Paton numbered two: "As we met at the banquet full of joy each in the other, to the tune of applause and all that ..." She went on to articulate feelings about Iwanek that she never expressed with any other person in the movement, due primarily to the passage of the New Zealand open records law, flawed as it was. "If the people there really understood what it meant that we met, well and good. For me it was the establishment on earth of a long hope that there would come someone who knew and cared to the necessary extent. You came." Iwanek also reinforced Paton's hardening belief that social workers had no place in the AAC.

Several months later, in December 1986, Paton's disgust at the increasing participation of nonadopted persons in AAC activities boiled over and prompted her to type a four-page, single-spaced "Open Letter" denouncing the program for the May 1987 AAC national conference, to be held in Boston.[94] She had looked almost in vain for adopted people who would be participating in the conference; she could only find two, and those were among the ranks of the AAC leadership. After all these years, she noted despairingly, the program lacked "a dominant presentation from the point of view of adopted people." Paton firmly believed that professionals should discuss matters concerning adoption, but they should do so at their own annual meetings "rather than at our conferences which are suppose to be helping the thousands and thousands of suffering people in our world to have permanent and profound assistance." Worse, she found no references in the program to the most important subjects: how to get adoption records open, the motivation for sealing the records in the first place, and the issue of illegitimacy.

Finally, Paton used the "Open Letter" to address the question of whether there existed "an adoption syndrome, a combination of traits embedded in the adopted person," which she depicted as "passive, hostile, and dependent."[95] In extreme cases, Paton asserted, such behavioral traits could result in arson or murder. This controversial issue had first come to public attention in September 1977 when author and adoption therapist Betty Jean Lifton wrote a letter to the editor of the *New York Times* pointing out that "Son of Sam" serial killer David Berkowitz was adopted and asserting that that fact played an important role in explaining his criminal behavior.[96] David Kirschner, a clinical psychiatrist, coined the term "adopted child syndrome" in 1978, defining the syndrome as a cluster of behaviors that included theft, pathological lying, learning disabilities, fire setting, promiscuity, defiance of authority, preoccupation with excessive fantasy, lack of impulse control, and running away from home.[97] In her letter Paton made no mention of Lifton or Kirschner, noting instead that she had written about this issue in an article that had appeared in a 1955 issue of the *Western Journal of Surgery, Obstetrics and Gynecology*. Further research she had conducted on development of the brain in adult adoptees confirmed her belief in its reality. She concluded, "there need be no dispute about the existence of the syndrome." Paton's "Open Letter" fell on deaf ears. There is little evidence that it had any effect on the 1987 AAC national conference in Boston, though Paton believed that it had provoked many people.[98]

In 1988, at the age of eighty, Jean Paton went "through a rather awful, quiet disturbed year" in a deep depression, set off by a minor event that roused in her "a fantasy of abandonment."[99] It came as a complete surprise. Paton thought that she had weathered successfully the psychological malaise of "genealogical bewilderment" those lifelong feelings of rejection, confusion, and low self-esteem that had periodically sapped her self-confidence and her ability to stay on task and to forge long-term friendships.[100] One of the reasons for her surprise, Paton admitted, was that she never let herself become too aware of her feelings of abandonment; she was too busy "caught up in the lives of others," which allowed her to avoid direct contact with her interior self.[101] Another part of the problem, she recognized, was her "deep and constant denial."[102]

It took Paton three months to figure out what was wrong: that she had unearthed her "bottom forgotten experience, yes of abandonment."[103] She lived in a trance throughout the summer and then "wrestled with this situation as with a devil or an angel." Paton took the rest of the year to shake it off, "until it broke like a fever."[104] But, Paton confessed, she should have known better. As she acknowledged to one correspondent, "All of us in adoption are slow growers."[105] Two years later, looking back on her life after the depression, she saw "great effort and courage, but also a vast sea of immaturity." Still, Paton found the experience ultimately a positive one. She had learned of the "frantic desire people have to cover it up, to never see it again, no matter how it influences our lives, shortens them, pushes in our margins so that we can cope."[106] Just as important, Paton had finally "walked up to the door of my terror at the age of four months and opened it."[107] She now believed that "I am truly open through all of myself" and attributed her good fortune to her strong physique and perseverance.[108] And yet Paton felt she remained alone intellectually. No matter how many people she knew, no matter how close psychologically she felt toward others, "when it came to thinking things through and getting a perspective, I am truly alone."[109]

Aiding Paton's recovery from depression was a friendship she developed for a short period—in 1988 and 1989—through an extensive correspondence with the AAC's newly elected president, Kate Burke. Paton met Burke at the 1988 AAC regional conference in Atlanta. There, Burke enthusiastically embraced Paton. She told her that she had admired Paton for many years, had read everything she wrote, and was in total agreement with her. On parting, Burke promised to write Paton.[110]

In her first letter, Burke informed Paton that now that she was president of the AAC she found herself "lost and frustrated" because the "AAC seems to have drifted away from its constituents." On the issue of social workers, Burke felt they were irrelevant to the adoption reform movement. She did not hate them; she was not afraid of them; nor would she be rude to them. She simply believed that "they have nothing to do whatsoever with the fight to open our records." As to her future plans for the AAC, Burke vowed to return the organization "back to the people it belongs to—the adoptee and birthparent (and adoptive parent, I suppose)." She recognized that this would be an uphill battle. The AAC was an organization that merely hosted conferences. Unfortunately, Burke ruefully confessed, conferences were the only means by which the AAC supported itself, "and in spite of the professionals, they are a forum for the Triad to gather and network."[111]

Paton responded enthusiastically to this kindred spirit. She declared, "Every inch of your letter sounded good to me."[112] But then, characteristically, Paton qualified her exuberance by adding, "except that part about the rationale of the conferences." She agreed with Burke that money was needed, but not for conferences. Instead, Paton declared that if the AAC followed Orphan Voyage's example, sufficient funds could be raised through a newsletter. More radically, Paton put forth the novel idea that "social work should pay for what they have done." She explained that movement leaders should ask adoption agencies for contributions to fund their adoption reform work. The AAC also needed to stop depending on professionals and "eat humble pie."

A month later, Burke responded, "I love writing to you, Jean," because "it gives me an opportunity to sit back and take an overview of what is going on."[113] She had many ideas. With Joe Soll, author, psychiatrist, adoption reformer, and director of the Adoption Counseling Center, Burke had decided that Paton should attend the next AAC conference in New York City. She was needed there "to make us look at ourselves a little harder." The organization would provide financial help, if necessary, and grant her free registration. In her first letter, Paton had warned Burke that if she attended the New York conference, she would reprise her San Antonio performance and wear chains: "I could not attend otherwise."[114]

Burke assured Paton that she could wear them. She added that the speech she was going to give in New York would "rattle THEIR chains." Burke was planning to announce a march on Washington. She believed that such an event would serve to both unite the movement in an unprecedented manner, and secondarily, garner extensive media attention. A successful march would dissolve the egos and political factionalism that bedeviled the AAC. She asked Paton for advice on the Washington march. Burke ended the letter by stating that at the upcoming AAC executive board meeting in San Francisco she was going to force its members to make a statement of purpose. If the board decided that the AAC's mission was only to educate and put on conferences then, she declared, she would resign.

Paton wrote Burke back immediately, urging her not to resign too hastily if things did not go her way at first. She readily admitted that Burke was faced with serious problems, but cannily suggested that instead of resigning, she put crucial matters to a vote of the membership after some discussion; that method of circumventing the leadership, said Paton, would be more effective and more helpful than a resignation.[115] To Mary Iwanek, Paton reported enthusiastically that Burke was "a very intelligent and rather worldly person" who was going to demand a clear statement of purpose. Paton predicted that "sparks will be flying."[116]

As for Burke's idea of a march on Washington, Paton threw cold water on it. She noted that the idea had first been raised as early as May 1986 at the Milwaukee AAC conference, and then was bought up again a year later, suggesting that it was just an old idea not worth pursuing. But setting aside that objection, Paton mused hypothetically: What if the march was taken up? She answered with a series of pessimistic questions: Were there sufficient people intelligent enough to work out all the details? Would enough people show up? What if it rained? Were adopted people experienced enough? Was the march too big of an event to attempt? Paton wished that the movement had conducted smaller marches in the past in order to be ready for such a big one as Burke was proposing. In short, based on her long experience, Paton offered Burke little encouragement about the plans for a march on Washington by members of the adoption triad.

Undeterred, Burke replied to Paton three weeks later with news that left her "extremely excited and also a trifle scared."[117] She had convinced the AAC board to issue a statement of purpose for open records and also a strong statement against the Levin Bill for a national adoption registry, should he reintroduce it in Congress. The AAC was also going to declare the first week in August of 1989 as "National Open Records Week," which would be celebrated by a march on Washington, D.C., beginning in New York City during that last week of July and ending in the nation's capital during the first week of August. Moreover, the board approved working on a five-year plan to lobby all of the state legislatures to open adoption records. Burke exulted, "the poor board didn't know what hit them. They came to do the same boring stuff they had been doing for years and left vibrating with new energy and ideas. It was truly Triad members taking charge of their destiny." She added that the meeting broke up with "everyone referring to 'the old AAC' and 'the new AAC.'"

Paton's response to Burke's successful meeting with the AAC board was strangely muted. She did not offer her congratulations, but instead attempted to put herself in the place of the board members as they realized that their destiny was at long last in their own hands. Rhetorically, she asked, "How did they come to think otherwise."[118]

Most of her letter, however, was devoted to two more criticisms of the AAC. The first one concerned the subject of fees for service and paid consultants. As early as 1959, Paton announced her philosophy toward the place of money in adoption: she did not believe in charging adult adoptees for counseling or any other services involved in helping people in their search for natal family members.[119] Twenty years later and more experienced, Paton had shifted her view on fees slightly: it now involved a moral calculus, a position that remained constant for the rest of her life. Money, she believed, was necessary to carry on the business of helping adult adoptees, and thus people were entitled to be paid for working.[120] Still, Paton declared in 1982, she had never taken any money for personal use. "I do not believe in charging for wisdom, for caring, for a bit of listening time."[121] She believed that people who dealt with "our brethren in affliction" had an obligation to them, which was all the greater because they knew of their pain.[122] She increasingly juxtaposed her own financial practices with those of the new, commercial breed of paid consultants. Paton admitted that she took membership fees for many years, but justified them as a necessary expense for the paper and postage of Orphan Voyage's newsletter, *The LOG*, and her research trips across the country.[123]

However, by the late 1970s, Paton feared that some search consultants were now demanding unreasonable prices, which could lead to "making profit out of someone's misery, a dastardly thing to do."[124] To help make her point, Paton was fond of quoting from the pages of William Langland's *Piers Plowman*, the late medieval English allegorical poem, on priests receiving "indulgences" from people who confessed to them:

Ye who feast upon the sins of men
Unless ye shed tears of compassion on them
Ye shall vomit up with torments
Those meats you now feast upon amid pleasure.

Paton even had coined her own saying for this type of behavior: "There's no money in cure."[125]

Paton was particularly alarmed with the increasing popularity of the California group Independent Search Consultants (ISC), founded in 1979 by adoption reformer Patricia Sanders. ISC was a nonprofit corporation, with certified consultants across the country (one had to be an expert searcher to be certified by ISC). When a searcher contacted ISC, the person was put in touch with a consultant who was knowledgeable of that particular area or state. The ISC consultant also provided the client with the name of a search group, if one was available.[126] Paton respected Sanders and her work for adult adoptees, but nevertheless believed that there was no need "for such a pretentious organization." In particular, Paton objected to ISC's exorbitant fees, singling out the $15 per half hour it charged. Not only was this an outrageous sum to Paton, but inherent in the process was the temptation for the participants to think that the consultant was indispensable to the task. In contrast, Paton believed that those engaged in "the art of helping" should encourage adult adoptees to conduct the search themselves, with guidance.[127] For Paton, the process of searching was just as important to an adult adoptee's psychological health and sense of identity as the end result of reuniting with original family members.

By the mid-1980s, Paton not only was objecting to profiteering by paid expert searchers and consultants, but was pronouncing them "quite unacceptable" because the practice divided the movement between volunteers and experts.[128] Three years later, in 1988, she noted with alarm that some AAC board members were also acting as paid consultants: Paton had discovered that the new editor of the AAC newsletter had applied to be a paid intermediary consultant with the Georgia Welfare Department. Although the application was eventually turned down by the Georgia legislature, the incident provided Paton with "clear evidence of my speculations about Pat Sanders' Search Consultants (the AAC editor is one of her group)." She concluded that the ISC was "clearly a cult acting within the AAC but not responsible to it, infiltrating wherever it can."[129] To Peggy Dorn, founder of the Dallas branch of Orphan Voyage, Paton asserted that the AAC should "divest itself of all board members who are consultants." She suggested that the AAC issue a statement that no paid searchers were to be policy makers, extending the rule down to regional directors. Paton perceived a conflict of interest in the two roles of paid consultant and activist for opening adoption records. She observed to Dorn, "those who make this kind of money don't want the records open, and that is understandable."[130] Opening adoption records would deprive them of an important source of income. Every year, she informed Burke, subscribers of *The LOG* were able to read Orphan Voyage's detailed financial report, which had been validated by the IRS. Paton added, "Now that I live at the poverty level these reports to [the] IRS are not needed."[131]

The second policy that Paton criticized the AAC for was its refusal to recognize able people in the movement, specifically its rejection of Lori Carangelo's request that she be allowed to list the organization as one of her liaisons. Carangelo had been involved in adoption reform for more than twenty years. On December 17, 1968, Carangelo had given birth in Connecticut to an infant boy. According to Carangelo, several weeks thereafter, while feeling distraught and feverish, she sought temporary care for him, but social workers in the Children's Center, an adoption agency in Hamden, Connecticut, tricked her into signing a revocation of her parental rights. Over the course of the many years Carangelo thereafter spent searching for her child, she was radicalized by the sealed adoption law governing her son's adoption.[132] In 1989, two years after being reunited with her son, she founded Americans for Open Records (AmFOR) and began publishing "The Open Record," a militantly anti-adoption newsletter dedicated to abolishing the system of sealed adoption records.[133] To Burke, Paton praised a proposed law to open adoption records, which Carangelo's group had pro-

posed, for having as much substance on one page "as any single page I have seen."
She suggested that the AAC should open its board to people who acted separately from the organization. Paton herself had always welcomed such liaisons
with anybody, such as Carangelo, "who was hitting the nail with the hammer." It
was what the AAC needed, Paton urged. The AAC "should give its blessing" to
Carangelo's request.[134]

Burke's response, almost two months later, on March 24, was defensive and
acerbic.[135] In January 1989 the AAC had mailed out an election ballot with the
names and credentials of six nominees for three director-at-large positions, the
majority of them paid consultants.[136] Burke justified the right of AAC members
who also were employed by ISC to run for national office by pointing to their
selfless behavior. Many of them, Burke declared, were leaders of adoption search
and support groups who put in long hours of volunteer work for the AAC.
Burke denied they overcharged adult adoptees, maintaining that most of them
performed a search for free or for a nominal amount. Turning to Lori Carangelo
and AmFOR, Burke disagreed with Paton's high opinion of the fiery adoption
activist and instead roundly criticized her. She accused Carangelo's literature
of being "filled with wrong information—and flat out lies." Her inflammatory
letters and telephone calls, Burke informed Paton, had already lost the AAC
sympathetic legislators in several states, including Texas. In short, Burke stated,
she personally felt that what Carangelo was doing was "hurting the Adoption
Reform Movement and not helping."

In a veiled warning to Paton to stop her critical approach to adoption reform,
Burke declared, "As long as we concentrate on what is wrong with the AAC or
any other organization we are going to stay dead in the water." She asked Paton,
"How about we look at some of the things we have done right and what we will
be doing right in the future?" On the whole, Burke believed that reform was
beginning to look up; her job was "to concentrate and nurture those seeds of activism instead of going backwards." She vowed that she was not going to spend
her time making the AAC "perfect" while accomplishing nothing. Burke reiterated that the AAC was going to march on Washington, D.C. Recognizing the
sharpness of tone, Burke closed her letter with an attempt to make amends and
reassure Paton that they were on the same side. She apologized and brushed off
her criticism as rambling. In truth, Burke wrote, she considered Paton a friend
and had just poured out what was in her heart. She so much wanted to achieve
the goal of access to adoption records. She quickly assured Paton that in her
presidential address, at the AAC conference in New York City, she was going to
set people straight about the organization's mission: "We are not a search and
support group. . . . Search is not why we exist. That is why other groups exist.

We exist only to change the adoption laws. We must stop confusing the two." She looked forward to seeing Paton in New York and closed the letter "Fondly."

Burke's March 24 letter to Paton marked a fatal turning point in their collegial relationship. It arrived right after an exchange of letters between Paton and Pat Sanders exacerbated tensions over the issue of paid consultants to new heights. Sanders again defended the right to be a member of ISC and a candidate for national office in the AAC, and she emphatically denied there was a conflict of interest between fighting for opening the records and being a paid searcher. She used as a prime example Kate Burke, who "totally supports herself by her search fees, and yet does an incredible amount of energetic and untiring work as AAC President, on a volunteer basis, of course."[137] Paton must have been shocked by the extent of Burke's dependence on search fees for her livelihood. She must also have read with mounting horror and disbelief Burke's understanding of the AAC's mission. Paton never thought the answer to the problems of adult adoptees was simply opening adoption records, and it was never her intention that the AAC be solely dedicated to that purpose. The month before, she had sent Burke the bylaws she had written up for the AAC in 1979 and summed them up as emphasizing "a focus on affliction and on communication, on the importance of people with special talents to all of us."—in short, a national organization helping people reunite with their natal kin, just like Orphan Voyage

In her reply to Burke, Paton never directly addressed the issues of paid search consultants or Burke's supposed misunderstanding of the AAC's mission.[138] But the extent of Paton's distress can be gauged by the fact that she devoted the first page of her letter to philosophy, what might be called "Paton's First Principles." Burke had inadvertently struck Paton in her most vulnerable spot. She had asked Paton to give up her critical faculties in defense of adult adoptees, the very essence of Paton's lifelong calling. In response to such an unprecedented attack, Paton attempted to explain the difference between herself and "others," which now obliquely included Burke. She explained that "the world of affliction in which we all live" tested the human spirit. We are "privileged to learn the fears and the destructiveness in which all live," but in the course of the work "we become specialists." Reiterating her long-standing belief that there was an inherent difference between adult adoptees and others in society, Paton noted, "Our superficial resemblances to others belie the cavern within." She added, "Though we may shout to our fellow men, they hardly ever hear us." Consequently, "some of us come to value the spiritual bonding of reaching out in the darkness and finding someone else there." It was this quasi-religious feeling for her fellow afflicted, adopted persons that Paton declared was "the base from which I try to be practical." It had turned her "far more earnest about many things that most people enjoy." This had resulted, Paton continued, in constant rejection of most of the ideas and projects she had ever introduced; nevertheless, people grudgingly respected her. She had come to accept being rejected, but vowed that "I will never turn my back on my brothers and sisters—as I call my adopted counterparts."

Paton then turned to her own personal history and recounted that fateful night early in her career when "the social work officialdom in Harrisburg, Pennsylvania" warned her off from identifying too closely with adopted children. "Don't carry this too far, Jean," they advised her. She couldn't sleep that night. The next day, Paton "heard the envelopes plopping to the floor through my mail slot, the envelopes that contained the questionnaires that became *The Adopted Break Silence*. That night I decided I would choose my siblings, and I have never turned away from that choice." The lesson that Paton drew from this experience was that "social work sent me to Coventry," but being ostracized and abandoned by her peers did not crush her; instead, she was strengthened. And thus her education began. These experiences were "repeated and repeated, and repeated." And, Paton implied, Burke was just another brick in the wall.

Paton then got down to her practical side and returned to criticizing the AAC for failing to reach out and encourage people who were engaged in adoption reform efforts, though not connected to the AAC. Paton specifically named Sandy Musser, an adoption activist and reunited birth mother. Paton had known Musser for thirteen years, initially in 1976 as a member of Orphan Voyage seeking advice, then in 1978 as coordinator for the Pennsylvania/South Jersey branch of CUB, and the following year as the author of one of the first birth parent books, *I Would Have Searched Forever*.[139] Musser held a special place in Paton's heart. She repeatedly praised Paton's accomplishments for adoption reform and was one of the first persons to refer to her as the "Mother—of our Movement."[140] She had gone on to found the Adoption Triangle Ministry and advocated for the unconditional opening of adoption records. Like Paton, Musser objected to the AAC inviting William Pierce to speak before the national meeting in Boston in 1987 and had written the leadership denouncing the decision. Such a letter could not have endeared her to the board, and when Musser approached the AAC for help she had been rejected. To Burke, Paton declared this an "indescribable decision." She again criticized the AAC for wrongly emphasizing "the Board, the social work liaison, the annual conference." But, she told Burke, it was not just the Musser decision that Paton found discouraging. From the very start of the AAC, "Competent and concerned people had found no place in it, either nationally or within the local groups."

Paton then struck a new note, stating that her "main feeling" about the AAC was that it was too "complacent and respectable." Whereas almost twenty years earlier Florence Fisher had been the wild-eyed radical and Paton the sober, responsible reformer, Paton now denied the label, declaring "I am not respectable." As evidence, she cited the buttons she circulated with the slogan "Bastards are Beautiful" and the fact that they remained popular year in and year out. And yet, she continued, the AAC would neither discuss the issue of illegitimacy nor use the word "freedom." Paton felt this "strange, and until those words can be let into the door we will continue to go in circles." They were difficult words "for people born on the limb and shackled in one's early years." It made adult adoptees a "difficult and thorny people hard to help, but there is a way."

Paton attended the AAC-sponsored summer March on Washington, but her heart was not in it. She walked halfway across the Memorial Bridge in 100-degree heat to greet the marchers, but her feet got itchy and she turned back before they arrived. Paton did say a few words at what was termed the "Speak-Out," but then quickly returned to her hotel because of the heat. A month later, Paton wrote Mary Iwanek, "I simply do not plan to go on any more trips."[141] Instead, she was going to write a series of books, including a volume of letters and one that she was thinking of calling "The Tragedy of Adoption." She was also going to publish *The LOG* after indexing it. In addition, Paton announced that she would take up sculpture again and reorganize her office. In September, she vowed to her good friend (and future literary executor) Molly Johnson that she would not attend any more AAC regional or national meetings. She declared that it was "impossible for me to any longer countenance being a sort of figure-head at conferences, 'Look, she is the one who started it.' As if that were all I had ever done." Paton's alienation from the AAC was fueled by a growing feeling of neglect, a sense that no one in a leadership position in the AAC took her seriously. She stated, "AAC had never once asked my views." Paton believed that the reason for being overlooked by the AAC was because her ideas were contrary to the dominant social work paradigm on adoption. In Paton's opinion, the AAC leadership "would rather do anything than cross social work."[142]

Alienated from both the national AAC leadership and its policies, and sensing her influence was waning, Paton decided to withdraw from attending any more AAC conferences. She had always been a loyal conference attendee, participating regularly in both national and regional conferences. But by the mid-1980s, Paton preferred the regional conferences. At the 1986 regional conference in Louisville, Kentucky, at which she gave a paper on sealed adoption records, Paton waxed enthusiastic on the emotional closeness of the participants and the reasonable cost of the fees. There was a price to be paid, however: the regional conferences were also more difficult emotionally. To Mary Iwanek, she declared, "there is so much pain when these people meet together, and it oozes through my skin. And my myelin sheath is thinner than it once was. I have no techniques of denial left in me."[143] The 1988 AAC regional conference in Atlanta, which Paton referred to as "Orphan Voyage territory," also won her wholehearted approval. She appreciated its small size (only about sixty people attended) and the fact that the attendees were mature, responsible individuals who displayed little egoism. There were few men in attendance, four or five, but Paton spoke with all of them. She also made several important contacts, including a typist for her manuscripts and a potential publisher for her many book projects. Among friends and admirers at the regional, Paton received what she always craved: respect and attention.[144]

14

Straight Ahead

I have more or less decided that nothing will work for us until we build structures in society that translate into how much we care for each other.

—JEAN PATON, 1998

During the 1980s, Jean Paton devoted an enormous amount of time to the American Adoption Congress—leading it, criticizing its activities, and attending its annual conferences. But Paton never confined herself to a single issue or organization, and this period of her life was no different, as she also carried on her lifelong efforts to educate the public about the problems of adopted people and fought for adoption reform in numerous ways. Although there was much continuity in Paton's ideas and actions, she was able to change her mind about long-held intellectual positions, support other adoption activists' fresh ideas, and think up new ways to strengthen the lives of adopted persons.

Although she often complained that she was slowing down, in 1980 the seventy-two-year-old Paton kept up a schedule of a person half her age. She received around 1,500 letters annually—half were inquires and half told of Orphan Voyage members' problems—which she dutifully attempted to answer.[1] She still traveled extensively. In 1980, even with summer allergies and a bad September cold that lingered into mid-October, she gave several local talks on adoption reform, including one at a daylong workshop in Grand Junction, Colorado, about the "blended family."[2] At the invitation of Illinois adoption activist Sandra Lott, she also traveled to Illinois and then Indiana, where first she met with adoption reform leaders and with CUB member Carole Anderson.[3]

Paton continued to fight for adoption reform creatively, on many diverse fronts. She remained convinced that an important way to improve the lives of adult adoptees was to establish permanent institutions, both practical and symbolic: witness her serial creation of the Life History Center, Orphan Voyage, and the American Adoption Congress. Late in life, she explicitly stated this heretofore unarticulated belief: "I have more or less decided that nothing will work for us until we build structures in society that translate into how much we care for each other."[4] A new example of Paton's efforts to build such structures was the Adoption Memorial, an idea that she first broached in early 1983.[5]

Given that Paton had just celebrated her seventy-fourth birthday in December, it is perfectly logical to conclude that the source of this idea was a sense of her own mortality. But that would be a mistake. Paton had a robust constitution and was in relatively good health. She experienced only minor ailments during her long life: an abscessed tooth, a stiff neck, an aching back (for which she had been seeing a chiropractor for over a year).[6] Though her hair was turning grey, it was still not white.[7]

Rather, Paton had been thinking about the idea of the Adoption Memorial for some time. She could not erase from her mind all the numerous tragic events she had heard about. Paton recalled several of these to Patricia Murphy, a birth mother and former CUB coordinator in New England. There was the case of the adult adoptee who, after finding his father's grave, "lay on it and pounded it with his fists." Another adopted person went to the family cemetery and demonstratively "longed for a shovel." One birth mother, who later married and had several other children, requested that she be buried with only a notebook "in which she had written the name and date of birth of that first child." To these cases, she added the many adoptees who had committed suicide and the birth mother who swallowed poison several years before her daughter found the family. In short, Paton was "weary of wiping the tears here at my correspondence desk" as a result of reading about how often "adoptees find that their birthparents had died or even the reverse."[8]

But it was the emotional dedication of the Vietnam Veterans Memorial three months earlier, in November 1982, that prompted her to act.[9] The Adoption Memorial, she wrote author Warren Siegmond, would honor "the memory of all those who died unreconciled."[10] Emulating the designer of the Vietnam Veteran Memorial, Maya Lin, whose "memorial aesthetic is the revelation of loss and reaffirmation of stability, both self and national," Paton wanted to give recognition to people who had been hurt by discovering that members of their birth families had died before they could meet them.[11] The memorial would allow the bereaved to "open their grief to the outside and let it flow away from them."[12]

Paton had no illusions that the task would be easy. From the outset, she worried about commercialism in the movement, fearing that "ambitious folks" would try to "take it over and spoil it," either by promoting themselves or by making money from it.[13] But her concern was far outweighed by her zeal for the venture. To one CUB birth mother, Paton confided, "I don't think anything has moved me as much as this tragedy, even more than the rejoicing of reunion." This was because, she continued, a person was not alone in a reunion, while in death, one was. It was another important reason why a memorial was needed.[14]

Paton began building the Adoption Memorial slowly. She sent preliminary statements about it to close friends. She also placed a notice in the *Open A.R.M.S. Quarterly* announcing that Orphan Voyage was underwriting "a memorial to those in the adoption population who have died without the opportunity of reconciliation with the person or persons they have lost or could not find because of the sealed record in adoption."[15] In recognition of this tragedy, which, she said, involved "hundreds of thousands, perhaps a few million" triad members, Orphan Voyage was donating in the name of Rebecca Smith (Marion Carson) a thousand dollars to begin the work. Carson, the notice stated, was a longtime friend of Paton's. They had been "crib-mates": she had been born several years earlier in the same maternity hospital as Paton. Carson had searched for her mother but found her too late; she was already dead. When Carson passed away, she donated $1,000 to Paton for whatever purpose she deemed appropriate. Paton had chosen the Adoption Memorial. She ended the notice with a plea for cooperation and understanding of the importance and significance of the project. "It does represent the more painful side of the adoption experience," she wrote, "and many will be repelled. But I believe we deny our own worth, and reduce our own reunion achievement if we have no sorrow to give to those who experience the ultimate tragedy—death without reconciliation."[16]

To private correspondents, Paton outlined the form the Adoption Memorial would take. She would collect statements from people whose relatives had died and ask them to contribute to the program. She would then insert these statements "carefully into a special notebook, something highly presentable." She also began corresponding with an artist to render a preliminary illustration for a more solid memorial, though as a sculptor she had a pretty good idea of what such a structure should look like.[17] By the spring of 1984, Paton had begun preparing a brochure, containing a statement, illustrative letters, and a reproduction of a sketch from *The Adopted Break Silence*, for the actual memorial; she recognized that potential contributors needed the incentive of seeing the real thing.[18]

Despite Paton's ardor for the project, the response to the idea was tepid. Paton could understand people's apathy: death was unpalatable to most people, even if it was universal.[19] Still, a year after she first broached the idea to Sieg-

mond, she confessed to Murphy that Murphy had been the only person to respond to Paton's ad in the *Open A.R.M.S. Quarterly*.[20] But although Murphy
was an army of one, immediately taking charge and suggesting numerous strategic and tactical details crucial to making the memorial a success, little progress was made.[21] Another year passed. In 1985, Murphy announced that she had
reunited with her daughter and at age forty-two had been diagnosed with lung
cancer.[22] When Paton responded, she expressed the hope that chemotherapy
would bring Murphy back to health and congratulated her on the wonderful
news that she had been reunited with her daughter. She informed Murphy that
the reason she had delayed replying was because she was depressed, due partially to the abysmal lack of response to the proposal for an Adoption Memorial.[23]

In 1986, Murphy died. Her death deprived Paton of her strongest supporter and a major source of ideas for creating the Adoption Memorial. She
abruptly decided to return a large donation to one of the few people who had
supported the project. Paton explained to the donor that the memorial would
take too much energy at her late stage of life. Nor could she figure out a way
to encourage a critical mass of young people to take an interest in "the esoteric
subject of death." Although not giving up on the Adoption Memorial entirely,
Paton admitted that she was no longer actively promoting it. She added that an
emissary from Florence Fisher had offered to take over the memorial, but she
declined, distrusting Fisher. It was Paton's opinion that ALMA made "a lot of
money on their program" and that the memorial would have been used in the
same manner.[24] In the following decade, only a few people contacted Paton to
express interest in the Adoption Memorial, and Paton lowered her sights.[25] To
one correspondent, who thanked her for "recognizing that my grief is valid and
real,"[26] Paton replied that she had come to believe that "something on a smaller
scale" would have to do for the moment and that it would have to grow gradually, as knowledge of the cause became more widely known.[27] By 1998, Paton
envisioned "replicas of the Memorial all over cemeteries, and on postcards, and
stationary, letterheads, media pictures." She herself was going to build a small
replica of the Adoption Memorial and place it on her front lawn.[28]

In addition to the Adoption Memorial, Paton supported the creation of institutions that sustained adoption reform. In 1988, Molly Johnson, a close friend
of Paton and coordinator of Orphan Voyage in Jacksonville, Florida, put forward an idea reminiscent of Paton's Hospitality Network, a plan to identify
people willing to open their homes to adoptees who needed to travel to another
state during their search for first family members. Like the Adoption Monu-
ment, it never got very far.[29] Johnson sent Paton a draft of the project, describing
it as "a safe house" in which individuals in unfamiliar cities with limited financial

resources, who were actively searching for members of their original families, "might find support and shelter."[30] It was to be called Paton House, which surprised the "mother" of the movement. As she said, "I know I am old enough (80 in about a week) to be memorialized, none the less it is startling."[31] By July 1989, Johnson had received $175 in donations and volunteers had contributed eleven places to stay—ten in the United States and one in Ontario, Canada.[32] She had a thousand flyers printed for the upcoming AAC national convention planned in April 1990. Johnson's goal was to get the AAC board to accept Paton House as a service organization, a proposal she successfully pushed through.[33]

Along with institutions, symbols, and rituals, holidays can act to solidify social groups. In addition to her Museum of Orphanhood exhibit, whose purpose was to inform the public that "orphans and bastards are valuable people," Paton had seized on the idea of overcoming the stigma of illegitimacy through distributing buttons that read "Bastards are Beautiful." She first distributed them at the AAC conference in 1979. They were a form of self-assertion, she informed Joan Vanstone, founder of the Canadian search group Parent Finders, by personalizing the issue and forcing other people to think about the injustice. By way of example, Paton recalled the reaction of a man at the airport who caught sight of her "Bastards are Beautiful" button and did a double, then a triple take. She conjured that "he is still losing sleep over the shock of it all." Similarly, a young black woman inspected her button as Paton hurried for her plane and, with her face lit up in a smile, called after her, "Do you really mean it?"[34]

Some adopted people objected to the buttons, finding them offensive and untrue. Adult adoptee Jerry Stapleton contradicted Paton. He declared that bastardy made people ugly, unpleasant, and miserable by denying them their normal human development. By coining a slogan that was false, it encouraged "more and more 'slutting' and 'bastardmongering.'" Stapleton suggested more appropriate sayings, such as "'I Want My Real Mother' or 'The Only Thing That Comes from a Cabbage Patch Is Sauerkraut.'"[35] Paton patiently brushed aside Stapleton's objections. She declared that he should view the buttons as a weapon. She used herself as an example. When people made cracks, Paton told Stapleton, she turned to them and said, "I am one," and they were startled. Talking about their pains, she declared, would get people in the movement nowhere. "But if we can assure society that it is damaging itself by damaging us, well that is another story."[36] It was in that spirit that Paton quickly endorsed Adoption Triangle Ministry's founder Marsha Riben's suggestion that a campaign be started to encourage adult adoptees to wear two carnations on Mother's Day.[37] She remembered that in her teenage years she wore multiple carnations, for her three mothers.[38]

As sociologist Amitai Etzioni notes, in addition to solidifying existing groups, holidays and rituals can also function to "work out a new relationship between society and a member group, and in the process, advance and ritualize a change in the belief of those involved." A prime example is the establishment of a holiday honoring the late Dr. Martin Luther King, Jr.[39] Similar in purpose, in 1990, a support group of birth mothers from the Seattle area created Birth Mother's Day "to remember and honor ourselves as mothers." Paton received a letter from the holiday's founders, Mary Marsh, a nurse who had relinquished a baby girl in 1978, and Lovina de Fierro, who explained the origin and history of the event and requested that Paton initiate a Birth Mother's Day for Orphan Voyage members. Marsh and del Fierro were quick to define the holiday as "a ceremony—not a rally, a picket, or a demonstration." Although these other activities had their time and place, this was not the intention of Birth Mother's Day. Instead, its purpose was to

gather birth mothers together to remember our sorrow and our pain. It is intended to take back our name as birth-givers and mothers. It is intended to be a time to celebrate the birth of our lost children—something most of us have been robbed of. . . . It is about compassion and celebration. It is a way of bringing our story, and our existence to the larger community who is unaware of the depths of this experience.[40]

Marsh and del Fierro went on to describe the ceremonial nature of the day's activities. Gathered into a circle, the birth mothers sang, lit candles, and listened to a poetry reading. In the past year, they added a drum and an anthem. The birth mothers were presented with corsages and a table had been set up for their children's photos; empty frames signified the children about whom mothers had no information. Paton must have nodded her head in silent assent as she read the sentence "Our pain, our stories, and our joy cannot be told by others"; it echoed her basic message down through the years to adult adoptees, social workers, and birth mothers.

Paton replied enthusiastically to Marsh and del Fierro. She sent them references to people and birth mother groups who she thought would be interested in commemorating the holiday, as well as a pamphlet she had written, "Whom Do You Seek?"[41]

The pamphlet powerfully affected Marsh. She wrote Paton that she had "never thought about 'search' in the context of the human need and desire for reconciliation." Now, she interpreted reconciliation as a process, which made any particular outcome less essential. Marsh concluded from this that "one could experience rejection and still accomplish this process." It also explained better the psychological drive behind searching in the first place. Marsh liked "Whom Do You Seek" so much that she informed Paton that she and del Fierro were going to include a portion of it in the ceremony's presentations. She included the excerpt for Paton's approval:

[Some] say those whose parents are in the wilderness, and the parents themselves, should never ask about each other. And the traces, the footprints, the markers, the names, all these should be hidden, blotted out, burned.

[Yet] there are things that cannot be eradicated as long as there is any life at all. The desire for reconciliation lives in every human heart, for each of us has lost someone, somewhere, sometime. This desire is ineradicable, permanent, and is summoned powerfully and frequently in the give and take of life. We can count on it. And we need it, for it makes us both civil and human. Society needs it, too. It needs its citizens to be reconciled with one another.

Reconciliation brings something new into the lives of the reconciled. It civilizes the wilderness, removes our fears of it by disarming the ghosts of the past. It substitutes plain human faces for fancies and brings the beginning of wisdom to those who dared to seek reconciliation.[42]

With Paton's help and Marsh's energy and organizational skills, the idea for a national celebration for birth mothers took off. In 1993, Marsh submitted a proposal to the AAC to bring the idea of the Birth Mother's Day ceremony to its next convention in Cleveland, and "to her astonishment" the proposal was accepted. There she gave a workshop, which included a reading of the excerpt from "Whom Do You Seek."[43] In the following years, birth mother ceremonies spread through the United States and Canada and were held in Cleveland, Cincinnati, and Dayton, Ohio; Cambridge, Massachusetts; Minneapolis and St. Paul, Minnesota; Cando, North Dakota; and Victoria, British Colombia; the ceremony was given prominent coverage in the *New York Times*.[44] Paton viewed this development as of "the greatest importance" and interpreted it as an encouraging sign of local efforts to advance the cause of adoption reform.[45]

As the self-appointed ombudsman of the movement, Paton also kept her finger on the pulse of contemporary events concerning adoption and birth mothers and never hesitated to make her views known. One trend that caught her attention was the national mania for the dolls known as Cabbage Patch Kids, the popularity of which in December 1983 caused a near riot in Charleston, West Virginia, when 5,000 people attempted to purchase them at Hills Department Store in time for Christmas. Coleco, the manufacturer, sold more than 2.5 million of them that year, making it the most successful new doll launch in the history of the toy industry. What accounted for Cabbage Patch Kids' remarkable success? Some suggested that it was the very homeliness of the dolls; others believed it was their uniqueness: no two looked alike. But their real distinctiveness was that they could not be bought; they could only be "adopted." Each doll came with a certificate of adoption from Babyland General Hospital, where "doctors" and "nurses" had watched over them until they were ready to be placed with loving families. Each certificate stated the baby's computer-generated name and birth date and had to be signed and returned to Babyland by the new "parent" to authenticate the adoption process.[46]

As early as March 1983, both CUB and the AAC lodged protests with Coleco against the Cabbage Patch Kids.[47] Paton was late with her bitter commentary on the Cabbage Patch Kids craze, which was eventually published in the spring of 1984.[48] Never, she observed, in all her many years of helping adopted people find members of their birth families, had she ever seen such a cultural appreciation of how important roots were. Finally, these dolls demonstrated that this issue matters to adoptees, after all. "We do have roots," she sarcastically declared, "and they arise in a patch of cabbage out there somewhere." Paton mockingly concluded by bestowing a blessing on "the profit motive, and its sensitivity to the true needs of the culture."[49]

Abortion was another, more serious, national issue, which Paton continued to oppose. During the ten years after *Roe v. Wade* (1973), many states passed regulations to restrict access to abortion. In the wake of the election of Ronald Reagan to the presidency, however, anti-abortionists resorted to violence, firebombing an abortion clinic in 1982. Two years later, the number of violent incidents climbed to twenty-five.[50] The escalation of the war against abortion coupled with Paton's long-term interest in the issue, galvanized her to play the peacemaker by writing a letter to her local newspaper. Paton stated that both supporters and opponents of abortion wrote "from outside of the experience" and thus the discourse was abstract, despite the passion they invested in the issue. She then noted, almost as an aside, that most people who favored abortion actually found it distasteful and, in a tart comment on the double standard, pointed out that "in order for a woman to become pregnant, somebody else participates." Paton then came to the heart of her message: adopted people, the majority of whom were born out of wedlock and were the most likely to be aborted, had not been and were glad of that fact. This was why, she explained, adopted people read the arguments about a woman's right to an abortion with mixed emotions. Paton declared that adopted people knew what mothers suffered to bring them into the world: "their abandonment by society, their loss of status, their years subsequent to adoption, which were full of pain for the loss of their child." Instead of arguing and marching about abortion, Paton declared, people's energy would be better expended "by devising programs of love and care for women in the pregnancy predicament which would help them keep their children and raise them with love." She complained that although such programs existed elsewhere, singling out Vancouver, British Columbia's cooperative homes of mutual assistance for young, single, pregnant women, none existed in her home county of Delta, Colorado, because "too many people simply want to use these women as brood mares for children they may themselves adopt." Paton concluded by asking aloud why the anti-abortion advocates attack pregnant women and "leave the men also responsible for the pregnancies intact and unchallenged?"[51]

During the early 1980s Paton's attitude toward opening adoption records underwent a significant change. As she lost faith in her own adoption registry, the Reunion File, and despaired at the AAC's failure to lobby for open records, Paton became more militant on the subject. By the early 1980s, she began to speak out in her own voice, advocating that the records be opened and, for the first time, participated in a public demonstration against sealed records. In July 1983, Paton and a few like-minded friends decided to enter a float in the annual Delta County, Colorado, parade. On a flatbed truck, two women sat on chairs at a table. Paton had draped herself in chains; adoption activist Anita Seitz wore a judicial black robe while holding a judge's gavel. The "judge" had her arm extended with her hand on a locked file cabinet, labeled "Birth Records, Adoption." Some months later, Paton complained to her good friend Joan Vanstone of the complacency in the U.S. movement. According to Paton, the worst form of this complacency was that it set up "adoption conferences at which the sealed record does not come up for discussion."[52]

In May 1985, at the American Adoption Conference in Jacksonville, Florida, Paton gave her first public talk devoted solely to the problem of sealed adoption records.[53] It was divided into three parts: the effect of sealed adoption records on adult adoptees, its effect on society, and solutions to the problem of sealed records. Paton began her talk by noting that various studies had demonstrated that adoptees were underachievers academically and experienced significantly higher levels of anxiety and feelings that their lives were out of control than the general population, though the cause of these problems still remained unclear. She ventured an explanation. Paton had become persuaded that it was "somewhere in the brain" that these inhibitions arose.[54] As Paton explained in her talk, she had become convinced of the relationship between the brain and adult adoptees' dysfunctional behavior. She provided a detailed explanation: "There are inhibitory centers in all brains, human or otherwise. We all have inhibitions. The difference for adopted people is that the inhibitory areas in the brain are increased, are spread about, and come to have a dominance over their lives." According to Paton, much of the increase in adult adoptees' inhibitions was owing to "the sealed adoption record, and by the cultural ramifications of the policy of the sealed record." The mechanism by which this occurred began early in life, when the adoptee began to wonder where his first family was and yet was told not to look for them. Thus, "the very prong of the adoptee's curiosity, by which he should grow, is blunted at the outset. And this area of inhibition spreads by association."

Paton hastily added that her explanation was not meant to demean adult adoptees. What she was trying to get across to her listeners was that "adopted people are not *born* that way." In an invisible way, the deck was stacked against the young adopted person just starting out in life. Arrayed against the adopted person was the sealed record, its restraints enforced by the adoption agency and reinforced throughout society "in the attitudes of the general public, and the local legal profession and the judge next door." No young person could stand up to the weight of such negative societal forces, and thus it was hardly surprising that the result was inhibition. "And when the brain says 'No' to inquiry you do not grow, you do not move and you do not ask and you do not learn." The message was loud and clear, and the child was subdued.

Expanding on this point with specific examples about what goes on in the brain of adopted persons as they mature, Paton explained that as adopted people moved into the wider world they discovered it was populated by family figures connected to their own origins and birth. But, for them, these figures were "very vague, ghosts, phantoms." This was because adopted people lacked photos of their birth parents, except for a canned description of them from the adoption agency, such as "'Your mother was 5' 4", had blue eyes, and liked sports.'" The lack of specificity, Paton declared, led adopted people to be beset by what she wittily called "non-identified flying objects." These "threatening ghosts" interfered with the natural tendency of the mind to explore, resulting in stunted growth. Remarkably prescient of developments later in the decade in neuroscience with the new techniques of functional brain imaging, Paton said she hoped someday scientists would begin "to take pictures, electrograms, micrograms, whatever is required about the brain of the adoptee."[55] This would not only reveal the inhibitory areas of the brain but also identify sources of repression. By viewing the zones of repression in their charts and diagrams, Paton predicted, scientists would in the future be able to identify which brain was an adopted person's. Paton believed that the relief an adopted person felt at the point of a reunion—"the signs of great joy, the sobs and the shakings," the sense of peace and security—confirmed her theory about repression and inhibition in the brain. For it was with the moment of reunion that "the missing piece has fallen into place. The prohibited one appears and one is not destroyed. An excessive fear is overcome forever."

Turning to the second part of her talk, Paton admitted that it was more difficult to portray the injuries that the sealed adoption record did to society. She attempted to do so by presenting a diagram consisting of concentric circles. The inner circle represented society—its orderliness, stability, and continuity. The outer circle was the boundary that separated people from the wilderness. Adoptees and other unnamed outliers lived in the area between the two circles, which she called "the margin of society." Society was where established kinship resided between people who shared common genetic factors. In the margin of society existed people who lacked a social relationship between the generations of kinship. The larger the number of people in this part of the circle, the less stable was society. According to Paton, sealed adoption records had created more anxiety and uncertainty, resulting in societal instability.

How had this state of affairs arisen? Paton believed that its origins stretched as far back as Plato, who advocated that the family be abolished and that children be raised by the appointed mentors of the state. These ideas then found a home in America's long-standing history of utopian idealism, beginning with such nineteenth-century communitarian projects as New Harmony. But it was twentieth-century East Coast liberals whom Paton accused of building "a utopia out of babies who were born inconveniently," destroying in the process their kinship and heredity:

> The sealed record acted as a concerted attack on the kinship family, from the ideology of the people who believed in building "one world" for the purpose of peace and who believed that family loyalties would interfere with developing a "one world" mentality . . . Those folks on the east coast [sic] who sat down and said "To create one world, we must destroy the family and its small loyalties," succeeded perhaps more than they anticipated. Society seems to have no way of defending itself against those who would destroy it.

The sealed adoption record scheme succeeded in large part because, Paton declared, "the appetite for babies overcame people's basic instincts to preserve society and its institutions." But Paton held out hope for the future. None of this utopianism was inevitable or necessary. Adoption could return to its traditional manner of openness, where people "could go and see [their records] and know who they were." Returning to the tradition of open records would not only restore adopted people's lives but also restore society, by strengthening the genetic family and an appreciation of heredity.

The third point Paton addressed was the future: if adoption records were opened, what then? Did the utopian experiment of sealed records have anything of value to teach adopted people? Paton answered affirmatively. The movement to open the records revealed the true nature of the instigators and motive behind those people responsible for closing them originally. The legislation was "pushed into a special direction by people who were childless, and by people, largely men, who wished to avoid the sight of a child they had brought into the world." They tried to escape the unhappy consequences of an unacceptable part of their lives and therefore set out to destroy "the structure of society, its necessary kinship, ancestry and heredity provisions." More positively, an unintended consequence of the sealed adoption records legislation was the discovery of "the orphan, the outcast," the illegitimate bastard. Through studying and analyzing the adoption situation, "which has no racial limitation and has little regard for character or behavior," Paton had unearthed the virtues and social function of orphans. Her research had revealed that

> almost all the great literature of the world was written by people who were orphaned—whether by death, illegitimacy, exile or neglect of parents, whatever. When you are outside of the settled order of things you have a different perspective. It's open out there, the air is thinner and there are fewer clouds. You can find universal values which you can give back to society. But also if you are on the margin, it is a little scary. You are glad to know that there is a settled society back there in town.

Paton ended her talk by rallying adoption activists to keep fighting to open the records. She advocated protests and use of the media, and she encouraged activists to be both graphic and realistic, using as examples her protest in Delta, Colorado, the Adoption Memorial, and the Hospitality Network. Paton told triad members not to be discouraged by the large amount of money needed for legislative lobbyists or afraid of the majesty of the law, "but to stand quietly and with the dignity that comes from understanding, and say that changes must come." She was unsure whether adoption records would ever be opened on the basis of "our 'rights' or because we are miserable" and suggested that perhaps the only way was to show society what it was losing by destroying the genetic family. She warned against the therapeutic society. If the social order continued on its present course, "we will not have a society but a dictatorship, with experts who try to substitute for what we have lost. The picture is already in our sights."

By the end of the decade, Paton's dislike of professionals and her advocacy of open records came together forcibly as she denounced "people getting doctorates." She was "weary of so many initials" and wondered if anything more could be accomplished in the movement with such professionals. As she had been lamenting for the past thirty-five years, what was missing from the conversation was the "true voice from the mouths of the adopted." As an illustration, she pointed to a newsletter from a Colorado adoptive parent group, which was filled with articles by professionals "specializing in the inability of adopted people to bond." She pointedly complained, "*not one word* in any of it about the cure, which is open records now." Paton found such a state of affairs tragic and oppressive.[56]

As Paton more actively campaigned for opening adoption records, she gradually turned against open adoption. Before the 1970s, open adoption performed by a licensed adoption agency was a rare event, lacking any underlying theoretical rationale, though evidence suggests that in Florida in the 1940s, for example, nearly 40 percent of independent adoptions involved some contact, however brief, between birth parents and adoptive parents.[57] The first theoretical description of what would be called open adoption was published in 1964 by H. David Kirk, a professor of sociology at the University of Waterloo.[58] Four years later, in 1968, Paton was the first person to use the term "open adoption," though she meant only that adoptive parents should talk openly to the child about his or her original parents.[59] The actual practice of open adoption was a result of profound sexual, constitutional, and demographic changes in American society during the 1960s and early 1970s, which led to a crisis in the practice of traditional adoption: the decline in the availability of white, out-of-wedlock infants for adoption.[60] As early as 1971, the staff at the County of Los Angeles Department of Adoptions was breaking down the barriers separating birth and adoptive parents by permitting birth mothers to choose an adoptive couple from among several applicants.[61] By 1974, adoption agencies in California, Minnesota, and Nebraska had also begun to experiment with offering birth parents alternatives to traditional closed adoption.[62]

Despite Kirk's prescience, it was not until March 1975 that the concept of "open adoption" was invoked for the first time in its modern sense, by social science researchers Annette Baran, Reuben Pannor, and Arthur D. Sorosky. A paper Baran read before the annual meeting of the American Orthopsychiatric Association defined and advocated an open adoption as "one in which the birth parents meet the adoptive parents, participate in the separation and placement process, relinquish all legal, moral, and nurturing rights to the child, but retain the right to continuing contact and to knowledge of the child's whereabouts and welfare."[63]

When Paton first heard about Baran's idea about open adoption, she thought "it was a very creative solution to a difficult human problem." But because it emanated from Soroksy's research team, Paton was distrustful of the proposal. She was unsure of what he was up to due to his legitimate birth status and her dislike of experts "promulgating methods for adoption."[64] Paton's criticism was unfair. In the paper, Baran identified adoption professionals as being at the center of the problem facing adult adoptees because they refused to acknowledge that the era of secrecy—sealing records, protecting adoptive parents, matching babies, and resolving unwed mothers' psychological conflicts—was over.[65] Two years later, Paton had warmed to the idea, stating to one correspondent that she was strongly against adoption "except under the open plan."[66] Writing to Lee Campbell, CUB's president, Paton endorsed open adoption and suggested that birth mothers should begin to practice it by offering themselves to women with infertility problems and to potential adoptive parents willing to adopt on an open basis.[67] Paton had witnessed such a program being discussed in a Toronto birth mothers' support group she had visited.[68]

By 1980, however, Paton's positive view of open adoption had begun to change. In a major revision of her outlook, she wrote birth mother Lucy Pare stating that she had always thought open adoption "awkward." By this Paton meant that any birth mother entering into an open adoption would always feel inferior and humiliated, having to meet "face-to-face the people who are able to raise her child and she presumably is not." Paton did not believe that it was "a livable thing, except in some rare cases," where the adoptive parents loved the birth mother in addition to the child.[69] Nor was she alone in her misgivings about open adoption. Fellow reformer Betty Jean Lifton also expressed doubts:

> I think I'm much more conservative than a lot of my social worker friends who are all for open adoption. But as an adoptee, I have all kinds of questions about how it will work. When you're on one side with your adoptive family, you have a certain security. If you have this other known family, I don't know what that does to your identity with your adoptive family. It's such a delicate balance— how much they talk about it, how much or how often they tell you. It's very hard for people to be wise psychologically when they're emotionally involved. Yet it seems to me a healthy child would want to see those other parents.[70]

Nevertheless, the practice of open adoption spread slowly and quietly across the nation, attracting little public comment, positive or negative, from adoption officials or the mass media. The attention of adoption activists and their critics was focused on the legal and legislative battles over unsealing adoption records.

Beginning in 1983 and accelerating throughout the 1980s, however, open adoption became one of the most contested issues within the adoption reform movement. In July 1983 Paton, coming full circle, turned against open adoption, finding herself on the side of the psychoanalytic psychiatrists she loathed, along with William Pierce, president of the National Committee for Adoption and a longtime opponent of open records. To Marilyn Hipp, Paton declared that "open adoption under the sealed record is a pretense and a sham." Paton now believed that ultimately open adoption did not improve birth mothers' happiness. Instead she favored family preservation, and advised Hipp that "we should help them keep their babies, and I mean help."[71]

Not for the first time, Paton's ideas were diametrically opposed to those of the professional social work community. In 1984 adoption reformers Reuben Pannor and Annette Baran advocated that the traditional, closed system of adoption should be abolished and be replaced by open adoption. This radical proposal first appeared in an article that Pannor and Baran published in *Child Welfare*. The practice of "secrecy, anonymity, and mystique surrounding the traditional adoption of the past," they proclaimed, "must not be perpetrated but must be replaced by a form of adoption that practices openness and honesty, and thereby permits a healthier and psychologically sounder adoption practice." It was now their firm belief that "all adoptions should fall within the open adoption framework."[72] In 1986, the Child Welfare League of America, at its biennial meeting in San Francisco, passed a resolution endorsing open adoption as long as a consensus existed among all members of the triad.[73]

Paton viewed this trend with great alarm. Writing to Berkeley, California, feminist and adoption reformer Janine Baer, she disagreed with Baer's positive assessment of open adoption. What troubled Paton was the substitution of open adoption for the movement's main focus: open records. She viewed open adoption as a novel, utopian scheme focused on the future, while the solution to the problems of adoption could only be found "by curing the ills of the past"— that is, by opening adoption records. Advocating open adoption was putting the cart before the horse. In addition, Paton believed that the movement's energies would be better spent on keeping babies connected with their families of origin. Paton thought that was especially hard work because of the many forces pushing for children to be adopted, yet the goal of family preservation had to be attempted "for the good of society as well as us."[74] Two years later, she repeated her doubts about open adoption to Sandy Musser, concluding her letter by harshly criticizing the reasons for its popularity: "It is about ten times easier to do open adoption than to look at the results of the seal and try to do something about those. People are just lazy, and then they invent so many excuses and substitutes for cleaning house."[75]

In 1990, as open adoption gained the support of adoption agencies nation-wide, Baran and Pannor reversed themselves, repudiating open adoption as an alternative to traditional or confidential adoption and calling instead for a form of guardian adoption. They addressed their statement to Paton, asking that she publish it in her newsletter. It began by calling for an end to traditional adoption, defining it as the relinquishment of children to a new set of parents and the severing of all rights of the birth parents as a final, irrevocable act. They then wrote:

> Open adoption, which we helped pioneer, is not a solution to the problems inherent in adoption. Without legal sanction, open adoption is an unenforceable agreement at the whim of the adoptive parents. Instead, we propose a form of guardianship adoption that we believe would be in the best interests of all concerned, with special benefits for the adoptee for it would decrease the abandonment/rejection issue and permit the child to know the birthparents as real people who cared about him but could not raise him.[76]

Paton thought it "a good statement" but scoffed at their request to print it. She noted to Australian adoption activist Anna Coffey that such an appeal revealed how out of touch Baran and Pannor were with her, since Paton had discontinued publishing *The LOG* almost a decade earlier.[77] Nor was the statement particularly earth-shattering. Six months earlier, Paton had arrived at a similar conclusion. Summing up the logic of her many years of experience and research, Paton declared to Coffey that babies should not be separated from mothers, except under extraordinary circumstances or death, and traditional adoption should not be permitted to destroy a child's ancestry or knowledge of his original family. "So we are left with guardianship or whatever it should be called." She added that there should be no change of name and the child should know this original name, "for indeed it is *his.*" The law governing these guardianships should be minimal. It should simply confer upon the acting parents the rights necessary to perform their duties.[78]

In 1991, Paton elaborated on her understanding of guardianship in commenting on the psychologist Dr. Randolph Severson's brief book, *A Letter to*

Adoptive Parents . . . On Open Adoption.[79] Severson strongly advocated open adoption within a framework of courage, compassion, and common sense. By courage Severson meant that adoptive parents had to be brave enough to meet the birth parents rather than give into their fears of the unknown. Adoptive parents expressed compassion by staying in touch with the birth parents once they had met. Finally, adoptive parents exercised common sense by recognizing and honoring the child's need to have their birth parents provide them with a photo, talk with them, and occasionally tell them that they love them. Conversely, birth parents demonstrated "the same wisdom in their heart," by providing that picture and communicating with the child "in a way that does not overwhelm the child or intrude too much on the [adoptive] parents." For Severson, common sense meant that "adoption is not dual parenting."[80]

But Paton rejected Severson's major premise: open adoption, which to her appeared ineffective. After much thought, Paton had come to the conclusion that open adoption would not reduce adoptive parents' fears: only guardianship could do that. There was also something superficial about Severson's characterization of open adoption. For Paton, what was best for adopted people was "to maintain a significant relationship with those they left behind," not to simply provide the child with a photo and worry about "intruding" on the adoptive parents. Although she endorsed the three characteristics that Severson found most admirable about open adoption—courage, compassion, and common sense— it was only because they "combine in a natural fit in guardianship situations and in no other format." Paton declared that "after almost forty years of looking straight at the reality of adoption I know the cures for what we have done can be brought about only by Guardianship, an indisputable form of openness which we now approach."[81]

As these anti-adoption views reveal, Paton was becoming more radical with her advancing age. Another illustration of Paton's increasing radicalization, as well as her strength of character to stand up for what she believed in, was her steadfast support of Lori Carangelo when almost everyone in the movement turned against her. It is not clear whether it was Carangelo's extreme anti-adoption views and demand for unconditional access to adoption records or her cavalier attitude toward appropriating other adoption reform groups' names without permission in support of her ideals that caused the animosity between her and other reformers. Perhaps it was both. But on New Year's Day 1989 Carangelo shot a rocket across the bow of the adoption reform movement. She bypassed the leadership of the AAC, CUB, ALMA, Orphan Voyage, and all the other adoption organizations and crafted a bill calling for the opening of adoption records unconditionally, which she sent to fifty state lawmakers who, she claimed, would simultaneously introduce it in their legislatures.[82] In her cover letter she denounced "compromise legislation" (the first time the phrase was used) referring to voluntary mutual consent adoption registries, noted the medical and psychological damage done to adopted children before their twenty-first birthday, called the sealed adoption record unconstitutional and un-American, and proclaimed the year 1989 as "The Year of the Adopted American Revolution."[83]

In February 1989, Paton received a letter from her friend, CUB founder Mary Anne Cohen, asking her if she was aware that Carangelo was using Paton's name on AmFOR literature and letterhead. Cohen advised Paton against allowing this. Carangelo, said Cohen, had boundless enthusiasm and money but lacked common sense. According to Cohen, Carangelo had misled Connecticut legislators with her mailings, which set back the cause of open records. Her actions had made it much more difficult for adoption activists to convince legislators that they were not loonies. Cohen pleaded with Paton to read Carangelo's material very carefully and to consider her record of alienating numerous adoption reform group leaders before supporting her. She concluded that although Carangelo's activism was needed, it had to be done the right way if it was going to have a good effect.[84]

Paton disagreed with Cohen. Yes, she was well aware that her name was being used on AmFOR's literature. She had given Lori permission to use her name. And no, she was "not going to withdraw" her name.[85] Paton then explained her support of Carangelo. She had read her bill proposing to open adoption records and thought it "the most intelligent page I have read on that subject. It shows much perspective. That it could irritate a lot of people I have no doubt. Have people reached the point where they will accept smoothie Pierce more than the rough-skinned Lori?" In addition to the merit of Carangelo's legislative proposal, Paton identified with her being ostracized. Paton told Cohen that she herself had been "in the doghouse here and there" for many years and was not about to "turn her back on anyone active in the movement who may be stepping on a few toes and doing some damage, along with some good work."

Six months later, Paton repeated her sentiments about Carangelo to Molly Johnson. Carangelo had recently visited Paton, she said in her letter, and she had found Carangelo to have "intelligence, energy, conviction, and she cares." She asked rhetorically, "What more do people want?" Paton then went on to enumerate the similarities between Carangelo and herself:

> When I started this work, there were all kinds of things said about me, some of which still reverberate through the years, unchanged. I think it is very reprehen-

sible for any of us to blackball a person on a relatively small matter, and hang on to it grimly year after year. The Movement has lost more than a few people through one or another process of exclusion. I think this is one of the things, perhaps the most important factor, in the Movement having accomplished so little for a decade. It is time we stopped.[86]

Until the day she died, Paton continued to fight for her radical reform agenda.

15

The Great American Tragedy

I have seen tragedy every day of my life in this work.... The only way I have been able
to do this is by a combination of actions: Do what I can, try to love as many people
as possible, broaden my perspective constantly . . . , study continuously, communicate
honestly and openly.

—JEAN PATON, 1995

During her last decade, Jean Paton's life continued very much in the same path
as always. She read widely in subjects connected with adoption reform and
fought hard for the cause she had dedicated her life to for the past forty years.
She made new intellectual discoveries, altered her reform focus while continuing to champion the opening of adoption records, and focused on new causes.
She made new friendships and new enemies. None of these activities deviated
much from the way she had always lived her life. What did change was how
Paton assessed her life's work. She grew bitter, prompted in part by the fact that
her poverty, caused by her long-term service to the adopted community, worsened even as the income of adoption search consultants and therapists grew, and
in part by her belief that few, if anyone, appreciated her past service or valued
her counsel. Nothing hurt Paton more than the fact that no one listened to her.
With some exceptions—a few members of Bastard Nation and leading reformers in Canada, New Zealand, and Australia—a new generation of American activists barely acknowledged her existence, which led Paton to look to history to
ultimately vindicate her pioneering role and give her the recognition and respect
that she believed she deserved. A striking illustration of the new generation of
reformers' amnesia, bordering on callousness, and Paton's growing bitterness
and alienation from the American adoption reform movement was her breaking
off from the American Adoption Congress, the organization she helped create
more than twenty years earlier.

Her relationship with the AAC hit bottom in the early 1990s over the question of registering for a conference. At the start of the new decade, Paton confided to birth mother Carol Komissaroff that the AAC "only used me for my name" and that she attended the national conferences "not be a real part of them" but to socialize: "to meet people and be met by people." Paton declared that she was not going to attend any more conferences.[1] Nevertheless, a year later, she couldn't resist the camaraderie and emotional uplift of attending a conference and requested a table in the book room–exhibit area at the April 1991 AAC national conference in Garden Grove, California.[2] Gayle Beckstead, a Simi Valley, California, search consultant and the AAC conference registrar, informed Paton that requests for table reservations must be accompanied by a paid conference registration. She explained that the room where the book exhibit was being held that year was small and had filled quickly, and thus it was necessary to procure another book room on the second floor. Beckstead would await Paton's instructions.[3]

Beckstead's letter angered Paton. She replied that that she was "astonished" by it. She had no plans to register. Consequently, she half threatened and half observed that since she had been invited to attend a book-signing party, she would be forced to carry her own books around the conference in a knapsack. The injustice of demanding a paid registration from the mother of the movement overwhelmed her: "After the many years during which I subsidized the development of the movement, and thereby impoverished myself, I had no thought of creating paid employment for so many people in the adoptee population." She deduced from their action that she was "not exactly wanted," but informed Beckstead that she planned to attend anyway for the benefit of those people who wanted to talk to her. She ended the letter with a threat that when people asked her why she was carrying her books on her back, she would reply that it was because the AAC had denied her a table.[4]

Beckstead referred Paton's angry missive to Pat Sanders, the AAC conference chair, who replied to Paton, expressing the conference committee's own "astonishment" on learning that she did not plan to register for the April conference.[5] The committee members, Sanders wrote, had thought Paton's failure to register was an oversight. She punctiliously informed Paton that every person who attended, in whatever capacity, had always registered. Thus, "we asked nothing out of the ordinary from you, only the same as that asked of any other attendee." Moreover, Sanders added, conferences produce revenue for the AAC; if the organization was to effect change and maintain a national presence, the reality was that it must have operating capital. Sanders attempted to soften the AAC's strict policy on registration by apologizing if Paton "felt slighted in any way." She should never doubt that the AAC respected and admired greatly her contributions to the movement over the years. Her perfunctory apology and words of tribute were immediately followed by two paragraphs of attack. First, she qualified her praise by noting that Paton's contributions and impoverishment were not unique. There were "many, many people who have given (and continue to give) time, money and energy to adoption reform." Second, she noted that Paton was not alone in having limited funds. Everyone in the movement, Sanders declared, sacrificed more time and money than they could afford. "But that is the choice we make." Sanders was also puzzled by the oblique reference Paton had made to subsidizing the movement and by providing paid employment. Undoubtedly still smarting over Paton's earlier accusation that the head of Independent Search Consultants had a conflict of interest, Sanders denied that anyone in the AAC was paid for their services; it was totally made up of volunteers. Finally, Sanders asserted that Paton was always welcome at AAC conferences, and flatly contradicted her statement that she had been denied a book table. "You were only asked to register, as were all attendees." Sanders was at a loss to understand why Paton had taken exception to the AAC's request, though she said she remained available to discuss the matter with Paton by mail or phone, if she so desired.

Paton never replied. Instead, she attended the 1991 AAC conference in Garden Grove, California, without registering. Two months later, writing to her friend Dirck Brown, founder of the adoption reform organization PACER, Paton believed that some AAC people in leadership positions were miffed by her action. She mused that they were incapable of understanding "the life history and events leading up to one's financial condition after the age of eighty."[6]

Four years later, encouraged by her friend, Canadian clinical social worker and adoption reformer Ray Ensminger, Paton contemplated attending another national conference.[7] But for a number of reasons, she had grave doubts. She felt "like a real outsider." No one in the AAC was willing or able to accept her ideas about what should be done. The AAC had a wrong idea about her: they thought, "I am a nice person who helped the thing get started. What they do not know is that I am not particularly nice, and that I have never stopped growing in my thoughts about our problems." Another point holding Paton back from attending was the unappealing conference program. Out of the seventy-three panels, she could identify only one workshop with which she felt "simpatico." For the rest, "the stench of professionalism" darkened her desire to attend. Topping off everything was the "registration affair," which still rankled. This was more of a practical problem. As she said to her friend Molly Johnson, "Pat Sanders does not let me have a book table, because I am not registered. I believe I have paid my way over the years, and resent having to pay." Paton believed that including her at the conference added value to it; by her very presence people attended. Yet Paton found it impossible to allow the AAC leadership to pass judgment—to put herself in a position to be censored—on a future paper, for example that she might want to submit.

By this time, the mid-1990s, there was little hope for any rapprochement between Paton and the AAC. Her recollection of the early days was colored by the present. To Mary Anne Cohen, she confided that the AAC "has never belonged to me. It was taken from me at the outset, like candy from a baby." She no longer held a position in the organization where she could influence policy and had been prevented from speaking to members directly at AAC board meetings. This had not stopped her, and she had made herself heard by other means, but none of her suggestions had been acted on. Casting herself as the misunderstood radical, Paton chalked it up to the fact that people were unable to "grasp or accept the extreme nature of my perspective." The present situation was no better. Although many of the old guard were gone, which Paton considered an improvement, the new Turks were impatient and did not comprehend why resorting to such things as task force suggestions were ineffective. She confessed that she really was not in touch with what was going on, but in any case she had little hope for the AAC. In short, she concluded, "I have definitely given up on the AAC."[8]

As the dustup over the 1991 AAC conference demonstrated, poverty had begun complicating Paton's life. Indeed, as early as 1977 she complained of being personally impoverished and unable to travel to California because of a lack of money; only Orphan Voyage memberships were keeping her afloat.[9] Paton gained some breathing room in the 1980s by selling off some of her California property and sheltering it in money market accounts, which brought her income slightly above the poverty level.[10] But with the discontinuance of *The LOG* her Orphan Voyage membership plummeted, and she again complained of her inability to travel.[11] What particularly rankled was that people thought her wealthy. She complained to Diana Vickery that she "had a false reputation in the Movement of being a woman of means because I seemed always to be spending money." But, she explained, "it was mostly capital, which I no longer have available." The truth was that "if interest rates go down my income will be near the poverty level."[12] By 1987, her income was so small that Paton was relieved of "the onerous task of filling out an income tax form." She did not look forward to going on Old Age Assistance, and vowed that since she anticipated living at least another decade she would have to be frugal.[13] In 1991, she begged off attending a CUB conference for lack of money, "even though all the big names are going to be there." But as Paton confessed to Carol Gustavson, founder and president of Adoptive Parents for Open Records, she was "weary of big names, even of mine, when we must, absolutely encourage those who are coming along."[14] To Carole Anderson, the president of CUB, she detailed her financial woes in May 1991. Her income was down to $350 a month, supplemented only by a $400 subsidy from the state of Colorado for heating expenses and a tax rebate. And, although she did own her home, it had to be reroofed the previous winter. In addition, she had substantial dental work done in the recent past, which had not been covered by Medicare. On the whole, Paton told Anderson, her home was comfortable and she was in good health, but she simply could not undertake the expense of travel.[15]

Paton did not tell Anderson everything about her health. She neglected to reveal that she had also scheduled cataract surgery to implant a new lens in her right eye. Off and on over the past couple of years, Paton had complained about the darkness of the house, not realizing that the problem was her eyesight. The operation was entirely painless, and Paton recovered rapidly from the procedure. By May 1991, medication had reduced the swelling in her cornea, and she declared, "there was much more light, the colors of all objects, including the sky and the distant mountains are deepened."[16] Her only complaint was the eye medicine, which she referred to as a nuisance, "drops, drops, drops."[17] Six months later, Paton had a second successful cataract operation on her left eye.[18]

Neither poverty nor old age and its accompanying aches and pains slowed down Paton's inquiring mind. For decades she had advocated family preservation—that it was important for children to have knowledge of their original family as early as age twelve—and she had more recently repudiated both traditional adoption and open adoption in favor of some form of guardianship. Between 1990 and 1995 Paton announced, as if it were a revelation that she had shifted her intellectual focus from the adult adoptee to the adopted child. In late 1990 she announced to her New Zealand friend Mary Iwanek that she was "putting her focus on the childhood years of adopted people" and wondered "why I did not do that from the first."[19] Several weeks later, Paton described this new idea to adoption activist Carol Gustavson: "Children must learn early, realistically, whom they are descended from. They must!" Chastising herself she continued, "I should have focused on that from the outset. It is a mystery to me how I missed it for so long."[20] A month later, Paton characterized the idea of focusing on the childhood years to Joyce Pavao, Harvard research fellow and adoption therapist, as "something of a leap forward" and "of the utmost importance." She continued to kick herself for neglecting the young child and instead "somehow got involved in older people from day one, and left it there for this long time."[21] Paton believed that there was no way for society to make up for the lost years, and considered its neglect of the childhood years "a Great American Tragedy."[22]

Paton's shift in focus from adult adoptees to children emerged from both experiential and intellectual sources. Her participation in public service activities in Delta County, the local community surrounding Cedaredge, gave Paton a firsthand look at the problems affecting children. There she attended meetings of the Health Board and the Crisis Line, and learned of a child who was dying for lack of medical attention while her parents prayed, and watched helplessly as this child was "snatched into adoption rather than trying to help the family stay together." It was these "mammoth" tragedies, she wrote to Molly Johnson, that made her "realize what a CHILD REALLY IS AND HOW IT OPERATES." And, she added, it was the disregard of "the real nature of the children that is behind the troubles in adoption."[23]

Paton's newly focused attention on the childhood years was reinforced by her wide interdisciplinary study of psychology and science. Years earlier, she had read the work of Swiss developmental psychologist and philosopher Jean Piaget, who placed great importance on the education of young children, and she lamented that Piaget was "perhaps never as well-known as he might have been."[24] More recently, she had delved deeply into the development of infant-parent bonds, reading a number of books, all of which stressed the importance of prenatal life to social, emotional, behavioral, and language development.[25] These works had convinced Paton that children needed a connection with those with whom they had made a bond with while still in the womb.[26] Following from this insight, she now believed that children "should have, not information, *but contact* in childhood. Otherwise they will never will be able to weave in their heritage, their ancestry, their kindred into the intertwining parts of their lives as they grow."[27]

In addition to works of infant psychology, Paton continued to read studies of the brain. She regularly collected articles that might shed light on or support her theory about the relationship between the brain and the problems of adopted people. In 1987, Paton wrote to John Zimmerman, a professor and research psychiatrist at the University of Colorado Health Science Center in Denver, after reading about his work in the field of biomagnetism and the brain.[28] She told Zimmerman about her conviction that from a very early age the wiring in the brain of adoptees, as a result of the sealed adoption record, was responsible for a syndrome "best described as the 'PHD Phenomenon,' that is: passive, hostile and dependent."[29] In 1990, Paton noted an article reporting the use of magnetic resonance imaging (MRI) technology, which collected precise, live, color pictures of the brain; the article suggested that dyslexia in children was linked to a lack of development of four distinct regions of the brain.[30] She immediately wrote Dr. George Hynd, chair of the Division for Exceptional Children in the College of Education at the University of Georgia, who was one of the researchers of the MRI study, outlining her hypothesis about the inhibitions that adopted people labor under and her conclusion that "the problem has to be in our brains." Now that researchers actually could look into people's brains, Paton hoped that she had aroused Hynd's interest and he would pursue the hypothesis as developed in more detail in her publication "The Influence of the Sealed Record," which she enclosed.[31]

Paton's immersion in the problems of children through her community volunteer work, reinforced by extensive reading in brain research and infant psychology, led to major revisions in her thinking about adoption. In many ways, these changes were simply a natural culmination of several trends of her thought. Throughout her life, Paton had emphasized the importance of kinship and family preservation and the detrimental psychological effects—traumatic neurosis—of sealed adoption records. With her new emphasis on the crucial importance of childhood, she began to highlight an earlier theme—the failure of adopted children to have knowledge of or to connect with their natal parents before the age of eighteen, and various social organizations efforts to destroy kinship ties—and the resulting cruelty of adoption, which led to reinforcing her anti-adoption views.

In 1991, Paton revisited her conspiracy theory of the origins of sealed adoption records. In a letter to the editor of the *Denver Post*, she hotly rejected a Colorado's judge's statement that records came to be sealed for reasons of family preservation and to protect those born out of wedlock from the stigma of illegitimacy. Instead, she asserted that they came to be sealed through "a scheme to undermine and to eventually destroy the institution of the natural family" as it had been traditionally known in America. The conspirators believed that "only by destroying the natural family could our society and others enter into the Brave New World, enter into a One World Scheme."[32] Instead of the liberal social workers of the 1930s and 1940s, she asked her readers to "remember what Russia did to the family, or at least tried to do."[33] According to Paton, these plotters were joined in the conspiracy by sociologists, who made this foreign ideology popular on college campuses; by biologists, who denied the importance of heredity while stressing the significance of the environment; and by the growth of juvenile courts, whose purpose was to replace the work of the family and let the state discipline its children.[34]

Later, Paton revealed the headquarters of this conspiracy and identified new, modern-day conspirators.[35] Dismissing Bill Pierce and the anti–open records organization the National Council for Adoption as "on the way out," she identified Minneapolis as the "new focus of Power for the Seal," where the country's "enthusiasts for adoption" gathered. As evidence, Paton pointed to the new non-offensive language copyrighted by the Children's Home Society of Minnesota social worker Marietta Spencer for use in adoption; the recently published Search Institute's study of adolescent adoptees, which found the majority of adopted teens psychologically healthy; a conference on adoption held in the Twin Cities by social workers and ethicists, which urged the removal of the stigma of relinquishment and declared birth mother searchers to be anti-adoption; and the recent publication of a pro-adoption magazine, *Adoptive Families*, aimed at adoptive parents. Naming names, Paton condemned Rita Simon, a professor in the School of Public Affairs at the Washington College of Law at American University and author of a twenty-year longitudinal study of transracial adoption, for her conclusion that such adoptions did not have any special problems.[36] Similarly, she dismissed Elizabeth Bartholet, a Harvard Law professor, as overrated.[37]

On considering the ethics of adoption, Paton saw its cruelty ever more starkly. She provided two examples. The first came from a paper read at the recent Minneapolis conference on adoption ethics, which described the callous refusal by an orphanage to provide a female adult adoptee with information about her first mother even though the mother had been dead for over twenty-five years and the adult adoptee herself was close to death. The second example Paton took from a letter written by a Wyoming birth mother who was searching for her child. She wrote, "When I went to my father and told him I was pregnant, he whipped me, put a blindfold over my eyes and took me to the maternity home." Paton concluded from these two incidents that "it is time for us to focus on the brutality that inheres in adoption under the seal. We all know it is there. Let us educate the ethicists."[38]

During the 1990s Paton undertook two major projects to educate not only ethicists about the evils of adoption, but also her beloved community of adult adoptees as well as the general public. The first venture was the publication of a collection of primary source narratives to be called *Voices of Our Own: Orphan Voyage Letters, 1945–1985*, with an introduction and commentary by Paton.[39] The project went nowhere; she knew too much about her topic, and its complexity overwhelmed her.[40] The second project Paton hit upon was publication of "the one volume" which contained "all the answers," *The LOG*, where everything of significance about the movement was covered.[41] But it quickly dawned on her that publishing *The LOG* was a very large undertaking that was beyond her financial means.[42]

Instead of a book of letters or a published collection of *The LOG*, Paton created another newsletter in June 1993, which she named *A Proper Response: To the Situation in Adoption*. In the first issue, she explained that the title had evolved from her new insight about the importance of childhood. Adoptive parents now held the key to the movement's success. Paton believed that adoptive parents, encouraged by liberals, had been responsible for traditional adoption and the sealed records, but it was also adoptive parents who now recognized the need for change. Consequently, the proper response for activists was "to persuade them (and others) of the extent and depth of the change that is absolutely basic for the sound and healthy growth of children, and for the protection from grief of women who bear children in circumstances that make it problematic for them to raise them without aid." This was a different problem from that facing adult adoptees, who needed adoption records to be unsealed and the stigma "that has cruelly mistreated them for so many years" to disappear from society at large. *A Proper Response* would address these topics as well as current issues in adoption reform.[43]

In the first issue of *PR*, Paton addressed a scandal involving her longtime friend, adoption activist Sandy Musser, who was indicted in March 1993 and convicted four months later on federal charges of fraud and criminal conspiracy for illegally obtaining confidential government information from her foundation's investigator, Barbara Moskowitz. Musser had used identifying information stolen from the Social Security Administration to aid in completing reunions of adoption triad members. On October 1, Musser was sentenced to serve four months in Marianna Federal Prison in Florida for defrauding the government.[44] She was unrepentant. Casting herself in the role of a civil rights martyr, Musser declared, "These are immoral, unconscionable laws, and I believe in what we are doing. Did Rosa Parks break the law when she sat in the front of the bus?"[45]

The scandal rocked the adoption reform movement. Kate Burke, president of the American Adoption Congress, expressed concern that Musser's case would lessen the credibility of adoption activists who were working for reform. She was quoted in the *New York Times* as saying she hoped that "legislators will not think this is a bunch of gangsters."[46] Similarly, an unsigned editorial supported by the board of directors of Orphan Voyage of Alabama denied Musser was martyr or a hero, declared their lack of support, and called her "an opportunist whose time had come." Musser, the editorial continued, had cast the movement in an unfavorable light, which reflected badly on all adoption reformers. It concluded, "To hold Sandy Musser up as a martyr does nothing to further the cause for Open Records in adoption."[47]

Support for Musser, though not widespread, was immediate and strong. On the online service Prodigy, members of adoption support groups spread the news of Musser's indictment and organized writing campaigns in her defense to Florida newspapers. Adoptive parent Jane Nast roused adoption activists by urging them to seize the opportunity "to let the public and legislators know that we believe closed records are unconstitutional and we all stand together to support Sandy and to restore the civil rights of those connected with adoption." Penny Partridge established the Musser Legal Defense Fund. Other adoption activists, such as Lori Carangelo, supported Musser through correspondence and letters defending her actions to federal authorities. From New Zealand, Methodist minister and adoption researcher Keith C. Griffith wrote President Bill Clinton, expressing his repugnance "that in any democracy a person may have to break a law to discover the truth about themselves" and pleading for adoption law reform.[48]

Paton strongly supported Musser.[49] Initially she urged that a bulky amicus brief be sent to the court to educate the judges.[50] A month later, in July 1993, Paton wrote Attorney General Janet Reno, calling upon her to consider the fact that the adopted population was forced to pay fees for search assistance before Reno took any further action on Musser's indictment. She provided Reno with a brief history of adoption records policy, noting that records had been open for inspection to all parties prior to the mid-1940s and then were sealed. Paton urged Reno to restore the earlier practice of open records "promptly, and the practice of closure ceased at the earliest date." She noted that she was often referred to as the "the mother of the movement" to open adoption records, and that she had studied the problem for the past forty years on a daily basis. As a result, Paton informed Reno, she was intimately acquainted with adult adoptees, who had suffered a large loss in personal development as a result of the policy of sealed adoption records. It was a human tragedy, said Paton. It was only in this context that the effort to reunite adopted people after separation should be viewed. Consequently, Paton reiterated, it was her "strong conviction that an examination of the cultural climate of adoption should be undertaken in advance of any further procedures in the indictment which has been placed on Musser."[51]

A second issue that Paton campaigned against was the Uniform Adoption Act (1994) drafted by the National Conference of Commissioners on Uniform State Laws (NCCUSL). After five years of intense debate the commissioners recommended that adoption court records should be sealed for ninety-nine years. The best method for the release of identifying information, they concluded, was a voluntary mutual consent adoption registry.[52] Paton warned her

readers about this "terrible proposal."[53] Singling out the ninety-nine-year stipu-
lation, she sarcastically remarked that the NCCUSL "will then reopen them so
that eager beavers of the genealogical profession can scan the yellowed papers
and do their job." She then stated the obvious: "We will all be dead by the time
the 99 years are up."[54]

A third issue Paton tackled was the failure of the feminist movement to take
up the cause of birth mothers. Throughout her life as an adoption reformer,
Paton had taken little notice of the women's liberation movement because of
its longtime indifference to the plight of birth mothers. In late 1993, however,
she received a letter from Patricia Ireland, the president of the National Organization of Women (NOW), addressed to "Dear Friend," soliciting money and
requesting her to join the group.[55] But instead of tossing NOW's fund-raising
appeal into the wastebasket, Paton wrote Ireland and published the letter in *A
Proper Response*. In her letter to Ireland, Paton stated that NOW promoted
several causes (economic equality, reproductive freedom, civil rights for lesbians
and gays), but "there is one cause you never list, that is never covered in your
print-outs, and perhaps never will be": the cause "of women in permanent grief
from having surrendered their children to adoption." She wondered, "Why is
this matter so hush-hush with you?" She asked whether birth mothers were
seen as a handicap to the cause of women's liberation, "Does not your compassion flow toward them, or have you none to give?" Paton concluded, "I think
NOW is diminished by this neglect."[56]

In a subsequent issue of *A Proper Response*, Mary Marsh, one of the founders of Birth Mother's Day, concurred with Paton's critical view of NOW, noting
that she and other feminist birth mothers had put similar questions to such
groups many times before and received "no satisfactory answer." She then offered a sophisticated critique of the women's movement, noting that it was not
monolithic, that it included a spectrum of lifestyles among women who called
themselves feminists. Yet Marsh asserted that she had received "more understanding as a birthmother from radical lesbian feminists than from corporate
NOW-type women." Marsh found it "comforting that Jean, an adoptee, would
even bother to challenge NOW about their ignoring birthmothers."[57]

Long-standing medical issues that reappeared in 1993 did not deter Paton
from publishing *A Proper Response*. Her arthritis—"a little gremlin lurking inside me," which typically afflicted her left hand—began to act up again.[58] She
made an appointment with an internist-gerontologist, who, fresh out of medical
school, had established a practice in nearby Palisade, Colorado. After a physical
exam, Paton began taking three different analgesics, one of which, the doctor
assured her, would make a difference.[59] Soon thereafter, Paton reported to Betty

Wheeler that she no longer woke up in the morning with her left shoulder and hand hurting. She attributed her relief to the medication and declared "so now I have joined the drug club." Paton also joined an exercise program at the Recreation Center in Delta, Colorado, and began lifting weights to strengthen her shoulder.[60] Later that year, her enthusiasm for exercise broadened to include a special swimming class that, as she put it, was "designed for old ladies with aching joints."[61] By the end of the year, Paton reported that she had slowed down more than she had expected at her age and attributed it partly to depression. But her arthritis was being held in check, and though she had recently fallen and injured her knee, the "lovely" swimming "pool was just the thing for it."[62] In early 1994, two weeks after her eighty-fifth birthday, Paton acknowledged to Mary Iwanek that she had "less stamina and less decisiveness" than earlier in her life, but declared that she could "still think about as well as ever" and was "not falling into Alzheimer's thank goodness."[63]

In the following three years, Paton focused her wrath on social workers' persistent callousness and the pernicious social consequences that followed in their wake. Still stung by the way social workers ostracized her for "attacking the profession," she criticized them for not caring "enough about the individual client to see his pain."[64] Paton also denounced them for being responsible for the sealed record policy in adoption. She dared those who objected to the policy to emulate her and quit the profession; she thought it "impossible to change things from within."[65] And, although Paton did make an exception for a small number of social workers—10 percent, mostly older ones, ready to retire—whom she thought could be educated, she held out little hope for the rest, "no matter how hard they try. They are just too legitimate."[66] She was now of the opinion that the social work profession had to be "replaced by something quite different" if society were to benefit from its services. History had demonstrated that the power that social workers wielded in the lives of adopted people resulted in "much, much destructiveness . . . and they seem not even to see it. It is really the great American Tragedy." Paton also suggested that in addition to changing the profession of social work, "the academic world has to be changed also—all the sociologists and psychologists, and anthropologists, as well, to name a few" because all these professions were responsible for social work's policies. But such changes would take forty or fifty years, and she would not live to see them.[67]

What Paton particularly objected to in social work was its emphasis on therapy. During the first half of the twentieth century, the profession was deeply rooted in psychoanalytic theory and the medical model. Harshly criticized in the 1960s for viewing different lifestyles as deviant and for ignoring the needs, difficulties, and positive attributes of oppressed groups, social work—and psychotherapy itself—moved away from its reliance on classical psychoanalytic techniques and grew more diverse. By the 1990s, the profession had expanded to encompass many forms of psychotherapy. One authority stated that treatment "may be short term or long term in nature and involve discharge planning, case management, and linkage to community and social resources, as well as the support of or modification of long-standing personality or interpersonal difficulties."[68]

Paton, along with many others, did not distinguish between the various forms of psychotherapy and lumped them together. This tendency to view all therapies as similar was due to what the historian Eva S. Moskowitz has documented as the exponential growth in America after World War II of the "therapeutic gospel," which she defines as not just a philosophy "but a faith, a program for individual and social development" whose chief tenets are that happiness, wealth, and success "must be measured with a psychological yardstick."[69] The adoption support groups of the 1970s were just the tip of the iceberg of an unprecedented expansion in the number of organizations that brought people together to work on personal issues, rediscover their feelings, and find their identity. In the 1980s, the American Psychiatric Association's *Diagnostic and Statistical Manual of Mental Disorders* had identified a problem it labeled "identity disorder," which consisted of "severe subjective distress regarding inability to integrate aspects of the self into a relatively coherent and acceptable sense of self." No adopted person in the 1970s had imagined that asking the question "Who am I?" would end up classified as an official psychiatric disorder. With the advent of such TV talk programs as the *Phil Donahue Show* and *Oprah*, confessing one's personal problems—a messy divorce, an alcohol problem, or the search for a birth parent—became a form of mass entertainment. In the United States today, there are more than three million recovery and/or self-help groups. The adoption reform movement was deeply implicated in the therapeutic gospel, as self-help books with titles such as *Adoption Encounter: Hurt, Transition, Healing* lined bookstore shelves.[70]

Paton was a longtime critic of psychoanalysis, and her views on psychotherapy and adoption in the 1990s were complicated, sometimes contradictory, and easily misunderstood. To one correspondent, she declared that she did not actually disapprove of therapy, citing her own positive experience with Otto Rank, who "helped [me] get back into the world," for which she had "always been grateful." She conceded that some modern therapists empathized with adult adoptees. She contrasted Nancy Verrier's strong conviction about the importance of searching for first family members with her own therapist, Jessie Taft, who failed to make any such suggestion. Had Taft encouraged her to search, "I could have been into the clear much earlier in my life. But, she, too, was an adoptive parent! It was a misfortune for me."[71] Similarly, Paton initially approved of a psychologist named Marlou Russell, who gave a lecture on "Adoption: The Lifelong Impact" and sponsored a discussion of "the emotional/psychological aspects of adoption."[72] Upon receiving a flyer advertising the event, Paton wrote Russell, stating that although she believed that "therapeutics with adopted people" was questionable as long as adoption records remained sealed, "consultation and education on adoption issues is another matter entirely, and I believe it should be done often by those who have perspective."[73]

The key to understanding Paton's apparently contradictory remarks about therapy is to recognize that throughout her life she made a sharp distinction between the causes of an adoptee's psychological trauma and its cure. As she wrote Janine Baer, a feminist adoption activist, "I find the necessary therapy for the adoptee to be for his traumatic, not his character, neurosis. That makes it a very different scheme." Reiterating her understanding of Abram Kardiner's work on traumatic neurosis, Paton believed that the psychological problems of adult adoptees were the result of environmental factors, in particular sealed adoption records, rather than dysfunctional interior psychological processes. Therapy for the latter she referred to as "character" or "reality" therapy, and asserted that "reality therapy cannot be used with records under the seal. It is that simple."[74] Paton believed that "growth experiences" in the lives of adult adoptees—the need to search, for example—were impossible to experience under "reality therapy," which she identified with "professionalism and fees."

In a piece entitled "Therapeutic Hesitancy," Paton provided readers with her most detailed critique of therapy's ineffectiveness. She wrote it in reaction to the rapid, mushrooming business of counseling adult adoptees, which she "put on par with counseling people in prison with life sentences."[75] She was convinced that therapy failed to help adopted people due to its faulty methodology—the talking cure. From what Paton could tell, "something goes on in these encounters, the problems are recognized," but therapists using this method with adopted persons fail to solve their problems. Paton attributed the lack of success to the analyst's failure to acknowledge "an adopted person's interest in background information or to the existence of sealed records." This "aura of avoidance" extended even to those adult adoptees in the movement "turned counselors and therapists," who "should know better." Had not their own search experience taught them this?

Paton proceeded to elaborate on the proper form of "therapeutic services toward people who are in bondage toward the sealed record." Special processes had to be developed in which both the expert and the person receiving therapy joined together. Paton suggested that both of them might need "to go to the local library, to the local court house, to the local newspaper, and present their interests in obtaining information." She urged that that these actions had to be done repeatedly in order for the adopted person to grow and mature. As an example, Paton recalled her employment as a social worker in rural Pennsylvania. She had entered a county court house with a sixteen-year-old girl who was under her supervision. Paton asked for and received the court papers that had brought the young girl many years earlier into the state's care. She turned these documents over to her. Paton then wrote: "She read them through, and as we left the court house she was aglow with quiet happiness." She believed that the young girl's "quiet happiness" was due to her learning why she had been separated from her parents and beginning "to know who she was and had been." Through this process, Paton believed, "she could the better learn about who she was to become." Paton never deviated from insisting that adult adoptees depend as much as possible on themselves, not experts.

Paton's dissatisfaction with mainstream therapy was not due simply to its methodological shortcomings and ineffectiveness. She denounced the "several thousand therapeuticians" who worked on adult adoptees' problems for avoiding the real issue of opening adoption records.[76] "I disbelieve in post-adoption therapeutics, which yammers away in the counseling interview, but leaves the source of cure still under the seal in the agency and the courthouse .... To engage in such activities is to deny the pain of the adopted person, and therefore once again to fail him/her at a point of crisis."[77] Paton asked what good was therapy to an adopted person who desired to search for his first family, "prohibited by law, if the law is not changed?" It was the "prohibition itself that [was] the demon behind the problem," and therefore it was the "the prohibition itself which needed to be done in."[78] If that political goal was achieved, Paton declared, it "would cure a great proportion of the difficulties." But she doubted that would ever happen.[79] When Paton heard that Senator Carl Levin was again proposing his National Reunion Registry bill in Congress, to be administered by the Department of Health and Human Services, with high fees, mandatory counseling, and consent required from adoptive parents, she thundered, "the trend to confront each searching adopted person with nothing but counseling and therapy makes me sick to my stomach."[80] Moreover, Paton had always viewed the reunion process as a healing process. She was astonished to see "a whole new population of therapists trying to heal us without a reunion."[81] Several years later, Janine Baer asked Paton whether she still believed in the power of a reunion to heal adult adoptees. Paton replied, "I don't know what else heals us. It releases potentialities that have been under wraps for many years. I think that is healing."[82]

Paton also became fed up with the misuse of her early work by psychiatrists and repudiated two theoretical perspectives that by the 1990s had become axiomatic among adoption professionals and academics.[83] The first was the idea that adoption was a lifelong process or that adoption had a lifelong impact on a person. Books with such titles as *The Adoption Life Cycle: The Children and Their Families through the Years* and *Being Adopted: The Lifelong Search for Help* provided triad members with psychosocial models of adoption adjustment broken down into phases, or stages, from infancy to young adulthood.[84] Paton interpreted this as meaning "you never get away from adoption as a causative element in your life" and declared "it simply is not so." She criticized the experts, who had "thoroughly misunderstood" her inductive hypothesis in *The Adopted Break Silence* that at certain times in their lives adult adoptees keep searching for their roots until they are satisfied. This did not mean that "an adopted person must go to the therapist all their life because 'adoption is a lifelong process,'" or that they "have to keep on attributing to adoption a lifelong influence on their lives." What her book did say was that if adult adoptees had information on how to locate members of their first family, they searched and then went on with their lives. Of course, if they were prevented from obtaining the information that would enable them to discover their kin, they might keep searching. But without such impediments—by which Paton of course meant sealed adoption records—most adopted people, after finding their roots, moved on with their lives.[85]

The second theory Paton criticized was the use made by experts of Elisabeth Kübler-Ross's five-stage grief cycle that occurred when people realize they had a terminal illness or faced a catastrophic personal loss or disaster.[86] In 1979 Pam Lamperelli, a psychiatric social worker, and Jane M. Smith, a nurse and human sexuality counselor, studied nineteen unwed mothers and reported that relinquishing a child for adoption produced a "parallel grief" reaction akin to that experienced by a person who loses a loved one through death or separation. They concluded that these mothers were suffering from separation anxiety and were grieving for the infant they had relinquished. Lamperelli and Smith argued that Elizabeth Kübler-Ross's morphology of mourning and grief was analogous to the experience of unwed mothers who had given up their children for adoption. Both groups went through a process of denial, anger, guilt, depression, preoccupation with the lost person, bargaining, and finally acceptance. Lamperelli and Smith believed that unwed mothers accepted the relinquishment of the child fairly quickly and, with counseling, could move on with their lives. Many adoption reform activists, however, denied that birth mothers could ever overcome the psychological damage inflicted by relinquishing a child for adoption without either opening the records, conducting a successful reunion, or practicing open adoption.[87]

Paton claimed that experts' misreading of Kübler-Ross's theory distorted "the true nature of adoption." Cutting to the heart of the difference between her ideas and those of the therapeuticians, she asserted, "The stages of grief, . . . do not apply to a physical separation of two people, a mother and her child, who remain in this life. It applies to the event of death, which is utterly distinct from an adoption separation." The signing of adoption relinquishing forms, Paton noted sardonically, "did not send either an adopted person, or her birth mother, to the realm of the angels, but leaves them among us, presentable to each other in the future here on earth."

Along with therapists' methodological shortcoming, ineffectiveness, and failure to condemn sealed adoption records, Paton denounced them for profiting at the expense of adult adoptees. To Rod Holm, an adoptive father and author, Paton declared, "Therapy is the name of the game today, and the blind professionals are hopeful of having a good and profitable life in this fashion."[88] In her opinion, they all had a conflict of interest. If they were truly concerned about their clients they should seek to open adoption records, but that would jeopardize "their status, their grants, and salaries."[89] However, she expected the professionals to make money from adoption reform, "as they always have and always will." What really hurt Paton were the activists, such as Nancy Verrier and Betty Jean Lifton, who administered therapy to adult adoptees and searchers, such as Pat Sanders, who charged for their services. Paton considered such activities unethical, and believed that such people wanted to earn "some cash because [they] have no idea what else to with [their] adoption life."[90] To one correspondent she declared that when she began the Life History Study Center, it had never occurred to her that the work "would encourage people to make money off of their brothers in adoptions." Even though her own poverty sometimes bothered her, "it never appealed to me to make money off my brethren in affliction except for the actual costs of the office and proper appurtenances."[91]

Paton's unhappiness with the adoption reform movement's confidence in professionals and therapy came to a head in 1998 with the announcement of an upcoming conference, "Demystifying the Adopted-Life Experience," sponsored by Philadelphia's Adoption Forum. Although triad members predominated at the conference, the vast majority of them were social workers, with professional credentials strung after their names: "MSW, LCSW"; "MA, CSW";

"BA, CSW." Also featured as speakers were a psychotherapist and a doctoral candidate described in the conference flyer as a "senior psychoanalytic candidate." The conference talks also reflected the movement's takeover by experts preaching the therapeutic gospel, with topics such as "Getting Ready to See the Social Worker," My Life as an Adoptee/Adoption Professional," and "I'm Fine and I'm Certainly Not Angry."[92] Paton exploded at Abigail Lovett, president of the Adoption Forum and vice president of the AAC, stating that she had been "disturbed" for three days after receiving the flyer announcing the conference. She deplored, "most of all, the distractions of therapy" and demanded that Lovett focus the conference on "ourselves [and] what we have lost." Paton angrily summed up what was wrong with the conference:

> A stinging swarm of women wanting to have initials after their names, wanting to have "employment that matters" are swarming on us little colonials, who have nothing to say about what is done to us. Our childhood matters not, let the child be bewildered until he is 18 or perhaps 21, and then send him or her to therapists all his life long. And let us not forget what happens to the mother, whose grief cannot be assuaged by Kubler-Ross.[93]

Paton's deep dissatisfaction with the adoption reform movement's dependence on professionals and therapy reinforced her repudiation of the institution of adoption. She had already endorsed guardianship in place of adoption. Now Paton went beyond guardianship as she put forward a series of proposals that would prevent the removal of children from their birth parents and, if the children were relinquished, make the eventual reunion easier. She publicly advocated that children must keep their original names if they had to be transferred to new homes; they must maintain an active connection to their original families; and babies must be kept with their mothers after birth and nursed (if possible). She urged that mothers and children not be separated, "even if we must devise help for the mother that is different from adoption." To carry out the idea, Paton called for a nationwide group of individuals to supervise the plan. These compassionate and wise "counselors," as Paton dubbed them, would be stationed in every county of every state to assist "a problem pregnancy moving toward completion." In addition to their compassion and wisdom, the counselors would also have been born out of wedlock themselves and have connections to wealthy patrons, who would be willing give abundant financial aid. Paton also urged that all social agencies that held adoption records should have "Open Houses, inviting all those whom they have separated to return for the processes of reunion." Paton believed that if the agencies enacted the Open

Houses policy and it were well advertised it would erase the societal prejudice against keeping children with their original families and signal the end of the state sealing of records. She concluded with the prayer "And may I be forgiven for my many years of blindness."[94]

In 1994 Paton sent a letter to *US News and World Report*, which expressed her anti-adoption view succinctly: "No ADOPTION at all." Paton reported to her friend Rosemary Sever that these few words undercut "all the fancy non-solutions the various parts of the movement come up with," referring probably to open adoption. Stopping all adoptions had the added benefit in Paton's mind of taking "most of the search money and the therapy money out of the picture. These people who have been supporting themselves this way will have to go to work." She anticipated heated criticism for her anti-adoption stance but said she was unworried; she even welcomed it. Paton declared that she was going to send her letter to newspapers as well to give her idea added publicity."[95]

As an alternative to adoption, and in combination with her new emphasis on the value of childhood, the 1990s found Paton reemphasizing the crucial importance of kinship and the preservation of the nuclear family. Even though she herself had not been born into what she called "a genetic family," its significance had been bred into her, she wrote one correspondent, a result of her having grown up in the large Paton family, with its frequent reunions at one or another of the relative's farms where there was plenty of food and ball games. She was treated as one of the family because, as she discovered decades later, the extended family "believed I was Dr. Paton's natural child."[96] Thus imbued with the importance of genetic family ties, Paton as early as 1958 lamented the changes that American kinship was experiencing and the negative consequences of adoption.[97] In 1983, she published in *Genealogy Digest* a short piece entitled "The Disappearance of Kinship," lamenting the destruction of kinship ties around the world as a result of adoption and divorce, as children's links to their past were broken.[98]

But it was in the 1990s when Paton's role as the Paul Revere of the nuclear family became a central preoccupation, as she warned whoever would listen of its decline, identified its enemies, and suggested methods for its preservation. She was outraged at the culture's redefining the word "family" to mean unrelated people living together in a household. In a manifesto, Paton denounced the use of the word when "applied to skimpy associations of a few people in one house." Such usage ignored the "fabulous definition of what can be, a stalk for the life of children, and appl[ied] it to any little effervescence of human cohabitation." For Paton, "a house which has no procreation is not a house for a family. It is a house for a small gathering of folks who are fearful and uncertain. Let the family return in its full sense again."[99] To another correspondent, Paton identified the enemies of the nuclear family as the same ones who promoted sealed adoption records and were enthusiastic about adoption. They despised the kinship family and thought it outmoded, conflict ridden, and especially "a barrier to ONE WORLD." She declared, "I have had a belly-full of utopianism" that could only be supported by the theories of the therapists, "to help us limp through our uncertain lives." As an example, Paton cited R. D. Laing, the Scottish psychiatrist who linked mental distress to a dysfunctional family upbringing, as one of those therapists who became "famous and admired because of his denigration of the kinship family."[100] Paton was also critical of the United Nations Convention on the Rights of the Child, which she asserted failed to mention kinship when it discussed adoption. She admitted that the convention did, however, talk about the rights of children and their ability to decide just about anything, "except adoption, which was always, 'in the best interests of the child'" a phrase that in essence was a "manual to deprive poor families of their children."[101]

In Paton's opinion, volunteer organizations, rather than state intervention, were necessary to preserve the deterioration of the nuclear family. She provided as an example a Palm Beach, Florida, church that formed a committee to interview and support deserving women whose families were at risk. Similarly, she commended an idea promulgated by an organization known as CASA, Court Appointed Special Advocates for Children, whereby court-appointed special advocates chosen from a pool of citizen volunteers were given the authority to go into a home where there was a report of abuse or neglect, work with the family, and report back to the court.[102] Paton also approved of a program that called on volunteers to assist in homes where there was a new baby and an inexperienced or young mother.[103] Paton's concern for preserving kinship ties became all consuming. Even when a book was published containing first-person accounts stressing the complexity, importance, and healing ability of reunions for birth mothers with their adopted children, Paton criticized it for not addressing the question "What about the rest of the family?"[104]

As Paton continued in 1994 to send out *A Proper Response*, she put the rest of her Colorado acreage on the market and contemplated selling her house and moving to Arkansas. It was a difficult decision. Cedaredge had been the most beautiful place she had ever lived, and she had called it her home for twenty-five years. Paton described Cedaredge as her "salvation and comfort."[105] But several factors eventually pushed Paton out of Cedaredge, including her tough financial situation. Even though Paton owned her house outright, the cost of living was much lower in Arkansas, and she anticipated living for at least another decade.[106] In addition, maintenance of the property had become onerous: "the snow, water problems, the septic tank, and all that goes with country living" had become just too much for the two old women.[107] Several other factors pulled Jean and June to the small town of Harrison, Arkansas. Prior to moving to Colorado, June had lived in Harrison a long time; she knew practically everyone, including the folks in the next county, from her fifteen years of nursing. Paton was pleased to think that they would know their neighbors and that they would not be isolated.[108] In addition, Paton boasted to her friend Margaret Lawrence that Harrison was "one of the 100 best small towns in America to live in."[109]

In 1995, Paton sold the Cedaredge home on contract, allowing them to stay as long as they wanted. Paton had already purchased a house in Harrison, which June visited in March 1996.[110] Three months later, they packed up and moved. Paton reported that "without friends, real friends, we could not have made it." One remarkable birth mother packed up all her files in shipping boxes, loaded them into a van and took them to the post office. She did the same for Paton's library of a thousand books. Over two days, the rest of their possessions were put into a U-Haul by a dozen or more friends who went through the entire house "like ants through a pile of sugar, filling box after box after box, taking out of our hands anything we were trying to add to the collection." Paton was awed by the experience; it reminded her of an old-fashioned "barn–raising on a farm." She was gratified that the same thing happened in reverse when they arrived in Harrison due to June's earlier contacts.[111] The four-bedroom older house that they moved into in mid-June was on a quiet street in a hilly part of Harrison.[112]

Selling off her Cedaredge property, packing up and moving, and settling into her new home had little effect on Paton's productivity. In 1994, Paton created another pin, oval in shape, red on white in color, with a single word, BIRTHISM, emblazoned on it. She explained that it signified that adopted people throughout their lives were subjected to social discrimination simply because they were born out of wedlock.[113] Despite Paton's having discontinued The LOG, people continued to contact Orphan Voyage, discovering her name in an adoption self-help book, being referred to by an adoption search group, hearing of the organization by word of mouth, or reading about her in an adoption newsletter. In 1997, for example, Shea Grimm, the legislative chair of the newly created, radical adoption rights organization, Bastard Nation, came across an old speech Paton had made while Grimm was reading a back issue of Chain-of-Life, a feminist adoption reform newsletter. In 1991, Paton had traveled to Washington, D.C., and spoke in front of the Lincoln Memorial at an open adoption records rally. In the speech, Paton had denounced a new piece of legislation calling for a confidential intermediary system, sponsored by an adoptee search organization in Denver. Paton's firm belief that any law that prevented adult adoptees from the unconditional freedom to access their adoption records was a message that Bastard Nation, the new radicals of adoption reform, found useful. Grim commented on the group's Internet discussion list:

> I almost cried when I read this, and I'm [a] fairly steely-eyed, hardened of heart individual. Some of those who we have been arguing with have called us arrogant, naïve, and inexperienced. Is that what they would call the now 87-year-old mother of adoption reform, who is expressing our same sentiments. . . . I submit that the adoption reform movement has caved. They have forgotten what it meant to be impassioned and they have turned away from what brought us all here in the first place.[114]

During the period 1994–1995, Paton received over 900 letters requesting help. She responded by making referrals by mail or discussing the issues by telephone. Perhaps feeling a little insecure, she asked rhetorically how an eighty-seven-year-old woman could have any idea about what was going on in the adoption reform movement. Her answer was to communicate with the outside world, as she had always done. Paton told her readers that "communication was my salvation," citing, "phones, travel, newsletter distribution, publicity here and there, and eventually a large mailing list." Although she had discontinued some of this activity, she still received mail and phone calls, as well as several adoption newsletters from groups all around the country, which she read carefully.[115]

Nor did Bastard Nation escape Paton's censure. Although in 1996 she had "some admiration for [its] youthful energies," Paton found it "basically weak" because its members were unwilling to consider what happened to the adopted child.[116] In February 1997, she reacted with disbelief that Bastard Nation justified opening adoption records "only as a civil right, empty of connections with other people, including our birth mothers and fathers, and other relatives." Plaintively, Paton asked, "What is the struggle for?" For Paton, the purpose of opening records was to connect with family members and heal the trauma that separation had created and the resulting psychological problems. Speaking in Bastard Nation's language, she asked, "Is it a right we are not going to use?" If not, was it because adult adoptees were so strong they would just go ahead and use the information or was it perhaps because they were too weak to use the information?[117]

Adding immensely to Paton's censorious opinion of the adoption reform movement's direction was her view that its leaders disregarded her advice and failed to appreciate her accomplishments. She despaired at her helplessness but was resigned to the fact that there was little she could do about it. Paton informed Mary Iwanek in 1995 that she still wrote letters and commented on issues, but she no longer was permitted at conferences to "engage in meaningful conversation with the leadership. They go their own way, because they think it has worked and will continue to work." She no longer had the energy or stamina to fight the movement's leadership.[118] Paton was particularly sensitive, one might say overly sensitive, to not being accorded the recognition for her pioneering activities in adoption reform, which demanded dedication, intense labor, and financial sacrifice. She complained to Joan Wheeler that "people are very much unaware of what I have accomplished, and how much work I have done." She specifically denounced the AAC "for never giving me credit, do not even seem to know what I did."[119]

Yet Paton had a tendency to ignore actions that did recognize her pioneering accomplishments. In 1996, on the occasion of CUB's twentieth anniversary, President Bonnie Bis honored her with a certificate of appreciation that enumerated the many services Paton performed in her long career. The inscription praised her in a variety of categories. As an educator, Jean Paton "taught everyone that adopted children grow up." She "has enriched us all with her insight, her analysis, her warmth, sometimes her gentle chiding, and always a wonderful sense of humor." As the conscience of the movement, Jean Paton "insists on pointing out the truth, not hiding it or hiding from it." And as an ombudsman and reformer, Jean Paton "has been the ultimate voice for adoptees and a friend to us all. She is neither a birthmother nor an adoptive mother but she is truly the Mother of the Adoption Reform Movement."[120] Paton never mentioned this honor in her newsletter and did so only once in her correspondence.

Like many who dwell on perceived affronts to their many achievements, Paton became very concerned about her place in history. She expressed "astonishment" and took exception to hyperbolic statements from regional leaders such as Susan Darke, who claimed that she, Darke, had made the "long walk alone in the dark when there was no one to help" her. She pulled Darke's file, read it thoroughly, and wrote to remind her about the extensive correspondence that they had had almost thirty years earlier, beginning with Darke's phone call and the substantial help Paton had afterward rendered her. She reminded her that it was Paton who organized the American Adoption Congress "and from that time on no one was alone." She indignantly informed Darke that she exaggerated greatly if she believed "that without you there would be no movement," and concluded from her ignorance of Paton's pioneering role in the movement that "all of us should know the history of the movement, and perhaps a little enlightenment is due."[121]

Paton followed her own advice to Darke and did her best to enlighten the readers of *A Proper Response* about her place in the history of the adoption reform movement. She did this in a number of ways. Using *A Proper Response* as a vehicle, she began providing capsule histories of her life in conjunction with her plan to publish two books, a diary of the years of her transition from social work to adoption reform (1950–1953) and a collection of issues of *The LOG*. The diary, Paton explained, described a time of "fierce conflict" in which she asked "very probing questions and found few answers." It was during this period, she continued, that she studied science for two years at the University of Pennsylvania, supporting herself through part-time work. These years Paton thought of "as the best of my life" because during that time she "learned to think." Learning to think like a scientist trained her for her future work as an adoption reformer, though she did not know it at the time. The second book project, the publication of *The LOG of Orphan Voyage*, Paton promoted as "the single source of information on the effort to build a movement to question the sealed record," thus subtly revising the historical record. More accurately, she described its original purpose as "the bold, but almost innocent effort I made to find someone who would share my thoughts, and help me in the development of mine." Instead, she found a community of adopted people, who down through the years shared her experiences. If only Paton could get *The LOG* published, its historical contents would demonstrate to the world her importance to adoption reform. But the cost was prohibitive. She thus began a campaign to raise money for its publication, ostensibly for public education, not personal aggrandizement. As she stated, "I would like, more than I can express, to find a way to have the *LOG* printed up so that more people can know how long we have tried."[122] By 1997, Paton had contacted a local printer, received an estimate on the cost of the project, and began to solicit financial support from her readers to get the project "off the ground."[123]

In keeping with her role as self-appointed historian of the adoption search movement, Paton took it upon herself to correct inaccurate portrayals of its history. She took to task sociologist Katarina Wegar for stating that the movement was "essentially an outgrowth and an extension of the civil rights movement of the 1950s."[124] On the contrary, Paton declared, "we did not grow out of the civil rights movement, but out of our own hunger for roots." In particular, she continued, the adoption reform movement between 1953 and 1972 "was under the almost exclusive promotion by Jean Paton, and between 1972 and 1979 it was added to by the impulses from Florence Fisher. Then in 1979 it grew into the American Adoption Congress." The real history, Paton emphasized, was buried and hidden in the archives of Orphan Voyage and in Fisher's files. But it also could be found in *The LOG*, her correspondence, and in a "book, due to come out this October, from Harvard University Press, by Dr. Wayne Carp of Ta-coma."[125] Almost a year later, Paton informed the readers of A Proper Response that "my principal anticipation at this time is awaiting the release of Family Mat-ters, a history of the movement to open adoption records, by Prof. E. Wayne Carp of the Pacific Lutheran University in Tacoma, Washington."[126] The press had sent her the manuscript of Family Matters, and she had written a blurb, stating that "the lives of millions of people will be influenced by this book."[127]

My book, Family Matters, turned out to be controversial. Before receiving any of Paton's correspondence or interviewing her, I was asked to be the key-note speaker at the 1998 annual meeting of the AAC held in Bellevue, Wash-ington. As I gave my talk, AAC members were feverishly devouring my book, where they discovered, among other things, that I had criticized psychological interpretations of maladjustment in adult adoptees; expressed skepticism of the unscientific conclusions of adoption researchers Arthur Sorosky, Annette Baran, and Reuben Pannor; and favored a national adoption registry. Things got hot during the question-and-answer period, as a number of AAC members took me to task for what they interpreted as my hostility to the adoption re-form movement. In truth, I was not hostile but ignorant and rather naïve about movement politics. I had told Paton as much in thanking her for publicizing the forthcoming publication of Family Matters in A Proper Response.[128] News of my divisive performance at the AAC conference reached Paton. One correspondent informed her that "Carp turned out to be a wolf in the henhouse," though she quickly added, "that may be a bit too strong, but [he] certainly caused some consternation."[129] Betty Jean Lifton was even more blunt, warning Paton "to stay away from him."[130] Nevertheless, Paton defended me. She noted in A Proper Response that "some in the AAC are aghast" at my talk and at Family Matters. Although Paton admitted that she, too, was taken aback by my apparent un-awareness of many movement events, she planned to remedy that when I visited her. More positively, she asserted, "[Carp] has given us widespread publicity, and if all of us do not agree with it, at least we have been recognized for what we have done, and history will decide our fate."[131]

Even before my trip to Harrison, Paton had sent me seven boxes of her cor-respondence, and word had spread in the movement that she had chosen me as her biographer. This, too, provoked controversy. Lifton wrote Paton denouncing my keynote address at the AAC annual meeting and criticizing Family Matters. In particular, Lifton was angry that I had described her background inaccurate-ly and had not interviewed her and other adoption reformers. "Some historian," she harrumphed. More seriously, she deplored the second half of Family Matters for discrediting "the adoption reform movement and the work of many people in it—including myself." Lifton expressed surprise that Paton had written a blurb for the book, and suggested that she could have done so only if she had not read the last half of the book. She was saddened at hearing that Paton had turned her archives over to me and hoped she would change her mind and get them back.[132] But Paton also received support for her decision. Author and adoption activist L. Anne Babb wrote, "I've heard that E. Wayne Carp is preparing your biography," and declared, "He's a good writer and I'm pleased to know that this is a work in progress. Congratulations! How wonderful to be honored."[133]

A few days later, Paton replied to Lifton, defending me as her biographer. She declared that she had read the book in page proof carefully and that she had disagreed with it on two basic issues.[134] But, she continued, "I did not see that [Carp's] attitude toward your work and Baran et al should prevent me from communicating with him." Paton noted my intense interest in her "correct role in the adoption reform movement, on which he has become considerably enlightened since he received my files to review (They have not been assigned to him for keeps). So, it is entirely rational, reasonable and judicious of me to receive him here in Harrison, Arkansas."[135]

After a wonderful week of being interviewed in Harrison, Arkansas, in June 1998, Paton must have made up her mind that I would make an ideal biographer. In some ways, she was predisposed in that direction. After reading *Family Matters*, Jean was of the opinion that I had some intelligence and concluded perhaps that I could make a contribution to historical understanding:

> I did get some new orientation from your book about my own work. You emphasized that it began about something we could do for ourselves, and for creating and demonstrating the existence of a special population. I had not thought of it exactly that way, but it strikes me that it is a correct assessment, and I am comfortable with it.[136]

In addition, *Family Matters* expressed viewpoints that were compatible with Paton's worldview. For example, it was critical of experts, such as Arthur Sorosky and his research associates, and skeptical of the discipline of psychology and psychoanalysis. But perhaps most important, and unknown to me at the time, my proposal to write the life of Jean Paton arrived at a critical time in her life, when she was feeling unrecognized and unappreciated. In her letter to Betty Jean Lifton she detailed how professional social work had ostracized her, with the result that "no student of adoption could have an understanding of my work." She also noted that the movement had shunned her, citing as evidence that no student could have learned about her or her work from reading the

Decree, the AAC's newsletter, because neither she nor her work was ever mentioned there. Referring to our intense weeklong talks, Paton wrote afterward that "it was something as if I was emerging from a grave, where the ostracism put me so long ago. . . . So now that will be corrected."[137] In short, Paton saw me as "a genuine historian"[138] with access to a prestigious university press, who would finally tell her story, which had been withheld by friend and foe alike; and, because I was not involved in the adoption reform movement, I would tell that story without bias or prejudice. As she said, "I really am not looking for justification, but simply an honest place in history."[139]

Epilogue

> I have always been certain that we bastards and associates are very important people to society, that our message should therefore be voiced with the greatest clarity and honesty. This I have tried to do, it appears so, with my life. It seems to be almost endless.

—JEAN PATON [1993–1994]

Paton died in 2002 at age ninety-three. Death came unexpectedly, surprising her friends. In relatively good health, she had begun to slow down and take it easy. But in January 1998, Paton experienced what she described as a slight stroke and was rushed to the hospital in her "nightgown and morning wrap," where she was stabilized for a week. Medical authorities informed her that she had suffered a TIA, a transient ischemic attack, that produced strokelike symptoms but no lasting damage. She was given the medication Cumadin (warfarin), a blood thinner, which is used to prevent blood clots.[1] Paton was unfazed by this threat to her health. In the last years of her life, she enjoyed telling her friends, "My doctor says to me 'you can make it into the hundreds.'"[2] Still, in thinking back about the causes of her stroke, she mused that beyond the fact that she was growing old, part of her illness was a result of "the accumulation of what it is like to have to work hard to overcome an ostracism," never being "permitted to get into 'respectable' publications."[3] She believed that to avoid further complications to her health she had "to lessen my intensity, if that is possible" and was glad that her companion, June Schwantes, had spent a lifetime as a professional nurse.[4]

Around this time, sensing her mortality perhaps, Paton decided to draw up her will. She left all of the assets of Orphan Voyage, including her books and correspondence, to her close friend Molly Johnson, stipulating that Johnson was to maintain these resources or place them in a suitable archive interested in preserving them. All of her other possessions she left to June. Paton included a living will, publicly stating that she did "not wish to be maintained in a vegeta- tive state."[5] In 2000, however, Paton reported that her doctor considered her "close to the picture of health."[6] When people were told her age, "they drop their jaws in disbelief."[7]

In her last years, Paton found some time for activities unconnected with adoption reform. One of her chief enjoyments was sitting in her backyard. A neighbor regularly mowed her front yard, but Paton forbade him from touching the grass behind her house. Much to her delight, the yard quickly became overgrown with plant life. Wild vegetation abounded, with "a specially lovely grass about four feet tall, and lovely to look at." Paton researched it and discovered it was Indian Grass. She would cut bunches of the flowering stalks, bring them into the house, and enjoy a long-lasting bouquet. The ninety-year-old Paton "loved sitting out back and just watching things grow."[8] Not one for formal religion, she nevertheless joined a Presbyterian church in 1999. Writing to adoption activist Betty Allen, Paton explained why she had not joined a church before this time. "I have found that the theology needed by orphans is far removed from some of the older ways of looking at things. Christianity belongs to us, does it not? Who are all these legitimate people who have taken it over?" She characterized it as "a small church, just the right size for my tastes," presided over by a liberal pastor. Although Paton worried that the church authorities desired to acquire another ten acres and build a larger structure, she was content to attend this "warm congregation" as long as it remained as it was. She justified her decision to join by declaring that "I have seen an immense correlation between search for parents and search for God. When we forbid one, we discourage the other."[9] She also continued to write poetry and found time to sculpt in clay, which was "really my true love."[10]

Still, most of Paton's time in those last years was occupied by some aspect of adoption reform. Spurred by her desire to leave a historical legacy, she spent much time sorting and organizing her vast correspondence and files. In part, this work was done to prepare her archive to mail the bulk of it to me, so that I could write her biography. In part, Paton wanted to write her own book, which she humorously characterized as one that "had a thousand titles." Writing was hard for her, however, not least because she was now ninety years old. She lamented, "I am still as sluggish about any real work. I spend too much time in a chair looking at TV. I know spring will help, and I continue in what seems to be a protracted vacation."[11] But Paton was hampered in writing for long stretches of time by a new development: numbness in a few of her fingers.[12] By the beginning of the year 2000, the dead sensation in her hands had developed into full-blown carpal tunnel syndrome, which became increasingly painful. Paton took to wearing a special glove which, by preventing her from undue use of her right hand, allowed her to continue to type.[13] In this way, she spent some time working on her book. But, although Paton detected some order beginning to appear, she lamented that "I have become so slow with everything."[14] In April 2001, she wrote to Annette Baran that much of her time was now spent "in the deeps of planning rather than doing," in particular conceiving of "the two books" of which she could think of the details, but "they are still waiting for me, tugging at my hands."[15]

Paton might have slowed down, but her mental and critical faculties were as sharp as ever. She continued to pursue research into psychoneurology, searching for a reason in the brain why adopted people lost their energy "after the trauma of separation from the mother."[16] In *Discover* magazine, a popular science and technology monthly, Paton found an article that explained a child's stress as a response to the brain sending signals to the sympathetic nervous system, setting off a "fight or flight" response, where adrenaline and cortisol were secreted from the adrenal glands. Paton underlined the following paragraph:

> This is all well and good—unless the perceived threat persists. In that case, adrenaline washes out of the body quickly, but cortisol may linger for days, weeks, or even years, keeping the immune system and other important functions depressed. Children are especially vulnerable to stress. . . . In the long term, too much cortisol can slow down a child's growth, brain development, and sexual maturation.[17]

These were the exact characteristics that Paton had been attributing to adult adoptees for decades. She also enthusiastically recommended Candace Pert's book, *Molecules of Emotion*. Pert, a research professor in brain biochemistry at the Georgetown University School of Medicine, propounded a theory that neuropeptides and their receptors carry information in a vast network, linking the material world of molecules with the nonmaterial world of the psyche. Her views on mind-body cellular communication provided strong scientific support for the idea that the power of peoples' minds and feelings affects their health and well-being.[18] Paton summed up her work by stating that Pert had discovered scientifically that "our problems are in our cells."[19]

Paton continued to keep close tabs on the adoption reform movement. During the late 1990s, several major developments had occurred. In 1996, Tennessee became the first state in the union to pass an open records law since records were first sealed in the 1950s. The law was challenged in the courts, but in *Doe v. Sundquist*, the Tennessee Supreme Court upheld the rights of adoptees to see their birth records. In 1998 and 2000, respectively, Oregon and Alabama also passed legislation opening adoption birth records unconditionally. Activists viewed these legislative developments with hope, seeing in them a trend toward openness in adoption that would lead to a revolution in adoption practice and policy.

Paton was much less optimistic. In the twilight of her career as an adoption reformer, she held to her earlier skepticism about the efficacy of legislation to effect adoption reform. To Denny Glad, the architect of the Tennessee open records law, Paton wrote, "I have come to the belief that there is no cure for us in the law (even in Oregon?) but it can only come by our showing society that we of this adoption population love one another." The way to do this, she suggested, was by specific programs, such as her own Adoption Memorial and Paton House. If these programs were enacted, "we would not be full of apologies and guilt in approaching search. We would somehow be welcomed. Oh, that is what we need!" Unfortunately, Paton continued, the response to her proposals was pitiful.[20] To other correspondents, she declared that "the entire program of changing the sealed record" through the law would not alter the damage already done to children separated from their parents. Paton continued to castigate herself for omitting from her many decades of adoption reform the childhood of adopted people. "It was the forward search that mattered," she wrote.[21] To Betty Wood, Paton lamented, "My most uncomfortable thought is what am I going to say when all the laws have passed in our favor, and yet we have done nothing to help the children of adoption know the truth about themselves until they are 18 or 21."[22]

As individuals and institutions recognized Paton for her work in adoption reform, Paton accepted them modestly. The only one that pleased her immensely was the Orphan Voyage Memorial, an Internet website created by Alice Syman to honor Jean Paton and her work. Syman, a personal friend of Paton's and a longtime supporter of open records for adopted persons, had founded Orphan Voyage of Arizona in 1987 before moving to Florida in 1997 and organizing Orphan Voyage at St. Augustine. Syman wanted the movement to remember that Paton "started the adoption reform movement, then AAC, ALMA, Bastard Nation and hundreds of search and support groups sprang up around the country. Wasn't long before they got so caught up in their individual operations that they began to forget who helped them get their start—Jean Paton, Not ALMA, Jean Paton!"[23] Syman announced the website in an e-mail on April 13, 2000, addressed to "Adoption Triad Member," with instructions on how to sign the Guest Book.[24]

By December, approximately fifty people had signed the memorial. Many of the comments supported opening adoption records, voiced encouragement, and thanked Paton fervently for her lifelong dedication to adoption reform. Typical of the sentiments expressed online was "Paula" who wrote, "Jean keep up the wonderful hard work and HAPPY BIRTHDAY." Brenda S. Herron from Blacklick, Ohio, declared that she "couldn't imagine what this world would be like if there weren't caring folks like Jean!!!! God Bless Her!!" Similarly, Deb Godek from Pittsburgh stated, "From the bottom of my heart and depths of my soul, THANK YOU for cutting the path for those of us who did not have to walk alone in our journey to be whole. May God bless you in His Care. May you find comfort in His Love."[25] Although Paton did not have access to the Internet, Syman contacted the librarian in Harrison, Arkansas, and persuaded her to call Paton and show the memorial to her. According to Syman, Paton "was overwhelmed by it, couldn't imagine anyone caring enough about her and her work to go to such lengths to recognize it as I did." After Paton's initial visit to the Harrison library, Syman printed the memorial guest book entries and sent them to her. Paton "always acted as if she felt unworthy of the praise that was heaped upon her."[26]

In May 2001, Paton received the Baran-Pannor Award for Excellence in Open Adoption from the American Association of Open Adoption Agencies at its biannual conference in Traverse City, Michigan, hosted by Jim Gritter and Catholic Human Services of Traverse City. Annette Baran had written Paton informing her of the honor and requested her attendance at the conference. Paton politely turned down the offer to attend due to her age, which had limited her ability to travel. She told Baran that she had long been aware of Gritter's advocacy for open adoption. True to form, however, Paton could not resist speaking truth even to the people who were honoring her. Paton thought that the "Open people," as she referred to Gritter's group, needed to take just one more step—which she did not identify, but by which she probably meant abolishing adoption, open or otherwise. She held out little hope that they would do so. "I also realize that people cannot envision taking a step when they already feel their toes point only to a yawning precipice beneath them, just ahead." Nevertheless, she did "appreciate the recognition by the Conference and shall treasure it."[27]

Despite these tokens of appreciation and honor, Paton remained keenly sensitive to any historical error or slight of her rightful place in history and was prepared to set the record straight. Such was the case in 2000 when Abigail Lovett, with the help of Kenneth Watson, wrote a short history of the adoption reform movement for the AAC house organ, the *Decree*. In describing Paton's pioneering role, they referred to her "lonely" challenge. On seeing the account, Paton fired off a letter to Lovett, denouncing this "travesty of our AAC reported history," exclaiming, "Believe me, that is the wrong word." Paton admitted that she might have been lonely before she started the Life History Study Center, but never after. She asserted, "I was utterly immersed in correspondence and field trips from then forward."[28] But in describing Paton's challenge as "lonely," Lovett was not referring to Paton's calling as the self-appointed ombudsman and spokesperson for adult adoptees and birth mothers. Rather, she meant that as a pioneer in adoption reform Paton had had few allies. In this quest Paton was indeed lonely.

In her letter to Lovett, Paton stated a truth that has been overlooked by many historians who view the movement as a two-stage process, with Paton first coming on the scene in the 1950s, then a hiatus, and then Florence Fisher in the 1970s. As Paton wrote: "Can you really believe that without this incessant labor there would be an organization today?" Paton meant that Fisher, as well as other reformers, reaped what Paton had continuously sowed for twenty years previously. Many thousands of the adult adoptees who responded to Fisher were the same people who had either corresponded with Paton or had been sensitized to adoption reform issues from newspaper and magazine articles written about and by her. Moreover, Paton was directly responsible for getting Fisher started by putting her forward at the Milan Conference in 1971 and had given the group CUB seminal encouragement and advice in 1976. In Paton's opinion, the next twenty years had seen declension in adoption reform, which was undoubtedly a result of the newer reformers not following her advice. Singling out legislative breakthroughs championed by the new generation of adoption reform leaders, Paton declared they were nothing to boast about. Referring to the criminal penalties adult adoptees were subjected to for violating Tennessee's open adoption records law, Paton mordantly noted that they faced potential imprisonment. As for voluntary mutual consent adoption registries, they were characterized by long delays. Even in Canada, which had more experience with such registries, adult adoptees had to wait up to six years for service. Paton found the law ineffective and believed that the adoption reform movement had chosen the wrong strategy. Returning to her perennial war against therapy and her more recent belief in the importance of early childhood, Paton wrote, "We jump up and down with excitement over the new laws," but by the time the records were opened it was too late: the psychological damage had been done. She viewed the consequences with alarm: "We will remain at the mercy of the several thousand sites where we may be therapeutized. It will be lifelong."

For the remainder of her life, Paton continued to be concerned about her rightful place in history. Five days before she died, she wrote a letter to the editor of the *C.U.B Communicator* correcting a professor's statement that the movement started in the 1970s. Sarcastically, Paton asked, "What was I doing in

1953?" She then again reminded the audience of her importance: "without the work of forming groups, the massive correspondence with individuals, the field trips, plus my own influence on Fisher, there would be no movement. . . . And what about the origins of CUB? Did you know I suggested there be such a group? Mary Anne Cohen and Lee Campbell came forth from Massachusetts and CUB began."

On March 27, 2002, Jean Paton died suddenly of a heart ailment at the North Regional Medical Center in Harrison, Arkansas. On April 1 a simple service was held in Harrison, officiated by the Reverend Carl McCormick. Paton was interred at Maplewood Cemetery.[29] The mainstream media ignored her passing. Tributes came from adoption triad members. In the *C.U.B Communicator*, three birth mothers paid homage to Paton and captured the various qualities that made her a force to be reckoned with for five decades in the adoption reform movement. In describing her personal encounters with Jean Paton, CUB president Karen Vedder caught her indomitable spirit. When Vedder attended her very first CUB meeting, she recalled, "I'll always remember the first time I saw Jean Paton—she was sitting in a light as if an angel descended from heaven. I was in awe of her—her courage, her intelligence, her whole being." Years later, at CUB's twentieth-anniversary conference, Vedder was on a ferry to Boston when she spotted a lone figure hiking along the dock.

> She appeared to be elderly, yet walked with purpose and a strong stride. As the admirable senior got closer, I recognized Jean Paton, so determined in her gait, showing no fear. She appeared confident of who she was and where she was going. It was in that moment that she became my role model. I decided that I want to be just like her when I reach my eighties—vital, self assured, independent, filled with words of wisdom, and not afraid to walk in strange places.[30]

Lee Campbell, founder of CUB, remembered the radical, controversial Paton, her "sheer raw passion" that no one in the movement could match, not even Campbell, who confessed she was "plenty intense in 'my day.'" Recalling their correspondence when she was just starting to organize CUB, Campbell declared that all her interactions "with this dynamo were through the snail mail she meted out as rapid-fire as a casino card dealer." Every word of those letters "packed a punch. Jean Paton always made me stop and think, and think some more. She was an inspiration." Remembering the first time she met Paton in the flesh, Campbell recalled the radical: "Jean hobbling into a banquet room, trailing a ball and chain behind her. In person, she was clearly no less afraid of controversy than she was in print."[31]

In honoring Jean Paton, Mary Anne Cohen, cofounder of CUB, birth-mother activist, and poet, saw deepest into this remarkable woman. Cohen be-gan by paying tribute to Paton's historical role, noting that "before Jean Paton there was no adoption reform. We owe a huge debt to the courage and foresight of this lone adoptee who dared to 'break the silence' about how it feels to be adopted and denied one's heritage." She recounted the many "firsts" that Paton was responsible for: creating the first support network, Orphan Voyage; being the first to suggest that birth mothers have their own group; the first to claim "bastard as a term of pride," with her 1970s "Bastards are Beautiful" buttons. Cohen then singled out Paton's exceptionally self-sacrificing altruism. Paton was "unique in the adoption reform movement in that she did not seek personal fame, money, or ego gratification. Jean devoted her personal efforts to the good of all touched by adoption, without asking for anything in return." And unlike many in the movement, Cohen recognized that Paton "was not just a reformer, she was a poet, philosopher, and accomplished sculptor and visual artist. . . . She was truly a Renaissance woman. She brought wisdom and a profound spiritual view to adoption that many others missed. She went deep into the mystery of adoptee as outsider, gadfly, oracle, and prophet to the larger society." Cohen concluded by declaring that "Jean fought the good fight with compassion, grace, intellect, and soul. May she be met in heaven by all her family, both by adoption and birth. May we continue her good work here on earth. Rest in peace, Jean. You were one 'Beautiful Bastard.'"[32]

Paton believed that when all was said and done, her "good fight" had been worth it. Reflecting on her life, she thought about the various career paths that had been open to her. Paton remembered that her vocational testing in Phila-delphia recommended that if she were younger she should go into surgery. This might have satisfied "the very strong engineering element" in her, she mused, but it was not for her. The only alternative Paton could think of would be to work in sculpture, which she loved. But ultimately, she concluded, adoption reform had been the best vocational choice she could have made:

Nothing I can think of would give me the comfort, peace, the warmth to think of people here and there, from Alaska to S. Africa to England, even France!, with whom I have shared and to whom I have given something of the abun-dance that has come to me in this work. Nothing I can conceive of would have made more demands and given me to more people than what I have done.[33]

Notes

Preface

1. That same year, Jean Paton, ever the intrepid researcher, had contacted me in regard to an obscure article I had written in the *Journal of Sociology and Social Welfare* about sealed adoption records, which I subsequently sent her. E. Wayne Carp, "The Sealed Adoption Records Controversy in Historical Perspective: The Case of the Children's Home Society of Washington, 1895–1988," *Journal of Sociology and Social Welfare* 19, no. 2 (1992): 27–57.

2. JP to E. Wayne Carp, 20 May 1993, in the author's possession.

3. E. Wayne Carp to JP, 13 Sept. 1996, in the author's possession.

4. JP to E. Wayne Carp, 16 Sept. 1996, in the author's possession.

5. Author, personal letter to JP, 15 Oct. 1996. A back operation postponed my visit to Harrison, AR, until June 1998.

6. Later, JP would write about my "glow of joy at finding the wide coverage in the materials I have squirreled over the years." See JP to L. Anne Babb [July 1998] [no folder]. See also JP to Betty Walter, 19 July 1998 [no folder], for similar sentiments.

7. A few words about my use of the term *birth mother* and other terms are in order here. As I have written in *Family Matters*, all language is historically constructed and emotionally charged. For example, in the 1970s, Lee Campbell, founder and president of CUB, turned the neologism *birth mother* into a single word in her campaign against the stigma of illegitimacy, while activist and author Lorraine Dusky hated the term, declaring that it made her "sound like a baby machine, a conduit, without emotions." *Birthmark* (New York: M. Evens, 1979), 75. Forty years later, the term is still hotly disputed. See the blog Adoption Critique, "The Power of Words . . . And an Adoptee Rights Petition," http://adoptioncritic.com/2011/04/29/words-and-adoptee-rights-petition/ (accessed August 12, 2013). I have chosen a middle way: As a historian it is my duty not to sanitize or censor the past, and thus I use the terms *birth mother, birthmother, birth family, birth parents,* even *natural family,* when used by the historical actors themselves or when the historical context calls for it. At other times, I have use a variety of terms, ranging from the neutral terms *natal family, natal parents, kinship family,* and *genetic family,* to the

terms favored by adoption activists, such as *first mother, first parents, first family, original parents,* and *original families.*

8. *ABS,* 3.

9. Erik Erikson, *Identity: Youth and Crisis* (New York: W. W. Norton, 1968), 188, 235; Paul Roazen, *Erik H. Erikson, The Power and Limits of a Vision* (New York: Free Press), 86–92.

10. I have paraphrased some of the ideas in Vicki L. Eaklor, *Queer America: A People's GLBT History of the United States* (New York: New Press: 2008), 3–5.

Introduction

1. The quote is from "Memorial Notice," *The Triad Tribune of Canada* 2 (Summer 2002): 2. Keith Griffith to author, e-mail, 17 Feb. 2003, in possession of the author. I am indebted to Sir Keith Griffith for sending me the "Memorial Notice." There are, however, numerous factual errors in it, including the dates of her conversion experience, the beginning of Orphan Voyage, and the name of the School of Social Work where she earned her MSW. See E. Wayne Carp to Keith Griffith, e-mail, 17 Feb. 2005, ibid.

2. R. L. Jenkins, "On Adopting A Baby," *Hygeia* 13 (Dec. 1935): 1066.

3. "The Epidemic of Adoption," *Living Age* 294 (Sept. 8, 1917): 632.

4. On language see, Jenkins, "On Adopting A Baby," 106; "The Epidemic of Adoption," 632.

5. Peter Romanofsky, "The Early History of Adoption Practices, 1870–1930" (PhD diss., University of Missouri, 1969), 67–69; Peter W. Bardaglio, *Reconstruction the Household: Families, Sex, and the Law in the Nineteenth Century South* (Chapel Hill, University of North Carolina Press, 1995), 170–74.

6. Social workers also were responsible for this linkage. See Agnes K. Hanna, "The Interrelationship Between Illegitimacy and Adoption," CWLA, *Bull* 16 (Sept. 1937): 4. The few existing studies indicate a range of 35–61 percent of adoptions involved children born out of wedlock. See E. Wayne Carp, "The Sealed Adoption Records Controversy in Historical Perspective," *Journal of Sociology and Social Welfare* 19 (June 1992): 39.

7. Henry H. Goddard, *The Kallikak Family: A Study in the Heredity of Feeblemindedness* (New York: Macmillan, 1912); Hamilton Cravens, *The Triumph of Evolution: American Scientists and the Hereditary-Environment Controversy, 1900–1941* (Philadelphia: University of Pennsylvania Press, 1978), 47–48; William Haller, *Eugenics: Hereditarian Attitudes in American Thought* (New Brunswick, NJ: Rutgers University Press, 1968), 106–7.

8. Butler, "The Burden of Feeble-Mindedness," National Conference of Charities and Correction, *Proceedings* (Baltimore, 1907): 4.

9. Child Welfare League of America, *Standards for Adoption Service* (New York: Child Welfare League of America, 1958), 14.

10. Carp, *Family Matters,* 113–16. See also Ellen Herman, *Kinship By Design: A His-*

tory of Adoption in the Modern United States (Chicago: University of Chicago Press, 2010), 148–50; Rickie Solinger, *Wake Up Little Susie: Single Pregnancy and Race Before Roe V. Wade* (New York and London: Routledge, 1992), chap. 3.

11. Clark Vincent, "Illegitimacy in the Next Decade: Trends and Implications," *Child Welfare* 43 (Dec. 1964): 515.

12. Elaine Tyler May, *Barren in the Promised Land: Childless Americans and the Pursuit of Happiness* (New York: Basic Books, 1995), 127–40, quotation on 129.

13. Margaret Marsh and Wanda Ronner, *The Empty Cradle: Infertility in America from Colonial Times to the Present* (Baltimore: Johns Hopkins University Press, 1996), 186–87.

14. Sophie van Senden Theis, "Adoption," *Social Work Year Book* 4 (New York: Russell Sage Foundation, 1937), 23; I. Evelyn Smith, "Adoption," ibid. 9 (1947), 24; Kathy S. Stolley, "Statistics on Adoption in the United States, *Future of Children* 3, no. 1 (Spring 1993): 28.

15. Michael Schapiro, *A Study of Adoption Practice*, vol. I (New York: Child Welfare League of America, 1956), 10.

16. Ann Fessler, *The Girls Who Went Away: The Hidden History of Women Who Surrendered Children for Adoption in the Decades Before Roe v. Wade* (New York: Penguin, 2006); Barbara Melosh, *Stranger and Kin: The American Way of Adoption* (Cambridge, MA: Harvard University Press, 2002), chap. 3; Solinger, *Wake Up Little Susie*, chap. 3. See also Melissa Ludtke, *On Our Own: Unmarried Motherhood in America* (Berkeley and Los Angeles: University of California Press, 1997).

17. JP to Judge John N. McMullen, 25 Feb. 1991, folder: Intermediary—Co; JP to David Reed, 23 Apr. 1984 [no folder].

18. *OV*, 51–52.

19. JP to David Reed, 23 Apr. 1984 [no folder]; JP to Judge John N. McMullen, 25 Feb. 1991, folder: Intermediary—Co.

20. JP to Mr. Downing, 9 May 1978, folder: MI.

21. Carp, *Family Matters*, chap. 4

22. Deutsch quoted in ibid., 116.

23. Ibid., chap. 4.

24. Ibid., 112–13.

25. Robert Coles, *Erik Erikson: The Growth of His Work* (New York: Da Capo, 1970), xiv.

Chapter 1

1. *OV*, 9; quotation from Paton, interview, 25 June 1998, Tape 1, Side A (transcript, 2).

2. Raymond O. Ensminger, "Pioneer For Adoption Reform," *Exchange* 2, no. 4 (1984): 4.

3. JP, "About the Director," 1 Aug. 1958, folder: Correspondence with Magazines, 1957–1958.

4. JP, "The Orphan and Society," 23 May 1973 [no folder].

5. JP, "About the Director," 1 Aug. 1958, folder: Correspondence with Magazines, 1957–1958; JP, "The Orphan and Society," 23 May 1973 [no folder].

6. Dan P. McAdams, Ruthellen Josselson, and Amia Lieblich, "Introduction," in *Identity and Story: Creating Self in Narrative*, ed. Dan P. McAdams, Ruthellen Josselson, and Amia Lieblich (Washington, D.C.: American Psychological Association, 2006), 304; quotations on 4.

7. Ibid., 4.

8. Jean Paton, interview by author, tape recording, Harrison, AR, June 26, 1998, hereafter cited as JP, interview. Like most families and unwed mothers of the time who feared the stigma of illegitimacy, Emma registered at the Women's Hospital under the assumed name of Cassie Emerson (made up from the reversed initials of her given name). (Ruth Edwina Emerson, Photostat Copy, Certificate of Birth, No. 10079, Dec. 27, 1908, Michigan Department of Health, Lansing, Michigan). In *My Mother Lost and Found: A Tale of Reconciliation* (Cedaredge, CO: n.p.), n.p., Paton mistakenly states that her mother's name in Women's Hospital was Cassie Edwards. Similarly, nowhere on the birth certificate was her name recorded as "Baby Edwards" or "Baby Emerson." See Emerson, Photostat Copy, Certificate of Birth.

9. Ensminger, "Pioneer," 3.

10. There is no evidence outside of the family's contention to support Paton's belief that J. J. Hill had an illegitimate son or, if he had an illegitimate son, he was James or Jim Kittson. What is known is that Paton's mother identified Paton's biological father as "Jim Kittson." She does not mention J. J. Hill. See Emma [Steiner] to Jean Paton, May 18, 1955, [no folder]. It is not clear where JP got the idea that J. J. Hill was Kittson's father. Nevertheless, by 1980, JP claimed that "Kittson" was Jim Kittson's mother's name and that Jim Kittson's father's name was "Hill," and Hill was "one of the robber barons." JP to Nancy Otto, 14 Apr. 1980, Folder: TX – OTTO, Nancy. Paton made a veiled reference to Kittson in an interview, but made no mention of his illegitimacy. Instead, Paton stated that after long study she was convinced that her father was "the natural son of one of the robber barons." Ensminger, "Pioneer," 4. Sixteen years later, Paton's reasoned conviction about Kittson's birth status had turned to unassailable truth. She wrote that "there is no question, none whatsoever" that "my father, James J. Kittson was the off-child of James Jerome Hill, builder of the Great Northern Railroad." JP to the author, 30 Mar. 2000. Contra Paton, his biographers describe him as a devoted family man. See Michael P. Malone, *James J. Hill: Empire Builder of the Northwest* (Norman: University of Oklahoma Press, 1996), 19; Albro Martin, *James J. Hill: The Opening of the Northwest*, reprint (St. Paul, Minnesota Historical Society Press, 1991), 256. See chap. 5.

11. JP, interview, 26 June 1998, Tape 3, Side B (transcript, 72). JP also mentions Viola's visits to her in the maternity home in JP, "How Old is Four," *A Proper Response: To the Situation in Adoption* 2, no. 2 (Sept. 1995). According to Paton, Emma often sang Brahms's Lullaby and other nursery tunes to her during those four months. Jean Paton, interview by the author in Harrison, AR, 26 June 1998, Tape 3, Side B (transcript, 72).

Of course, Paton could not have remembered this experience. I regret not asking her if she had heard it directly from her mother.

12. JP, *My Mother Lost and Found* [n.p.]; quotations on [1, 2].

13. Paton, interview, 25 June 1998, Tape 1, Side A (transcript, 1); Henry Dean, Photostat Copy, Death Certificate, No. 2929, 6 May 1911, Detroit Department of Health, Division of Vital Statistics, Lansing, Michigan.

14. Jean Paton-Kittson to Joseph Califano, June 1979, enclosure, "Background information on Jean Paton-Kittson," folder: DC–Hew–CB. See also JP to BJ, 25 Jan. 1982, folder: MD–Jacobs 1980s, where she states, "I was marked permanently by the time I was three, both to the hatred of suffering, and the sight of healing."

15. More than eight decades later, JP mentioned that the foster family's name was Pettit. JP, "How Old is Four," *A Proper Response* 2, no. 2 (Sept. 1995).

16. JP, interview, 27 June 1998, Tape 6, Side A (transcript, 149). See, for example, Mary Ruth Colby, *Problems and Procedures in Adoption*, Children's Bureau Pub. 262 (Washington, D.C.: Government Printing Office, 1941), 6; Alice Leahy, "Some Characteristics of Adoptive Parents," *American Journal of Sociology* 38 (January 1938): 557.

17. JP, interview, 25 June 1998, Tape 1, Side A (transcript, 1).

18. Photograph of JP's home, 122 Normal St., Ypsilanti, Michigan, n.d., in possession of the author; Barney Everitt, Bill Metzger, and Walter Flanders founded the E-M-F Company in 1908, and soon the company was "the largest employer in Detroit and was producing more cars than any other company in the United States other than Ford." The Studebaker Brothers purchased the company in 1910. See Anthony J. Yanik, *The E-M-F Company: The Story of Automotive Pioneers Barney Everitt, Bill Metzger, and Walter Flanders* (Warrendale, PA: Society of Automotive Engineers, 2001), vi.

19. JP, interview, 25 June 1998, Tape 1, Side A (transcript, 1, 3). *OV*, 9.

20. JP to Mary Paton, 8 July 1921, and JP to Dr. Paton, n.d. [no folder].

21. JP to Henry H. Work, 20 Nov. 1967, folder: Miscellaneous 1960s.

22. JP, interview, 27 June 1998, Tape 6, Side A (transcript, 149–50).

23. Ibid., 150. 151

24. Ibid..

25. Psychologist H. J. Sants coined the term, referring to the plight of children who have uncertain, little, or no knowledge of one or both of their birth parents. Sants argued that genealogical bewilderment constituted a large part of the additional stress that adoptees experienced that is not experienced by children being raised by their birth parents. See H. J. Sants, "Genealogical Bewilderment in Children with Substitute Parents," *British Journal of Medical Psychology* 37 (1964): 133–41. See also Erich Wellisch, "Children Without Genealogy—A Problem of Adoption," *Mental Health* 131, no. 1 (1952): 41–42. A critique of the concept can be found in Kimberly Leighton, "Addressing the Harms of Not Knowing One's Heredity: Lessons from Genealogical Bewilderment," *Adoption & Culture* 3 (2012): 63–107.

26. JP, interview, 25 June 1998, Tape 1, Side A (transcript, 4).

27. Ibid.

28. Both quotations from Ruthena Kittson [JP], "The Vocabulary of Social Orphanhood" (unpublished paper, 1954), n.p.

29. JP to Selma Chesler, 4 May 1977. In 1993, Paton would soften her opinion and write that "I always have felt closer to Holyoke than to Wisconsin, and remain so." JP to Mary Budd, 5 Sept. 1993, folder: Mt Holyoke.

30. JP, letter to the author, 22 May 2000; Kittson, "Vocabulary of Social Orphanhood." See also JP to W. Stephen Jeffrey, 18 Dec. 1986, folder: Mt Holyoke. Jeffrey was Mount Holyoke College's Director of Development.

31. JP to Ruth Wallis, 12 Mar. 1958. The other was the fact that her chosen profession of social work failed to help her get to the bottom of her confusion (ibid.).

32. I have been able to piece together Thomas Paton's approximate date of death from his undated obituary, which identifies JP as living in Washington, D.C. See Obit. "Dr. Paton, Dean of City Doctors, Taken By Death," [Ypsilanti Daily Press, n.d.]; JP's résumé identifies her as working in the nation's capital in mid-1935–1938. JP, "Resume" [Aug. 1951] [no folder].

33. JP to Friends of the Alumnae Association, 5 Jan. 1991, folder: Mt Holyoke.

34. JP to Editor, Mt. Holyoke Alumnae Quarterly, 25 Feb. 1991, folder: Mt Holyoke.

35. JP, "Focus," January 1962, Release 1C, [no folder]; JP, letter to author, 14 July 2000. JP refers to Elizabeth DeSchweinitz as Beth McCord. McCord was her middle name. See NASW Foundation, "NASW Social Work Pioneers, Elizabeth DeSchweinitz," http://www.naswfoundation.org/pioneers/ElizabethdeSchweinitz.htm (accessed July 15, 2011).

36. JP, "Resume" [August 1951] [no folder]; Paton, interview, 25 June 1998, Tape 1, Side A (transcript, 6).

37. She took a course in the mathematics of statistics, including its calculus underpinnings, and her MA thesis was "a comparison of two time series." JP to Anna Coffey, 21 Apr. 1987, folder: New Zealand—Coffey, Anna.

38. Paton taught herself bookkeeping. See JP to Sammi Eaton, 16 July 1981, folder: Eaton, Sammi; JP to Marilyn Hipp, 15 July; JP, interview, 26 June 1998, Tape 4, Side A (transcript, 90–91).

39. JP, interview, Tape 1, Side A (transcript, 9, 10).

40. JP, letter to author, 14 July 2000.

41. Virginia P. Robinson, ed., Jesse Taft: Therapist and Social Work Educator, a Professional Biography (Philadelphia: University of Pennsylvania Press, 1962), 37, 41–48, 67, 193.

42. JP, letter to author, 14 July 2000. The reference to sculpture and therapy can be found in JP to B. A. Timmer, 22 Feb. 1980. Late in life, Paton recounted that Taft had said, "'I think you would like clay.' I don't know where she got that. But how right she was." JP, interview, 26 June 1998, Tape 4, Side B (transcript, 100).

43. JP, letter to author, 14 July 2000.

44. Ibid. For background and the history of the Bank Street School, see "A Brief History: Bank Street College," http://www.bankstreet.edu/gems/about/ABriefHistory.

pdf (accessed August 11, 2009). For Paton's experience there, see JP, letter to author, 14 July 2000

45. JP was undoubtedly introduced to Rank by Taft, who had a long personal relationship with him. See Jesse Taft, *Otto Rank: A Biographical Study based on Notebooks, Letters, Collected Writings, Therapeutic Achievements, and Personal Associations* (New York: Julian Press, 1959), ix–xiv; Roy J. deCarvalho, "Otto Rank: The Rankian Circle in Philadelphia, and the Origins of Carl Rogers' Person-Centered Psychotherapy," *History of Psychology* 2 (May 1999): 3.

46. JP to Anita J. Faatz, 21 Nov. 1967 [no folder].

47. JP to Janine Baer, 25 Mar. 1992.

48. All of the information and quotations in this paragraph and the next two are from JP, "County Commissioners and Child Welfare," *Survey Midmonthly* 78, no. 10 (October 1942): 300–301. For the journal's description as the "bible" of social work, see Clarke A. Chambers, *Paul U. Kellogg and the Survey: Voices for Social Welfare and Social Justice* (Minneapolis: University of Minnesota Press, 1971), 245.

49. In 1962, Paton made a passing reference to the *Survey Midmonthly* article, noting that she "did not fully, consciously realize the strong dissident note, against professionalism that this came out of me so clearly on the page, at that early time in my development." In her interpretation, she was clearly "upholding the value of general institutions against welfare statism." She concluded playfully that "apparently, I had smelled the grass in a distant field and hungrily began to move in that direction." "Focus," January 1962, Release 1C; JP, letter to author, 14 July 2000.

Chapter 2

1. JP to Amram Scheinfeld, 1 Oct. 1954, folder: Response to Sat. Rev. Ads.; JP, "Resume." [Aug. 1951] [no folder].

2. JP, "Resume" [August 1951] [no folder]. Paton supported herself between 1942 and 1943 in a series of odd jobs, including working as a caseworker at the Philadelphia Child Guidance Clinic, a job which she returned to after graduation.

3. JP to B. A. Timmer, 22 Feb. 1980; JP, letter to author, 14 July 2000. Paton first received instruction in sculpture in her home from Jane Austin, an art student at the Corcoran Gallery of Art, Washington, D.C., at an unknown date. JP, "Reunion," leaflet, n.d. [no folder].

4. JP to Louise Whitfield, 17 Feb. 1956, folder: SC.

5. JP to Bev Fisher, 12 Feb. 1977.

6. JP to Mary Doyle, 30 June 1976.

7. JP, interview, 26 June 1998, Tape 4, Side B (transcript, 99); emphasis in the original.

8. JP to Katherine Gordon, 28 Sept. 1982.

9. JP to Carole Anderson, 11 July 1980, folder: CUB—Carole Anderson. In an earlier account, JP also described it as a transformative moment in her life, one she never

forgot. From that day forward, she declared, "I never fail to see the element of death dealing in closed adoption, in final surrender, in sealed records, and I cannot accept it." JP, "Our First Steps Together toward Illegitimacy," Jan. 1962, FR, 1B, 3.

10. JP to Karla Holbrook, 15 Mar. 1996.

11. JP to Editor, *Good Housekeeping*, 7 Oct. 1949, folder: Correspondence with Magazines 1949–1953.

12. Ibid.

13. Paton never sent the actual article, only the idea for the article. See Nancy Goodman to Jean M. Paton, 14 Oct. 1949, ibid.

14. JP, "Adoption Comes of Age," unpublished manuscript, folder: ibid. The article was eventually published in *OV*, 28–31.

15. Ibid., 4–6.

16. See Arthur L. Rautman, "Adoptive Parents Need Help Too," *Mental Hygiene* 33 (July 1949): 424–31. Paton's article appears without attribution to *Mental Hygiene* in *OV*, 28–32. Paton had broached the same idea to an editor at *Good Housekeeping* three weeks earlier, on 7 Oct. 1949.

17. *OV*, 31.

18. JP, Letter to the Editor, *New York Times*, 8 Nov. 1949, reprinted in "History Page," *The LOG*, November 1974 [n.p.].

19. JP, Diary entry, 8–15 Jan. [1950], "A Reasonably Complete Copy of Notebook Used from January 1950 through 9/17/53," folder: Search for Direction, 1950–1953, hereafter cited as folder: SFD. Unless otherwise stated, all diary entries are from this folder.

20. Jean Paton, interview by the author in Harrison, AR, 26 June 1998, Tape 4, Side B (transcript, 102).

21. Quotations from JP, diary entry, evening of 28 Jan. [1950].

22. Diary entry, 22 Jan. [1950].

23. JP, Letter to the Editor, *New York Times*, 7 Jan. 1950, folder: SFD. Two pages long, it was really more of an op-ed piece than a letter to the editor.

24. Diary entry, evening of 15 Jan. [1950].

25. Diary entries, 29 Jan.–4 Feb. and 5–11 Feb. [1950].

26. Diary entry, 5 Feb. [1950]; on smoking, see diary entry, evening of 12 Feb. [1950].

27. (New York: Duell, Sloan & Pearce, 1949); Diary entry, 19 Feb. [1950].

28. Diary entry 12–18 [Mar. 1950].

29. Diary entry, 27 Feb. [1950]. Paton's entry states that she was trying to recapture the mood of the previous week.

30. Diary entry, evening of 19 Feb. [1950].

31. Ibid.

32. Paton spelled Mattison's name in the diary entry phonetically as "Madison." She must have heard it that way in the din of the New Year's Eve party. She spells the name correctly in the acknowledgments to *The Adopted Break Silence* (Philadelphia: Life History Center, 1954), 4.

33. Marc Stein, *City of Sisterly and Brotherly Loves: Lesbian and Gay Philadelphia, 1945–1972* (Chicago: University of Chicago Press, 2000), 21–35.

34. "Kendall" quoted in ibid., 32.

35. Marquez quoted in Enrique Krauze, "In the Shadow of the Patriarch," *New Republic* 240 (Nov. 4, 2009): 41.

36. John D'Emilio, *Making Trouble: Essays on Gay History, Politics, and the University* (New York: Routledge, 1992), 18.

37. Diary entry, afternoon of 7 Jan. [1950].

38. Martin Meeker, *Contacts Desired: Gay and Lesbian Communications and Community, 1940s–1970s* (Chicago: University of Chicago Press, 2006), 6.

39. Diary entry, evening of 5 Mar. [1950].

40. Diary entry, 5–11 Mar. [1950].

41. Diary entry, 14 Mar., "very late" [1950].

42. Ibid.

43. Diary entry, 26 Mar. [1950].

44. Diary entry, 4 Apr. [1950].

45. Ibid.

46. Ibid.

47. Diary entry, 13 Apr. [1950].

48. Diary entry, 18 Apr. [1950].

49. Diary Entry, Evening of 5 Feb. [1950], folder: ibid.

50. JP, "To the Editor," *Social Casework* 23 (May 1950): 209. A JP diary entry for 5 Feb. [1950] states that some "brief remarks" by JP about social workers and social action had appeared in the serial *Social Work Journal*. This is inaccurate. I was unable to locate anything written by JP in any volume of *Social Work Journal*.

51. Diary entry, 12–18 Mar. [1950].

52. Diary entry, 22 Mar. [1950].

53. Diary entry, 26 Mar. [1950].

54. Diary entry, 2–8 Apr. [1950].

55. For the clay book see, diary entry, 25 Apr. [1950].

56. *Baltimore Evening Sun*, 3 May 1950; diary entry, 7 May [1950].

57. Oliver W. Larkin, *Art and Life in America*, rev. and enlarged ed. (New York: Holt, Rinehart and Winston, 1960), 486–87, quotation on 487; Wayne Craven, *American Art: History and Culture* (New York: Harry N. Abrams, 1994), 585–94. On the change of the function of art from the 1930s to the 1950s, see Barbara Haskell, *The American Century: Art and Culture, 1900–1950* (New York: W. W. Norton, 1999), 372.

58. Diary entry, 19 May [1950].

59. Diary entry, 4 June [1950].

60. Diary entry, 20 May [1950].

61. Diary entry, 10 Oct. [1950].

62. Diary entry, 28 May [1950].

63. JP to Pitirim Sorokin, 26 June 1950, folder: SFD. There ensued a series of let-

ters between Sorokin and Paton, in which Paton took a more measured tone and semi-apologized for having used language that might have affronted him. See Pitirim A. Sorokin to JP, 1 July 1950, folder: SFD; JP to Pitirim Sorokin, 26 July 1950, folder: ibid. Nevertheless, Paton published a highly critical review of Sorokin's book in *Survey* (Sept 1950).

64. Diary entry, 13 June [1950]; The *Survey* (December 1950): 568–69.

65. Diary entry, 15 July [1950].

66. Diary entry, 16 July [1950].

67. Diary entry, 13 July [1950].

68. Diary entry, 16 July [1950].

69. JP, "Resume" [Aug. 1951] [no folder]; Diary entry, 3 Jan. 1951.

70. All the information and quotations in the rest of this paragraph are from David G. French to JP, 4 Apr. 1951, ibid.

71. Ibid.

72. Bauman is best known for pioneering the development of nonverbal psychological evaluation instruments for blind or visually impaired people. Her increasing interest in the subject led her to establish a psychological testing and vocational guidance service for blind persons. Throughout her lifetime, she was honored with many awards, and in 2002 Bauman was inducted into the Hall of Fame: Leaders and Legends of the Blindness Field. "Mary K. Bauman," http://www.aph.org/hall_fame/bios/bauman.html (accessed August 25, 2009).

73. JP to Anna M. Baetjer, 5 July 1951, folder: SFD.

74. Diary entry, 15 July [1951].

75. Abraham Flexner, "Is Social Work a Profession?" *Proceedings of the National Conference on Charities and Correction* (Chicago: Hildmann Printing Co., 1915), 576–90.

76. Flexner, "Is Social Work a Profession?" 585; JP, diary entry, 15 July [1951].

77. Michael Richter, Tabitha Jacobs, Corinne Senky, and Jennifer Marshall, "Strong Vocational Interest Inventory," http://workforce.cup.edu/sweeney/P721%20SVIB.pdf (accessed August 23, 2009). Developed by Edward K. Strong, a professor at Carnegie Institute of Technology between 1919 and 1923, this was the first widely used career assessment test. The original test was designed for men only; a version for women was developed in 1933.

78. Jean Paton [n.d], folder: SFD. Interestingly, Paton scored relatively low in the categories "author" and "social worker." The Strong Vocational Interest Test for women can be found at my blog, *The Biography of Jean Paton*, jeanpaton.com.

79. JP to Mary Nauman, 8 July 1951, ibid.

80. Ibid.

81. JP to Mary Bauman, 2 Aug. 1951, ibid. As a token of her gratitude and admiration, Paton gave Bauman "a beautiful plaque" of unknown design (perhaps one of Paton's own pieces of sculpture). Bauman told Paton that she took the gift home and placed it in "an appropriate setting and where it will become a delightful part of that leisure time enjoyment which I can never achieve at the office."

82. Diary entry, 4 Aug. [1951].

83. JP to Mary Bauman, 30 Aug. 1951, ibid.

84. JP to Mary Bauman, 12 Oct. 1951, ibid.

85. Diary entry, 21 Nov. [1951].

86. Diary entry, 22 Nov. [1951].

87. Diary entry, 27 Nov. [1951].

88. JP to Mary Bauman, 29 Mar. 1952, folder: SFD.

89. JP to Frederick E. Smith, 27 Feb. 1952, ibid.

90. JP to William Seifritz, 1 Feb. 1952, folder: Gem.

91. William Seifritz to JP, 1 Feb. 1952, folder: ibid. The letter is handwritten on the back of Paton's letter to him of 1 Feb. Paton considered this letter "rather special, as I remembered it quite well, and did not want it to disappear." JP, letter to author, 26 Nov. 1998 (in possession of the author). JP also wrote to Edmund W. Sinnott, professor of biology and Dean of the Graduate School at Yale University but received no reply. See JP to Edmund W. Sinnott, 20 Feb. 1952, folder: SFD.

92. JP, letter to author, 26 Nov. 1998 (in possession of the author).

93. They were Edmund W. Sinnott, professor of biology and dean of the graduate school at Yale University; Professor Frederick E. Smith, professor of zoology at the University of Michigan; and Dr. Nathan S. Kline, Director of Research at Worcester State Hospital in Massachusetts. See JP to Edmund W. Sinnott, 20 Feb. 1952, folder: SFD. Sinnott never replied. JP to Frederick E. Smith, 27 Feb. 1952, ibid; Smith responded favorably to Paton. His general conclusion, which she proudly repeated in the future, was that she was "embarked upon a professionally perilous journey, but one which had good potentialities." Frederick E. Smith to JP, 17 Mar. 1952, ibid. For the extended exchange between JP and Kline, see JP to Mary Bauman, 29 Mar. 1952, ibid.; JP to Nathan S. Kline, 3 Mar. 1952, ibid.; Nathan S. Kline to JP, 5 Mar. 1952, ibid.; JP to Nathan S. Kline, 8 Mar. 1952, ibid.; Nathan S. Kline to JP, 3 July 1952, ibid.; JP to Nathan S. Kline, 9 July 1952, ibid.

94. Diary entry, 10 Oct. [1950].

95. JP to Jackie Wolf, 27 Mar. 1969, folder: Adopt. Parents Wolf

96. JP to Mrs. Jerome Wolf, 24 July 1963, folder: Adopt. Parents Wolf. JP only learned about the cover story after her adoptive mother's death. Ibid.

97. JP to Rita Atkins, 8 Sept. 1986.

98. JP to Sally Nance, 8 July 975.

99. JP to Mary Bauman, 20 May 1952, folder: SFD.

100. Fred L. Kuhlmann, "Intestate Succession by and from the Adopted Child," *Washington University Law Quarterly* 28 (1943): 221–50, esp. 227–31. In discussing Michigan, Kuhlman emphasizes the inadequacy of its adoption inheritance laws and notes "a surprising degree of dissimilarity among the statutory provisions." Ibid., 231.

101. Paton, interview, 26 June 1998, Tape 3, Side A (transcript, 55).

102. See "Six Ways to Compute the Relative Value of a U.S. Dollar Amount, 1774 to Present," http://www.measuringworth.com/calculators/uscompare/result.php (ac-

cessed September 7, 2009); Historical Income Tables—Families, Table F-7, Type of Family, All Races by Median and Mean Income: 1947 to 2006, "Female Householder, No Spouse Present," http://www.census.gov/hhes/www/income/histinc/f07ar.html (accessed September 7, 2009).

103. JP to Gladys Comstock, 19 Jan. 1953, folder: SFD. Comstock expressed disappointment at Paton's departure, though she understood "her situation in doing just the things you want to do." Gladys Comstock to JP, 5 Feb. 1953, ibid.

104. In contrast to her detailed notes of her first year at the university, Paton did not record anything about her experience during the 1953 spring term. For evidence that Paton took anthropology, see JP, "P's notes" 28 Feb. 1953–2 May 1953, ibid; JP to Goodwin Watson, 26 Aug. 1953, ibid. For the other courses, see OV, 24. Paton appears to have exaggerated slightly the amount of time she was actually enrolled taking classes at the University of Pennsylvania. Although she repeatedly claimed that she spent two years there—indeed, she claims they were the happiest two years of her life—the extant documentary record suggests that she was only enrolled for one and a half years.

105. See the exchange of letters between JP and Earl W. Count, 1 Apr. 1952, folder: SFD; Earl W. Count to JP, 25 Apr. 1953, ibid; JP to Earl W. Count, 14 May 1952, ibid; JP to Earl W. Count, 30 Dec. 1952, ibid; diary entry, 31 Dec. 1952. Count was a professor at Hamilton College.

106. JP to Gladys Comstock, 7 Feb. 1953, ibid.; JP, interview, 26 June 1998, Tape 3, Side A (transcript, 56).

107. See Goodwin Watson to JP, 14 Aug. 1953, folder: SFD; JP to Goodwin Watson, 26 Aug. 1953, ibid.

108. Paton had met McConaughy at Mount Holyoke. In 1953, McConaughy was teaching summer school at Rutgers University. JP, "Other Voices," Release (1), August 1957 BN. That study would become The Adopted Break Silence: The Experiences and Views of Forty Adults Who Were Once Adopted Children (New York: Vantage Press, 1954).

109. OV, 24. For a similar statement, see JP, interview, 26 June 1998, Tape 4, Side A (transcript, 89).

110. JP to Mrs. Erroll B. Abell, 24 Mar. 1955, folder: Responses to Sat. Rev. Ads.

111. Ibid.

Chapter 3

1. ABS, Appendix, "Some Further Details on the Study Method," 166. Paton stated that she ordered letterhead in July 1953. Ibid. JP, "The Program of the Life History Study Center," Supplement, September 1953 BN. This document appears to be a draft for a leaflet promoting the Center. In various places, Paton mistakenly dates the opening of the Life History Study Center as September 1953; in one source she gives the precise date of September 16. "Center Traces Life Patterns for Adopted Adults," Philadelphia Inquirer, 26 Nov. 1955. Paton also frequently stated that the Center began in the fall of 1953. See JP to Deloris Murray, 28 Jan. 1955 [no folder]. For similar statements, see JP

to Lee Campbell, 30 Aug. 1977; JP to Karen Rowland, 1 Oct. 1975; JP to Cindy Birnbaum, 9 Mar. 1982. However, other evidence demonstrates conclusively that the Life History Study Center was operating in August. See *ABS*, 6.

2. *OV*, 25.

3. JP to Sandy Musser, 31 Oct. 1981.

4. *ABS*, 6–7.

5. JP, "The Program of the Life History Study Center," brochure, 20 Oct. 1953 [no folder].

6. Ibid.

7. JP to Saturday Review Assn., Inc., 14 Aug. 1953, folder: Correspondence with Magazines 1949–1953; hereafter referred to as CM 1949–1953. See also, Joan Beletsis to JP, 9 Sept. 1953, folder: CM 1949–1953; JP to Joan Beletsis, 18 Sept. 1953, ibid.

8. *OV*, 39. But see H. David Kirk's letter of 16 Sept. 1953 to JP for evidence that the ad must have started running sometime before September 19. H. David Kirk to JP, 16 Sept. 1953, folder: Kirk.

9. JP, "Adoption Life History Study" [n.d.], ibid; quotation from *OV*, 39.

10. JP, "Adoption Life History Study" [n.d.], folder: CM 1949–1953.

11. JP, "Progress Report," 15 Dec. 1953, folder: Response to Sat. Rev. Ads.

12. I am withholding identity of this person. The letter can be found written in JP, "Progress Report," 15 Dec. 1953, ibid. In her reply of 21 Dec. 1953, Paton declared, "Please do not feel any guilt about it." Ibid.

13. JP to Remington Rand, 30 Sept. 1953, folder: CM 1949–1953. Remington Rand officials replied to Paton and a meeting was set. See JP to Martha Everett, 20 Oct. 1953, ibid. I have been unable to find any documentation that the meeting took place. The information on Remington Rand is from James Cortada, *Before the Computer: IBM, NCR, Burroughs, and Remington Rand and the Industry They Created, 1865–1956* (Princeton, NJ: Princeton University Press, 1993), 233–35.

14. JP, "Registration Specifications," 3 Oct. 1953, ibid. Soon thereafter, JP contacted the Pennsylvania Secretary of State, requesting the regulations to take out a copyright in her own name or the name "Life History Study Center." JP to Secretary of State, 4 Dec. 1953, ibid. She also felt that the need of a good lawyer and eventually contracted with Joseph Head Jr., of the law firm Swartz, Campbell, and Henry, who registered the Center as a business in January 1954 with the Commonwealth of Pennsylvania. Joseph Head, Jr., to JP, 4 Jan. 1954, folder: Correspondence with Magazines, 1954–1956; hereafter cited as CM 1954–1956. See also *ABS*, 167. Apparently, Head rendered additional service because Paton mentions him in her acknowledgments to *ABS*, where she thanks "Joseph Head, Jr., attorney, for help in approving parts of the text" (4).

15. JP to Martha Everett, 28 Oct. 1953, folder: CM 1949–1953.

16. JP to Margaret Wagenhals, 30 Oct. 1953, ibid.

17. JP to D. Edgar, 29 Oct. 1953, folder: ibid.

18. JP, "To Those Who Answered the First SRL Notice (9/17 issue)," 14 Nov 1953 [nofolder].

19. JP, "Dear Adopted," Thanksgiving Day 1953, BN.

20. JP to Martha Everett, 13 Nov. 1953, folder: CM 1949–1953.

21. Margaret H. Wagenhals to JP, 14 Dec. 1953, ibid.

22. Day Edgar to JP, 2 Nov. 1953, ibid.

23. Janet Hotson Baker to JP, 10 Nov. 1953, ibid.

24. Leola Michaels, "We Like Lots of Children," *Parents Magazine*, January 1946, 26–27, 73, 75–77; Harry Bell, "We Adopted a Daughter," *Saturday Evening Post*, 16 Aug. 1952, 22–23, 70, 72–73. See also Carlton E. Morse, "We Want Her for Always," *Parents Magazine*, December 1951, 46–47.

25. To reassure adoptive parents that adoption was safe, adoption stories stressed the scientific nature of the modern adoption process. See, for example, "Scientific Adoption," *Today's Health* 28 (August 1950): 24–25.

26. JP to Editor, *Scientific American*, 21 Dec. 1953, folder: CM 1949–1953.

27. John D'Emilio, *Sexual Politics, Sexual Communities: The Making of a Homosexual Minority in the United States, 1940–1970* (Chicago: University of Chicago Press, 1983), 9.

28. JP to Charles Scribner's Sons, 7 Nov. 1953, folder: CM 1949–1953. JP requested that her poem be published in addition to her adoption study.

29. MCJ to JP, 19 Nov. 1953, ibid.

30. JP to Macmillan and Company, 4 Dec. 1953, ibid. The description and name of the poem are first mentioned in a letter to the Macmillan Company in the context of a mix-up about returning the manuscript to Paton. See JP to R. L. Wilton, 27 Oct. 1954, folder: CM, 1954–1956. For the non-return of the manuscript, see a series of letters between JP and R. L. Wilton and his replies during 1954 and 1955 in ibid.

31. [Invoice], Dec. 16, 1953, ibid.

32. Hazel to JP, handwritten note on Constance Carr to JP, 3 Dec. 1954, [n.d.], folder: Publicity for ABS.

33. Art Linkletter, as told to Cameron Shipp, "The Secret Reason Why I Love Kids," *Woman's Home Companion*, December 1953, 33, 53, 54, 66–67; quotation on 66. Linkletter discovered the identity of his birth parents through the intercession of the FBI during a World War II security background check. Ibid., 66.

34. Ibid., 32, 54.

35. JP to Art Linkletter, 30 Nov. 1953, folder: CM 1949–1953.

36. Linkletter probably did not sympathize with Paton's project. In his first autobiography, written in 1960, Linkletter expressed conflicted emotions about his abandonment by his birth parents, with resentment at their rejection winning over the desire to be reunited. See Art Linkletter with Dean Jennings, *Confessions of a Happy Man* (New York: Bernard Geis Associates, 1960), 15–16. In his second autobiography, written some twenty years later, Linkletter explicitly rejected the adoption reform movement's goal of opening adoption records for the purpose of reuniting family members on the grounds that it could be harmful. He did, however, endorse the revealing of medical information to adult adoptees. See Art Linkletter, as told to George Bishop, *I Didn't Do It Alone: The Autobiography of Art Linkletter* (Ottawa, IL: Caroline House Publishers, 1981), 48.

37. (New York: The Free Press, 1964).

38. H. David Kirk to JP, 16 September 1953, folder: Kirk. Kirk addressed the letter "Dear Sir." Paton took no umbrage. It was a common error in an era when women infrequently occupied the top position in any organization. See, for example, Robert E. Kingery to JP, 21 Sept. 1954, folder: Publicity for ABS; (Mrs. A[lice] Lapon to JP, 27 Mar. 1955 [no folder]; Ward Greene to JP, 29 Jan. 1954 [no folder].

39. JP to H. David Kirk, 21 Sept. 1953.

40. Kirk's letter is missing. The statement is apparent from JP's letter to Kirk, 29 Sept. 1953, ibid.

41. JP to H. David Kirk, 29 Sept. 1953.

42. All the information and quotations in this paragraph are from H. David Kirk to JP, 1 Dec. 1953, folder: Kirk.

43. All the information and quotations in this paragraph are from JP to H. David Kirk, 3 Dec. 1953 [no folder].

44. Ibid.

45. For Kirk's letter, see H. David Kirk to JP, 9 Dec. 1953, folder: Kirk. He canceled their planned meeting. For Paton's comments on the definition of adoption, see JP to H. David Kirk, 12 Dec. 1953.

46. JP to H. David Kirk, 12 Dec. 1953.

47. See JM, "Announcement, The ABS," 9 Dec. 1953, folder: CM 1949–1953. I have been unable to locate any documents explaining how Paton settled on the title.

48. Paton, *ABS*, 168. She had received sixty-four inquiries from the *Saturday Review of Literature* ads; in response, she sent out fifty-two questionnaires in reply, and received forty back. Ibid. JP to Richard Palmer, 20 Mar. 1954.

49. JP to Mrs. H. William Taeusch, 20 July 1954; JP to Mrs. H. William Taeusch, 4 Oct. 1954; JP to Lee R. Steiner, 20 July 1954, folder: NY–NEVD Jan 20 '55 & '59.

50. See Valentina P. Wasson, *The Chosen Baby* (Philadelphia: J. B. Lippincott, 1939), a national best-seller. For more on this book, see chap. 4, at note 84.

51. Carol Prentice, *An Adopted Child Looks at Adoption* (New York: D. Appleton-Century Co., 1940); Eleanor Gallagher, *The Adopted Child* (New York: Reynal & Hitchcock, 1936).

52. JP, "Meditation upon the Release of ABS: Containing Some Information on the History of Adoption in the US," [n.d], folder: Basics (Abstracts). Paton stated the same idea in *ABS*, 179.

53. *ABS*, 3.

54. Ibid.

55. Ibid., 6.

56. Ibid.

57. Ibid., 11–13.

58. Ibid., 14–53.

59. JP to Katherine Gordon, 28 Sept. 1982.

60. JP to Jeanette Kammen, 10 Oct. 1967. Paton was replying to the information that

the St. Paul Library had referred to her book as "The Adapted Break Silence." Jeanette
Kammen to JP, 29 Sept. 1967, ibid.

61. Ibid., 114.

62. Ibid., 125.

63. Ibid., 136.

64. Ibid., 160.

65. Jean Paton, interview by the author in Harrison, AR, 27 June 1998, Tape 5, Side B,
(transcript, 135).

66. JP, "Extended Concerns in the Adoption Problem," *Western Journal of Surgery, Obstetrics, and Gynecology* 63, no. 6 (June 1955): x.

67. The next three paragraphs and quotations, except where noted, are all derived
from JP, "Life History Method," August 1954, folder: Life History and Death.

68. See E. Wayne Carp and Anna Leon Guerrero, "When in Doubt, Count: World
War II as a Watershed in the History of Adoption," in *Adoption in America: Historical
Perspectives*, ed. E. Wayne Carp (Ann Arbor: University of Michigan Press, 2002), 188–
93, 201–10.

69. *ABS*, 158 (emphasis in the original).

70. Ibid., 158–59.

71. E. James Liberman, *Acts of Will: The Life and Work of Otto Rank* (New York: Free
Press, 1985), 196.

72. JP to Elizabeth de Schweinitz, 7 Jan. 1954, folder: Book Reviewing. Paton identified Schweinitz to be the author in a personal note dated 27 Aug. 1999, in possession of
the author.

73. JP, "Adoption Consultation," April 1954, folder: CM 1954–1956.

74. All the information and quotations in this and the next two paragraphs are from
JP, "The Adoption Project of the Life History Study Center," 30 Jun. 1954, folder: CM
1954–1956. The "others" Paton referred to were "present and prospective adoptive parents, and relatives and friends of both." Ibid.

75. JP to John L. Dusseau, 10 Jan. 1954, folder: CM 1954–1956. The other sentence
was, "See enclosed preparation announcement."

76. For an excellent description of the circumstances surrounding the background of
the W. B. Saunders Company and the publication of Kinsey's book, see James H. Jones,
Alfred C. Kinsey: A Public/Private Life (New York: W. W. Norton, 1997), 536–42.

77. John L. Dusseau to JP, 14 Jan. 1954, folder: CM 1954–1956.

78. JP to Prudence Michael, 24 Feb. 1972. Paton at some later date ordered a second
printing of 2,000 copies. Because the plates for the first printing were reused, the price
of the second printing was half of the first. Ibid.

79. Even before she finished writing *The Adopted Break Silence*, Paton began marketing the book. Indeed, sometime in December 1953, she had written to the American
Association of Psychiatric Social Workers announcing the publication of *The Adopted
Break Silence* and soliciting a review in the *Journal of Psychiatric Social Work*. The review
editor invited JP to send him a review copy. See Marcene P. Gabel to JP, 29 Dec. 1953,

folder: Publicity for ABS. In the same month, Paton wrote to the Girl Scouts of the United States of America and to the Camp Fire Girls. Helen Rowe to JP, 7 Jan. 1954, ibid. Rowe was the National Associate Director of the Camp Fire Girls. Mrs. Lewis A. DeBlois to JP, 30 Dec. 1953, ibid. Both organizations turned down Paton's solicitation to call attention to the publication.

80. JP to Librarian, 19 Aug. 1954, folder: CM 1954–1956; JP to the Philadelphia Art Alliance, 26 Aug. 1954, ibid.; JP to Library, 26 Aug. 1954, ibid.

81. JP, "Advance Orders for 'The Adopted Break Silence,'" 7 Aug. 1954, ibid.

82. JP to the Editor, 30 Aug. 1954, ibid. Paton suggested that a small city, such as Ypsilanti, probably contained many adopted people, and she said she was thinking of doing a study of the adopted people of the city.

83. "Adoption Study by Miss Paton to Be Released," *Ypsilanti Daily Press*, 7 Sept. 1954, ibid.

84. JP, "Pre-publication publicity," [n.d.], ibid. The academic departments were specifically in Pennsylvania, New Jersey, Maryland, Virginia, and Washington, D.C.

85. JP, "From Psychologists Directory," [7 Sept. 1954], ibid.

86. Paul Popenoe, *Modern Marriage*, 9 Oct. 1954. On Popenoe's career, see Molly Ladd-Taylor, "Eugenics, Sterilization, and Modern Marriage in the USA: The Strange Career of Paul Popenoe," *Gender and History* 13, no. 2 (August 2001): 298–327; Wendy Kline, *Building a Better Race: Gender, Sexuality, and Eugenics from the Turn of the Century to the Baby Boom* (Berkeley and Los Angeles: University of California Press, 2001), 140–56.

87. Oren A. Loenz to Sirs, 9 Oct. 1954, folder: Responses to Sat. Rev. Ads.

88. JP to Oren Lorenz, 12 Oct. 1954, ibid.

89. JP, "NOTE 'The Adopted Break Silence' is being mailed to reviewers this week," 5 Nov. 1954, folder: CM 1954–1956.

90. David Riesman, *American Journal of Sociology* 59 (1954): 379–83.

91. All quotations from Riesman, "Aging," 379.

92. JP to David Riesman, 16 Nov. 1954, folder: Responses to Sat. Rev. Ads.

93. David Riesman to JP, 22 Nov. 1954, ibid.

94. JP to C. B. Murray, 28 Jan. 1955 [no folder]; Deloris Murray to JP [January 1955], folder: CM 1954–1956. Paton addressed her letter to Deloris Murray's married name: Mrs. C. B. Murray.

95. "On Radio," *New York Times*, 20 Jan. 1955. The host of the show, psychologist Lee R. Steiner, described it as having a "a large following of intelligent listeners who buy books." Lee R. Steiner to The Publicity Director of the Life History Center, 1 Jan. 1954, folder: NY–NEVD Jan 20 '55 & '59. Paton gave many excuses and postponed appearing on the radio show for nearly a year. For the convoluted discussions, see ibid.

96. Garry Cleveland Myers, "Once Adopted Children Tell Their Experiences," 25 Jan. 1955, King Features Syndicate, Inc. [no folder]. Undoubtedly, the review was a product of an exchange of correspondence that took place a year earlier between the general manager of King Features Syndicate, Ward Greene, and JP. Greene had seen the ad in

Saturday Review of Literature and asked for more information about *The Adopted Break Silence.* He gave as his reason that he was an adoptive parent and that he was engaged in writing a book about adoption. See Ward Greene to JP, 29 Jan. 1954, folder: Publicity for ABS. For Paton's reply, see JP to Ward Greene, 21 Feb. 1954, ibid.

97. JP to Elizabeth Taeusch, 5 Feb. 1955. Skodal had written several articles on adoption. See for example, "The Mental Development of Adopted Children Whose True Mothers Are Feeble-Minded," *Child Development* 9, no. 3 (September 1938): 303–8; "Children in Foster Homes: A Study of Mental Development," *Studies in Child Welfare* 16, no. 1 (1939): 1–156.

98. Constance Carr to JP, 3 Dec. 1954, folder: Publicity for ABS.

99. Hazel to JP [n.d.]. (handwritten) on Constance Carr to JP, 3 Dec. 1954, ibid.

100. Ernest Osborne to JP, 15 Dec 1954, ibid.; JP to Ernest Osborne, 17 Dec. 1954, ibid.

101. JP to Edika L. Lauer, 9 Aug. 1954, ibid.

102. Henrietta L. Gordon to JP, 12 Aug. 1954, ibid.

103. JP to Henrietta Gordon, 13 Sept. 1954, ibid.

104. Mary D. Paasch to JP, 31 Aug. 1954, ibid.

105. Madelyn C. Waterbury to JP, 30 Aug. 1954, ibid. Two weeks later, the editor of the *Social Work Journal* solicited from Paton a copy of *The Adopted Break Silence,* stating that the journal would mention it and, if space warranted, review it. Russell H. Kurtz to JP, 13 Sept. 1954, ibid. It is apparent that Paton read the editor's letter hastily because in February she asked him whether she should send him a review copy. See JP to Editor, *Social Work Journal,* 9 Feb. 1955, ibid.

106. "For Brief Mention," *Social Work Journal* 36, no. 1 (January 1955): 27, ibid.

107. JP to Editor, *Social Work Journal,* 9 Feb. 1955, ibid.

108. JP to Mental Health Personnel, [early and late Feb]. folder: CM 1954–1956.

109. JP to Members of the Ministry, 14 Feb. 1955, ibid.

110. In a separate ledger, Paton recorded how many copies she sold of *The Adopted Break Silence,* who purchased them, the date of purchase, and from which state. The exact count was 1,179 copies. By 1976, when the record breaks off, 1,670 copies had been sold. [JP], *Sales and mailing record—"Adopted Break Silence" with accounts & receipts.*

Chapter 4

1. JP to Ruth G. Gagliardo, 14 Jan. 1954 [no folder]. Four months later, Paton wrote to her first supervisor at the Children's Aid Society in Philadelphia that she was thinking of participating in larger-scale studies in the Midwest. JP to Beth de Schweinitz, 4 May 1954, folder: Book reviewing.

2. Except where otherwise noted, all the information and quotations in this paragraph are from JP, "Announcement of a New Adoption Study," 3 Dec. [1954], folder: Correspondence with Magazines, 1954–1956, hereafter cited as CM 1954–1956.

3. JP, "Announcement of a New Adoption Study," 3 Dec. [1954], folder: CM 1954–1956.

4. Quoted in *OV*, 53. I have not been able to locate this announcement in JP's papers. In *OV*, 41–42, Paton claimed that a letter, highly critical of her methodology, from "a reader in Washington, D.C." was the "prime mover to continue my plans," resulting in her decision to embark upon a second adoption study. Paton responded extensively to this letter in *OV*, 42–48. However, Paton misrepresents the chronology and contents of the letter. The letter was from Richard B. Barker of the Barker Foundation, a child-placing agency licensed in Washington, D.C., and Maryland. It was dated March 1, 1955, three months *after* Paton announced the second study. Moreover, Barker praised *The Adopted Break Silence*. He thought it contained "a great deal of meat" and called it "fascinating" and "very thought provoking." Barker even contemplated making the book required reading for the foundation's adoptive parents, going so far as to ask Paton about the possibility of receiving a discount for purchasing the book in wholesale quantities. He concluded by asking whether she would be interested in being the featured speaker at the foundation's annual meeting of adoptive parents. Although Barker asked four methodological questions, the letter could hardly be viewed as a hostile one. See Richard B. Barker to JP, 1 Mar. 1955, folder: Barker Foundation. In contrast to the extensive reply to these four questions that she provided in *OV*, 42–48, Paton gave short shrift to them in her reply to Barker the following week. See JP to Richard B, Barker, 7 Mar. 1955, ibid.

5. Quoted in *OV*, 53.

6. Paton had talked to a few people for *The Adopted Break Silence*, but they had been selected from the correspondence and lived nearby. See ibid., 54.

7. Ibid.

8. Garry Cleveland Myers, "Once Adopted Children Tell Their Experiences," *Royal Oak (MI) Daily Tribune* [ca. 15 Feb. 1955]; Tom Starr to JP, 7 Mar. 1955 [no folder]; "Michigan Adoption Study Making Good Progress," *Oxford (MI) Leader*, 25 Feb. 1955.; Tom Starr to JP, 7 Mar. 1955 [no folder]. Starr sent Paton both newspaper articles. Ibid.

9. JP to Joan William, 9 Dec. 1959, folder: Angellar.

10. JP to Esther [Reed], 18 Aug. 1958, folder: Reed. For the complications of the birth certificate, see above 316n8.

11. The R. L. Polk & Co., producer of the Polk city directories, dominated the industry, and by the 1930s was producing more than 1,000 city and suburban directories. Today, it is a multinational business. See R.L. Polk & Co., "Company History," http://www.fundinguniverse.com/company-histories/R-L-Polk-amp;-Co-Company-History.html (accessed July 15, 2011). JP relied on the Polk directories all her life and recommended them to triad members.

12. *OV*, 56.

13. For a more elaborate description of this event, see chapter 5.

14. JP to Budd Gaugher, 11 Feb. 1971; JP, *OV*, 56. "Cursory" from JP to Donovan Folkerts, 8 July 1974.

15. JP to Betty Tschopp, 8 Nov. 1955, folder: Misc. 1950s; JP to Betty Tschopp, 25 Jan. 1956, ibid.

16. *OV*, 56. The investigator had found Viola as a result of her replying to one of his letters. See JP to Mary Bearden, 9 Jan. 1976.

17. *OV*, 63–83; JP mentions the snowstorm on p. 74.

18. These interviews are discussed in more detail in chapter 5.

19. JP to Theodore Reich, 24 Oct. 1972, folder: MO.

20. *OV*, 86.

21. Ibid., 86–87.

22. JP to Elizabeth Taeusch, 26 Mar. 1955; JP to Goodrich Schauffler, 27 Mar. 1955. One of the few documents that mentions where Paton's mother lived can be found in [Emma Steiner] to JP, 15 May 1958 [no folder].

23. JP to Miriam Buncher, 24 Mar. 1955, folder: MI.

24. JP to Deloris Murray, 28 Mar. 1955 [no folder].

25. *OV*, 87.

26. JP, *My Mother Lost and Found: A Tale of Reconciliation* (Cedaredge, CO: Orphan Voyage, 1981), n.p.; JP to Deloris Murray, 28 Mar. 1955 [no folder]. On Eddie Steiner's illiteracy, see [Emma Steiner] to JP, 18 Sept. 1958 [no folder].

27. JP to Sidney Green, 27 Oct. 1970; JP to Margaret X [Bonnie Jacobs], 26 Dec. 1974, folder: MD–Jacobs 1974; JP to Jean Gehrmann, 22 June 1991. See also Emma Steiner to JP, 18 Sept. 1958, [no folder], where Emma states, in reference to JP's father, that "I loved only one man"

28. JP to Sidney Green, 27 Oct. 1970.

29. JP to Linda Shipley, 20 Aug. 1998. See also JP to Jean Gehrmann, 22 June 1991. The intense erotic feelings felt by blood relatives upon meeting as adults have been labeled "genetic sexual attraction" (GSA). The term was first coined in 1987 by Barbara Gonyo, founder of a Chicago-based support group for adult adoptees, Truth Seekers in Adoption. Barbara Gonyo, "Genetic Sexual Attraction," *American Adoption Congress Newsletter* 4, no. 2 (1987): 1. See also Maurice Greenberg, "Genetic Sexual Attraction," in *Adoption and Healing*, Proceedings of the International Conference on Adoption and Healing (Wellington: New Zealand Adoption Education and Healing Trust, 1997), 100–104.

30. JP to Miriam Buncher, 24 Mar. 1955, folder: MI.

31. JP to Mrs. Nash, 21 Feb. 1968.

32. JP to Jackie Wolf, 27 Mar. 1969, folder: Adopt. Parents, Wolf.

33. JP to Deloris Murray, 28 Mar. 1955 [no folder]. See also JP to Elizabeth Taeusch, 26 Mar. 1955; JP to Mrs. Nash, 21 Feb. 1968.

34. JP to Goodrich Schauffler, 27 Mar. 1955.

35. JP to Deloris Murray, 28 Mar. 1955 [no folder].

36. JP to Miriam Buncher, 9 Apr. 1955, folder: MI.

37. JP to Eleanor Campbell, 8 June 1955.

38. [Emma Steiner] to JP, 27 May 1955 [no folder].

39. [Emma Steiner] to JP, 5 June 1955 [no folder]. I have been unable to identify just who this "lady friend" of Paton's was that Paton might take her to Michigan to meet Emma.

40. [Emma Steiner] to JP, 14 Aug. 1955 [no folder].

41. Emma Paton quoted in JP to Marion Carson, 7 July 1955.

42. JP to Elizabeth Taeusch, 5 May 1955.

43. JP to Eleanor Campbell, 8 June 1955.

44. JP to Marian Carson, 9 May 1955.

45. Unnamed supervisor quoted in *OV*, 121. See also Gary K. Hill, "Adoptees Have a Right to Know Parents, Says Paton," *Houston Chronicle*, 6 Nov. 1975, sect. 5, p. 2.

46. JP to Evelyn Zeimeta, 19 Mar. 1981, folder: Inquires 1981–1982.

47. JP to [name withheld], 14 June 1955, folder: Misc 1950s. I am respecting Paton's promise to this adult adoptee that she would never use her name or any fact told her. Ibid.

48. JP to Betty Tschopp, 25 Jan. 1956, ibid.

49. JP to Betty Tschopp, 19 Mar. 1956, ibid.

50. JP to Anna Marie Przybylak, 14 Oct. 1959.

51. JP to Sidney Green, 27 Oct. 1970.

52. JP, "I Went To Michigan," 23 Mar. 1955, CM 1954–1956. Perhaps hoping for repeat sales or forcing new readers to purchase her first book, Paton wrote that the new study "will assume at least a degree of familiarity with the adoption concepts which were first examined in 'The Adopted Break Silence.'" This strategy, however, may have backfired and discouraged new readers from purchasing the book.

53. "Michigan Adoption Study Reports," *Oxford (MI), Leader*, 25 Mar. 1955.

54. "'We Want to Know Names,' Adopted Say," *Detroit News*, 24 Apr. 1955, 14E.

55. "Ye Town Crier" *Menominee (MI) Herald-Leader*, 28 Apr. 1955, folder: MI, Menominee—Herald-Leader Apr '55.

56. I will quote from the more accessible *OV*, though the thirty-five-page section first appeared in "Three Trips Home" (1960).

57. JP quoted in *OV*, 129.

58. Ibid., 135–47.

59. Paton quoted in [Jean Worth], "Ye Town Crier," *Menominee (MI) Herald-Leader*, 28 Apr. 1955, folder: MI, Menominee—Herald-Leader Apr '55. Worth is identified by Paton in a LHSCR, "Michigan Field Trip Completed," 12 May, 1955, folder: Publicity for ABS.

60. *OV*, 162.

61. Paton included four pages of descriptive material with the flyer. See, for example, JP to Child Caring Institutions in Pennsylvania (listed in state directory), Memo, 20 July 1955, folder: CM 1954–1956.

62. JP to Booksellers, Memo, 1 June 1955, ibid.; JP to New Jersey social councils,

church workers and private schools, also to libraries for the attention of the above and others, Memo, 12 Aug. 1955, ibid; Invoices for *Popular Mechanics, Pennsylvania Farmer, Cupid's Destiny,* and the *Christian Register* can be found in ibid. Paton also advertised again in the *Saturday Review of Literature.* Ibid.

63. *OV,* 41; JP, "Reprinting of 'The Adopted Break Silence,'" 20 Aug. 1955, ibid.

64. JP to Mrs. William Rex [Child Study Association], 19 Feb. 1955, folder: Publicity for ABS; H. T. Friermood [National Council of the Young Men's Christian Associations], 15 Apr. 1955, ibid; Majorie Nicholson [Reader's Digest], 19 Aug. 1955, ibid.; Otto Zausmer [*Boston Globe*], 21 Dec. 1955, ibid.

65. Albert Wiggam, "Explore Your Mind," *Detroit Free Press,* 12 May 1955. The columns had been collected and published as *Let's Explore Your Mind* (New York: Pocket Books) in 1949. Biographical details about Wiggam can be found in Christine Rosen, *Preaching Eugenics: Religious Leaders and the American Eugenics Movement* (New York: Oxford University Press, 2004), 128–31.

66. Paton quoted in [Helen Lowe], "Center Traces Life Patterns for Adopted Adults," *Philadelphia Inquirer,* 26 Nov. 1955. Paton identified Lowe as the reporter. JP to Helen Lowe, 3 Dec. 1955, folder: Phila. Inquirer, 11/55. Paton believed Lowe was the birth mother of a child, Ruth, whom she had placed for adoption while working as a social worker. See JP to Ruth Anne Wruck, 9 June 1999, ibid.

67. Paton described the project as "adoption research from the point of view of the adult." See JP, "Adoption Study Field Trip" [n.d.], folder: Publicity for ABS. In the only mention I can locate of her activities on this trip, she reported that she met for three hours with a group of about twenty adoptive parents in a question-and-answer session. She thought it a good experience. See JP to Pat Patterson, 4 Aug. 1955.

68. Gesell Institute, "New Report Tells Results of Adoption," *Washington Post,* 15 Dec. 1955.

69. H. David Kirk to JP, 14 July 1955, folder: Kirk.

70. JP to H. David Kirk, 18 July 1955, ibid.

71. *Western Journal of Surgery, Obstetrics and Gynecology* 63, no. 6 (June 1955): viii, x, xxi.

72. JP to Feature Editor, 11 Aug. 1955, folder: Publicity for ABS.

73. Iago Galdston, "How Social Is Social Work," folder: Responses to Sat. Rev. Ads. See also JP to Iago Galdston, 7 Apr. 1955, ibid.

74. JP to Iago Galdston, 8 Aug. 1955, ibid

75. JP, "Points of Planned contact on October field trip, (Sept. 30–Oct. 15)" BN. Paton originally planned to go for only two days to the St. Louis area. See JP, "Adoption Study Trip in St. Louis Area," folder: CM 1954–1956.

76. JP, "Post-Adoption Registration Service Opens," 26 Oct. [1955], folder: Publicity for ABS.

77. JP, "The Program of the Life History Study Center," Leaflet, 21 Sept. 1955, folder: CM 1954–1956. As early as January 1955, Paton was referring in private correspon-

dence to the Center as a "communications center" or a "clearing house." See, for example, JP to Deloris Murray, 28 Jan. 1955 [no folder].

78. JP to Women's Editors of California newspapers [1 June 1955] [no folder]. Writing to the Indian anthropologist Ruth Sawtell Wallis, Paton gave several reasons for moving to Ojai, including her feeling of comfort there, her increasing dislike of East Coast weather, proximity to Los Angeles' library resources and contacts, and that her mailing list to adult adoptees was as strong in California as anywhere else. JP to Ruth Wallis, 25 Jan. 1956.

79. All quotations and information in this and the next three paragraphs are from JP, "Pain Versus Tragedy," June 1956, LHSCR, BN.

80. All the information and quotations in this paragraph are from "What the Center Is," August 1956, Report, BN.

81. All the information and quotations in this paragraph are from JP, "'Three Silences': An Expression of the Center's Present Orientation," 13 Aug. 1956, LHSCR, BN.

82. All the information and quotations in this paragraph and the next are from JP, "Anastasia in America," LHSCR, 20 Feb. 1957, BN.

83. Illinois Children's Home and Aid Society, "The Chosen Child," *Home Life for Childhood*, new series, 5 (July–August 1926): 15.

84. Philadelphia: J. B. Lippincott, 1939. For more on this volume and the notion, see Carp, *Family Matters*, 95–96; Herman, *Kinship by Design*, 275.

85. JP, "Time Is Slow Here," Annual Report, 13 Aug. 1956, BN; JP, "Growth and Development," Annual Report, 13 Aug. 1956, ibid. The annual report is made up of five pages, unpaginated, with clearly delineated sections on each page.

86. JP, "Materials and resources at the Center," [August 1956], BN. For the announcement of the new title to "Three Trips Home," see JP, "Backwards and Forwards," May 1957, ibid.

87. Quotation from JP, "Growth and Development," Annual Report, 13 Aug. 1956 [n.p.], BN; JP, "Fall Field Trip Schedule," 1 Aug. 1956, LHSCR, BN.

88. JP, "Growth and Development," Annual Report, 13 Aug. 1956 [n.p.], BN.

89. JP, "Interim Release of the Life History Study Center," 1 Aug. 1956, ibid.

90. Ibid.

91. JP, "Time Is Slow Here," Annual Report, 13 Aug. 1956, BN.

92. JP, "Interim Release of the Life History Study Center," 1 Aug. 1956, ibid.

Chapter 5

1. The ad read in part, "ANASTASIA IN AMERICA. Studies in American adoption cast light on problems of identity." JP to *Saturday Review*, 26 Jan. 1957, folder: CM 1957–1959. See also Helen Dardaganis to JP, 20 Feb. 1957, ibid.

2. There were ten questions in the form she devised. Paton defined the adoption fantasy as "the idea that an individual becomes possessed by, usually during childhood or adolescence, but sometimes later, that the parents who raised him, and whom he has

presumed to be his physical parents, were not his physical parents." JP, "Adoption Fantasy," 1 Feb. 1957, ibid

3. JP, "The Adopted Break Silence," Flyer, 20 Nov. 1957, ibid.

4. Ibid; JP, "Special Information Sheet," 20 Nov. 1957, ibid. The institute's name later was changed to the Gesell Institute of Human Development. For biographical information on Ames and Ilg see, Henry Fountain, "Louise Ames, 88, a Child Psychologist, Dies," *New York Times*, 7 Nov. 1996; Walter Waggoner, "Dr. Francis L. Ilg, Authority and Writer on Child Behavior," ibid., 28 Jul. 1981.

5. Between 24 October and 6 November, Paton planned on stopping at San Pedro, Long Beach, Pasadena, Los Angeles, San Diego, and La Mesa. JP, "First California Field Trip," 14 Oct. 1957, folder: CM 1957–1959.

6. JP, "Bridey Bridey," August [19]57, LHSCR (2), BN. See also JP to Madalyn Murray, 7 Feb. 1958, folder: CM 1957–1959.

7. JP, "The Pursuit of Anxiety," LHSCR, 1 May 1958, BN. For her reasons for moving to Acton see ibid.

8. For the list of books, see the entry "Partial List of Books Read, (1956–1959)" at E. Wayne Carp's blog, *The Biography of Jean Paton*, at Jeanpaton.com. In addition, Paton read for the first time a number of books written by or about adopted or orphaned individuals, including William March's 1954 novel *The Bad Seed*, and *A Cornish Waif's Story*, an autobiography of the pseudonymous Emma Smith, who had been born out of wedlock and abandoned by her family. William March, *The Bad Seed: A Novel* (Hopewell, NJ: Ecco Press, 1954). Emma Smith (pseud.), *A Cornish Waif's Story: An Autobiography* (New York: Dutton, 1956).

9. An extended discussion of this subject can be found in E. Wayne Carp, "Jean Paton, "Christian Adoption, and the Reunification of Families," *Journal of Christian Legal Thought* 2, no. 1 (Spring 2012): 20–22. The entire article can be found at http://www.clsnet.org/document.doc?id=357.

10. See C. Colburn Harvey, *The Story of Ypsilanti* (S.I.: s.n, 1923); James Thomas Mann, *Ypsilanti: A History in Pictures* (Chicago: Arcadia, 2002); JP to Delores Murray, 28 Mar. 1955, [no folder].

11. JP to Agnes Baker, 23 Apr. 1973; Paton claimed that until the age of twelve she "had a pervasive and happy faith, and nothing I have been able to do since could undo it." JP to Ruth Wallis, 24 Mar. 1956.

12. JP to Ruth Wallis, 12 Mar. 1958.

13. JP to Rev. Richard Byfield, 6 Feb. 1961.

14. Ibid.

15. JP, "From the Center's Notebook," Release, Oct. 1958, folder: CM 1957–1959.

16. JP to Marilyn Hipp, 8 Jan. 1983.

17. JP to Kay Rachford, 10 Aug. [1977].

18. JP to Geneva Ferrozzo, 2 Feb. 1982, folder: Ferrozzo, G. "God is Love," 1 John 4:8.

19. JP to Sidney Green, 14 Sept. 1971; JP to Bill Lumley, 5 Dec. 1975. According to Yigal Levin, "most modern scholars assume that Joseph must have adopted Jesus in some

form or another." See Levin, "Jesus, 'Son of God' and 'Son of David': The 'Adoption' of Jesus into the Davidic Line," *Journal for the Study of the New Testament* 28, no. 4 (2006): 415–42. But this is a contested idea. For a learned view that the historical Jesus was fatherless, see Andries Van Aarde, *Fatherless in Galilee: Jesus as Child of God* (Harrisburg, PA: Trinity Press International, 2001), 77, chap. 5. Paton's definition of a social orphan comes from an untitled essay written "after '67."

20. JP, "Jottings," Feb. 1, 1961, folder: Reunion 1960–1962.

21. Ibid. (emphasis in the original).

22. OV, 116–17. For scholarly support of Paton's view, see Aarde, *Fatherless in Galilee*, chap. 6.

23. JP to Bill Cody, 10 Sept. 1979.

24. OV, 117.

25. JP to Sidney Green, 14 Sept. 1971; JP to Bill Lumley, 5 Dec. 1975.

26. JP to Sidney Greene, 14 Sept. 1971.

27. Except where noted, all quotation and information in this paragraph are from JP, "Jonathan Edwards Returns," Life History Study Center, November 1957, News Release, folder: Life History Center for "Reunion" Program. Paton admitted there were other types of adoptions, but she favored Christian adoptions. Ibid.

28. JP to Selma Chesler, 20 Feb. 1966.

29. JP to Katherine Gordon, 28 Sept. 1982.

30. JP to Joanna G. Schenk, 28 Oct 1955, folder: MA.

31. Célestin Musekura, *An Assessment of Contemporary Models of Forgiveness* (New York: Peter Lang, 2010), chap. 1. Musekura dates the earliest psychological study of forgiveness to a dissertation in 1984. Ibid., 18.

32. Wilhelm and Marion Pauck, *Paul Tillich: His Life and Thought*, vol. 1 (New York: Harper & Row, 1976).

33. Andrew S. Finstuen, *Original Sin and Everyday Protestants: The Theology of Reinhold Niebuhr, Billy Graham, and Paul Tillich in an Age of Anxiety* (Chapel Hill: University of North Carolina Press, 2009), 1–2; quotation on 2.

34. Paul Tillich, *The New Being* (New York: Charles Scribner's Sons, 1955). The other two volumes, both published by Scribner's, were *The Shaking of the Foundations* (1948) and *The Eternal Now* (1963). For Paton's notes, see JP, "Tillich, Paul, 'The New Being,' Scribner's 1955," folder: Method of Benevolence.

35. A copy of the sermon was in Paton's possession. Paul Tillich, "Forgiveness," 21 Feb. 1954 (SERMON SERIES, Series 1953–54, no. 12 [Philadelphia: Unitarian Church of Germantown]). It was later published as "To Whom Much Is Forgiven," in Tillich, *New Being*, 2–14. The published version omits the first two-sentence paragraph of the original sermon, in which the only significant addition is that the Pharisee is identified as "Simon." Otherwise, the published version is identical to the original sermon. For the convenience of readers, references are to the published version.

36. Luke 7: 36–47 in Tillich, *New Being*, 4.

37. Ibid., 5.

38. Ibid., 7.

39. Ibid.

40. Ibid., 7–8.

41. Ibid., 13.

42. JP, "Boundaries of Affliction, Commentary 2," 1 Aug. 1961, Reunion Release, BN.

43. *OV*, 52. Although *OV* was published in 1968, it was written between 1955 and 1959, much closer to the time of Paton's experience described here.

44. JP to Connie Dawson, 2 Sept. 1991, folder: Dawson, Connie.

45. JP to Dr. Eleanor Scott, 15 Oct. 1955, folder: 1950s Misc.

46. Ibid.

47. JP, "The Bright Journey," Dec. 1958, LHSCR, folder: Life History Center for "Reunion" Program.

48. JP to Jo Anne Ernest, 16 May 1977, folder: KY—Ernest, Jo Anne.

49. JP to Mariellen Self, 2 Oct. 1978.

50. JP to Bonnie Jacobs, 28 July 1970, folder: MD—Jacobs 70–71.

51. JP, "From the Center's Notebook," October 1958, LHSCR, BN.

52. JP to Jo Anne Ernest, 16 May 1977.

53. JP, "From the Center's Notebook," LHSCR, October 1958, BN. Paton did not elaborate on this religious metaphor, except to compare the experience of the search to entering upon psychoanalysis: "one should not lie upon the couch without some shred of faith to await the day of one's departure." Ibid.

54. JP to Mary Sobczyk, 9 Dec. 1955.

55. JP to Mariellen Self, 2 Oct. 1978.

56. JP to Nancy Sitterly, 14 Sept. 1979, folder: CT—Hart Daube Sitterly; JP to Nancy Sitterly, 16 Jan. 1980, ibid.

57. JP to Rose Mary Sever, 15 Jan. 1993, folder: Sever, JM.

58. JP to Gloria Veillon, 16 Nov. 1983, folder: LA—Veillon, Gloria.

59. JP to Pat Hinchey, 27 Aug. 1979, folder: Hinchey.

60. JP to Lynn Greiner, 13 May 1982.

61. JP to Pat Hinchey, 27 Aug. 1979, folder: Hinchey.

62. All information and quotation in this paragraph, unless otherwise stated, are from JP, "REUNION: A Program of the Life History Study Center," Leaflet, June 1958 [no folder].

63. JP, "News at the Center," Aug. 1958, BN.

64. All the information and quotations in this paragraph are from JP, "Hill House" [n.d.], ibid. Paton also referred to this structure as "Reunion cottage." See JP, "For 1959," 10 Jan. 1959, folder: CM 1957–1959.

65. See JP to Ernestine Mejia, 23 Sept. 1975, folder: Mejia, E.

66. See, for example, JP to Elizabeth Taeusch, 8 June 1955, folder: Taeusch; JP to Mary Sobczyk, 8 Nov. 1955.

67. JP to Marion Carson, 15 Jan. 1957, folder: Carson, Marion E.; JP to Florence

Kneller (Fitch), 21 Jan. 1957, folder: Kneller (Fitch), Florence. James Kittson worked for Burroughs for four years.

68. JP to Donna Collom, 3 Sept. 1974.

69. JP to Mrs. Jesse Reed, 15 Mar. 1958, folder: Reed; JP to Jeanette Kamman, 23 Feb. 1958, folder: Kamman.

70. See the series of letters to Ruth Wallis. JP to Ruth Wallis 7 Dec. 1956, folder: Wallis; JP to Ruth Wallis, 18 Dec. 1956; folder: ibid.; JP to Ruth Wallis, 2 Jan. 1957, folder: ibid.

71. Michael Malone, *James J. Hill: Empire Builder of the Northwest* (Norman: University of Oklahoma Press, 1996), 15. See also, Albro Martin, *James J. Hill and the Opening of the Northwest* (St. Paul: Minnesota Historical Society, 1976).

72. JP to Jeanette Kamman, 25 Apr. 1958, folder: Kamman. See also, JP to Jeanette Kamman, 23 Feb. 1958, folder: ibid. Kamman sent Paton clippings about the Hill family.

73. JP to Prudence Michael, 25 Apr. 1973.

74. All quotations and information about Hill's affair are from JP to Donna Collom, 3 Sept. 1974.

75. JP, "News at the Center," August 1958, LHSCR, BN.

76. JP, "Three Trips Home" Progress Report [n.d.], ibid.

77. JP, "Adoption in Existence," 11 July 1959, folder: CM 1957–1959. Paton stated that the three pieces were to be considered "the second study of adopted adulthood to be issued by the Life History Study Center." Ibid. See also JP, "Adoption in Existence," 24 July 1959, ibid. A decade later, Paton would publish "Three Trips Home" as *Orphan Voyage*.

78. See Elizabeth Alston, to JP, [7 Apr. 1959], folder: CM 1957–1959; Harold Martin to J. H. Reed, 3 Mar. 1959, ibid.

79. JP to The Editors, McCall's, 30 Mar. 1959, ibid.

80. JP to The Editors, American Mercury, 28 Aug. 1959, folder: ibid. JP was referring to Martha Vansant's article, "The Life of the Adopted Child," which appeared in the February 1933 issue of the *American Mercury*.

81. All the information and quotation in this and the next paragraph are from JP, "How to Change the World," 1 Nov. 1958, BN.

Chapter 6

1. Gen. 16:12 (King James version).

2. Deut. 23:2.

3. Sir. 23:24–26.

4. I have relied heavily on the excellent study by John Witte, Jr., *The Sins of the Fathers: The Law and Theology of Illegitimacy Reconsidered* (New York: Cambridge University Press, 2009), 11–16. Witte demonstrates conclusively that these biblical passages condemning illegitimacy have been misinterpreted.

5. See chapter 2.

6. *Western Journal of Surgery, Obstetrics and Gynecology* 63, no. 6 (June 1955): viii, x, xxi.

7. (New York: Elizabeth Ann Guild, 1927). By 1931, Britton put the worldwide sales at 110,000 copies. Robert H. Farrell, *The Strange Deaths of President Harding* (Columbia: University of Missouri Press, 1966), 65. Historians are divided on the truthfulness of Britton's claim that Harding fathered her child. Farrell, *Strange Deaths of President Harding*, presents the strongest case against her, though he makes no allowance for the bias inherent in Harding's staunchest supporters and accepts their statements at face value. Francis Russell supports Britton's claim. See his *The Shadow of Blooming Grove: Warren G. Harding and His Times* (New York: McGraw-Hill, 1968).

8. Britton placed this information, under the title "Six Burly Men," prominently before her book's frontispiece and book title. Britton, *President's Daughter*, n.p. Farrell, *Strange Deaths of President Harding*, 56.

9. JP to Madalyn Murray O'Hare, 29 Apr. 1957.

10. Of the several biographies of O'Hair, the most scholarly is by Bryan F. Le Beau, *The Atheist: Madalyn Murray O'Hair* (New York: New York University Press, 2003). Written in a journalistic style but packed with valuable historical information is Ann Rowe Seaman, *America's Most Hated Woman: The Life and Gruesome Death of Madalyn Murray O'Hair* (New York: Continuum Press, 2005). Another popular account is Ted Dracos, *Ungodly: The Passions, Torments, and Murder of Atheist Madalyn Murray O'Hair* (New York: Free Press, 2003).

11. Jane Howard, "The Most Hated Woman in America," *Life*, June 19, 1964, 94.

12. For additional biographical details on Murray, see "The Atheist and the Christian: Madalyn Murray O'Hair, Jean Paton, and the Stigma of Illegitimacy in the 1950s," *The Journal of the Historical Society* 12, no. 2 (June 2012): 206.

13. Murray's second son was the result of her romance with Michael Fiorillo, an aeronautical engineer and coworker at the Glenn L. Martin Aircraft plant. See Le Beau, *Atheist*, 33; Seaman, *America's Most Hated Woman*, 34–35.

14. Murray to JP, 26 Apr. [1957].

15. The information that Murray worked at the Children and Family Aid Society of Baltimore County comes from Seaman, *America's Most Hated Woman*, 38.

16. Murray to JP, 26 Apr. [1957]. In the fall of 1957, Murray enrolled in Howard University's Graduate School of Social Work, supported by a grant from the National Institute of Mental Health. See Seaman, *America's Most Hated Woman*, 39.

17. Murray to JP, 26 Apr. [1957].

18. The three other works Paton recommended were Everett V. Stonequist, *The Marginal Man: A Study in Personality and Culture Conflict* (New York: Charles Scribner's Sons, 1937); Kingsley Davis, "Illegitimacy and the Social Structure," *American Journal of Sociology* 45, no. 2 (September 1939): 215–33; and Kingsley Davis, "The Forms of Illegitimacy," *Social Forces* 18, no. 1 (October 1959): 77–114.

19. All information and quotations here are from JP to Madalyn Murray, 29 Apr. 1957.

20. Murray to JP, 3 June [1957]. Paton sent her Britton's address the next month. See JP to Madalyn Murray, 22 July 1957.

21. Unless otherwise noted, the information and quotations in this and the next three paragraphs are from Murray to JP, 28 July 1957. (emphasis in the original).

22. JP to Madalyn Murray, 18 Sept. 1957.

23. JP, "The Sulphur Mountain Conference," 15 Jan. 1958, folder: CM 1957–1959. See also, JP, "The Sulphur Mountain Conference," January [19]58, ibid.

24. JP, "The Sulphur Mountain Conference," January [19]58.

25. JP to Madalyn Murray, 7 Feb. 1958, ibid.

26. JP, "A New Home," March 1958 BN. No additional correspondence relating to the Sulphur Mountain Conference on illegitimacy has been found.

27. See JP, "Report on the Attempt to Arrange a Conference for Persons Afflicted with Illegitimacy," folder: CM 1957–1959.

28. Unless otherwise noted, all quotations and information in this and the next two paragraphs are from JP, "Humiliating the Unmarried Mother," Release, November 1958, ibid.

29. Josie Svanhuit, "The American Caricature of the Unmarried Mother " *Canadian Welfare* (December 1955): 246–49.

30. Editors, *American Mercury* [to JP], [n.d], folder: CM 1957–1959; JP to The Editors, *McCalls*, 30 Mar. 1959, ibid: Elizabeth A. Alston [to JP], [mailed 7 Apr. 1959], ibid.

31. JP, "Life History Study Center, Field Trips Resumed," Release, 10 Apr. [1959], folder: CM 1957–1959.

32. Ibid.

33. JP, [n.t.], 22 July 1959, ibid.

34. Except where noted, all the information and quotations from this and the next four paragraphs are from Murray to JP, 18 July 1959.

35. Le Beau, *Atheist*, 38; Seaman, *America's Most Hated Woman*, 40.

36. Seaman, *America's Most Hated Woman*, 40, citing Murray's oral interview in 1971 to two Baylor University historians. However, Seaman expresses doubts at Murray's account. She suggests that Murray may have dropped out of Howard because "graduate schools almost never expel students except for cheating, theft, or some other serious infractions." Ibid,. 347n.40

37. JP to Madalyn Murray, 18 July 1959.

38. All the information and quotations in this paragraph are from Murray to JP, 4 Aug. [1959]. (emphasis in the original).

39. JP, "A New Cradle for the Illegitimate?" 7 Sept. 1959, folder: CM 1957–1959.

40. All quotation in this paragraph are from Murray to JP, 20 Oct. 1959.

41. Le Beau, *Atheist*, 37–39; Seaman, *America's Most Hated Woman*, 41–43.

42. Murray to JP, 20 Oct. [19]59, (emphasis in the original: triple underlined).

43. All the information and quotations in this paragraph are from JP to Madalyn Murray, 25 Oct. 1959.

44. JP, "Remembered," *Los Angeles Times*, 24 Dec. 1959, folder: CM 1957–1959.

45. John E. B. Merriman to JP, 27 Dec. 1958, ibid.

46. JP, "(personal)," 6 Feb. 1963, Blue Notebook.

47. JP to Selma Chesler, 22 Apr. 1968, folder: Chesler.

48. JP to Mary Malefyt, 22 Apr. 1969, folder: Book Reviewing.

49. JP to Selma Chesler, 20 Feb. 1966.

50. JP to Minnie J. Sigdestad, 9 Nov. 1959, folder: ND.

51. All of the information and quotations in this paragraph are from JP to Marie Norton, 29 Oct. 1959, folder: Miscellaneous 1950s.

52. JP to Ruth Wallis, 26 Jan. 1958.

53. Ibid.

54. JP to Mildred Smith, 5 Jan. 1959.

55. Jesse to JP, 17 July [1960], in JP, "Motivations and Forecast: An Exchange of Letters" [26 July 1960] [no folder; sent to author by JP].

56. Ester to JP, 17 July [1960], in ibid.

57. Except where noted, all the information and quotations in this paragraph are from JP, "Reunion and Identity" [25 Oct. 1960] (Acton, CA: Life History Study Center) [n.p.].

58. All the information and quotations in this paragraph are from Madalyn Murray to JP, 20 Oct. 1960.

59. All the information and quotations in this paragraph are from JP, "Tempo Rubato," 1 Feb. 1961, BN.

60. JP, "Clinical Aspects of Adoption," 1 Feb. 1961, BN.

61. For Hoffman, see "Traumatic Neurosis," http://www.answers.com/topic/traumatic-neurosis (accessed December 15, 2009).

62. Diane Casoni, "'Never Twice without Thrice': Outline for Traumatic Neurosis," *International Journal of Psychoanalysis* 83 (February 2002): 137–59.

63. For information about Kardiner's work and life, I am indebted to William C. Manson, *The Psychodynamics of Culture: Abram Kardiner and Neo-Freudian Anthropology* (New York: Greenwood Press, 1988), esp. chap. 1.

64. 2nd ed. (New York: Harper & Brothers, 1947).

65. JP to Abram Kardiner, 29 July 1956, folder: 1950s Correspondence. In this letter, Paton referred to Kardiner's book simply as "War Neurosis." The first edition of *War Stress and Neurotic Illness* was titled *The Traumatic Neurosis of War* (New York: Harper & Brothers, 1941). JP cleared up any possible of confusion about which edition she was referring to by stating in a second letter that the only work she had read of Kardiner's was *War Stress and Neurotic Illness*. See JP to Abraham Kardiner, 30 Dec. 1959, folder: 1950s Correspondence.

66. JP to Abraham Kardiner, 30 Dec. 1959, folder: ibid.

67. Except where noted, all the information and quotations in this paragraph are from JP, "Clinical Aspects of Adoption," 1 Feb. 1961, BN (emphasis in the original).

68. This incident can be found in Kardiner, *War Stress and Neurotic Illness*, 388.

69. JP, "Encircling Fog," Apr. 1961, BN; JP, "Acton's Parting Gift," 14 May 1961, folder: Reunion 1960–1962; quotation from "Acton's Parting Gift," ibid.

70. JP, "Village Life, I" 7 June 1961, folder: Reunion 1960–1962.

71. Robert Coles, *Simone Weil: A Modern Pilgrimage* (Reading, MA: Addison-Wesley, 1987).

72. Leslie Fiedler, "Introduction," in Simone Weil, *Waiting for God* (New York: Harper & Row, 2009; orig pub. G. P. Putnam's Sons, 1951), 26.

73. Simone Petrement, *Simone Weil: A Life* (New York: Random House, 1976), chap. 8; Francine du Plessix Gray, *Simone Weil* (New York: Viking 2001), chap. 5.

74. Weil, *Waiting for God*, 68.

75. I have relied here on the works previously cited by Coles, Gray, and Petrement for information about Weil.

76. Gray, *Simone Weil*, 24.

77. Simone Weil, *The Need for Roots: Prelude to a Declaration of Duties toward Mankind*, trans. Arthur Wills (New York: G. P. Putnam's Sons, 1952).

78. Coles, *Simone Weil*, 102.

79. The first sentence of *Need for Roots* states, "The notion of obligations comes before that of rights, which is subordinate and relative to the former." Weil, *Need for Roots*, 3–9; quotation on 3. For insightful remarks on Weil's *Need for Roots*, see E. W. F. Tomlin, *Simone Weil* (New Haven, CT: Yale University Press, 1954), 54–58.

80. Simone Weil, "Beyond Personalism," trans. Russell S. Young, *Crosscurrents* 2, no. 3 (Spring 1952): 59–76. In her copy of the article, Paton underscored Weil's statement "Rights naturally depend on force" (ibid., 66). From Paton's notations, which include mention of an "orphan exhibit," it is clear that she did not read Weil's article at the time of its publication but instead in the early 1960s, well after *The Need for Roots*. The article can be more easily accessed in *The Simone Weil Reader*, ed. George A. Panichas (New York: David McKay Co., 1977), 313–39, under the title "Human Personality."

81. Gray, *Simone Weil*, 98.

82. Weil, *Waiting for God*, 66–67. With some small changes in language, the passage is quoted in Gray, *Simone Weil*, 98–99.

83. Weil, *Waiting for God*, 68–69. The quotations in this paragraph are from JP, "The Affliction Process," 10 June 1961, BN.

84. JP to Mary Doyle, 30 June 1976. Paton follows Weil in this sentiment. Weil states, "The Book of Job is a pure marvel of truth and authenticity from beginning to end. As regards affliction, all that departs from this model is more or less stained with falsehood." *Waiting for God*, 120.

85. JP, "The Affliction Process," 10 June 1961, BN.

86. Weil, *Waiting for God*, 135.

87. Gray, *Simone Weil*, 223.

88. For the Daughters of Bilitis, see Marcia M. Gallo, *Different Daughters: A History of the Daughters of Bilitis and the Rise of the Lesbian Rights Movement* (New York: Carroll & Graf, 2006).

89. JP, "Readers of THE LADDER," *The Ladder:A Lesbian Review* 12 (October–November 1969): 39, 40. Because of editorial problems, the article appeared as a letter

to the editor. See Barbara Grier to JP, 6 June 1969. A copy of Paton's article can be found in folder: Baer, Janine.

90. Barbara Grier to JP, 8 Feb. 1969.

91. JP to Barbara Grier, 25 Feb. 1969.

92. Grier to JP, 1 Mar. 1969. (ellipses in the original).

93. JP to Barbara Grier, 2 June 1969. (emphasis in the original). Paton never got around to writing the longer serious piece on affliction. Earlier, she had three short Reunion Releases on affliction. See JP, "The Boundaries of Affliction," 22 July 1961, Release, folder: Reunion 1960–1962; JP, "Boundaries of Affliction, Commentary 1," 1 Aug. 1961, Release, ibid.; JP, "Boundaries of Affliction, Commentary 2," 1 Aug. 1961, Release, ibid

94. JP, "Focus for 1962," 13 Nov. 1961, BN.

95. JP, "The Response to 'Focus,'" Jan. 1962, FR, IA, p. 1, folder: Reunion 1960–1962.

96. Many years later, Paton explained that *Manon Lescaut* expressed "more deeply and completely than anything I have heard sing or played the emotion which is pointed to by the name." JP, "Art for Our Souls," *A Proper Response: To the Situation in Adoption* 2, no. 2 (September 1995).

97. JP, "Our First Steps Together toward Illegitimacy," Jan. 1962, FR, IB, 3. JP then shared some personal history, revealing her experience in 1947 at the New Hampshire Children's Aid Society with the unwed mother she interviewed. See chapter 2.

98. JP, "Notice to Mailing List," 6 Feb. 1962, FR, folder: Reunion 1960–1962.

99. JP, "Enduring Colonials," 15 May 1962, FR, ibid. For both the physical and mental or emotional symptoms of menopause depicted by physicians, see Judith A. Houck, *Hot and Bothered: Women, Medicine, and Menopause in Modern America* (Cambridge, MA: Harvard University Press, 2006), 66.

100. John S. Haller Jr. and Robin M. Haller, *The Physician and Sexuality in Victorian America* (Urbana: University of Illinois Press, 1974), 134–35. See also Carroll Smith-Rosenberg, "Puberty to Menopause: The Cycle of Femininity in Nineteenth-Century America," *Feminist Studies* 1 (1973): 58–72.

101. Houck, *Hot and Bothered*, 68–71, 85–86, 95.

102. JP, "Enduring Colonials," 15 May 1962, FR, folder: Reunion 1960–1962.

Chapter 7

1. JP, "Orphan Voyage: a program of mutual aid and guidance for social orphans," 1 Sept. 1962, folder: Reunion 1960–1962.

2. All the information and quotations in this and the next paragraph are from Madeline Hill [JP], "Is Illegitimacy Inferiority?" June 1962, FR.

3. Paton was no stranger to Schechter's work. In 1960, Paton had sent Schechter a copy of *The Adopted Break Silence*. JP to Marshall D. Schechter, 15 June 1960. Schechter had already read *The Adopted Break Silence* and told JP that he had incorporated parts of it in his paper. See Marshall Schechter to JP, 24 June 1960.

4. Schechter had sent her an offprint of his seminal 1960 article "Observations on Adopted Children," *Archives of General Psychiatry* 3 (July 1960): 21–32

5. JP, "Enduring Colonials," 15 May 1962, FR, folder: Reunion 1960–1962.

6. Ibid. Two months later, however, writing an open letter to "adoptive parents" under the name of Viola Dean, Paton criticized Schechter's paper, finding parts of it "entirely unacceptable." What irritated Paton was Schechter's failure to distinguish between agency and independent placement. Paton's tone is bitingly sarcastic, thus raising some doubt about how wholeheartedly she approved of Schechter's work at this time. See Viola Dean [JP], "A Look Inside Official Adoption Research," June 1962, FR. In December 1962, Kirk wrote Paton, complimenting her "very challenging" statement, "Letter to an Adoptive Parent." He requested permission to include it in his soon-to-be-published work, *Shared Fate: A Theory of Adoptive Relations.* He was pleased, he told JP, to "make reference to your devoted and incisive mind." H. David Kirk to JP, 17 Dec. 1962, folder: Kirk.

7. JP, "Enduring Colonials," 15 May 1962, FR, folder: Reunion 1960–1962.

8. Ibid.

9. Harold Grotevant, "The Integrative Nature of Identity: Bringing the Soloists to Sing in the Choir," in *Discussions on Ego Identity,* ed. J. Kroger (Hillsdale, NJ: Erlbaum, 1993), 137.

10. All the information and quotations in this paragraph are from JP, "Orphan Voyage: A program of mutual aid and guidance for social orphans," 1 Sept. 1962, folder: Reunion 1960–1962.

11. JP, "September Letter of the Orphan Voyage, 11 Sept. 1962, BN.

12. JP to Leona Bayer, 7 Oct. 1962, folder: Bayer, L.

13. Except where noted, all the information and quotations in this paragraph are from JP, "September Letter of the Orphan Voyage," 11 Sept. 1962, BN.

14. JP to Leona Bayer, 7 Oct. 1962, folder: Bayer, L.

15. Except where noted, all the information and quotations in this paragraph are from JP, "September Letter of the Orphan Voyage," 11 Sept. 1962, BN.

16. Initially, Paton's stationery was headed "The Orphan Voyage." See, for example, JP to Leona Bayer, 7 Oct. 1962, folder: Bayer, L.

17. See, for example, JP, "The use of the word 'Orphan,'" 14 Mar. 1979 [no folder]; JP to James Swain, 12 July 1994.

18. JP to Marion Morris, 16 Feb. 1966.

19. Ibid.

20. This quotation and the next are from JP, "The use of the word 'Orphan,'" 14 Mar. 1979 [no folder].

21. JP to James Swain, 12 July 1994.

22. Except where noted, all the information and quotations in this paragraph are from JP, "What Is the Orphan Voyage?" 11 Dec. 1962, BN.

23. Paton's use of the word "overweening" was purposeful. It is from a Middle English word meaning "to be arrogant."

24. Except where noted, all the information and quotations in this paragraph are from JP, "Illegitimacy and the Artist," 11 Dec. 1962, Orphan Voyage Release, BN.

25. JP to Ladd Z, 27 Feb. 1970, folder: [Budd] Gauger.

26. Ibid.

27. JP to Pamela Biagi, 24 Feb. 1975.

28. JP to Sue Brostrom, 31 Oct. 1977, folder: Brostrom.

29. All the information and quotations in this paragraph are from JP, "Letter to the Orphan Voyage," 22 Jan. 1963, BN.

30. JP, "'Reunion' Resources" [1963], BN.

31. JP, "From the ship's log," 25 Jan. 1963, BN. This is JP's first use of the word "log," used later as the name of Orphan Voyage's newsletter, *The LOG of Orphan Voyage*.

32. All information and quotations in this paragraph are from JP, "(personal)," 6 Feb. 1963, BN.

33. Mel Gussow, "Odd Man In," *Newsweek*, 4 Feb. 1963; Mel Gussow, *Edward Albee: A Singular Journey* (Milwaukee, WI: Applause Theatre Books, 2001), 14. Unknown to her readers, Paton chose Albee because she had a special relationship with him: Albee had been one of the forty adult adoptees that Paton used in her sample for *The Adopted Break Silence*.

34. All the information and quotations in this paragraph are from JP, "Albee Go Home!" 16 Feb. 1963, BN.

35. Although Arendt achieved fame with the publication of the now-classic *The Origins of Totalitarianism* (1951), it is often forgotten that her 1929 dissertation was written on the concept of love in the thought of Saint Augustine, under the direction of existentialist philosopher-psychologist Karl Jaspers. A great admirer of Arendt, Paton was familiar with a number of her works, including *The Origins of Totalitarianism; Between Past and Future: Six Exercises in Political Thought* (New York: Viking, 1961); and *The Human Condition*, 2nd ed. (Chicago: University of Chicago Press, 1998; 1st ed., 1958). See JP to Hannah Arendt, 17 Sept. 1962, folder: 1960s Correspondence.

36. Arendt, *The Human Condition*, 238.

37. Ibid., 240.

38. See chapter 5. The parable is in Luke 7:36–47.

39. JP, "Albee Go Home!" 16 Feb. 1963, BN.

40. JP, "Arising Out of Adoption," 13 Mar. 1963, ibid.

41. JP, "Hill House," 6 Apr. 1963, ibid.; JP, "Hill House Meeting," 6 May 1963, ibid.

42. Ruthena Kittson [JP], "Hill House says," 1 Aug. 1963, ibid.

43. See Chapter 4. Except where noted, all the information and quotations in this and the next paragraph are from JP, "The Chosen Child," 1963, BN.

44. Carp, *Family Matters*, 90–98.

45. Søren Kierkegaard, *Either-Or*, 2 vols. (Garden City, NY: Doubleday, 1959), vol. 2: 181.

46. Benda quoted in JP, "The Chosen Child," 1963, BN.

47. JP, "Developments ——," 25 Oct. 1963, ibid.

48. JP and Marie Lewis, "By-Laws of Orphan Voyage," 15 Mar. 1964, 1, folder: Orphan Voyage Bylaws. Paton, Lewis, and Joan Williams were named as directors of the corporation, but only Paton and Lewis signed the document. Ibid.

49. Ibid., 2.

50. Ibid., 3.

51. Ibid., 3–4; quotations on 3, 4.

52. Ibid., 1–4; quotation on 3.

53. Ibid., 4; quotations on 4.

54. Except where noted, all the information and quotations in this and the next three paragraphs are from JP, "The Gentle Balm of Approbation," 24 Oct. 1963, BN. Paton completed the journey by plane. Ibid.

55. Jackie Germann, "'Foundlings Should Get Background,'" *St. Paul, MN, Pioneer Press,* 29 Sept. 1963, folder: MN—Minneapolis Star/St. Paul Pioneer.

56. Peter Ritter, "Jeanette Kammen's Library of Orphans," http://www.citypages.com/2001–11–21/news/jeanette-kamman-s-library-for-orphans/2/ (accessed November 27, 2011).

57. JP, "Developments——," 25 Oct. 1963, BN.

Chapter 8

1. Except where noted, all the information and quotations in this paragraph are from JP, "Developments - - - - -," 25 Oct. 1963, BN.

2. JP, interview by the author in Harrison, AR, 26 June 1998, Tape 5, Side A (transcript, 114).

3. JP, "Eastern Field Trip," 27 Dec. 1963, BN.

4. JP to Bonnie Jacobs, 4 Aug. 1995, folder: MD-Jacobs 1994 to Present.

5. The phrase "nothing fancy" is from JP to Mara Jane Thorne, 21 May 1981, folder: AR-Thorn.

6. JP, "You can Participate" [1964], BN.

7. All the information and quotations in this paragraph are from JP, "Current Projects" [1964], ibid.

8. June Schwantes, interview by author in Harrison, AR, 23 May 2009, Tape 1, Side A. See Karl A. Olsson, *Quality of Mercy: Swedish Covenant Hospital and Covenant Home: Seventy-Fifth Anniversary, 1886–1961* (Chicago: Swedish Covenant Hospital, [1961?]), n.p.

9. Schwantes, interview, Tape 1, Side A; "Schwantes is August volunteer of the month at NARMC Auxiliary," *Harrison (AK) Daily Times,* 18 Aug. 2005; Emory A. Massman, *Hospital Ships of World War II: An Illustrated Reference to Thirty-Nine United States Military Vessels* (Jefferson, NC: McFarland & Co., 1999), 360. Massman notes that that although the *Bountiful* was three and one-half miles off ground zero for the first blast, Navy tests revealed there was only minor radiological contamination, and later the ship was declared "radiologically safe." Ibid.

10. "Northwest Baptist Association," http://www.nwbaptist.net/#MissionTrip (accessed June 14, 2010).

11. Schwantes, interview, Tape 1, Side A.

12. JP to Miriam Morris, 16 Feb. 1966. Almost forty-five years later, Schwantes told a slightly different story. She recalled that soon after the jeep incident, Jean stopped by her house rather than vice versa (Schwantes, interview, Tape 1, Side A). Given the wide disparity in the dates of the statements and Paton's proclivity to guard her privacy, it is more than likely that her version is more accurate.

13. JP to Marion Morris, 16 Feb. 1966,

14. Schwantes, interview, Tape 1, Side A.

15. "Schwantes is August volunteer of the month at NARMC Auxiliary."

16. JP to Marion Morris, 16 Feb. 1966.

17. See Valerie Jenness and Kimberly D. Richman, "Anti-Gay and Lesbian Violence and Its Discontents," in *Handbook of Lesbian and Gay Studies*, ed. Diane Richman and Steven Seidman (Thousand Oaks, CA: Sage, 2002) 403–14.

18. Lillian Faderman, *Surpassing the Love of Men: Romantic Friendship and Love between Women from the Renaissance to the Present* (New York: William Morris, 1981), 23–42; Faderman, *Odd Girls and Twilight Lovers: A History of Lesbian Life in Twentieth Century America* (New York: Columbia University Press, 1991), chap. 1.

19. Regional characteristics perhaps also played a role, though it is difficult to document for Paton and Schwantes. But clearly Arkansas citizens in the 1940s and 1950s were not as hostile to gays and lesbians as they would become in the last decades of the twentieth century. For a remarkable work on "queer" Arkansas, see Brock Thompson, *The Un-Natural State: Arkansas and the Queer South* (Fayetteville: University of Arkansas Press, 2010), esp. part 3.

20. Schwantes, interview, Tape 1, Side A. Schwantes related how in the 1990s she was repeatedly stopped in the street when she returned to Harrison, Arkansas, by camp alumni, who asked her fondly, "Don't you remember me, Miss June?" One camper, now grown up, refused to accept payment for repair work he had done for Schwantes because he could not possibly charge "Miss June."

21. Paton, interview, 27 June 1998, Tape 5, Side B (transcript, 116).

22. Esther D. Rothblum and Kathleen A. Brehony, eds., *Boston Marriages: Romantic but Asexual Relationships among Contemporary Lesbians* (Amherst: University of Massachusetts Press, 1993), 5.

23. Naomi B McCormick, *Sexual Salvation: Affirming Women's Sexual Rights and Pleasures* (Westport, CT: Praeger, 1994), 57.

24. Ibid.

25. Paton, interview; Schwantes, interview, Tape 1, Side A.

26. Rothblum and Brehony, *Boston Marriages*, 5.

27. Nancy Sahli, "Smashing: Women's Relationships before the Fall," *Chrysalis* 8 (Summer 1979): 25.

28. Except where noted, all the quotations and information in the paragraph are from JP to Lucille Hood, 1 Jan. 1965.

29. Denis Johnson, *In Search of Swift* (Dublin: Hodges Foggis, 1959).

30. JP, "Open House at Orphan Voyage," 18 Sept. 1964, BN. The open house was scheduled for October 3–11, 1964.

31. Ibid. Paton was proud of the phrase "persons of unsocial birth," writing in ink along the margin, "First time this was used here or anywhere?"

32. Robert Johnson, "Good Evening," *Memphis Press-Scimitar*, 2 Apr. 1965, sect. 2, p. 19.

33. JP, "Open House at Orphan Voyage," 18 Sept. 1964, BN.

34. All the information and quotations in this and the next paragraph are from JP, "Bible Belt," 15 Jan. 1965, ibid.

35. All the information and quotations in this and the next two paragraphs are from JP, "Bible Belt—Part II," April 1965, Issues and Events, ibid. "April" is crossed out and Paton has inked in "May."

36. JP, "Recently," April 1965, Issues and Events, ibid.

37. Schwantes, interview, Tape 1, Side A.

38. Ibid.

39. JP to Ester Reed, 24 May 1965, folder: Reed.

40. Robert Johnson, "Good Evening!" *Memphis Press-Scimitar*, 2 Apr. 1965, sect. 2, p. 19.

41. Christopher P. Manfredi, *The Supreme Court and Juvenile Justice* (Lawrence: University Press of Kansas, 1998), chaps. 3–4, quotation on 121.

42. John Morton, "Great While It Lasted: The National Observer, That Wonderful Weekly, Couldn't Survive Financially," *American Journalism Review*, December 2002, http://findarticles.com/p/articles/mi_hb3138/is_10_24/ai_n28962038/ (accessed July 31, 2010).

43. All the information and quotations in this paragraph and the next two are from JP, "Babies and Lawyers," Topical Release, May 1965, BN.

44. "Father to Face Jury in Kidnap of His Children," *Memphis Commercial Appeal* [February 1967], folder: TN, Memphis.

45. JP to Joseph Bearman, 9 Feb. 1967, ibid.

46. Kenneth A. Turner to Ruthena Kittson [JP], 14 Feb. 1967, ibid.

47. JP to Kenneth A. Turner, 27 Feb. 1967, ibid.

48. Kenneth A. Turner to JP, 3 Mar. 1967, ibid.

49. R. Kittson [JP], "Adoption Comes to Light," March 1966, ibid. Sants's article appeared in the *British Journal of Medical Psychology*.

50. Ruthena Kittson [JP], "Conference," *The LOG*, March 1966, BN].

51. Ruthena Kittson [JP], [comparison of Orphan Voyage and Adoptees Anonymous], *The LOG*, May 1966, ibid.

52. Ruthena Kittson [JP], "A Very Busy Time," March 1966, ibid.

53. Ruthena Hill Kittson [JP], "Final Note," *The LOG*, August 1966, ibid. Paton had stated "the illusion of adoption is lifting" as early as June 1966. See R. K. [Ruthena Kittson, JP] [n.t], *The LOG*, 15 June 1966, ibid.

54. R. K. [Ruthena Kittson, JP] [n.t], *The LOG*, 15 June 1966, ibid.

55. Leslie J. Reagan, *When Abortion Was a Crime: Women, Medicine, and Law in the United States, 1867–1973* (Berkeley and Los Angeles: University of California Press, 2003), 223–24. The Society for Humane Abortion was founded in 1961 by Patricia Maginnis as the Citizens Committee for Humane Abortion Laws. Harvard University, "Society for Human Abortion. Records: Finding Aid." http://oasis.lib.harvard.edu/oasis/deliver/~sch00916 (accessed August 10, 2010).

56. Quotation from JP to Rowena Gurner, 19 May 1966, folder: TN, Memphis. I have been unable to locate the earlier April letter, but it can be surmised from Gurner's response, dated 28 Apr. 1966, folder: Abortion.

57. "Psychiatrists Support Abortion Law Change," *Washington Post*, 15 Oct. 1967, folder: Hillsdale MI 12/92.

58. Ruthena Hill Kittson [JP], "C. R. I.—A Preliminary Statement," 15 June 1966, [*The LOG*], BN.

59. Ibid.

60. JP, "Application for Membership on the Committee for Reconsideration of Illegitimacy," 5 July 1966, folder: Kammen, Jeanette; Ruthena Hill Kittson [JP], "C. R. I.—A Preliminary Statement" [*The LOG*], 15 June 1966, ibid.

61. JP, "Final Note, *The LOG*, August 1966, ibid.

62. JP to Mildred Smith, 7 July 1958; JP to Mildred Smith, 5 Jan. 1959; JP to Mildred Smith, 9 Jan. 1962; JP to Leona Bayer, 5 Jan. 1962.

63. JP to Mildred Smith, 28 Aug. 1968. Founded in 1949, Vantage Press is still in business. See "Vantage Press," http://www.vantagepress.com/ (accessed August 11, 2010).

64. JP to Leona Bayer, 15 Aug. 1967. Paton admitted to Bayer that hers was "a better title from some points of view, not from others." Ibid. See also JP to Elizabeth Taeusch, 15 Aug. 1967.

65. Lee Campbell to Jean Paton, 12 Oct. 1976; JP to Lee Campbell, 26 Oct. 1976.

66. JP to Lee Campbell, 26 Oct. 1976.

67. JP to Debbie Fomento, 10 July 1978.

68. JP to Linnea Johnson, 2 May 1980; JP to Harold Miller, 28 July 1980. Yet despite repeated rejections, Paton persisted in attempting to see her book published by a commercial press. In 1982 she submitted a copy of *Orphan Voyage* to Moody Press, a well-established publisher of inexpensive Christian books. And, once again, she received both praise for having written "a touching and informative account" and another rejection. Phillip Johnson, the Press's trade book editor, explained that Moody sought only books that conveyed "a distinctly evangelical message," suggesting that *Orphan Voyage* would "best be handled by a secular press." Phillip R. Johnson to JP, 10 Dec. 1982, folder: Gordon, Katherine. Paton's reaction to the rejection was acidic. She wrote one correspondent, "It seems to me that nobody wants to touch the bastard, in print, anyway. No room in the inn." As to Moody Press's suggestion that Paton try a secular press, she dismissed the idea to the same correspondent as hopeless, at least when it came to publishers in the Northeast. See JP to Katherine Gordon, 17 Dec. 1982.

69. John Hope Franklin and Evelyn Higginbotham, *From Slavery to Freedom*, 9th ed. (McGraw-Hill, 2010).

70. See Laurie B. Green, *Battling the Plantation Mentality: Memphis and the Black Freedom Struggle* (Chapel Hill: University of North Carolina Press, 2007), chaps. 7 and 8.

71. David R. Goldfield, *Black, White, and Southern: Race Relations and Southern Culture, 1940 to the Present* (Baton Rouge: Louisiana State University Press, 1990), 215.

72. James T. Patterson, *Grand Expectations: The United States, 1945–1974* (New York: Oxford University Press, 1996), 565–68, quotation on 568.

73. JP to Regina Adams, 6 Sept. 1972, folder: WI.

74. JP to Joan Smith, 12 Mar. 197.

75. JP to Regina Adams, 6 Sept. 1972, folder: WI. See also JP, "Black and White," *The LOG*, September 1977, n.p., ON.

76. JP to Regina Adams, 6 Sept. 1972, folder: WI. Ibid.

77. JP to Preston Wilcox, 22 July 1977, folder: Afram. In the same letter, Paton expressed surprise that black social workers were willing to work within the modern institution of adoption because "it is a colonialist, if not racist, practice under the sealed records." Ibid.

78. JP, "Black and White," *The LOG*, September 1977, n.p., ON.

79. Except where noted, all the information and quotations in this and the next paragraph are from JP, "Lesson from Memphis," 2, *The LOG*, November 1968, ibid.

80. JP, "Black and White," *The LOG*, September 1977, n.p., ibid.

81. JP to Joan Smith, 12 Mar. 1971.

82. JP to Sandy Sperrazza, 3 Jan. 1995.

83. JP to Janine Baer, 26 Dec. 1995.

84. Ibid.

85. Ibid.

86. JP, "Enduring Colonials," FR, 15 May 1962, BN.

87. JP to Joan Williams, 10 Jan. 1967, folder: Angellar.

88. JP, "Lesson from Memphis," *The LOG*, November 1968 [no folder], 2A, ON.

89. Ibid.

90. White Rescue Service, "Atrocities Committed By SUN" [1966?], folder: TN, Memphis.

91. L. H. Brown, "Are All Men Created Equal?" [1966?], ibid.

92. There is a copy of Fox's letter "Who Sold Slaves?" [n.d], in ibid. The author's name can be found in Paton's letter to the editor, 23 Nov. 1966, ibid.

93. Paton wrote her letter on 23 Nov. 1966. See Ruthena Kittson [JP] to Editor, 23 Nov. 1966, ibid. It was published in the *Memphis Commercial Appeal*, signed as Ruthena Kittson: "Slaves to Routine," 4 Dec. 1966, ibid.

94. Memphis Public Library, *Four on Poverty*, Special Program Series [26 Oct.–16 Nov. 1965], ibid.

95. Ruthena Kittson [JP] to James B. Wray, 23 Nov. 1965, ibid.

96. "Unintended Problem of Poverty-Eaten Slums Is Costing All Memphians More by the Year," *Memphis Commercial Appeal*, 2 Dec. 1967. The article was motivated less by liberalism than by the high cost of welfare to taxpayers.

97. Except where noted, all the information and quotations in this and the next two paragraphs are from JP to The Editor, 4 Dec. 1967, folder: TN, Memphis.

98. JP, "A Modest Proposal," Orphan Voyage Release, November 1967, ibid. For the media linking of the Watts Riot and the Moynihan Report, which predicted devastating social consequences to the black family as a result of high rates of illegitimacy and welfare, see Ellen Herman, *The Romance of American Psychology: Political Culture in the Age of the Experts* (Berkeley and Los Angeles: University of California Press, 1996), 206.

99. All the information and quotations in this paragraph are from JP, "A Modest Proposal," Orphan Voyage Release, November 1967, folder: TN, Memphis. Paton sent a copy of "A Modest Proposal" to another newspaper, the *Memphis Press-Scimitar*, upon hearing that it was going to run a series on the subject of illegitimacy. See JP to Kay Pitman, 14 Feb. 1968, ibid.

100. JP, "Can August Have Been So Long Ago?" Orphan Voyage Release, 30 June 1967 [no folder].

101. Ibid.

102. Carol Rolloff, "Orphans Acquire Past," *St. Paul Pioneer Press*, 16 Sept. 1967 [no folder]; Molly Ivins, "Who Are Their Real Parents?" *Minneapolis Tribune*, 15 Sept. 1967 [no folder].

103. "Aide: Adopted Have Right to See Parents," *Minneapolis Star*, 27 Apr. 1967 [no folder]. JP made a copy of this newspaper article and distributed it.

104. Ivins, "Who Are Their Real Parents?"

105. Information about Mondloh, Hagen, and Paton are from ibid.

106. Rolloff, "Orphans Acquire Past." The woman who enjoyed shocking people could not help adding that adoptive parents also were disturbed by the same ghost: the "slut of a woman who might turn up and ruin everything." Ibid.

107. JP, "Plans," *The LOG*, May 1968 [no folder].

108. JP to Jeanette Kammen, 23 Oct. 1967; Jeanette Kammen to JP, 13 Nov. 1967.

109. Taylor Branch, *At Canaan's Edge: America in the King Years, 1965–1968* (New York: Simon & Schuster), chap. 39, esp. 733.

110. All the quotations in this paragraph are from JP, "Plans," *The LOG*, May 1968 [no folder].

111. JP, "Dear fellow crew members and shore patrol," *The LOG*, 20 Nov. 1968 [no folder].

112. See for example, JP to Florence Kneller, 23 Feb. 1970, folder: Kneller (Fitch), Florence; JP to Jayne Askin, 8 June 1993.

113. JP to Florence Kneller, 25 Feb. 1970, folder: Kneller (Fitch), Florence.

114. JP to Anni-Brita Lewis, 16 June 1969, folder: Lewis, 1968.

115. JP to Selma Chesler, 16 June 1969.

Chapter 9

1. Information about the conference comes from a flyer in *National Adoptalk* 7, no. 2 (March–April 1971): n.p.

2. Green had contacted Paton as early as October 1970 asking for her help in approaching the Louise Wise adoption agency for information about his adoption and birth parents. See JP to Sidney Green, 27 Oct. 1970.

3. JP, "Interviews and Phone Calls—Florence Eigenfeld," 24 Mar. 1971, 13 Apr. 1971, 12 May 1971, folder: Eigenfeld; FF to JP, 8 Apr. 197[1], ibid.

4. Grace Lichenstein, "Adoptive Parents Lose Lenore Suit," *New York Times*, 28 Apr. 1971.

5. Francis X. Clines, "Legislature Votes 30-Day Limit for Natural Mother in Adoption," ibid., 11 May 1971. Fisher favored an alternative bill, which would have provided birth mothers with counseling and given her the right to reclaim her baby within three to nine months, depending on the age of the infant. Sidney Fields, "The Pawns in Adoption," *New York Daily News*, 14 Apr. 1971; Governor Nelson Rockefeller vetoed the Pisani bill, which had passed the New York legislature.

6. JP to FF, 24 Mar. 1971, folder: Eigenfeld.

7. FF to JP, 8 Apr. 197[1], ibid.

8. JP, "Interviews and Phone Calls—Florence Eigenfeld," 24 Mar. 1971, 13 Apr. 1971, 12 May 1971, folder: Eigenfeld; FF to JP, 8 Apr. 197[1], ibid.

9. Virginia Woolf, *Mr. Bennett and Mrs. Brown* in *The Captain's Bed and Other Essays* (New York: Harcourt, Brace and Co., 1950), 96.

10. JP, "Interviews and Phone Calls—Florence Eigenfeld," 24 Mar. 1971, 13 Apr. 1971, 12 May 1971; FF to JP, 8 Apr. 197[1], ibid.

11. Theo Wilson, "Adoption Underground on the March," *New York Daily News*, 12 July 1971; "Won't Somebody Tell Me Who I Am?" ibid., 13 July 1971; "She Heard the Scream and Came to Their Aid," ibid., 14 July 1971; "The Muzzle Is Finally Coming Off," ibid., 15 July 1971.

12. JP to BJ, 19 Apr. 1971, folder: MD—Jacobs 71–72.

13. FF to JP, 24 Aug. 1971, folder: Eigenfeld.

14. JP to FF, 25 Aug. 1971, ibid.

15. It was at times like these Paton wished she had a more intricate organizational structure, such as a board of directors to help shoulder the load and make decisions. JP to BJ, 28 May 1971, ibid.

16. JP to Theo Wilson, 10 Aug. 1971, folder: Theo Wilson, *New York Daily News* Article.

17. "Flaming Manifesto" quote in JP to BJ, 28 Aug. 1971, folder: MD—Jacobs 71–72. See also JP to Genevieve Ringius, 24 Aug. 1971.

18. Jean Paton-Kittson, "The American Orphan and the Temptations of Adoption: A Manifesto" (Cedaredge, CO: Orphan Voyage, 1971), n.p.

19. Ibid.

20. JP, Interviews and Phone Calls, 23 Aug. 1971, "Florence Eigenfeld," ibid.

21. FF to JP, undated [received 24 Aug. 1971], ibid.

22. Lorraine Dusky, e-mail message to author, 27 Oct. 2008; JP to Sally Nance, 17 Mar. 1975; JP to Myrna McNitt, 24 Aug. 1984. Paton initially demurred, and requested instead that Fisher take to Italy only the copies of Paton's two books that she already owned and distribute some Orphan Voyage leaflets. JP to FF, 25 Aug. 1971, folder: Eigenfeld.

23. FF to JP, 26 Feb. 1972, folder: Eigenfeld (ellipses in the original). Fisher believed the conference a failure. In addition to reporting on Paton's "Manifesto," she stated that though David Kirk's presentation was eloquent, it was "almost totally disregarded and that the audience "could care less" about her own presentation. Ibid.

24. FF, interview by author, New York, NY, May 23, 2011, hereafter cited as FF, interview.

25. Carole Williams, "Retired Social Worker Believes in Open Records for Adopted," *Toledo (OH) Blade*, 31 Oct. 1971.

26. JP to MAC, 7 July 1977.

27. Paton had heard about the audience's negative response from correspondents other than Fisher. See JP to Sally Nance, 17 Mar. 1975; JP to Myrna McNitt, 24 Aug. 1984.

28. JP to William Deautreill, 8 Mar. 1973.

29. Selig Adler, "New Organization Helps Persons Given Up for Adoption Find Their Natural Parents," *National Enquirer*, 3 Dec. 1972; Jolyon Wilde, "Group that Helps Persons Adopted as Infants Find Natural Parents Gets 2,600 Letters in Response to Enquirer Story," ibid., 47 [December 1972], folder: Rowland, K.

30. JP to William Deautreill, 8 Mar. 1973; JP to Agnes Baker, 9 Jan. 1973.

31. JP to BJ, 2 Sept. 1973, folder: MD—Jacobs 71–72. See also JP to Joanne L. Frankwich, 8 Aug. 1975, folder: Frankwich.

32. JP to BJ, 30 Apr. 1971, folder: MD—Jacobs 71–72.

33. Ibid.

34. JP to Bill Deautrill, 1 June 1973.

35. (Fawcett Press, 1973).

36. Paton's inscribed copy in possession of the author.

37. JP to BJ, 14 June 1973, folder: MD—Jacobs 71–72.

38. Fisher, *Anna Fisher.*

39. JP to BJ, 11 June 1973, folder: MD—Jacobs 71–72.

40. JP to BJ, 14 June 1973, folder: ibid.

41. Jean Frazier, "Adoption Cancels a Basic Right," *Michigan State Journal*, 17 June 1973, F-2. See also Virginia Kern, "Search for Self," *Jacksonville (FL) Times-Union*, 3 June 1973.

42. Ibid. See also K.P.S., "Adoptees' Manifesto Sensible," *Birmingham (AL) News*, 10 June 1973.

43. Paton thought Fisher was "very good" on the *Today* show. JP to Judy Rosemarin, 19 June 1973.

44. For the cases, see, *State ex rel. John Thomas Lewis and Jerry D. Rothstein vs. Lutheran Social Services of Wisconsin and Upper Michigan*, Wisconsin Supreme Court, August term, 1970; Robert C. Burrell to JP, 7 Feb. 1973, folder: Rothstein, Jerry; JP, *The LOG*, Apr. 1973 (n.p..

45. *St Louis Post-Dispatch*, 1 Nov. 1972, reprinted in *The LOG*, Apr. 1973; JP, "Calendar of Events, 1973, second half," *The LOG*, Oct. 1973, n.p.

46. Annette Baran to JP, 12 Jan. 1973, folder: Baran/Sorosky. For the reply, see JP to Annette Baran, 16 Jan. 1973, folder: Sorosky, Dr. Arthur.

47. Reuben Pannor to JP, 16 July 1973, folder: Sorosky, Dr. Arthur.

48. JP to Annette Baran, 16 July 1973, folder: Baran et al Sorosky.

49. Reuben Pannor to JP, 16 July 1973, folder: Sorosky, Dr. Arthur.

50. JP to Annette Baran, 16 July 1973, folder: Baran et al Sorosky.

51. This paragraph and the quotations are from Lynn Lilliston, "Who Am I? Adoptees Seek Right to Know," *Los Angeles Times*, 22 July 1973, pt. 10, pp. 1, 14–17.

52. All the quotations in this paragraph and the next one are taken from *The LOG*, October 1973, n.p.

53. Except where noted, all the information and quotation in this paragraph and the next are from BJ to JP, 15 Oct. 1973, folder: MD—Jacobs 71–72.

54. BJ to JP, 26, June 1970, [no folder]; BJ to JP, 2 July 1970, ibid.

55. According to Lawrence, she founded the Adoption Study Project in late 1969 in response to a request from the psychiatric community to ask adult adoptees to evaluate adoption laws and practices. Margaret McDonald Lawrence, "Adoption: Realities and Illusions," unpublished paper (Southeastern Region, AAC, 12 Mar. 1988), 1, [no folder]. Lawrence would later be elected to serve on the American Adoption Congress's first board of directors along with Jean Paton and Anne Silber. See chapter 13.

56. This paragraph and the quotations are from JP to BJ, 26 Dec. 1973, MD—Jacobs 71–72.

57. *Time*, 24 June 1974, 81; Hal Aigner, *Faint Trails: A Guide to Adult Adoptee–Birth Parent Reunification Searches* (Greenbrae, CA: Paradigm Press, 1987), 67.

58. Hal Aigner, *Adoption in America: Coming of Age* (Greenbrae, CA: Paradigm Press, 1986), 2–3.

59. Mary Ann Jones, *The Sealed Adoption Record Controversy: Report of a Survey of Agency Policy, Practice, and Opinions* (New York: Child Welfare League of America, 1977), 29–30.

60. BJ to JP, 12 Dec. 1972, folder: MD—Jacobs 71–72.

61. JP to Jean Wandres, 30 July 1973.

62. JP to Agnes Baker, 19 June 1973; JP to Judy Rosemarin, 19 June 1973. Paton mollified her resentment by telling herself that "there is my mouthpiece talking about my File." JP to Judy Rosemarin, June 19, 1973.

63. JP to Betty Jean Lifton, 23 Jan. 1975.

64. Quoted in JP to Kathy and Maxine Demeris, 27 Aug. 1975, folder: MN-LINK-Demeris.

65. BJ to JP, 7 June 1974, folder: MD-Jacobs 1974.

66. JP to BJ, 13 June 1974, ibid.

67. All the quotations are from JP to Betty Mattson, 1 Oct.1975.

68. JP to Penny Partridge, 3 Sept. 1974, folder: PA Philadelphia.

69. JP to Betty Jean Lifton, 23 Jan. 1975.

70. JP to Penny Partridge, 25 Feb. 1975, folder: PA Philadelphia.

71. JP to Agnes Baker, 8 Jan. 1973.

72. JP to BJ, 31 Mar. 1975, MD—Jacobs 71–72.

73. JP to Harold Miller, 10 July 1976.

74. Carp, *Family Matters*,148–54.

75. Ibid. Along with articles in professional journals, they published in the mass-circulation magazine *Psychology Today*. See Annette Baran, Arthur D. Sorosky, and Reuben Pannor, "The Dilemma of Our Adoptees," *Psychology Today* 9 (Dec. 1975): 38.

76. Carp, *Family Matters*, 148–54.

77. All quotations from JP, "The Controversy over the Sealed Record in Adoption: A Psychological Investigation," Sorosky, Baran, and Pannor's "Conclusions" quoted in *The LOG*, Dec. 1973, n.p.

78. JP to Arthur Sorosky, 29 Oct. 1973.

79. "The Controversy over the Sealed Record in Adoption: A Psychological Investigation," Sorosky, Baran, and Pannor's "Conclusions" quoted in *The LOG*, Dec. 1973, n.p.

80. JP to Arthur Sorosky, 29 Oct. 1973.

81. JP to Arthur Sorosky, 15 Nov. 1973.

82. This paragraph and the quotations are from JP to Arthur Sorosky, 24 Apr. 1974. The article was "Who Are My Real Parents," by Jeanie Kasindorf.

83. This paragraph and the quotations are from Arthur Sorosky to JP, 29 May 1974, folder: Baran/Sorosky.

84. All quotations and information in the next two paragraphs are from JP to Arthur Sorosky, 5 June 1974, ibid.

85. This paragraph and the quotations are from Arthur D. Sorosky to JP, 8 July 1974.

86. This paragraph and the quotations are from JP to Arthur Sorosky, 15 July 1974.

87. "Samuel Andrew Stauffer," *Dictionary of American Biography*, 1956–1960, Suppl. 6 (New York: Charles Scribner's Sons, 1980), 604; *New York Times*, 25 Aug. 1960 (obituary).

88. JP to Nancy Otto, 26 Feb, 1981.

89. See Arthur D. Sorosky to JP, 10 Sept. 1974; Arthur D. Sorosky to JP, 17 Dec. 1974.

90. Sorosky, Baran, and Pannor, "Reunion of Adoptees and Birth Relatives," 195–206; quotation on 203.

91. Ibid., 196–97, 205.

92. Ibid., 203–4.

93. All the information and quotations in this paragraph are from JP to Arthur Sorosky, 27 Dec. 1974.

94. Except where noted, all the information and quotations in this paragraph and the next one are from Arthur D. Sorosky to JP, 8 Apr. 1975.

95. For Sorosky's ignorance of the history of his profession's involvement in adoption issues, see Carp, *Family Matters*, 128-37.

96. All the information and quotations in this paragraph are from JP to Arthur Sorosky, 13 Apr. 1975.

97. All the information and quotations in this paragraph are from ibid.

98. JP to Betty Jean Lifton, 23 Jan. 1975.

99. Betty Jean Lifton to JP, 27 Feb. 1975.

100. All quotations from JP to Betty Jean Lifton, 3 Mar. 1975.

101. Betty Jean Lifton to JP, 30 Apr. 1975, ibid.

102. JP to Betty Jean Lifton, 9 May 1975, ibid.

103. JP to Katie Berg, 8 Aug. 1975.

104. This paragraph and the quotations are from "SOROSKY et al Speak," *The LOG*, Summer 1975, n.p.

105. This paragraph and the quotations are from ibid.

106. JP to Budd Gaugher, 11 Feb. 1971; JP to Mary Bearden, 9 Jan. 1976.

107. See, for example, JP to Bonnie Orkow, 10 May 1990, folder: Intermediary—Co.

108. JP to Anna Przybylak, 14 Oct. 1959.

109. JP, [n.t.] "25th Anniversary Issue," *The LOG* [Spring 1978]: 3.

110. All of the information and quotations in this paragraph are from JP to BJ, 19 Apr. 1974, folder: MD—Jacobs 1974.

111. Cindy Skauge to JP, 29 Sept. 1988, folder: ND; JP to [Cindy Skauge], 24 Oct. 1988, ibid. See also JP to Steve Acquafresca, 21 May 1991, folder: Intermediary—Co.

112. JP to Howard Kennison, 17 July 1990, folder: Intermediary—Co.

113. JP to Stephen R. Silva, 5 May 1978, folder: Search.

114. JP to [Judge] John N. McMullen, 25 Feb. 1991, folder: Intermediary—Co.

115. JP to Patty O'Gorman, 12 July 1978, folder: MN–O'Gorman.

116. JP to Stephen R. Silva, 5 May 1978, folder: Search.

117. JP to Joan Vanstone, 22 Sept. 1975, folder: Vanstone, Joan (1).

118. Originally the organization was known as "Birthright." See "Warm's History," http://www.warmsearch.org/history.html (accessed February 18, 2009).

119. Ibid.

120. JP to William Gage, 12 Jan. 1991, folder: Intermediary—Co.

121. JP to BJ, 23 Aug. 1978, folder: MD—Jacobs 78–79.

122. JP to Agnes Ingram, 5 Nov. 1979; JP to Joan Vanstone, 12 July 1978, folder: Vanstone, Joan (2).

123. JP to Joan Vanstone, 12 July 1978, folder: Vanstone, Joan (2).

124. JP to Eddie Rizk, 14 Dec. 1978, folder: WA, Seattle—WARM. Paton conceded that she was fortunate in being offered another position. Ibid.

125. Ibid.

126. Ibid. Paton came away from the meeting with WARM believing she had acquitted herself well. See JP to BJ, 23 Aug. 1978, folder: MD—Jacobs 78.

127. JP to Posie Beamish, 15 Jan. 1976.

128. JP to Betty Jean Lifton, 26 Jan. 1976. These exceptions could be counted on one hand, and included such people as Marilyn Peers in Halifax, Nova Scotia, who worked with Joan Vanstone of Parent Finders in Canada. See JP to Julie Frankel, 28 May 1976.

129. JP to Posie Beamish, 15 Jan. 1976.

130. JP to Lee Campbell, 7 Oct. 1976.

131. Ibid.

132. JP to Michael Haag, 4 Nov. 1976.

133. Ibid.

134. JP to Tina Caudill, 30 June 1976, folder: MI–OTWAX, Frances.

135. JP to Joan Vanstone, 30 Mar. 1976, folder: Vanstone, Joan (1).

136. JP to Posie Beamish, 15 Jan. 1976.

137. JP to Michael Haag, 29 May 1976; all quotations in this paragraph are from ibid.

138. JP to Kathy Demers, 3 Apr. 1976, folder: MN—LINK—Demers.

139. JP to Ileen Weber, 7 Aug. 1976, folder: MO.

140. JP to Lee Campbell, 30 Aug. 1977.

141. JP to Kathy Demers, 3 Apr. 1976, folder: MN—LINK—Demers.

142. All the information and quotations in this paragraph are from JP "Successor to Coordinator??" *The LOG*, Sept. 1977 [n.p.] (emphasis in the original).

143. All the information and quotations in this paragraph are from JP, [n.t.] "25th Anniversary Issue," *The LOG* [Spring 1978]: 2 (emphasis in original).

144. Washington Adoptees Rights Movement, "The Annual Report," *Mediator* 4, no. 2 (May 1980): 5.

145. JP to BJ, 25 Jan. 1982, folder: MD—Jacobs 1980s.

146. JP to Jay Swearingen, 27 Feb. 1989.

Chapter 10

1. See, for example, *Los Angeles Times*, 23 Oct. 1973, sec. 4, pp. 1, 5; 6 Mar. 1974, sec. 4, pp. 1, 15. After West Coast newspapers and mass-circulation magazines repeatedly featured stories about the adoption search movement, the East Coast news media finally took notice of the phenomenon in the spring of 1975. Carp, *Family Matters*: 161–62.

2. See, for example, *Los Angeles Times*, 12 May 1974, sec. 4, p. 3; 11 Aug. 1974, sec. 1, p. 1; 10 Sept. 1974, sec. 2, p. 1; 15 Sept. 1974, sec. 2, p. 9.

3. "Searching for Myself," *Seventeen*, November 1971, 118–19, 148.

4. Jeanie Kasindorf, "Who Are My Real Parents?" *McCall's*, May 1974, 53; Lorraine Dusky, "The Adopted Child Has a Right to Know Everything," *Parents Magazine*, October 1975, 40–43, 64; Gordon S. Livingston, "Search for a Stranger," *Reader's Digest*,

June 1970, 85–89; Elizabeth Pope Frank, "We're a Family Again," *Good Housekeeping*, October 1977, 111, 224–27.

5. "I Found My Mother," *Cosmopolitan*, June 1974, 60, 62, 134, 137, and 142. The story was written "as told to" by Lorraine Dusky, a pioneer of the adoption reform movement. For background, see Lorraine Dusky, "Helen Gurley Brown Gave Early Ink to Adoption Reform," [Birth Mother,] First Mother Forum, http://www.firstmotherforum.com/2012/08/helen-gurley-brown-gave-early-ink-to.html (accessed August 14, 2012).

6. JP to Georgia Toney, 22 Sept. 1975, folder: Anderson, Georgia; JP to Helen G. Brown, 5 June 1974, folder: Cosmopolitan 1974.

7. JP to Barry Reiman, 5 June 1975, folder: Brown, Dale.

8. JP to Arthur Sorosky, 5 June 1974, folder: Baran/Sorosky.

9. JP to Nelson Rockefeller, 19 Sept. 1971, folder: Correspondence 1970s. JP signed the letter Jean Paton-Kittson. See Francis X. Clines, "Legislature Votes 30-Day Limit for Natural Mother in Adoption," *New York Times*, 11 May 1971; Lesley Oelsner, "Adoption: Toward a Limit on Natural Mother's Claim," *New York Times*, 25 Apr. 1971.

10. JP to Charlene Kemp, 5 Feb. 1974.

11. JP to MAC, 23 Aug. 1975.

12. JP to MAC, 22 July 1976. See also JP to MAC, 28 June 1976.

13. *Pursuit* 1, no. 1 (May 1976): 3, 4.

14. [Massachusetts] "ALMA Meeting," Adoptee Liberty Movement Association, *Bulletin* (May 1975): 2.

15. See, for example, "An ALMA International Reunion Registry Databank 'A match'—Between Simon Divorn, a natural mother, New Jersey & Jane Wolfe, adoptee, New York," *The ALMA Tenth Anniversary Christmas Album* (1971–1981): 5.

16. JP, *The LOG*, Summer 1975.

17. MAC, e-mail message to author, 30 June 1998; MAC to JP, 28 Apr. 1975; JP to MAC, 5 May 1975.

18. MAC, e-mail messages to author, 30 June 1998 and 25 Feb. 2009.

19. JP to Betty Jean Lifton, 10 Oct. 1975; *The LOG*, Summer 1975.

20. For a sample of Cohen's numerous letters, see, MAC to JP, 5 May 1975; MAC to JP [May–June 1975]; MAC to JP, 19 Aug. 1975; MAC to JP, 3 Sept. 1975, ibid.; MAC to JP, 1 Oct. 1975.

21. JP, "Announcement," 27 Nov. 1975, (emphasis in the original), [no folder].

22. MAC, "Letter to My Sisters," reprinted in "Special Release," 26 Feb. 1976, folder: C.U.B. It is difficult to pinpoint the exact date when Mary Anne Cohen wrote "Letter to My Sisters." The original has been lost, and Cohen does not remember when she wrote it. MAC, e-mail message to author, 25 Feb. 2009. It is clear from surviving correspondence in JP's papers that as late as 9 Feb. 1976 Paton had not "firmed up" her ideas about what form the Orphan Voyage network would take, though she hoped that "mothers can get together into some kind of loose organization, and call on me for whatever help" they

needed. See JP to Karen and Posie Rowland, 9 Feb. 1976, folder: Rowland, K. Similarly, on the same day, Paton confessed to Cohen that she was going forward and sending out leaflets to birth mothers, but did not feel that she should be "entirely in charge of this new undertaking." She simply wanted to assist in every way she could. JP to MAC, 9 Feb. 1976.

23. JP, "Untitled letter," 26 Feb. 1976, folder: C.U.B. In addition to Mary Anne Cohen's "Letter to My Sisters," the Special Release was accompanied by three of Paton's 1950s Life History Study Center writings on unmarried mothers, demonstrating her support for them and her recognition of their pain.

24. JP to Betty Jean Lifton, 4 Jan. 1976 (emphasis in the original). See also JP to MAC, 5 May 1975.

25. Judith S. Modell, *Kinship with Strangers: Adoption and Interpretations of Kinship in American Culture* (Berkeley and Los Angeles: University of California Press, 1994), 172. The first meeting took place in the church, not in Campbell's home (Lee Campbell, e-mail to author, 15 Mar. 2009). Cf. Modell, *Kinship with Strangers*, 172.

26. Lenore Hatch [Lee Campbell], Circular Letter, "Concerned United Birthparents, Inc.," July 1976, folder: Campbell, Lee. Campbell used a pseudonym to protect her husband and young children from harassment. Lee Campbell to JP, 13 Aug. 1976, ibid.

27. Concerned United Birthparents, "Bylaws," Article III, ibid.

28. JP to Lee Campbell, 7 Aug. 1976, ibid.

29. Lee Campbell to JP, 13 Aug. 1976, ibid.

30. Ibid. Two years later, Campbell affirmed that CUB members "remain the child's progenitor and thus find the term 'birthparent' both accurate and sensitive to our place in the child's existence." *C.U.B. Communicator* (June 1978), n.p.

31. Ibid. Of course, there was no way that CUB could force adoptive parents to inform their children of the contents of a Release of Protection form. In 1977, Bill H.5200, the legislation that CUB crafted for the Massachusetts legislature, was tabled in committee after opposition from adoptive parents, who feared that it was an opening wedge for birth parents to reclaim their children. "H.5200," *C.U.B. Communicator*, Dec. 1977, n.p., ibid.

32. JP to Lee Campbell, 7 Oct. 1976, ibid.

33. Lee Campbell to JP, 12 Oct. 1976, ibid.

34. JP to Lee Campbell, 30 Aug. 1977, ibid.

35. JP to Lee Campbell, 8 May 1978, ibid.

36. Ibid.

37. Lee Campbell to JP, 2 Sept. 1977, ibid.

38. JP to Lee Campbell, 29 Sept. 1977, ibid.

39. Ibid.

40. JP to Lee Campbell, 2 June 1978, ibid.

41. *C.U.B. Communicator*, December 1977, n.p., folder: Campbell, Lee.

42. Lee Campbell, telephonic discussion with author, Oct. 31, 2011; Lee Campbell, e-mail message to author, 1 Nov. 2011.

43. MAC to JP, 17 June 1977. Cohen added, "I don't have any 'hard-line' policy that nobody should try to contact the adoptive family—I believe in personal freedom—but it's not for me." Ibid.

44. "Submitted by Lee Campbell," *C.U.B. Communicator*, November 1977, 3.

45. "Voting Results," *C.U.B. Communicator*, October 1977, 1, folder: Campbell, Lee. Over time, CUB's met the issue head-on with a more positive position toward searching. It later hosted search workshops and, as one commentator has noted, published "a list of 'search buddies,' a directory of search groups, and information about CUB's reunion registry." See Modell, *Kinship with Strangers*, 172.

46. Lee Campbell to JP, 21 Aug. 1978.

47. See, for example, JP to MAC, 17 Nov. 1976; JP to Lee Campbell, 26 Oct. 1976; JP to Phyllis Gurdin, 8 Apr. 1977; JP to Steve Peck, 21 June 1979; JP to Alison S. Ward, 30 Nov. 1981.

48. JP to MAC, 24 Aug. 1978.

49. *OV*, 94–95.

50. JP to MAC, 6 Aug. 1976.

51. JP to Lee Campbell, 21 Nov. 1977.

52. JP to MAC, 17 Nov. 1976; JP to Luana Whitefox, 26 June 1981, folder: MA—Whitefox, Luana.

53. See, for example, JP to MAC, 29 Oct. 1975; JP to MAC, 23 Mar. 1977; JP to Julie Frankel, 15 Aug. 1977.

54. JP to Linda Lape, 2 Nov. 1992.

55. JP to Lee Campbell, 21 Nov. 1977; JP to Linda Crenwelge, 21 Jan. 1990. Paton elaborates on the dangers of adolescence in *OV*, 94–97.

56. JP to Lee Campbell, 21 Nov. 1977.

57. JP to Lee Campbell, 29 Sept. 1977.

58. JP to Lee Campbell, 29 Nov. 1977. See also JP, "The Magic Age of 'Eighteen,'" *The LOG*, Spring 1978, n.p.

59. JP to Susan Darke, 12 Apr. 1977, folder: Drake, Susan. The difference in Darke's name from the folder is a result of Paton's having transposed the letters of Darke's name to Drake on the folder label.

60. JP to Lee Campbell, 21 Nov. 1977.

61. JP to MAC, 17 Mar. 1981, folder.

62. Ibid.

63. JP to Linda Lape, 2 Nov. 1992.

64. JP to Lee Campbell, 8 May 1978.

65. JP to Lee Campbell, 24 Aug. 1978.

66. Ibid.

67. According to Campbell, three years later an adoptive mother and CUB member, in an attempt to help her, wrote Michael's adoptive parents to introduce Campbell. After receiving the letter, they contacted Campbell. A week after meeting Campbell, they invited her to their home to meet Michael. Soon thereafter, both families shared a

Thanksgiving dinner and were later invited to Michael's eighteenth birthday party. Lee H. Campbell, "The Birthparent's Right to Know," *Public Welfare* 37 (Summer 1979): 27; e-mail to author, 15 Mar. 2009; phone call with Campbell, 16 Oct. 2011.

68. Ellen Herman, *Kinship by Design: A History of Adoption in the Modern United States* (Chicago: University of Chicago Press, 2008), 279; Carp, *Family Matters*, 140.

69. JP to Clare Marcus, 26 Jan. 1987.

70. On ideas about Paton's leadership, I have been deeply influenced by, and have borrowed liberally from, Jim Collins, *Good to Great* (New York: HarperCollins, 2001), 45–46, 63.

71. JP to Molly Johnson, 17 June 1983.

72. JP, "Personal Page," *The LOG*, Spring 1971, n.p.

73. JP to Lee Campbell, 26 Oct. 1976.

74. JP to Peggy Dorn, 30 July 1976, folder: TX—Peggy Dorn. Paton born in Ypsilanti, a major stop on the Underground Railroad, would have been familiar with the concept from early childhood. James Mann, "Historically Speaking: A Look at Ypsilanti's Role in the Underground Railroad," http://www.annarbor.com/news/ypsilanti/a-look-at-ypsilantis-role-in-the-underground-railroad/ (accessed November 27, 2011).

75. JP, "A spare outline of the growth of two adoption groups," *The LOG*, Summer 1974, n.p. Paton visited the McCurdys before testifying in the Rothstein case. Ibid.

76. Ibid.

77. See chapter 9.

78. JP, "Groups," *The LOG*, February 1975, n.p.

79. Ibid.; JP to Sidney Moss, 24 Nov. 1975.

80. JP, "Groups," *The LOG*, February 1975, n.p.; quotation from ibid.

81. JP to Sidney Moss, 24 Nov. 1975.

82. Joan E. Vanstone to JP, 5 July 1976, folder: Vanstone, Joan (1).

83. Ibid.

84. JP to Molly Johnson, 17 June 1983.

85. JP to Molly Johnson, 11 Mar. 1985.

86. JP to Molly Johnson, 17 June 1983.

87. JP to Nancy Schmitt, 14 Nov. 1978, folder: D.C.—Schmitt, Nancy.

88. JP to Bill Deautreill, 1 June 1973, folder: Deautreill, William.

89. JP to Nancy Schmitt, 15 May 1974, folder: D.C.—Schmitt, Nancy.

90. JP to Bill Deautreill, 1 June 1973, folder: Deautreill, William.

91. JP to Ernestine Mejia, 26 Sept. 1975, folder: Mejia, E. Paton tried several other solutions to the problem of dual membership fees until giving up in 1982 and simply charging a national fee and leaving the groups alone. See JP to Susan Darke, 17 Feb. 1977, folder: Drake, Susan; JP to Harold Bauer, 27 Mar. 1981.

92. JP, *The LOG*, June 1972, n.p.

93. Ibid.

94. Ibid.

95. Ibid.

96. JP to Georgia Toney, 22 Sept. 1975, folder: Anderson, Georgia; JP to Bill Deautreill, 25 Sept. 1975, folder: Deautreill, William. In May 1975, Paton said she had twenty groups and listed by hand fifteen locations down the side of a letter, including New York, Boston, Philadelphia, Washington, D.C., Detroit, Columbus, Minneapolis/St. Paul, Dallas, Topeka, Denver, Los Angeles, San Francisco, Portland, Seattle, and Tacoma.

97. Francesca Polletta, *Freedom Is an Endless Meeting: Democracy in American Social Movements* (Chicago: University of Chicago Press, 2002), 6, 202.

98. JP to MAC, 22 Aug. 1975.

99. JP to Bill Deautreill, 12 Feb. 1976, folder: Deautreill, William. See also JP to Betty Jean Lifton, 26 Jan. 1976, for an even earlier expression of JP's intent to give up on the group idea.

100. JP to Karen Rowland, 15 Mar. 1976.

101. JP to Linda Overand, 1 Nov. 1976, folder: PA, Pittsburgh—Overand.

102. JP to Peggy Dorn, 30 Mar. 1977, folder: TX—Peggy Dorn.

103. JP to Bill Deautreill, 12 Feb. 1976, folder: Deautreill, William.

104. Ibid.; JP to MAC, 15 Dec. 1976.

105. JP to MAC, 15 Dec. 1976.

106. JP to Linda Overand, 1 Nov. 1976, folder: PA, Pittsburg—Overand. For the two-year figure, see JP to Nancy Sitterly, 9 Dec. 1980, folder: CT—Hart Daube Sitterly; JP to Harold Bauer, 27 Mar. 1981. For quarreling groups, see also JP to Betty Wheeler, 16 Nov. 1976; JP to Peggy Dorn, 30 Mar. 1977, folder: TX—Peggy Dorn; JP to Nancy Schmitt, 6 Feb. 1978, folder: DC—Schmitt, Nancy.

107. Nancy Sitterly to JP, 30 Nov. 1980, folder: CT—Hart Daube Sitterly.

108. All the quotations in this paragraph are from JP to Nancy Sitterly, 9 Dec. 1980, ibid.

109. All the quotations in this paragraph are from JP, "The Essential Nature of the Orphan Voyage program," *The LOG*, February 1976, n.p.

110. JP to MAC, 22 July 1976.

111. JP to Phyllis McFarland, 22 Sept. 1976.

112. JP to Agnes Ingram, 6 Sept. 1976.

113. JP to Mary Doyle, 30 June 1976; Simone Weil, *Waiting for God* (New York: Harper & Row, 1951), 120.

114. JP to MAC, 22 July 1976; JP to Chris Framton, 6 Sept. 1976.

115. JP to MAC, 15 Dec. 1976.

116. For JP's emphasis on the importance of the personal touch, see JP to Sidney Moss, 24 Nov. 1975; JP to Linda Overand, 1 Nov. 1976, folder: PA, Pittsburgh—Overand.

117. JP to Phyllis McFarland, 22 Sept. 1976.

118. JP, "The Growth of the Movement," *The LOG*, October 1978, n.p. The statement was written on 14 Sept. 1976.

119. JP to Phyllis McFarland, 22 Sept. 1976; JP to MAC, 22 July 1976.

Chapter 11

1. JP to Ann Patterson, 30 Aug. 1976; JP to Carl Callaway, 10 Sept. 1976.

2. JP to Havoc Franklin, 7 Oct. 1976, folder: Canada, Toronto—Fall '76 Great Debate.

3. JP to Betty Wheeler, 16 Nov. 1976. For a full account of "The Great Debate," see E. Wayne Carp, "A Revolutionary in the Making: Jean Paton and the Early Decades of the Sealed Adoption Records, 1949–1977," *Adoption & Culture* 3 (2012): 50–52.

4. Ibid.

5. Americans for Open Records, "'Mother' of the Open Records and Anti-adoption Movement for the Past 50 Years has Died at 93," http://www.amfor.net/OpenRecord/?8 (accessed March 16, 2009).

6. Jackie Germann, "'Foundlings Should Get Background,'" *St. Paul (MN) Pioneer Press*, 29 Sept. 1963, folder: MN—Minneapolis Star/St. Paul Pioneer.

7. See JP to Fred Stephens, 2 Dec. 1957, folder: Miscs 1950s; JP to Joe Pyne, 15 Feb. 1968, folder: 1960s Correspondence; JP to the Editor, *Denver Post*, 4 Dec. 1969, ibid.; JP to Thomas J. Dodd, 15 July 1964, folder: Washington, D.C.

8. JP to the Editor, *Denver Post*, 4 Dec. 1969, folder: 1960s Correspondence.

9. Carp, *Family Matters*, 42–43.

10. Ibid., 58–70. E. Wayne Carp, "Adoption and Disclosure of Family Information: A Historical Perspective," *Child Welfare* 74 (January–February 1995): 217–41. Carp, *Family Matters*, 55.

11. *ABS*, 7; OV, 53.

12. Paton quoted in "Ye Town Crier," *Menominee (MI) Herald-Leader*, 28 Apr. 1955, folder: MI, Menominee—Herald-Leader Apr '55.

13. JP to Marion Carson, 15 Jan. 1957; all quotations, ibid.

14. JP to Madalyn Murray O'Hair, 22 July 1957 [no folder].

15. See chap. 2.

16. The phrase "Mutual Registration" and "Matching File" can be found in the Life History Study Center's pamphlet, "Reunion" (1958), folder: Life History Center.

17. Paton had taken a correspondence course on computers with RCA. See JP to George Jarvis, 24 Jan. 1968, folder: Thies, Merry; JP to Judy Rosemarin, 19 June 1973.

18. JP to Jeanette Kammen, 26 Sept. 1966.

19. JP to George Jarvis, 24 Jan. 1968.

20. Carp, *Family Matters*, 142.

21. Fisher quoted in Caroline Drewes, "Liberation Movement for the Adopted," *San Francisco Examiner and Chronicle*, 26 Aug. 1973.

22. Donna Cullom, "The President's Message," *The Searchlight*, Issue 1 (July 1974), [n.p.], folder: Cullom, Donna.

23. All the information and quotations in this and the next two paragraphs are from JP [n.t.], *The LOG*, October 1973.

24. See, JP to Thomas Patterson, 21 May 1970, folder: 1970s Correspondence; JP to

Editor, *Minneapolis Tribune*, 26 Feb. 1971, ibid. For a discussion of these two letters, see Carp, "Revolutionary," 40–41. A third letter defended opening adoption records from the charge that such a policy would encourage a black market. JP felt that, on the contrary, opening the records would encourage adoption. See JP to Stan Rothstein, 18 Mar. 1974, folder: 1970s Correspondence.

25. Quote from Dorothy Gardner, "Adopted Children Search for Identity," *St. Louis Post-Dispatch*, 1 Nov. 1972, reprinted in *The LOG*, April 1973 [n.p]. Paton also excoriated adoption agencies for opposing unsealing the records and defending social work confidentiality.

26. JP to Joanne Small, 4 June 1975, folder: DC.

27. *The ALMA Searchlight*, Summer 1976: 2.

28. Ibid.

29. Debra D. Poulin, "The Open Adoption Records Movement: Constitutional Cases and Legislative Compromise," *Journal of Family Law* 26 (1987–1988): 400.

30. *ALMA Soc'y, Inc. v. Mellon*, 601 F.2d 1225 (2d Cir.) *cert denied*, 100 S. Ct. 531 (1979), 1232.

31. JP to MAC, 6 Aug. 1976.

32. JP to BJ, 18 Apr. 1979, folder: MD—Jacobs 78–79.

33. Ibid.

34. Ibid.

35. JP to Linda Burgess, 6 June 1977.

36. Theo Wilson, "Adoption Underground on the March," *New York Daily News*, 12 July 1971; "Won't Somebody Tell Me Who I Am?," ibid., 13 July 1971; "She Heard the Scream and Came to their Aid," ibid., 14 July 1971; "The Muzzle Is Finally Coming Off," ibid., 15 July 1971.

37. JP, "Reunion File," *The LOG*, Summer 1971 [n.p.].

38. JP, "History Page," ibid., November 1974, [n.p.].

39. JP, "Announcements," ibid., Summer 1975 [n.p.].

40. JP to Bill Lumley, 7 Feb. 1977.

41. JP, "Application for Membership in Orphan Voyage," 18 Mar. 1974, folder: Carlisle.

42. FF, *The ALMA Searchlight*, June 1975: 1, 2; quotation on 1.

43. See, for example, FF, "*THE SEARCH IS OVER!!!*," ibid., Summer 1976: 5–9.

44. *The ALMA Searchlight*, June 1975: 2.

45. JP to Judy Rosemarin, 19 June 1973. See also JP to Nancy Otto, 14 Sept. 1981.

46. JP, "A Challenge to Divisiveness in the Movement," *The LOG*, June 1977 [n.p.].

47. JP, "History Page," ibid., November 1974 [n.p.].

48. JP to Nancy Otto, 14 Sept. 1981.

49. JP, "A Challenge to Divisiveness in the Movement," *The LOG*, June 1977 [n.p.].

50. JP to Lee Campbell, 29 Sept. 1977; JP to Lee Campbell, 30 Aug. 1977.

51. In 1976, Vilardi started an independent registry, Soundex within ALMA, in protest of Fisher's commercialism. See JP to Anna Halbach, 27 Aug. 1979. It would be free, in contrast to the $20 fee for ALMA's registry. International Soundex Reunion Registry,

"ISSR Fourth Annual Report," November 1982, VWBP, box 63, folder 7. Fisher would brook no competition, however, and in 1978 she excommunicated Vilardi from ALMA. "Annie" Florence Fisher, "Memorandum to ALMA Coordinators, SOUNDEX," 6 Mar. 1978 [n.p.], folder: Reunion File (History). For its history, see Tony Vilardi, "The Origins of ISSR," History of ISSR, (http://www.isrr.net/history.shtml) (accessed March 26, 2009).

52. JP to Theresa Montgomery, 16 June 1977.

53. JP to Nancy Otto, 14 Sept. 1981.

54. JP to Nancy Otto, 8 Dec. 1981.

55. International Soundex Reunion Registry, "ISSR Fourth Annual Report," Nov. 1982, VWB, box 63, folder 7.

56. Abigail Van Buren, "Group Links Birth Mothers, Adoptees," 2 Nov. 2, 1983, http://www.isrr.net/History/After1stDearAbby.pdf (accessed March 27, 2009).

57. Today it is known as the National Committee on Early Childhood, Adoption, and Dependent Care. See Academy of Pediatrics, "National Committee on Early Childhood, Adoption, and Dependent Care," http://www.aap.org/visit/cmte15.htm (accessed February 4, 2011).

58. Joseph H. Davis, "Who Am I? The Adoptee's Search for Identity," *California Pediatrician*, September 1974, 4, reprinted in *The LOG*, November 1974 [n.p.]. For the subsequent collaboration between Davis and Paton, see Carp, "Revolutionary in the Making," 45–48.

59. Donna Cullom, "The Time Has Come," *The LOG*, February 1975 [n.p.].

60. JP, "Adoptees' Case Goes to Trial," ibid.

61. *Yesterday's Children v. Kennedy*, 569 F.2d 431 (7th Cir. 1977), *cert denied* 1978.

62. Muriel Marshall, "Do Adopted Adults Have Rights to Records?" *Grand Rapids (CO) Daily Sentinel*, 21 Feb. 1975, reprinted in *The LOG*, Spring 1975 [n.p.]. See also JP, "About the Illinois Court Case," *The LOG*, Fall 1975: [n.p.]; JP [n.t.], *The LOG*, February 1976 [n.p.]

63. "Access to Personnel Records," *The LOG*, Summer 1975 [n.p.].

64. Joan [Vanstone], "A Report from Vancouver, Canada," *The LOG*, Fall 1975 [n.p.].

65. JP, "Reading Matter," *The LOG*, October 1975 [n.p.].

66. JP [n.t.], *The LOG*, February 1976 [n.p.]

67. JP, "THE LAW AND US," *The LOG*, February 1977 [n.p.].

68. JP, "Ten Point Program" March 1977 [no folder].

69. JP, "A CHALLENGE TO SUPERFICIALITY IN THE MOVEMENT," *The LOG*, June 1977 [n.p.].

70. "Sealed Files in Adoption: Are They Christian?" *The LOG*, September 1977 [n.p.].

71. JP to Glenda Winkler, 9 Dec. 1976.

72. JP to Betty Wheeler, 16 Apr. 1976.

73. JP to Marion Morris, 19 Jan. 1978.

74. JP to Michael Haag, 28 Nov. 1978.

75. Ibid.

76. JP to Betty Wheeler, 16 Apr. 1976.

77. Ibid.

78. JP to Joan Vanstone, 12 July 1978, folder: Vanstone, Joan.

79. Ibid.

Chapter 12

1. JP to author [2000], personal communication.

2. The evidence for this can be found in JP to Richard Pancoast, 18 Mar. 1954, folder: Publicity for ABS. During her temporary absence from home her mail had been forwarded to her at 3212 Topping Road, Madison, Wisconsin. Paton also mentions her visit to the Midwest in JP to Ward Greene, 21 Feb. 1954, ibid.

3. Jean M. Paton and Ruth Oliver Hill to Elton J. Morrison, 2 Feb. 1954 [no folder; copy sent to author].

4. Elton J. Morrison to Jean M. Paton and Ruth Oliver Hill, 17 Feb. 1954, folder: Publicity for ABS.

5. JP to Elton J. Morrison, 1 Aug. 1954, ibid. For another early example around this time of Paton's role of ombudsmen, see her letter to the editor of *McCall's* about Swiss twins, one of whom a nurse had exchanged by accident at birth and placed with another family. JP to Otis Wiese, 5 Aug. 1954, folder: CM 1954–1956. The article in question is Madeleine Joye, "My Son Was Not My Son," *McCalls*, August 1954, 30–31, 120, 122, 124, 127–28. Joye later published a book on the matter, *He Was Not My Son* (New York: Reinhart, 1954)

6. JP, "The Green Market in Adoption," 4 Nov. 1955, ibid.

7. See chapter 11 for details.

8. The bill was revised and reintroduced on 9 Feb. 1966 as H.R. 12727, the Adoption Opportunity Act. See H.R. 12727, 89th Congress, 2nd Session, folder: Washington, D.C.

9. Unless otherwise noted, all the information and quotations in this and the next paragraph are from JP, "Mr. Zablocki (and who else) Proposes," Orphan Voyage Topical Release, [17 Jan. 1966], folder: ibid.

10. Clement J. Zablocki to Ruthena Hill Kittson [JP], 3 Feb. 1966, ibid. JP corrected Zablocki's reference to her "letter" to "memo only."

11. Ruthena Hill Kittson [JP] to Clement Zablocki, 17 Feb. 1966, ibid.

12. JP, "Mr. Zablocki (and who else) Proposes" [1966], ibid.

13. JP to Alan Cranston, 14 May 1975, folder: ibid. See also JP to Cranston, 14 June 1974, folder: ibid.; JP to Alan Cranston, 1 July 1974, ibid. Cranston replied to JP, saying that he was corresponding with several groups that dealt with the problems of adopted adults. See Alan Cranston to JP, 5 June 1975, ibid.

14. All quotations are from Joanne Small to Jean Paton, 16 July 1975, folder: DC.

15. Roberta Ross [Joanne Small] to Walter F. Mondale, 16 July 1975, ibid. For JP's

reply, see JP to Roberta Ross [Joanne Small], 25 July 1975, ibid. See also JP to Roberta Ross [Joanne Small], 17 Nov. 1975, folder: ibid. Paton also wrote numerous letters to Mondale. For the letters and Mondale's replies during 1975, see the Walter Mondale folder.

16. All quotations from JP to Nancy Schmitt, 20 Dec. 1977, folder: DC.

17. Ibid., 230, 231; Debora Spar, *The Baby Business: How Money, Science, and Politics Drive the Commerce of Conception* (Boston: Harvard Business School Press, 2006), 27. See also Margaret Marsh and Wanda Ronner, *The Empty Cradle: Infertility in America from Colonial Times to the Present* (Baltimore: Johns Hopkins University Press, 1996), 229, 230.

18. Richard Lacayo, "Whose Child Is This?" *Time*, 19 Jan. 1987, 57.

19. Martha A. Field, *Surrogate Motherhood: The Legal and Human Issues*, expanded ed. (Cambridge, MA: Harvard University Press, 1990), 5. Abraham, for example, impregnated the handmaiden Hagar, who gave birth to Ishmael (Gen. 16:1–4, 15; 30: 1–10).

20. JP, "Statement . . . before the Ethics Panel, of H.E.W.," 8 Dec. 1978, folder: D.C.—Ethics Panel. It was typical of Paton to misidentify the Board.

21. U. S. Department of Health, Education, and Welfare, Ethics Advisory Board, *HEW Support of Research Involving Human In Vitro Fertilization and Embryo Transfer: Report and Conclusions* (Washington, D.C.: Government Printing Office, 1979), i, 81, 106. The positive recommendation was qualified with many provisos. See chap. 6, pp. 100–114. Whether the Ethics Board read Paton's statement is open to question. The announcement of the public hearing, printed in the *Federal Register*, a copy of which was in JP's possession, announced that the deadline for submission of statements was December 1. JP's statement was dated a week later, December 8, the day of the hearing. *Federal Register*, vol. 43, no. 210, 30 Oct. 1978. Her statement is not included in the Ethics Board's massive Appendix, which contains its many reports, but no public statements. See U.S. Department of Health, Education, and Welfare, Ethics Advisory Board, *Appendix: HEW Support of Research Involving Human In Vitro Fertilization and Embryo Transfer* (Washington, D.C.: Government Printing Office, 1979).

22. "Model State Adoption Act and Model State Adoption Procedures," *Federal Register* (Washington, D.C.: Government Printing Office, 1980), vol. 45, no. 33, pp. 10622–10691. The National Conference of Commissioners on Uniform State Laws usually proposes model statutes, which do not have the force of law. The commissioners are a group of law school deans, professors, judges, and practicing lawyers appointed by state governors. When completed, the model state law is then presented to the states as a prototype, which each state is then free to adopt in whole, in part, or not at all as their particular needs and interests dictate. *Black's Law Dictionary*, 5th ed., s.v. "Model Act."

23. Title II of the law stated that its purpose was "to facilitate the elimination of barriers to adoption and to provide permanent and loving home environments for children who would benefit by adoption, particularly children with special needs." See "Child Abuse Prevention and Treatment Reform Act," *Federal Register* (Washington, D.C.: Government Printing Office, 1978), vol. 43, p. 92.

24. Department of Health, Education, and Welfare, "Model State Adoption Act and Model State Adoption Procedures; Request for Comment," *Federal Register*, vol. 45, no. 33, 15 Feb. 1980, 10648.

25. JP to Elaine Schwartz, 24 June 1978, folder: D.C.—Hew—CB; JP to Susan Weber, 29 June 1978, folder: D.C.—Hew—CB.

26. Paton mentions this information in a letter to Califano. See JP to Joseph Califano, 29 June 1978, folder: ibid. Susan Weber's title from http://www.danya.com/dlc/welfareChild/beforeStart/authors.asp (accessed April 19, 2009).

27. JP to Joseph Califano, 29 June 1978, folder: D.C.—Hew—CB.

28. All quotations from JP, "Background Information on Jean Paton," n.d., enclosure to Joseph Califano, 29 June 1978, ibid.

29. JP to Joseph Califano, 29 June 1978, folder: ibid.

30. Joseph Califano, "Charter: Model Adoption Legislation and Procedures Advisory Panel," 11 Aug. 1978, Memo, ibid.; Diane D. Broadhurst and Elaine J. Schwartz, "The Right to Know," *Public Welfare* 37 (Summer 1979): 6. (Laurie Flynn of the North American Council on Adoptable Children served as the representative for adoptive parents. Ibid.)

31. *Federal Register*, vol. 45, no. 33, 15 Feb. 1980; both quotations on 10691.

32. Carp, *Family Matters*, 186.

33. Mary Jo Rillera, *Adoption Encounter: Hurt, Transition, Healing* (Westminster, CA: Triadoption Publications, 1987), 28. Although the vast majority of commentators objected to the Model Act in general, its open records provisions were favored by 57 percent. Ibid.

34. Edwin Watson to Member Agencies and League Board, memorandum, 10 Apr. 1980, Child Welfare League of America Records, Box J, 10–11; Social Welfare History Archives, University of Minnesota; Edwin F. Watson to League Board and Member Agencies, memorandum, 2 Sept. 1980, ibid., 7. In January 1981, the U.S. House of Representatives sent a resolution to the Secretary of HEW expressing its disapproval of certain provisions of the proposed Model State adoption legislation, including the provision requiring automatic opening at the request of adult adoptees of confidential birth records, court records, and adoption agency records. "Bill Summary & Status 97th Congress (1981–1982) H. RES. 36 CRS Summary," http://thomas.loc.gov/cgi-bin/bdquery/z?d097:HE00036:@@@D&summ2=m& (accessed July 9, 2011). The Model State Adoption legislation was withdrawn.

35. JP to Janine Baer, 6 May 1993. Paton's annotated copy of the "Model State Adoption Act and Model State Adoption Procedures," as published in the *Federal Register*, can be found in folder: D.C.—Hew—CB.

36. JP to Diane D. Broadhurst, 22 May 1980, ibid.

37. JP, "A Commentary on the Model State Adoption Act—A Proposal" (Cedaredge, CO: Orphan Voyage, 1980), 2.

38. Ibid., 2–3.

39. Ibid., 1.

40. Ibid., 4.

41. Ibid., 4–5.

42. Ibid., 7.

43. Ibid.

44. Ibid., 5, 6; quotation on 6.

45. Ibid., 9.

46. Ibid., 10.

47. Ibid.

48. Carl Levin, "On the Issues: Adoption and Foster Care," http://levin.senate.gov/issues/index.cfm?MainIssue=AdoptionandFosterCare (accessed March 30, 2009). In addition, in 1981 Levin authored the first ever adoption expense tax-deduction law. Ibid.

49. The bill was offered by Senator Levin as a floor amendment to H.R. 2977, the proposed Domestic Violence Prevention and Services Act. The Senate rejected it by a vote of 58–27 on 25 Aug. 1980. See Alan Cranston to Eileen Ling, 24 Aug. 1981, folder: DC—Levin, Bill.

50. JP to Harold Miller, 21 Feb. 1980.

51. Ibid.

52. JP to Jack Atkinson, 23 Feb. 1981.

53. All quotations in this paragraph are from JP to Jackie Parker, 26 Mar. 1980, folder: Levin—P.C. Council Coalition for Chris Youth.

54. It is curious that Levin himself never mentioned the words "computer" or "computerized" in connection with his proposal during the hearing or in the statement placed in the record.

55. U.S. Senate, Committee on Labor and Human Resources, Subcommittee on Aging, Family, and Human Services, *Adoption in America, 1981: Hearing before the Subcommittee on Aging, Family, and Human Services of the Committee on Labor and Human Resources, United States Senate, Ninety-seventh Congress, First Session, on a Bill to Examine the Progress That Has Been Made in the Adoption Procedures in America, July 23, 1981* (Washington, D.C.: Government Printing Office, 1981), 83–85; "minimal" on p. 85 (hereafter cited as *Adoption in America, 1981*).

56. Ibid., 86.

57. Ibid., 85–86.

58. JP to Jeremiah Denton, 26 June 1981, folder: DC—Levin, Bill.

59. Quotations here and in the next paragraph from JP, "A Basic Guide to the After-Adoption Reunion Experience," (Cedaredge, CO: Orphan Voyage, 1975), n.p.

60. *Adoption in America, 1981*, 120.

61. Ibid.

62. Ibid., 123.

63. JP to Joseph Harrington, 22 Jan. 1982, folder: KS—Harrington, Joseph.

64. For the opposition to the bill see, *Adoption in America, 1981*, 93–94, 109–10.

65. For the senators' objections, see ibid., 108–9; Joseph D. Harrington, "Legislative Update on Sealed Adoption Records," *Public Welfare* 39 (Spring 1981): 31. Levin re-

introduced a similar bill in January 1988, where it again met with defeat. See Jeffrey Rosenberg, "1988 Survey of State Laws on Access to Adoption Records," *Family Law Reporter* 14 (16 Aug. 1988): 3019.

66. Carl Levin to JP, 10 Aug. 1982.

67. JP to Gloria Veillon, 15 Aug. 1982, folder: Hipp.

68. Harrington, "Legislative Update," 55–56; Jeannine J. Fay, "The Mutual Consent Voluntary Adoption Registry," *Rutgers Law Journal* 18 (Spring 1987): 674–76; Joseph D. Harrington, "Adoption and the State Legislatures 1984–1985," *Public Welfare* 44 (Spring 1986): 25; Rosenberg, "1988 Survey of State Laws," 3019.

69. JP to Margaret Hutchinson-Betts, n.d. [July–August 1986?], folder: VT—Parents for Private Adoption.

70. JP to Clare Marcus, 28 Jan. 1987.

71. JP to Margaret Hutchinson-Betts, n.d. [July–August 1986?], folder: VT—Parents for Private Adoption.

72. JP to Marge Brower, 20 Aug. 1986, folder: IA/NE—Johnson S.

73. JP to Jackie Parker, 3 Feb. 1988, folder: Levin: P.C. Council Coalition for Chris Youth.

74. JP to Carl Levin, 30 Jun. 1988, ibid. Paton also took the opportunity to deplore the restrictions on sibling searches, and repeated her strictures on counseling, which she declared was "only the devil's foot in the door. The devil has many feet, but this is one of those most firmly-planted ones." Ibid.

Chapter 13

1. JP, *The LOG*, July 1968.

2. For Deutreill's background, see William Deautriell to JP, 17 Sept. 1975, folder: Deautriell, B.; William Deautriell to JP, 28 June 1976, ibid.

3. William Deautriell to JP, 31 Mar. 1973, ibid; William Deautriell to JP, 17 Sept. 1975, ibid.

4. William P. Deautriell to Karen M. Rowland, 16 Mar. 1976.

5. Karen M. Rowland to William Deautriell, 22 Mar. 1976. See also interlineations in William P. Deautriell to Karen M. Rowland, 16 Mar. 1976.

6. JP to Karen Rowland, 15 Mar. 1976.

7. JP quote in JP to Victor Thayer, 2 July 1976; JP to Joan Van Stone, 2 June 1776, folder: Van Stone, Joan (1).

8. JP to Karen Rowland, 15 Mar. 1976. See also JP to Victor Thayer, 2 July 1976.

9. JP to Joan Van Stone, 2 June 1776, folder: Van Stone, Joan (1).

10. JP to Edith Ward, 30 Apr. 1976, folder.

11. All the information and quotations in this and the next paragraph are from JP, "A Plan for a National Conference of Some Members of the Adoption Triangle," *The LOG*, Spring 1978. For information on Anne Silber, see "An Empty Chair," http://www.bastards.org/bnpress/imjn-19990924.html (accessed July 23, 2011).

12. All the information and quotations in this and the next paragraph are from JP, "Meditation of a Coordinator in the Spring of 1978," *The LOG*, 25th Anniversary Issue, Spring 1978, 5.

13. JP, "Retirement," ibid., 11.

14. JP to Edith Ward, 30 Apr. 1976.

15. I have been unable to locate this letter. However, it can be easily reconstructed from the replies of some of the recipients. See for example, Sue Minnis to Anne Silber, 14 Apr. 1978, Box 1, in JPP, UF; Rae Johnson to Anne Silber [April 1978], ibid.

16. Ann Keck to Anne Silber, 28 Apr. 1978, ibid. For similar sentiments, see Susan C. Darke to Anne Silber, 28 May 1978, ibid.; Sue Minnis to Anne Silber, 14 Apr. 1978, ibid.

17. See, for example, Karen L. Tinkham to Anne Silber, 4 June 1978, ibid.

18. See, for example, Marianne Lippold to Anne Silber, 31 May 1978, ibid.; Ty Stroudsburg to Anne Silber, 17 Apr. 1978, ibid.

19. All the information and quotations in this paragraph are from Anne E. Silber to Dear———[23 May 1978], ibid. Silber described this phrase as "a verbal bouquet." Ibid.

20. *"WE HAVE A START!!!" The Adoption Format and Digest* (October 1978): 1; "Report of the American Adoption Congress First International Congress, May 4–7, 1979" [n.d.], 2, ibid.

21. All of the information and quotations in the next two paragraphs are from JP to Nancy Schmitt, 14 Nov. 1978, folder: DC—Schmitt, Nancy.

22. Nancy Schmitt to JP, 17 Nov. 1978, ibid.

23. JP to Nancy Schmitt, 14 Nov. 1978, ibid.

24. All the information and quotations in this paragraph are from Nancy Schmitt to JP, 17 Nov. 1978, ibid.

25. Nancy Schmitt to JP, 17 Nov. 1978, folder: DC—Schmitt, Nancy.

26. JP to Nancy Schmitt, 21 Nov. 1978, ibid.

27. "Report of The American Adoption Congress First International Congress, May 4–7, 1979" [n.d.], 2, JPP, UF.

28. Untitled enclosure, 16 Nov. 1979, Nancy Schmitt to JP, 17 Nov. 1978, folder: ibid.

29. Margaret Lawrence to JP [June 1979], folder: MD—Jacobs 1979. The letter is on letterhead stationery and unsigned. It is stamped "as received June 13, 1979."

30. Nancy J. Schmitt and Virginia Rader, "American Adoption Congress," 22 Feb. 1979, folder: AAC—Misc.

31. Anne E. Silber to JP [date stamped 7 Feb. 1979], JPP, UF.

32. All of the information and quotations in this paragraph are from, JP, "Suggested By-Laws for the American Adoption Congress," 23 Mar. 1979, folder: Orphan Voyage By-Laws. Apparently, the AAC did not accept Paton's bylaws, for immediately after the inaugural 1979 AAC conference, the board of directors appointed a committee to draft bylaws for its membership. See "Report of The American Adoption Congress First International Congress, May 4–7, 1979" [n.d.], 15, JPP, UF.

33. JP [n.t.], *The LOG*, March 1979.

34. Except where noted, all the information and quotations in this paragraph are from

"The American Adoption Congress, First International Conference, May 4–7, 1979, Program," folder: AAC—Misc.

35. Silber resigned from the board of directors on 22 Feb. 1979, and Schmitt had been named to replace her. See "Report of The American Adoption Congress First International Congress, May 4–7, 1979" [n.d.], 2, JPP, UF.

36. The other speakers in order of appearance were Lee Campbell (CUB), Annette Baran (coauthor of *The Adoption Triangle*), and Penny Partridge (an adoptive parent and founder of the group Adoption Forum).

37. "Report of The American Adoption Congress First International Congress, May 4–7, 1979" [n.d.], 3, JPP, UF.

38. JP to Marianne Lippold, 18 May 1979, folder: IA—Lippold.

39. JP, "Orphan Voyage Founder Attends Convention," *The LOG*, June 1979, ON.

40. JP to Marianne Lippold, 18 May 1979, folder: IA—Lippold. Margaret Lawrence informed JP that the soup ladle was Linda Burgess's gift to her "because there was no way she was going to stand up there and not hand you something—and it was something you could use in the cabin." Margaret Lawrence to JP [June 1979], folder: MD—Jacobs 1979.

41. JP, "Orphan Voyage Founder Attends Convention," *The LOG*, June 1979, ON.

42. The only fly in the ointment that Paton mentioned to Lippold was a proposal by Cullom and Western regional coordinator Eddie Rizk to have membership in the organization determined by groups rather than individuals. Paton feared that such a course would lead to tyranny and censorship. She promised her correspondent, "We will have none of that." JP to Marianne Lippold, 18 May 1979, folder: IA—Lippold.

43. JP, "Orphan Voyage Founder Attends Convention," *The LOG*, June 1979, ON.

44. Darke quoted in ibid.

45. Rae Johnson to Nancy [Schmitt], Sharon [Forbes], Virginia [Rader], Dirk [Brown] Eddie [Rizk], Margaret [Lawrence], and Jean [Paton], 8 May 1978, "Memorandum: A.A.C.," folder: Campbell, Lee. See also Rae Johnson to Lee Campbell, 8 May 1979, ibid.

46. JP, "Moving On From the American Adoption Congress Meeting," *The LOG*, June 1979, ON.

47. Margaret Lawrence to Dirck Brown, 23 May 1979.

48. "*SUMMARY,*" "Report of The American Adoption Congress First International Congress, May 4–7, 1979" [n.d.], 15, JPP, UF; "*QUESTIONNAIRE,*" 19, ibid.

49. All the information and quotations in this paragraph are from Margaret Lawrence to Dirck Brown, 23 May 1979. See also Margaret Lawrence to Dirck Brown, 28 May 1979.

50. For the membership of the bylaws committee, see "Report of The American Adoption Congress First International Congress, May 4–7, 1979" [n.d.], 15, JPP, UF.

51. JP to Virginia Rader, 14 Sept. 1979, folder: DC—Cub Rader.

52. Colleen Hogan to JP, 21 Aug. 1979 [no folder].

53. JP to Nancy Sitterly, 3 Nov. 1979.

NOTES TO PAGES 239–45

54. All the information and quotations in this paragraph are from JP to Marion Rebecca Carson, 7 Jan. 1981, folder: Carson, Marion, E.

55. JP to Jay Swearingen, 11 May 1981.

56. JP to Jay Swearingen, 4 Nov. 1981.

57. For JP's statement that she attended the Kansas City conference, see JP to Penny Partridge and others in the AAC, 7 Jan. 1982, folder: CO—Misc. Late 70s–Early 80s. JP mentions her honorary membership in a letter dated July 1981. JP to Penny Partridge, 8 July 1981, folder: Conference—AAC 80–93. She received a second "Certificate of Award for A.C.C. Honorary Lifetime Membership," dated 20 May 1983, at the 1983 AAC San Antonio Conference.

58. JP, "The Adoption Colony" (Cedaredge, CO: Orphan Voyage, 1983), n.p.

59. Bob O'Dell, "AAC Convention 'Puts It All Together' at K.C.," *Open A.R.M.S. Quarterly* 1, no. 2 (Summer 1981): 1.

60. JP, "Update," *The LOG*, July 1981, n.p.

61. O'Dell, "AAC Convention 'Puts It All Together,'" 1.

62. Ibid.

63. Penny Callan Partridge, "New AAC President Greets Members," *Open A.R.M.S. Quarterly* 1, no. 3 (Fall 1981): 1.

64. All of the information and quotations in the next two paragraphs are from JP to Penny Partridge, 8 July 1981, folder: Conference—AAC 80–93.

65. All of the information and quotations in this paragraph are from JP to Penny and others in the AAC, 7 Jan. 1982, folder: CO—Misc. Late 70s–Early 80s.

66. JP to Jay Swearingen, 30 Jan. 1982. See also JP to Jay Swearingen, 1 Feb. 1982. Paton was unable to locate the AAC bylaws that she wrote in 1979, which is extremely unusual. Perhaps she misplaced the document. I discovered it not in a folder pertaining to the AAC, but in one labeled "Orphan Voyage Bylaws." Paton eventually found the bylaws and sent a copy to then–AAC president Kate Burke. See JP to Kate Burke, 3 Jan. 1989, folder: CA—Burke, Kate.

67. JP to Jay Swearingen, 10 Mar. 1982.

68. Ibid.

69. JP to Mary Jane Brinkos, 5 Apr. 1982, folder: Conference AAC—80–93.

70. JP to AAC Board Members et al, 9 Apr. 1982, ibid.

71. All of the information and quotations in this paragraph come from JP, "Advance copy of a memo to the AAC Board of Directors," 15 Apr. 1982, ibid.

72. "Minutes of First Meeting of Directors of the American Adoption Congress," June 1981, JPP, UF.

73. Ibid.

74. Joseph D. Harrington to Tom Allington, 26 Mar. 1982, ibid.

75. JP to All, 20 Apr. 1982, ibid.

76. The only substantive remark came from Betty Jean Lifton, who took issue with Paton's term "afflicted people." Betty Jean Lifton to JP, Apr. 1982, ibid. See also Elizabeth Scott to JP, 19 May 1982, for dialogue and mild disagreement, ibid.

77. JP to Jayne Askin, 21 Apr. 1982.

78. Patricia Dorner, e-mail to author, 28 May 2009; JP to Kate Burke, 24 Nov. 1988, folder: CA—Burke, Kate.

79. JP to William Brow, 13 Sept. 1983.

80. JP [n.t.], [19]82, folder: Conference—AAC 80–93. It is not clear whether this opening sentence, part of a two-page, handwritten document, was delivered to a group of people at the conference or was simply a note to herself.

81. JP to Patty O'Gorman, 21 Jan. 1983, ibid.

82. JP to Sophie Elvert, 15 July 1983, JPP, UF. See also JP to William Brow, 13 Sept. 1983.

83. See Patty O'Gorman to Sophia Elvert, 6 Jan. 1983, folder: Conference—AAC 80–93; Margaret Lawrence to JP, Kermit Karns, Jay Swearingen, and Patty O'Gorman, 10 June [19]83, ibid.

84. JP to Jay Swearingen, 14 Mar. 1983, ibid.

85. JP to Lynn Greiner, 2 June 1983.

86. JP to Joan Vanstone, 20 Jan. 1984, folder: Vanstone, Joan (1).

87. JP to David Reed, 23 Apr. 1984 [no folder].

88. JP to Jayne Askin, 25 June 1984.

89. JP to David Reed, 23 Apr. 1985 [no folder].

90. JP, "Suggested By-Laws for the American Adoption Congress," 23 Mar. 1979, folder: Orphan Voyage By-Laws.

91. JP to Sally File, 31 July 1984, folder: NM.

92. JP to Mary Iwanek, 26 Mar. 1986, folder: New Zealand (Mary Iwanek).

93. Mary Iwanek to JP, 19 May 1986, ibid. Iwanek quickly added that she also "met a large group of dedicated people," though it is not clear whether she meant dedicated people among "the professionals" or other adoption activists.

94. All of the information and quotations in the following paragraph comes from JP, "AN OPEN LETTER on the Proposed Agenda for the 1987 AAC National Conference," 11 Dec. 1986 [no folder].

95. Ibid.

96. Lifton called for the opening of adoption records to prevent future recurrences of such crimes by adult adoptees on society. Betty Jean Lifton, "'So That Adoptees Do Not Have to Vent Their Rage,'" New York Times, 19 Sept. 1977..

97. David Kirschner, "'Son of Sam' and the Adopted Child Syndrome," Adelphi University Society for Psychoanalysis and Psychotherapy Newsletter (1978): 7. See also David Kirschner, "The Adopted Child Syndrome: Considerations for Psychotherapy," Psychotherapy in Private Practice 8 (1990): 93–100; David Kirschner, "Understanding Adoptees Who Kill: Dissociation, Patricide, and the Psychodynamics of Adoption," International Journal of Offender Therapy and Comparative Criminology 36 (1992): 323–33.

98. JP to MAC, 24 Jan. 1987 [no folder].

99. JP to Sandy Lott, 27 Dec. 1990.

100. See H. J. Sants, "Genealogical Bewilderment in Children with Substitute Parents," British Journal of Medical Psychology 37 (1964): 133–41.

101. JP to Jeanelle Pasternack, 13 Jan. 1994, folder: Pasternack-Livingston, Jeanelle.

102. JP to Linda Shipley, 20 Aug. 1998.

103. JP to Carol Gustavson, 25 Apr. 1990, folder: Gustavson-II.

104. JP to Marcy Axness, 8 July 1995; JP to Linda Shipley, 20 Aug. 1998.

105. JP to Sandy Lott, 27 Dec. 1990.

106. JP to Carol Gustavson, 25 Apr. 1990, folder: Gustavson-II.

107. JP to Linda Shipley, 20 Aug. 1998.

108. JP to Marcy Axness, 8 July 1995.

109. JP to Sandy Lott, 27 Dec. 1990.

110. JP to Mary Iwanek, 28 Oct. 1988, folder: New Zealand (Mary Iwanek).

111. All of the information and quotations in this paragraph are from Kate Burke to JP, 19 Nov. 1988, folder: CA—Burke, Kate.

112. All of the information and quotations in this paragraph are from JP to Kate Burke, 24 Nov. 1988, ibid.

113. All of the information and quotations in this paragraph, unless otherwise indicated, are from Kate Burke to JP, 29 Dec. 1988, ibid.

114. JP to Kate Burke, 24 Nov. 1988, ibid.

115. JP to Kate Burke, 3 Jan. 1989, ibid.

116. JP to Mary Iwanek, 5 Jan. 1989, folder: New Zealand (Mary Iwanek).

117. All of the information and quotations in the following two paragraphs are from Kate Burke to JP, 21 Jan. 1989, folder: CA—Burke, Kate.

118. JP to Kate Burke, 31 Jan. 1989, ibid.

119. JP to Joan Williams, 3 Dec. 1959, folder: Angellar.

120. JP to Wendy Bischoff, 9 Jan. 1979.

121. JP to Mary Bumpus, 16 Apr. 1982.

122. JP to Linda Crenwelge [Nov.–Dec. 1990].

123. JP to Kay Russell, 14 Nov. 1985.

124. JP to Wendy Bischoff, 9 Jan. 1979. See also JP to Molly Johnson, 27 Oct. 1989.

125. The poetry of *Piers Plowman* and Paton's saying can be found in JP to Mary Bumpus, 16 Apr. 1982. As early as 1955, JP mentioned Langland's *Piers Plowman* favorably in connection with reconciliation of adult adoptees in a letter to anthropologist Ruth Wallis. See JP to Ruth Wallis, 6 Sept. 1955. For other references to this particular stanza in *Piers Plowman*, see JP to Robin Ropar, 9 Oct. 1985.

126. Pat Sanders to JP, 12 Feb. 1980. ISC is still in existence, and its mission statement is quite similar to Sanders's 1980 description. See its web page at http://www.iscsearch.com/ (accessed July 22, 2009).

127. JP to Pat Sanders, 18 Feb. 1980.

128. JP to Kay Russell, 14 Nov. 1985.

129. JP to Mary Iwanek, 28 Oct. 1988, folder: New Zealand (Mary Iwanek).

130. JP to Peggy Dorn, 21 Dec. 1988. See also JP to Molly Johnson, 27 Oct. 1989.

131. JP to Kate Burke, 31 Jan. 1989, folder: CA—Burke, Kate.

132. Lori Carangelo, *The Ultimate Search Book: Worldwide Adoption and Vital Records* (Bountiful, UT: Heritage Quest, 1999), xii. See also Lori Carangelo, "Alive in My Heart

(A Reunion Story)," http://www.loricarangelo.com/ReunionStory.html (accessed July 22, 2009).

133. Biographical information on Carangelo comes from Jessica DelBalzo, "Lori Carangelo: Her Lifelong Quest for Human Rights," *Maternal Instinct* (2001). http://www.loricarangelo.com/Maternal Instinct.html (accessed October 27, 2008); Chris Janis, "Woman Fights to Open Birth Records," *New Haven Register*, 30 Jan. 1989, http://www.amfor.net/OpenRecord/Jan_Feb_1989_07.jpg (accessed January 5, 2011); Carangelo, "Alive in My Heart."

134. JP to Kate Burke, 31 Jan. 1989, folder: CA—Burke, Kate.

135. Unless otherwise noted, all of the information and quotations in the next two paragraphs are from Kate Burke to JP, 24 Mar. 1989, ibid.

136. Susan Lovett, "American Adoption Congress Ballot" [n.d.], ibid.

137. Pat Sanders to JP, 12 Mar. 1989.

138. All of the information and quotations in the next six paragraphs come from JP to Kate Burke, 28 Mar. 1989, folder: CA—Burke, Kate.

139. Sandy Zimmerman to JP [November 1976], folder: Musser; Sandy Musser to JP, 29 July 1978; Sandra Kay Musser, *I Would Have Searched Forever*, (Plainfield, NJ: Distributed by Haven Books, 1979, Announcement, July 1979, folder: Musser.

140. Sandy Musser to JP [October 1981], Folder: Musser. Musser repeated the phrase without the hyphen in a 1986 letter, a copy of which she sent to Paton. See Sandy Musser to AAC Board and regional Directors, 14 Oct. 1986.

141. JP to Mary Iwanek, 18 Aug. 1989, folder: New Zealand (Mary Iwanek).

142. All of the information and quotations in this paragraph come from JP to Molly Johnson, 16 Sept. 1989.

143. JP to Mary Iwanek, 19 Nov. 1986, folder: New Zealand (Mary Iwanek).

144. JP to Mary Iwanek, 28 Oct. 1988, ibid.

Chapter 14

1. JP to Nancy Corey, 7 Apr. 1981, folder: MN—MN-ALMA.

2. JP, *The Adoption Circle*, Fall 1980 [no folder].

3. Becky Emmons, "Reconciliation Is the Name of Her Game," *South Bend (IN) Tribune*, 2 Oct. 1980.

4. JP to Lori Carangelo, 26 July 1998 [no folder].

5. JP to Warren Siegmond, 24 Feb. 1983. See also JP to Sandy Musser, 18 Oct. 1983.

6. JP to Mildred Smith, 5 Jan. 1959; JP to BJ, 1 July 1975, folder: MD—Jacobs—1974. Paton attributed the source of the neck and back problems to her having been hit by a car in childhood, and said they had slowly worsened over the years. She also noted "a tingling and numb hands." See JP to Joan Vanstone, 11 Dec. 1979, folder: Vanstone, Joan (1). She assured Vanstone that the pain was minimal, but admitted that she hated pain, and that just a little would drive her to seek help. Ibid.

7. JP to Marion Morris, 19 Jan. 1978.

8. Quotations from JP to Patricia Murphy, 11 Jan. 1984.

9. Quotations from JP to Warren Siegmond, 24 Feb. 1983. See also JP to Jay Swearingen, 8 Dec. 1983.

10. JP to Warren Siegmond, 24 Feb. 1983.

11. Quotation from Erika Doss, *Memorial Mania: Public Feeling in America* (Chicago: University of Chicago Press, 2010), 130.

12. JP to Linda Lipscombe, 24 Feb. 1984.

13. JP to Allison Ward, 21 Sept. 1983. See also JP to Sandy Musser, 5 Oct. 1983.

14. JP to Joyce Villanueva, 27 Jan. 1984, folder: LeeCampbell, Joyce [Villanueva], CUB.

15. JP, "Orphan Voyage Begins Memorial," *Open A.R.M. S. Quarterly* 3, no. 4 (Winter 1983).

16. All the information and quotations are from ibid.

17. JP to Joan Vanstone, 20 Jan. 1984, folder: Vanstone, Joan (1).

18. JP Marilyn Hipp, 18 May 1984; JP to Patricia Murphy, 6 June 1984, folder: Musser.

19. JP to Jay Swearingen, 8 Dec. 1983; JP to Joyce Villanueva, 27 Jan 1984, folder: LeeCampbell, Joyce [Villanueva], CUB

20. JP to Patricia Murphy, 11 Jan. 1984, folder: Musser.

21. See, for example, Patricia Murphy to JP, 3 Jan. 1984, ibid. See also Paton's reply. JP to Patricia Murphy, 11 Jan. 1984, ibid.

22. Patricia Murphy to JP, 7 Apr. 1985, ibid.

23. JP to Patricia Murphy, 22 Apr. 1985, ibid.

24. JP to Leona Umphrey, 14 Mar. 1986. Uncharacteristically, Paton apparently misspelled Umphrey's name. In an earlier letter (12 Nov. 1985), the one in which the check arrived, Paton spelled her name "Humphrey." But there is no question that the second letter was addressed to Umphrey, and the folder was so labeled. It is unclear whether Paton ever returned Umphrey's donation.

25. See Marsha Riben to JP, 14 Sept. 1987; Patti Jo Kubinski to JP [November? 1992], folder: Kubinski, P. J.; Becky Wheeler to JP, 26 Mar. 1996, folder: Walter, Betty. In 1992, Paton mentioned two other people who expressed an interest in the Adoption Memorial: Edith Wagner and Lynn Lape. See JP to Patti Jo Kubinski, 18 Nov. 1992.

26. Patti Jo Kubinski to JP [November? 1992].

27. Both quotations can be found in JP to Patti Jo Kubinski, 18 Nov. 1992.

28. JP to Lori Carangelo, 26 July 1998 [no folder].

29. Originally JP got the idea for the Hospitality Network in 1980 from Pat Allard's wish for "a hotel strictly for the use of our movement." JP interpreted this into "Hospitality for traveling and searching orphans" and referred to it as a hospitality network. JP, "Projects and Dreams," *The LOG*, October 1980. A year later, JP identified sixteen cities in ten states and Toronto, Canada, as Hospitality Network locations, though "no one was using it yet." See JP, "Participation Page," *The LOG*, Spring 1981. See also JP, "The Influence of Sealed Adoption on the Individual and on Society" (Cedaredge, CO: Orphan Voyage, 1987).

30. Molly Johnson, "Paton House" [16 Dec. 1988].

31. JP to Molly Johnson, 17 Dec. 1988.

32. Molly Johnson to JP, 14 July 1989.

33. JP, "Paton House" [n.d.], ibid. There are two documents headed "Paton House." The one referred to here is not printed on Orphan Voyage of Jacksonville letterhead, like the other one, which is date-stamped 16 Dec. 1988 and signed "Molly."

34. JP to Joan Vanstone, 18 May 1979, folder: Vanstone, Joan (1). JP had also created another pin that read "I LIVE IN THE ADOPTION COLONY."

35. Jerry Stapleton to JP, 30 Mar. 1985.

36. JP to Jerry Stapleton, 14 June 1985, ibid.

37. "What We are and What We are Not," Seek and Find 1, no. 1 (July 1980): n.p. in The LOG (Spring 1981), n.p.

38. JP, "Marsha Riben," The LOG (Spring 1981), n.p.

39. Amitai Etzioni, "Holidays and Rituals: Neglected Seedbeds of Virtue," in We Are What We Celebrate: Understanding Holidays and Rituals, ed. Amitai Etzioni (New York: New York University Press, 2004), 20–21.

40. All of the information and quotations in the rest of this paragraph are from Mary Marsh and Lovina del Fierro to JP, 28 Feb. 1992, folder: Marsh, Mary.

41. I have been unable to locate this publication. All the information and quotations about it are from Mary Marsh to JP, 9 Dec. 1992, ibid.

42. Jean Paton-Kittson, "Excerpt from 'Whom Do You Seek'" [n.d.], ibid.

43. Mary Marsh to JP, 9 Dec. 1992, ibid.

44. "Day for Those Who Gave Up Their Babies," New York Times, 8 May 1994; JP to Editor, Adoption Network News, 16 Mar. 1994, folder: Ceremonies; Adoption Network News, "Birthmother's Day Ceremony," (March–April 1994); Audrey Scammell, "Annual Mother's Day March," 9 May 1993, folder: Scammell.

45. JP to Betsy Norris, 1 July 1998.

46. Otto Friedrich and Robert Carney, "The Strange Cabbage Patch Craze," Time, 12 Dec. 1983. The idea of Babyland came from Xavier Roberts, an artist who traveled from his Georgia mountain home to regional crafts fairs selling the original "Little People," hand-stitched dolls. The dolls were not (and still are not) referred to as being sold, but "adopted." When demand for the kids increased, Roberts opened Babyland General Hospital in Cleveland, Georgia. Clint Williams, "Buying Mania Is Over, but Cabbage Patch Kids Still Going Strong," Seattle Post-Intelligencer, 25 Sept. 1999, p. E7. For the Babyland website, see http://www.cabbagepatchkids.com/ (accessed October 5, 2011).

47. Coleco sent representatives to talk to CUB president Lee Campbell but ignored her suggestions, including that the company change the wording on the forms from "adopting papers" to "presenting papers." For the controversy, see William Hoffman, Fantasy: The Incredible Cabbage Patch Phenomenon (Dallas: Taylor Publishing Co., 1984), chap. 4; quotation on 155.

48. Paton wrote her commentary in December 1983. See JP, "Cabbage Patch Dolls Send a Message All Their Own," 7 Dec. 1983, folder: CO—Misc. Late 70s–Early 80s. I have quoted from the published version, which is identical.

49. JP, "Cabbage Patch Dolls Send a Message All Their Own," *Open A.R.M.S. Quarterly* 4, no. 1 (Spring 1984): 4.

50. For a detailed discussion on the tactics and strategy of abortion opponents during the 1980s, see N. E. H. Hull and Peter Charles Hoffer, *Roe v. Wade: The Abortion Rights Controversy in American History* (Lawrence: University Press of Kansas, 2001), 210–22. See also JP to the Editor, *Grand Junction (CO) Daily Sentinel,* 21 Oct. 1983, reprinted in Illustrations.

51. JP, "Avoid Abortion: Aid Women," Letter to the Editor, *Delta (CO) Courier Independent,* 28 Mar. 1985.

52. JP to Joan Vanstone, 20 Jan. 1984, folder: Vanstone, Joan (2). According to Paton, the movement was afflicted with two other lesser forms of complacency. A wrongheaded belief that anger at Bill Pierce was a sufficient response to the movement's enemies and its happy association with social workers. Ibid.

53. Paton published the talk two years later. See JP, "The Influence of Sealed Adoption." Unless otherwise indicated, all the information and quotations in the next five paragraphs are from ibid. (emphasis in the original).

54. Paton's interest in the brain was of long standing. See JP to Wilder Penfield [1959], folder: Brain.

55. See Marcus E. Raichle, "Behind the Scenes of Functional Brain Imaging: A Historical and Psychological Perspective," *Proceedings of the National Academy of Scientists* 95 (February 1998): 766.

56. JP to Maureen Peer, 9 Apr. 1990.

57. For the early history of open adoption in the United States, see Carp, *Family Matters,* 197–98; and Ellen Herman, *Kinship by Design: A History of Adoption in the Modern United States* (Chicago: University of Chicago Press, 2008), 227–28.

58. H. David Kirk, *Shared Fate: A Theory and Method of Adoption and Mental Health* (New York: The Free Press, 1964), 154 and n. 3; Carp, *Family Matters,* 198.

59. *OV,* 96 and n. 20.

60. Carp, *Family Matters,* 200–202.

61. Lynn J. Witkin, "Bridging the Gap: Natural Parents and Adoptive Families," *Social Work* 16 (October 1971): 96.

62. Ruth G. McRoy, Harold D. Grotevant, and Kerry L. White, *Openness in Adoption: New Practices, New Issues* (New York: Praeger, 1988), 15–16.

63. Annette Baran, Reuben Pannor, and Arthur D. Sorosky, "Open Adoption," *Social Work* 21 (March 1976): 97. I will quote from the published version of the talk. Detailed notes of Baran's talk suggest that there was little change between the two.

64. JP to Betty Jean Lifton, 3 Mar. 1975.

65. Baran, Pannor, and Sorosky, "Open Adoption," 97.

66. JP to Cal Callaway, 1 June 1977.

67. JP to Lee Campbell, 30 Aug. 1977.

68. JP to Cal Callaway, 1 June 1977, folder: Callaway, Cal.

69. JP to Lucy Pare, 11 Apr. 1980.

70. Lifton quoted in Children's Home Society of California, *The Changing Picture of*

Adoption (San Francisco: Children's Home Society of California, 1985), 39.

71. JP to Marilyn Hipp, 15 July 1983. A week later, in a follow-up letter to Hipp, Paton modified this view, stating she was "not entirely opposed to open adoption."

72. Reuben Pannor and Annette Baran, "Open Adoption as Standard Practice," *Child Welfare* 63 (May–June 1984): 245.

73. Ibid., 318. Two years later, in its 1988 revision of adoption standards the Child Welfare League of America added a totally new section, recommending to its member agencies that open adoption "be an integral part of all adoption services." CWLA, *Standards for Adoption Service*, rev. ed. (New York: CWLA, 1988), sect. 0.10.

74. JP to Janine Baer, 27 Sept. 1985. See also JP to Janine Baer, 30 Oct. 1985; JP to Wendy Redmond, 16 Dec. 1986, folder: Redmond, Wendie E. Canada.

75. JP to Sandy Musser, 26 June 1989.

76. I have been unable to locate Baran and Pannor's statement to Paton. The quotation is from "Annette Baran: Pioneer of Open Records," http://familypreservation.blogspot.com/2008/07/annette-baran-pioneer-of-open-records_19.html   (accessed January 3, 2011).

77. JP to Anna Coffey, 22 June 1990, folder: New Zealand: Coffey, Anna.

78. JP to Anna Coffey, 5 Dec. 1989, ibid. (emphasis in the original).

79. Severson had asked his publisher to send Paton a copy of the book. The publisher requested Paton to provide "a written review of the book," parts of which, she hoped to use as a blurb. See Christina Swan to JP, 18 June 1991, folder: Hope Cottage.

80. Randolph Severson, *A Letter to Parents . . . On Open Adoption* (Dallas: Cygnet Designs, 1991), 1, folder: ibid.

81. All quotations are from Edwina Hill [JP] to Christine Swan, 2 July 1991, folder: ibid.

82. Progress was slow. Carangelo published a running account of the progress—or lack of progress—the bill was making in the state legislatures. See Lori Carangelo, "Repeal! 5 States Begin Repeal Bid," http://www.amfor.net/OpenRecord/Jan_Feb_1989_04.jpg, and "Repeal! 5 States Begin Repeal Bid," http://www.amfor.net/OpenRecord/?71 (accessed January 5, 2011).

83. Lori Carangelo, "An Open Letter Mailed to Legislators Nationwide on a Proposal to Repeal Sealed Records Laws," 1 Jan. 1989, http://www.amfor.net/OpenRecord/?79 (accessed January 5, 2011).

84. MAC to JP, 14 Feb. 1989, folder: Cohen, Mary.

85. The quotations in this paragraph are from JP to MAC, 15 Mar. 1989.

86. JP to Molly Johnson, 7 Jul. 1989. JP declared her support for Carangelo in several other letters. See, for example, JP to Linda Crenwelge, 21 Jan. 1990 and JP to Janine Baer [July 1991].

Chapter 15

1. JP to Carol Komissaroff, 3 Jan. 1990.
2. Gayle Beckstead to Sellers and Exhibitors, 4 Feb. 1991, folder: AAC Misc.

3. Gayle Beckstead to JP, 2 Mar. 1991, ibid. Biographical information on Beckstead from "Adoption Are You My Mother," *Time*, 9 Oct. 1989, http://www.time.com/time/magazine/article/0,9171,958698–2,00.html (accessed December 23, 2010).

4. JP to Gayle Beckstead, 7 Mar. 1991, folder: AAC Misc.

5. All of the information and quotations in this paragraph are from Pat Sanders to JP, 14 Mar. 1991, ibid.

6. JP to Dirck Brown, 18 June 1991.

7. All of the information and quotations in this paragraph are from JP to Molly Johnson, 20 Jan. 1995. In 1988, Ensminger was vice president of the AAC.

8. All of the information and quotations in this paragraph are from JP to MAC, 22 Dec. 1995. For additional criticisms of the AAC, see JP to Carol Gustavson, 19 Nov. 1995, folder: Gustavson—II; JP to Betty Jean Lifton, 8 Aug. 1996 [no folder].

9. JP to Michael Haag, 14 Mar. 1977.

10. JP to BJ, 23 Dec. 1980, folder: MD—Jacobs 1980s; JP to BJ, 17 Dec. 1982, ibid.

11. JP to Jay Swearingen, 18 Nov. 1982. See also JP to Bill Cody, 29 Sept. 1982; JP to BJ, 1 Feb. 1983, folder: MD—Jacobs 1980s.

12. JP to Diana Vickery, 25 Feb. 1985.

13. JP to Jay Swearingen, 18 Feb. 1988; quotation from ibid. "Old Age Assistance," was part of Title I of the 1935 Social Security Act, which would provide cash payments to poor elderly people, regardless of their work record. ElderWeb, "Social Security Act Creates National Old-Age Assistance," http://www.elderweb.com/node/9667 (accessed August 3, 2011).

14. JP to Carol Gustavson, 13 May 1991, folder: Gustavson—II.

15. JP to Carol Anderson, 7 May 1991, folder: CUB—Carol Anderson. At the end of 1990, a dentist had installed a new, full upper plate and a partial lower one. Paton declared that she had only four teeth left to hold the lower plate. See JP to Alice Syman, 27 Dec. 1990, folder: Syman, Alice. But to another correspondent, she reported that she still had six teeth. JP to Carol Gustavson, 25 Jan. 1991, folder: Gustavson—II.

16. JP to Carol Gustavson, 13 May 1991, folder: Gustavson—II. See also JP to Jean Gehrmann, 21 Jun. 1991. Jean. Paton first mentioned the cataract surgery in January 1991. JP to Carol Gustavson, 25 Jan. 1991, folder: Gustavson—II. See also JP to Betty Wheeler, 8 Jul. 1991. In November 1991, Paton had the left eye lens replaced also. See JP to Connie Dawson, 19 Nov. 1991.

17. JP to Carol Gustavson, 13 May 1991, folder: Gustavson—II.

18. JP to Connie Dawson, 19 Nov, 1991. See also JP to BJ, 22 Jun. 1992, folder: MD—Jacobs 1994 to Present. Almost as an aside, Paton also mentioned that she had a small cancerous spot removed from her forehead. Ibid. See also Molly Johnson to JP, 19 May 1992.

19. JP to Mary Iwanek, 16 Dec. 1990, folder: New Zealand (Mary Iwanek).

20. JP to Carol Gustavson, 25 Jan. 1991, folder: Gustavson—II. Paton would later date this important insight to "late in the year 1992." See JP, "Babies What Do They

Know, *A Proper Response: To the Situation in Adoption* 2, no. 2 (Sept. 1995): 2. (hereafter referred to as *PR*).

21. JP to Joyce Pavao, 11 Feb. 1991, folder: Pavao, J.; all quotations are from this source.

22. JP to Joyce Pavao, 18 May 1992, ibid.

23. JP to Molly Johnson, 26 Oct. 1990 (caps in the original); all quotations from this source.

24. JP to Mary Iwanek, 16 Dec. 1990, folder: New Zealand (Mary Iwanek).

25. Thomas Verny, *The Secret Life of the Unborn Child* (New York: Summit Books, 1981); T. Berry Brazelton and Bertrand G. Cramer, *The Earliest Relationship: Parents, Infants, and the Drama of Early Attachment* (Reading, MA: Addison-Wesley, 1990); David B. Chamberlain, *Babies Remember Birth: And Other Extraordinary Discoveries about the Mind and Personality of your Newborn* (Los Angeles: J. P. Tarcher, distributed by St. Martin's Press, 1988).

26. JP, "Babies What Do They Know," *PR* 2, no. 2 (Sept. 1995): 1.

27. JP to Anna Coffey, 12 July 1993, folder: New Zealand—Coffey, Anna.

28. Carl Raschke, "Biomagnetism Promises Sharper Brain Images," *Colorado Business* (May 1985): 34.

29. JP to John Zimmerman, 27 Oct. 1987, folder: Cook, Annabelle.

30. Hal Strauss, "Color 'Maps' of Brain Allow New Look at Dyslexia," *Grand Junction (CO) Daily Sentinel*, 16 Jan. 1990. Paton also intuited a relationship between adoption and attention deficit hyperactivity disorder (ADHD). She attended local parent meetings and even besieged a local psychologist, attempting to draw attention to the connection, but no one would listen. The parents only wanted information about the correct drug dosage for their children. JP to LaVonne Stiffler, 30 Dec. 1992

31. JP to George Hynd, 17 Mar. 1990, folder: Brain. Paton states this more explicitly in JP to LaVonne Stiffler, 30 Dec. 1992. Twenty years later researchers are finally catching up to Paton. At the March 2012 Rudd Adoption Research Program at the University of Massachusetts, the keynote speaker, Megan R. Gunnar, spoke on "Post-Institutionalized Children Become Teenagers: Early Deprivation and the Developing Teen Brain."

32. In Aldous Huxley's dystopian novel no one has a family.

33. Paton is referring to the attempt by the Bolsheviks to subsume the family under the socialist state. George M. Day, "The Family in Soviet Russia," *Social Forces* 16, no. 4 (May 1938): 556–61.

34. JP to The Editor, Denver POST, 25 Dec. 1991, reprinted in *PR* 2, no. 4 (May 1996).

35. Except where noted the information in this paragraph comes from JP, "New Focus of the Opposition," *PR* 1, no. 3 (September 1994).

36. Rita J. Simon and Howard Altstein, *Adoption, Race, and Identity: From Infancy to Young Adulthood* (New Brunswick, NJ: Transaction Publishers, 1992).

37. Paton misidentified Bartholet as associated with the discipline of biology. Her dismissive remark about Bartholet was prompted by a keynote address the Harvard professor delivered at Duke Law School on April 8, 1994, in which she advocated reforming current adoption law to allow childless couples to adopt more easily and endorsed reproductive technologies such as in vitro fertilization clinics and surrogacy brokers. The talk was eventually published as "Beyond Biology: The Politics of Adoption and Reproduction," *Duke Journal of Gender Law and Policy* 2 (1995): 5–14.

38. JP, "Is It Ethical to Be Brutal?," *PR* 1, no. 3 (September 1994).

39. Diana Edwards, "Program Plan," February 1989, ibid.

40. JP to Diana Edwards, 4 Sept. 1989, ibid.

41. Ibid.

42. Ibid.

43. JP, *PR* (June 1993).

44. Musser's prison sentence did not begin until November 1, 1993. Sandy Musser, *To Prison with Love: the True Story of an Indecent Indictment and America's Adoption Travesty* (Cape Coral, FL: The Awareness Press, 1995), 152.

45. Lori Carangelo, *Born Losers: Billion Dollar Babies in America's Foster Care, Adoption, and Prison Systems* (Palm Desert, CA: Access Press, 1999), 162–67.

46. Burke quoted in Tamar Lewin, "Women Convicted of Fraud in Efforts to Find Adoptees," *New York Times*, 30 July 1993.

47. [Leah Wesolowski], "Musser Convicted," *(Alabama) Orphan Voyage News* 2, no. 1 (Winter 1994): 1–3, folder: Leah Wesolowski. In a letter to Musser, Paton disassociated herself from the views of the Alabama branch of Orphan Voyage, noting that she did not supervise groups that took the name of Orphan Voyage, nor had she even seen the editorial. JP to Sandy Musser, 12 Apr. 1994, folder: Musser. Musser replied to the editor and the board, defended her action, denied she was a martyr, and donated money to the organization. Orphan Voyage of Alabama refused to accept Musser's donation, claiming it would be hypocritical. See Sandy Musser to Leah and Orphan Voyage Board, 6 Apr. 1994, and Orphan Voyage of Alabama's reply in *(Alabama) Orphan Voyage News* 2, no. 2 (1994), folder: Leah Wesolowski.

48. Jane Nast to Support Groups, "About Sandy Musser," 12 Apr. 1993, folder: Musser; Carangelo, *Born Losers*, 166, 165; Keith C. Griffith to President Clinton, 30 Nov. 1993, folder: Griffith, Keith.

49. Ever true to her principles, Paton criticized Musser's empire building and the exorbitant fees she appeared to be charging for helping adult adoptees search for their original families. For Paton's criticism of Musser's activities, see JP to Sandy Musser, 15 Jan. 1991; JP to Sandy Musser, 31 Jan. 1991; JP to Keith Griffith, 8 Mar. 1994; JP to Sandy Musser, 12 Apr. 1994.

50. JP, 3 June 1993, quoted in Carangelo, *Born Losers*, 164.

51. JP to Janet Reno, 12 July 1993, *PR* [June 1993], n.p.

52. Uniform laws or acts do not have the force of law. They are drafted and promulgated by the National Conference of Commissioners on Uniform State Laws, the members

of which are appointed by state governors. Their purpose is to make the law consistent among the states when existing statutes display wide disparities. A uniform law is expected to embody a public consensus about how the legislature ought to respond to some given problem. Once a uniform law is completed, the states are then free to adopt the law in whole, in part, or not at all as their particular needs and interests dictate. The success of a uniform law is measured by how many states adopt the measure. *Black's Law Dictionary*, 5th ed., s.v. "Uniform Laws or Acts." To date only one state, Vermont, has adopted the Uniform Adoption Act. "The Vermont Statutes Online," http://www.leg.state.vt.us/statutes/chapters.cfm?Title=15A (accessed January 25, 2011). For the text of the 1994 Uniform Adoption Act, see "Uniform Adoption Act (1994)," http://www.law.upenn.edu/bll/archives/ulc/fnact99/1990s/uaa94.htm (accessed August 1, 2011).

53. JP, *PR* 1, no. 2 (September 1994).

54. Both quotations are from JP, "Why Would Anyone Want to Destroy Kinship," *PR* 1, no. 3 (December 1994). Paton was not alone in protesting the Uniform Adoption Act; both the AAC and CUB also protested it. See "The Uniform Adoption Act," http://en-cyclopedia.adoption.com/entry/Uniform-Adoption-Act-UAA/363/1.html (accessed January 25, 2011).

55. Patricia Ireland, "Dear Friend" [n.d.], folder: NOW.

56. JP to Patricia Ireland, 30 Nov. 1993, *PR* 1, no. 1 (June 1993). A second letter soliciting money caused Paton to write Ireland again, repeating her sentiments. See JP to Patricia Ireland, 7 July 1994, folder: NOW. Paton received a reply from Loretta A. Kane, NOW's Special Projects Director. Kane curtly informed Paton that "NOW's position in reproductive freedom is clear. NOW supports every woman's right to make her own reproductive decisions." If Paton had additional questions, she could write Kane for further clarification. Loretta A. Kane to JP, 25 Aug. 1994, ibid. JP responded to Kane, but after reciting her long list of accomplishments for the cause of birth mothers and adult adoptees, asked Kane no questions and briefly restated her earlier critical views of NOW. See JP to Loretta Kane, 30 Aug. 1994, ibid.

57. Mary Marsh, "Feminists and Adoption Reform," *PR* 1, no. 2 (September 1994), n.p. Marsh proposed an ancient Polish toast to Paton that translated to "May you live one hundred years," which she thought a fitting tribute to "Jean Paton, who continues to lead the long fight for adoption reform, like those ancient Celtic warrior women who fought with equal strength and fury beside their men." Ibid.

58. JP to Molly Johnson, 5 Mar. 1993.

59. JP to Betty Wheeler, 23 July 1993.

60. JP to Betty Wheeler, 9 Sept. 1993.

61. JP to Connie Dawson, 5 Oct. 1993.

62. Ibid.; quotation from JP to Carol Gustavson, 15 Dec. 1993, folder: Gustavson—II.

63. JP to Mary Iwanek, 8 Jan. 1994, folder: New Zealand (Mary Iwanek).

64. JP to Abigail Lovett, 1 Jan. 1997.

65. Ibid.

66. JP to Joyce Pavao, 11 Feb. 1991.

67. Quotation from JP to Carole Anderson, 1 June 1989, folder: CUB—Carole Anderson; JP to Janine Baer [July 1991].

68. Eda G. Goldstein, "Psychosocial Approach," in *Encyclopedia of Social Work*, 19th ed., ed. Richard L. Edwards et al. (Washington, D.C.: National Association of Social Workers Press, 1995), 3: 1948–1954, esp. 1950–1951.

69. Eva S. Moskowitz, *In Therapy We Trust: America's Obsession with Self-Fulfillment* (Baltimore: Johns Hopkins University Press, 2001), 2.

70. Mary J. Rillera, *Adoption Encounter: Hurt, Transition, Healing* (Westminster, CA: Triadoption Library, 1987).

71. Both quotations in JP to Janine Baer, 25 Mar. 1992.

72. Marlou Russell, Invitation to "Adoption: The Lifelong Impact," [n.d.], folder: Russell, Marlou.

73. JP to Marlou Russell, 30 Sept. 1993, ibid. Two years later, Paton refused to provide Russell with information about Orphan Voyage for inclusion in her book because of fundamental differences in perspective about the nature of therapy for adult adoptees. See JP to Marlou Russell, 23 Oct. 1995, ibid.

74. JP to Janine Baer, 25 Mar. 1992.

75. JP to Jon Ryan, 5 Dec. 1992.

76. JP to Connie Dawson, 1 Feb. 1991.

77. JP, "Therapeutic Hesitancy," *PR* 1, no. 3 (September 1994). The piece was written earlier. Although undated, JP mentioned it to Jon Ryan. See JP to Jon Ryan, 5 Dec. 1992. In addition, a copy of "Therapeutic Hesitancy" is attached to a letter written to Molly Johnson in 1992. See JP to Molly Johnson, 19 May 1992.

78. Ibid.

79. JP to Connie Dawson, 1 Feb. 1991.

80. JP to Mary Iwanek, 12 Apr. 1990, folder: New Zealand (Mary Iwanek).

81. JP to Linda Brown, 11 Apr. 1990.

82. JP to Janine Baer, 28 Mar. 1997.

83. Except where indicated, this paragraph and the next are based on JP, "Lifelong Impact," *PR* (August 1997).

84. Elinor B. Rosenberg, *The Adoption Life Cycle: The Children and Their Families through the Years* (New York: The Free Press, 1992); David M. Brodzinsky, Marshall D. Schechter, and Robin Marantz Henig, *Being Adopted: The Lifelong Search for Help* (New York: Doubleday, 1992).

85. JP, "Lifelong Impact," *PR* (August 1997); JP, "Is Adoption Lifelong?" *PR* 1, no. 3 (September 1994). See also JP to Rod Holm, 20 Apr. 1997, folder: Holm, Rod.

86. Elizabeth Kübler-Ross, *On Death and Dying* (New York: Scribner's, 1969). There is little evidence to support the existence of stages of mourning or the corollary that if the stages are not followed completely, there is cause for alarm. See George A. Bonanno, *The Other Side of Sadness: What the New Science of Bereavement Tells Us about Life after Loss* (New York: Basic Books, 2009).

87. Pam Lamperelli and Jane M. Smith, "The Grieving Process of Adoption: An Application of Principles and Techniques," *Journal of Psychiatric Nursing and Mental Health Services* 17 (October 1979): 24–29, quotation on 24; Carp, *Family* Matters, 207.

88. JP to Rod Holm, 20 Apr. 1997.

89. JP to Connie Dawson, 1 Feb. 1991.

90. JP to BJ, 7 Nov. 1994, folder: MD—Jacobs 1994 to Present.

91. Both quotations are from JP to Jon Ryan, 5 Dec. 1992.

92. Adoption Forum, "Call for Proposals: 'Demystifying the Adopted-Life Experience,'" October 1998, folder: Lovett, Abigail.

93. All quotations are from JP to Abigail Lovett, 16 Oct. 1998.

94. JP, *PR* 2, no. 2 (September 1995).

95. JP to Rosemary Sever, 12 Jan. 1994. See also JP to Gov. John Engler, 11 Apr. 1995, reprinted in *PR* 1, no. 4 (April 1995).

96. JP to Janine Baer, 8 Aug. 1991. Apparently all of the Paton family members believed and accepted without prejudice the idea that the good doctor had had an illicit affair. Ibid.

97. JP, "Kinship and the Child of Yore," August 1958, BN.

98. JP, "The Disappearance of Kinship," *Genealogy Digest* 13, no. 4 (February 1983).

99. JP, n.t., 30 June 1992 [no folder].

100. JP to Janine Baer, 24 Mar. 1995.

101. JP to Judy Taylor, 22 Apr. 1994.

102. CASA's current website states that the citizen volunteer advocates for "children who have been already removed from their homes due to parental abuse and neglect." http://www.casaforchildren.org/site/c.mtJSJ7MPIsE/b.5301295/k.BE9A/Home. htm (accessed March 13, 2011).

103. JP to Linda Lape, 2 Nov. 1992.

104. JP to Linda Brown, 11 Apr. 1990. The book was *Birth Bond: Reunions between Birthparents and Adoptees: What Happens After* (Far Hills, NJ: New Horizon Press, 1989).

105. JP to Gretchen L. Van Hoosier, 1 Mar. 1994.

106. JP to BJ, 21 July 1995, folder: MD—Jacobs 1994 to Present.

107. JP to Anna Coffey [April 1997], folder: New Zealand Anna Coffey.

108. JP to BJ, 22 Dec. 1995, folder: MD—Jacobs 1994 to present; JP to Lori Carangelo, 1 Jan. 1996.

109. JP to BJ, 22 Dec. 1995, folder MD—Jacobs 1994 to present.

110. For the purchase of the Harrison, AR, house, see JP to Carol Gustavson, 16 Nov. 1993, folder: Gustavson—II; for the move, see JP to Molly Johnson, 20 Mar. 1996.

111. The "ants" quotation is from JP to BJ, 13 Dec. 1996, folder: Lawrence. See also JP to Anna Coffey [1999?] folder: New Zealand Anna Coffey; JP to Betty Jean Lifton, 2 July 1996 [no folder]. Paton mailed most of her files to Harrison. See JP to Nancy Iacobucci, 14 May 1996. She sent her orphan library to a friend of Molly Johnson's in North Carolina. JP to BJ, 13 Dec. 1996, folder: Lawrence.

112. JP, "Change Is the Order of the Day," *PR* 2, no. 3 (January 1996).

113. JP, "Follow-Up," *PR* 1, no. 3 (September 1994).

114. Shea Grimm, "BEST: Ranting, Raving, and the Mighty Jean Paton," 28 Jan. 1997, folder: Bastard Nation.

115. JP, "Growing Old in the Country," *PR* 2, no. 3 (January 1996). For Paton's views on the computer revolution, see at E. Wayne Carp's blog, *The Biography of Jean Paton*, at jeanpaton.com.

116. JP to Connie Dawson, 19 Mar. 1998, [no folder].

117. JP to Janine Baer, 28 Feb. 1997, folder: Baer, J. Paton received her information about Bastard Nation from Baer. See Janine Baer to JP, 17 Feb. 1997, ibid.

118. JP to Mary Iwanek, 3 Jan. 1995, folder: New Zealand (Mary Iwanek).

119. JP to Joan Wheeler, 2 Jan. 1990, folder.

120. Concerned United Birthparents, "Jean Paton," 12 Oct. 1996, folder: Carp.

121. JP to Susan Darke, 6 Mar. 1995, folder: Drake, Susan. Paton's admonishment of Darke was perhaps owing to the fact that this was the second time that Darke had slighted Paton's contribution to the movement. See JP to Susan Darke, 25 Aug. 1986, ibid.

122. JP, "Foreseeing Changes," *PR* 2:2 (Sept. 1995). See also JP, "Change Is the Order of the Day," *PR* 2, no. 3 (Jan. 1996).

123. JP, "The Adoption Archives of Orphan Voyage," *PR* (Aug. 1997). The printer gave JP an estimate of $6,000 for 2,000 copies (500 in hardback and 1,500 paperback). The response for financial support was tepid, which Paton interpreted as indicating "do not do it." See JP to E. Wayne Carp, 18 June 1999, in possession of the author.

124. The quotation is from William Feigelman and Arnold R. Silverman, *Chosen Children: New Patterns of Adoptive Relationships* (New York: Praeger, 1984), which Wegar quoted in her book, *Adoption, Identity, and Kinship: The Debate over Sealed Adoption Records* (New Haven, CT: Yale University Press, 1997).

125. JP, "The Adoption Archives of Orphan Voyage."

126. JP [n.t.], *PR* [May 1998].

127. *Family Matters*, back dust jacket. JP to Joyce Seltzer, 1 Dec. 199[7], enclosure, folder: Carp.

128. E. Wayne Carp to JP, 5 Nov. 1997, in the author's possession.

129. Marcy Axness to JP [Apr. 1998].

130. Betty Jean Lifton's remarks can be found in JP to Marcy Axness, 20 July 1998.

131. JP [n.t.], *PR*, [July] 1998.

132. Betty Jean Lifton to JP, 12 Apr. 1998, folder: BJ-AAC-Carp.

133. L. Anne Babb to JP, 7 July 1998 [no folder].

134. These issues were my evaluation of the importance of kinship and the origins of sealed adoption records. See JP to E. Wayne Carp, 27 Mar. 1998, in possession of the author

135. JP to Betty Jean Lifton, 19 Apr. 1998, folder: BJ-AAC-Carp.

136. JP to E. Wayne Carp, 15 Dec. 1997, in possession of the author.

137. JP to Betty Walter, 19 July 1998 [no folder].

138. JP to Nancy [no last name], 22 May 1998 [no folder].

139. JP to E. Wayne Carp, 5 Sept. 1997, in possession of the author.

Epilogue

1. JP to Lori Carangelo, 18 Feb. 1998; JP to Betty Walter, 9 Mar. 1998; JP to Nancy [Iacobucci], 22 May 1998 [no folder]; National Institute of Health, "Warfarin," http://www.ncbi.nlm.nih.gov/pubmedhealth/PMH0000634/ (accessed March 15, 2011).

2. JP [n.t], *PR*, [July] 1998.

3. JP to E. Wayne Carp, 10 Apr. 1998, in possession of the author.

4. Ibid.

5. JP, "Last Will and Testament of Jean M. Paton" [n.d., no folder]. The quotation is from JP [n.t], *PR*, [July] 1998.

6. JP to E. Wayne Carp, 30 July 2000, in possession of the author; JP to Nancy Verrier, 13 Jan. 2000 [no folder].

7. JP to Nancy Verrier, 13 Jan. 2000 [no folder].

8. JP to E. Wayne Carp, 6 Oct. 1999, in possession of the author; see also JP to E. Wayne Carp, 1 Sept. 1999, ibid.

9. JP to Betty Allen, 26 Sept. 2000.

10. JP to E. Wayne Carp, 22 June 2001, in possession of the author

11. JP to E. Wayne Carp, "near end" November 2000, ibid.

12. JP to E. Wayne Carp, 6 Oct. 1999, ibid.

13. JP to E. Wayne Carp, 21 Jan. 2000, ibid.; JP to E. Wayne Carp, 14 Apr., 2000, ibid.

14. JP to E. Wayne Carp, 21 Jan. 2000, ibid.

15. JP to Annette Baran [16 Apr. 2001], ibid.

16. JP to E. Wayne Carp, 1 Oct. 1998, ibid.

17. Meredith F. Small, "Family Matter," *Discover* (August 2000): 66–71; quotation on 69. The article also stated that children who had many kin connections were both taller and heavier for their age than children with few relatives: ibid., 71. JP sent a copy of the article to me on 18 July 2000.

18. JP to E. Wayne Carp, 4 Nov. 1999, in possession of the author; JP to Nancy Verrier, 13 Jan. 2000 [no folder]. Candace B. Pert, *Molecules of Emotion: The Science behind Mind-Body Medicine* (New York: Scribner's, 1997). Biographical information on Pert can be found at "Candace Pert, PhD," http://www.candacepert.com/biography.html (accessed April 27, 2011).

19. JP to E. Wayne Carp, 4 Nov. 1999, in possession of the author.

20. JP to Denny Glad, 8 July 1999, folder: Tenn—Glad. JP went out of her way to clarify that it was Tennessee's open records law, not Glad herself, that was the source of her pessimism. Over the years, JP had "found that as I pursue the truth of something,

people have the feeling, the thought that I am attacking them, so hard does my mind operate on some subject." This included her housemate, June Schwantes, "who does not realize that I am just acting as if I were in chemistry class, seeking answers." Ibid.

21. JP to Nancy Verrier, 13 Jan. 2000 [no folder].

22. JP to Betty Allen, 26 Sept. 2000.

23. Alice Syman, e-mail to author, 10 Nov. 2010.

24. Originally the website was to be a fulfillment of Paton's Adoption Memorial project. The announcement was titled "Memorial to Deceased Adoptees and Birthparents (on the Internet)." Its purpose was explained as follows: "We are constructing a memorial site dedicated to adoptees and birth parents that died before the chance of meeting the one they lost to adoption. It will be called ORPHAN VOYAGE MEMORIALS. A memorial like this had long been the dream of Jean Paton, Mother of the Adoption Reform Movement in this country." See Cheryl Richmond, forwarding Alice Syman's e-mail to multiple recipients, 26 Apr. 2000, in possession of the author.

25. "Orphan Voyage Memorial," http://www.geocities.ws/orphanvoyage1953/geobook.html (accessed July 16, 2012). For the updated memorial, see "Orphan Voyage Memorial" http://www.geocities.ws/orphanvoyage1953/jean.html (accessed July 16, 2012).

26. Both quotations are from Alice Syman, e-mail to author, 10 Nov. 2010. Before the website was taken down, a few years after Paton's death, the site had been visited more than 6,000 times. Alice Syman, e-mail to author, 11 Nov. 2010. Syman was forced to take the site down when Yahoo began charging a monthly maintenance fee for the website and she lost the technical support for maintaining it. Alice Syman, e-mail to author, 10 Nov. 2010. But it can still be found at "Orphan Voyage Memorial" http://www.geocities.ws/orphanvoyage1953/jean.html (accessed July 16, 2012).

27. JP to Annette Baran, 16 Apr. 2001, copy in possession of the author. Paton's plaque was packed up with all the other trappings of the conference. It languished out of sight in a storage closet for a couple of months until Baran brought the oversight to Gritter's attention. He sent the plaque on to Paton, which arrived in November 2001. Jim Gritter, e-mail to author, 11 Apr. 2011; JP to E. Wayne Carp, 15 Nov. 2001, in possession of author. I am indebted to Jim Gritter for generously sharing with me the background and details of this incident in JP's life.

28. JP to Abigail Lovett, 21 Aug. 2000 [no folder]; Lovett letter was an enclosure. JP to E. Wayne Carp, 26 Aug. 2000, in possession of the author. Quotations in this and the following paragraph are from JP's letter to Lovett.

29. "Memorial Notice," *The Triad Tribune* of Canada, issue 2 (Summer 2002): 2.

30. Karen Vedder, "Tribute to Jean Paton," *CUB Communicator* (Spring–Summer 2002).

31. Lee Campbell, "Tribute to Jean Paton," ibid.

32. MAC, "Tribute to Jean Paton," ibid.

33. JP to E. Wayne Carp, 31 Jan. 2000, in possession of the author.

Index

AAC (American Adoption Congress), 1, 17, 45, 259, 267, 269, 275, 300, 301, 308: and Birth Mother's Day, 265; bylaws of, 235–36, 239, 243, 246, 372n32; creation of, 228–29, 231–36; early history of, 238–39, 240, 241, 243–44, 373n42; and *Family Matters*, 302; first conference of, 236–38; fourth conference of, 245; honors JP, 235, 237, 240, 245; and JP conference registration, 279–80; and Kate Burke, 249–51, 254–55; and march on Washington, D.C., 250–251, 254, 257, 298–99; and Margaret McDonald Lawrence, 355n55; on opening adoption records, 251; third conference of, 240–41; on Uniform Adoption Act (1994), 385n54

Abortion, JP views of, 266–67

Ackley, Norman B., 173

Acton, CA, 76, 107, 128

Adolescence (Hall), 187

Adopted Break Silence, The (Paton), 1, 24, 36, 50–51, 53, 54, 55, 68, 72, 101, 119, 120, 126, 132, 149 203, 256, 261, 293; marketing of, 40–41, 51–52, 53–55, 328–29n80, 333n52; reviews of, 51–52, 54, 75, 64–65, 75, 329--30n96; sales of, 55, 63–64, 330n110; title of, 327n47

Adopted Child, The (Gallagher), 44

An Adopted Child Looks at Adoption (Prentice), 44

Adopted Child Syndrome, 248

Adoptees, 21–22, 37, 38, 39, 45–47, 64, 66, 122, 172, 260; and access to adoption records, 200; on birth mothers, 179–80; characteristics of, 74; on contact with minors, 185–88; culture compared to gay culture, 40; and illegitimacy, 145–47, 203; and inheritance law, 32, 323n100; and intermediaries, 165, 238; JP on, 49–50, 52–53, 70, 93–94, 106–7, 148–49, 168–69, 192–93, 206, 220–21, 229, 230, 255–56, 267–69, 282–83, 307, 310; meet with JP, 126–27; and Model State Adoption Act (1980), 221; pain of, 67–69, 71; and Presbyterian Church, 225; and reunions, 81–82, 147–48, 167; and search consultants, 253; therapy for, 289–92

Adoptees and adoption records, 159, 267–69. *See also* Adoption records

Adoptees' Liberty Movement Association. *See* ALMA

Adoptees in Search, 180, 219

Adoption: and African Americans, 142–44; and Attention Deficit Hyperactivity Disorder, 383n31; black market, 213; compared to juvenile court, 136; history of, 2–5; and illegitimacy, 88; JP on, 43–44, 46, 138–39; stigma of, 37; and tax deduction, 214–15

Adoption agencies: JP's criticism of, 175–76, 365n25; and sealed adoption records, 176–77, 200

Adoption Assistance and Child Welfare Act (1980), 222

Adoption Counseling Center, 250

"Adoption in Existence: Three Studies" (Paton), 85

Adoption fantasy, 74, 335n2

Kittson, Ruth, (pseudonym of JP), 83–84
Komissaroff, Carol, 279
Kostyshak, Maria, 18
Kübler-Ross, Elisabeth, 293–94, 295, 386n86

Ladder, The: A Lesbian Review, 111–12
Ladies Home Journal, 39–40
Ladner, Joyce, 142
Laing, R. D., 297
Lamperelli, Pam, 293–94
Langland, William, 252, 376n125
Lauer, Edika, 54, 55
Lawrence, Margaret McDonald, 153, 162, 171,
    190, 231, 235, 236, 298, 355n55, 373n40;
    criticizes American Adoption Congress,
    238–39; criticizes Florence Fisher, 162;
    criticizes JP, 160
Lesbians, 24–25, 111–12
A Letter to Adoptive Parents . . . On Open
    Adoption (Severson), 274–75
Levin, Carl, 227, 292, 222, 370–71n65, 370n48,
    370n49, 370n54; and Adoption Identifi-
    cation Act (1981), 223, 226
Liberal Education for Adoptive Families, 245
Life History Study Center 1, 6, 9, 34, 64, 65,
    22, 260, 310; creation of, 35–37; and
    FOCUS program, 87, 103, 112, 113, 115;
    growth of, 72–73; and Identity program,
    104; mission of, 35–36, 40, 49–50, 66;
    name of, 35; publicity for, 38, 39–40; and
    Reunion program, 75, 103, 113
Lifton, Betty Jean, 174, 244, 248, 294, 375n96:
    on E. Wayne Carp, 302–3; on open
    adoption, 272; praises Arthur Sorosky,
    169–70
Lifton, Robert Jay, 169
Linkletter, Art, 41 326n33, 326n36
Listener, The (radio program), 77
Livingstone, David, 119
Loeb, Martin, 53
LOG of Orphan Voyage, The (Paton), 1, 193,
    137–38, 301
Lonely Crowd, The (Riesman), 53
Los Angeles Times (newspaper), 178
Lott, Sandra, 525
Louise Wise adoption agency, 51
Lovett, Abigail, 295, 309
Lowe, Helen, 334n66
Lumley, Bill, 205
Lutheran Children's Friends Society, 147
Lutheran Social Service of Minnesota, 148

Macmillan Company, 41, 326n30
Maginnis, Patricia, 350n55
Manon Lescant (opera), 344n96, 113
Marcus, Clare, 189
Marquez, Gabriel Garcia, 24
Marsh, Mary, and Birth Mother's Day,
    264–65; honors JP, 385n57; on National
    Organization of Women, 288
Mass-market magazines and the adoption
    reform movement, 178–79
Mattison, Dorothy, relationship with JP, 24–
    25, 26–27, 320n32
May, Rollo, 203
McCall's (magazine), 85, 95, 165, 178, 367n5
McConaughy, Mary, 33, 324n108
McCord, Elizabeth, 15. See also DeSchwein-
    itz, Elizabeth
McCormick, Carl, 311
McCormick, Naomi, 131
McCurdy, Laverne, 190
Meeker, Martin, 24
Memphis, TN, 129, 134–35, 141
Mental Hygiene, 21, 38, 39
"Method of Benevolence, The" (Paton), 85
Metzger, Bill, 317n18
Milwaukee Urban League, 142
Mixed Families (Ladner), 142
Model State Adoption Act (1981), 217, 219–22,
    225, 368n22, 368n23, 368n33, 368n34
Molecules of Emotion (Pert), 307
Mondale, Walter, 215–16
Mondloh, Ray, 148
Montesquieu, Charles—Louis de Secondat,
    Baron de La Brède et de, 132
Moody Press, 316–350n68
Morison, Alton and John Tschudy custody
    case, 212, 213
Moskowitz, Eva S., 290
Mount Holyoke College, 12–13
Murphy, Patricia, 260; and Adoption Memo-
    rial, 262
Murray v. Curlett (1963), 89
Murray, Deloris N., 54
Murray, Jon Garth, 89, 91
Murray, Madalyn, 91–92, 94–95, 96–-100,
    103–4, 201, 341n36; on emigration to the
    Soviet Union, 99–100
Murray, William J. III, 89
Museum of the American Orphan, 193
Museum of Orphanhood, 159, 203, 263
Museum School of Manchester, NH, 18